Introduction to Business

CONCEPTS & APPLICATIONS

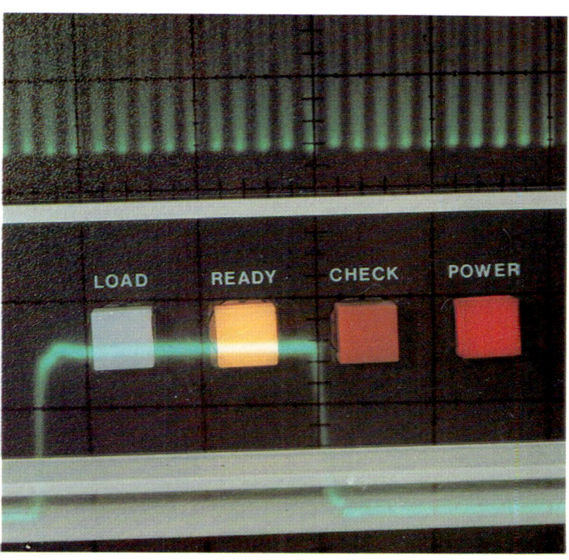

abschwarten-
Tee trinken!

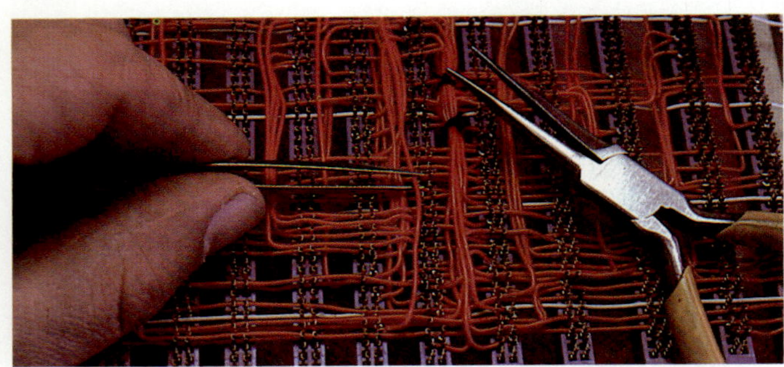

WATKINS

WEST PUBLISHING COMPANY

Saint Paul New York Los Angeles San Francisco

Introduction to Business

CONCEPTS & APPLICATIONS

STEVEN L. MANDELL
Bowling Green State University

SCOTT S. COWEN
Case Western Reserve University

ROGER LEROY MILLER
University of Miami

50 West Kellogg Boulevard
P.O. Box 3526
St. Paul, Minnesota 55165

Printed in the United States of America

Library of Congress Cataloging in Pubication Data
Main entry under title:
Introduction to business.
Includes index.
1. Business enterprises—United States.
2. Business enterprises—United States—Case studies. I. Mandell, Steven L. II. Cowen, Scott S. III. Miller, Roger LeRoy.
HF5343.I57 658:.00973 80-27003
ISBN 0-8299-0393-3
1st Reprint—1981

Copy Editor: Rebecca Smith
Artwork: Barbara Hack with Brenda Booth
Composition: The Clarinda Company

Photo Credits appear on page 593.

To my in-laws
John and Alice
Roscoe and Tee
S.L.M.

To Lynn and Amanda
S.S.C.

A study guide has been developed to assist you in mastering concepts presented in this text. The study guide reinforces concepts by presenting them in condensed, concise form. Additional illustrations and examples are also included. The study guide is available from your local bookstore under the title, *Study Guide to Accompany Introduction to Business: Concepts and Applications*, prepared by Steven L. Mandell.

CONTENTS

PART I

The Environment of Business 1

12

PRICING 271

13

MARKETING CHANNELS 289

14

PART IV

15

18

RISK AND INSURANCE 415

PART V

Quantitative Decision Making 437

23

INTERNATIONAL BUSINESS 529

24

BUSINESS IN THE THE WORLD OF TOMORROW 555

25

PREFACE

There is an old saying among experienced business people that "in order to learn business you have to do business." This book was written with this saying in mind. As such its objective is to provide students with a broad *conceptual and applied* overview of business. Students are not only introduced to important business concepts, but also get to see the practical application of these in the "real" world through such companies as Procter and Gamble, IBM, DuPont, Republic Steel, Merrill Lynch, and twenty other major American business organizations. The book is unique in its approach and every effort has been made to make it readable, interesting, and relevant. This perspective should enrich the students' learning experience and allow professors more flexibility in teaching.

A Unique Text

In thinking back over our educational and teaching experiences, each of us has concluded that the learning experience for us and our students was most meaningful when there was an opportunity to practice or apply what we were studying in the classroom. There is nothing like an actual example to assist students in visualizing and understanding the application of a particular business concept. In our attempt to bridge the gap between theory and practice, we have developed one of the really unique features of this book—the "Applications," or case illustrations, found at the end of each chapter. Each Application, written in the context of a real company, shows how a corporation implements the concepts presented in a chapter. For example, Chapter 10—Production Management—describes, in general terms, how companies produce their products. The chapter closes with an Application from IBM Corporation that describes how the company manufactures a computer system. The Application concludes with a section on career opportunities with IBM in the field of production and discussion questions that focus on the circumstances described in the Application.

The Applications are the heart of this book, but they are not the whole story. Several other important and unique features are included in each chapter.

- **Objectives, Outline, Key Terms** Every chapter opening includes a brief list of learning objectives, a chapter outline, and key terms presented in the chapter. These key terms are again highlighted by boldface type in the body of the chapter, and a complete glossary of terms appears at the end of the text.
- **Lead-in Article** Each chapter opens with an article that contains a humorous or interesting story related to the specific chapter topic. These articles invoke student attention, act as a motivator, and acquaint students with some of the more popular business literature.
- **Highlight Boxes** Periodically throughout the chapter we have included in shaded boxes, anecdotes—some real, others fictional—related to a particular concept discussed in the chapter. These Highlights serve to solidify concepts and provide other practical examples of what is being discussed.
- **Point-by-Point Summary and Questions for Review** At the end of every chapter, there are chapter summaries and questions for review that require more than rote answers so the students are encouraged to really think about the material presented in the text. Answers to these question are presented in the Instructor's Resource Guide.
- **Applications and Career Opportunities** As previously mentioned, we feel these will emerge as the hallmark of the book. They enable the students to understand how concepts learned in the chapter may be applied to a real business. And, to give the students more practical information, the Applications also describe entry-level job opportunities with the companies.
- **Business in Action** Each of the six parts of the book features a full-color portfolio we have called "Business in Action." The color photos illustrate pertinent business situations that add another facet to the practical and applied approach of the text.

This textbook was written with the student in mind. Technical jargon has been minimized, and every effort has been made to provide a reading level, writing style, and format to maximize student reading comprehension and pleasure. The book is divided into six parts that follow a logical sequence of material beginning with the environment of business (Part I) to a study of management principles (Part II), management functions (Parts III and IV), and decision-making tools (Part V) to looking at business in the future and career-planning issues (Part VI).

Supplemental Materials

We realize that most introduction to business teachers face a difficult task in finding the time to teach all of the varied subjects required in an introductory business course. To ease the preparation and teaching burden of instructors and to aid students in synthesizing and understanding the masses of material available to them, a number of supplemental materials have been prepared to accompany this text.

Instructor's Resource Guide, Test Banks, Transparencies, and Transparency Masters

Professor Raymond Tewell of American River College has prepared a very comprehensive, informative, and helpful resource guide. Contained in this resource guide is a course overview that includes a course syllabus, course outlines, grading guidelines, and film suppliers. Each chapter of the resource guide follows a format that includes objectives, brief outline, key terms, expanded outline, answers to the end-of-chapter questions, hints to instructors, expanded lectures, and films.

In addition, there are two Test Banks available each consisting of true-false and multiple choice questions. Both of these Test Banks are also available in a computerized testing format—**WESTEST.** Finally, to further enhance our total educational package, actual transparencies are available as well as many transparency masters.

Student Study Guide

The study guide for this text was prepared by Professor Mandell and closely adheres to a structured learning approach. Each chapter begins with a summary of the main points contained in the corresponding chapter in the textbook. The student is then requested to answer a series of objective questions relating to the chapter material. Following each question is the answer with a short explanation of why it is the correct answer. This structured approach facilitates students' learning and reinforces the concepts and practices read in the textbook and covered in class. In addition to the structured learning feature, the study guide also contains other objective-type questions, a glossary, and several mini-cases. These mini-cases supplement the applications in the book and require students to apply their knowledge in a decision-making setting.

ACKNOWLEDGMENTS

Many individuals and companies have been involved in the development of material for this book. The corporations featured in the Applications of this book have provided invaluable assistance; to each we express our appreciation. In addition, we would like to thank a number of individuals at our respective universities for the extraordinary jobs they have done in helping us: Rod Harris, Parvez Sopariwala, Brad Bogar, Lynn Cowen, Linda Stillabower and David Schlactus in manuscript research and preparation; Norma Morris and Wendy Grant for administrative assistance; and Marcia Strachan for typing. A special thanks to Rebecca Smith, our copy editor, who had the task of editing the final manuscript.

A significant contribution to this book was also made by numerous individuals throughout the country who reviewed our book during the different stages of production. The criticisms, suggestions, and encouragement offered by these reviewers are deeply appreciated. The contributions of the following people have added immensely to the text:

David E. Arant
Los Angeles Harbor College

John S. Bowdidge
Southwest Missouri State University

Eugene L. Britt
Grossmont College
California

Saul Candelas
El Paso Community College

Mel Choate
North Seattle Community College

Michael Cicero
Highline Community College
Washington

Jack Denson
Fullerton College
California

Nicholas Grunt
Tarrant County Jr. College
Texas

Robert W. Higgins
Middlesex County College
New Jersey

Thomas M. Huddleston
Northern Virginia Community College

Jack Kapoor
College of Dupage
Illinois

Allen D. Kartchner
Utah State University

Doug Mollenkopf
Southwest Texas State University

Jack W. Partlow
Seminole Community College
Florida

Norman Petty
Central Piedmont College
North Carolina

Enrique Ruelas
Foothill College—California

John I. Seitz
Oakton Community College—Illinois

Leon J. Singleton
Santa Monica College—California

Thomas D. Smith
University of Northern Colorado

Raymond Tewell
American River College—California

Angelo H. Trippy
Erie Community College
New York

Our personal thanks to each of you.

Finally, we want to add a special word of thanks to the editorial and production people at West Publishing Company for their many contributions in developing our manuscript and converting it into a polished, finished product.

PART I

KEMMONS WILSON

What better example of the role of the businessperson in the U.S. economy than Charles Kemmons Wilson, head of Holiday Inns of America. When he was thirty-eight, Wilson took his wife and five children in the family station wagon to Washington DC. En route, they stayed in motels that grated on Wilson's nerves, uncomfortable and overpriced with no restaurants nearby. As a result, Wilson designed the ideal motel—120 bright rooms with telephone and air conditioning, a restaurant, a swimming pool, parking facilities, and no charge for kids sharing their parents' room. The motel was named Holiday Inn after a 1942 movie. Two years later, in 1953, four Holiday Inns dotted the main highways into Memphis.

With visions of a national chain, Wilson approached the "biggest-thinking" man he knew, Wallace Johnson, a fellow Memphis builder. They incorporated Holiday Inns of America in 1954. Today there are over 1,500 Holiday Inns in every state and many foreign countries. Holiday Inns of America is still dominated by Kemmons Wilson, and his Memphis headquarters supplies and monitors every franchise.

The Environment of Business

OBJECTIVES

☐ To trace the evolution of business from the Stone Age to the Middle Ages
☐ To understand why people have always found it perfectly natural to trade with one another
☐ To discuss the profound changes that the industrial revolution made in the way business was transacted
☐ To explain in brief the free-enterprise argument that business indirectly produces societal well-being
☐ To discuss the role of business in a volatile and highly interrelated world, where one action creates a multitude of reactions

OUTLINE

ARTICLE *Wrong Tactic Root of Auto Industry's Ills*
THE EARLIEST TRANSACTION
A HISTORY OF BUSINESS
Egyptian Trade
Antibusiness Sentiment
Merchant Cities
The Roman Empire
Business in the Middle Ages
The Industrial Revolution
Business and the Development of America
MODERN BUSINESS AND THE FREE-ENTERPRISE SYSTEM
The Systems Point of View
The Business Life Cycle
The Decline and Fall of Businesses
APPLICATION *Anheuser-Busch Companies, Inc.*

KEY TERMS

BARTERING
BUSINESS LIFE CYCLE
COMPETITION
ENVIRONMENT OF BUSINESS
EXCHANGE
MERCHANT CITY
MONOPOLY
PRODUCTIVITY

THE EVOLUTION OF BUSINESS

Wrong Tactic Root of Auto Industry's Ills

ART BUCHWALD
Toledo Blade, May 20, 1980, p. 17.

It is no longer a secret that the American automobile companies are in a lot of trouble. They blame their woes on foreign imports, government emission standards, high interest rates, and gasoline prices. Very few will admit the real problem, and that is that people aren't buying American cars.

The auto companies, for all their expertise do not understand the consumer. They are making an appeal to his patriotism, offering rebates, and giving away autographed footballs.

It doesn't work. I don't wish to be presumptuous by telling the giant U.S. manufacturers how to move their cars, but this is a crisis and I believe they need all the help they can get.

What the American auto companies have to do is change their tactics and play hard to get.

This is how a dealer should treat a prospective buyer who comes into the showroom:

"Can I help you, sir?"

"No, I'm just looking."

"Go right ahead. None of these models is for sale anyway."

"What do you mean none of these models is for sale?"

"There is a six-month waiting list for anything you see in the showroom."

"I don't believe it."

"You haven't heard about the shortage then?"

"What shortage?"

"There is going to be a big shortage in American automobiles in the next three years. We're only going to be able to take care of our regular customers, and they're going to have to take whatever we give them."

"But I need a new car."

"Everyone needs a new car, but there are just so many to go around. I'm terribly busy now. Perhaps you might try a foreign-car dealer. I understand you can get a cheap import right away."

"But I don't want a cheap import. I want an American car."

"Everybody does. What makes you think you're so special that you should have one?"

"I'm an American and I have a right to own an American car."

"If you're going to become churlish, you can leave the showroom right now. We don't have to put up with someone with a bad temper."

"I'm sorry I lost my head. If I gave you a $500 rebate, would you sell me a car?"

"Sir, we don't accept bribes. There are people who have been waiting over a year for one of our cars. Even if Henry Ford himself called up and told us to give you one, we wouldn't do it."

"I don't want to beg. But I'm a salesman and I need an automobile for my work. Please give me a break. I'll take anything you have in stock."

"Occasionally we do make exceptions for hardship cases. But we'll need a letter from your employer certifying that the automobile will be used for business and not for pleasure."

"I'll get it."

"And then we'll also need three references from people attesting that you are of good character and worthy of driving one of our models."

"I'll give them to you now."

"And finally, you will have to sign a paper promising you will never reveal to a living soul that we sold you a car out of turn."

"My lips are sealed."

"Come into my office. I don't want anyone to see us concluding this sale."

"You're a good man, and I'll never forget this."

"If you don't mind. I can't stand a groveling customer."

Buchwald's tongue-in-cheek article does reflect the situation between a prospective buyer and seller if the article demanded was scarce. The following chapter will illustrate how business operates in the modern-day world.

In the early days of civilization, people discovered that they could share the fruits of other people's labor as long as they were willing to give up a part of the fruits of their own labor. Trade was a personal and rather modest matter until the industrial revolution during the eighteenth century, which mechanized production and permitted large quantities of goods to be produced and thus sold at low prices. Businesspeople became very prosperous, but their economic power frightened many people. To counteract this fear and distrust, the governments of most developed countries became guardians of the public interest. Modern businesses now operate in a complex environment far different from the circumstances of early trade.

In this chapter we examine the evolution of business. First we trace its evolution from the Stone Age to the Middle Ages, when the products that were traded were handmade. Then we analyze the effect of the industrial revolution on society and the changes in trade and attitudes that it created. Last we view the complexities of business today and attempt to understand the contribution it makes in spite of an environment that is at best indifferent and at worst hostile.

The Earliest Transaction

At best, scholars can only speculate about how business started. Taking a little poetic liberty, we might reenact one of the earliest business transactions as follows.

Imagine yourself a cavedweller. You adjust your bearskin and tighten your hand around your long spear. Your stomach churns in hunger. From your cover behind a bush, you see a big animal in the field, coming toward you. Slowly you pull the spear back and get ready for the throw. The animal nears. Suddenly it pulls its head upright, ears pointed. Quickly you raise and throw your spear, but too late. The animal veers away and lopes across the field. Imagine your dismay at having to go hungry another night.

From behind a distant bush, another hunter jumps up quickly, with a strange stick in his hand, curved in an arc with something tied to each end. As you watch, the stranger takes another, shorter stick and threads it on the thing tied between the ends of the large stick. He raises the whole contraption, pulls on the short stick, and it flies away from him. As the stick falls to earth, it hits the animal you missed. What magic is this? You look carefully at the contraption, then slip quickly away.

Filled with thoughts of what you just saw, you do not notice the stranger following you. You see a curved stick lying on the ground and pick it up. You pull your hand tool from your makeshift belt and start chipping away. Now it is time for the stranger to be amazed. Never has he seen wood cut so carefully and with such ease.

The stranger jumps out from behind a tree, curved stick in hand. Although surprised, you stand dead still, having seen what the pointed stick can do. The stranger relaxes and lowers the stick. He seems attracted by the tool you have in your hand. He reaches for it, but you pull back, firmly grasping your ax. This upsets the stranger. You gesture at him, pointing at the curved stick. He looks down at his bow and slowly starts to raise it. You, likewise, start to lift your ax. For a moment, both of you hold on to your possessions and then, as if by signal, let go. Each of you has a new tool.

No doubt some similar type of motives were involved in the earliest **exchange.** Someone saw a tool being used by a stranger that did a better job than his own, but the stranger would not part with his possession without some sort of compensation or exchange. An exchange of goods that does not involve the use of money, called **bartering,** is one of the oldest methods of acquiring goods and services.

A History of Business

While cavedwellers still roamed the forests of Europe, cities were well established in the Far East. There began what we now think of as "business." Imagine yourself at that time, making deals for wool, spices, soda, silver, or ointments. You would know very well to conduct the affairs of business—drawing up contracts, making partnerships, and defending your rights in court. By 2500 BC you might have been forming a trading company to explore some distant territory. It certainly would not be the same type of company we see today but rather an agreement among traders with similar interests to share in the risks and expense of an expedition, with the understanding that they would also share in the profits if they were successful.

Even in these times, you would have found it helpful to keep track of the things you owned and traded, as well as some of your more important business transactions. Some of the earliest clay tablets uncovered by excavators list business dealings. One might have explained why you needed more space for your business and constituted a contract to rent a more suitable location. You might have agreed to pay so much silver a year, some in the form of a down payment and the rest in easy installments. Yet another tablet might have been the letter you wrote to a colleague preparing a caravan, expressing your concern over providing enough food for the donkeys and enough guards to protect the venture.

If one of your customers lacked cash, you might have gone ahead and given him the goods right away in exchange for a note promising to pay the required sum later. Or perhaps you heard of a particularly good business opportunity in Egypt but did not have the funds to get the donkeys, ships, people, and provisions together. You might have visited someone of better means and asked to borrow the money. Naturally, you would have been willing to share some of your bounty in return for the use of his or her money. After all, that person would face a sizable risk of losing all of it if you were overcome by robbers on the journey.

EGYPTIAN TRADE

If you had gone ahead with this venture to Egypt, you would have been surprised by the different environment you faced there. Egypt at this time was made up of small communities, each largely self-sufficient. Trade was limited to items required in everyday life, and there was little need for a businessperson of your type. An Egyptian might bargain with a leather worker for a pair of sandals to protect her feet from the hot sands or for a leather water bag. Or perhaps she needed a covering for her chair or another basket for carrying farm produce from the field and storing seeds for next year's crop. The floor she sat on to eat may have been wearing out, or she might have wanted local carpenters to make a chair, bed, or table.

You would have been disappointed to learn that each Egyptian community had craftworkers who could supply these everyday needs. There was little place for someone like you traveling the countryside, plying your wares. In times of good harvest, however, you might have been able to trade some of your wares—weapons, musical instruments, drinks, horses, bulls, cattle, and perhaps fine-quality wood—for the excess corn offered by local rulers. Hence, in farming communities, your trade would have been limited to dealings with those who had the excess produce to barter with—more often than not, the heads of communities.

ANTIBUSINESS SENTIMENT

As a businessperson in a farming community, you would have noticed an important distinction between the types of transactions you would enter into and those that farmers would. Farmers traded or bartered because they needed the goods to maintain their households. They had little time to engage in "business." Not being tied to the land, you could trade or barter because you saw profit to be made. More often than not, you did not require the personal use of the goods you bought but rather sold them to others. You undertook ventures and deals because the farmers were either unwilling or unable to do so. By leading expeditions into distant realms, you were able to obtain honey, wax, and furs for use by your customers at home. Naturally, you expected a higher price for these goods than what they cost you. After all, you had taken the time, trouble, and risk that others had not.

This extra effort was not always obvious to farmers, who toiled hard in the fields to make a living. They looked with suspicion on people who earned their living by activities like bookkeeping, forecasting needs, and strange dealings with even stranger traders. In fact, most agrarian economies in ancient times frowned on business. City-states like Athens, Sparta, Egypt, and Rome looked on it as a dishonorable activity. In Athens, sea trading was much too lowly an activity for one of pure Athenian blood. Merchants like you were forced to live at the port where your ships docked and were prevented from engaging in political affairs or marrying anyone with Athenian blood.

Plato, the well-known Greek philosopher, disdained merchants. In his concept of the perfect state, Plato gave them a status little better than that of cobblers or masons and devised methods that would prevent them from rising to power or engaging in political affairs. In fact, businesspeople in Athens could enter political circles only by owning land, a reflection of the agrarian values of the time. In Egypt, political office could be gained only after refraining from trade for ten years. Unfortunately for merchants like you, this antibusiness sentiment was adopted by the later Roman Empire, which humbled business with controls, as well as by the Roman Catholic Church, which preached the evils of business profit throughout the Middle Ages.

MERCHANT CITIES

It is no wonder, given the prejudices of agrarian cities, that businesspeople like you jumped at the chance to become citizens of **merchant cities,** which supported and encouraged commerce. The success of such cities is well documented in history. Corinth saw its glory sometime between 800 and 450 BC. The intricate columns known as Corinthian, adopted by the Greeks and Romans, provide only a suggestion of the beauty and splendor befitting a city whose ships traded around the Mediterranean. Carthage was another merchant city that amassed great wealth from trading. Rulers seeking to do battle would come to these cities for ships and money to finance their war campaigns.

The wealth of merchant cities was unequaled until modern times. Nevertheless, gold was not a substitute for iron, and wealth alone was not enough to defend them from outside attacks. Even with mighty navies, treasuries full of metals of all kinds, and fortifications filled with hired troops of many nations, merchant cities eventually fell to the poor agrarian nations. Although they lacked wealth, agrarian societies tended to have greater determination and military strength.

THE ROMAN EMPIRE

Although businesspeople in Rome were unable to obtain powerful political positions, there were endless opportunities for business during this time. Businesspeople were given government contracts to build dams and aqueducts, to construct buildings, and to collect taxes. Some merchants were engaged in the very profitable baking business or built lamps, cut jewels, made pottery, manufactured tools, wove cloth. There was always a need for goods and military supplies for the great legions of armies supported by the Empire. Some merchants followed behind the conquering armies, buying the bounty taken by soldiers from captured cities.

In spite of the Roman Empire's vast wealth and power, it fell to barbarians invading from the north. Its collapse was not without repercussions. The lack of a central authority in Europe left a void, which was filled by aristocrats. They grew strong and independent as local

Highlight The Great Hanseatic League

Merchants in the Middle Ages often banded together in what were called merchants' guilds, whose interests were mainly self-regulation of trade. Often they found themselves in competition with guilds of skilled craftworkers. In fact, in London in 1200, one merchants' association succeeded in persuading the King that the Weavers' Craft Guild should be abolished.

A lot of merchants joined the Hanseatic League (see Exhibit 1.1), which was to become the most far-reaching international organization of merchants during that era. The best-known members of this league were the Hansa of London and those of the Teutons. The Hansa of London had by the end of 1350 gotten all of its members royal protection. Any member could go to any spot in England and stay there for forty days, all the while trading and making income.

Many historians and economists believe that increased trade among towns and nations contributed to the downfall of feudalism.

EXHIBIT 1.1 The Hanseatic League

The Hanseatic League during the Middle Ages encompassed over 70 towns throughout Europe and England. It was the most far-reaching international organization of foreign merchants.

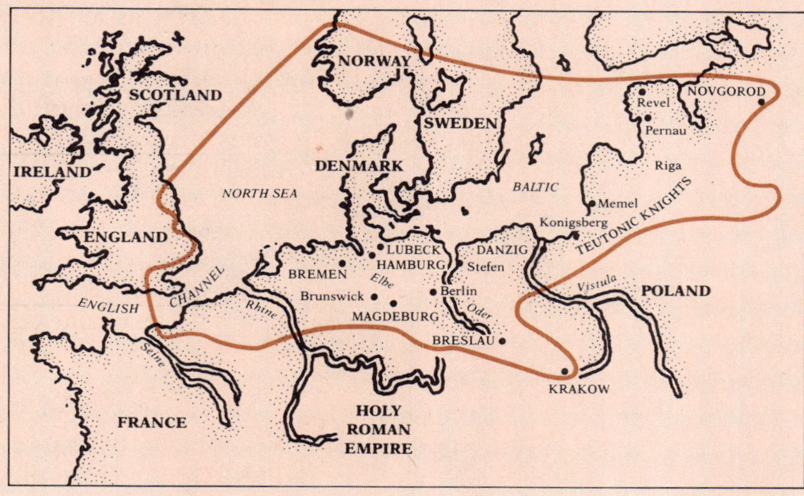

peasants turned to them for the protection no longer afforded by the Roman Empire. Over time the aristocrats, surrounded by their local populace, developed into self-sufficient feudal societies.

BUSINESS IN THE MIDDLE AGES

Feudal life revolved around the land. The cooperation required to produce food guaranteed that there was little time or need to engage in other activities. Common pasturage and meadowland, community plowing and harvesting, and common maintenance of roads all made the village a true community.

Within the medieval village, trade was limited to those things essential for production of food staples and for maintenance of the township. Each town had people who specialized in the production of crafted goods necessary for day-to-day life—metalsmiths, who made tools from iron; bakers, who made bread (an important staple at the time); millers, who ground wheat into flour; woodcutters, weavers, and tanners. In short, this was the same sort of self-contained environment common in ancient Egypt.

Some trade, however, was essential to these feudal towns. Iron was needed for the plows. The type of stones used in the mill to grind flour was not usually found near the village. Metal weapons for the local militia were also rarely produced from within. Salt for preserving meats and fish had to be obtained from the sea or mined.

Although these towns tolerated trade brought about by necessity, there was very little tolerance for merchants. The Middle Ages was a time of religious fervor, and peasants were taught by the Church not to seek enrichment and personal gain (nor was there much time in the daily routine to be concerned with thoughts of "making a living"). The Church could see no valid reason why someone who did nothing to improve an article should charge a higher price for it than the maker. A capitalistic way of life was hardly possible when accumulated earnings were, by Christian edict, to be given away or spent.

Thus businesspeople had no status in the Middle Ages. They were vagabonds of sorts, traveling from one town to another, buying products cheaply in times of surplus and selling them dear in other towns in times of need. Since, by the nature of their business, they received more than they started out with they challenged the religious tenets of the time. Their meager attempts to eke out an existence put them in peril of public disfavor. It was only in the development of modern-day merchant cities, reminiscent of ancient Corinth and Carthage, that businesspeople found a more favorable environment.

THE INDUSTRIAL REVOLUTION

The events that later became known as the industrial revolution were possible only because of a change in the religious and social beliefs prevalent in the Middle Ages. By the 1700s, people had become more receptive to experimentation and scientific (rather than religious) attempts to explain the natural order about them. Tradition, which had opposed change in favor of age and precedent, held less importance. It was only then that the inventions so characteristic of the industrial revolution were developed and put to practical use.

In England during the mid-1700s, demand for products was high, and the potential rewards for productive inventions were great. The wealth and power that had long been in the hands of the aristocracy began once more to accumulate with the merchants. Armed with their new wealth, these businesspeople backed new inventions, put them to practical use, and reaped the rewards of their efforts. The success of the cotton factories during this time is a prime example of the wealth to be obtained through invention and ingenuity.

The Beginnings of Mechanization

Tools could help a hand work better, but machines did the work of many hands, performing many times the work of a normal laborer in less time. This meant that goods made with the use of machines were cheaper. The demand for these cheaper goods was greater than the sup-

Highlight Industry Comes to America: The Case of Textiles

Before 1812, there was almost no manufacturing in the United States. Only 7 percent of the population lived in urban areas. The only real industry to speak of was the textile industry. But even by 1810, two-thirds of all textile manufacture was still a cottage business. Samuel Slater had made some heroic attempts in the 1790s to develop a mechanized weaving industry in Providence, Rhode Island, but he failed.

A big change occurred in the textile industry when the embargo of 1807 was enacted by Congress. This embargo prohibited American vessels from sailing to foreign ports in an effort to force England and France to respect American neutrality. The main effect it had, however, was to force America to produce many of the products that it had been importing. The effects were quickly felt in the textile industry. In 1808 there were only fifteen textile mills; by 1809 there were almost ninety.

The growth in the textile industry was to be short-lived, however. The War of 1812 and its massive blockage of American ports ended with the Peace of Ghent in 1814. Britain started exporting to the United States again. The textile industry had to wait until the Waltham System of Clothweaving, developed by Mr. Lowell, was better refined. A couple of years later, his use of power mills and a system that used low-cost, well-supervised labor finally gave the textile industry a boost (see Exhibit 1.2).

EXHIBIT 1.2 American Textile Mill

The cotton textile industry became a part of New England industrial life. This scene shows calico being printed. Calico was a coarse, plain-weave cotton cloth first imported from Calicut, India to England. (Historical Pictures Service, Chicago)

ply, which spurred more production and began an endless cycle.

Laborers had at first feared the increasing use of machines, but their fears were allayed as the demand increased for their skills in running these machines. These laborers now spent much of their time in factories instead of farming the land, so they required money in the form of wages in order to obtain food and clothing from others. At first, they were rewarded in wages as well as such other items as drink, clothing, and corn sold at cheaper prices. Soon, however, these "extras" were discontinued, and workers became increasingly dependent on wages to provide the wherewithal to supply their daily needs.

The Beginnings of Urbanization

Poor farmers in outlying towns, who had for years eked out meager existences on the land, became attracted to the industrial towns with dreams of the money to be made. The landlords, who for centuries had maintained control over the peasants by virtue of their control over the land, began to lose authority. The migration of peasants became so great, in fact, that many of the remaining farmers could hardly find anyone to work the land.

As the use of machinery increased and hence production, so did demand; and as demand increased, so did production in response. This economic growth had beneficial effects in the towns where factories were established. The factory workers' increased wages supported stonemasons, carpenters, corn dealers, butchers, storekeepers, and other businesspeople of every kind and description. The industrial revolution had a profound effect on society.

BUSINESS AND THE DEVELOPMENT OF AMERICA

America was discovered by a businessperson who wanted to find a better trade route to India. Once the New Land had been found, business interests helped to establish the colonies and develop trade. It was, in fact, the dispute over what types of business were allowed and which trade was legal that led Americans to seek independence from the British Crown. Once the United States had been established as a separate nation, business was responsible for the development of the industrialized cities of the North and the farming plantations in the South. Business, in short, was America's "reason for being."

If we were to make a comparison to the past, we would have to compare the United States to the ancient merchant cities of Corinth and Carthage or to the trading cities of the Hanseatic League. America is a country for businesspeople, supporting and encouraging business much as the merchant cities did in ancient times. Like those cities, too, this support and encouragement has its rewards. It has helped to make America one of the strongest and wealthiest nations on earth.

Modern Business and the Free-Enterprise System

The power of landlords was based on their control of the land; the power of merchants was based on their ability to trade the goods people wanted. If they had a **monopoly** on trade, if nobody else in their area controlled land or goods, their power was enhanced. However, the manufacturers who soon rose to meet the high demand for products normally had no exclusive control over resources or supplies. Their success was based on the productive and competitive use of machines.

In attempting to satisfy their own desires for wealth, these businesspeople were forced to apply the most inventive techniques to production processes in the most efficient way—in order to sell their products at the cheapest prices possible. The one who sold the same-quality product for the lowest price got virtually all the business.

These efforts resulted in greater **productivity**—the more efficient use of equipment, resources, and labor to produce more goods. In short, their efforts resulted in a better society. This notion—that individuals following their own self-interest will incidentally and necessarily benefit society—was suggested by Adam Smith in *The Wealth of Nations*. He pictured this process as "an invisible hand" leading businesspeople to answer society's needs while attempting to satisfy their own. This notion is one of the basic foundations underlying our present economic system. Business, by seeking to increase its wealth in the form of profits, must serve consumers and benefit society.

THE SYSTEMS POINT OF VIEW

It is easy to see from this extremely brief history we cannot talk about the development of business without considering the environment that surrounds it. In prehistoric times, there was no government, little social order, and not much of an economic system; life was "catch as catch can." In Egyptian times, business was limited to bartering among local people for the necessities of life, and the economic system was tied to the land. In the Middle Ages, the religious beliefs, the social order of the towns, and the need for cooperation all affected how business efforts were treated. It was not until the industrial revolution that wealth was slowly transferred from the aristocracy to the merchants and factory owners and that society encouraged the practical application of inventions—all of which allowed business to expand in the marketplace.

Today it is especially important to take into account the environment surrounding business. The **environment** consists of all the things that affect business efforts but that are largely out of its control:

1. One element of the business environment that is extremely important is **competition,** the rivals who are producing similar products and vying for the same customers.
2. Another element is the government, which has grown in regulatory authority in recent years; business needs to be aware of the regulations that affect its operations from its initial establishment and throughout its productive life.
3. The state of the economy can also affect business, by either stimulating or suppressing sales.
4. Most importantly, the way people perceive businesses and their products affect their ability to suceed in the marketplace.

A business cannot be evaluated simply by looking at its environment; it must be evaluated by carefully considering the interaction of it parts. However, the functions of business have become so specialized that some parts of a company often do not recognize the important functions being performed by other parts. For example, the accounting department may have trouble collecting payments due on credit. Its subsequent efforts to collect may be in stark contrast to marketing's efforts to improve customer relations and increase patronage.

A business functions as a set of different parts, but the parts nevertheless work together toward a common goal, within the constraints imposed by the environment. The goal? Success in the marketplace!

Highlight The Life Cycle of Palmer's Bike Shop

Joe Palmer liked to repair bicycles when he was a kid. When he got older, he continued repairing bicycles for other people in his garage as a sideline. He eventually decided to open a bike repair business and it became very successful.

One day a representative from a large bicycle manufacturing company stopped by Joe's house and asked him if he would like to sell new bikes. Joe agree. Since he was the only bike dealer in his small town, his business was soon booming. He decided to open a storefront operation downtown. Business tripled in just one year.

Unfortunately, Joe started to have staffing and hiring problems. He didn't have enough space to handle all of his workers. With his profits, he bought a large building. Just when he was finally getting things settled, two other bike stores opened in town, one of them a very good one. His business dropped. No matter what he did, he could not keep the same volume he had before the competitors moved into town. His business was so big he couldn't cut his overhead expenses down sufficiently to prevent bankruptcy. He sold out at a loss.

Joe is now living in a small town twelve miles away. His business? A new laundry company.

THE BUSINESS LIFE CYCLE

A business almost inevitably undergoes a cycle of success. From the initial birth, it grows, matures, and over time declines. This process, known as the **business life cycle**, can be important in explaining a firm's success or the change in the environment that eventually led to its downfall.

A new business is often established because it has developed a new process or technology. Its unique properties propel it into the marketplace rapidly. As awareness of its product grows, the business grows. But over time, other businesses develop with their own version of the process or technology, attracted by the demand and opportunity in the market. This increases the competition for customers, and many weaker companies fall by the wayside. Finally, the same process that guaranteed the company success when it was first established can cause its decline and fall. If the business becomes complacent, a new business with a better process may soon put it out of business.

The American Steel Industry

We can use the business life cycle to explain the growth and decline of major businesses in America. For example, the steel industry, when it was first established, had superior technology and processes, which made it quite competitive with other makers of metal products at the time. As the demand for steel increased, the manufacturers expanded production and increased their wealth. Soon they were firmly entrenched, a market for their products virtually assured. This stage of maturity, lasted until the late 1960s. Presently, however, the American steel mills are having their position in the market challenged. Foreign steelmakers, who have invested in new technologies and have made production more efficient, can sell their product at a lower price than permitted by the old equipment in U.S. mills. Unless the U.S. steel industry responds to the challenge by updating equipment and trimming operations, it could face the decline side of its business cycle.

The American Auto Industry

A similar state of affairs is prevalent in the automobile industry. When automobiles first arrived, they were unique and in constant demand. Production could hardly keep up with orders. So vast was the potential market that automobile manufacturers were able to establish huge factories and employ thousands of workers. But other competitors entered the market, and they increased the competition for customers by manufacturing variations. Soon the market was saturated, and most people had at least one car. Some families were able to buy two cars when supplies began to increase relative to demand. Presently, however, the automobile manufacturers are facing changing environmental conditions that will affect their ability to remain competitive.

The energy crisis, which puts demands on manufacturers to build smaller, more energy-efficient cars, and foreign competition, which manufactures these cars efficiently, will strain the American automobile industry in the near future. Chrysler Corporation nearly went bankrupt because it had been slow to respond to the changing environmental conditions in which it did business. The mistake was costly and nearly fatal.

THE DECLINE AND FALL OF BUSINESSES

The lesson to be learned from the systems approach and the business life cycle is that a firm must always be on the lookout for changes in the environment that could affect its ability to compete in the market. It must watch competitors to see what efforts they are making to gain customers and respond to those efforts. It must be aware of changing supplies of raw materials. It should evaluate how new government policies may affect market success. Finally, and most importantly, the business must always be on the lookout for customer satisfaction. In the final analysis, a business that is unable to respond to the needs of its customers or to changes in its environment will eventually decline and fall.

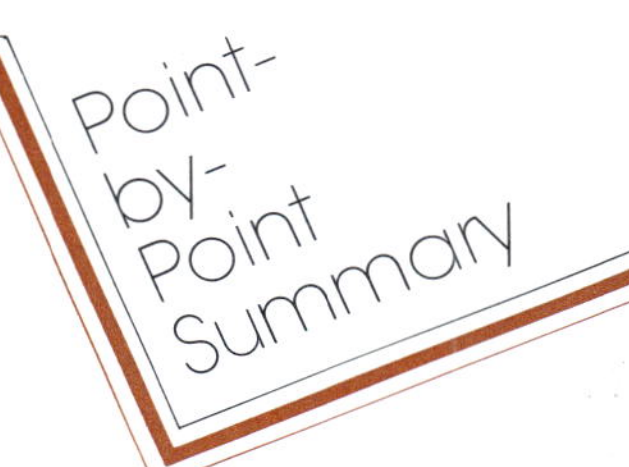

- Business is transacted by people who are willing to trade for the efforts of others by giving up a part of their effort.
- Even as early as 2500 BC, trading companies were being formed; not as we think of trading companies today, but rather as agreements among traders with similar interests. As trade developed, precious metals such as gold and copper became the medium of exchange, which meant that all trade was transacted in terms of these metals.

- In the Middle Ages, trade was mainly confined to village communities; and within the village, trade was limited to those things essential for production of food staples and for maintenance of the township. The heavy religious influences encouraged people to look down on merchants, because they violated religious tenets by attempting to make a profit from trade.
- The characteristics of trade were radically changed with the industrial revolution, which introduced machinery into the production process. These machines could do the same tasks as humans but much more efficiently and quickly. This change reduced the cost of production and made products easily available to the masses. Most of the workers displaced by the machines were put to work supervising them, and all benefited from the increased productivity created by the machines.
- As a result of the industrial revolution, many peasants moved to the industrial towns—so many, in fact, that the remaining farmers had difficulty in finding people to work the land.
- The economic growth, caused by the increased demand and production had beneficial effects on the towns with factories. The factory workers' increased wages supported stonemasons, carpenters, storekeepers, and other businesspeople.
- Business and the free-enterprise system are perfectly compatible. The free-enterprise system encourages business to be productive or go under. The result is better products at lower prices, so that consumers' dollars can go further in satisfying their wants.
- Businesses all over the world exist in a changing environment. In the old days, trade only required two people who wished to exchange the fruits of their individual efforts. Today, a business must always be on the lookout for changes in the environment that could affects its ability to compete in the market. A business that is unable to respond to the needs of its customers or to changes in its environment will eventually decline and fall.

1. Why do you think it is necessary to trade the fruits of your efforts for the fruits of other people's efforts?
2. What benefit do you think ordinary consumers got from the industrial revolution?
3. Do you agree with Adam Smith's statement that individuals would incidentally benefit society if they followed their own self-interests? Why?
4. What developments have caused businesses today to be more concerned about what is happening around them, as compared to business, say, in the Middle Ages?

APPLICATION

Anheuser-Busch is a good example of a company evolving and adapting to environmental changes over time. In fact, the company that today is the world's largest producer of beer nearly failed to survive through its fifth birthday.

HOW IT ALL STARTED

Georg Schneider's tiny St. Louis brewery opened in 1852 and nearly collapsed in 1857. Competitors stepped in and saved it, however. They renamed it Hammer & Urban and began expanding. The expansion was financed by a loan from Eberhard Anheuser, a successful soap manufacturer.

In 1860 Hammer & Urban failed again. Anheuser shouldered the debt of the firm and reluctantly became a brewery owner. The following year, Eberhard Anheuser's daughter, Lilly, married a young St. Louis brewery supplier named Adolphus Busch. In 1864 Busch decided to join his father-in-law's brewery as a salesperson and sold his own brewery business. His hard work earned him a position as a partner and later as president of the company. Because it was his driving force that turned the company into an industry giant, Busch is considered the real founder of Anheuser-Busch.

Young Busch dreamed of manufacturing a beer that would be enjoyed by a national market, appealing to virtually every taste preference. This was an unusual

Anheuser-Busch Companies, Inc.

dream in a time when local beers and breweries abounded. To realize this ambition Anheuser-Busch created a network of railside icehouses to cool cars of beer being shipped long distances. Busch later launched the industry's first fleet of refrigerated freight cars. When additional methods were needed to safeguard the beer's freshness, Busch applied the then-new concept of pasteurization to his beer.

In 1876 Busch and a close friend, Carl Conrad, worked together to develop a new beer using time-consuming Old World methods. The beer was called Budweiser. It is still made the same way today. Busch also had a flair for advertising. In 1879 the company became Anheuser-Busch Brewing Association, with some 105,234 barrels in annual sales. In 1901 the company manufactured over a million barrels of beer.

Upon his father's death in 1913, August A. Busch, Sr. took charge. He faced three major crises in succession—World War I, Prohibition, and the Great Depression. His main efforts were therefore directed at the survival of the company. During Prohibition, he focused the company's expertise and energies on producing corn products, baker's yeast, ice cream, commercial refrigeration units, and truck bodies. In an attempt to manufacture nonalcoholic beverages, the company also introduced Bevo, a malt-derived beverage, and a number of carbonated soft drinks, including Carcho, Kaffo, Buschtee, Grape Bouquet, and Busch Ginger Ale. These products enjoyed various levels of success, but all were eventually discontinued after Prohibition was repealed.

Another Anheuser-Busch product introduced at this time, baker's yeast, was a great success. So successful were sales of baker's yeast that a second plant was opened in 1931 at Old Bridge, New Jersey. The company eventually became the nation's leading producer of baker's yeast.

After the war, Anheuser-Busch established eight branch breweries

April 7, 1933—Left to right, Adolphus Busch III, August A. Busch, Sr. and August A. Busch, Jr. celebrate the repeal of prohibition by preparing the first case of relegalized Budweiser for shipment to President Franklin D. Roosevelt.

and diversified into family entertainment, real estate, can manufacturing, transportation, and major league baseball. In the late 1960s and 1970s, Anheuser-Busch opened its tenth brewery and introduced Michelob Light, Natural Light, and Wurzburger Hofbrau beers. In an effort to gain more control over its operations, it added new can-manufacturing and malt-production facilities. It also created a new Busch Gardens theme park.

ADAPTATION AND SURVIVAL

It is not hard to see how environmental pressures can affect a firm in the marketplace. Imagine the trauma of a beer manufacturer facing Prohibition! In order to survive, Anheuser-Busch was forced to adapt, altering the very nature of its business and applying the expertise it had gained in making and distributing beer to other profit-making opportunities. The astounding success of its yeast-manufacturing efforts is a good example. The use of its newly gained expertise in the manufacture of refrigerated cars is another.

It was not until the repeal of

Prohibition that Anheuser-Busch regained its footing and the competitive edge that would guarantee its long-range success, but it was Anheuser-Busch's ability to respond to environmental change that guaranteed its survival. Today, Anheuser-Busch's diversification serves the same purpose. By expanding into areas unrelated to beer production, such as family entertainment and real estate, Anheuser-Busch is able to offset difficulties brought on by environmental factors affecting any one area.

CAREER OPPORTUNITIES

Anheuser-Busch offers a number of different areas for new employees. Naturally, there are jobs related to the production of beer, but since Anheuser-Busch is so diversified, a number of other areas are available as well.

An example of a traditional entry-level position in Anheuser-Busch might be that of a market research analyst, a staff function in support of beer production and sale. The entry-level marketing research analyst is responsible for assisting management in making decisions regarding brand positioning, advertising, packaging, and product acceptability. The analyst is also responsible for identifying new product opportunities. By meeting with market planning and brand-marketing management, the analyst helps define issues of concern to future marketing efforts. The analyst proposes a study, coordinates the collection and tabulation of data, analyzes the data using the latest quantitative methods, and presents the results of the research to management orally and in writing. Management can then use this new information to refine its marketing plans.

FOR DISCUSSION

1. What adverse environmental factors did Anheuser-Busch have to face in the early part of the twentieth century?
2. Besides brewing beer, Anheuser-Busch is involved with the manufacture of baker's yeast, family entertainment, real estate, and transportation services. Why do you think Anheuser-Busch diversified from its original and still-principal business of brewing and selling beer?
3. Based on your general knowledge, what future does Anheuser-Busch face in the beer market?

OBJECTIVES

- ☐ To distinguish between profit as a rate of return on sales and profit as a rate of return on investment
- ☐ To compare pure capitalism with pure socialism
- ☐ To apply the laws of demand and supply to the selling activities of businesses
- ☐ To identify the ways competition can be restricted and monopolies can be formed
- ☐ To define the social responsibility of businesses to customers, employees, and stockholders

OUTLINE

KEY TERMS

BARRIER TO ENTRY
CAPITAL COST
CAPITALISM
CAPITALIST
ENTREPRENEUR
EQUILIBRIUM PRICE
LAISSEZ-FAIRE
LAW OF DEMAND
LAW OF SUPPLY
MONOPOLISTIC COMPETITION
MONOPOLY
OLIGOPOLY
PRIVATE ENTERPRISE
PROFIT
RETAINED EARNINGS
RETURN ON INVESTMENT (ROI)
SOCIALISM

BUSINESS, CAPITALISM, AND SOCIAL RESPONSIBILITY

The Buzzword Is Capitalism

DANIEL SELIGMAN
Fortune,
October 8, 1979.

Bernd Heinrich, professor of entomological sciences at the University of California at Berkeley, cautions the readers of his new book on bumblebees not to draw morals to human society. We propose to defy Professor Heinrich and draw a moral or two. The world he depicts in *Bumblebee Economics* (Harvard University Press, $17.50) is ordered far more logically than the world we keep seeing on the seven o'clock news. The reason is that the bumblebees, unlike virtually all those characters on the news, do not believe in capitalism.

This judgment may seem surprising since bee societies look as though a lot of planning has gone into them, and some writers have identified them as essentially socialist in organization. However, Professor Heinrich makes it clear that the dominant economic themes in bumblebee life are initiative and competition and that—just as Adam Smith said it would—the competition of individually motivated units benefits the society as a whole. That planned look is actually Smith's "invisible hand" at work.

Bumblebee colonies may be viewed as factories whose operations require steady supplies of both pollen and nectar. To secure both resources, bumblebees must get out and forage, sometimes going as far afield as several miles. The optimization of gains from foraging is critical to the survival of the colony.

It turns out that gains are, in fact, optimized by a high degree of specialization among the foragers. Some bumblebees concentrate on pollen, some on nectar; most forage for both—but virtually all have a major and minor specialty in the type of flower visited. Professor Heinrich demonstrates that this rather elaborate division of labor is not based on any plan but reflects the individual experiments of bumblebees with different flowers. For each one, the flowers that yield the highest "profit"—the most pollen or nectar at the least expenditure of effort—get to be revisited the most.

Heinrich also demonstrates that the colony as a whole does best by having each bumblebee doing the best he can. If some members of the colony "sub-optimized," e.g., by taking less from flowers in order to leave more pollen or nectar for their colony mates, the amounts left behind would be taken by bees from other colonies.

Finally, *Bumblebee Economics* delineates a world without inflation. There is no inflation because the same amount of labor always leads to accumulation of the same amount of capital (the pollen and nectar). The author notes pointedly: "Strikes, used in the human system to increase by force the value of labor, are impossible. In the bee's world, scabs are legion. . . ." And there are no guidelines.

As this review of the book, *Bumblebee Economics,* indicates, bees seem to operate in a world of competition. As we shall see in this chapter, competition is only one aspect of our capitalist system.

The business of America *is* business. In our system of allocating resources, privately owned, privately operated businesses attempt to satisfy people's demands because of the lure of profits. When businesses provide more, different, and better products and services, consumers voluntarily choose to purchase them over and over again. Consumers believe that by doing so they are making themselves better off, that they are attaining a higher standard of living.

In this chapter we look at the role of profits in business and the economy, the way our economy works, and the social responsibility of business today. Keep in mind throughout, however, that we are not referring to an abstract, unreal concept called business. We are referring to the place where you just got your shoes repaired, the store where you just purchased a shirt, the company that made the car you're driving, and the people who decide which records and films are to be produced.

Business and Profits in America

The role of a business in this country is to make profits. To some people, *profit* is a dirty word; however, when viewed in a more objective light, profits may appear quite different. A roundabout example will show you what we mean.

Say you stop at a fruitstand to buy oranges. You are not forced to buy any, but if you decide to pay the stated price of, perhaps, $3.50 for a twenty-pound bag, you must think they are worth at least $3.50. If you buy the oranges, you can't spend that $3.50 for anything else you might want. So the amount of money you give the fruitstand owner for the bag of oranges is equal to, at a minimum, the value you place on those oranges.

The amount of money that the fruitstand owner had to pay to provide you with those oranges—rent, wages, cost of goods, insurance, and the like—is the total cost. The difference between those expenses and what you paid the fruitstand owner is the profit. Thus **profit** is the difference between the value that individual consumers place on the products or services they buy and the costs that the providers of those products or services incur in supplying them. Viewed in this light, profits are beneficial. They indicate the value that consumers place on the products and services they buy. And remember that this principle applies to the work of one person as well as to the work of a giant corporation.

By the way, profits don't end up stashed away in a safe somewhere. For example, the fruitstand owner might use part of the profits to enlarge the stand. Fully 45 percent of all profits are plowed right back into business as **retained earnings,** or corporate savings. Thus most of those profits are reinvested in America so that we can enjoy more jobs and a higher standard of living in the future.

TAKING RISKS AND EARNING PROFITS

In a capitalist society, those who take risks by starting and operating businesses are called **entrepreneurs.** *Entrepreneur* is derived from a French word meaning "someone who undertakes a venture." An entrepreneur is also a **capitalist**—a person who provides money for a business.

Many critics of our society have claimed that capitalists are parasites. To understand the problem in such an attitude, ask yourself whether you would lend money to a person to start a business if you were not promised a reward. You could always spend that money on something you want or earn interest on it in a savings account. Furthermore, you could lose your money altogether if the business fails, so you might want a reward for the risk you are taking. Entrepreneurs are rewarded with profits.

The lure of higher profits directs entrepreneurs to invest their money in those areas of the economy where people want more goods and services. The lure of increased profits also causes entrepreneurs to abandon certain sectors of the economy when consumers no longer consider an industry's product desirable. It did not take long for entrepreneurs to stop investing in horse carriages when automobiles became popular. They were willing to invest capital in the automobile industry because it offered higher profits.

MEASURING PROFITS CORRECTLY

Unfortunately, the term *profit* has many different meanings. A company that makes $100 million in one year may seem tremendously successful. However, that figure says nothing about profitability. For one thing, to compare today's profits with the profits a firm made ten years ago is meaningless, unless today's profits are reduced by an inflationary factor. Over the past ten years we have experienced about 100 percent inflation—in consumer dollars as well as profit dollars.

A lot of people go wrong by thinking of profits as a percentage of sales. The sporting goods store's profit of 50 percent on a tennis racket may sound like a lot, but that figure is merely the markup on the wholesale cost of the tennis racket. The overhead that the store owner must pay may eat up 10 points of that 50 percent; labor costs may eat up another 10 points; insurance and losses from shoplifting may take away another 10 points. In addition, the firm may have outstanding loans that it has to pay interest on. The percentage left over may be mighty small indeed.

From an investor's point of view, the markup means absolutely nothing. What is important is the bottom line—profits—after taxes and all other expenses are taken out. That figure must then be compared to the total investment in the business. Thus the only meaningful measure of profits is the annual rate of **return on investment (ROI),** expressed as a percentage. ROI is computed by dividing net profits by the total amount invested in the business. If a company's bottom line reads $5 million in earnings but the investment is $200 million, the rate of return is a mere 2$\frac{1}{2}$ percent.

Highlight Adam Smith: Founder of Modern Economics

In 1776, the Declaration of Independence was drafted in Philadelphia, an eloquent statement setting forth a doctrine of political freedom for the American colonies In the same year, *An Inquiry into the Nature and Causes of the Wealth of Nations* was published. Its author was Adam Smith. Like the Declaration of Independence, Smith's work stressed freedom—economic freedom.

Adam Smith was born in Scotland and studied at Oxford University in England, but he acquired much of his knowledge from out-of-class reading. In addition to economics, his interests ranged from physics and astronomy to literature and the arts. After leaving Oxford, Smith became a lecturer in literature and philosophy at the University of Glasgow in Scotland. Eventually he was appointed professor of logic and philosophy (at that time economics was called moral philosophy).

Smith was the first major advocate of economic freedom. He talked in terms of "free" or "unrestricted" market actions in the economy. He believed that people's self-interest would lead them to do what was best not only for themselves but also for the economy and society as a whole. This idea underlies Smith's doctrine of the "invisible hand." According to Smith, the economy is guided as if by an invisible hand when all individuals are allowed to do what they want to improve their standard of living. Since the invisible hand is at work at all times, there is no need for government help to make things run smoothly.

Another term used to describe Adam Smith's basic theory of economics is *laissez-faire,* a French term that means "do not interfere." To be sure, Smith recognized that government should do certain things for people. It should provide for national defense, domestic tranquility, and the like. But it should not hinder economic activities in any way.

Most economists consider Adam Smith the founder of modern economics. He pointed out the benefits of unrestrained competition in an economy free from government interference and the benefits of the division of labor. His writings eventually convinced many people that governments should not only stay out of domestic economic activities but also refrain from involvement in international economic dealings.

Competition and Capitalism

Given freedom of choice, most people make exchanges to better themselves. In doing so, they specialize, seeking out, for example, the highest-paid occupation. In general, this is how economic decisions are made in the United States. Under the American economic system, known as capitalism, people own the means of production (whether their own labor or machines) and decide themselves how to use them.

CAPITALISM

The concept of capitalism is usually associated with Adam Smith, an eighteenth-century economist. In his book *The Wealth of Nations,* Smith described a system in which government had little to do with economic activities. He said that individuals would pursue their own self-interests but that in doing so they would increase the well-being of the entire nation.

Obviously, capitalism in such a pure form has never existed. Capitalism today must be defined more realistically. Throughout this book, we describe **capitalism** as the economic system in which individuals own the productive resources of the society and have the right to use those resources in whatever manner they choose, within the limits of the law.

Private Enterprise

Another characteristic of the capitalistic system is the freedom of individuals to choose economic activities for whatever resources they own. This idea, called **private enterprise,** allows people to seek whatever occupations they want without restrictions. Again, this description applies to the purely theoretical aspects of a capitalistic system. Just try to become a doctor without first graduating from medical school and getting a license.

Many people view private enterprise as supporting a laissez-faire system. As Smith outlined it in *The Wealth of Nations,* a **laissez-faire** system lets each person go his or her own way to maximize personal self-interest; the government does not restrict a person's actions unless that person physically harms others. Thus, theoretically, productive resources in a private enterprise system are generally directed toward their best uses. For example, people tend to work at jobs that pay them the most. In doing so, they contribute the most they can to the material well-being of society.

This does not, of course, mean that people seek only to maximize their income in choosing an occupation. Many people choose occupations because the work is pleasant, the colleagues are nice, or it allows them to help people in need. But other things being equal, most people choose the higher-paying job.

The Role of Government

Even a purely capitalistic system has a role for government. The government protects the rights of individuals, especially in their control over property. In *The Wealth of Nations,* Smith described in some detail the role of government in a capitalistic system. For example, he talked about the government's need for national defense. To pay for this, government must levy taxes.

Today, the accepted role of government has expanded, even in capitalistic countries. Most governments take an active role in providing welfare for those in poverty. The government's role as the provider of education is accepted virtually everywhere. And the increasing problems of pollution and degradation of the environment have brought with them increased amounts of government regulation.

Capitalism versus Socialism

At the opposite end of the spectrum from capitalism is **socialism.** *Socialism* means many things to many people, but in its purest form the state owns the major productive resources. To be sure, socialism is not a new idea. As far back as 2100 BC, in a place called Sumeria, the state owned most of the land and kept records of all business transactions.

Exhibit 2.1 shows a comparison of some of today's economic systems based on how centralized decision making is. At one extreme is pure capitalism (complete decentralization), and at the other is pure socialism. All real-world systems fall somewhere in between these two pure forms.

COMPETITION

The private enterprise system is based on competition among businesses: Each business attempts to capture as large a share of the market as possible while trying to make as much profit as possible.

Maximizing Profits

Businessowners try to maximize profits by making a product or offering a service that appeals to a sufficiently large number of people to get a market. Once that market has been established, the goal is to expand it, thereby increasing profits. This can be done by improving the product or service so that it will appeal to new customers. Or the price can be lowered by reducing costs. Lower prices help induce more customers to buy.

Of course, this is only a model of business behavior. In reality, businessowners do not have perfect information about how consumers will respond to their products or changes in price. If they set the price

EXHIBIT 2.1. Degree of Centralization in Representative Economic Systems

On the extreme right-hand side of the diagram we find pure capitalism, which no country follows. On the extreme left-hand side is pure socialism, which again no country follows. In the middle are all of the world's economies: U.S.S.R., the United Kingdom, Mexico, and the United States are just a few that are shown, with the United States being closer to capitalism, of course, than any of the others and the U.S.S.R. being closer to socialism.

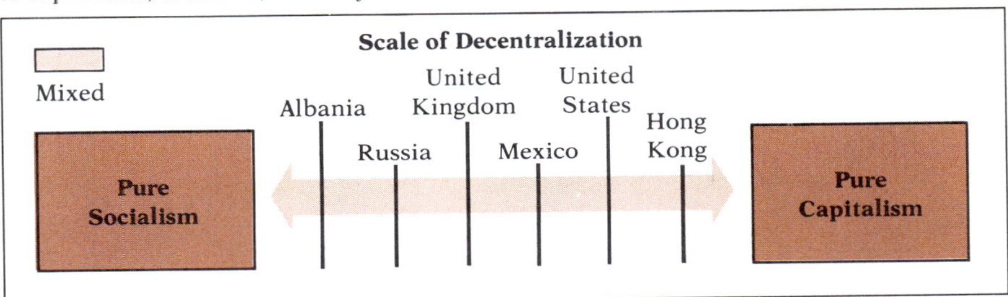

either too high or too low, they may lose profits. Thus they must constantly seek a profit-maximizing price for their products or services.

Another element in the drive to maximize profits is competition. No businessperson can long use more capital and labor than is absolutely necessary. Some competitor will use fewer resources, thereby cutting costs and prices. As a result, the inefficient producer will be driven out of business. Therefore, the more competition there is in our economy, the better we will use our limited resources.

Quality and Variety

Increased competition also leads to higher-quality products with less variation in quality at a given price level. Producers always compare the good qualities of their products to the lack of quality in competitors' products. Consumers, in attempting to have the highest standard of living possible, are not content to buy a lower-quality product when a higher-quality product is available for the same price. All they need to know, either by word of mouth or media advertising, is that the higher-quality product exists somewhere else. The competition to win consumer favor gradually improves quality in the industry as a whole.

Competition, and certainly increased competition, almost invariably leads to a larger variety of goods and services as well. Every potential competitor in a market looks for an area in the marketplace that has not yet been fully exploited. Thus competition forces producers to seek ways to satisfy the specialized demands of consumers. Take the example of automobiles. Ignoring all of the varieties of cars available from the big car makers, consider the specialty car makers. Different manufacturers produce car kits, replicas of antique cars, convertibles, elongated limousines. You may criticize the frivolousness of some of the products in the marketplace, but that is a separate issue. All we can say is that competition leads to more variety because of the attempt to satisfy more demands. We cannot determine, at least not here, whether such demands are valid or in the best interests of society.

Supply, Demand, and Price

THE LAW OF DEMAND

People in business may not always know it, but all of their actions in every market are determined by supply and demand.

Simply put, the **law of demand** states: As the relative price of an item falls, a larger quantity will be bought; as the relative price of an item rises, a smaller quantity will be bought (see Exhibit 2.2). For example, as the price of imported automobiles rises relative to domestic cars, fewer imports will be sold. As the relative price of calculators falls, the quantity demanded will rise.

The law of demand exists because no person has unlimited income. Nobody can ever buy everything that he or she wants to buy. Suppose that you want something very much—so much that you consider it a necessity. If its relative price rises and rises, eventually you will not be

EXHIBIT 2.2 The Law of Demand

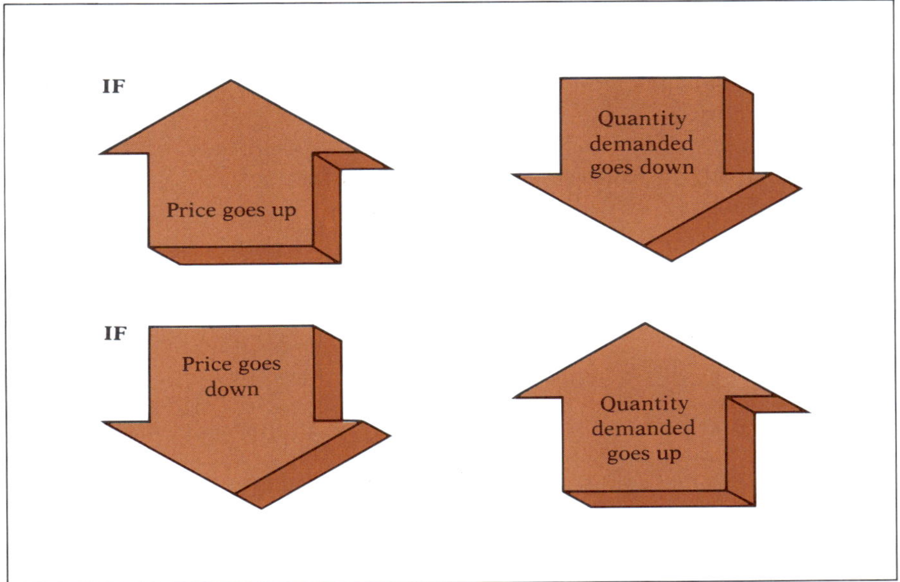

able to keep buying the same quantity, no matter how much you want it. At some point, you would have to reevaluate how much you need it.

For example, suppose that the money you have to spend each week remains the same but that the price of Big Macs keeps rising. There is no way that you can keep buying a Big Mac every day and still buy the same amount of other things. In order to keep eating a higher-priced Big Mac every day, you will have to give up something else. At some point you will no longer be willing to cut back on your purchase of other things. You will cut back on your purchase of Big Macs, perhaps buying one every other day.

THE LAW OF SUPPLY

The law of demand alone is not enough to explain what determines the prices of things that people buy. It states only that people will purchase more at lower prices than they will at higher prices. It does not explain the price for an item or why that price may change. In order to complete the picture, it is necessary to look at the opposite side of demand, the side concerned with the producers or suppliers who provide the things people want to buy.

Assume that you are the owner of all the McDonald's restaurants in a given area. You must have land to build the restaurants on, employees to serve your customers, meat, buns and sauces, grills, refrigerators, and other equipment. You must pay taxes and insurance. And you must pay for the repair and upkeep of each restaurant and all its equipment. But the price you are charging for Big Macs covers all your costs and gives you a profit. According to the law of demand, if you decided to raise the price, the number of hamburgers you sell—and your profits—would fall. But at the higher price, you might be willing to build new stands, hire additional workers, and buy additional equipment. In other words, you could afford to take on any higher costs per hamburger in order to increase the quantity supplied (sold).

This is essentially the **law of supply:** At higher prices, suppliers are willing to supply more than at lower prices. The law of supply applies to entire industries, as well as single suppliers. For example, at a higher relative price for all hamburgers, *potential* operators—that is, those who are operating fast-food restaurants now—might be attracted to the business. At a higher price, they would see the opportunity to make larger profits.

PUTTING DEMAND AND SUPPLY TOGETHER

As the price of a good or service goes down, the quantity demanded rises and the quantity supplied falls. As the price goes up, the reverse is true. Is there a price at which the quantity demanded and the quantity supplied will meet? Yes. The price of any good or service will find a level—the **equilibrium price**—at which the quantity demanded and the quantity supplied are the same. Neither has any tendency to change unless something else changes.

WHAT DETERMINES PRICE?

Supply and demand are important aspects of the economy that affect the prices of things people buy, but prices are not really determined by supply and demand. They are determined by the underlying *forces* that determine supply and demand. On the demand side, those forces include people's tastes, preferences, values, and customs. On the supply side, they include natural resources, the ability to produce, and the costs of production.

On the other hand, the interworkings of supply and demand do not always determine price. Many prices in the economy are fixed by government rules. In some cases, one must distinguish between a legal and an illegal price of a good. If there is a complete ban on some good, such as heroin, there is no legal price. And the illegal price will tend to be quite high given the restrictions on supply and the huge risks involved in selling the product.

The Lack of Competition

Adam Smith once said, "People of the same trade seldom meet together, even for merriment and diversion, but the conversation ends in a conspiracy against the public, or in some contrivance to raise prices."* Adam Smith was referring to a lack of competition in our economy—monopoly.

*Adam Smith, *An Inquiry into the Nature and Causes of the Wealth of Nations* (1776; New York: Modern Library Edition 1937), p. 128.

Highlight The First Monopolists: The Medieval Guild

The medieval guild was probably one of the first examples of monopoly. Guilds developed among craftworkers, probably around the start of the 1200s, and were found in middle-size towns of about 25,000 people. There were many types of guilds, including the Glovers' Guild, the Hatters' Guild, and the Scribners' Guild. Typically, a guild was run by a master or several masters who voluntarily agreed to set up a system of rules that would govern the conduct of other craftworkers and, more importantly, the conduct of anyone attempting to enter that particular craft in that particular town.

Herein lies the restrictive nature of the guilds: To prevent entry into the particular craft in which the guild masters were making money, they required a long apprenticeship for anyone who wanted to become a journeyman (master craftworker). The apprenticeship was ostensibly designed to ensure the adequate training of journeymen, but as an aside, it also prevented them from entering the profession "too" rapidly, hence maintaining the incomes of the guild masters at levels they thought appropriate to their station in life.

The guild masters were essentially establishing themselves as a single seller of a particular type of service and its products. They attempted to prevent competition *within* the guild by specifying, for example, how many threads per inch had to be in a piece of cloth, how the cloth had to be shrunk, how much buttons had to weigh, and what type of production techniques could be used. In fact, in certain places it was necessary for craftworkers to keep their windows open so that passersby could easily see if they were cheating on the guild's production-technique restrictions. Ostensibly, these monitoring techniques were used to establish "standards" and to protect the guild's "good name."

MONOPOLY

When you turn on lights to read, you are using the output of the electric power company in your area. Because there is only one power company for you to buy electricity from, that company is called a **monopoly.** The word *monopoly* comes from the Greek words *monos,* meaning "one" or "single," and *polein,* meaning "to sell."

Most electric power companies are monopolies because an agency of the government has granted them the sole rights to operate in certain geographical areas. You and your friends could not pool your money, buy a small generator, and sell electricity to people in your neighborhood. That would be illegal, because government regulations do not allow it. Furthermore, some monopolies—like first-class mail service—are owned by the government as well as controlled by it.

Although there are many ways to become a monopolist, few work in the long run. In the first place, a monopoly implies that there is little or no competition. Thus there must be some reason why other people are barred from setting up competing companies. These obstacles to competitors are called **barriers to entry.**

One barrier to entry is government regulation. It is impossible to enter the electric utility business where another is already operating, because the government does not permit it. One cannot start a telephone system, because the government will prevent it. The most obvious barriers to entry, therefore, are legal ones.

Another barrier to entry is the cost of getting started—**capital costs.** Setting up an electric power company—building a dam, buying generators, stringing power lines—is so costly that it does not pay to

Highlight How to Get Taken by a Taxicab

One way to attempt to obtain monopoly profits is to foreclose entry into the market by legal means. If a law can be passed that requires a license to be obtained in order to do business in a particular industry, those in the industry prior to the licensing restriction will obtain monopoly profits.

A clear-cut case of the monopoly power of licensing restrictions can be seen in the market for taxi services throughout the United States. In many, if not most, cities a license must be obtained in order to operate a taxi. In New York City this license is called a medallion. Before 1937 in New York, the taxicab industry had free entry. The price of taxi medallions was near zero, since they were given to anyone who wanted to operate a taxi. Little by little, the city began to restrict its issuance of new medallions. And little by little, anyone wishing to buy a medallion from the then-current owner had to pay a higher and higher price to purchase it. As the market price went up, those who had obtained the medallions at a lower price were treated to increases in their net worth. At the beginning of the 1980s, the market price of a medallion was $30,000.

compete with an existing firm. The same is true of telephone service.

Ownership of essential raw materials can also provide a barrier to entry. A classic example is the diamond industry. De Beers Consolidated Mines of South Africa controls the export of 80 percent of all the world's diamond output. An example from the past is the Aluminum Company of America (ALCOA). At the turn of the twentieth century, it controlled almost all of the basic sources of bauxite, the major ore used to produce aluminum. For many years, ALCOA was able to retain its near-monopoly in aluminum because it would not sell bauxite to any potential competitor.

FORMS OF MONOPOLY

When a business has a true monopoly selling a good or service, that business is, by definition, an entire industry. There are few pure monopolies, but there are several less-pure forms of monopoly in the United States today. These less-stringent forms of monopoly have more than one seller of a good or service. Economists call the two most common forms oligopoly, which has only a few sellers, and monopolistic competition, in which many sellers sell slightly different products.

Oligopoly

An **oligopoly** is a market structure characterized by a few firms that depend on one another. The main characteristic of an oligopoly is that any change in one firm's output or price influences the profits and sales of its competitors. One of the most basic observations about an oligopolistic industry is that when one firm changes its prices, others generally follow suit immediately.

There are several obvious oligopolies in the American economy. The automobile industry is dominated by three large corporations—

General Motors, Ford, and Chrysler. Although the steel industry has numerous firms, the four largest account for more than 60 percent of the industry's capacity each year. Exhibit 2.3 lists other industries in which the four largest firms produce 80 percent or more of the total industry output. The firms in all of these industries are oligopolies.

The fact that the four largest companies produce most of an industry's output does not necessarily mean the situation should be changed. In fact, a surprising aspect of the general criticism of oligopolies is that there is often little proof of their harmful effects. To define an industry as oligopolistic says nothing about an *alternative* market structure and what the *costs* of creating such an alternative might involve.

Monopolistic Competition

In the 1920s and 1930s, economists became increasingly dissatisfied with talking only about the extremes of market structure—perfect competition and perfect monopoly. They started to develop theoretical and practical research on some sort of middle ground. The most popular and best-received theory was that of monopolistic competition.

Monopolistic competition is defined as a situation in which a relatively large number of producers offer similar, but slightly different, products. Obvious examples are such brand name items as toothpaste, cosmetics, and gasoline. Each firm within these industries has some special product identity, even though the differences between its products and its competitors' products may indeed be very small.

In monopolistic competition, each producer has such a small part of the industry that it faces neither the total industry demand nor even a *large* part of it, as an oligopolist does. Still, each monopolistic competitor has some control over the price of its product. That control is

EXHIBIT 2.3. Oligopolies

Industry	Percent of industry output produced by four largest firms
Primary aluminum	100%
Passenger cars	99
Locomotives and parts	97
Steam engines and turbines	93
Sewing machines	93
Electric lamps (bulbs)	92
Telephone and telegraph equipment	92
Gypsum products	84
Synthetic fibers	82
Cigarettes	80

Source: United States Senate, Subcommittee on Antitrust and Monopoly Concentration Ratios in the Manufacturing Industry.

slight, however, because many substitutes—other brand name products—are available.

The Social Responsibility of Business

A standard definition of social responsibility is management's consideration in its decision making of social effects in addition to purely economic effects. Most businesses want to be socially responsible, but they are caught in a bind. For one thing, it is very difficult to tell exactly *what* is best for society as a whole. Our society is made up of some 250 million unique individuals. What is good for some may be bad for others.

Suppose you are the head of a major corporation, and you realize that the smokestacks from your factories are polluting the surrounding environment. In order to be socially responsible, you get together with your company managers and tell them to put all of the necessary antipollution equipment on the smokestacks. Your accountant then informs you that if this is done, your costs will rise by 12 percent. Since you are in a highly competitive industry, your profit margin is only 10 percent. You can't raise the price to cover the cost of the new equipment because then you won't be able to sell your product in the competitive market. If you go ahead anyway with your socially responsible ideas of eliminating pollution, you will end up causing the company to take a loss. Will the stockholders in your company be willing to lose money for the sake of what you consider to be socially responsible actions? Will employees be willing to forgo pay increases or even lose their jobs as a result of decreased sales? Will consumers pay a higher price for your product instead of purchasing, let's say, a very similar product from a

lower-priced competitor? It would be naive to expect the answer to any of these questions to be yes.

The term *socially responsible* means different things to different people. As long as we live in a world of scarce resources, any action will have a cost associated with it. The difficult task of a business leader is to decide which actions are worth the cost to society and which groups should pay for such costs. Those who attempt to be too socially responsible may end up going out of business.

DEFINING THE RESPONSIBILITIES OF BUSINESS

In addition to its responsibilities as a whole, business has some responsibilities toward specific groups.

Customers

The customer is supposedly king or queen in America's competitive system. In the long run, the customer holds all of the cards. A business that provides a shoddy product at a high price, using false advertising, will eventually be forced out of business by competition.

But in the shorter run, it is possible for businesses to dupe customers, particularly by using incorrect or fraudulent advertising techniques. Clearly, business does have a social responsibility to minimize situations in which unsuspecting, uninformed customers can be "taken."

Numerous other tenuously legal or quasi-legal sales techniques are considered unethical by reputable businesspeople. For example, bait-and-switch techniques, in which customers are lured into a store by the advertisement of an unreasonably low-priced item and then immediately induced to purchase an item at a much higher price, cannot be considered a part of good business behavior.

In short, the social responsibility of business to customers consists of presenting fair and accurate information on availability, price, quality, and other important attributes of the product or service and providing what was promised when promised and how promised.

Employees

In a highly competitive society, it would seem that competition for employees would prevent socially irresponsible behavior toward them. But again, this is a long-run concept of competition. In the short run, employees, particularly those with insufficient information about job alternatives, may end up bearing the brunt of unethical business behavior.

In many situations, employers cannot make a decision that will satisfy everyone. For example, assume that an employer has decided to promote individuals only on the basis of merit. Should a senior employee who has worked for the firm for twenty years not be promoted simply because a new "whippersnapper" who has worked for the firm for one year can do the job better? This is not an easy situation to comment on, even from afar.

And what about a situation in which an employer knows that spending $1 million to install additional safety equipment will reduce the probability of accidents to workers by 10 percent? Should the equipment automatically be installed? What if installing the equipment raises production costs and hence prices so much that sales fall and workers have to be laid off? A tradeoff may be involved—more safety and fewer workers on the job.

The most we can say about the social responsibility of a business to its employees is that job offers should be explicit, detailed, and complete. People should know what they are getting into before they take a job. Working conditions should enhance the welfare of all workers, including prospective employees. And finally, all employees should understand explicitly the ways in which they can expect to be promoted within the structure of the business organization.

Stockholders

Stockholders are the ultimate claimants to anything left over after a corporation has paid all contractual expenses. Some might say that a business's only responsibility is to maximize the stockholders' rate of return on investment. But even if this were the case, and many do not agree that it is, the corporation should still be expected to present accurate and detailed financial information to its actual and potential stockholders.

How many times have you heard about a land scheme or an oil swindle? Investors have lost literally millions of dollars in such activities by unscrupulous corporations. Financial scandals, however, seem to be fewer today than in the past. Numerous laws restrict the ability of corporations to provide actual or potential investors with fraudulent information. Moreover, a number of government agencies and professional organizations oversee financial ethics in today's business world. Finally, certified public accountants and lawyers working with corporations can now be held liable for misinformation that they knowingly allow to be published.

In short, then, the social responsibility of business to its stockholders is to provide accurate and timely information about its financial affairs.

CONSUMERISM

Until recently, the public and the government were content to allow Adam Smith's famous invisible hand to guide the welfare of the nation. Times have changed, however, and the dictum *caveat emptor*—let the buyer beware—no longer seems appropriate. The age of consumerism is upon us. Heralded by the exposés of Ralph Nader and his Raiders, picked up by presidents and politicians, and furthered by continued popular support, active control of business practices by the government has become a reality in practically every state. Business can no longer assume that it is the buyer's responsibility to find out whether a product is safe or whether advertising has been fair. Now business must make sure that its products are safe. If a business fails in this task, it can now be sued, and its managers and officers can even be put in jail. We are clearly in the age of consumerism, in which consumers actively participate in exposing and rectifying abuses by American businesses.

Consumer Rights

Consumers have recently obtained rights that they have never before enjoyed. In 1962, John Kennedy sent the first consumer-protection program to Congress. In that message, he stated four consumer rights:

- *The right to safety* A protection against goods that are dangerous to life or health
- *The right to be informed* A provision not only for discovering fraud but also for making rational choices
- *The right to choose* A restatement of the need for many firms in a competitive market and for protection by government where such competition no longer exists
- *The right to be heard* A guarantee that consumer interests will be considered when government policy decisions are being made

Several presidents have added other rights. For example, Lyndon Johnson added:

- *The right to a decent environment*

Gerald Ford added:

- *The right to consumer education*

Finally, most consumer representatives would add one more right:

- *The right to reasonable redress for damages incurred when dealing in the marketplace*

Consumer Responsibilities

It would be unfair to list a set of consumer rights without indicating that consumers have responsibilities too. No president has yet come out with a list of them, and probably no two consumer organizations would agree on the same set of responsibilities. Nonetheless, there are some obvious areas of responsibility that most of us would not disagree about:

- A responsibility not to steal

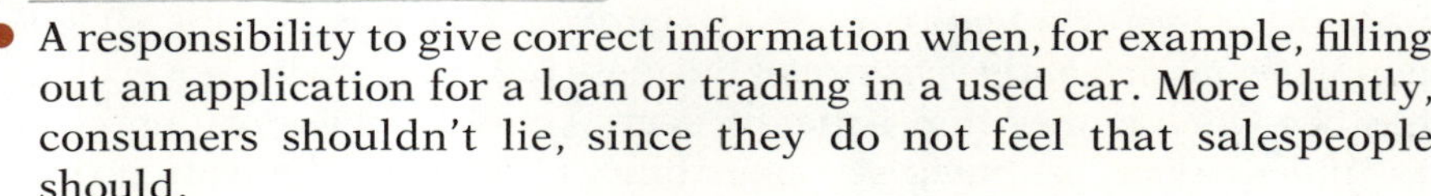

- A responsibility to give correct information when, for example, filling out an application for a loan or trading in a used car. More bluntly, consumers shouldn't lie, since they do not feel that salespeople should.

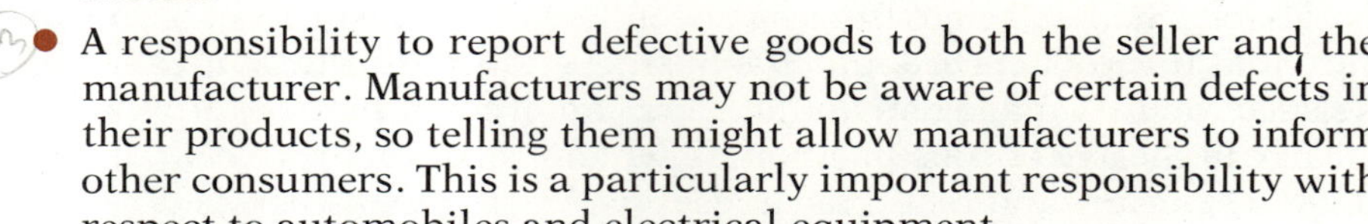

- A responsibility to report defective goods to both the seller and the manufacturer. Manufacturers may not be aware of certain defects in their products, so telling them might allow manufacturers to inform other consumers. This is a particularly important responsibility with respect to automobiles and electrical equipment.
- A responsibility to report wrongs incurred in consumer dealings. These should be reported to appropriate government agencies and to private organizations responsible for monitoring the marketplace.

BUSINESS AND THE ENERGY CRISIS

In the fall of 1973, the United States faced its first energy crisis with the embargo on Persian Gulf oil being sent to this country. Since then we have been subjected to an energy roller coaster. Business, to be sure, acts in a dual role in our continuing energy problem: It suffers from the lack of adequate energy sources (which may exacerbate the unemployment problem because of the resulting plant shutdowns), and business, or at least certain businesses, can be considered a contributor to our energy problem because of its tremendous use of energy.

Prior to 1973, business in America did indeed treat energy as if it were an unending input into the economy's production processes. Electricity and gasoline and oil products were relatively cheap. It is therefore understandable that businesses (and consumers) used more and more energy.

Today, even without an explicit goal of energy conservation, businesses are being forced to find ways to conserve energy in order to keep the prices of their products competitive. To be sure, American businesses have a duty to act consistently with government rules about the use of energy. But even more, American business has a duty to its stockholders and owners to continue to seek lower-cost production techniques as long as they pay off.

THE PUBLIC'S VIEW OF AMERICAN BUSINESS

Monopoly, shoddy products, bribery, high prices—the list of abuses goes on and on. Many people think about American business only in the above terms and do not think about the many good products at reasonable prices that American businesses provide. And the problem is getting worse. In 1968, 70 percent of those surveyed by the firm of Yankelovich, Skelly and White agreed that "business tries to strike a fair balance between profits and the interest of the public." By 1977, only 15 percent agreed. Louis Harris's surveys found that in 1968, 55 percent of those surveyed had "a great deal of confidence in the people in charge of running major companies." By 1977, that figure had dropped to 18 percent.

The public's knowledge about the profitability of the corporate sector probably makes corporate management shudder. A survey done in February 1980 by Opinion Research Corporation of Princeton, New Jersey, determined that the public's estimate of the average manufacturer's *after-tax* profit was 32 percent, up from a 1976 estimate of 29 percent. The public's estimate is six times the actual rate of after-tax profit. According to the same firm, more than half the public believes that business as a whole is making too much profit. Furthermore, 60 percent of the public believes government should put a limit on corporate profits rather than allowing companies, even in industries where there is fierce competition, to make all the profit they can.

What can business do today to improve its image? There is no simple answer. But one of the ways business leaders have attempted to change their image is by establishing business codes.

BUSINESS CODES: ETHICS ABOVE ALL

Specific codes of ethics for various industries have been enacted as guides to ethical behavior. These codes provide a road map for socially responsible business activity. There are three types of business codes:

- Professional codes for occupational groups, such as doctors, dentists, lawyers, and accountants
- Advisory group codes, which government agencies usually propagate.
- Business association codes designed for use by everyone in the same industry.

Let's look at the two most important.

Occupational Codes

Codes of ethics for everyone who engages in the business of medicine, law, accounting, engineering, and dentistry have been around for many years. These codes provide for behavior standards, and members of such occupations usually must abide by them. One word of warning is in order, however. Numerous research studies have shown that many aspects of such ethical codes are included to eliminate or restrict competition among members of a given profession. The longstanding, but now defunct, ethical code against advertising in the legal profession was shown to be a rather adroit ploy to prevent young lawyers from competing with established lawyers who already had reputations and many referrals. The same can be said for the strictures against advertising in medicine, pharmaceuticals, and optometry. Indeed, studies have shown

Highlight Bribery: Doing Business Abroad

A few years ago, when the huge Lockheed Aircraft payoffs to foreign officials were uncovered, many Americans were shocked. It appeared that American corporations were engaged in the seedy business of bribing public officials in order to get business. However, in some countries and in some types of business, firms are expected to bribe foreign officials in charge of granting large contracts. If the U.S. government is effective in preventing American companies from competing in this manner, companies in other countries will be able to get more business by continuing to engage in payoffs. In some respects, a bribe to a foreign official in order to obtain a license, the right to deal, a large contract, or any other "favor" is not so different from a Christmas present to a company's best domestic customers.

that when advertising is not allowed, the prices of products and services are invariably higher than when advertising is allowed.*

Business Codes

As we pointed out above, many specific industries have their own codes of ethics. In addition, the Better Business Bureau and the Chamber of Commerce attempt to improve the ethics and public image of business.

The National Better Business Bureau, established in 1916, now has local affiliates in all major cities and counties. The Better Business Bureau has a multiple purpose:

- To provide consumers with information on products and selling practices
- To provide businesspeople with a source of local standards for acceptable business practices
- To provide a technique for mediating grievances between consumers and sellers

Because the Better Business Bureau has no enforcement powers, all of its actions must be voluntary. And because the Better Business Bureau depends on the business community for its membership, it cannot afford to put any more pressure on those in business than it puts on consumers. The weaknesses in the voluntary system were felt most strongly when the consumer movement began to press for protection against not only fly-by-night, illegal, fraudulent firms but also marketing practices generally accepted by the business community. When consumers began to seek redress for damages suffered from exaggerated advertising, ineffective warranties and guarantees, safety hazards, and poor choices, the private business organization was unable to police its members effectively.

But the Better Business Bureau has survived, and it continues to

*Lee Benham, "The Effect of Advertising on the Price of Eyeglasses," *Journal of Law and Economics* 4 (October 1972):337–352.

thrive as it seeks to improve communication with consumers. For example, the Better Business Bureau's arbitration program has been expanding. It is now attempting to deal more effectively with the issue of consumer redress for grievances against sellers and producers of goods and services.

FREE ENTERPRISE VERSUS SOCIAL RESPONSIBILITY

You might get the impression after reading this chapter that there is a basic antagonism between the precepts of free enterprise and the notion of social responsibility. There is indeed a contradiction between unfettered competition and what we believe is necessary for ethical business behavior today. We no longer live in a world in which business can do as it pleases. Business now has an increased awareness of its ethical responsibilities, which is clearly a step in the right direction. Business codes, although often self-serving, nonetheless provide guidelines for how business must act in today's world.

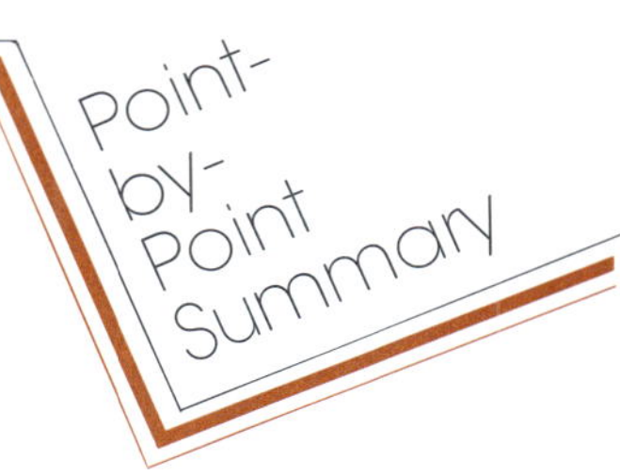

- Profit is the difference between total costs and total revenues and thus the difference between the value that consumers place on products and the costs that suppliers incur.
- Profits are the rate of return to entrepreneurs for taking risk and must be expressed as the annual rate of return on investment, in percentage terms. Absolute profits, to be comparable to previous years, must be corrected for inflation.
- Capitalism is an economic system in which private individuals own the productive resources of society and have the right to use those resources in whatever manner they choose, within the limits of the law. In contrast, socialism concentrates ownership of the major productive resources in the hands of the state.
- The law of demand, simply stated, is that there is an inverse relationship between quantity demanded and relative price.
- Demand is a function of income. As income goes up, the demand for most products also goes up.
- The law of supply, simply stated, is that quantity supplied and relative price are directly related.
- At the equilibrium price for a product or service, quantity supplied equals quantity demanded. Any shocks moving this price away from its equilibrium will be met with countervailing forces pushing it back to equilibrium.
- In the real world, there are several market structures that involve less-than-perfect competition: pure monopoly, in which there is a

single seller; oligopoly, in which there are a couple of sellers; and monopolistic competition, in which there are many sellers, each with a specific monopolistic product trade, such as a brand name.

- Businesses do have a social responsibility, but defining that responsibility is extremely difficult because of tradeoffs. Some actions help certain members of society but hurt others.
- One way that business leaders have attempted to change the image of business in America is through the promulgation of codes of ethics, which may take the form of professional codes, advisory group codes, or business codes.
- Unfortunately, professional codes have served, in many instances, simply to restrict competition within the occupation.

Questions for Review

1. Every quarter (every three months), the profits of America's largest corporations are reported in the press. Typically, a statement like the following will appear: "Oil company profits leap 42 percent." How would you analyze newspaper reports of increases in corporate profits in a dispassionate, scientific manner? How would you decide, if you were an investor, whether your corporation was yielding a satisfactory rate of return?
2. Imagine yourself in a world where profits were illegal. How would resources be allocated? Is there any way that people could be rewarded for taking risk in such a world?
3. What is the difference between pure capitalism and capitalism as it exists in the United States today?
4. Imagine you are Adam Smith. You seek a limited role for government in a capitalistic system. Nonetheless, you know that government is necessary. Make a list of what you would consider the basic roles of government.
5. How are resources allocated in a socialistic system?
6. "The higher I charge, the more money I make." Do you think this businessperson understands the law of demand? Why or why not?
7. When is your body weight in equilibrium? How can you relate the concept of body weight equilibrium to the concept of an equilibrium price?
8. List the ways to become a monopolist. Which way seems to be the easiest and most certain?
9. What is the difference between oligopoly and monopolistic competition? Would you rather be an oligopolist or a monopolistic competitor?
10. How would you define the social responsibility of businesses toward customers?
11. Is it ever true that a socially responsible action by a businessperson can harm certain members of society? Give an example.

Business in Action

PORTFOLIO I: THE ENVIRONMENT OF BUSINESS

NEW HOLLAND

TR85

NEW HOLLAND

NEW HOLLAND

COMMITTEE ON
GOVERNMENT
REGULATIONS

APPLICATION

General Dynamics Corporation

Tomahawk ground-launched cruise missile test.

Aerospace systems, marine systems, telecommunications and electronic systems, data systems. They are all part of General Dynamics, which is perhaps the epitome of a wide-ranging corporation built on the fundamentals of capitalism that also relies on government as a major source of revenue for its products. A study of General Dynamics will also show how a small group of individuals could form a company that would later grow to over $3 billion in annual sales.

HOW IT ALL STARTED

In 1899—before Kitty Hawk, before the Model A, and before the technological boom in America—a group of engineers and scientists began exploring new marine products at a firm called the Electric Boat Company. In 1900, that company delivered its first submarine to the U.S. Navy.

On April 24, 1952, General Dynamics Corporation was created as a successor to the Electric Boat Company. At that time there were three divisions—Electric Boat, Electrodynamic, and a subsidiary, Canadaire, Ltd. Three years later, the General Atomic Division became an operating unit. Today the company has fifteen operating units, many of them the result of mergers with formerly independent corporations.

DIVISIONS OF GENERAL DYNAMICS

A few of General Dynamics' operating units are described in detail here; the rest are listed in Exhibit 2.4.

The Stromberg-Carlson Corporation

This division is headquartered in Rochester, New York and operates out of San Diego. It was once a separate entity, formed in 1894 in Chicago. In the 1920s, it established itself as a radio producer, and then it entered the radio, phonograph, and high-fidelity fields. In June 1955, the Stromberg-Carlson Company became the Stromberg-Carlson Corporation of General Dynamics.

During the 1950s, the Stromberg-Carlson Division continued its work in telecommunications, intercommunication systems, and electronics for defense. It remains one of the leaders in telephone switching equipment and is also a large manufacturer of telephones for both offices and residences.

The Electric Boat Division

The predecessor of General Dynamics built the first U.S. submarine, the USS *Holland*. It also built the first nuclear-powered submarines. One of them, the *Nautilus*, made the first transpolar underwater cruise from the Pacific to the Atlantic. The *Skate* twice navigated submerged over the North Pole, and the *Seawolf* set an underwater endurance record, remaining completely independent of the atmosphere for sixty consecutive days. In the 1970s, the division worked on the *Ohio*, the first of the huge Trident ballistic missile submarines.

One of the oldest of General Dynamics' units was Electrodynamic, which became part of the Electric Boat Division. Electrodynamic made the motors for nuclear-powered submarines. It also made motors for luxury liners in the 1950s and 1960s.

Building Products and Resources

One of the major areas of General Dynamics' expansion has been into building products and resources. It has three companies in Chicago: Material Service Corporation, Marblehead Lime Company, and Freeman United Coal Mining Company. Material Service is the Chicago area's largest supplier of concrete and concrete pipe used in construction and road building. The Marblehead Lime Company is the largest lime producer in the United States, operating six plants. It sells most of its lime to the American steel industry, which uses over 80 percent of Marblehead's 2- to 3-million-ton annual production. Plants are located to serve the steel market. The Freeman United Coal Mining Company has four underground and two surface mines in Illinois. In a normal year it produces between 7 and 8 million tons of coal. General Dynamics considers Freeman of extreme importance because of the long-range energy needs of this country.

THE GROWTH OF GENERAL DYNAMICS

General Dynamics is a company that grows as it needs to grow. When something becomes too big to handle on a piecemeal basis, a

EXHIBIT 2.4 Other Divisions of General Dynamics

Division	Product
Convair	space vehicles, aircraft and missiles
Fort Worth	military planes
Pomona	tactical missiles and weapons systems
Electronics	automatic test equipment and tactical data and range systems
General Dynamics Communication Company	nonutility telecommunications
DatagraphiX, Inc.	computer output and microfilm
American Telecommunications Corporation	telecommunications equipment
Asbestos Corporation Ltd.	high-grade long fiber asbestos

new division or subsidiary is started. This was clearly the case with Data Systems Services. In addition, when the corporation sees an area where demand is growing, it does not hesitate to start a new division or to acquire another company to serve that demand. Its decisions to enter the building products and resources areas and additional electronic and data-processing areas were based on such a perception. Management also seems to have a distinct desire to rely less on government contracts.

CAREER OPPORTUNITIES

General Dynamics is a big company, with fifteen operating units and more than a hundred branches and offices across North America and overseas. Somewhere between 80,000 and 90,000 people are working for the company at present. The management of General Dynamics talks in terms of "broad corporate career paths for anyone being well-trained in business systems and management techniques."

There are entry-level jobs in all fifteen units of General Dynamics. A business student might enter the corporation in

- Accounting/finance (all divisions except American Telecommunications Corporation)
- Business/economics (all divisions except American Telecommunications Corporation)
- Computer science (eight divisions)
- Operations research (seven divisions)
- Sales marketing (Stromberg-Carlson Corporation, General Dynamics Communications Company, and DatagraphiX, Inc.)

Students with an Associate of Arts or an Associate of Science degree (two-year degrees) will find numerous entry-level jobs at General Dynamics in computer sciences and sales marketing. In particular, the graduate with an A.S. degree in computer science who has taken numerous business and economics courses will find quite a few job opportunities at General Dynamics.

FOR DISCUSSION

1. How can a company like General Dynamics simultaneously be built on the fundamentals of capitalism but rely so heavily on the government as a major source of revenue?
2. Why would a company with so many divisions have them scattered throughout the United States? Wouldn't it be cheaper to run the company if the divisions were in one location?
3. Which divisions of General Dynamics do you believe will grow the fastest in the 1980s?

OBJECTIVES

- ☐ To distinguish among sole proprietorships, partnerships, and corporations
- ☐ To understand the advantages and disadvantages of these three most common forms of business organization
- ☐ To understand the definition, use, and limitations of limited partnerships
- ☐ To explain how a corporation is formed and organized
- ☐ To understand the benefits of Subchapter S corporations and closely held corporations
- ☐ To understand the costs and benefits of forming a closely held corporation
- ☐ To distinguish between vertical and horizontal mergers

OUTLINE

KEY TERMS

ARTICLES OF INCORPORATION
BOARD OF DIRECTORS
CHARTER OF INCORPORATION
CLOSELY HELD CORPORATION
COMMON STOCK
CORPORATION
FRANCHISE
FRINGE BENEFITS
HORIZONTAL INTEGRATION
LIABILITY
LIMITED PARTNERSHIP
MERGER
MONEY CAPITAL
PARTNERSHIP
SHORT-TERM WORKING CAPITAL
SOLE PROPRIETORSHIP
SUBCHAPTER S CORPORATION
VERTICAL INTEGRATION

TYPES OF BUSINESS ORGANIZATION

Facts on Federal Chartering

Wall Street Journal, September 28, 1978.

For some years now there has been a movement afoot for federal chartering of corporations. Ralph Nader has contributed public visibility to the movement, and men such as the former chairman of the SEC, William L. Cary, have contributed respectability. Part of their argument is that the existing competition among states for corporate charters results in a "race for the bottom," a race that is won by supplying charters that inadequately protect stockholders. Delaware has been singled out as leading a "movement towards the least common denominator." Its liberal corporate code allegedly attracts managements by allowing them to expropriate stockholder wealth and explains the predominance of Delaware in the market for corporate charters.

Until now proponents of federal chartering have faced two main problems. One is that the clamor for federal chartering has not come from investors. The suspicion naturally grew that its proponents were primarily engaged in creating certain impressions about management as a basis for another federal power grab. The other is the remarkable study by Professors Michael Jensen and William Meckling at the University of Rochester. They concluded that the main threats to stockholders' wealth are federal laws and rules that diminish the value of securities by reducing the property rights of the owners. In this context federal chartering was like suggesting that the fox guard the chicken house.

Now advocates of federal chartering face a third problem—an empirical one. In a study for the Managerial Economics Research Center at the University of Rochester, Peter Dodd and Richard Leftwich tested the claim that competition among states for corporate charters results in a reduction of stockholders' wealth. If managers seek out weak state charters for the purpose of reducing stockholder protection, the price of the stock will drop when the decision to reincorporate is announced and people take into account the increase in the expected cost of management's expropriation.

Dodd and Leftwich examined reincorporations of New York Stock Exchange firms during the 1927–77 period, including 242 switches to Delaware, and found that when the decision to reincorporate was announced, the price of the stocks rose. They conclude: "The evidence presented here lends no support to the arguments that stockholders are harmed by management's choice of state of incorporation. In fact, when managements initiate a change in state of incorporation to a more permissive state, such as Delaware, stockholders earn abnormal positive returns."

Dodd and Leftwich propose an alternative hypothesis to explain management decisions to change the state of incorporation, one that is consistent with the empirical evidence that it actually tends to increase share values. In chartering decisions as in plant location decisions, managements seek to reduce the expected costs of the firm's production, investment and financing activities. The attraction of Delaware may lie less in the charter and more in the reduction of uncertainty that is the product of the long history of established precedents and predictable rulings of the Delaware judiciary.

Empirical science has a way of disarming rhetoric. Now that the debate has been moved to the empirical level, perhaps it will become clear whether the central purpose of federal chartering is to protect stockholders against management, or to require that managements pay more attention to the effects of their decisions on "outside constituencies" and less on profits for stockholders.

Who should run corporations is not a trivial question. As this article indicates, Ralph Nader believes that the federal government should be in charge of legally chartering corporations. In this chapter, we will look at how corporations are formed today and compare their structure with other legal forms of business.

Suppose that you have been tinkering with electronic equipment since the age of seven. By now you can take apart and reassemble radios and television sets without difficulty. In fact, you are so good at repairing electronic equipment that you have been fixing your friends' portable radios and old television sets. An idea comes to you: Why not make some money? Why not do electronic repairs for other people and charge for your work? Why not start a business?

Starting a Business

To start a business, you need to make potential customers aware that your services are available for a fee. One way to do this is by word of mouth. That is, you tell your friends and relatives, who tell their friends that you are in the repair business. Another way to make your business known is to have business cards printed and distribute them in the area. Yet another way is to buy advertising space in the local newspaper. A three- or four-line advertisement in the classified section would probably cost no more than a few dollars a week. You can also run what is called a space ad in a nonclassified section of the paper, but that costs more. Once you get customers, information about your business will spread if they are satisfied with your work.

BUYING EQUIPMENT

As your number of customers increases, you may want to buy more sophisticated equipment to handle more complex problems and to do work faster. To buy new equipment, you will need money. Perhaps your parents or a friend will lend you **money capital**—the cash you need to buy equipment to increase the income you earn from your business.

You will also need replacement parts. At first, you might buy parts as you need them for a specific job. But if you need certain parts for many jobs, you may want to have a supply of them on hand so that you do not have to go to a supply shop for each job. When you have inventory, you have money tied up in it. Of course, your customers will repay you for the parts as you use them.

Sometimes you may find you need major parts for a repair job. These parts may take more capital than you have on hand, and so you might face the problem of obtaining **short-term working capital**—the money you need only until you have finished the job and the customer has paid. If you had a well-established business, you might get a bank loan. You could also ask the customer to pay in advance, but this might not be convenient for the customer. In addition, most of the other electronic repair shops in the area probably do not require prepayment for major repairs. For you to do so would put you at a competitive disadvantage. Hence, you look for short-term working capital from whomever will loan it to you. Some friend might agree to do so if you are willing to pay him or her interest. Obviously, the cost of borrowing is a business expense.

KEEPING RECORDS

From the start of your business, you need to keep records. You need to know how much money you are making and how much you may owe in taxes. Of course, you may not be making enough profit to owe taxes. Nevertheless, you need a record of all of your expenses and receipts. Basically, your profit is the difference between your expenses and receipts.*

TAKING RISKS

As a businessperson, you are taking many risks. For example, if you spend part of your savings to pay for advertising and equipment, you are risking money. You may not get sufficient business to cover these costs. Whenever you buy inventory, you are taking a risk. Your business could drop off so that you never use the parts, and you could be forced to sell them at a loss. Whenever you buy a major part for a repair job, you are running a risk that your customer may refuse to pay the bill. Even if you are left with a radio or television set, you may not be able to sell it for enough money to cover your costs.

You are even taking a risk with the time you spend to set up the business. It takes time to think about what to do, write the ads, set up the bookkeeping. That time has a value. You could have used it to do something else, including working for someone else for a wage.

Note that if you work for somebody else, essentially you take only the risk of not being paid. As a worker, you take little risk. As an entrepreneur (a businessperson), you take many risks. However, you expect to make a profit as a reward for taking them.

Sole Proprietorships

The business we have just described is the oldest, most basic, and most common type of business organization. A **sole proprietorship,** also called an individual proprietorship, is a business owned by one person. Today there are more than 10 million sole proprietorships in the United States. You may know of hundreds in your area—beauty parlors, fruitstands, repair shops, drugstores, hobby shops, liquor stores. Many doctors, dentists, lawyers, and accountants also practice as sole proprietors.

There are many advantages to operating a sole proprietorship, including the following:

1. *Control over all profits* As sole owner, the proprietor gets all of the profits, because he or she takes all of the risks.
2. *Pride of ownership* A person who is his or her own boss and makes the business whatever it is can take full pride in owning it.

*Actually, not all of the difference is profit. After all, your time is worth something. You could be working for somebody else and making income. Therefore, you should pay yourself a wage equal to what you could earn elsewhere. This can be counted as part of the cost of doing business. If you add it to your other expenses and subtract the total from receipts, you get a truer measure of what economists call (economic) profit.

3. *Ease of starting the business* Since the proprietor makes all decisions, starting a proprietorship is less difficult than types of businesses that require agreement with other people.
4. *Freedom from corporate income taxes* A proprietor does not pay corporate income taxes. Of course, he or she does have to pay personal income taxes on profits, but these taxes may be lower than those for a different type of business organization.

Obviously, a proprietorship has disadvantages as well. They must be less important than the advantages, however, or proprietorships would not be so widespread in the United States.

1. *Responsibility for all losses* As sole owner, the proprietor bears the risk of all losses.
2. *Limited capital* The proprietor is limited by his or her own funds and those that others will lend. This is perhaps the greatest disadvantage. It is very difficult for a business to grow with little capital.
3. *Unlimited liability* The proprietor has **liability,** or legal responsibility, for all debts and damages incurred in doing business. For example, if the proprietor of a repair service wired a television set incorrectly and it blew up, he or she could be held responsible and sued for damages. If someone were injured, the legal responsibility might extend to all of the proprietor's personal wealth.

Partnerships

Let us now suppose that your repair business is doing very well. You find that you do not have time to see your friends or go to the movies. You have several choices. You could refuse to take on more business. You could discourage business by charging higher prices. Or you could expand your business. One way to expand is to take on a partner (or hire an employee). If you also want to buy more sophisticated equipment, you should look for somebody whose skills complement yours and who has money to put into business expansion. When you find this person, you can make a proposal to share ownership of the business. That is, you offer to form a partnership.

A **partnership,** or general partnership, is any business that two or more individuals own and operate for profit. A written agreement is usually drawn up when a partnership is formed. You probably know of numerous partnerships in your area. Many lawyers, doctors, and dentists, as well as small retail stores, are partnerships.

Partnerships are formed because they offer advantages not found in a sole proprietorship:

1. *More capital* A partnership combines the capital of two or more people and thus makes more money available to operate a larger and perhaps more profitable business. If each partner has a good credit rating, a partnership can generally borrow more money than a sole proprietorship.

2. *Greater efficiency* Each partner can specialize in certain aspects of the business, thereby making it more efficient.

A partnership also has disadvantages:

1. *Unlimited liability* Complete legal responsibility is a major disadvantage in a sole proprietorship. As a partner, however, one is responsible for the debts of other partners as well as his or her own.
2. *Shared profits* Obviously, since partners share the risks of the business, they also share the profits. But in many situations, one partner may feel that he or she has contributed more than the other.
3. *Possible disagreement* Disagreements about necessary decisions can lead to severe problems in running the business. Often such disagreements prevent any decision, causing the business to miss a very profitable opportunity.

Limited Partnerships

A special form of partnership is the **limited partnership,** which permits someone to invest in a business without responsibility for management and without liability for losses beyond the initial investment. The limited partner does have the right to share in the profits, however.

The creation of a limited partnership is a public and formal proceeding that must follow requirements set forth by law. Contrast this with the informal, private, and voluntary agreement that usually suffices for a general partnership. In forming a limited partnership, two or more partners must sign a certificate setting forth the following information:

- Company name
- Character of the business
- Location of the principal place of business
- Name and place of residence of each member
- Duration of the partnership
- Amount of cash and agreed-on valuation of any other property contributed by each limited partner
- Share of profits or other compensation that each limited partner is entitled to receive

See Exhibit 3.1 for a sample certificate of limited partnership.

Limited partnerships have largely become popular because of high federal income-tax rates, particularly on corporations. Limited partners can deduct expenses or losses from other income and still be protected from personal liability. Although limited partnerships were originally conceived to accommodate only a few limited partners, there have been limited partnerships that assemble hundreds of them.

EXHIBIT 3.1 A Sample Certificate of Formation of a Limited Partnership

The undersigned, being desirous of forming a limited partnership under the Act of ________, entitled "The Uniform Limited Partnership Act", hereby make and sign the following certificate for that purpose:

I. The name under which the partnership is to be conducted is "Sunnyside Dairy Company."

II. The purpose of the partnership shall be to engage in the general dairy business, together with all other business necessary and related thereto, including the purchase, processing, manufacture, sale, and distribution of milk, cream, and other products which may conveniently be handled with such products.

III. The location of the partnership's principal place of business is ________.

IV. The names and places of residence of the general and limited partners are:

John Smith	General Partner	[*Address*]
Harold Jones	General Partner	[*Address*]
Frank Brown	Limited Partner	[*Address*]
George Green	Limited Partner	[*Address*]

V. The partnership shall continue for an indefinite term.

VI. The limited partners have contributed the following cash to the partnership:

Frank Brown	$10,000
George Green	$10,000

VII. Each limited partner may make any additional contributions to the capital of the partnership as may from time to time be agreed upon by the general partners.

VIII. Each limited partner may make those withdrawals from his capital account as may from time to time be agreed upon by the general partners.

IX. By reason of their contributions the limited partners shall receive the following percentages of the net profits of the partnership:

Frank Brown	10 percent
George Green	10 percent

X. In the event of the retirement, death, or insanity of a general partner, the remaining partners shall have the right to continue the business of the partnership under the same name by themselves, or in conjunction with any other person or persons they may select.

IN WITNESS WHEREOF, we have hereunto set our hands and seals this ________ day of ________, 1965.

________________ [*Seal*]
General Partner

________________ [*Seal*]
General Partner

________________ [*Seal*]
Limited Partner

________________ [*Seal*]
Limited Partner

Other Forms of Business Organization

There are several other forms of business organization, but space allows detailed discussion of only one—corporations. Among the others, one of the most common is the cooperative, which is owned by members who share the profits. Perhaps the most popular cooperatives are those made up of consumers or farmers.

Government-owned and government-operated corporations are another type. They include the postal service and many public utility companies (water, gas, and electric).

Corporations

In terms of the volume of business transacted in the United States today, by far the most important type of business operation is the corporation. Corporations provide most of the goods that people buy. Although they constitute only 10 to 12 percent of all business firms, they collect almost 75 percent of all business receipts.

The corporate form made possible large-scale business. It was a key to the development of American industry and to America's growth as the most industrial nation in the world. In fact, some corporations are larger than the economies of many nations. Exhibit 3.2 lists the ten largest industrial corporations in the United States.

A **corporation** is an artificial being with a distinct existence separate from the human beings who control it. That is, it enjoys many of the same legal powers, such as the rights to buy and sell property, enter into contracts, and sue or be sued. In other words, it is a legal entity.

FORMING A CORPORATION

Let's suppose your repair business has grown until you have several partners and have converted your garage into a workshop. Now you would like to rent a store to make your business more visible. You would like to buy the latest automated repair equipment, charge a little

EXHIBIT 3.2 The Top Ten Industrial Corporations (Ranked by Sales)

Rank '79	Rank '78	Company	Sales ($000)	Assets ($000)	Assets Rank	Employees Number	Employees Rank
1	2	Exxon (New York)	79,106,471	49,489,964	1	169,096	9
2	1	General Motors (Detroit)	66,311,200	32,215,800	2	853,000	1
3	4	Mobil (New York)	44,720,908	27,505,756	3	213,500	6
4	3	Ford Motor (Dearborn, Mich.)	43,513,700	23,524,600	5	494,579	2
5	5	Texaco (Harrison, N.Y.)	38,350,370	22,991,955	6	65,814	50
6	6	Standard Oil of California (San Francisco)	29,947,554	18,102,632	7	39,676	113
7	9	Gulf Oil (Pittsburgh)	23,910,000	17,265,000	8	57,600	63
8	7	International Business Machines (Armonk, N.Y.)	22,862,776	24,529,974	4	337,119	5
9	8	General Electric (Fairfield, Conn.)	22,460,600	16,644,500	10	405,000	3
10	12	Standard Oil (Ind.) (Chicago)	18,610,347	17,149,899	9	52,282	75

Source: *Fortune* May 5, 1980 p. 276.

less than similar business, and capture a larger share of the market. But you do not have the capital to do all of these things.

What you want are financial backers who will let you use their money and not bother you about how you run the business. You do not want more partners, because then you would have to consult with them about every detail of the business. If you form a corporation, you can sell shares of stock in the business to raise capital. The shares represent ownership rights to a certain proportion of the corporation's profits.

Before you start a corporation, you must do two things. First, you must *register the corporation* according to state and federal laws. (Most state laws are similar, although they vary according to the type of corporation being formed.) Usually a lawyer draws up the **articles of incorporation,** which state the name, address, and purpose of the corporation; the names and addresses of the initial board of directors; the number of directors; and the amount of capital to be put into the corporation (see Exhibit 3.3). The articles of incorporation and an application for a certificate or **charter of incorporation** are sent to the appropriate state or federal agency. If the articles comply with the laws, a charter will be granted.

The second thing you must do is *choose a board of directors.* Every corporation must be controlled by a **board of directors** that is elected by the stockholders, the people who own the corporation. Although they are responsible for supervising and controlling the corporation, the directors do not generally perform daily business operations. Rather, the board selects company officers—a president, vice president(s), secretary, and treasurer—to run the business. Exhibit 3.4 shows how a typical major corporation is organized.

Once you have registered the corporation and chosen its directors, you can raise capital by selling stock. Basically, shares of stock represent ownership rights to the profits of the corporation. You would probably sell shares of **common stock** in your new corporation. If it became large, you might find that its stock would be traded in a local over-the-counter stock market and listed in the local newspapers. Should it continue to grow, it would be traded on a regional exchange and might eventually be traded on one of the national exchanges. (Chapter 17 describes in more detail the types of stocks and stock markets.)

Selling stock is not the only way for your corporation to raise capital to develop or expand. You could also sell debt—that is, issue bonds. You could also reinvest some (or all) of the profits in the business rather than distribute them among the stockholders.

PROS AND CONS OF CORPORATIONS

There are four major advantages to the corporate form of business:

1. *Greater capital* A corporation can raise more capital than either a sole proprietorship or a partnership because of the stockholders' limited risk.
2. *Limited liability* Many people consider this the major advantage of

EXHIBIT 3.3 A Sample Articles of Incorporation

ARTICLES OF INCORPORATION

OF

____
(name of corporation)

We, the undersigned, of full age, for the purpose of forming a corporation under and pursuant to the provisions of Chapter 301 Minn. Statutes, known as the Minnesota Business Corporation Act, and laws amendatory thereof and supplementary thereto, do hereby associate ourselves as a body corporate and adopt the following Articles of Incorporation:

ARTICLE I

The name of this corporation is: ________________________________

____

Note: The corporate name must end with "Incorporated," "Inc." or "Corporation" or contain "Company" or "Co." not immediately preceded by "and" or "&."

ARTICLE II

The purposes of this corporation are: ________________________________

____

____

____

____

ARTICLE III

The period of duration of corporate existence of this corporation shall be:

____

Note: The duration may be perpetual or for a specified period of time.

ARTICLE IV

The location of the registered office of this corporation in this state is:

____

Note: Give street or post office address, city or town, county and zipcode number.

ARTICLE V

The amount of stated capital with which this corporation will begin business is:

____

Note: The stated capital must be at least $1000.

ARTICLE VI

The total authorized number of shares of par value is: ____________________

and the par value of each share is: ______________________________

The total authorized number of shares without par value is: ________________

____

ARTICLE VIII

The description of the classes of shares, the number of shares in each class, and the relative rights, voting power, preferences and restrictions are as follows: ____________________

____

the corporate form of business. If a corporation goes bankrupt or is sued, stockholders generally cannot be asked to pay more than the value of their stock, and they pay by having the market value of their stock reduced or eliminated.

3. *Unlimited life* When the principals in a sole proprietorship or partnership die, their business ceases to exist. A corporation, however, can exist as long as it remains profitable. The life of the corporation is not affected by the death of its owners, because the shares are transferable.

EXHIBIT 3.4 Organization Chart for General Motors Corporation

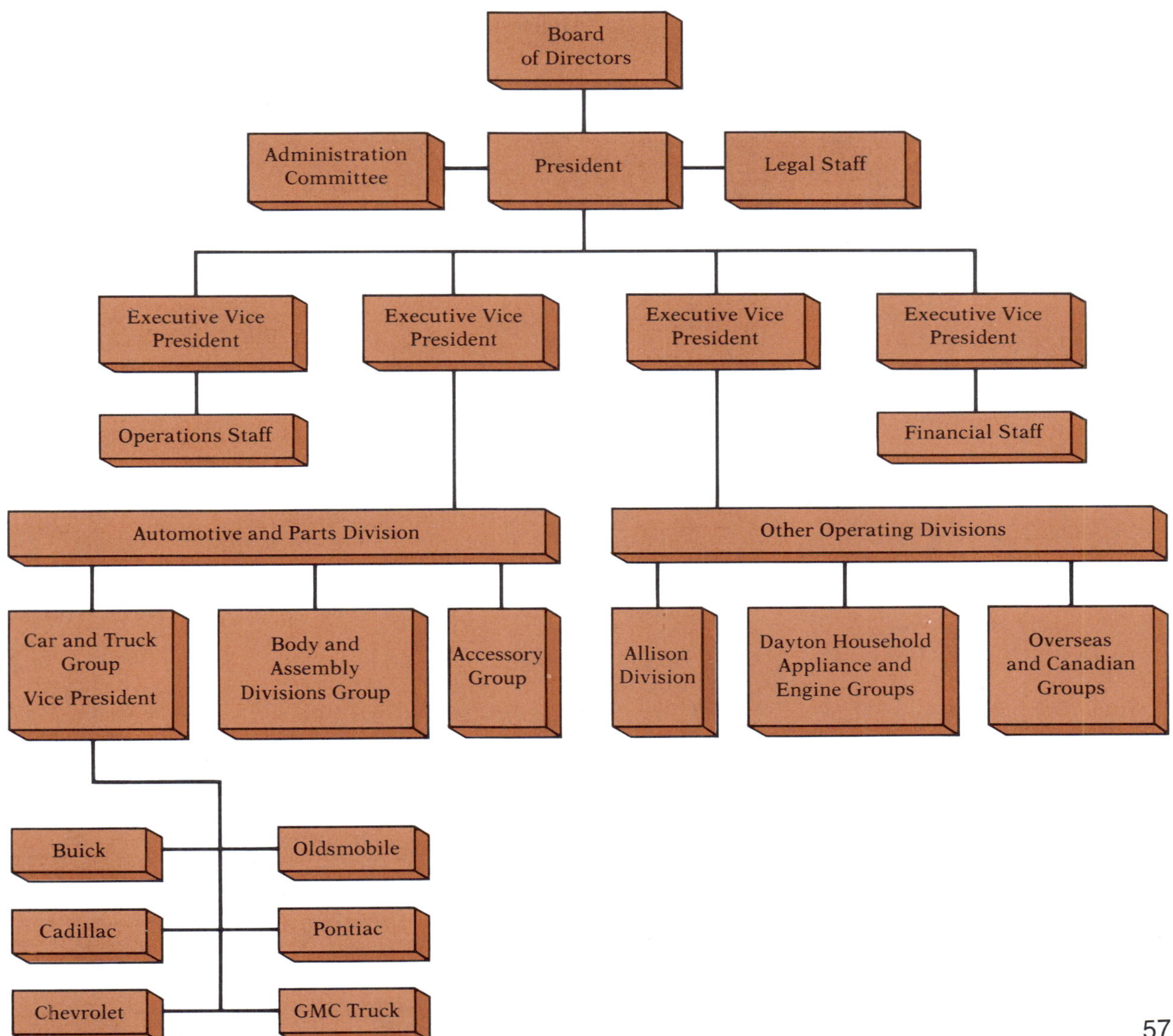

4. *Specialized and professional management* Corporations, because of their size, can hire professional managers to run them. Most smaller sole proprietorships and partnerships have to use generalized management personnel.

The corporate form of business has two chief disadvantages:

1. *Increased taxes* The federal income tax on corporations, a problem that proprietorships and partnerships do not face, is levied on the profits of all corporations. In addition, some states and localities tax corporation profits or property. A state may also tax a corporation for the right to carry on business within its boundaries. Exhibit 3.5 compares the tax liabilities of partnerships and corporations.
2. *Increased government control* Since corporations are chartered by

EXHIBIT 3.5 Tax Considerations in Partnerships and Corporations

Tax Aspect	Partnership	Corporation
1. Federal Income Tax	Partner is taxed on proportionate share of partnership income, even if not distributed; the partnership files information returns only.	Income of the corporation is taxed; stockholders are also taxed on distributed dividends. Must file corporate income tax forms.
2. Accumulation	Partners taxed on accumulated as well as distributed earnings.	Corporate stockholders not taxed on accumulated earnings. There is, however, a penalty tax, in some instances, that the corporation must pay for accumulations of income.
3. Capital Gains And Losses	All partners taxed on their proportionate share of capital gains and losses.	Corporation taxed on capital gains and losses. There is no special deduction to reduce taxes for any excess of long-term gains over short-term losses, but there is a special rate.
4. Exempt Interest	Partners are not taxed on exempt interest received from the firm.	Any exempt interest distributed by a corporation is fully taxable income to the stockholders. Exempt interest can come, for example, from municipal bonds.
5. Pension Plan	Partners are not eligible for an exempt pension trust. The firm cannot deduct payments for partners except under what is called a Keogh Plan.	Employees and officers who are also stockholders can be beneficiaries of a pension trust. The corporation can deduct its payments to the trust.
6. Social Security	Partners do not pay social security tax, but often must pay a self-employment tax.	All compensation to officers and employee stockholders subject to social security taxation up to the maximum.
7. Death Benefits (excluding those provided by insurance)	There is no exemption for payments to partners' beneficiaries.	Benefits up to $5,000 can be received tax free by stockholders' and employees' beneficiaries.
8. State Taxes	In many states, the partnership is not subject to state income taxes.	The corporation is subject to state income taxes (although these taxes can be deducted on federal returns).

Highlight 40% of World's Top Economic Units Are Firms, Not Nations

NEW YORK (AP)—Nearly 40% of the 100 biggest economic units in the world are corporations, not countries, according to a study released Tuesday by the Conference Board.

According to the rankings by 1978 data, General Motors Corp. sales of $63.2 billion made it the largest corporation in the world and the 23rd largest economic unit. Its sales were larger than the economic output of Yugoslavia, whose gross national product was $55.6 billion, but less than Romania with a GNP of $67.4 billion.

Exxon Corp. with sales of $60.3 billion was ranked as the second largest corporation and 24th largest economic unit in 1978. But it would jump much higher in the rankings based on 1979 data.

"With 1979 sales of $84.4 billion, Exxon already has emerged as the world's largest corporation and would move into 16th place, surpassing East Germany and Iran," said John Hein, author of the analysis.

Among other top-ranking corporations, Royal Dutch Shell and Ford Motor Co. were ranked 30th and 31st, respectively, which made them smaller than Indonesia but bigger than Austria.

Hein noted that in compiling the list double-counting was inevitable since a company's sales automatically are a part of a country's GNP. Also he said the positions were only approximate because of estimates used in translating currencies into dollars for comparison purposes.

The survey is published in the May issue of Across the Board, the nonprofit business research organization's monthly magazine.

The 10 largest companies and their sales and world economy rankings, after GM and Exxon, included: Royal Dutch Shell, 30th ($44 billion); Ford 31st ($42.8 billion); Mobil, 38th ($34.7 billion); Texaco, 42nd ($28.6 billion); British Petroleum, 43rd, ($27.4 billion); Standard Oil of California, 47th, ($23.2 billion); National Iranian Oil Co., 49th ($22.8 billion); and International Business Machines, 52nd ($21.1 billion.)

Los Angeles *Times* May 5, 1980

government agencies, the government is generally more concerned with corporate activities than with those of other forms of business. There are numerous laws and enforcement procedures that affect corporations but not partnerships or proprietorships.

Nevertheless, the advantages of a corporation often outweigh its disadvantages, especially for large companies. Exhibit 3.6 compares partnerships and corporations to give you a better idea of their advantages and disadvantages.

TAXING A CORPORATION

Corporations can exist only as long as consumers buy their products, employees make their goods, stockholders (owners) buy their stocks, and bondholders buy their bonds. Corporations per se do not do anything. So who really pays the tax on corporate income? Some economists say that corporations pass their tax burdens on to consumers by charging higher prices. Other economists believe that it is the stockholders who bear most of the tax. The debate is not yet settled, but in either case, if you are a consumer or a stockholder, you may end up paying for any increase in corporate taxes.

Subchapter S Corporations

Corporations that want to avoid corporate income taxes while retaining all of the advantages of a corporation, particularly limited legal liability, may be able to qualify under Subchapter S of the Internal Revenue Code. A **Subchapter S corporation,** sometimes known as a tax-option corporation, is basically taxed like a partnership. It need only file a return that allocates income among the shareholders, regardless of dividend distributions. As owner of the electronic repair shop for example, you might decide to incorporate as a Subchapter S corporation. All of the profits (or losses) would be passed through to you, and you would have to pay only personal federal income taxes (and perhaps state income taxes) on your profits.

The Subchapter S corporation does have some disadvantages. One of the most important is the limit on the amount of income that can be placed in pension plans to permit corporate shareholders to shelter income from personal income taxes.

EXHIBIT 3.6 Partnerships versus Corporations

Characteristic	Partnership	Corporation
1. Method of Creation	Created by agreement of the parties.	Charter issued by state—created by statutory authorization.
2. Legal Position	Not a separate legal entity in many states.	Always a legal entity separate and distinct from its owners—a legal fiction for the purposes of owning property and being party to litigation.
3. Liability	Unlimited liability (except for limited partners in a limited partnership).	Limited liability of shareholders—shareholders are not liable for the debts of the corporation.
4. Duration	Terminated by agreement of the partners, by the death of one or more of the partners, by withdrawal of a partner, or by bankruptcy.	Can have perpetual existence.
5. Transferability of Interest	Although partnership interest can be assigned, assignee does not have full rights of a partner.	Shares of stock can be transferred.
6. Management	Each general partner has a direct and equal voice in management unless expressly agreed otherwise in the partnership agreement. (Limited partner has no rights in management in a limited partnership.)	Shareholders elect directors who set policy and appoint officers.
7. Taxation	Each partner pays pro rata share of income taxes on net profits, whether or not they are distributed.	Double taxation—corporation pays income tax on net profits, with no deduction for dividends, and shareholders pay income tax on disbursed dividends they receive.
8. Organizational Fees, Annual License Fees, and Annual Reports	None.	All required.
9. Transactions of Business In Other States	Generally no limitation.	Normally must qualify to do business and obtain certificate of authority.

Highlight Double Taxation

The after-tax profits of a corporation are taxed again when stockholders pay taxes on dividends received or on realized capital gains. If you receive $1,000 in dividends, you have to declare it as income, and you must pay taxes at your marginal rate. But before the corporation paid you those dividends, it had to pay taxes on all of its profits, including any that it put back into the company or did not distribute in the form of dividends. Eventually the new investment made possible by those retained earnings—profits not given out to stockholders—will be reflected in the increased value of your stock. When you sell your stock, you will have to pay a capital-gains tax on the difference between what you paid for the stock and what you sold it for. In this sense, corporate profits are taxed twice.

For example, say that sale of a product yields $2 in revenues and that the cost of producing it is $1. That means the before-tax profit is $1. If the tax rate on corporate profits is 46 percent (or 46 cents on the dollar of profit), the after-tax profit is 54 cents. If this amount is given to stockholders as a dividend, they must pay, at minimum, the federal personal income tax on it. If the tax is 50 percent, they have to pay 27 cents of the dividend in taxes. Thus $1 of corporate profit yields 27 cents in stockholders' pockets.

Nevertheless, Subchapter S status can be beneficial in several situations:

1. When the corporation has losses, Subchapter S status allows shareholders to use the losses to offset other income.
2. When the stockholders are in a lower tax bracket than the corporation, Subchapter S status causes the entire corporate income to be taxed in the shareholders' bracket, whether or not it is distributed. This is particularly attractive when the corporation wants to accumulate earnings for some future business purpose.
3. The taxable income of a Subchapter S corporation is taxable only to those who are shareholders at the end of the corporate year, when that income is distributed.
4. Shareholders in a Subchapter S corporation can give some of their stock to other members of the family who are in a lower tax bracket.
5. A Subchapter S corporation can still offer some tax-free corporate benefits, which can mean federal tax savings to the shareholders. (These are explained in more detail a little later.)

Closely Held Corporations

The **closely held corporation** is one whose shares belong to members of a family or relatively few people. Usually they are personally known to one another. Because there is such a small number of shareholders, there is no trading market for the shares.

In practice, a closely held corporation is operated like a partnership. A single shareholder or a close-knit group of shareholders usually are the directors and officers. In the eyes of the law, however, it is still a corporation, subject to any special laws governing closely held corporations in the particular state in which it is chartered.

Incorporation for Individuals

Sometimes an individual may want to incorporate, either as a closely held corporation or a Subchapter S corporation. Only those who have substantial outside income that can be funneled through the corporation—not salaried income—can take advantage of incorporation, however. (In general, payments from which Social Security and federal withholding taxes have been deducted cannot be deposited into the corporation as corporate income.) A family cannot incorporate simply because it is a family; it must be engaged in a bona fide business from which it receives nonsalaried income.

Those stipulations aside, just about anyone in any state can start a corporation. There are, however, numerous expenses associated with starting and running such a venture:

1. *Lawyer's fees* These can range from a minimum of $250 to as much as $3,000.
2. *Accountant's fees* It can cost several hundred dollars to establish a bookkeeping system for a corporation.
3. *Fees to the state* The state may require an annual corporate fee ranging from a few dollars to several hundred dollars.
4. *Unemployment insurance taxes* Even if the corporation has only one employee and is clearly set up for tax reasons only, it still must pay unemployment insurance taxes, either to the state in which it is registered or to the federal government.
5. *Employer's contribution to Social Security* Even those who are a salaried employee of some other company "contribute" to Social Security. This contribution is nonrefundable and seems to be on the rise.
6. *Annual legal and accounting fees* Many forms must be filed for corporations (for retirement funds in particular), and corporate records and minute books must be maintained. Typically an accountant or a lawyer does this. Annual fees for such services can run into many hundreds of dollars.

The major benefits of incorporating are being able to start a pension or profit-sharing plan and realizing some tax advantages associated with fringe benefits.

PENSION AND PROFIT-SHARING PLANS

The Internal Revenue Service (IRS) routinely allows pension plans consisting of two parts—a retirement plan and a profit-sharing plan. Up to 10 percent of an employee's gross salary in any one year can be put into the retirement plan; an additional 15 percent can be put into the profit-sharing plan. As an example, let's say that in the year after you have incorporated your repair business, you are able to take $50,000 as income. Your corporation could contribute $5,000 to your corporate pension plan and $7,500 to your corporate profit-sharing plan.

These contributions to the pension and profit-sharing plans would be tax deductible to the corporation but not taxable to you in the year you took them. You would pay taxes on those contributions only when you retired and took out the benefits. What makes this arrangement so advantageous is that most people are in a lower tax bracket after retirement. Moreover, they can earn interest on their deferred taxes (and the taxes on those earnings are deferred).

FRINGE BENEFITS

Anyone who starts a corporation can take advantage of a number of **fringe benefits,** providing items that might otherwise have to be bought with after-tax dollars.

Term Life Insurance

An individual who owns a corporation can purchase up to $50,000 of term life insurance every year with dollars out of the corporation. Because these dollars are a cost to the corporation, they are not taxable. If the person is in the 50-percent tax bracket, for example, he or she can buy $50,000 of term insurance for "50-cent dollars," which means that the cost of the insurance is essentially half what it would have been if it had been purchased outside the corporate structure.

Medical Plans

An incorporated individual can set up a comprehensive medical plan to cover virtually all kinds of medical expenses. Thus the corporation can pay for all medicines, dental work, and anything that relates to physical well-being. For someone with a large family, this comprehensive medical plan can mean substantial savings every year. Furthermore, the corporation pays these expenses with before-tax dollars, thereby reducing the tax bite. Of course, the benefit of a medical plan is reduced by the lack of itemized medical deductions from personal federal income taxes.

The Revenue Act of 1978 requires that a medical plan not discriminate among employees. In other words, if it is made available for the president of the corporation, it must also be made available for all employees in the corporation.

Disability Insurance

An individual can purchase through the corporation, with before-tax dollars, long-term disability insurance. Such insurance pays a certain amount of money every month if the person becomes disabled and is unable to work. Without the corporate umbrella, disability insurance would have to be bought with the individual's after-tax income.

Corporate Growth

The growth of large companies has become a topic of concern in both business and government. One major tool corporations use to become bigger is the **merger,** or the purchase of one firm by another. There are two basic types of mergers (see Exhibit 3.7).

Horizontal integration involves mergers of firms selling a similar commodity. If two shoe-manufacturing firms merge, that is horizontal integration. If a group of firms, all producing steel, merge into one, that also is horizontal integration.

Vertical integration occurs when one firm merges with either a firm it purchases an "input" from or a firm it sells its output to. Vertical integration occurs, for example, when an electric utility that uses coal purchases a coal-mining firm or when a shoe manufacturer purchases retail shoe outlets.

A third type of merger involves conglomerates. A conglomerate is a company that has many subdivisions dealing in totally different products. A good example is International Telephone & Telegraph, which produces and sells houses, radios, books, insurance, hotel services, and rental car services. It is now a multibillion-dollar corporation. You can see in Exhibit 3-8 all of its different aspects.

Franchises

The Federal Trade Commission has defined a **franchise** as "an arrangement in which the owner of a trademark, a trade name, or a copyright licenses others, under specified conditions or limitations, to use the trademark, trade name, or copyright in purveying goods or services." Franchise systems have also been described as organizations composed of distributive units established and administered by a supplier as a medium for expanding and controlling the marketing of its products.

Each franchise dealer is a legally independent, but economically dependent, unit of the integrated business system. Thus individuals with small amounts of capital can become entrepreneurs. Each franchisee (the holder of the franchise) can operate as an independent business yet have the advantages of a regional or national organization in obtaining products, advertising, and other services. Franchise systems also provide consumers with an opportunity to obtain uniform products

EXHIBIT 3.7 Mergers

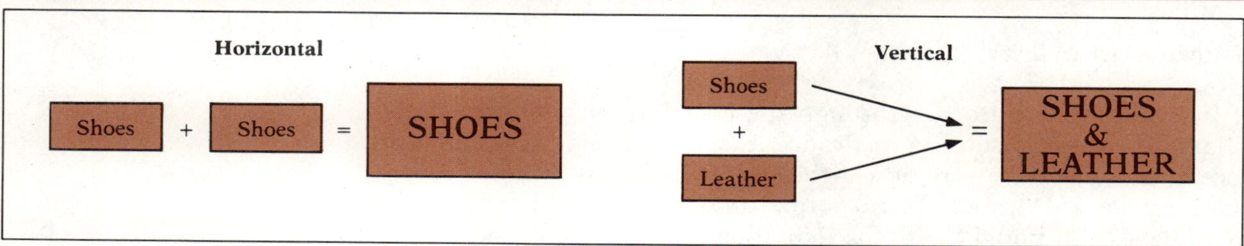

at numerous distribution points from small independent contractors. The system therefore seems good for the businessperson, good for the consumer, and good for the economy.

The use of franchises, which began in the early part of the twentieth century, has expanded rapidly in recent years. Between 1910 and 1940, franchising appeared in the automobile industry, sports, and the soft-drink bottling industry. Franchises now account for about 25 percent of all retail sales and over 13 percent of this country's gross national product.

There are three types of franchises: distributorships, chain-style businesses, and manufacturing or processing plants.

1. A distributorship exists when a manufacturing concern (franchisor) licenses a dealer (franchisee) to sell its product. Often a distributorship covers an exclusive territory.
2. A chain-style business operation occurs when a franchisee operates under a franchisor's trade name and is identified as a member of a select group of dealers who engage in the franchisor's business. The franchisee is generally required to follow standardized methods of

EXHIBIT 3.8 A Sample Conglomerate: Principal Subsidiaries of International Telephone and Telegraph Corporation

Abbey Intl. Corp
Abbey Life Assurance Co., Ltd.
Abbey Life Insurance Co. of Canada
Abbey Overseas Insurance Co., Ltd.
Abrasive Products Co.
Aerospace/Optical Div.
Aimco Div.
Automotive Products-North America
Automotive Distributors Div.
Automotive Electrical Prods. Div.
Hancock Indus., Inc.
Higbie Mfg. Co.
Thompson Metals Div.
United Plastics Div.
Avionics
Barton Instruments
Blackburn Co.
Cable Hydrospace Div.
Cannon Electric
Carbon Industries
J. C. Carter Co.
Communications Equip. & Systems Div.
Community Devel. Corp.
Consumer Specialty Prod. Div.
Continental Baking Co.
Contrell & Cochrane, Inc.
Controls & Instruments Div.
Defense Communications Div.
Eason Oil Co.
Educational Services, Inc.
Electro-Optical Products
Electron Tube Div.
Environmental Products Div.
Export Corp.
Federal Electric Corp.
Financial Corp.
Aetna Corp.
Industrial Credit Co.
Life Insurance Corp.
Thorp Corp
Fluid Handling
General Controls
Gilfillan Div.
Grinnell Corp.
Harper Div.
Hartford Fire Insurance Co.
Henze Service
International Standard Electric Corp.
IT&T Credit Corp.
Jennings
Kellog Credit Corp.
Lighting Fixture Div.
Marine & Recreation Div.
Meyer Industries
Payot, Inc.
Pennsylvania Glass Sand Corp.
Phillips Drill Div.
Pumps & Compressors Div.
Marlow
Pneumotive
Rayonier Inc.
Royal Electric Div.
Howard W. Sams & Co. Inc.
The O. M. Scott & Sons Co.
Semiconductors
Service Industries Corp.
The Sheraton Corp.
Southern Wood Piedmont Co.
Space Communications, Inc.
Surprenant Div.
Telecommunications
Teryphone Corp.
Thermotech
American Cable & Radio Corp.
Subsidiaries:
All American Cables & Radio, Inc.
Central America Cables & Radio, Inc.
The Commercial Cable Co.
Communications, Inc.—Virgin Islands
Corporate Communications Services, Inc.
Diversified Services, Inc.
Domestic Transmission Systems, Inc.
P T Indonesian Satellite Corp.
United States Transmission Systems, Inc.

Highlight Public Control of Corporations?

For many years Ralph Nader has been suggesting that since the public is affected so directly by corporate decision making, the public should be represented on the boards of directors of giant American corporations. Indeed, a number of corporations now have so-called consumer or public-interest directors.

However, critics of Ralph Nader point out that there is no such thing as one consumer interest or one public interest. We are a nation of more than 200 million consumers. Another criticism involves the fundamental philosophy of corporate organization. Is the corporation meant to be a quasi-public institution that operates for the benefit of its customers rather than for the benefit of its stockholders?

operation. Often the franchisor also requires that minimum prices be maintained. In addition, sometimes the franchisee is obligated to deal exclusively with the franchisor to obtain materials and supplies.

3. A manufacturing or processing plant arrangement is one in which the franchisor transmits to the franchisee the essential ingredients or formula to make a particular product. The franchisee then markets it either at wholesale or at retail in accordance with the franchisor's standards.

For the franchisor, a system of franchises is a highly effective means of gaining rapid market expansion and exposure with a minimum of capital outlay. Because franchisees invest their own money in the business, they have a strong incentive to make a profit. In most cases, the contract is written so that both the franchisee and the franchisor make a profit.

The franchisee gets the benefit of all of the franchisor's trade names and trademarks. In addition, the franchise carries with it goodwill and customer acceptance as well as the benefits of the franchisor's national advertising. The franchisee can obtain guidance from an experienced organization in areas such as site selection, operational know-how, and bookkeeping. For the franchisee, a moderate investment can develop into a prosperous business.

In short, the franchisee pledges money and service; the franchisor pledges aid and protection. In an economic context, franchising systems are clearly desirable for both parties. But there are some shortcomings—especially for the franchisee. Most problems occur after the franchise agreement has been entered into. Because there are usually a number of potential franchisees for every franchise operation, typical contract provisions favor the franchisor. The courts, hampered by a lack of case law or statutory law, have been very slow to protect the rights of franchisees.

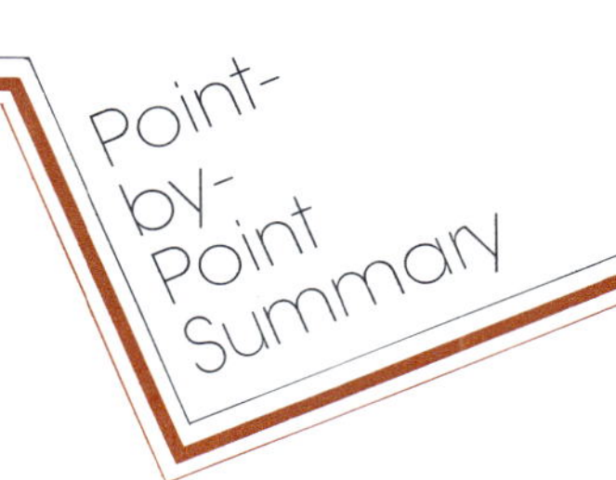

- The formation of any business requires money capital, often in the form of short-term working capital. In addition, every business must start keeping records for tax purposes and for the purpose of estimating profits that are made.
- Any entrepreneur who starts a business engages in risk taking. This risk taking is rewarded by profits.
- A sole proprietorship has the following advantages: the proprietor receives all of the money, pride of ownership, ease of starting, and freedom from corporate income taxes. But there are also disadvantages: the sole owner is responsible for all losses, there is limited capital, and the proprietor has unlimited liability, or legal responsibility.
- A partnership has the advantages of more capital and greater efficiency. However, the partners have unlimited liability, profits must be shared, and the partners may disagree.
- Limited partnerships allow investment in a business organization with limited liability for all limited partners.
- To form a corporation, it must be registered by drawing up articles of incorporation and applying for a charter of incorporation, and a board of directors must be chosen.
- The four advantages of a corporation are greater capital, limited liability for stockholders, unlimited life, and the availability of specialized and professional management. The disadvantages of a corporation are the payment of federal and state corporate profit taxes and increased government control.
- Corporations as such are not taxed, because a corporation is a legal fiction. It does not exist as a person exists. Thus only the stockholders, employees, and customers of corporations can be taxed.
- Subchapter S corporate status allows the stockholder to pass profits (and losses) directly into personal income and thus avoid paying taxes on corporate profits.
- One of the major benefits of incorporating for an individual is the ability to start pension and profit-sharing plans that shelter income from the tax collector. The numerous fringe benefits, including term life insurance, medical plans, and disability insurance, are another advantage.
- Corporations can expand by simple growth but also by merger with other corporations. There are two major types of mergers—horizontal and vertical. Conglomerates are mergers too.

1. What would be the reasons you might want to start your own business?
2. Why might someone decide to start a business as a sole proprietorship rather than as a partnership or a corporation?
3. Is there any way to start a corporation and avoid paying taxes on corporate profits?
4. What is the difference between a limited partnership and a regular, or general, partnership?
5. Under what circumstances might someone be interested in being a limited partner in a limited partnership?
6. There are far fewer corporations than partnerships and sole proprietorships. Nonetheless, they undertake the bulk of all manufacturing activity in the United States. Can you explain this anomaly?
7. What is the difference between the articles of incorporation and the charter of the corporation?
8. One of the disadvantages of forming a corporation is that the corporation incurs increased government control. Does this mean that partnerships and sole proprietorships do not come under government control? If your answer is no, what types of government controls do they encounter?
9. "Let's tax the hell out of those corporations and use the money for the people." Is it possible to "tax the hell" out of corporations?
10. What is meant by the double taxation of corporate profits?
11. Why would anyone want to be able to set up pension and profit-sharing plans? Why are fringe benefits a benefit to the person who starts a corporation? (Hint: What is the tax effect?)

APPLICATION

There are 12 to 13 million businesses in the United States. Most of them are partnerships or sole proprietorships. Nonetheless, the corporation is the dominant form of business organization in the United States simply because of its relative importance in generating the vast bulk of business revenues. We clearly live in a corporate world. United Technologies Corporation is a corporation that spans the entire United States as well as all of the oceans in the world. Its subsidiaries are found in Italy, Brazil, Malaya, Mexico, Switzerland, France, Singapore; in short, just about everywhere. It is a company that is growing. In 1972, its sales were $2 billion. In 1979, they had risen to $9.053 billion. In 1972, it was fifty-sixth on the Fortune 500 list of the largest industrial corporations in the U.S. By 1980, it had joined the top ten corporations in America. Today, it has almost 200,000 employees working in more than 300 plants around the world.

United Technologies Corporation

THE ORGANIZATION OF UNITED TECHNOLOGIES

United Technologies comprises numerous major operating organizations plus a research center, as well as a multitude of subsidiaries. It basically divides itself into three groups:

1. *Power Group* This group has a multitude of companies which deal in industrial gas turbines, rocket engines, motors and boosters, as well as aircraft engines.
2. *Carrier Group* The products developed in this group cover air conditioning and related equipment. It also handles power recovery turbines for natural gas and petroleum processing, and for the petrochemical and chemical industries.
3. *Electronics Group* This is the newest group, established in November 1979. It produces major electronic components and systems for military and commercial markets, including automotive, appliance, telecommunications, construction, aerospace, industrial control, and data processing.

SELECTED DIVISIONS OF UNITED TECHNOLOGIES

Pratt & Whitney Aircraft Group

The largest unit of United Technologies is Pratt & Whitney Aircraft Group, which designs and builds commercial and military engines. Keeping in line with today's concern over energy conservation, this group has adapted energy conservation technology for application to marine propulsion, gas compression and electric power generation.

Pratt & Whitney Aircraft was founded in 1925. By 1930, 90 percent of the nation's commercial transports were powered by Pratt & Whitney engines. Over half of the aircraft engines used by United States forces in World War II were produced by Pratt & Whitney. Over 40 percent of those used by the Allies were of a Pratt & Whitney Aircraft design. In the 1940s, this company shifted its concern to the construction of jet engines. In 1953, it introduced the J57, which set a new standard of performance and reliability for turbojets. Since the J57 the company has built the J75, J60, J52 and J58. The first Boeing 707 was powered by a JT3, which was derived from the company's J57. This marked the beginning of America's era of commercial jet travel.

Pratt & Whitney Aircraft's JT-8D Engine.

Corporate Structure within Pratt & Whitney The corporate structure within Pratt & Whitney is such that there are four principal units:

1. Commercial Products Division
2. Government Products Division
3. Manufacturing Division
4. Pratt & Whitney Aircraft of Canada

Each division has its own line and staff functions. About 50,000 persons work for the Pratt & Whitney Aircraft Group.

Otis Group

When one thinks of elevators, one often thinks of Otis. The elevator industry was started by Otis in 1853, based on an elevator safety device Elisha G. Otis had invented in 1852. Otis introduced the escalator in 1899. This group installs from 20,000 to 25,000 new elevators and escalators annually, thus accounting for one-half of the Otis Group's dollar revenues. The other half is from the servicing of almost 600,000 Otis elevators and escalators that have already been installed.

An International Company Seventy-two percent of the volume of Otis comes from its international sales and servicing, with the remainder from the United States. The company has representation in more than 130 countries and branches or majority-owned subsidiaries in 53 of the larger countries with significant elevator business.

The Takeover by United Technologies In November 1975, United Technologies became the majority shareholder of the Otis Corporation when it purchased 70 percent of the outstanding common stock. A complete merger was accomplished in July 1976. According to company information, the merger was sought to broaden the commercial and industrial portion of United Technologies' total activities. One of the goals of United Technologies has been to reduce its relative dependence on government contracts. In fact, United talks about "good business balance" in all areas. Today, only 20 percent of the company's revenues come from government.

Organization of the Company The manufacturing end of Otis is done out of twenty-nine worldwide plants. The field work, including marketing, installation, and service, is carried out through a network of Otis-owned regional branch offices. The company is organized into four geographical elevator operating units. It has almost 50,000 employees.

Electronics Group

This group was formed from the assets of a number of corporations.

Within the group there are four entities: Mostek Corporation, Essex Group, Automotive Group, and Controls Group. This group was formed in 1979 in an effort to consolidate all of United Technologies' efforts in electronics.

Mostek Corporation Because it is the leading member of the semiconductor industry, the acquisition of Mostek Corporation was considered a feather in United Technologies' cap. This corporation is based in Carrollton, Texas. It pro-

EXHIBIT 3.9 Management of United Technologies Corporation

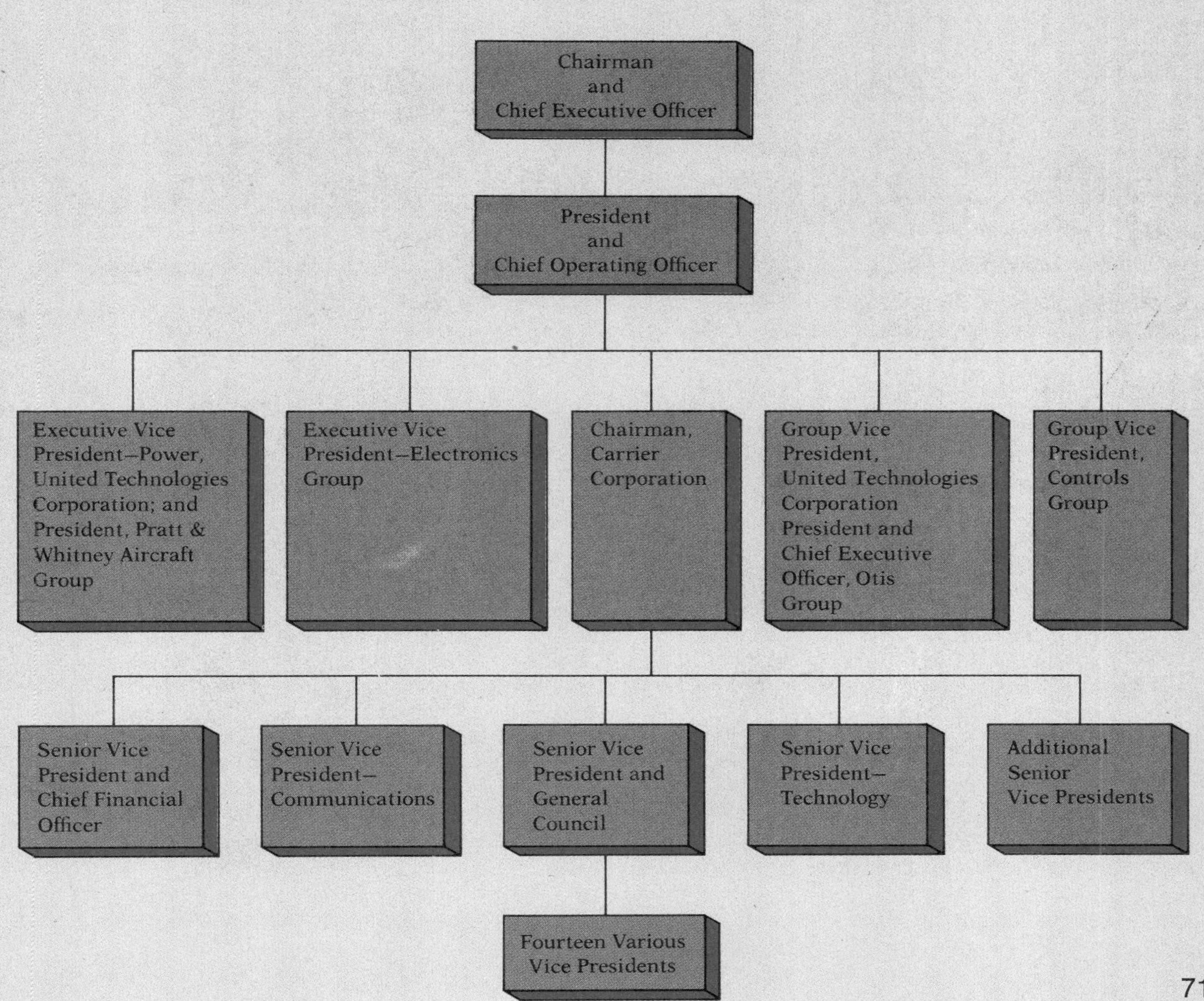

duces microelectronic components and systems with primary emphasis on data processing and telecommunications. It is the world's largest producer of memory circuits. Additionally, it makes microprocessors and microcomputers. Its major competitors are Intel Corporation, Texas Instruments, Motorola Semiconductor, and several Japanese manufacturers. By the end of 1979, Mostek employed over 7,000 workers.

MANAGEMENT OF UNITED TECHNOLOGIES CORPORATION

It would be impossible to put down the entire management structure of such a vast multinational corporation. United Technologies Corporation, though, is managed in a way similar to many other large multinational firms. Consider the organizational structure.

ENTRY-LEVEL JOBS

A company with 200,000 employees operating 330 plants obviously has numerous entry-level jobs at any moment in time. While most of the career opportunities are in technical fields relating all the way from jet engines to fuel cells to heliocopters to rocket propulsion, a large number of entry-level jobs are in the business area. Indeed, company brochures point out that "if you can meet our high standards and your educational background is in engineering, science, business or one of many other professional fields, you may find opportunities for an exciting career in one of our divisions or subsidiaries."

Given the vast range of products and services that United Technologies sells, marketing is clearly an important aspect of the company's entire operation. Additionally, the financial aspects of such a large organization are so large as to boggle the mind. Modern financial techniques are utilized throughout the organization. An entry-level accountant, for example, could look ahead to the possibility of making numerous career advances in such a large organization.

FOR DISCUSSION

1. Do you think that United Technologies could have grown as big as it has become using a partnership form of business organization? Why or why not?
2. Do you think that United Technologies' subsidiaries are complete corporations unto themselves?
3. Do you think that United Technologies has full ownership of all of its subsidiaries in other parts of the world?

OBJECTIVES

- ☐ To understand why businesses have been allowed to pollute and the major government regulations controlling pollution
- ☐ To understand the nature of government regulation in the areas of consumer and employee protection
- ☐ To describe how the Sherman Antitrust Act and other antitrust acts prevent businesses from restraining trade, or monopolizing
- ☐ To understand the difference between state court systems and the federal court system
- ☐ To define the major criminal activities affecting business
- ☐ To outline the requirements for a legal contract
- ☐ To understand, at least basically, what the laws of property and torts are all about

OUTLINE

ARTICLE *Coal Town's Choice: Clean Air or Jobs*

TO PROTECT THE ENVIRONMENT

TO PROTECT THE CONSUMER

TO PROTECT THE WORKER

TO PRESERVE COMPETITION

The Sherman Antitrust Act

The Clayton Antitrust Act

The Federal Trade Commission Act

The Robinson-Patman Act

ARE BUSINESSES OVERREGULATED?

The Legal Environment of Business

Types of Law

The Court System

Some Basic Law Affecting Business

APPLICATION *Bethlehem Steel Corporation*

KEY TERMS

APPELLATE COURT
BURGLARY
CASE LAW
CEASE-AND-DESIST ORDER
COMMON LAW
COMMON PROPERTY
CONSIDERATION
CONTRACT
CONTRACT LAW
CRIMINAL LAW
CUTTHROAT PRICING
EMBEZZLEMENT
ENVIRONMENTAL IMPACT STATEMENT
FORGERY
GENERAL-JURISDICTION TRIAL COURT
INFERIOR TRIAL COURT
LARCENY
PERSONAL PROPERTY
PRICE DISCRIMINATION
REAL PROPERTY
ROBBERY
STATUTE LAW
TORT

BUSINESS, GOVERNMENT, AND THE LAW

Coal Town's Choice: Clean Air or Jobs

Reprinted from "U.S. News & World Report"

DILLES BOTTOM, Ohio

A bitter environment fight that has plunged this tiny Appalachian mining town into despair demonstrates in microcosm the problems frustrating efforts to increase use of America's most plentiful fuel—coal.

Residents of Dilles Bottom began looking for boom times two years ago, when President Carter told the nation that coal was a key to ending U.S. addiction to foreign oil. He proposed doubling coal output by 1985.

Plans were announced for up to 16 new mines that would provide thousands of jobs in coal-rich areas of Ohio, Pennsylvania and West Virginia.

EARLY HOPE

Optimism spread quickly through the sooty villages and back roads of Appalachia. In Dilles Bottom, a settlement of some 500 persons about 20 miles southwest of Wheeling, W.Va., many took out installment loans on new cars and furniture on the promise of better days ahead.

But the boom soon turned to bust. Demand for the region's high-sulfur coal has declined as utility companies, under increasing pressure from the Environmental Protection Agency to cut smokestack emissions, have turned to cleaner-burning coal from the West.

The result: Coal companies have closed at least 10 mines in the region and plan to shut others, adding to the thousands of miners already idled. A vast supply of fuel is going unused.

Over all, the United States has 218 billion tons of coal that can be mined with existing technology—a 273-year supply measured against current use of about 800 million tons a year.

The conflict squeezing Dilles Bottom raises the issue of whether the U.S. can satisfy its energy needs quickly and still preserve its environment.

In these parts, where some miners have been out of work for more than six months, people are not certain that coal and clean air are compatible.

Says George Haggerty, who was laid off five months ago from the North American Coal Company's No. 3 mine: "What's the use of having clean air if everybody's going to starve to death?" He adds bitterly: "We're going to be out of work and out of food but, by God, at least we can breathe!"

Carol Glass, president of a United Mine Workers women's auxiliary that collects and distributes food to families of idled mine workers, says few other jobs are available. She observes: "If you want money, you work in the mines, and when that's gone, you pray."

Hundreds of miners who have avoided layoffs are working shortened shifts; some are down to three days a week.

"When you're used to making $1,200 to $1,500 a month, you have bills to match," says Charlotte Walters, whose husband is working a curtailed shift.

Many miners have sold off land, cars, campers and other belongings because they no longer could meet payments.

A miner with a family may get up to $400 a month in state unemployment benefits for 26 weeks, compared with daily pay of $75. After that? Welfare and food stamps for those who qualify.

Many miners, however, won't accept government aid. Diets have suffered.

No one has starved, says Martha Underwood, a member of the women's auxiliary, adding: "But some have come in here saying that they were down to a bag of beans or a can of soup. Some don't look too healthy."

RARE ALLIANCE

With miners unable to pay bills and purchase more than bare necessities, merchants report that business has dropped off dramatically. Some have had to let sales personnel go. Hard times in Dilles Bottom and other communities have spawned a rare alliance among miners, coal companies and public utilities, which charge that federal air-pollution rules are too strict and are causing irreparable harm to the region's economy.

Utility spokesmen insist that technology needed to clean up Ohio coal is unproven and too costly. The EPA, however, responds that technology is available and that it is economically feasible to burn high-sulfur coal.

Until this impasse is resolved, miners in Dilles Bottom and nearby areas are short on work and hope.

Haggerty, the jobless miner, now spends most of his time cutting firewood from a lot behind his mobile home. "But what's the use?" he says. "Nobody can afford to buy it."

The nation is indeed faced with a tradeoff: more clean air and fewer jobs, at least according to this article. Whether the tradeoff is real or imagined, government regulation does affect the way businesses work and how profitable they are, as we shall see in this chapter.

The average American ends up paying over 40 cents of every dollar earned to some form of government. Thus it would be difficult for any American to ignore the fact that government constitutes a large part of this nation's economic activity. But what is perhaps less understood is the role of government in regulating the affairs of private businesses.

Regulation of private business was relatively light until the 1930s. But since the Great Depression, government has grown. In the past, most government agencies merely carried out specific activities mandated by Congress, but they have gradually won increasing discretionary powers. Furthermore, starting in the late 1960s, an increasing number of new rules and regulations were established, along with new federal agencies. For example, seven new regulatory agencies, including the Consumer Product Safety Commission, the Environmental Protection Agency, and the Occupational Safety and Health Administration, were created in the early 1970s. And in the first four years of the 1970s, the number of pages doubled in the *Federal Register,* the primary document for notification of federal rules and regulations.

For better or worse, the result of all these changes is that no future businessperson can hope to enter the world of business without first understanding at least the rudiments of government regulation. These rules are intended to protect society, but they can hamper those who misunderstand them.

To Protect the Environment

One of the newest areas of government regulation involves controls on how the environment is used. In one sense, concerns about the environment are not new. For example, the English Parliament passed a number of acts that regulated the burning of soft coal in medieval England. And for hundreds of years there have been statutes allowing property owners to prevent pollution by neighboring factories. Beginning in the 1960s, however, Americans became more concerned than ever about pollutants in the air they breathe and the water they drink and swim in. Exhibit 4.1 describes the major environmental legislation in the United States.

In discussing pollution control, we must first ask a very important question: Why have people been allowed to pollute? The answer lies in the fact that nearly everyone has treated air and water as if nobody owns them. If no one person owns the air and water, it is to no one's *personal* advantage to make sure they are not polluted. Economists call this a common-property problem. That is, air and water have been **common property** owned by everyone and by no one.

On January 1, 1970, the National Environmental Policy Act was passed. It created the Council of Environmental Quality and mandated that an **environmental impact statement** be prepared for every recommendation or report on legislation or major federal action that would significantly affect the quality of the environment. The Environmental Protection Agency (EPA) now employs about 10,000 people to carry out

EXHIBIT 4.1 Major Federal Environmental Legislation

1899 REFUSE ACT
Made it unlawful to dump refuse into navigable waters without a permit. A 1966 court decision made all industrial wastes subject to this act.

1947 FEDERAL INSECTICIDE, FUNGICIDE AND RODENTICIDE ACT
Enacted to protect farmers from fraudulent claims of salespersons. Required registration of poisons.

1955 FEDERAL WATER POLLUTION CONTROL ACT
Set standards for treatment of municipal water waste before discharge. Revisions to this act were passed in 1965 and 1967.

1963 CLEAN AIR ACT
Assisted local and state governments in establishing control programs and coordinated research.

1965 CLEAN AIR ACT AMENDMENTS
Authorized establishment of federal standards for automobile exhaust emissions, beginning with 1968 models.

1965 SOLID WASTE DISPOSAL ACT
Provided assistance to local and state governments for control programs and authorized research in this area.

1965 WATER QUALITY ACT
Authorized the setting of standards for discharges into waters.

1967 AIR QUALITY ACT
Established air quality regions, with acceptable regional pollution levels. Required local and state governments to implement approved control programs or be subject to federal controls.

1967 FEDERAL INSECTICIDE, FUNGICIDE AND RODENTICIDE AMENDMENTS
Provided for licensing of pesticide users. (Further authority granted through 1972 revision.)

1970 NATIONAL ENVIRONMENTAL QUALITY ACT
Established Council for Environmental Quality for the purpose of coordinating all federal pollution control programs. Authorized the establishment of the Environmental Protection Agency to implement CEQ policies on a case-by-case basis.

1970 CLEAN AIR ACT AMENDMENTS
Authorized the Environmental Protection Agency to set national air pollution standards. Restricted the discharge of six major pollutants into the lower atmosphere. Automobile manufacturers were required to reduce nitrogen oxide, hydrocarbon and carbon monoxide emissions by 90 percent (in addition to the 1965 requirements) during the 1970s. Set aircraft emission standards. Required states to meet deadline for complying with EPA standards. Authorized legal action by private citizens to require EPA to carry out approved standards against undiscovered offenders.

1970 RESOURCE RECOVERY ACT
Authorized government assistance for the construction of pilot recycling plants. Authorized the development of control programs on national level.

1970 WATER QUALITY AND IMPROVEMENT ACT
Required local and state governments to carry out standards under compliance deadlines.

1972 FEDERAL WATER POLLUTION CONTROL ACT AMENDMENTS
Set national water quality goal of restoring polluted water to swimmable, fishable waters by 1983.

1972 NOISE CONTROL ACT
Required EPA to establish noise standards for products determined to be major sources of noise. Required EPA to advise the Federal Aviation Administration on acceptable standards for aircraft noise.

1972 PESTICIDE CONTROL ACT
Required that all pesticides used in interstate commerce be approved and certified as effective for their stated purposes. Required certification that they were harmless to humans, animal life, animal feed, and crops.

1974 CLEAN WATER ACT
Originally called the Safe Water Drinking Act, this law set (for the first time) federal standards for water suppliers serving more than twenty-five people, having more than fifteen service connections, or operating more than sixty days a year.

1975 FEDERAL ENVIRONMENTAL PESTICIDE CONTROL ACT AMENDMENTS
Established 1977 as the deadline for registration, classification, and licensing of approximately 50,000 pesticides. This deadline was not met.

1976 RESOURCE CONSERVATION AND RECOVERY ACT
Encouraged conservation and the recovery of resources. Put hazardous waste under government control. Disallowed the opening of new dumping sites. Required that all existing open dumps be closed or upgraded to sanitary landfills by 1983. Set standards for providing technical, financial and marketing assistance to encourage solid waste management.

1977 CLEAN AIR ACT AMENDMENTS
Changed deadline for automobile emission requirements from 1975 and 1978 to 1980–1981.

1977 AMENDMENTS TO CLEAN WATER ACT
Revised list of toxic pollutants and set new policies for review. Required that pollutants be monitored "by best available technology" that is economically feasible.

1977 FEDERAL WATER POLLUTION CONTROL ACT AMENDMENTS
Authorized extension of the 1972 regulations.

Highlight The Cost of Clean Air and Water

No longer are clean air and water easy to come by. Making them clean costs plenty for businesses, consumers, and taxpayers. The Environmental Protection Agency has estimated the costs of complying with environmental laws between 1977 and 1986:

Fuel and energy production	$97.8 billion
Motor-vehicle emissions	$92.1 billion
Government	$71.7 billion
Metal industries	$25.7 billion
Food processing	$16.0 billion
Chemical industries	$16.0 billion
Waste disposal	$15.2 billion
Soft-goods industries	$13.4 billion
Other industrial	$5.6 billion
Other manufacturing	$3.6 billion
Construction-material businesses	$2.5 billion
Service industries	$0.4 billion
TOTAL	$360.0 billion

"Good evening, sir. As you may know, the soaring costs of recent environmental-protection legislation have forced us to pass part of this burden along to the consumer. Your share comes to $171,947.65."

the directives of federal laws affecting the environment. One estimate projects that the federal government will spend $15 billion for environmental programs in 1982, an amount two-and-a-half times what was spent in 1975.

To Protect the Consumer

Americans seem more concerned today with the safety and reliability of products than ever before. The age of consumerism is here. Its goal is to protect people against bad buying deals in a society that is increasingly complex. Thus, active control of business by government has become a reality in almost every state in the nation. Business firms can no longer assume that it is the buyer's responsibility to know whether a product is safe, food is healthful, or advertising is accurate. The age of *caveat emptor* has now become the age of *caveat venditor*.

Numerous federal laws have been passed to provide more explicit directions on the duties of sellers and the rights of consumers. Exhibit 4.2 gives a rundown of major federal consumer legislation involving product safety, food and drugs, advertising, and credit.

In many cases, consumers are protected through direct regulation by administrative agencies. The Federal Trade Commission (FTC), for example, is foremost in federal consumer-protection activities; in fiscal year 1981 it will spend approximately 38 percent of its estimated $71 million budget for such activities. The FTC's five commissioners, appointed by the president for terms of seven years, have been given extensive enforcement responsibilities for a number of federal statutes. The commission can stop "unfair deceptive acts or practices" used to influence, inhibit, or restrict consumers unfairly in their purchasing decisions. Violations are punishable by law. For example, the FTC might issue a **cease-and-desist order** that prohibits General Motors from advertising fuel economy levels achieved by professional drivers without disclosing that information. Then the FTC can impose legal penalties against Ford and Chrysler as well if they advertise similar mileage tests without the disclosure that professional drivers have been used.

The FTC also engages in making sure that consumer products are completely and truthfully packaged and labeled and it is heavily involved in enforcing the Truth-in-Lending Act of 1968, as well as later amendments. Another important activity involves the prevention of **price discrimination** by sellers. In other words, the FTC attempts to enforce legislation that makes it illegal for one seller to sell the same product or service to two different buyers at two different prices.

The Department of Housing and Urban Development (HUD) is another agency that engages in consumer protection. For example, it can enforce federal standards for mobile-home construction and require that sellers of subdivided lots provide potential buyers with a legal description of the land, the legal owner, and its present condition. If the land is two feet under water in the Florida swamps, this must be indicated on a sales brochure.

EXHIBIT 4.2 Major Federal Consumer Legislation

1906 PURE FOOD AND DRUG LAW
Prohibits adulteration and mislabeling of food and drugs sold in interstate commerce. The Food and Drug Administration is responsible for enforcement.

1907 MEAT INSPECTION ACT
Requires inspection of meat packaging, slaughtering and canning plants.

1938 FOOD, DRUG, AND COSMETIC ACT
Put cosmetics and therapeutic products under FDA control. Expanded definition of mislabeling to include "false and misleading" labeling. The FDA was transferred from the Department of Agriculture to the Department of Health, Education and Welfare (now called the Department of Health and Human Services).

1939 WOOL PRODUCTS LABELING ACT
Requires that manufacturers' labels clearly state the type of wool and all other fibers making up 5 percent or more of the fabric content.

1951 FUR PRODUCTS LABELING ACT
Requires that fur products indicate on their labels the type of fur, the country of origin of an imported fur, whether the fur has been dyed or tinted, and if the garment is made from scraps of fur. Prohibits misbranding, false advertising, and false invoicing of fur products.

1953 FLAMMABLE FABRICS ACT
Forbade the shipment in interstate commerce of articles of clothing made from highly flammable fabrics.

1958 TEXTILE FIBER PRODUCTS IDENTIFICATION ACT
Forbade the false advertising and mislabeling of all textile products not covered under the Wool and Fur Products Labeling Acts.

1960 FEDERAL HAZARDOUS SUBSTANCES LABELING ACT
Required warning labels on all items containing dangerous household chemicals.

1962 KEFAUVER-HARRIS DRUG AMENDMENTS TO FOOD AND DRUG ACT
Required that manufacturers test the safety and effectiveness of all drugs before putting them on the market. Also required that the generic (or common) names of drugs be included on labels.

1966 NATIONAL TRAFFIC AND MOTOR VEHICLE SAFETY ACT
Required manufacturers to inform new car buyers of any safety defects found after manufacture and sale.

1966 FAIR PACKAGING AND LABELING ACT
Required honest and informative listings on package labels. Also authorized the secretary of commerce to limit "undue" proliferation of product package sizes. In 1972, the FTC further required that product origin, number of product contents, number and size of servings, and product use be clearly listed on labels.

1967 WHOLESOME MEAT ACT
Updated and stiffened inspection standards for slaughtering plants of red meat animals.

1968 CONSUMER PROTECTION CREDIT ACT (TRUTH-IN-LENDING)
Required creditors to provide the following to persons obtaining credit: statement of finance charges, time of disclosure, and annual percentage rates.

1969 CHILD PROTECTION AND TOY SAFETY ACT
Increased protection from mechanical and/or electrical hazards of children's toys.

1970 PUBLIC HEALTH SMOKING ACT
Prohibited radio and television advertising of cigarettes and required that warnings be listed on cigarette packages.

1970 FAIR CREDIT REPORTING ACT
Required consumer credit reporting agencies to use "reasonable" measures to guarantee accuracy of credit information. Specified that consumers be notified when an investigative report will be made. Also required that consumers, if denied credit, be given access to substance of all information in the reporting agency's file, as well as the sources and recipients of information (subject to certain limits).

1972 CONSUMER PRODUCT SAFETY COMMISSION ACT
Established the Consumer Product Safety Commission with power to set safety standards for consumer products, to require warnings by manufacturers, to require producers to give rebates to consumers, and to ban or recall products without a court hearing. The Commission can also impose criminal penalties on executives in firms who violate the act.

1977 FEDERAL HAZARDOUS SUBSTANCES ACT
Required labels listing hazardous substances be of a certain size and include such information as instructions for first aid, instructions for safe use and storage, and an accurate description of the dangers associated with using the product. This act is a revision of the Federal Hazardous Substances Labeling Act of 1960.

1977 MAGNUSON-MOSS WARRANTY ACT
Required that any product containing a warranty include a simple, complete and conspicuous statement listing the name and address of the warrantor, what is covered and for what amount, a step-by-step procedure for placing warranty claims, how disputes between parties will be settled, and the warranty's duration. This must be available to the consumer as purchase information.

1978 FAIR DEBT COLLECTION PRACTICES ACT
Regulated the debt collection practices of collectors. Made it unlawful, for example, to employ such practices as calling at unusual times, harassing or abusing persons, and making false claims or statements when collecting debts.

To Protect the Worker

In 1970, the Occupational Safety and Health Act was passed, and since then the Department of Labor has issued detailed safety standards for almost every industry. For example, there are standards that apply to electrical grounding, fire extinguishers, guards for machines, and exits from buildings.

Inspectors from the Occupational Safety and Health Administration (OSHA) frequently visit businesses to see if any rules have been violated. All inspections must comply with constitutional protections against unreasonable searches. Prior to 1978, however, inspectors were not required to obtain permission to enter work areas. In 1975, an OSHA inspector entered the customer-service area of Barlow's, Inc., an electrical and plumbing installation business. After showing his credentials, the inspector informed the president and general manager, Mr. Barlow, that he wished to conduct a search of the working areas of the business. Barlow, however, found out that no one had complained about the working conditions of his company; the inspector was randomly selecting businesses to search. Since the inspector did not have a search warrant, Barlow refused to permit the inspector to enter the working area. OSHA filed suit and successfully obtained an order requiring Barlow to admit the inspector. But even with the court order in hand, Barlow refused admission to the inspector. Barlow then went to court seeking a prohibition against the inspector for making a warrantless search, on the grounds that it violated the Fourth Amendment of the Constitution. Barlow obtained this legal prohibition, and it was upheld by the Supreme Court of the United States. Now OSHA inspections conducted without warrants are unconstitutional.

To Preserve Competition

One of the many aims of the U.S. government is to foster competition in the economy. To this end, many laws have been passed to eliminate business practices that seem to weaken competition or destroy it.

THE SHERMAN ANTITRUST ACT

The first major antitrust law passed by Congress was the Sherman Antitrust Act of 1890. Its most important provisions are:

> **Section 1:** Every contract, combination in the form of trust or otherwise conspiracy, in restraint of trade or commerce among the several states, or with foreign nations, is hereby declared to be illegal.
>
> **Section 2:** Every person who shall monopolize, or attempt to monopolize, or combine or conspire with any other person or persons to monopolize any part of the trade or commerce . . . shall be guilty of a misdemeanor.

Notice how vague the wording is. No definition is given for *restraint of trade* or *monopolize.*

Despite its vagueness, in 1906 the Sherman Antitrust Act was used to prosecute the Standard Oil Trust of New Jersey. At that time, Standard Oil controlled more than 80 percent of the nation's oil-refining

Highlight How OSHA Describes an Exit

OSHA, in an attempt to make sure that exits from buildings are safe, has provided the following definition of *exit:*

"A means of egress is a continuous and unobstructed way of exit travel from any point in a building or structure to a public way and consists of three separate and distinct parts: the way of exit access, the exit, and the way of exit discharge. A means of egress comprises the vertical and horizontal ways of travel and shall include intervening room spaces, doorways, hallways, corridors, passageways, balconies, ramps, stairs, enclosures, lobbies, escalators, horizontal exits, courts, and yards.

"Exit discharge is that portion of a means of egress between the termination of an exit and a public way."

capacity. Among other charges, Standard Oil was accused of cutting prices to drive competing companies out of business. It was also accused of obtaining preferential price treatment from the railroads for transporting its products, which enabled Standard Oil to cut prices.

Standard Oil was first convicted in a U.S. district court. The company then appealed to the U.S. Supreme Court. The Supreme Court ruled that Standard Oil's control of the oil market created an obvious "presumption of intent and purpose to maintain dominancy . . . not as a result from normal methods of industrial development, but by means of combination." (The Supreme Court's reference to combination meant taking over other businesses and obtaining preferential price treatment from railroads.) The Supreme Court forced the Standard Oil Trust to break itself into many smaller companies.

However, the Supreme Court ruling came about because the justices believed that Standard Oil had made "unreasonable" attempts to restrain trade. The fact that Standard Oil had the major share of the oil market did not matter. Rather, the problem was the way in which Standard Oil had acquired its share.

THE CLAYTON ANTITRUST ACT

The Sherman Act was so vague that a new law was passed. The Clayton Antitrust Act of 1914 prohibits or limits a number of specific business practices that were viewed as "unreasonable" attempts at restraining trade. Some of the more important sections of the Clayton Act are:

> **Section 2:** It is illegal to discriminate in price between different purchases [except in cases where differences are due to differences in selling or transportation costs].
>
> **Section 3:** Producers cannot sell on the condition, agreement, or understanding that the . . . purchaser thereof shall not use or deal in the goods . . . of a competitor or competitors of the seller.
>
> **Section 7:** Corporations cannot hold stock in another company where the effect . . . may be to substantially lessen competition.

Notice that these provisions outlaw practices that tend to lessen competition "substantially." Because it is not clear what *substantially* actually means, the courts have a difficult time interpreting the law.

THE FEDERAL TRADE COMMISSION ACT

The Federal Trade Commission Act of 1914 was designed to stipulate acceptable competitive behavior. In particular, it was supposed to prevent **cutthroat pricing**—aggressive competition in setting prices, which tends to eliminate too many competitors.

One of the basic features of this act was the creation of the Federal Trade Commission (FTC), which has the power to investigate unfair competitive practices. It can do so on its own or at the request of firms that feel they have been wronged. The FTC can also issue cease-and-desist orders where "unfair methods of competition in commerce" are discovered.

In 1938, the Wheeler-Lea Act amended the Federal Trade Commission Act. The amendment expressly prohibits "unfair or deceptive acts or practices in commerce." Thus the FTC engages in what it sees as a battle against misleading advertising, as well as the misrepresentation of goods and services.

THE ROBINSON-PATMAN ACT

In 1936, section 2 of the Clayton Act was amended by the Robinson-Patman Act. The Robinson-Patman Act was aimed at preventing producers from driving out smaller competitors by means of discriminatory price cuts.

The Robinson-Patman Act has often been referred to as the "Chain Store Act," because it was meant to protect independent retailers and wholesalers from "unfair discrimination" by chain sellers. It was the natural outgrowth of the increasing competition that independents faced when chain stores and mass distributors started to develop after World War I.

The essential provisions of the Robinson-Patman Act are as follows:

1. It was made illegal to pay brokerage fees unless an independent broker is employed. Often chain stores would demand a brokerage fee as a form of discount when they purchased large quantities of products directly from the manufacturer instead of going through a broker or wholesaler. Thus chain stores gained an unfair advantage over independents, who had to use a broker or wholesaler.
2. It was made illegal to offer concessions—such as discounts, free advertising, promotional allowances, and so on—to one buyer if the same concessions were not offered to all buyers. This provision was an attempt to stop large-scale buyers from obtaining special deals that would allow them to compete "unfairly" with small buyers.

3. Other forms of discrimination, such as quantity discounts, were also made illegal whenever they "substantially" lessened competition. However, price discrimination is not illegal if, in fact, price differences are due to differences in cost or are "offered in good faith to meet an equally low price of a competitor."
4. It was made illegal to charge lower prices in one location than in another or to sell at "unreasonably low prices" in order to "destroy competition or eliminate a competitor."

Are Businesses Overregulated?

The regulation of American business is increasing at an alarming rate. At least forty-one federal agencies in one way or another regulate the way business operates. In 1974, these agencies' costs were a mere $2.2 billion; the estimated cost for 1981 is $17.4 billion.

Administrative costs, however, are much smaller than the costs of compliance. One researcher found that in 1976 the total cost to business of federal regulation was $65.5 billion.* A 1979 study of forty-eight manufacturing firms by the Business Roundtable found that government regulations account for 10 percent of total capital expenditures.

To give you an idea of the burden that government regulation may impose, Exhibit 4.3 lists the government forms that a typical corporation must prepare and file.

The Legal Environment of Business

Not only are businesses governed by federal and state legislation concerning the environment, worker health and safety, and consumers, but they also function under legal rules of the game—business law. The law is the body of principles and rules that courts apply in deciding disputes. Thus, the study of business law is the study of these rules as applied to the business community.

TYPES OF LAW

There are several ways to look at the law. **Case law,** or **common law,** includes the rules of law announced in court decisions. It is sometimes called judge-made law. **Statute law,** on the other hand, is the law laid down by legislators. We have listed a number of statutory laws in Exhibits 4.1 and 4.2.

THE COURT SYSTEM

The United States has a dual court system, which means that it includes the state systems and one federal system. The word *court* comes from the Latin word *cors,* meaning "an open space near the king's palace." This is where disputants came to have their differences adjudicated by the king or by his representatives.

*Murray Weidenbaum, "On Estimating Regulatory Costs," *Regulation,* May/June 1978, p. 15.

EXHIBIT 4.3 Government Forms Required of a Typical Corporation

Agency	Form or Subdivision	Time to Fill Out Form
Federal		
Department of Commerce	Census of Manufacturers	8.0 hours
Office of Equal Employment Opportunity	Employer Information Report EEO-I	0.5
Federal Trade Commission	Division of Financial Statistics	0.8
Department of Labor	Log of Occupational Injuries and Illnesses	1.0
Department of Labor	Supplementary Record of Occupational Injuries and Illnesses	0.5
Department of Labor	Summary—Occupational Injuries and Illnesses	1.0
Department of Labor	Wage Developments in Manufacturing	0.5
Department of Labor	Employee Welfare or Pension Benefit Plan Description	1.0
Department of Labor	Employee Welfare or Pension Benefit Plan Description Amendment	1.0
Department of Labor	Employee Welfare or Pension Benefit Plan Annual Report	8.0
Department of Labor	Information on Employee Welfare or Pension Benefit Plan Covering Fewer than 100 Participants	—[a]
Department of the Treasury	Federal Tax Deposits—Withheld Income and FICA Taxes	104.0
Department of the Treasury	Unemployment Taxes	12.0
Department of the Treasury	Employer's Annual Federal Unemployment Tax Return	3.0
Department of the Treasury	Employee's Withholding Exemption Certificate	—[b]
Department of the Treasury	Reconciliation of Income Tax Withheld from Wages	24.0
Department of the Treasury	Report of Wages Payable under the Federal Insurance Contributions Act	64.0
Department of the Treasury	Return of Employee's Trust Exempt from Tax	1.0
Department of the Treasury	U.S. Information Return for the Calendar Year 1971	3.0
State of Illinois		
Industrial Commission	Application for Adjustment of Claim—Notice of Disputed Claims and Memorandum of Names and Addresses	—[c]

EXHIBIT 4.3 (Continued)

Agency	Form or Subdivision	Time to Fill Out Form
Industrial Commission	Employer's Report of Compensable Injury	—[c]
Industrial Commission	Memorandum of Names and Addresses for Service of Notices	—[c]
Industrial Commission	Notice of Filing Claim	—[c]
Employment Service	DOL-BES Form	—[d]
Division of Unemployment Compensation	Notice of Possible Ineligibility	—[e]
Division of Unemployment Compensation	Employer's Contribution Report	64.0
Department of Revenue	Retailers' Occupation Tax, Use Tax, County, Municipal Service Occupation and Service Use Tax Return	2.0
Department of Revenue	Employee's Illinois Withholding Exemption Certificate	—[b]
Department of Revenue	Monthly State Income Tax Payment Form	1.0
Department of Revenue	Application for Renewal of Resale Certificate Number	—[f]
State of California		
Department of Business Taxes	State, Local, and District Sales and Use Tax Return	2.0
State of New Jersey		
Division of Taxation	Resale Certificate	—[f]
Division of Taxation	Blanket Exemption Certificate	—[f]
City of Chicago		
Commission of Human Relations	Contractor Employment Practices Report	1.0
Metropolitan Sanitary District	Industrial Waste Surcharge Certified Statement	2.0
Metropolitan Sanitary District	Report of Exemption Claim or Estimate of Liability for Surcharge	1.0
Metropolitan Sanitary District	Computation of Initial Estimate of Liability for Surcharge	2.0
City of Los Angeles		
Department of Building and Safety	Application and Agreement for Testing Electrical Equipment	1.0
Department of Building and Safety	Application for Approval Labels	1.0

[a]Not available. [d]15 minutes per month.

[b]5 minutes per form. [e]15 minutes per form.

[c]1/2 hour each. [f]1 hour each.

Source: U.S. Senate Hearings, Subcommittee on Government Regulation. *The Federal Paperwork Burden,* 92nd Congress, Part 1, pp. 124–128.

State Court Systems

The court systems of the states vary, but there is a general pattern to the hierarchy of courts within each state (see Exhibit 4.4).

At the bottom of the hierarchy, every state has some type of trial court with limited jurisdiction over the matters it can consider. These so-called **inferior trial courts** are typically domestic-relations courts, which handle only divorce actions and child custody; local municipal courts, which handle mainly traffic cases; probate courts, which handle the execution of wills and the settlement of estate problems; small-claims courts; and justice-of-the-peace courts.

Cases involving state law most often originate in what are called **general-jurisdiction trial courts.** Cases involving corporate law, contract law, and criminal law start here.

Finally, there are **appellate courts,** or courts of appeal and review, in every state. These courts examine the record of the case on appeal and determine whether the trial court committed an error—but do not try cases. In other words, they look at questions of law rather than questions of fact.

The Federal Court System

The federal court system is similar in many ways to a typical state court system. It includes specialized courts, general trial courts, appellate courts, and the Supreme Court. Exhibit 4.5 shows the organization of the federal court system.

EXHIBIT 4.4 Organization of a Hypothetical State Court System

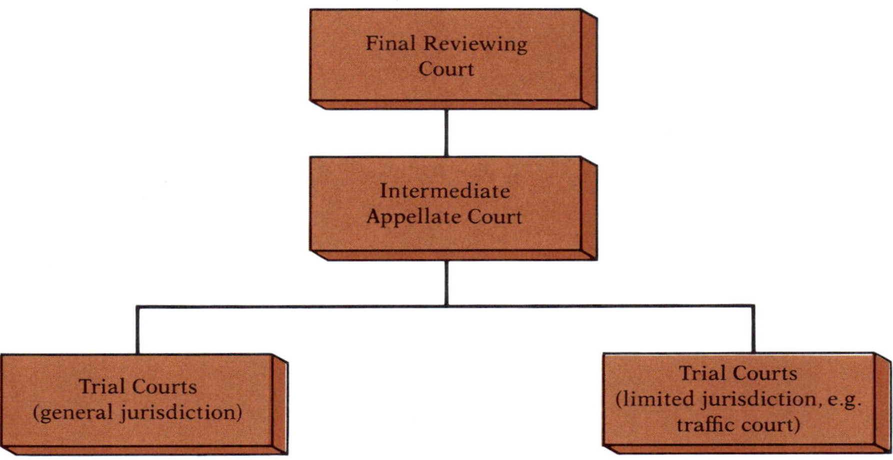

EXHIBIT 4.5
Organization of the Federal Court System

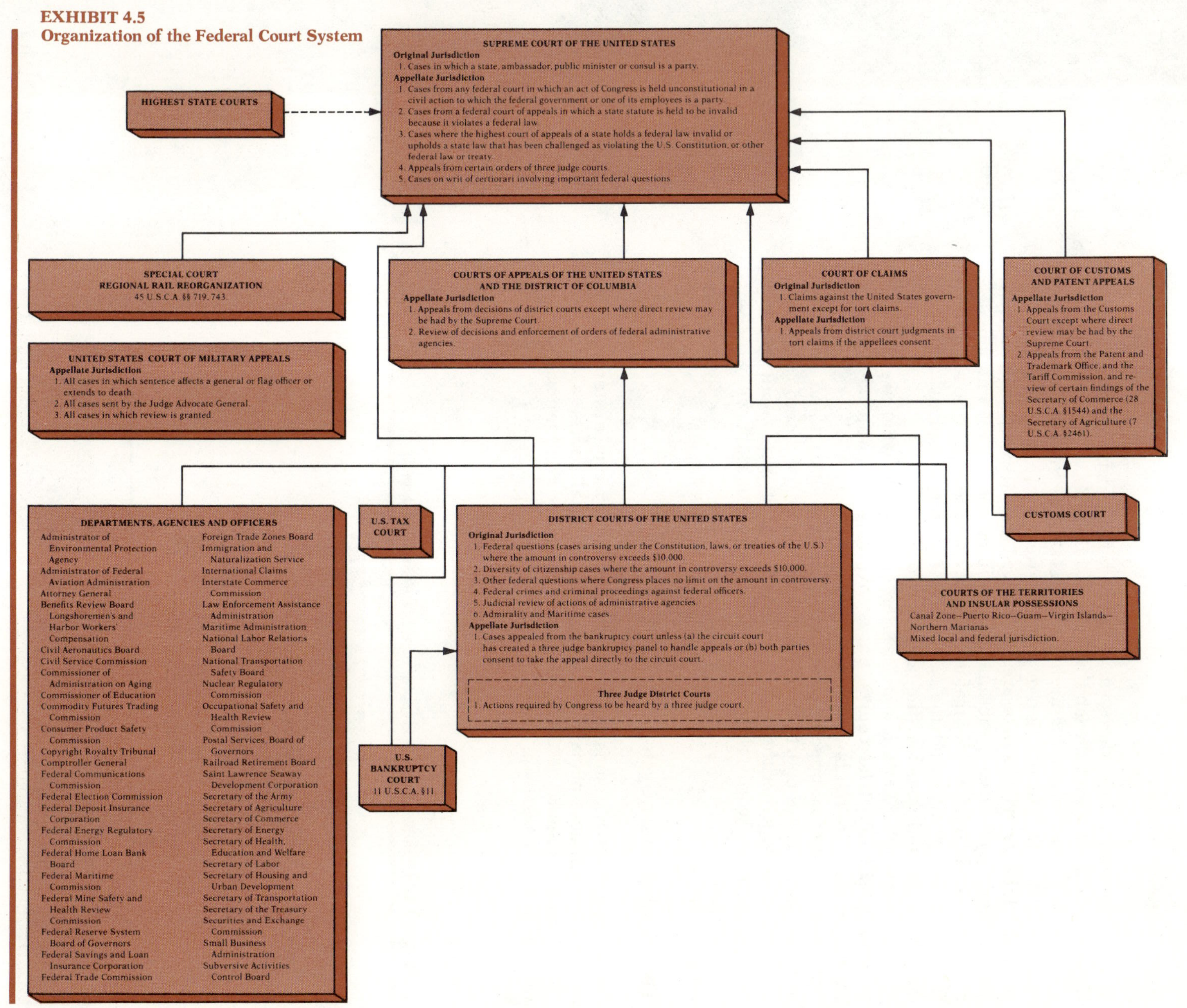

SUPREME COURT OF THE UNITED STATES
Original Jurisdiction
1. Cases in which a state, ambassador, public minister or consul is a party.
Appellate Jurisdiction
1. Cases from any federal court in which an act of Congress is held unconstitutional in a civil action to which the federal government or one of its employees is a party.
2. Cases from a federal court of appeals in which a state statute is held to be invalid because it violates a federal law.
3. Cases where the highest court of appeals of a state holds a federal law invalid or upholds a state law that has been challenged as violating the U.S. Constitution, or other federal law or treaty.
4. Appeals from certain orders of three judge courts.
5. Cases on writ of certiorari involving important federal questions.
HIGHEST STATE COURTS
SPECIAL COURT
REGIONAL RAIL REORGANIZATION
45 U.S.C.A. §§ 719, 743.
UNITED STATES COURT OF MILITARY APPEALS
Appellate Jurisdiction
1. All cases in which sentence affects a general or flag officer or extends to death.
2. All cases sent by the Judge Advocate General.
3. All cases in which review is granted.
COURTS OF APPEALS OF THE UNITED STATES AND THE DISTRICT OF COLUMBIA
Appellate Jurisdiction
1. Appeals from decisions of district courts except where direct review may be had by the Supreme Court.
2. Review of decisions and enforcement of orders of federal administrative agencies.
COURT OF CLAIMS
Original Jurisdiction
1. Claims against the United States government except for tort claims.
Appellate Jurisdiction
1. Appeals from district court judgments in tort claims if the appellees consent.
COURT OF CUSTOMS AND PATENT APPEALS
Appellate Jurisdiction
1. Appeals from the Customs Court except where direct review may be had by the Supreme Court.
2. Appeals from the Patent and Trademark Office, and the Tariff Commission, and review of certain findings of the Secretary of Commerce (28 U.S.C.A. §1544) and the Secretary of Agriculture (7 U.S.C.A. §2461).
CUSTOMS COURT
DEPARTMENTS, AGENCIES AND OFFICERS
Administrator of Environmental Protection Agency
Administrator of Federal Aviation Administration
Attorney General
Benefits Review Board
Longshoremen's and Harbor Workers' Compensation
Civil Aeronautics Board
Civil Service Commission
Commissioner of Administration on Aging
Commissioner of Education
Commodity Futures Trading Commission
Consumer Product Safety Commission
Copyright Royalty Tribunal
Comptroller General
Federal Communications Commission
Federal Election Commission
Federal Deposit Insurance Corporation
Federal Energy Regulatory Commission
Federal Home Loan Bank Board
Federal Maritime Commission
Federal Mine Safety and Health Review Commission
Federal Reserve System Board of Governors
Federal Savings and Loan Insurance Corporation
Federal Trade Commission
Foreign Trade Zones Board
Immigration and Naturalization Service
International Claims
Interstate Commerce Commission
Law Enforcement Assistance Administration
Maritime Administration
National Labor Relations Board
National Transportation Safety Board
Nuclear Regulatory Commission
Occupational Safety and Health Review Commission
Postal Services, Board of Governors
Railroad Retirement Board
Saint Lawrence Seaway Development Corporation
Secretary of the Army
Secretary of Agriculture
Secretary of Commerce
Secretary of Energy
Secretary of Health, Education and Welfare
Secretary of Labor
Secretary of Housing and Urban Development
Secretary of Transportation
Secretary of the Treasury
Securities and Exchange Commission
Small Business Administration
Subversive Activities Control Board
U.S. TAX COURT
DISTRICT COURTS OF THE UNITED STATES
Original Jurisdiction
1. Federal questions (cases arising under the Constitution, laws, or treaties of the U.S.) where the amount in controversy exceeds $10,000.
2. Diversity of citizenship cases where the amount in controversy exceeds $10,000.
3. Other federal questions where Congress places no limit on the amount in controversy.
4. Federal crimes and criminal proceedings against federal officers.
5. Judicial review of actions of administrative agencies.
6. Admiralty and Maritime cases.
Appellate Jurisdiction
1. Cases appealed from the bankruptcy court unless (a) the circuit court has created a three judge bankruptcy panel to handle appeals or (b) both parties consent to take the appeal directly to the circuit court.
Three Judge District Courts
1. Actions required by Congress to be heard by a three judge court.
COURTS OF THE TERRITORIES AND INSULAR POSSESSIONS
Canal Zone—Puerto Rico—Guam—Virgin Islands—Northern Marianas
Mixed local and federal jurisdiction.
U.S. BANKRUPTCY COURT
11 U.S.C.A. §11.

The nation's highest court is the Supreme Court. It consists of nine justices who, like all federal judges, receive lifetime appointments from the president. However, they must be confirmed by the Senate, and their behavior is always subject to review.

The Supreme Court is basically an appellate court. It can review any case decided by any of the federal courts of appeal. Many people are surprised to learn, however, that in a typical case there is no absolute right of appeal to the U.S. Supreme Court. Over 4,500 cases are filed with the Supreme Court each year, yet it hears an average of only 300.

SOME BASIC LAW AFFECTING BUSINESS

Some of the basic areas of the law that affect business are criminal law, contract law, commercial law, property law, the law of torts, and bankruptcy law.

Criminal Law

Businesspeople are concerned with **criminal law** for two reasons. First, businesses are often the target of criminals. The crimes of embezzlement, passing bad checks, shoplifting, and theft, for example, are costly for both businesses and consumers. Second, some criminal law applies directly to the activities of businesses and those who run them.

Fraudulently marking or altering a document to change the legal liability of another is **forgery.** If Brown signs Smith's name to the back of a check made out to Smith, Brown has committed forgery. Forgery also includes changing trademarks, falsifying public records, counterfeiting, and, in fact, altering any legal document.

Robbery is defined as forcefully and unlawfully taking personal property of any value from another. Picking pockets is not robbery, because the action is unknown to the victim.

Burglary is breaking and entering a dwelling with the intent to commit a serious crime.

Anyone who wrongfully or fraudulently takes and carries away the personal property of another is guilty of **larceny.** Many business-related crimes entail fraudulent conduct. Larceny is different from robbery because the latter involves force or fear. Therefore, picking pockets is larceny, not robbery.

Embezzlement is the fraudulent taking of property or money owned by one person but entrusted to another. It typically involves an employee who fraudulently appropriates money. Banks face this problem, and so do a number of businesses in which corporate officers or accountants "jimmy" the books to cover up the fraudulent taking of money for their own benefit. It does not matter whether the accused takes the money from the victim or from another party. If, as the comptroller of a large corporation, Henderson pockets a certain number of checks from third parties that were given to her to deposit into the account of another company, Henderson has committed embezzlement.

It is also a criminal act to obtain goods by means of false pretenses —for example, by buying groceries with a check that you know has insufficient funds to cover it.

The list of crimes affecting business could be extended for many pages. It includes swindles and confidence games; counterfeiting; false credit statements; false advertising; the use of false measures, labels, and weights; arson (burning to defraud insurers); the use of the mails to defraud; and receiving stolen goods.

Corporations, because they are "artificial persons" created by law, can also be held criminally liable for certain acts or omissions. Although they cannot harbor the criminal intent that is required for conviction of a crime, their officers can. The modern tendency is to hold corporations responsible if the penalty is a fine and if intent either is not an element of the crime or can be implied. Obviously, a crime such as perjury cannot be committed by a corporation but can be committed by a natural person, such as an officer of the corporation. Furthermore, crimes punishable by imprisonment or corporal punishment cannot be committed by corporations. However, when a statute allows a fine in addition to or in the place of these penalties, a corporation can be convicted of that crime. If, for example, a statute requires that adequate safety equipment be installed on machines and a corporation fails to do so—and if the result is the death of a worker—the corporation can be fined for committing criminal manslaughter. In addition, the officers of the corporation can be jailed for their conduct.

Contract Law

Contract law governs the relationships between people and those to whom they make promises. A **contract** is defined simply as any agreement between two or more parties that can be enforced in a court. Essentially, a contract is a promise that something shall happen or that something shall not happen in the future. The importance of such promises has been recognized for thousands of years, and they have been enforceable in courts for a very long time. Basically, a contract is enforceable if it includes all of the following elements:

1. *Agreement* The contract must be an agreement that includes an offer and an acceptance. That is, a party must offer to enter into a legal agreement, and another party must agree to the terms of the offer.
2. *Consideration* Any promises made by the parties must be supported by legally sufficient **consideration**—something of value. Legal consideration exists when something is intentionally exchanged for something else. Consider the following example: Jones says to his

son, "In consideration of the fact that you are not as wealthy as your brothers, I will pay you $1,000." This promise is not enforceable, because Jones's son is not giving any consideration to support it. Jones has simply stated his motive for giving a gift to his son.

3. *Contractual capacity* Both parties entering into a contract must have the contractual capacity to do so; that is, they must possess characteristics qualifying them as competent parties. Hence, they must be of legal age, not mentally insane, nor drunk.
4. *Legality* The contract must be made to accomplish some goal that is legal. Contracts that require either party to commit a crime are illegal.
5. *Absence of fraud* There has to be a genuine acknowledgement and understanding of the terms of the contract. The existence of fraud or undue influence makes a contract voidable.
6. *Form* The contract must be in whatever form the law requires. For example, certain contracts for the sale of goods above a value of $500 must be in written form. If they are in oral form, they are not enforceable by a court.

Commercial Law

A system of mercantile courts in England in the Middle Ages administered a law known as *Lex Mercatoria,* or the law merchant. This law was based on the customs of merchants, many of whom traveled from place to place to do business. And the Magna Carta made special provisions for merchants. One section states that all merchants should "have safe and secure conduct, to go out of, and to come into England, and to stay there, and to pass as well by lands as by water, for buying and selling by the ancient and allowed customs."

Even in the early courts, there was an idea that it was fairer to resolve disputes in the way they had been resolved before. Thus it became necessary to keep a written record of court proceedings. The law merchant eventually became part of common law and was incorporated into American law.

In the United States today, business transactions are covered by the Uniform Commercial Code (UCC). It views the entire "commercial transaction for the sale of and payment for goods" as a single legal occurrence having numerous facets. Consider a consumer who buys a refrigerator from an appliance store and agrees to pay for it on an installment plan. Different articles of the UCC cover the contract of sale, the processing of the check given as the down payment and the store's extension of credit to the consumer while retaining a right in the refrigerator (collateral). If the appliance company obtains the refrigerator from a manufacturer's warehouse, several other articles come into play. Every phase of commerce involved in the seemingly simple sale of and payment for goods is provided for in the UCC.

The Law of Property

Property is defined as anything with ascertainable value that is subject to ownership. Property would have little value if the law did not define the right to use it, sell it, and prevent trespassing on it. In the United States, the ownership of property receives unique protection under the law. The Bill of Rights states that "no person shall . . . be deprived of life, liberty, or property, without due process of law; nor shall private property be taken for public use, without just compensation." The Fourteenth Amendment to the U.S. Constitution states that "no State shall . . . deprive any person of life, liberty, or property, without due process of law."

To understand property law, one must distinguish between personal and real property. **Personal property** is a right or interest in personal things that are movable. Immovable property, such as land or houses, is called **real property.** Since personal property and real property differ significantly, the law has developed different sets of rules to deal with their acquisition and transfer of ownership.

Real property is always tangible (with physical substance), but personal property can be tangible or intangible. Examples of tangible personal property include a TV set, heavy construction equipment, or a car. Intangible personal property, such as stocks and bonds, represents some set of rights and duties but has no real physical existence.

As our society has changed, the concept of personal property has expanded to take account of new types of ownership rights. For example, gas, water, and telephone services are now considered property for the purpose of criminal prosecution when they are stolen or used without payment. Federal and state statutes protect against the copying of musical compositions. It is now a crime to engage in "bootlegging"—illegal copying for resale—of records and tapes. And the theft of computer programs is usually considered a theft of personal property.

The Law of Torts

Part of doing business today is the risk of being involved in a lawsuit. An employee injured on the job may attempt to sue the employer because of an unsafe working environment. The consumer who is injured while using a product may attempt to sue the manufacturer because of a defect in the product. The patient who has received negligent treatment may attempt to sue the doctor. The issue in all of these examples is alleged wrongful conduct by one person that causes injury to another. Such wrongful conduct is covered by the law of torts.

Tort law had its origin in early common law. Even today, when most other areas of the law have been codified in statutes, tort law is found primarily in the reports of court opinions. A **tort** can be defined simply as wrongful conduct by one individual that results in injury to another. It is difficult to find a more exact definition, because there are so many different torts, and torts cover the whole range of human activity.

Two notions—wrongs and compensation—serve as the basis of all torts. There are, of course, different types of wrongs. A crime is an act so wrong that it is considered to harm the state or society as a whole, as well as an individual victim. Therefore, the state prosecutes the criminal. A tort is a civil action in which one person brings a suit of a personal nature against another, and the state is not involved. On the other hand, there are some acts that might be considered morally wrong that are not wrong for the purposes of tort law. You and I might consider it wrong to be rude or ungrateful or to shirk our responsibilities, but this type of wrongful conduct does not constitute a tort.

In recent years tort law has been used to combat intentional interference with contractual obligations. A landmark case involved an opera singer, Joanna Wagner, who was under contract to sing for a man named Lumley for a specified period of years.* A man named Gye, who knew of this contract, nonetheless "enticed" Wagner to refuse to carry out the agreement, and Wagner began to sing for Gye. Gye's action constituted a tort because it interfered with the contractual relationship between Wagner and Lumley. In principle, any lawful contract can be the heart of an action for interference with contractual obligations, but the plaintiff must prove that the defendant actually induced a breech of the contract—not merely that the defendant reaped the benefits of a broken contract.

Bankruptcy Law

The U.S. Constitution provides that "the Congress shall have the power . . . to establish . . . uniform laws on the subject of bankruptcies throughout the United States."† Bankruptcy proceedings are therefore rooted in federal laws; bankruptcy courts are special federal courts; and bankruptcy judges are federally appointed. The original Bankruptcy Act was enacted in 1898 and amended by the 1938 Chandler Act. The last major revision occurred in 1978. It now covers every form of bankruptcy procedure available to individuals and organizations.

Bankruptcy law is designed to accomplish two main goals. The first is to protect debtors against frivolous suits by creditors, especially when the debtor is still able to recover. The second major goal is to provide a fair means of distributing a debtor's assets among all creditors. Bankruptcy law establishes priorities among creditors and prohibits the debtor from favoring one creditor over another.

Bankruptcy may occur voluntarily or involuntarily. For a voluntary bankruptcy, the debtor—whether a natural person, a firm, an association, or a corporation—files a petition. (Voluntary bankruptcy is pro-

*Lumley v. Gye, 118 Eng. Rep. 749 (1853).

†Article I, Section 8, Clause 4.

hibited for banking corporations, building and loan associations, insurance corporations, municipal corporations, and railroad corporations, which are subject to special laws.) Generally, a person can declare bankruptcy only once within a six-year period. A voluntary bankruptcy petition for a partnership requires that the petition be signed by all of the partners.

Involuntary bankruptcy occurs when creditors force a debtor into bankruptcy proceedings by filing a petition. Any natural person or any business or corporation owing $5,000 or more—except for farmers and nonbusiness corporations—can be petitioned into involuntary bankruptcy by creditors. As long as the debtor is generally not paying off his or her debts as they become due, involuntary bankruptcy can be initiated.*

*Bankruptcy Reform Act of 1978, Sec. 303(h) (1).

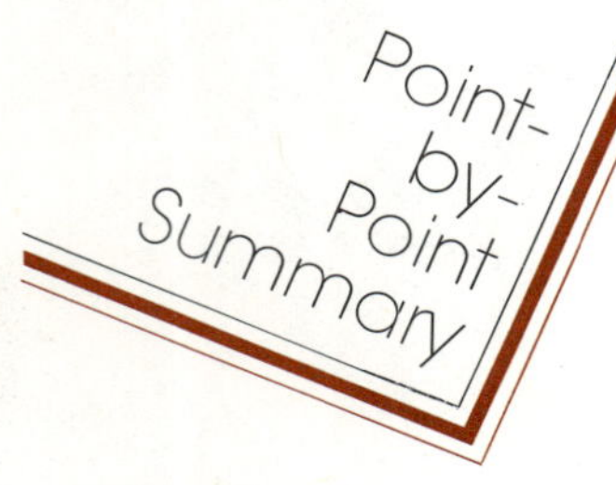

- Whenever property is owned by everyone—as common property—it is a potential pollution problem. One way to solve pollution problems is for government to legislate the socially correct use of common property, such as air and water.
- The Federal Trade Commission has been given extensive responsibilities for protecting consumers. It can issue cease-and-desist orders and impose fines on companies that engage in unfair business practices, and it can prevent price discrimination.
- The Occupational Safety and Health Administration is responsible for regulating business to protect workers, especially in regard to safety. However, OSHA inspectors must now have warrants in order to make inspections.
- The most important pieces of antitrust legislation are the Sherman Antitrust Act, the Clayton Antitrust Act, the Federal Trade Commission Act of 1914, and the Robinson-Patman Act.
- The legal environment of business includes laws handed down by the courts—case or common law—and laws handed down by legislation—statute law. Additionally, businesses are governed by rules established by federal and state agencies.
- Criminal law involves cases in which an individual or business commits some wrong against the state. Criminal law covers forgery, robbery, burglary, larceny, and embezzlement, among other things.
- Contract law governs the relationships between people and those to whom they make promises. A contract is any agreement that can be enforced in a court. In order to be enforceable, it must be an agreement, involve consideration, take place between responsible parties, be legal, involve no fraud, and be in the correct form.

- The most important body of law governing sales in the United States is the Uniform Commercial Code, which has been adopted by every state in the nation, except Louisiana.
- In applying the law of property, one must distinguish between personal and real property. Personal property is any thing or any interest in a thing that is movable. Real property, such as land and houses, is immovable.
- The law of torts covers wrongful conduct by one individual that results in injury to another. Business torts include infringement on trademarks, patents, and copyrights and malicious injury to business.
- Bankruptcy law is designed to protect debtors and to provide a fair means of distributing a debtor's assets among all creditors.

1. Why do you think pollution was not as serious a problem in the 1900s as it has been in the twentieth century? (Or was it?)
2. Under what circumstances would you, as a businessperson, not want to allow an OSHA inspector to enter your premises?
3. What are some of the ways that businesses can restrain trade? Which pieces of legislation prevent such practices?
4. How would you define cutthroat pricing? How could you spot it in the marketplace?
5. What is the distinction between contract law and criminal law?
6. Assume you own a business. A customer slips and falls on your premises and then sues you. What type of law is involved here?
7. One set of laws governs virtually all commercial sales in the United States. What is this set of laws called?
8. Is a stock personal or real property? Is it tangible or intangible? How would you classify telephone services? Are they rightfully property?

APPLICATION

Bethlehem Steel Corporation is 20 million net tons of raw steel. It is a corporation with 100,000 employees whose average hourly wage in 1979 was over $16. Bethlehem, which now faces serious competition from foreign steel industries, has responded by asking the government for help. At the same time, Bethlehem and other large steel-manufacturing companies have been asking the government to stop what they consider to be overregulation of their industry and of business in general.

BETHLEHEM'S ORGANIZATION

In 1904, Charles M. Schwab took the leadership of a small steel company along the banks of the Lehigh River in Bethlehem, Pennsylvania. Schwab was eventually joined by Eugene Grace, and together they formed one of the strongest management teams in American industry. After seventy-five years, their company was the second-largest steelmaker in America and the third-largest in the Western world. Although steel remains the company's primary product, it also builds and repairs ships and mobile offshore oil-drilling platforms. It has also begun to manufacture plastic products.

Bethlehem is a fully integrated company. To guard against shortages of raw materials, it mines ore and coal and quarries limestone, particularly for its own use. It also transports coal, ore, and limestone on the Great Lakes and bulk commodities between foreign ports and to and from the United States.

The company has eight steel-producing plants as well as sixteen other plants for manufacturing miscellaneous steel products. One of its plants produces only wire rope and related products, and another produces industrial fasteners.

Bethlehem has sales offices, mill depots, and supply stores at over eighty locations in the United States. The company sells quantities of steel products to dealers, jobbers, and steel service centers. Its plastics division sells mainly to distributors, except for industrial molded-plastic products, which are sold directly by its own sales force. It also has a very small export division that accounts for only 2 percent of total sales.

Although Bethlehem has not been known as an international company, it established in 1978 a wholly owned subsidiary, Bethlehem International Engineering Corporation (BIEC), that is expanding its program of engineering and technical services worldwide. Its first business venture was a proposal to the People's Republic of China for the development of an iron mine and related materials. BIEC additionally licenses know-how agreements, provides consulting services, and operates training services and project-management services external to Bethlehem.

THE GOVERNMENT AND BETHLEHEM

Steelmaking can be a dirty process, spewing pollutants into the air. Whether because of government regulation or a sense that it should help the community in which it is based, Bethlehem has for many years been involved in developing methods to reduce pollution from its mines, quarries, shipyards, and plants. Since 1950, Bethlehem has spent $800 million on an environmental program. This program is directed at complying with government regulations, but Bethlehem is not afraid to put up a fight if it feels government regulations are not cost-effective. In particular, one of the company's objectives has been to negotiate agreements with federal and state agencies to alter the timing and type of required controls. Bethlehem has anticipated expenditures of $600 million from 1980 to 1985 to satisfy the government's environmental restrictions.

Under certain circumstances, the company has been successful in obtaining delays in the implementation of environmental standards. Because of a 1977 flood at the Johnstown plant, the Environmental Protection Agency and the Pennsylvania Department of Environmental Resources postponed the company's necessary compliance with certain environmental controls at that plant.

In the environmental arena, Bethlehem and the government could be considered adversaries. But Bethlehem's keen desire to restrict imported steel keeps it working with the government. In an annual report issued in February 1980, Bethlehem's chairman, Louis W. Foy, pointed out that the percentage of imported steel in the United States had risen precipitously in the past two decades and that it was apparently going to rise further (see Exhibit 4.6). Foy was concerned with so-called dumping, in which a product is sold in another country at a lower price than in its country of origin. Said Foy, "I am hopeful that the federal government will take the action authorized . . . to put an end to the unfair trade practices that continue to take place in this country."

Clearly, the company faces a dilemma here. Its desire to use the government's power to combat unfair competition from abroad is in a sense inconsistent with its strong plea to reduce government regulation. Companies in a mixed economy are often in this same dilemma. On one hand, they see government doing a tremendous amount of harm to the business community; on the other hand, they see a benefit from employing government to restrict industrial practices in other countries, or even in their own, that harm them or their industry.

CAREER OPPORTUNITIES

Entry-level positions for recent college graduates within Bethlehem Steel Corporation are primarily in the Loop Course management training program. The program is divided into three stages: corporate orientation, plant orientation, and on-the-job training.

The first phase of training is the corporate orientation program. The purpose of this two-week segment is to indoctrinate the Looper in the many facets of Bethlehem Steel. Included are presentations on steel operations, mining, shipbuilding, accounting, and sales and visits to the steel plant in Bethlehem to become familiar with the

EXHIBIT 4.6 Steel Imports as a Percentage of Domestic Supply

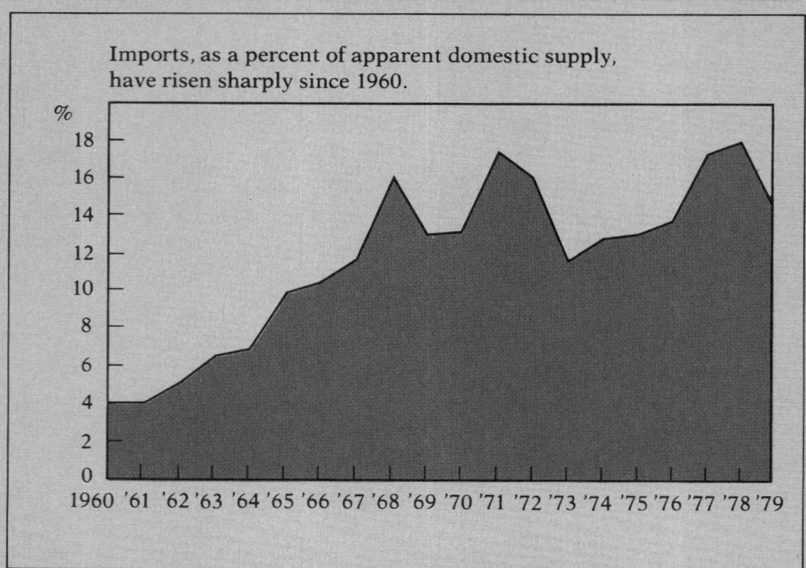

steelmaking process. The Looper gets a complete overview of the corporation and its environment in this phase.

The plant orientation emulates the first phase, but the Loopers travel to the facilities for which they were hired—mutually agreeable locations chosen through interviews and plant visits. The participants become familiar with the plant layouts, departments, and personnel before their actual job training gets under way.

Specific job training for each participant is the final phase of the program. The first and most important activity is the introduction to all of the people within the department and the breakdown of their assignments. The graduate then spends some time learning the job requirements of the position from the people who are doing the job. Through experience and confidence in the nature of the work, more responsibility is acquired. Although classified as a trainee for approximately two years, the graduate can perform many of the tasks associated with the position well before he or she completes the program.

Throughout the Loop Course, the graduate's progress is evaluated—for feedback about the graduate as well as the effectiveness of the training program.

FOR DISCUSSION

1. If you were a stockholder in Bethlehem Steel, would you be in favor of the company spending more than the required amount to satisfy environmental quality controls?
2. In what ways does Bethlehem Steel face overregulation by the government?

PART II

JOHN H. JOHNSON

John H. Johnson's rise to success began when he joined Supreme Life Insurance. As an assistant to the president, Johnson edited a monthly digest of company, local, and national news for blacks. Reader response within the company encouraged him to launch similar publications for general circulation. Tapping into a mailing to Supreme Life policyholders, he recruited 3,000 charter subscribers to the *Negro Digest,* which was patterned loosely after *Reader's Digest.*

Johnson's second publication adopted the picture format of *Life* and the credo "to provide positive images of blacks in a world of negative images." The first issue of *Ebony* hit the Chicago newsstands in November 1945, focusing on black achievements and success stories. In time, Johnson convinced major advertisers that his picture magazine provided direct access to a ripe new market, and *Ebony* was secure. By the mid-1970s, circulation ran well over a million, and ad revenues topped $10 million.

Management

5 Management Principles and Practices
6 The Structure and Design of Organizations
7 Human Relations
8 Human Resource Management
9 Management, Labor, and the Unions
10 Production Management

OBJECTIVES

- ☐ To distinguish between the art of management and the science of management
- ☐ To trace the history and development of management principles from the beginning of the twentieth century to the present
- ☐ To identify and describe the functions of management
- ☐ To describe the various management schools of thought and how each approaches the art of management
- ☐ To understand how the role of the manager has changed in the past and will change in the future

OUTLINE

KEY TERMS

CONTROLLING

DIRECTING

EMPIRICAL MANAGEMENT

GOAL

HUMAN-BEHAVIOR MANAGEMENT

MANAGEMENT

OPERATIONAL MANAGEMENT

OPERATIONAL PLANNING

ORGANIZING

PLAN

PLANNING

SCIENTIFIC MANAGEMENT

SOCIAL-SYSTEM MANAGEMENT

STAFFING

STRATEGIC PLANNING

TAYLORISM

MANAGEMENT PRINCIPLES AND PRACTICES

Management on the Gridiron

FLOYD G. LAWRENCE, *Industry Week*, November 1, 1976

"I'm not a manager but a teacher," reflects head coach Chuck Noll as our interview marks the halftime of a Pittsburgh Steeler practice session.

"And, if your management readers wonder how we motivate our players, I'm afraid they may be disappointed," he adds with a mischievous grin. "The answer is that we don't motivate players. If they don't have motivation when they come here, we drop them."

Whether manager or teacher, Chuck Noll set the National Football League (NFL) championship as the goal he would achieve through directing the efforts of others when he became the Steeler head coach in 1969. That year the team won only one game, and it was four years before the Steelers had a winning season.

During those years mere respectability—a more quickly achievable short-term objective—would have been welcomed by many. But newly appointed head coach Noll wasn't interested in that. His strategy was to build the Steelers girder by girder and rivet by rivet into a structure with the soundness and strength to rise to the pinnacle of professional football.

IMPROVE AS YOU CAN

A key tactic in the Noll plan was the player draft. "The problem in selecting talent is that the players available really are unrelated to the team. So if you go into the draft with the attitude that you are going to draft for a particular position, you are going to make mistakes.

"We always go into the draft with the idea that this is a completely separate entity, a way to stock the team in any way you can improve yourself. Because if you improve yourself in any way, you are going to get better. Even if you improve yourself in a position that you're already strong in, you're going to get better. So you make individual decisions that you feel are right from a long-range standpoint.

"The danger is that if you start making decisions that have long-term implications on a short-range basis, then you will end up with a bunch of pieces that don't fit. So in the building process you're looking longer-term. But as you go along, your drafting process becomes more efficient, because you're starting from a base where almost anybody can make the team and moving toward tighter and more selective requirements. You're in complete control because as your standards go up your performance goes up."

INDIVIDUALS TOTAL TEAMS

"In football a player is only as good as the others around him," adds coach Noll. "So to improve a team, what you've got to do is select the best individuals and then help them through training to become the best that they can. You can have a handful of players who are 'all-world' rated, but you still won't have a team unless every individual is effective.

"So a major part of what we're doing is a selection process—continually evaluating people. We search out men able to learn and willing to pay the price and make the sacrifices to excel in this very difficult profession.

"That's where motivation comes in," observes coach Noll. "We look for men who are self-motivated in the same way that we look for other essential elements of a good player. To contribute to the team he's got to have various skills and aptitudes and other qualities. One of them happens to be tremendous determination—the will to work and become the best that he can be."

EVALUATION UNDER STRESS

Picking talent is a process in which judgments have to be made on performance in a variety of circumstances. Some players function well, for example, in the quiet of the meeting room but their thinking processes fall apart in a pressure situation. Others are unimpressive in a meeting room but are stimulated and function magnificently under stress circumstances. "They're the men we call 'game players,' " explains coach Noll, "because the game situation is where they come into their own."

"We've experimented with personality testing to try to make the process more efficient and to cut down on the time," he adds. "It has some value in the case of college players whom we know little about and particularly if the result is exceptionally positive or negative. But it still reflects just one moment in time and is more a look back than a look ahead. Men can change, depending on what you do to help them help themselves.

"The football season compresses all of the emotions of life into a few short months—elation, despair, trauma, and stress. That takes special people. Not everybody can do it, and not everybody is willing to do it.

"That's why our selection process is so important and covers the physical, mental, and emotional dimensions of the man. It's all right there in a picture window, and we simply have to stay with a man long enough to test him in a wide variety of situations necessary to make those judgments."

MOTIVATION BACKFIRE?

There's clearly the possibility of high motivation leading to low morale if a player finds himself sitting on the bench. But it doesn't lead to hand-holding. "We're not necessarily interested in keeping his spirits up, but in performance. Each player knows that if he works hard enough he's going to play. He knows that we'll help him to improve and earn participation. If he has a different view of us and of himself, then he's not a player you want, and you look to move him.

"By the same token, we're not interested in getting players 'up' for a game. We don't want highs and lows but steady performance. And if players look at the season realistically, that's what you should get, because in the NFL there really are not 'weak' teams. The difference between winning and losing is very small.

"So if you look at the facts, you go into every game with respect for your opponents. You assume your opponents will be at their best, and you get ready to do your best.

"It's true in football—and I suspect the same is true in business—that your own mistakes are going to hurt you more than your competitor does," observes coach Noll. "You observe your competitor and you may learn from him. But your problem is your performance—the thing that you can control.

"If you spend all your time worrying about the other guy, all you're going to do is confuse yourself. You've got to be efficient in your preparation and prepare yourself to be the best."

A PROVEN WAY

Although the quarterback and middle linebacker may appear to be the "managers" on the field, coach Noll notes that in fact *every* player is trained to be a manager of his position—to assume responsibility for the function and to make the right decisions as circumstances unfold.

"There are so many variables in a football game that you can't begin to predict what's going to happen. Each player has to think right and direct himself in doing the right thing in the circumstances," he explains.

"Further, the load shifts from week to week, depending on your opponent. That means, in order to have a championship football team, your players individually have to be better prepared than your opponent to rise to the occasion, to shoulder the load rather than having a committee meeting to discuss who should do the job.

"You might say that we have participative management—we give the guy the right to voluntarily do it our way and expect him to voluntarily do it our way," smiles coach Noll. "But in fact we really do use both authoritative and participative techniques.

"What it comes down to is that our experience has given us a proven way to get something done, and we're going to assert ourselves and try to teach it that way. But if someone has a better way, we certainly don't want them to keep it to themselves. We are still learning all the time, too.

"So if I detect some resistance on the right way to do something, I try to get it out in the open. Only one of two things can happen: if the guy is right and his way is better, then that's the way we're going to do it; if he's wrong and I can prove to him that our way of doing it is the right way, then I've not only solved the problem but I've also made him a believer.

"The one thing you want to avoid is going on the defensive when somebody questions something. That will turn the two of you off in different directions when you need consensus. What we're after is finding the most efficient way and we don't care whose idea it is."

DELEGATING RESPONSIBILITY

The assistant coaches have the ultimate responsibility for deciding what has to be done and the best way to get it done, both in preparing for the season and for each game. They work with the players of their designated positions under the coordination of offensive and defensive coaches whom coach Noll refers to as "coordinators."

"Our preparation for a game is not one giant 'get one for the Gipper' meeting, but assistant coaches working with individuals on their tasks in facing that specific team. We'll change or add as we go along, so it makes a very live, vital emphasis on the practice field. It's not just routine and dreary. We're learning as we go along—the players, the coaches, and everybody. You can't have a championship football team without a championship organization from top to bottom.

"You never quit trying to improve and you never *can* quit trying to improve, because when you think you've arrived, you're starting downhill. You always have shortcomings, and if you want to be the best, you work on your shortcomings.

"That's not easy. It's human nature to go out and do the things you do best. So the tendency is for a good receiver to work on his catching. It's the rare receiver who works on his blocking. But those who work on their shortcomings and make them their strengths are the ones who are going to have the edge that makes them the best.

"What we're seeking to do is give the individual keys for self-analysis. We don't try to put the spotlight on somebody's weaknesses. We put the spotlight on his strengths and try to give him the insight to see his own weaknesses and the help to improve them.

"As individuals and as a team we're really dedicated to only one objective," concludes coach Noll, "to improve every time we go out on the practice field."

The principles of management described in this article are appropriate to managers in all kinds of organizations. What managers do and the principles guiding their actions are the topics of discussion in this chapter.

It is 9:15 on Monday morning. You don't mind your job as a copywriter in a large advertising agency, but Monday mornings are glum. You start to think, "Why am I here so early?" Then another thought occurs to you: "Why is it that my boss, the manager, is always here earlier than I am?" In fact, why is the boss considered to be a manager? What really is managing all about?" The best way to figure this out is to understand the "art" of managing.

The Art of Managing

In general terms, **management** is the achievement of organizational objectives through people, machines, material, and money. Of course, there are many aspects to management.

For one thing, the management of others is a process. Your hypothetical boss at the advertising agency must have skills in design, ad placement, and even copywriting, as well as full knowledge of how to promote an advertising campaign. Indeed, any boss should be familiar with all aspects of every job in his or her department in order to follow through on a project or task from beginning to end. Thus your hypothetical boss not only has to be familiar with the technical side of developing and promoting an ad campaign, but he or she must also have the ability to manage the people, money, and equipment necessary to get the job done.

Every manager must also be competent at leadership, delegation of responsibility, communication, financial planning, and a host of other skills. Together, these things constitute the discipline of management. Background and knowledge in a specific field coupled with the ability to perform day-to-day activities are the two key ingredients in the making of every successful manager.

A TYPICAL MANAGEMENT PROCESS

To get an idea of the scope of a manager's job, let's continue with the example of the advertising agency. Your boss must be able to hire salespeople to go out and obtain new clients or be able to solicit clients herself. If she does solicit new clients, she must be able to meet with them, help them define their problems, and point out their needs. Finally, she must determine whether her firm has the capability in terms of staff and talent to satisfy the client's needs and, if not, what she would have to do to make the firm capable.

Once the contract has been signed, your boss must gather people who can design the ad campaign to meet the needs of the client. This would involve getting copywriters, like you, to create a verbal message and art directors to create sets for the ad. Finally, it would require a project director to put ideas together into a feasible project. All along, your boss would be considering the financial aspects of the project. Does a particular ad campaign suit the financial needs of the client? Does it simultaneously allow for a sufficient profit for the company?

Throughout the entire project, your boss has to be able to get employees to work well together, a task called team building. She also has to get the workers to communicate well with one another, in part by listening. Team building and listening skills are such an important aspect of management that they are treated in more detail in Chapter 7.

Being a manager requires a wide range of knowledge, technical expertise, and working leadership skills. Management also requires shouldering tremendous amounts of responsibility. Your boss is responsible for the commercial and financial success of the project as a whole. She also has to make sure that your copywriting is done right, that your work is not substandard, and must be responsible for your well-being and the development and success of you and other employees.

WHAT MAKES A GOOD MANAGER?

What does it take to be a good manager? Certainly all of the skills mentioned above. But it takes something else too. Some people are simply born with the knack of managing in confused and complicated situations. You or someone you know could be extremely smart, do well in school, and never be a good manager. Certainly anybody can learn the technical skills of management, but some never develop the ability to get along well with people.

"Mr. Riordan is away from his desk."

Drawing by Stevenson; © 1976 The New Yorker Magazine, Inc.

Highlight Management Excellence: SASS and COPE

For years people have been trying to determine exactly what leads to excellence in management. Sociologists, psychologists, economists, and businessleaders have spent years observing and analyzing successful managers in hopes of finding the secret. The consulting firm of McKinsey and Company recently conducted some research into the area and concluded that good management takes a lot of SASS and COPE.

According to McKinsey, excellence in management is most often characterized by hard-working individuals who keep their lives and organizations simple. They don't fall into the trap of analyzing ideas to death. They are aggressive doers and entrepreneurs. They rely on simple communication, and they stress quality and customer service. These successful managers keep tight control over key aspects of the business yet allow and even encourage flexibility and initiative on the part of the people working for them. Finally, these managers establish simple goals, realizing that a well-motivated employee can add as much to profits as some new capital investments.

McKinsey listed the eight attributes of management excellence

- **S**imple form and lean staff
- **A** bias toward action
- **S**tress on one key business value
- **S**imultaneous loose-tight controls

and

- **C**ontinued contact with customers
- **O**perational autonomy to encourage entrepreneurship
- **P**roductivity improvement via consensus of employees
- **E**mphasis on doing what they know best

McKinsey may have a point. If COPE(ing) with the present situation doesn't appear to help, maybe managers should resort to a little SASS.

Even those who are born with a knack for managing must work to refine their skills. Most managers are constantly learning and relearning. Being a good manager means keeping up on all of the latest technical skills pertinent to one's field.

Some people are offended by the high salaries that some top managers receive but they are forgetting the tremendous emotional stress and pressures on managers—even those of small corporations or sole proprietorships. Imagine the pressure on the biggest manager of all—the President of the United States. The President must manage a massive bureaucracy made up of thousands of employees who are trying to satisfy the desires of hundreds of millions of individuals. As President Truman once said, "The buck stops here." Many people would crack under this kind of pressure. Thus management also requires the ability to work well under stress.

LEVELS OF MANAGEMENT

Anyone who is responsible for the performance of other people, even if it is only one other person, is technically a manager. There are basically three levels of management in most organizations—top, middle, and first-line (see Chapter 6). It is not always easy to distinguish among these levels for general purposes, but it is certainly possible to do so within the context of a single organization. For the time being, just keep in mind that these different levels exist and that the nature of the managing job differs according to the level. It is safe to conclude, however,

Highlight Why Top Managers Make So Much

Looking at Exhibit 5.1, you may ask yourself why top managers earn so much. They may not seem "that" good, but rest assured that they are good enough. And one thing is certain: They all work at very large corporations. This is a key to understanding why top management is often so highly paid.

Consider two businesses, one with sales of $1 million and one with sales of $100 million. A 5-percent error by the top management of these two corporations would have drastically different results on sales. A 5-percent error may reduce sales in the smaller company by $50,000, whereas it may reduce sales in the larger corporation by $5 million. Quite a difference, isn't it?

The top manager of a large corporation may be only marginally better than the top manager of a small corporation, but even a little mistake may make a huge difference in the profitability of the large corporation. Hence the high pay.

that the higher an individual is in the management hierarchy, the more pressure, responsibility, and power he or she has.

MANAGEMENT: ART OR SCIENCE?

There is no way to know for sure that a given person even with proper training, will manage well. We can only tell how well a manager has performed after the fact—that is, in retrospect. Thus management is a subjective skill.

Despite the subjective nature of management, there is a science to it, which includes all the technical aspects that any person can learn by reading books on how to handle all the details of business. This means that the science of management involves learning about accounting, production control, manpower planning, and the like.

In large part, the art of management relates to the "sixth sense"—sensing when to chew out an employee and when to praise, when to spend money on a new venture or to acquire a new client, when to step back and go slow. The art of management involves knowing what type of image to portray to clients, as a manager and as a company. The art of management can be fine-tuned, but it cannot be learned, at least not from books. At most, the skilled manager can learn to avoid mistakes that others have made and to review his or her own errors in order to make marginal improvements.

Thus we cannot say that management is either an art or a science. It usually is a combination of the two.

The History and Development of Management

Management, whether it is considered an art or a science, has existed since human beings began to control and manage the behavior of others. Management as a concept has been traced back to 1300 BC. Records from ancient cultures in Egypt, Greece, and China speak of the need for public administration and mention such desirable qualities for managers as honesty and unselfishness. In addition, these records identified some basic principles of management, that is, they set forth specific guide-

EXHIBIT 5.1 The Highest-Paid Executives in the United States

		Salary & bonus	Long-term income	Total com-pensation	Corporate Sales	Corporate Profits
		Thousands of dollars			Millions of dollars	
1. Frank E. Rosenfelt, pres. & CEO	Metro-Goldwyn-Mayer	$ 194	$4,869	$5,063	$ 491	$ 62
2. Rawleigh Warner Jr., chmn.	Mobil	902	3,411	4,313	47,900	2,010
3. Richard W. Vieser, exec. v-p.	McGraw-Edison	76	2,559	2,635	1,331	63
4. Barrie K. Brunet, exec. v-p.	Metro-Goldwyn-Mayer	121	2,330	2,451	491	62
5. Paul P. Woolard, sr. exec. v-p.	Revlon	630	1,738	2,368	1,718	153
6. Michel C. Bergerac, chmn., pres., & CEO	Revlon	900	1,439	2,339	1,718	153
7. William P. Tavoulareas, pres.	Mobil	770	1,543	2,313	47,900	2,010
8. R. M. Holliday, chmn.	Hughes Tool	286	1,838	2,124	805	85
9. Sidney J. Sheinberg, pres. & COO	MCA	330	1,654	1,984	1,266	139
10. James M. Beggs, exec. v-p.	General Dynamics	320	1,655	1,975	4,060	185
11. James D. Aljian, conslt. (1)	Metro-Goldwyn-Mayer	60	1,780	1,840	491	62
12. J. Robert Fluor, chmn., pres. & CEO	Fluor	638	1,146	1,784	3,543	99
13. E. Cardon Walker, pres. & CEO	Walt Disney Productions	245	92	1,521(6)	797	114
14. T. F. Bradshaw, pres.	Atlantic Richfield	524	992	1,516	16,677	1,166
15. Edward B. Walker III, exec. v-p.	Gulf Oil	425	1,067	1,492	26,137	1,322
16. O. C. Boileau, v-p. (2)	Boeing	167	1,171	1,338	8,131	505
17. Thomas D. Barrow, chmn. & CEO	Kennecott Copper	834	475	1,309	2,434	130
18. Jesse I. Aweida, chmn. & pres.	Storage Technology	500	796	1,296	480	40
19. Willard F. Rockwell Jr., chmn. (3)	Rockwell International	578	692	1,270	6,176	261
20. Lee A. Iacocca, pres. (4)	Chrysler	1,266	—	1,266	12,004	(1,097)

(1) Effective May, 1979
(2) Retired Jan. 10, 1980
(3) Retired Apr. 1, 1979
(4) Includes accrued portion of $1.5 million awarded upon employment

CEO = chief executive officer
COO = chief operating officer

Highlight Frederick Who?

By the late nineteenth century, mass-production technology was sweeping the country. More and more Americans were being employed in factories to produce goods. With the sudden increase of personnel, it became clear that American industry was ill prepared to administer and control employees.

Frederick W. Taylor was interested in this shortcoming. Beginning with just a few known management techniques, Taylor (an engineer) began numerous time-and-motion studies. With stopwatch in hand, he timed each separate movement a worker made while completing an assigned task. Taylor timed skilled and unskilled laborers. He compared the times of efficient and inefficient workers and noted possible causes of their effectiveness or lack of it. Next he studied the firm's managers and tried to measure their efficiency.

Naturally, Taylor's findings ruffled feathers in both camps. Management resented being scrutinized. Labor felt his findings would be used to make employees work harder for increased profits. But Taylor felt these charges to be unfounded. Maximum efficiency and increased production were not possible unless workers were content. Fortunately, his ideas were popularized by the press and educators. His treatise became standard practice throughout industry and provided the basis for modern industrial management techniques.

lines of how managers should manage. Through the years these principles, or guidelines, have been expanded and refined by many other people.

The most striking use of management principles has occurred in the Roman Catholic Church and military organizations, both of which have effectively used a hierarchical system based on specialization of activities (see Exhibit 5.2). Supervisors maintain very strict control over subordinates—clerics and soldiers—who work their way up the organizational ladder. At each step, they are given new responsibilities and new authority. Furthermore, as supervisors pass orders to lower-level "employees," they also pass on a doctrine of the organization that helps socialize employees to a certain type of accepted thought or behavior. In large part, these qualities of a hierarchical structure—specialization of task and responsibility and socialization to the organization's doctrine—developed because of the size of these organizations. Large, cumbersome organizations can easily lose focus and control without effective management.

As time continued, so did the refinement of management principles. But until 1911, few had successfully attempted to record or conceptualize these "passed-on" theories of management behavior. In 1911, Frederick W. Taylor published *The Principles of Scientific Management* and started a movement that became known as **Taylorism.** His premise was that management is most efficient when it follows a set of scientifically proven axioms. He advocated that management should

- Replace rule-of-thumb methods with scientific determination of each element of a job
- Select and train workers scientifically

- Cooperate with workers to accomplish work in accordance with scientific methods
- Divide responsibility more equally between managers and workers, with managers planning and organizing the work*

This approach was called **scientific management.**

Taylor's principles went a long way toward forming a general theory of management, yet they were too general to provide managers with guidelines for developing or using management principles. Frenchman Henri Fayol developed a more practical and comprehensive list of management principles that could easily be worked into a useful theory of management. Basically, Fayol believed that organizations perform six independent activities and that the effective management of these activities is based on fourteen general principles. Fayol's efforts laid the groundwork for the development of a comprehensive management theory. Public administrators, social scientists, mathematicians, psychologists, sociologists, and business managers added to his princi-

*F. W. Taylor, *The Principles of Scientific Management* (New York: Harper & Brothers, 1911), p. 7.

EXHIBIT 5.2 Managerial Hierarchies in the U.S. Army and the Roman Catholic Church

Managerial Hierarchy U.S. Army Versus Roman Catholic Church

U.S. Army	Roman Catholic Church
President	Pope
Joint Chiefs of Staff	Cardinals
5 Star General of the Army	Archbishop
4 Star General	Bishop
3 Star Lt. General	Monsignor
2 Star Major General	Priest
1 Star Brigadier General	Deacon
Colonel	
Lt. Colonel	
Major	
Captain	
1st Lieutenant	
2nd Lieutenant	
Warrant Officer 4	
Warrant Officer 3	
Warrant Officer 2	
Warrant Officer 1	
Sergeant Major	
Master Sergeant	
Sergeant 1st Class	
Staff Sergeant	
Buck Sergeant	
Corporal	
Private	

ples. Fayol's work gradually became an entire school of thought in the field of management.

Management Schools of Thought

Throughout time, many theories have been developed of how management does and should work. Practitioners and academicians have created theories revolving around their perceptions of management behavior, what it should be, and how it can best function. Over time, several schools of thought have evolved around these theories, including the four described here.

OPERATIONAL MANAGEMENT

The school of thought commonly referred to as the traditional approach to management—**operational management**—was fathered by Fayol. This school analyzes what managers do and, based on that analysis, develops principles of how managers should perform their functions. For example, Fayol found in his research that all managers, regardless of the organization they work in, perform five functions: planning, organizing, commanding, coordinating, and controlling. Fayol and others then focused on developing general guidelines for how these functions should be performed. Using their approach, a person who wants to learn what management is all about would simply sit down and make a list of some things that a manager ought to be doing, such as planning what workers should do, hiring new workers, and obtaining new clients. This person would read as much about the functions and principles of management as possible and use this knowledge to construct the list. Likewise, when this person was in a managerial position he or she would use this list of functions and principles as a guideline for managing employees and work.

EMPIRICAL MANAGEMENT

In contrast to operational management, the school of **empirical management** advocates a more practical approach to understanding what what management is all about. An expert using this theory of management simply drops in on a production operation, say a steel foundry or a bicycle manufacturing plant. He says to the owner, "I don't want to get in your way. Just let me hang around here for a week. I'm going to take some notes on what you guys are doing." If the owner agrees, this expert spends a week making a list of what's happening. Thus the expert knows what the manager is actually doing but knows little about what the manager should be doing. The empirical approach looks only at what managers actually are doing rather than at what should be happening. Unlike the operational approach, the empirical school of thought does not advocate predetermining lists of managerial functions and activities, instead people learn to be managers by doing and observing the activities of other managers.

HUMAN-BEHAVIOR MANAGEMENT

The logical followup to empirical management is to figure out the basis of how humans behave. Empirical management looks at what people do; **human-behavior management** looks at why people do what they do. It is the study, therefore, of interpersonal relationships and reactions. For example, if an expert went to the bicycle plant and determined that the manager put together a production team for ten-speed racing bikes, he would then try to find out how the team approach to building bikes affected the individual workers. The manager following this school of thought would be interested in understanding what motivates individuals to work, why individuals behave the way they do in certain situations, and how the manager's actions affect human behavior. The human behavior-oriented manager believes that the understanding of human behavior is as important to successful management as is the use of management principles. Thus, in managing people, the manager must be cognizant of how the application of these principles and how their actions affect worker behavior.

SOCIAL-SYSTEM MANAGEMENT

One of the most recently developed theories of management tries to take account of the other three. **Social-system management,** which is basically sociopsychological, shows how humans with different cultural backgrounds, needs, and expectations affect the nature and success of a group working together. Some experts label this the school of cooperative thought, because it is the cooperation of individual members of a team that managers must contend with. Noncooperation destroys team effort and often makes it impossible to get anything done. This school of thought is really an extension of the human-behavior school. However, in the human-behavior school the emphasis is on understanding the psychology of individual behavior while the social-system approach focuses attention on understanding the psychology of group behavior and how groups affect the managing process.

The Functions of Management

Managers, whatever the school of thought they ascribe to, tend to undertake five basic functions: planning, organizing, staffing, directing, and controlling. There may be others, of course, but these represent the major portion of a manager's job. Exhibit 5.3 presents an overview of the five basic functions.

PLANNING

Planning is the process of setting goals for the organization and developing strategies, or approaches, to accomplish them. A **goal** is something you would like to get accomplished in a particular time period. In other words, it is a target—something to strive for. Besides setting goals in the planning process, managers must also decide how they will go about accomplishing them. The course of action developed by the manager is called a **plan.**

In order for goals to be meaningful, they should be stated in as much detail as possible and should be quantified. A poorly stated goal: I would like to do well this semester in my courses. A well-stated goal: I would like to get an overall B average in my courses this semester;

EXHIBIT 5.3 An Overview of the Five Management Functions

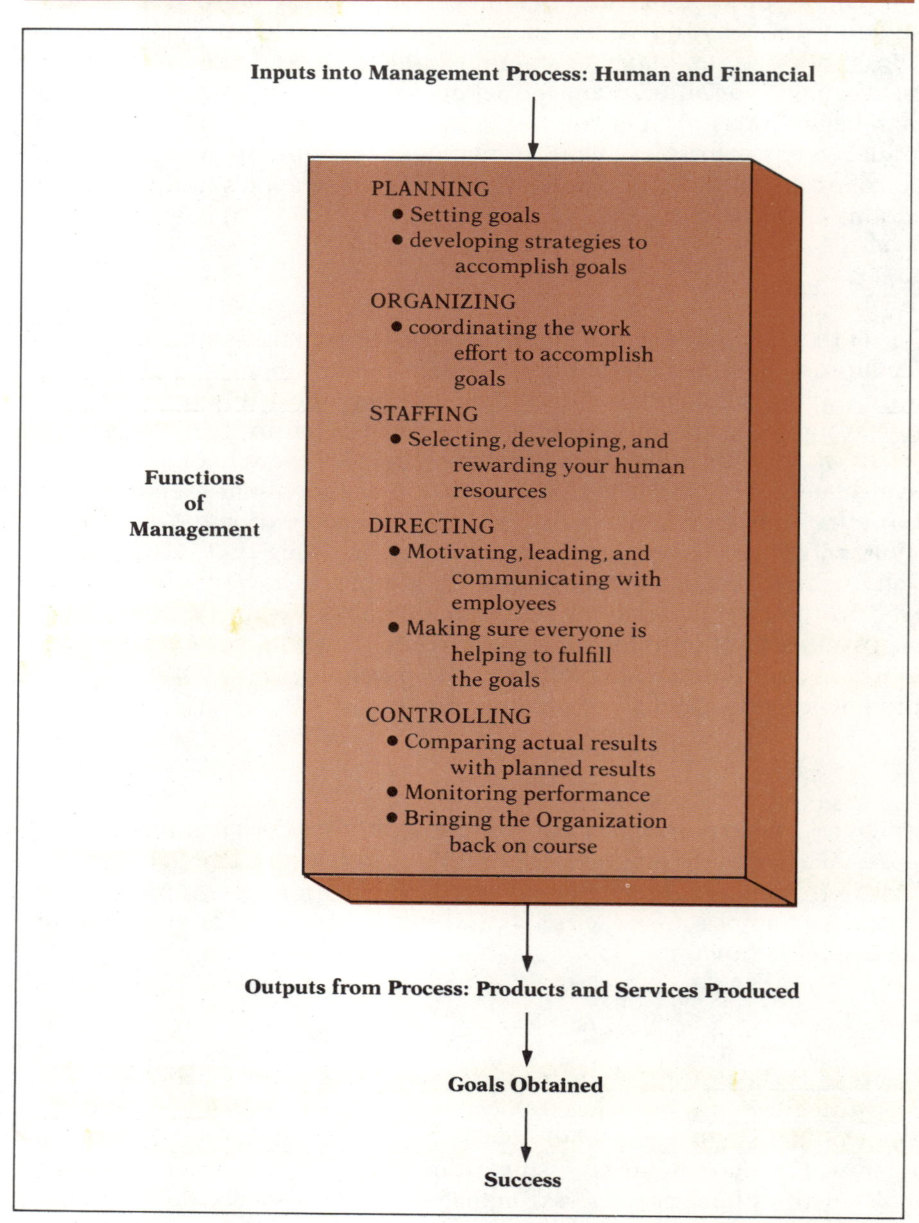

Inputs into Management Process: Human and Financial
Functions of Management
PLANNING
• Setting goals
• developing strategies to accomplish goals
ORGANIZING
• coordinating the work effort to accomplish goals
STAFFING
• Selecting, developing, and rewarding your human resources
DIRECTING
• Motivating, leading, and communicating with employees
• Making sure everyone is helping to fulfill the goals
CONTROLLING
• Comparing actual results with planned results
• Monitoring performance
• Bringing the Organization back on course
Outputs from Process: Products and Services Produced
Goals Obtained
Success

I'll try to get C in accounting and in finance and A in English and in history. Notice the difference between these two statements. One is broad and ill defined, but the other commits the student to a particular course of action. The "good" goal statement will also assist the student in evaluating his or her personal performance after the semester is completed. If the student does not meet the goal, it will be quite clear what went wrong.

Planning comes in two forms, **strategic planning** is concerned with the long term, and **operational planning** is concerned with the short term. The following example should help clarify the difference. Most of you who are reading this book are college students. As students, you are probably in constant need of spending money. Say that your goal is to alleviate this situation and that you have developed a long-range plan to meet this goal. You plan to pass all of your courses, graduate, and get a job that pays well. This long-range plan is a good one. You have a goal to achieve and have outlined a course of action to achieve success.

However, your rent must be paid in thirty days, not in three years. To pay the rent you need a short-range plan that brings in sufficient cash to match your expenses. You need a job that pays well and still leaves enough time to get your homework done. Because you worked two summers ago as a bike mechanic, you decide to open a bicycle repair shop on campus. You have the tools to do the work and the skills to do it.

In developing long-range and short-range plans, you have developed a course of action that meets both your immediate and long-range goals. This is the same task facing managers of organizations.

ORGANIZING

The managerial function of **organizing** involves coordinating the efforts of employees and assigning work activities in such a way that the goals of the organization can be accomplished. In short, it means getting everyone to work together for some common goal. The successful execution of plans and fulfillment of goals is often dictated by how effectively management organizes people for work. Disorganization can lead to inefficiency and ineffectiveness in the workplace, employee frustration and confusion, and eventually to business failure.

Great military leaders, such as General George Patton and German Field Marshall Erwin Rommel, achieved their reputation as much for their organizing skills as for their tactical abilities. Most of the great leaders in business, past and present, have the common characteristic of being good organizers. You too can benefit by being a good organizer, if only in the conduct of your own life. Exhibit 5.4 shows one method for coordinating your own resources and tasks.

Organizing is such an important management function that a large portion of Chapter 6 is devoted to it. Suffice it to say for now that the other management functions cannot effectively be performed unless the manager is adept at organizing.

EXHIBIT 5.4 A Personal Time Plan

Fixed Appointments			Items To Do
8:30	Class	A	Read two chapters in Intro. Business
9:30	Class	A	Study two hours for Spanish quiz
10:30		O	Wash clothes
11:30		B	Write parents
		O	Swim at gym
12:30	Lunch with friends	O	Call about part-time job
1:30	Class	O	Read some more of novel
2:30			
3:30	Dentist's Appointment		
4:30			
5:30			
Evening		**Key:**	A = do first B = do after A's O = fit in odd times

ORGANIZATION IS THE WATCHWORD

STAFFING

Staffing is the process of getting the best possible people to work with or for you. It includes recruiting and hiring the best-qualified people, compensating and promoting them, appraising their performance, and then developing their skills so they can do their job more efficiently.

Issues related to staffing are covered in more depth in Chapters 7 and 8, but an example of how staffing relates to the life of our hypothetical college student may give you an idea of the issues that are involved. Let's assume that you need some help to operate your bike shop. You need three employees, and six people have applied:

- *Norbert* Your roommate, who has no prior experience in repair but is a real nice guy
- *Jean* Your roommate's girlfriend
- *Jan* Your girlfriend
- *Tom* Your best friend, who has no mechanical skills at all
- *Mike* A total stranger who used to own a bike repair shop
- *Jack* Your cousin, who has experience but who you think is unreliable

As you can see, staffing is not always the easiest thing to do. Not everyone comes with the same qualifications, so staffing usually involves some difficult decisions.

DIRECTING

Directing is the process of supervising and guiding employees so that plans are completed and goals are accomplished. It involves motivating people so they will want to strive for excellence and establishing an effective communication network. Communication is essential. In order for people to perform, they must know exactly what it is that the manager wants them to do. Communication also makes it possible to become attuned to the needs and problems of employees.

Let's return to your bicycle repair business. By communicating well with your potential employees, you may find out that Mike's business folded due to lack of quality work. Jean has experience in racing and fixing motorcycles. Tom has experience running a cash register and doing books. Norbert doesn't really want the job; he only applied to get Jean to apply. Now whom do you think you should hire? Through effective communication, you have discovered the strengths and weaknesses of the applicants, and now you can use their talents to ensure the success of your company.

Motivating everyone to do the best job possible comes next. Often money itself is enough of a motivating factor. However, sometimes money is not enough, and other ways must be found.

CONTROLLING

Controlling is making sure that plans are completed and goals are achieved; plans alone do not assure that work will get done. Control is implemented by comparing actual results to planned results and correcting any significant differences. Managers can control their organizations by continually monitoring the use and performance of resources, especially people and money, and providing feedback to all concerned if the plan is not being fulfilled.

Control systems should not be punitive. That is, these systems are not designed to catch people doing a bad job and punish them. Instead, managers should try to provide employees with timely information about their performance to assist their self-development and to ensure that the organization keeps moving in the right direction.

Did you ever wonder why you have examinations or papers due during the semester? Besides the fact that they help the professors determine a final grade for you, they also help the professors exercise managerial control by monitoring your performance and determining whether you are learning what they had originally planned.

Some of the characteristics of an effective control system:

- Differences between planned and actual results are reported in a timely fashion.
- The system is as objective as possible so that feedback is not biased and reflects reality.
- Feedback indicates what actions should be taken to correct any unfavorable deviations from goals or plans.

EXHIBIT 5.5 Management Functions by Level

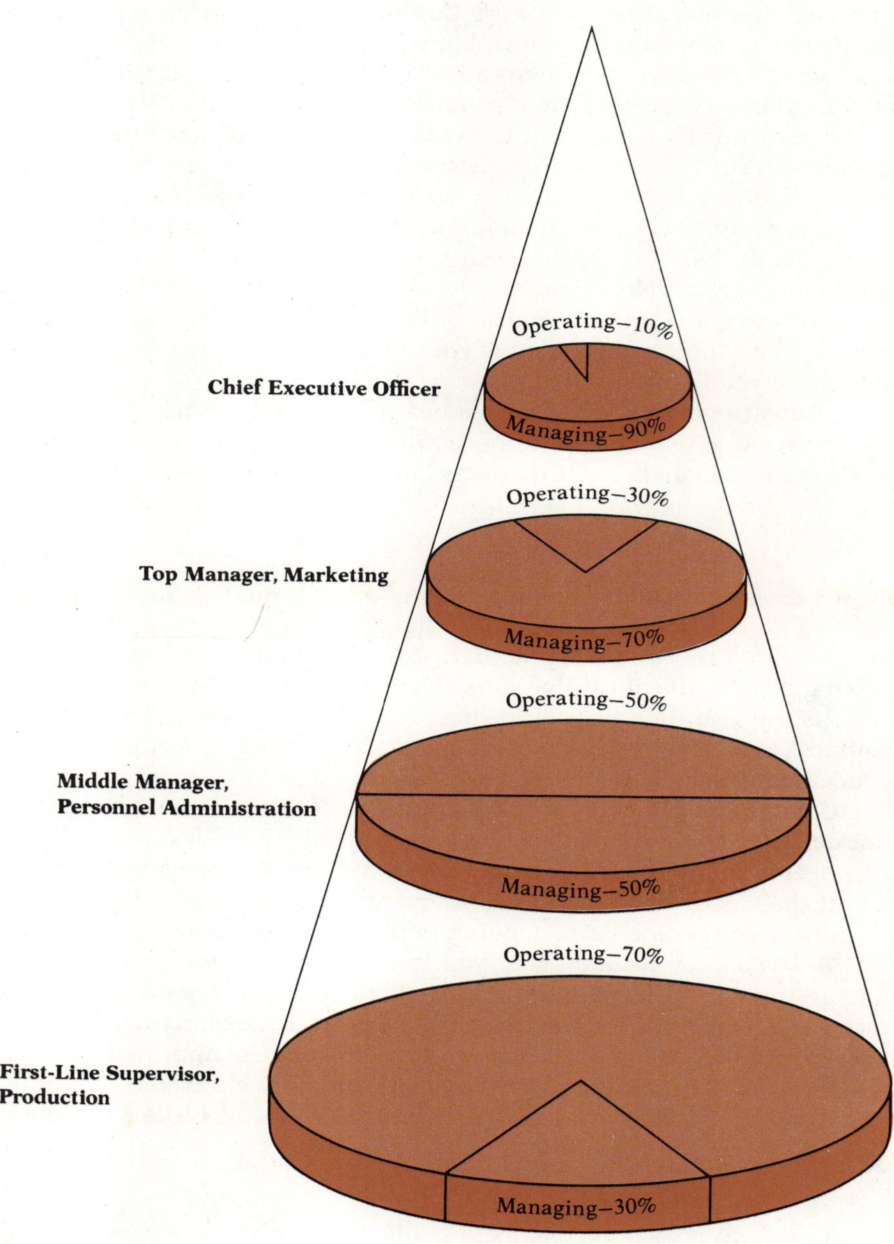

Source: Adapted from "The Time Management Cone," in R. Alec Mackenzie, *Managing Time at the Top* (New York: The Presidents Association, 1970). Copyright © 1972 by R. Alec Mackenzie.

MANAGEMENT FUNCTIONS AND THE LEVELS OF MANAGEMENT

Regardless of level, all managers get involved at one time or another with all the management functions. However, the relative amount of time spent on any particular aspect of managing depends on management level. For example, top managers spend the majority of their time planning, whereas lower-level managers are usually more heavily involved in controlling and directing. Exhibit 5.5 shows in a broad sense the relationship between management functions and management levels. The following table expresses in more detail the specific managing functions performed at each level along with the percentages of time spent for each function:

	Planning	**Organizing**	**Staffing**	**Directing**	**Controlling**
Chief Executive Officer (90%)	50%	10%	8%	15%	7%
Top Manager Marketing (70%)	23%	7%	7%	10%	23%
Middle Manager, Personnel (50%)	13%	6%	9%	9%	13%
First-Line Supervisor (30%)	4%	3%	6%	9%	8%

Management and the Changing Environment

Before unionism, before collective bargaining, before participative management, before the idea that management had to be attuned to the needs and desires of employees, management had virtually free rein in determining what employees did while on the job. Social responsibility, unfair labor practices, and government regulation of managerial power were unheard of. Today the process of management is far more complex because of the growing influence of notions of social responsibility, government regulation, and unionism.

Our society's concern with social responsibility has made it necessary for managers to consider the effect of their policies on the public at large, on investors, and on employees. Failure to consider their social responsibilities has meant trouble for some firms. For example, when General Motors started to manufacture the Corvair, public advocates like Ralph Nader questioned the car's safety to the point where production of the car had to be discontinued. Likewise, the perceived dangers inherent in nuclear power plants have caused public controversy and precipitated the formation of groups that have succeeded in stopping the construction of new nuclear plants.

Public interest in social responsibility has generated increased government regulation of industry. For instance, the Occupational Safety and Health Act created literally hundreds of regulations concerning what employees can and cannot do on the job. Regulations like these put constraints on managers and employees alike. Furthermore, they determine the environment that employees will work in.

Unions and unionism have also had a great impact on how managers manage. As explained in Chapter 9, management behavior in the past has had a role in the development of unions. For example, the United Farm Workers, led by Cesar Chavez, was formed in response to the injustices and unfair labor conditions imposed on the farmworkers of California and Arizona. By campaigning successfully for certain rights, American unions have had a significant effect on the relationship between management and labor.

- The two most important elements of the art of managing are the process of managing others and the discipline of management. Thus, managers must not only know how to plan, direct, and control the activities of employees, they must also be familiar with the technical aspects of the business.
- There has been some controversy whether management is a science, which is learned, or an art, which must come naturally. It seems that a certain type of person is the best suited to manage, although some of a manager's methods may be learned.
- Management principles help managers to be more effective and efficient. These principles serve as guidelines for managers in the performance of their jobs.
- Modern developments in management principles can be traced to Frederick W. Taylor and Henri Fayol. However, these principles have changed frequently through the years as we learn more about the art and science of management.
- Schools of management thought include operational management, empirical management, human-behavior management, and social-system management. The operational school looks at what managers ought to be doing as part of their job, while the empirical school studies what managers actually do in practice. In contrast, the human-behavior school and the social-system school focus attention on how the management process is affected by individual human behavior and group behavior, respectively.
- The main functions of management are planning, organizing, staffing, directing, and controlling. Planning is the process of setting goals for the organization and developing strategies, or approaches, to accomplish them. The managerial function of organizing involves coordinating the efforts of employees in such a way that the organization's plans can be accomplished. Staffing is the process of getting

the best possible people to work for the organization while the managerial function of directing is the supervision of employees so that plans are completed and goals accomplished. Finally, controlling involves comparing actual performance to planned performance to determine if plans and goals are being met and if not, why.

- Regardless of managerial level, all managers get involved at one time or another with all the management functions. However, the relative amount of time spent on any particular aspect of managing depends on management level.
- As government regulations and social responsibilities increase, the management process becomes more difficult and complex because managers do not have the free rein they once had in managing the business and its employees.

Questions for Review

1. Distinguish the process of managing from the discipline of managing. Why are both important?
2. Should management be considered an art or a science? Why?
3. If management is an art, why is there a need for management principles?
4. Why is there a need for a theory of management?
5. Which of the four major schools of management thought do you ascribe to? Why?
6. What is the difference between strategic and operational planning? Why are both important?
7. Which comes first: staffing an organization or determining what type of organizational structure to employ? Why?
8. What are the characteristics of good and bad control systems? Provide an illustration of how a control system works in an organization in which you are familiar.
9. Do you feel that the managerial functions must be performed in some set order? Explain your answer.
10. How do you think managing General Motors differs from managing the Mayo Clinic? How are the two tasks similar?

APPLICATION

For a great many people, 1899 was a momentous year. It came at the end of a century that had seen the United States grow from an emerging nation of fifteen states to a world power. That year was also the beginning of another significant chapter in U.S. history: This country was just beginning to reap international benefits from the industrial revolution. It was also the year that Republic Iron and Steel Company was born.

Republic Steel Corporation

Republic steel

HOW IT ALL BEGAN

The Republic Iron and Steel Company was the outgrowth of a merger of thirty-five smaller midwestern iron companies. In its early days, Republic attracted some interesting people, among them John "Bet-a-Million" Gates. Along with some associates, Gates bought into Republic with the idea of using it as the basis for a great steel empire. Although the strategy failed in the Panic of 1906, Republic Iron and Steel grew quickly.

By 1927, Republic was in the hands of Cyrus Eaton, one of this century's most active, eccentric, and brilliant empire builders. It was Eaton's desire to use Republic Iron and Steel as the nucleus for a vast midwestern steel company. In Eaton's view, this steel company would "rival U.S. Steel and whip the tar out of Eugene Grace's Bethlehem Steel."

Eaton's progress was impressive. In 1928 Republic combined forces with Steel and Tubes, Inc., which had plants in Ohio, New York, and Michigan, and merged with Trumbull Steel. Republic's own plants in Youngstown. Ohio gave Republic Iron and Steel much diversity. Union Drawn Steel, with plants in Ohio, Pennsylvania, Conneticut, Indiana, and Ontario, was added in 1929. The Republic Steel Corporation was officially born in 1930 as a result of mergers with three other steel and steel products companies.

Since then, Republic Steel has done better than most expected but worse than optimists like Eaton had hoped. Even before Republic's official birthdate, financial experts were predicting its death. Yet Republic has not died. Financially handicapped through most of the Depression, Republic nevertheless survived to grow in size and production capacity and continued to acquire smaller companies. During the 1960s, Republic's production of raw steel reached an all-time high of 10.7 million net tons (which was topped in 1973 with a total shipment of 11.3 million tons).

THE CURRENT CHALLENGE

Although Republic Steel never reached the goals of Cyrus Eaton, today it is this country's fifth-largest steel manufacturer. (For years, Republic was the third-largest steel company in America, but recent mergers of other financially troubled companies have reduced its proportional size.) Recently its sales reached an all-time high of $3.5 billion. Its corporate umbrella includes steel plants, steel and tubing divisions, and manufacturing, mining, and transportation interests.

However, in the face of rising inflation, a troubled auto industry, and increased foreign competition, Republic's steel shipments have declined to just over 7 million net tons per year. Many foreign steelmakers can get increased productivity for less money. Many believe that if this country's steel industry is to survive, even to compete successfully with foreign competition, it must expand, reinvest and increase labor productivity. To

Overall view of the 84-inch continuous hydrochloric acid pickling line in Republic Steel Corporation's new $250 million flat rolling mill complex in Cleveland, Ohio. The coils of sheet steel in the foreground were first hot rolled and then brought to an extremely clean state in the pickler. Carbon deposits and the mill oxide are removed in the pickling process in order to prevent them from being rolled into the steel in the cold rolling process. The pickling line, which has a trolley-type accumulator, is 750 feet long and can process up to 100,000 tons of hot rolled coils every month.

facilitate this resurgence, the industry will need effective management.

Thus Republic's Steel's goal is to build itself the best management team in the industry. Republic's Chief Executive Officer William De Lancey, has mapped out an extensive program to give the Cleveland-based steel producer a management team that can react to the unknowns of the 1980s. In a recent magazine interview, De Lancey commented on Republic's managerial philosophy. Excerpts from that interview:

We know Republic can't be the biggest steel company, but we don't want to be. We'd like to be the most profitable, but we must recognize that Republic has six separate steel plants, which are more costly to operate than one large facility. Republic, however, can be the best managed steel company, and with the strides we have already made in this direction, I see no reason why we can't accomplish our goal.

Our objective basically is to make satisfactory earnings. . . . [But] it is better for us to concentrate on those product lines and markets where we know we are good, where we know we are efficient, and where we believe we can maintain a competitive edge.

As one looks around Republic Steel today there appears to be a growing number of "younger" looking people in decision-making, responsible, managerial positions. Will you comment on this generation of management in relation to previous generations?

It's a striking difference. It really has to be understood to fully appreciate why it is I'm so dedicated to establishing a type of thinking and management approach that is appropriate for the times that we're now in.

We look for promising younger people and encourage them to exercise their abilities fully, letting them know we are not bound by the philosophy of the past—when it appeared that you had to be at least 55 or 60 years old to hold a position of much responsibility in a steel plant or in the corporate office.

How have the characteristics of the managers—such as ambition, character, confidence, technical competence in their area of specialty, and the ability to motivate people—changed today?

People at all levels are becoming better educated and as a result, aspirations and sensitivities increase. In this setting, old-fashioned motivational approaches become less satisfactory and, in some instances, even counterproductive.

Understanding people and what motivates them will be an increasing premier requirement for tomorrow's managers and executives.

What are the challenges that will face the managers of tomorrow?

Managers will have to be even better prepared to deal effectively with government officials at all levels and with the community. The 60s and, particularly, the 70s have made it abundantly clear that a company does not function in strictly an insular or commercial realm. A corporation has social and public responsibilities—and must be mindful to them.

Today's emerging managers should also be aware that we, in the steel business, have an uphill fight, particularly with respect to achieving satisfactory profitability and in generating adequate new capital. Among other things, this means that tomorrow's top executives must develop a comprehensive understanding of new managerial tools, particularly systems for utilizing computers.

One impression that comes through very readily is that Republic has been directing its activity in planning and analysis and that the computer is a vital part of this program.

This is one of the areas that really exemplifies the type of management approach Republic is following. It has the advantage of embodying a sound intellectual approach but in a very realistic, practical way.

One of the worst fates of planning is for it to be perceived as an ivory tower type of activity. That is not what we're doing. Our planning covers all aspects of the corporate activity. We have a broad master plan and a set of separate individual plans that fit into it. It is a most important part of the program that the managers who are governed by a plan have a major role in establishing their particular plan.

It's no secret that your principal objective, as Republic gets ready to enter the 80s, is to be the best managed steel company.

It's a broad objective. It starts with people and extends out to the methods they follow to get results. We have been achieving considerable success so far in finding and developing the people we need for the job.

We have also installed, in a practical way, procedures which we believe will allow us to optimize the kind of objective analysis and sound thinking which are vital in our business. We have already made great strides in this direction, especially in the administrative areas. We will continue to pursue this goal at all levels, including plant superintendents, supervisors, and operating foremen.*

*"Bill De Lancey's drive is aimed at building Steel's best management team" *33 Metal Producing,* January 1979.

William De Lancey makes it quite evident that Republic Steel is a company with a bright future. As he sees it, clear and innovative decision making, at all levels of management, is the key to Republic's continued success. To help direct managers, De Lancey has laid out a concise and consistent philosophy: Plan, analyze, replan.

De Lancey is quite sure that the marketplace has changed dramatically since he first entered it. Managing people and products, even helping managers to manage, has changed. The key now is for De Lancey and his team to develop a new breed of managers who can help get Republic Steel through the 1980s.

CAREER OPPORTUNITIES

Republic Steel hires people who have a degree in any fields related to business, science, or engineering and technology. Depending on degree and experience, an individual's first assignment might be in industrial engineering, production or maintenance supervision, sales/marketing, research and development, accounting, or mining operations.

Early in any employee's career with the company, he or she takes part in an orientation seminar on the company's organization, products, objectives, and philosophy. Normally an employee will rotate during the first two years among several jobs in his or her general area of interest, getting on-the-job training to supplement classroom sessions.

FOR DISCUSSION

1. Does De Lancey seem to view management as an art or a science? Defend your position.
2. Besides profit, what are some other ways of measuring management performance—according to De Lancey's philosophy?

OBJECTIVES

- ☐ To understand how companies are organized and why they are organized in a certain way
- ☐ To discuss the different models of organizations and their appropriateness in different business settings
- ☐ To understand the concepts of authority and responsibility and how these concepts relate to organizing
- ☐ To identify some of the mistakes commonly made in organizing
- ☐ To define the relationship among organizational structure, the management hierarchy, and goal setting

OUTLINE

KEY TERMS

AUTHORITY
BUREAUCRACY
CENTRALIZATION
CHAIN OF COMMAND
DECENTRALIZATION
DEPARTMENTALIZATION
FORMAL ORGANIZATION
FREE-FORM ORGANIZATION
FUNCTIONAL AUTHORITY
INFORMAL ORGANIZATION
LINE AUTHORITY
MATRIX ORGANIZATION
ORGANIZATION
ORGANIZATIONAL CHART
ORGANIZATIONAL CLIMATE
PROFIT CENTERS
RESPONSIBILITY
SPAN OF CONTROL
STAFF AUTHORITY
TASK FORCE

THE STRUCTURE AND DESIGN OF ORGANIZATIONS

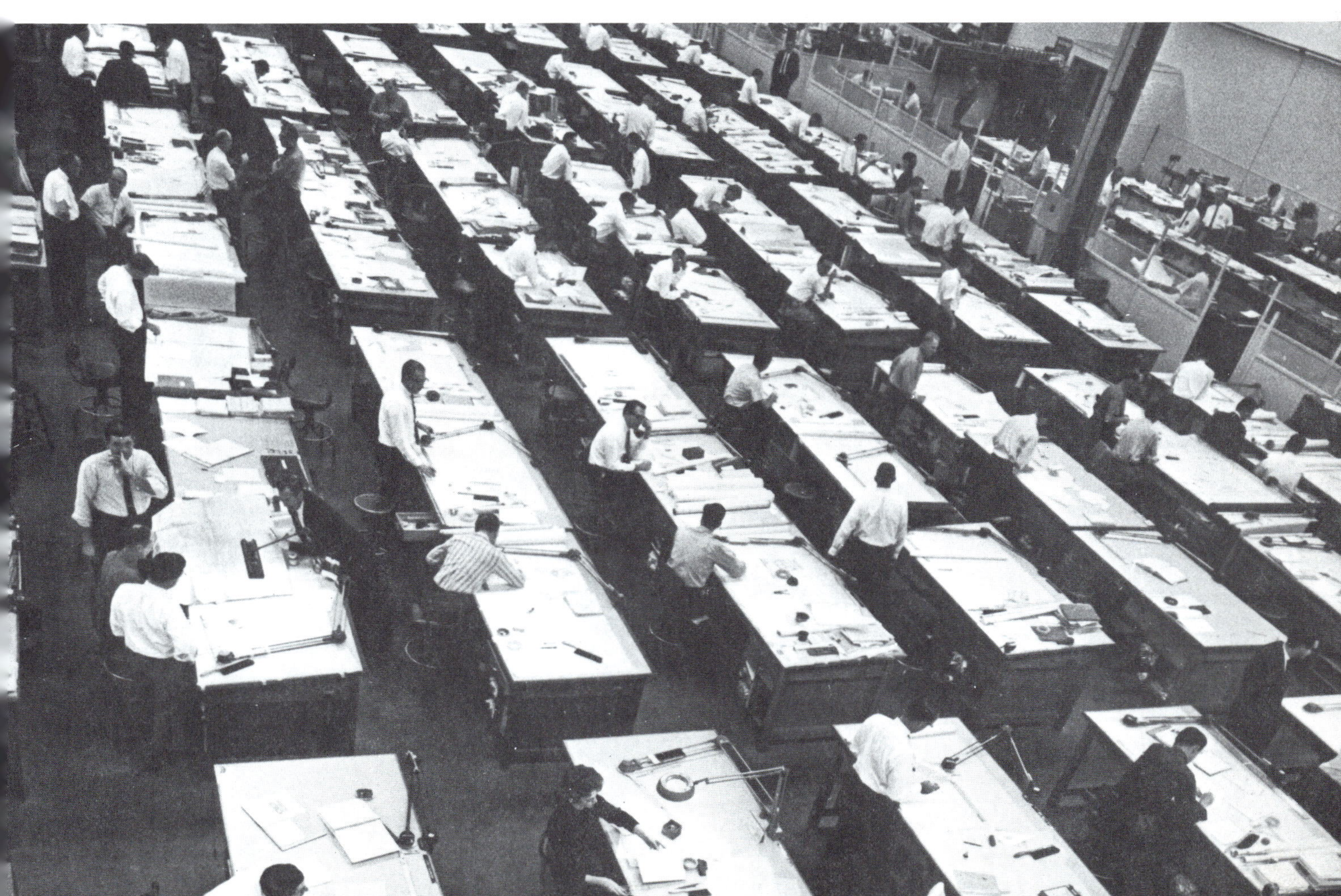

Form Follows Function . . .

JOHN YOUNG
Measure, April/May 1975

JOHN YOUNG, EXECUTIVE VICE PRESIDENT:

"Much can be visualized about how [Hewlett-Packard] works together by referring to the chart of the corporate organization. The balance we strive for is to preserve the flexibility and freedom of action characteristic of a small company with marketing, technological, and management strengths of a larger organization.

"The heart of the organization lies within the six product groups: Instruments, Computer Systems, Components, Medical, Calculators, and Analytical. These recently were expanded from four groups to better fit the businesses we are in, reflecting the dynamic nature of Hewlett-Packard and the measurement and computation field. No doubt we'll see more such changes in the future.

"Each product group is characterized by having a common sales force for all of its divisions' products on a worldwide basis except calculators, which has two. The task is to match our product offering to the applications needs of our customers.

"Other jobs of the group managers are to set overall targets and continually review performance. They also set the strategic direction for the business they are in, and insure that the product programs of the divisions are complementary and make that important 'contribution' to the customer that has so successfully characterized the company over the years.

"The overall corporate organization . . . has been designed to let the divisions and groups concentrate on the product activities that they uniquely can do without each having to understand and perform all the important administrative tasks of doing business on a worldwide basis.

"In particular, the administrative functions of the sales regions and the two international operations (Europe and Intercontinental) provide a broad 'umbrella' over all the field selling and international manufacturing activities of all product groups. Dealing with the tasks of billing and collecting from our customers, determining competitive pay rates in all of the countries where we employ people, and constantly monitoring our position in the major world's currencies are just a few examples of the critical services provided.

"More organizational elements are required to furnish the 'glue' that binds our overall activity together. Those elements include the Corporate Staff departments . . . While their individual functioning is complex and varied, they can be seen as having critical two-way communication ties to the organization as a whole. On the one hand the functional corporate staff office provides the policies and leadership for that function throughout the company. At the same time, they form an important upward communication path through the organization to make sure that a highly informed and expert voice is represented in the company's highest councils.

"Another vital element is . . . the forward planning and development functions represented by Corporate Development and the creation of major new product opportunities and basic technologies in [Hewlett-Packark] Labs. Although their primary mission is to serve as the company's vanguard in terms of planning and technology, they also provide a strong two-way channel of communication in those broad areas.

"The question remains: How does it all work together?

"I think any answer necessarily starts with the corporate objectives. These provide a common denominator that tells everyone what it is we are trying to do and, in general, how we should go about achieving it. Backing up these are the rather complete and formal policies for such areas as finance, personnel and marketing where, for legal and business reasons, specific procedures must be established and followed by everyone.

"The organization also has coordinating bodies that add to the team effort. First is the Executive Council which includes all Corporate Staff heads, group managers and top management of the corporation. Their monthly meetings deal with a wide variety of problems ranging from the business outlook to major policy changes.

"Another body, the Operations Council, has the often tough job of turning policy decisions into corporate action. Representing all the operations of the company, this closely knit team consists of the vice presidents of International and Marketing, the six group managers, the executive vice presidents, and the vice president of Administration. Meetings of the Operations Council are for a full day each month, and recent topics have ranged from a complete review of the compensation program for exempt employees to working out next year's planning cycle.

"Then there are the many gatherings of what might be called 'affinity' groups. These are largely informal in timing and structure but enormously important in terms of their ability to communicate ideas and to stimulate cooperative action over a wide front. Here would be included such get togethers as the twice-yearly general managers meeting, conferences of finance managers, personnel managers, engineering managers, EDP people—and so on. Special publications also serve many of these common-interest groups. The net effect is to share experiences, look for solutions to new problems, and to leave a common frame of reference for future decision making.

This article describes in detail how one large company has organized itself. The topic of this chapter is organizational design and structure. It is an important subject, because how a company organizes itself will have an impact on its performance.

You've gone to school for much of your life, no doubt. Thus you have been a member of an organization. And you will take a job when you finish school, if you haven't already had a number of them. Therefore, you have been or will be a member of another type of organization. It doesn't take much reflection to realize that many of the activities in our world are organized. **Organization** is simply the coordination of people doing different things to accomplish a common goal.

There are literally millions of different types of organizations, and they vary in structure, environment, and purpose. The structure and purpose of an organization dictates the type of people attracted to it and how they act within it. One of the challenges of management is to create an organizational environment in which they all perceive a mutual interest that leads them to pursue the goals and objectives of the organization. Thus a major task of management is to devise an organizational structure that facilitates the achievement of organizational goals while assuring that workers are properly motivated and directed. This chapter looks into some of the issues related to organizational structure and design; employee motivation is the topic of Chapter 7.

The Formal Organization

The "table of contents" for any organization is depicted in its **organizational chart.** This chart shows the official reporting relationships in a company, commonly referred to as the **chain of command,** and indicates how that company organizes its activities. All these things indicate the structure of the **formal organization.**

A typical organizational chart for a manufacturing company is shown in Exhibit 6.1. The company's board of directors has the ultimate responsibility for the successful functioning of the organization. Normally the board delegates responsibility for day-to-day operations to the president, who shares responsibility with the vice presidents, each of whom relies on managers to carry out the organization's functions. A typical organizational chart therefore takes the form of a pyramid—with top management, consisting of only a few individuals, at the apex and a broad base of general employees. The height of the organizational pyramid depends on the number and types of activities performed by the organization and on the number of employees assigned to each manager.

ACTIVITY GROUPS

Most organizations perform a number of different activities in the process of conducting their business. For example, a large company like American Telephone & Telegraph performs in several diverse areas, including production, accounting, personnel, and marketing. Even very small businesses perform a number of different activities.

In order to perform and manage diverse activities, most organizations departmentalize themselves. **Departmentalization** is the process of grouping activities and employees into identifiable areas of the organization. A department is usually headed by a manager who is responsible for the performance of his or her department and its employees.

Departmentalization normally occurs when the organization is performing enough activities that it becomes impossible or undesirable for one manager to oversee the daily operations of the entire business. Thus very large organizations tend to have many levels in their organizational structure. In these large companies, departments may even create their own departments, which in turn may require the creation of other subordinate groups. Each time new departments are formed, the organizational structure gets "taller."

Distinguishing One Group from Another

Imagine an organization that has departments within departments within departments. What should all these departments be called, and how can they be distinguished? Most companies overcome this problem by giving the same general label to all the departments at a particular

EXHIBIT 6.1 Sample Organizational Chart for a Manufacturing Company

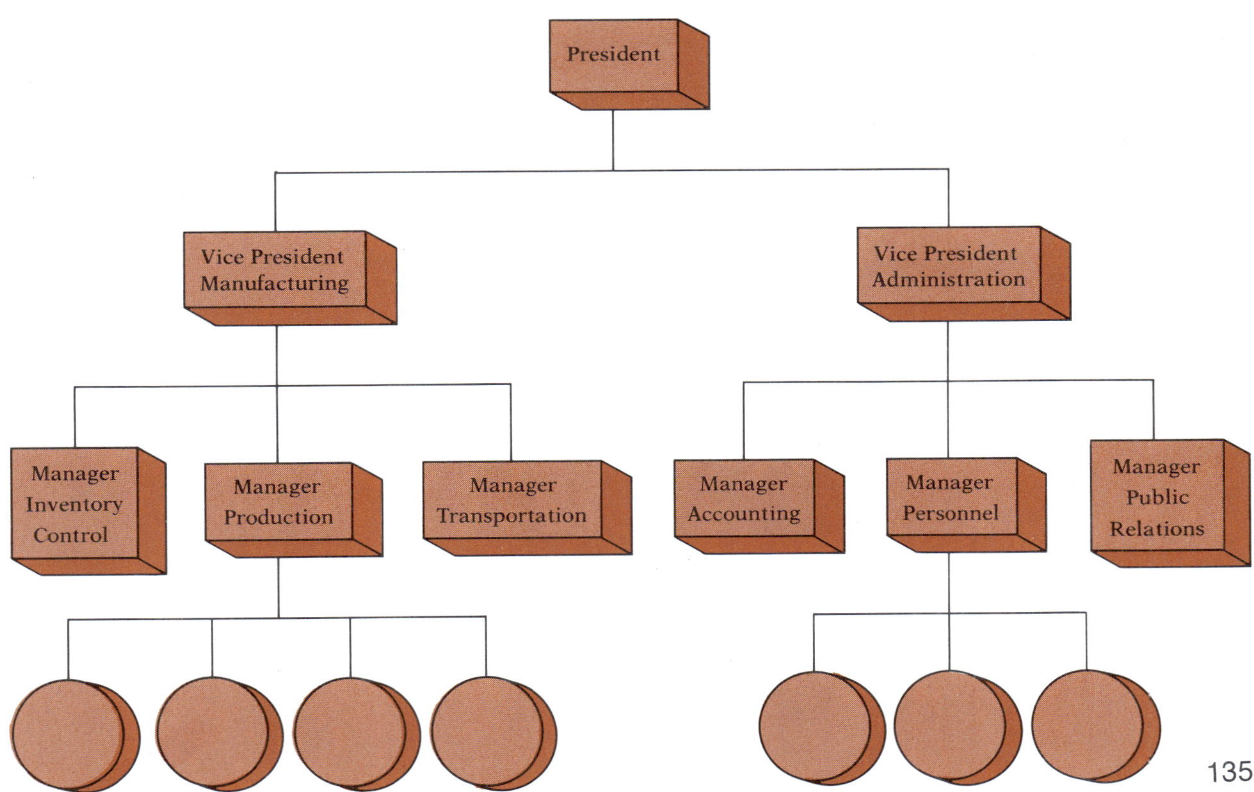

level. For example, The Pubpen Company is a typical medium-size company that publishes magazines and manufactures ballpoint pens. This company's organizational structure is depicted in Exhibit 6.2(a). At the top of the organization is the president and his staff. Since the organization is too large for the president to operate alone, she has decided to departmentalize. The first organizational or departmental level is referred to as the group level. This level consists of three groups, each headed by a vice president with responsibility for the performance of his or her group and its employees. Each group has been further divided to create a second organizational level, referred to as the divisional level. Divisional managers are responsible for what goes on in their divisions and report to the group vice president.

Obviously, this process of departmentalization can go on endlessly. Every time it occurs, a label for the new organizational level must be found. By the way, there is nothing sacred about the labels given to each grouping, and in fact, these labels may be quite different from organization to organization. For comparison, look at the organizational structure and labels used by the Executive Branch of the U.S. government (see Exhibit 6.2(b)).

EXHIBIT 6.2 Organizational Structure of the Pubpen Company (a), and the Executive Branch of the U.S. Government (b)

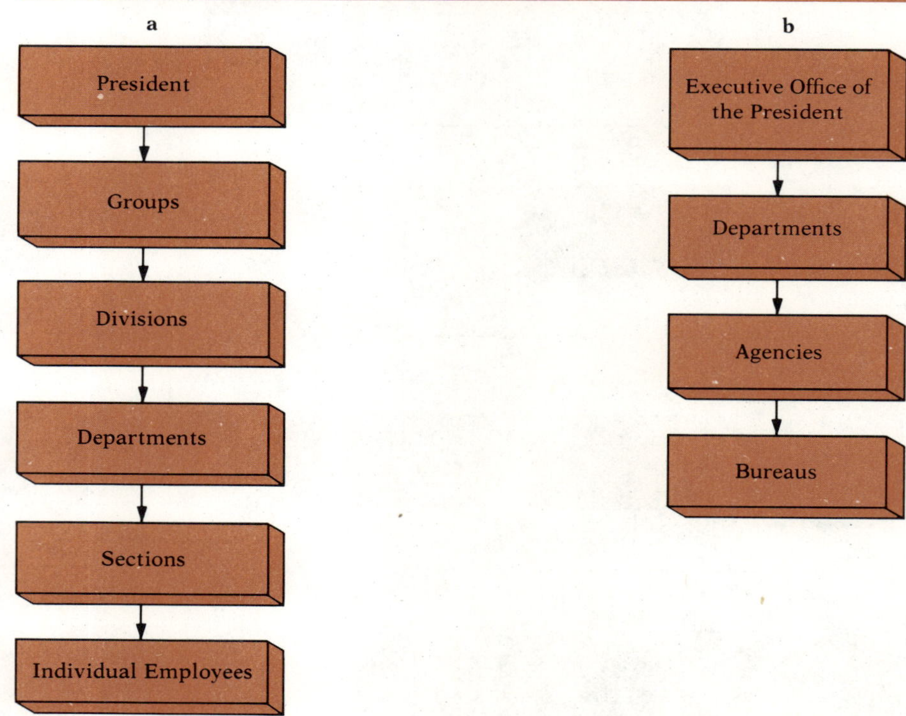

Grouping Activities

There are numerous ways to group activities within organizations. Two of the more frequently used are groupings by function and by product. The functional approach forms groups based on the function performed for the organization. Some of the most basic functions are accounting, production, personnel, sales, and finance. The functional approach is the most widely used basis for departmentalization.

In recent years, departmentalization by product or product line has become popular. This approach involves grouping together all activities related to a particular product. It is not uncommon to then departmentalize each product group by function. This basis of organization is typically used in manufacturing companies with multiple products.

There are many other bases on which organizations can structure themselves. These other methods range in complexity from organizing by numbers—forming departments based on the number of employees—to departmentalization by geographical areas served or by customer. How an organization groups its activities depends on the nature of the organization and its needs.

SPAN OF CONTROL

Another factor that influences the number of organizational levels is each manager's **span of control,** meaning the number of employees supervised by one person. The more people reporting directly to a manager, the more difficult it is for him or her to supervise and coordinate their efforts. Thus the number of employees assigned to one manager is a function of the manager's abilities and the abilities of the employees he or she directs.

The extent of the span of control affects the company's organizational structure. For example, a company with a large span of control (each manager is responsible for a large number of employees) normally has a "flat" organizational structure with only a few managerial levels. A limited span of control for each manager produces an increased number of managerial levels. Exhibit 6.3 illustrates the difference.

There is no magic number to determine the proper size of a manager's span of control, even though this problem has been studied quite often. One of the more interesting studies in this area was conducted by V. A. Gracicunas, a French management consultant, during the 1930s. Gracicunas studied subordinate-superior relationships in a number of organizations and developed a mathematical formula to determine a manager's span of control. Although his formula was never found particularly helpful in determining the proper size for a span of control, the logic he used was helpful in identifying some of the relevant factors. His studies and those that followed seem to indicate that a manager should not be directly responsible for more than seven subordinates and that the ideal span of control is probably between four and seven.

STRUCTURE, HIERARCHY, AND GOALS

It is important to understand that there is a direct relationship among organizational structure, the management hierarchy, and the goal-setting process. As you have seen, a company's management hierarchy parallels the organizational structure. For example, in a "flat" organization, the distinction between top, middle, and lower management is not too discernible or important, because there is unlikely to be much difference in the authority, power, and status of the managers. Any significant differences probably exist only between the top manager and all the other managers, since they are all at the same level. On the other hand, the management hierarchy becomes more noticeable in organizations that have a relatively "tall" structure. As the number of organizational and managerial levels increases, the difference between these levels becomes more pronounced. Eventually, the distinction between top, middle, and lower-level management emerges and becomes clarified.

EXHIBIT 6.3 Span of Control and Organizational Structure

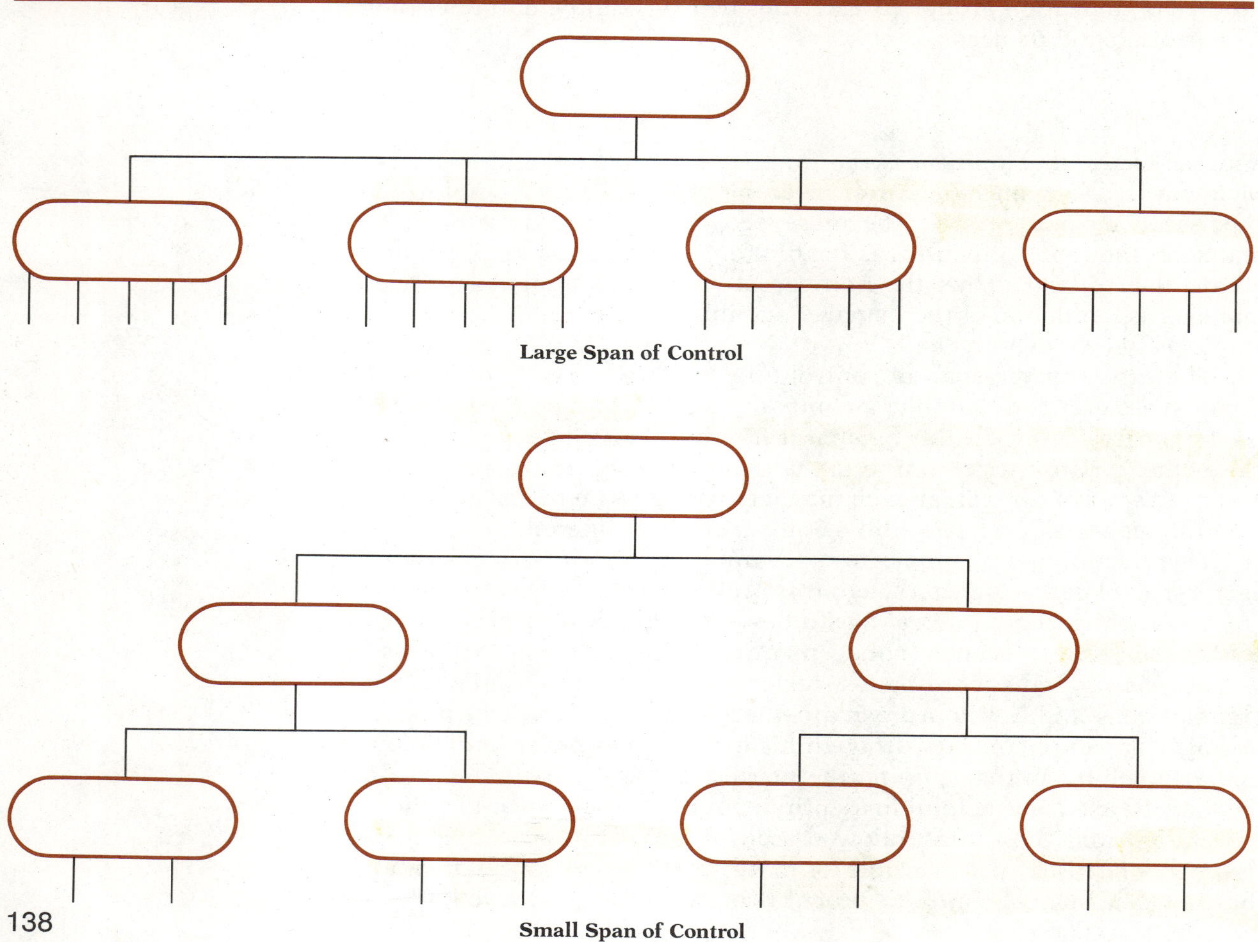

Business in Action

PORTFOLIO II: MANAGEMENT

LONGSHOREMEN'S UNION
LOCAL 10
ILWU
I. L. W. U.
SAN FRANCISCO

Highlight Moses and the Span of Control

"The thing thou doest is not good. Thou wilt surely wear away. . . ."

Exodus 18:17–26

If you were to read the entire passage in Exodus, you would realize that Moses' father-in-law is telling Moses that he is grossly over-extending himself as leader of his people. In effect, the father-in-law is advocating a span of control for the Israeli tribes.

As a leader, Moses dealt daily with all the problems in his "organization." Everybody reported to Moses. In order to manage his people more efficiently, Moses delegated some authority to other able leaders. He made some "rulers of thousands, rulers of hundreds, rulers of fifties and rulers of tens . . . ." These "rulers" judged and counseled their respective groups on "small-matters," saving the "great matters" for Moses alone.

Moses has much in common with his modern-day counterpart—the corporate/business manager. Imagine what would happen if all the employees of a large corporation, like IBM, reported directly to the president of the company. Besides dealing with top-level decisions, the manager might find himself involved with inventory problems in the stockroom. It would be ludicrous to run any organization this way. If so, the manager would "surely wear away," as Moses almost did. Thank Moses' father-in-law for the concept of span of control.

But how does the goal-setting process relate to organizational structure and the management hierarchy? Goals, which are established during the planning process, represent the things management would like to accomplish during a particular period of time. In reality, goals are set from the top down. Once goals have been established, they are communicated to managers at the next-lower level in the organization, and these managers establish goals for their departments. This process is repeated at all successive levels in the organization. The basic premise is that if all managers at all organizational levels establish goals for their own departments and subsequently accomplish them, the organization as a whole will accomplish the goals originally established by top management.

Concepts of Authority and Responsibility

The formal structure of an organization is closely associated with the concepts of authority and responsibility. **Responsibility** means being answerable or accountable for something; **authority** is the right to guide and direct the actions of others and to make decisions. For example, if you are the owner and president of a business, you have the authority, or right, to direct the actions of your employees, within reason, while they are at work. In addition, if the employees do not follow your instructions, you have the power to fire or demote them. Of course, you have the responsibility of fulfilling any contracts, whether or not you still have any employees to help you. As the boss, you also are in the position to delegate some of your authority to other people in the organization. For example, you may promote a machinist to be in charge of all the company's manufacturing operations. You may delegate to this person the authority to direct and guide the actions of the production workers.

Highlight "I Want This Dealership to Make $200,000 This Year"

Automobile dealerships, just like corporations, set goals and measure their performance against the goals. Consider Mighty Motors Auto Dealership. Mike Mighty, the owner, wants to earn $200,000 this year. At a meeting with the managers of the new-car department, the used-car department, and the service department, Mike and his managers figure out how much business each department must do to meet the $200,000 goal.

The managers then meet with their employees to translate this goal into department goals: How many cars must be sold? What models are more profitable? How much repair/body work will have to be completed before the overall goal is met? Monthly financial reports will show each department whether it is succeeding or failing in doing its part to achieve Mike Mighty's $200,000 goal.

There are different types of authority in an organization. Two of the most basic types are line authority and staff authority.

LINE AUTHORITY

Line authority is the most basic, fundamental type of authority in an organization. A line manager has responsibility for directing activities that are directly related to the firm's purpose for being in business. For example, in a typical manufacturing company the most fundamental line organization exists in the production area, because it is the production department that is responsible for producing the products sold by the company. A line organization is also characterized by the fact that management at one level has authority over employees at the next-lower level; thus the line of authority between superviser and subordinate is well defined.

As companies become larger, line managers usually find themselves performing more and more administrative tasks. This work is necessary to support their responsibilities but is auxiliary to the main objectives of the company. These administrative details fall into the areas of personnel (hiring and firing), accounting (determining in financial terms how the company is doing), and public relations (making the company look good).

STAFF AUTHORITY

When line managers have neither the time nor expertise to handle all administrative matters, organizations establish support functions and service departments to assist them. The managers who direct these functions have both line and staff authority. They have line authority in the sense that they have the right to plan, direct, and control the activities of people working in the staff department. However, with respect to the other departments and managers they work with, the staffer or service department employee only has staff authority. Thus **staff authority** gives staffers the right to provide assistance, support, and ad-

Highlight How Not to Do Staff Work

An example of the potential conflict between line and staff authority took place in a local hospital. The hospital administrator, pressured by increased costs and dwindling funds, decided to appoint his talented assistant to spearhead a committee to investigate ways to reduce costs.

The assistant, who had recently received a degree in hospital administration and management, assembled an impressive committee of statisticians, efficiency experts, organizers, planners, and budget personnel to assist him in his effort. This committee found many places to trim costs and distributed its findings to hospital employees.

The response to the report was extremely negative. Although the findings were accurate and the recommendations reasonable, hospital employees resented a "staff employee" telling them how to manage their own domain. The assistant had at no time tried to "sell" his recommendations to the line personnel. Nor had he even bothered to confer with them.

Distaste over how the project was conducted had a disastrous effect on the report—it failed due to lack of cooperation. The assistant had forgotten to pay attention to the subtleties of line and staff authority. Without the acceptance of the hospital employees, the report and its recommendations became a hollow document that never received the attention it might have deserved.

vice to other managers on request but does not give them the right to make other managers follow their wishes. Advice that a staffer provides must be accepted by line managers before it can be implemented.

Many times, the concepts of staff authority and functional authority are confused. **Functional authority** exists when a service department has the power to establish policies that must be followed by all employees in a particular area of the company. For example, the personnel manager usually has the functional authority to establish guidelines for hiring. In contrast, when the personnel manager is called in by another manager for advice on a particular personnel matter, the personnel manager is acting in an advisory capacity and thus has only staff authority.

RESPONSIBILITY

As indicated earlier, the concept of responsibility is closely related to authority. Managers who have authority also have responsibility for results—an obligation to ensure that the job gets done. Conversely, managers should not be held responsible for results unless they also have the authority to produce those results. Recall the earlier example where you put a machinist in charge of manufacturing operations. You could not reasonably hold this person accountable for results in production unless you delegated the authority to direct all facets of the manufacturing operation.

By the way, there is no way top management can ever totally delegate its responsibility for performance. In the final analysis, the overall performance of an organization is the responsibility of top management.

The Informal Organization

In addition to the formal organization developed by management, most companies have an **informal organization**—basically a system of communication created by groups of people with common interests. The structure of the informal organization can cut across formal organizational lines in any number of ways. For example, an informal group may be formed by people who live in the same neighborhood. Despite the fact that they are in different line and staff positions in the company, they communicate with one another and together may support or threaten the formal organizational structure.

Exhibit 6.4 provides another example of how the informal structure can affect the formal structure. The formal structure is depicted by solid lines; the informal structure, by dashed lines. As you can see, the dean is at the top of the organization and supervises the department chairs and the associate dean. The associate dean has several people working directly for her. But if, for example, a department chairperson has a question about a particular academic program, that person may go directly to the appropriate program director or faculty member to get a response rather than going through the associate dean.

The consequences of having an informal organization can be positive or negative:

EXHIBIT 6.4 Informal Contact in a Formal Organization

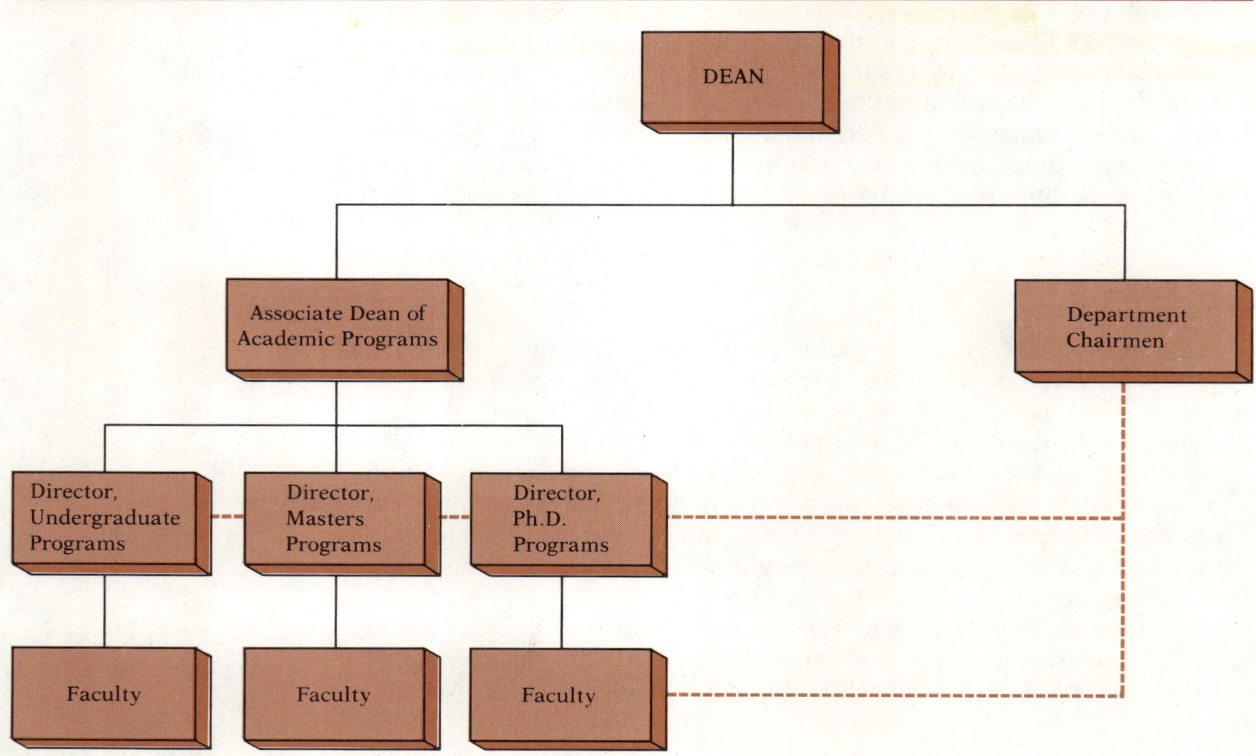

1. *Informal leaders* Sometimes informal groups recognize certain people as their informal leaders. These leaders may have more influence with the workers than formal leaders have.
2. *Worker standards different from the firm's* Informal group members sometimes develop standards of performance that are accepted by the majority of the group members but are in conflict with the formal standards.
3. *Communication by the "grapevine"* The flow of formal information and communication follows the organizational structure. When the formal system fails to meet the information needs of employees, an informal channel of communication known as a grapevine may develop to provide the desired information. The grapevine may pass information upward, downward, crosswise, or randomly throughout the organization, regardless of the formal chain of command. Sometimes communication through the grapevine is more efficient than through formal channels. However, the messages being transmitted may be no more than gossip and half-truths.

Practically all companies have an informal organization. Whether the informal organization works with or against the formal organization depends on whether the company's employees feel that their needs are being satisfied by the organization and that the goals and direction of the organization are compatible with their hopes and aspirations.

Models of Organization

CENTRALIZATION VERSUS DECENTRALIZATION

Numerous models of organizations exist to explain how organizations operate and are formed. Basic to any classification system, however, is the distinction between centralized and decentralized organizations.

A basic issue in organization is whether decision-making authority and responsibility are dispersed throughout the organization—**decentralization**—or are concentrated in the hands of top management—**centralization.** The traditional model in the United States has been centralization, but since the 1950s, decentralization has become more popular in the larger and more complex organizations. There are pros and cons to each pattern.

Decentralized organizations, such as IBM, Du Pont, General Electric, General Motors, and Hewlett-Packard, have the management philosophy that decision making should be delegated as far down the chain of command as possible. Decentralization is carried out by creating, under a central organization (normally corporate headquarters), a number of autonomous units. For example, in General Motors the major automotive divisions, such as Pontiac, Chevrolet, and Cadillac, are run as independent operating units with full responsibility for results and authority commensurate with that responsibility. These GM divisions are not only in competition with other car manufacturers but also with one another. Independent operating units in a decentralized company, sometimes referred to as **profit centers** or investment centers, are held accountable and responsible for their own profits and assets.

Since the 1950s, many large companies have become decentralized. The primary reasons include the following advantages:

1. *Improved decision making* Decisions are often made in a more timely manner in decentralized companies, because there are fewer managers involved in the decision-making process. Furthermore, the quality of the decisions is likely to improve, because decisions are made by those closest to the situation. These people are likely to have the best understanding of the problem at hand.
2. *Improved motivation of employees* The work environment in a decentralized company enhances the professional growth of employees and often motivates them to do a better job. In centralized companies, only a few employees have the opportunity to learn from being held accountable for the results of decisions. People who participate in making decisions often are more committed to the decisions and more motivated to achieve the expected results. Finally, the autonomy created by decentralization motivates managers in the major operating units to do a better job and gives them a feeling of being a big fish in a small pond rather than a little fish in a large pond.

Offsetting these advantages are the problems that can sometimes occur in a decentralized company:

1. *Operating inefficiencies* Decentralization often results in duplication of activities. In a centralized company, most of the staff and support functions are controlled centrally, which promotes uniformity and consistency in the performance of these activities and minimizes the number of people required to perform various jobs. However, in a decentralized company, each major operating unit requires separate staff and support functions. Thus instead of having a centralized personnel office, a decentralized company might have as many personnel offices as major operating units, resulting in a duplication of effort.
2. *Coordination difficulties* Decentralized companies may have trouble getting all the operating units to move in the direction planned by the corporate office. The autonomy created by decentralization may also result in communication problems and possible fragmentation of the organization. If a major operating unit becomes too independent, the corporate office might lose its identity, control, and influence in the operating unit.

Despite these potential problems, large companies continue to decentralize. In recent years, however, some companies have focused instead on refining their current mode of operation in an effort to increase organizational and managerial efficiency and effectiveness and to increase worker motivation and productivity. Thus some have experimented with newer organizational models.

BUREAUCRACY

The term *bureaucracy* is often used to describe big business and big government, usually with a negative connotation. Many times it is used to express anger and frustration over "red tape" and inefficiency. Unfortunately, the common use of the word *bureaucracy* is inaccurate and has caused people to lose sight of the fact that bureaucracy is a type of organization designed to accomplish administrative tasks by coordinating the work of many individuals.

Most of the original concepts of bureaucracy were developed by a German, Max Weber, who characterized **bureaucracy** as follows:

- Regular activities assigned to specific individuals as fixed duties
- A hierarchy of command (commonly referred to as the chain of command)
- A consistent system of rules and standards that cover how work is performed
- Fixed responsibilities for the managers
- Employment based on technical qualifications
- Protection from arbitrary dismissal
- Emphasis on attaining the highest degree of technical efficiency possible

This description should indicate that a bureaucratic organization is not an abnormality but a logical step in the development of large organizations. The challenge for managers is to understand the strengths and weaknesses of such a system and to make the organization as responsive to its workers as possible and as dynamic and adaptive as possible. The inherent danger of a bureaucratic organization is the tendency to become too rigid and to alienate employees and customers by treating them too impersonally.

NEWER MODELS OF ORGANIZATION

In recent years, the bureaucratic model has undergone substantial change. As the business environment has become more complex, organizations have had to change in order to survive. Three of the more common new models are free-form organization, task forces, and matrix organization.

Free-form Organization

According to some analysts, the primary task of management is to manage change. Thus the **free-form organization** reduces its emphasis on positions, departments, organizational charts, chains of command, rigid job descriptions, and the like. In place of the formal organization are operating units—some temporary, others permanent—that blend various functions and parts of the organization to take advantage of new opportunities. The static structure is replaced by an organization

Highlight Task Force: Target Downtown Cleveland

Cleveland, Ohio has rapidly been improving itself. Annoyed by unfounded media jokes and then shocked by its default on loans, Cleveland has the desire to polish its tarnished image. Luckily, the city is blessed with a wealth of human resources. Knowing this, Mayor George V. Voinovich has appointed a special task force to give him suggestions on improving the inner city and downtown.

People from all areas of the city and with diverse interests were appointed to this task force. Bankers, industrialists, merchants, professors, educators, doctors, and community leaders were asked to pool their knowledge and obtain ideas from local interest groups in order to come up with some viable plans to rebuild and revitalize their city.

After six months, the task force filed its report with the mayor. It was, of course, a long-range plan, encompassing everything from an enclosed shopping mall to transportation and public safety. With part of the plan underway, the "renaissance of Cleveland" is taking shape. This project will continue to be implemented, because it has the support of civic and industrial leaders who either served directly on the task force or provided input.

Once the task force's mission was complete, it was disbanded, and members went back to their normal jobs. But Cleveland had at its disposal, for one short period of time, some of its brightest talents studying a problem they all had in common—how to revitalize a city.

that is ready and willing to change in response to changes in the internal and external work environment.

The free-form structure is most likely to appear in organizations devoted to providing products or services on the frontier of public use, such as air pollution devices and electronics instruments. This type of structure would also be very appropriate in a "think tank" environment, where the emphasis is on high levels of employee interaction, creativity, and innovation. Several large companies, including Xerox, Textron, and Polaroid, have recently adopted the free-form structure in certain parts of the organization to enhance operating flexibility.

Task Forces

A **task force** is similar to an ad hoc committee—a temporary committee formed to accomplish a particular job that, when completed, eliminates the need for the task force. This device allows the organization to put together a group of select managers who can focus on a major problem or task with an intensity not possible among managers carrying out their normal duties. The people involved with a task force bring to the problem skills and training particularly appropriate to the task at hand. They usually have decision-making responsibility in addition to the responsibilities for planning, researching, and analyzing the problem under consideration.

Matrix Organization

A **matrix organization** is one that combines functional authority and project-management authority in the same hands. In the hypothetical organization shown in Exhibit 6.5, functional managers retain line authority over their own people, who may be assigned to project teams temporarily. The project teams, much like task forces, are formed on a temporary basis to work on particular projects. Once the project is completed, the team is disbanded, and members become eligible for assignment to other projects. Matrix organization is an attempt to integrate the task force concept with the traditional structure of an organization.

Matrix organizations are most often found in government and in public service (such as health care facilities). In organizations like these, a client's problem typically cannot be resolved by a single operating unit; instead, resolution of the problem might involve many units. As an example, consider the following:

> The client is an alcoholic. He has not worked for six months and has always had difficulty in holding a steady job. His family is currently on welfare, his wife is known to be psychologically disturbed, and his three children are very slow learners in school. One of the children has been arrested as a juvenile and is currently on probation.*

*L. Gray, "Matrix Organizational Design as a Vehicle for Effective Delivery of Public Health Care and Social Services, *Management International Review* 6 (1974): 78.

EXHIBIT 6.5 Sample Matrix Organization

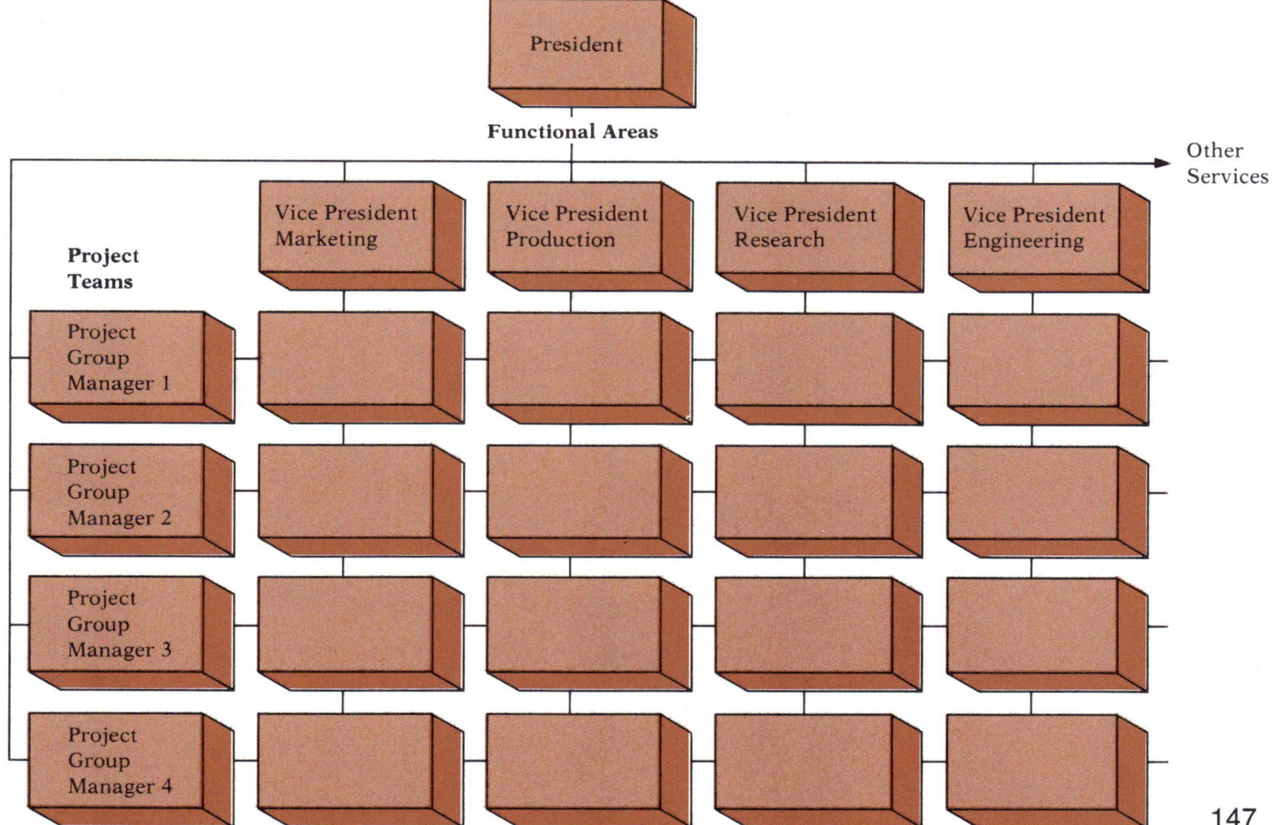

In a bureaucratic organization, this client would be treated by many separate agencies with little coordination. A properly structured matrix organization, like the one depicted in Exhibit 6.6, could adequately serve all elements of his problem.

Common Mistakes in Organizing

Is it possible to make mistakes in organizing? You bet it is! Many a company has suffered because it did not properly organize. Some of the most common mistakes are overstructuring, improperly defining reporting relationships, failing to state clearly who has what kind of authority responsibility, and failing to match authority and responsibility.

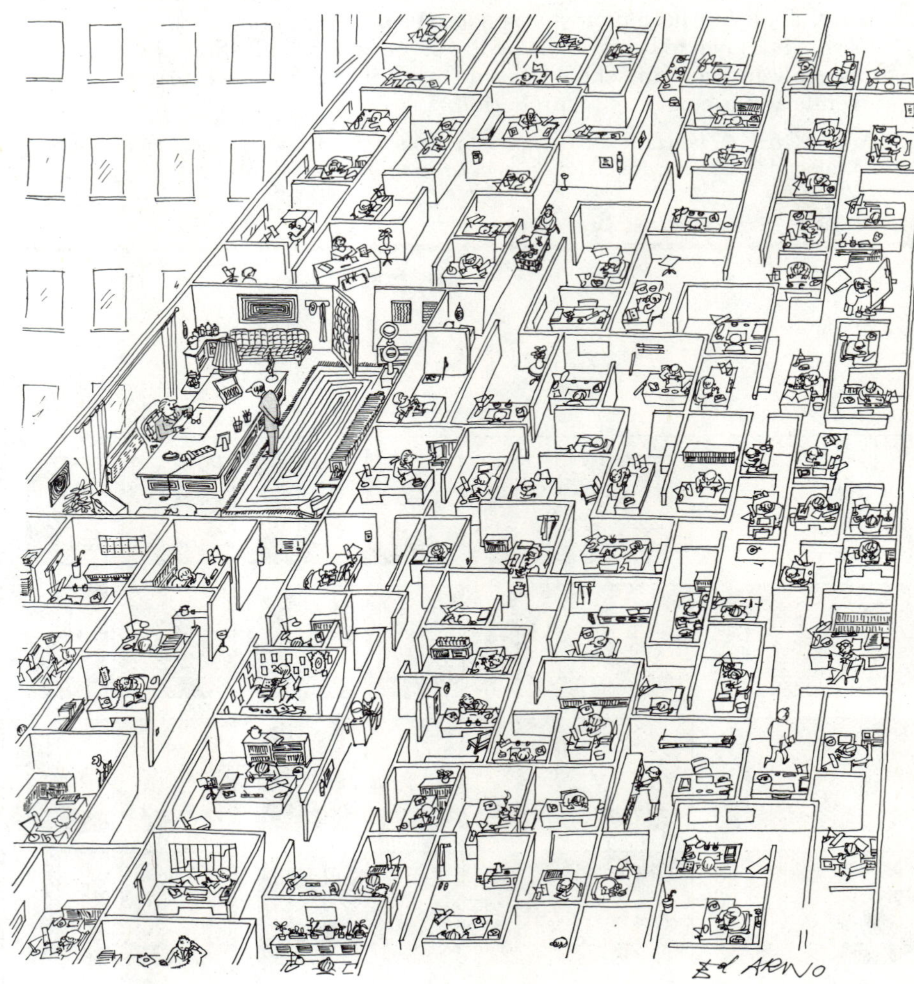

"I'm afraid a raise is out of the question, Benton, but in view of your sixteen years of service we are advancing you two spaces."

EXHIBIT 6.6 Matrix Organization in a Bureaucracy

Source: J. L. Gray "Matrix Organizational Design as a Vehicle for Effective Delivery of Public Health Care and Social Services," *Management International Review*, Volume 6 (1974): 80.

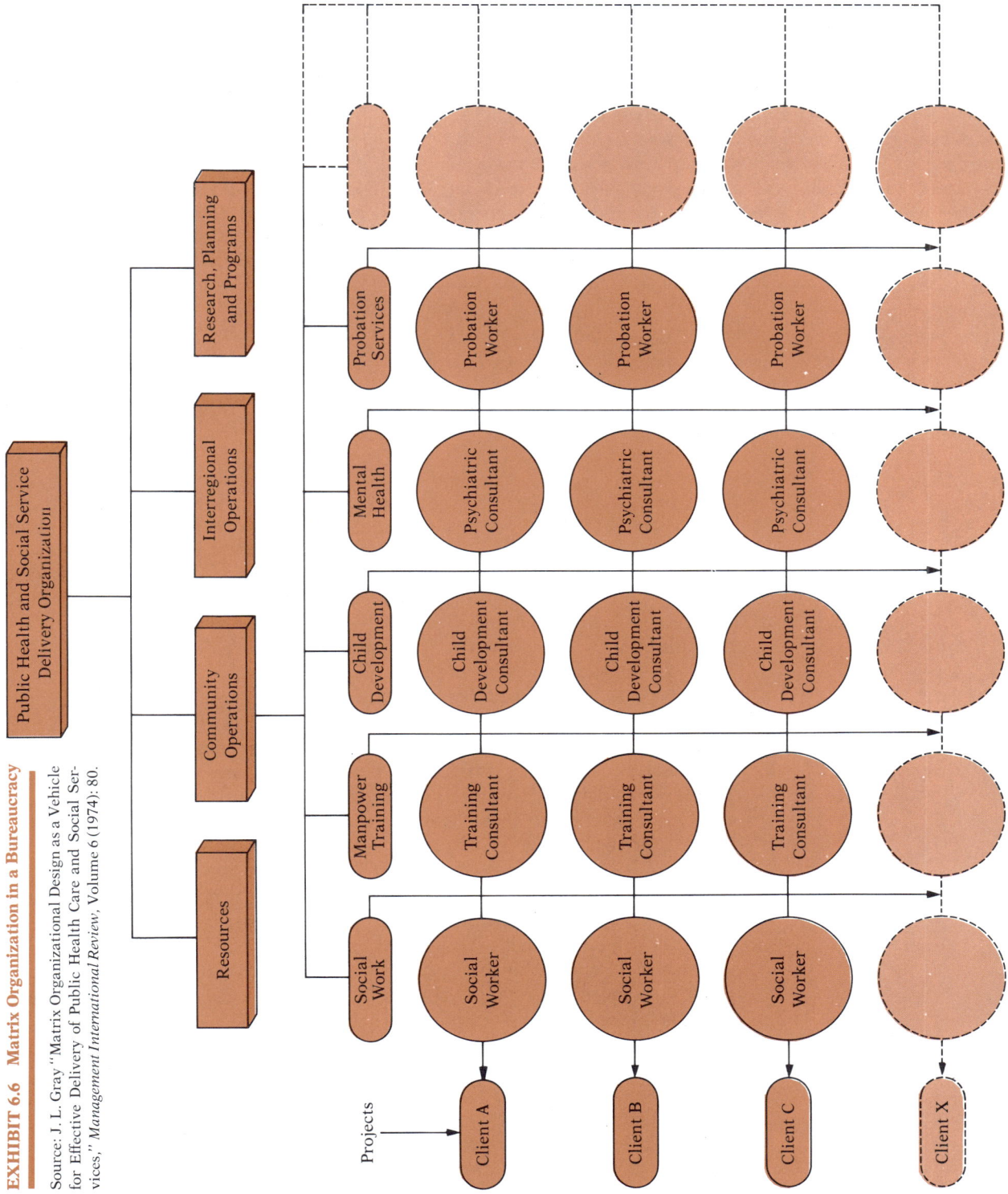

Highlight Misstructuring the Kitchen

Mary and John opened a French restaurant and hired a well-respected gourmet chef to oversee the cooking. But at the last minute, they decided to manage the kitchen themselves. In their eagerness to do everything just right, they instituted many rules about how the food was to be prepared, stored, served, and inventoried. Their overstructuring insulted the chef. He felt constrained and gradually developed a negative attitude toward the business. The result was that the restaurant flopped because of mediocre food.

Not wanting to lose their entire investment, John and Mary waited a few months and reopened. This time they hired several good chefs and allowed them to manage the kitchen. The result was chaos. Each chef felt his way was right. Because the chefs chouldn't agree on any guidelines, there were none. Veal cordon bleu was prepared three different ways, depending on which chef was cooking. Without any regulations to give some order to the kitchen, the chefs soon lost respect for one another and developed a negative attitude toward their job. The result? The restaurant failed again, because John and Mary had understructured their kitchen.

Maybe next time John and Mary will provide just the right amount of organization to get the cooking done.

Overstructuring usually occurs when an organization has established so many rules, procedures, and policies that it stifles creativity and innovation and discourages employee initiative. Such a situation is likely to result in inefficiency and have an unfavorable impact on a company's success. Many of the criticisms leveled at large bureaucratic organizations related to the frustration people feel when established rules and procedures hinder rather than help them.

Another critical mistake companies make in organizing is failing to define clearly reporting relationships. It is not uncommon to find an employee reporting to two or more bosses at the same time. This puts the employee in a very difficult position: Which boss's needs take priority? To avoid this problem, companies must establish reporting relationships that make sense and that are fully understood by managers and employees alike.

Closely associated with the above problem are the common mistakes of failing to specify who has what kind of authority and failing to match authority and responsibility. Pity the person who has the responsibility to accomplish a particular task but was not given proper authority. It would be difficult, if not impossible, for someone in that position to complete the job successfully, because he or she cannot control the factors that influence the outcome of the job. Another sorry case is the staff person who mistakenly believes he or she has line authority and cannot understand why nobody listens.

These mistakes and others like them are unfortunately quite common. Since they eventually create problems for the organization, managers try to anticipate in advance the positive and negative consequences of their organizational structure and eliminate the negative aspects as quickly as possible.

Organizational Climate

It would be unfair to end this chapter without some brief discussion of organizational climate. How a company organizes itself and how managers manage have an impact on how employees feel about their organization. **Organizational climate** is the quality of the environment within the organization and the impact of this climate on employees. Some companies have an environment that instills in workers a very positive attitude toward the company. Employees view their organization with pride and are likely to be more productive and loyal. In such a situation, the climate is considered healthy. Of course, there are also organizations with unhealthy climates that cause frustration and unhappiness in employees.

Organizational climate is not something that can be measured easily or with certainty. Nonetheless, a climate exists in every company, large or small, and one of the real challenges of management is to organize in such a way as to enhance the health of the organization. Therefore, in analyzing the effectiveness of an organizational structure and in designing organizations, as much attention must be paid to climate as to organizational charts and other such things.

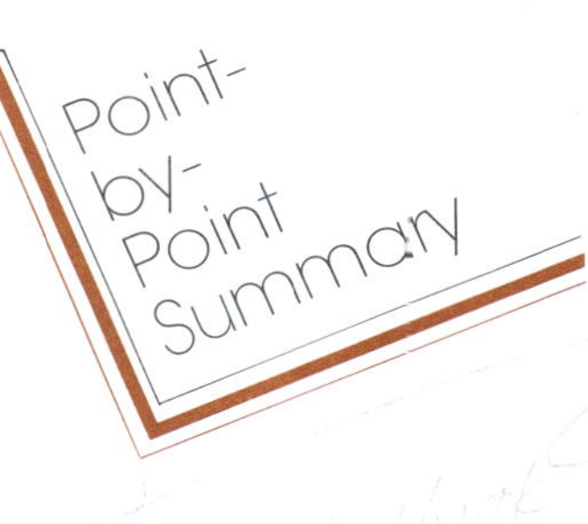

Point-by-Point Summary

- Organizations have formal structures that define the lines of authority and responsibility. Activities in organizations are usually grouped into departments on the bases of function and product. The process of departmentalization creates an organizational structure.
- There is an important and direct relationship among organizational structure, the management hierarchy, and goal setting.
- Within an organization's formal structure, authority can be line, staff, or functional, and the span of control can be large or small. Most organizations also have an informal structure, which dictates how communication and authority might bypass the formal routes.
- Organizations can be centralized, with decision-making authority in the hands of a few individuals at the top, or be decentralized (run as profit or investment centers), with authority for each center in the hands of that center's manager. The advantages of decentralization include improved decision making and employee motivation. The disadvantages of decentralization include duplication of effort and difficulties in coordinating activities.
- The bureaucratic form of organization was designed to assist in coordinating the tasks of many employees, but it can be unresponsive to individual needs
- Newer forms of organizational structure include free-form organization, task forces, and matrix organization.

- Some common mistakes in organizing are overstructuring, not properly defining reporting relationships, failing to clarify who has what kind of authority, and failing to match authority and responsibility.
- Organizational structure can have an impact on the organizational climate.

Questions for Review

1. Give an example of what might be a typical *formal* organizational design.
2. Discuss what *informal* structures might exist to bypass the formal structure outlined above.
3. In what ways might an informal structure be useful to managers?
4. What are the differences among line, staff, and functional authority? In what situations would each be appropriate?
5. What are the advantages and disadvantages of centralization and decentralization?
6. What are the strengths and weaknesses of the bureaucratic form of organization?
7. In what types of organizations would the new models of organization be effective?
8. Describe how an organization you are familiar with has been departmentalized. What mistakes, if any, has this organization made in designing its structure?
9. What impact do you feel decentralization has on organizational climate? What is the effect of centralization? A matrix organization?

APPLICATION

HISTORY

The Du Pont Company was founded in 1802 by Eleuthère Irénée du Pont de Nemours (1771-1834).

The story begins in France amidst the violence of the French Revolution of 1789. Control of the country alternated between mob rule and tyranny. Eleuthère Irénée's (pronounced ay-lu-tear, ear-in-nay) father, Pierre Samuel, was stripped of his government positions and pay. Turmoil continued in the streets of Paris during Robespierre's Reign of Terror, which began in 1793.

As an uneasy calm settled over Paris in the years immediately following the end of the Revolution, Pierre Samuel decided to take his family to America in 1797. He had hoped upon arrival to establish a colony in Virginia. This dream was never realized when scarcity of land and high prices became major obstacles.

Irénée was out hunting with a friend near Wilmington. Delaware, when he ran out of black powder. Angered by the high prices and poor quality he found when he tried to purchase more, he decided to try to establish a gunpowder mill in American to supply good quality powder that would meet the needs of the young, rapidly growing nation. After convincing his father that the idea was a promising one, Irénée and his brother Victor returned to France in 1801 and secured capital funds from investors there.

Du Pont Company

DU PONT
REG U S PAT & TM OFF
ESTABLISHED 1802

Back in America, Irénée searched for a suitable site for the powder mills. He decided on a parcel of land on the Brandywine Creek near Wilmington, Delaware. Construction of the mills began, and the first Du Pont Company powder went on sale in 1804. President Jefferson, anxious that America have its own supply of quality gunpowder, purchased Du Pont gunpowder. By the War of 1812, the Company had expanded to provide much of the U.S. military requirements.

In 1857, Lammot du Pont, grandson of Irénée, found a way to make black powder using sodium nitrate rather than potassium nitrate. The new product could outperform previous powders as a blasting agent. During the Civil War, the Company would be called upon to supply a large portion of the Union Army's powder needs.

During the 1880's Du Pont began producing smokeless powder, eventually becoming the country's only civilian producer of military powder. During World War I the Allies in Europe and then the U.S. Government turned to Du Pont for much of its smokeless powder.

After World War I, Du Pont began to diversify, into many new product areas, organic chemicals, synthetics, drugs, lacquers, household cement, film, crop protection chemicals, paints, textile fibers and plastics.

Today Du Pont's worldwide sales total more than $13 billion. The Company employs approximately 140,000 people worldwide and produces 1,700 products for industries as diverse as the automotive, pharmaceutical, agricultural, electronic and apparel.

ORGANIZATIONAL STRUCTURE

Exhibit 6.7 provides an overview of Du Pont's organizational structure. The chart shows how the industrial and staff departments are structured, depicts the key reporting relationships in the company, and provides insight into the management hierarchy. Interestingly

EXHIBIT 6.7 Du Pont's Organizational Chart

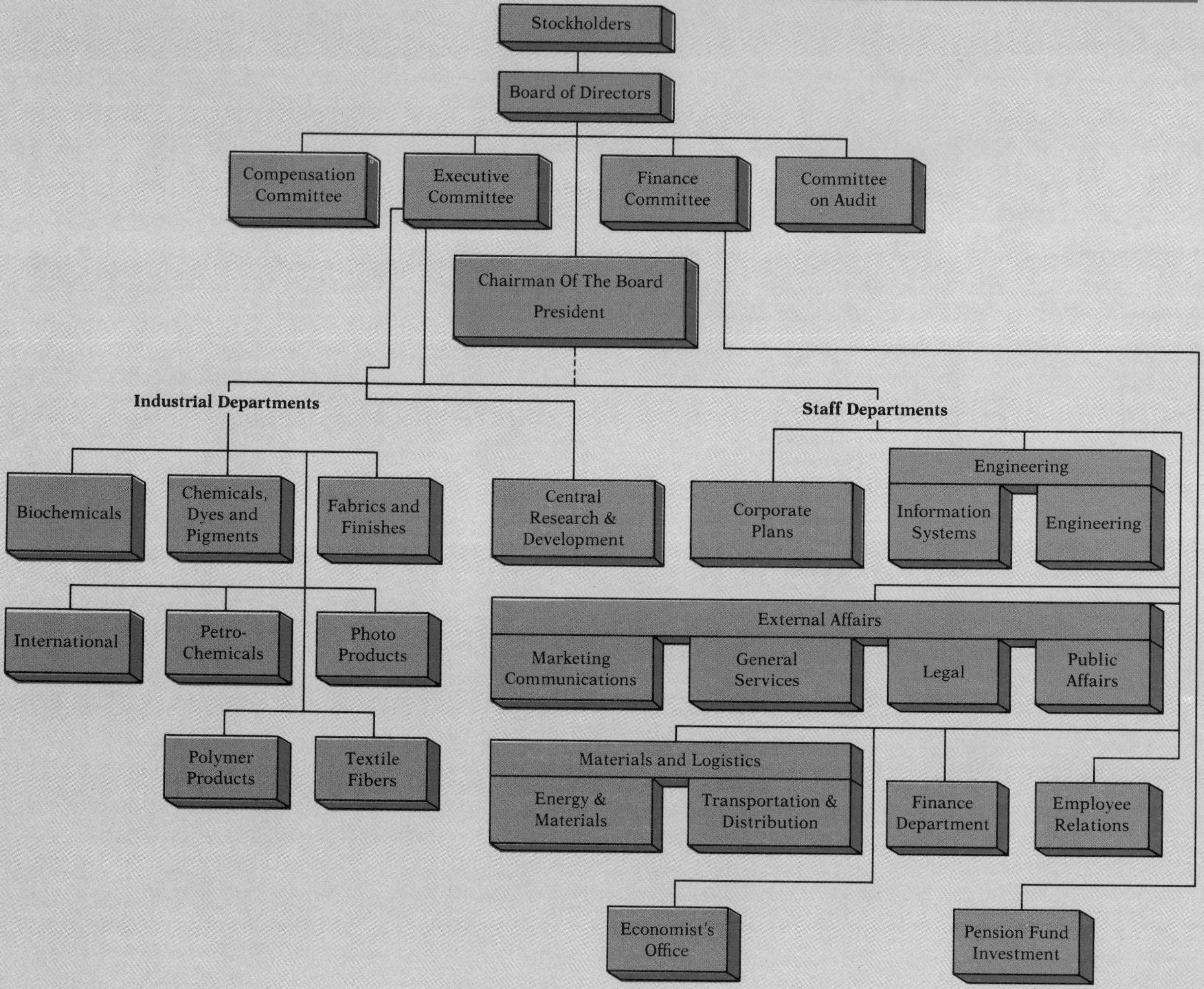

Stockholders

Board of Directors

Compensation Committee

Executive Committee

Finance Committee

Committee on Audit

Chairman Of The Board

President

Industrial Departments

Biochemicals

Chemicals, Dyes and Pigments

Fabrics and Finishes

International

Petro-Chemicals

Photo Products

Polymer Products

Textile Fibers

Central Research & Development

Staff Departments

Corporate Plans

Engineering

Information Systems

Engineering

External Affairs

Marketing Communications

General Services

Legal

Public Affairs

Materials and Logistics

Energy & Materials

Transportation & Distribution

Finance Department

Employee Relations

Economist's Office

Pension Fund Investment

enough, Du Pont's organizational structure shows characteristics of centralization, decentralization, and matrix organization all at once.

At the top of the corporate structure are the stockholders. Directly below the stockholders is the board of directors, which is composed of company executives and outside, independent people. The board of directors is responsible for managing the affairs and property of the company but is rarely involved in carrying out daily operations. Much of the board's work is accomplished through four standing committees. For example,

1. The Finance Committee is responsible for establishing financial policies, appraising the company's financial position and authorizing the expenditure of large sums of money.
2. The Audit Committee employs an independent C.P.A. firm to review the company's accounting procedures and to certify that all financial statements are prepared accurately and in accordance with established accounting principles.
3. The Executive Committee helps to insure that the firm is moving in the right direction. Their primary job is to establish operating principles and policies which management can use to guide them in their everyday work. Additionally the Executive Committee helps to develop and select the top management team that runs the firm, and then evaluates their performance.

   Finally, the Executive Committee is responsible for directing environmental and public affairs, research and development for the firm.
4. The Compensation Committee oversees and determines the company's compensation policies and sets compensation of executives who are Directors.

The chairmen of the board, or the chief executive officer (CEO), is charged with making sure that the functions of the board are carried out and is on several of the board's committees. The president, or chief operating officer (COO), is below the CEO and reports to the board of directors. The president is most directly responsible for making sure that the daily operations of the firm are successfully accomplished. It is his job to see that all staff and industrial departments function well.

Below the president, Du Pont is split into two major segments—staff and industrial—that are then subdivided into departments. The industrial departments represent the production side of the company; the staff departments provide administrative support to the industrial departments.

One thing this structure reveals is that Du Pont is centralized—in that the executive committee of the board of directors takes an active part in establishing goals and policies that guide Du Pont managers in their everyday work. In addition, certain staff departments serve the entire organization. Energy and Materials, for example, secures raw materials, equipment, and supplies for Du Pont's worldwide operations.

At the same time, Du Pont is decentralized. Each industrial department is run as a profit center. In an organization the size of Du Pont, it is impractical for higher management to get involved in the day-to-day operations of each department. Instead, the responsibility and authority to do so have been delegated to the top manager in each area.

At Du Pont, both staff and industrial departments also operate via a matrix process whereby business opportunities and/or problems are managed by tapping corporate resources. For example, a staff department such as Central Research & Development (CR&D) reports directly to a senior vice president on the Executive Committee; but the research and development function is closely coordinated with the specific industrial departments. The process permits, for example, the Company to manage R&D in the emerging life sciences areas where ultimate production and marketing responsibilities may be with either the Biochemicals, Photo Products or other industrial department. Hence, the R&D directors of each industrial department work directly, on a dotted line basis, with CR&D and have frequent interface with the Executive Committee.

In a more fundamental area, the Corporate Plans staff function reaches over the Company on a continuing basis. Managers often are tapped from industrial and/or staff departments to work on task forces which help identify needs, opportunities and strategic plans. In looking at the worldwide automotive industry, for example, all Du Pont industrial departments, with the exception of Biochemicals, have a stake in the changing design and down-sizing initiatives. As a result of a Corporate Plans study completed a few years ago, a Du Pont automotive group was formed to focus intra-departmental marketing, R&D, and related involvement with that important industry.

CAREER OPPORTUNITIES

Someone who has a degree in some area of business might begin work at Du Pont in either accounting and finance or data systems— at the corporate staff level or in one of the operating departments. Initial job assignments are intended to expose employees to the company's organization and to its financial, accounting, and data systems. Employees are assigned increasingly difficult and more responsible positions as they demonstrate their abilities. Du Pont offers to move employees between industrial and staff departments and between functional areas.

FOR DISCUSSION

1. What are the advantages and disadvantages of Du Pont's organizational structure?
2. Why are Du Pont's industrial departments treated as profit centers? What does being a profit center mean to the manager in each department?

OBJECTIVES

- ☐ To understand what motivates employees to work
- ☐ To identify and explain different leadership styles
- ☐ To describe practical approaches that management can use to increase employee motivation
- ☐ To identify and describe the major theories of motivation
- ☐ To understand the concept of organizational development and how it works in practice
- ☐ To identify your leadership style and to understand the consequences of that style

OUTLINE

KEY TERMS

ACHIEVEMENT THEORIES
EXPECTATION THEORIES
HAWTHORNE STUDIES
HUMAN RELATIONS
HYGIENE FACTOR
JOB ENRICHMENT
LEADERSHIP
MANAGEMENT BY OBJECTIVES (MBO)
MANAGEMENT STYLE
MANAGERIAL GRID
MOTIVATOR FACTOR
NEED HIERARCHY
ORGANIZATIONAL DEVELOPMENT (OD)
PARTICIPATION THEORIES
PRODUCTIVITY
PSYCHOLOGICAL THEORIES
THEORY X
THEORY Y
TRAIT THEORY

HUMAN RELATIONS

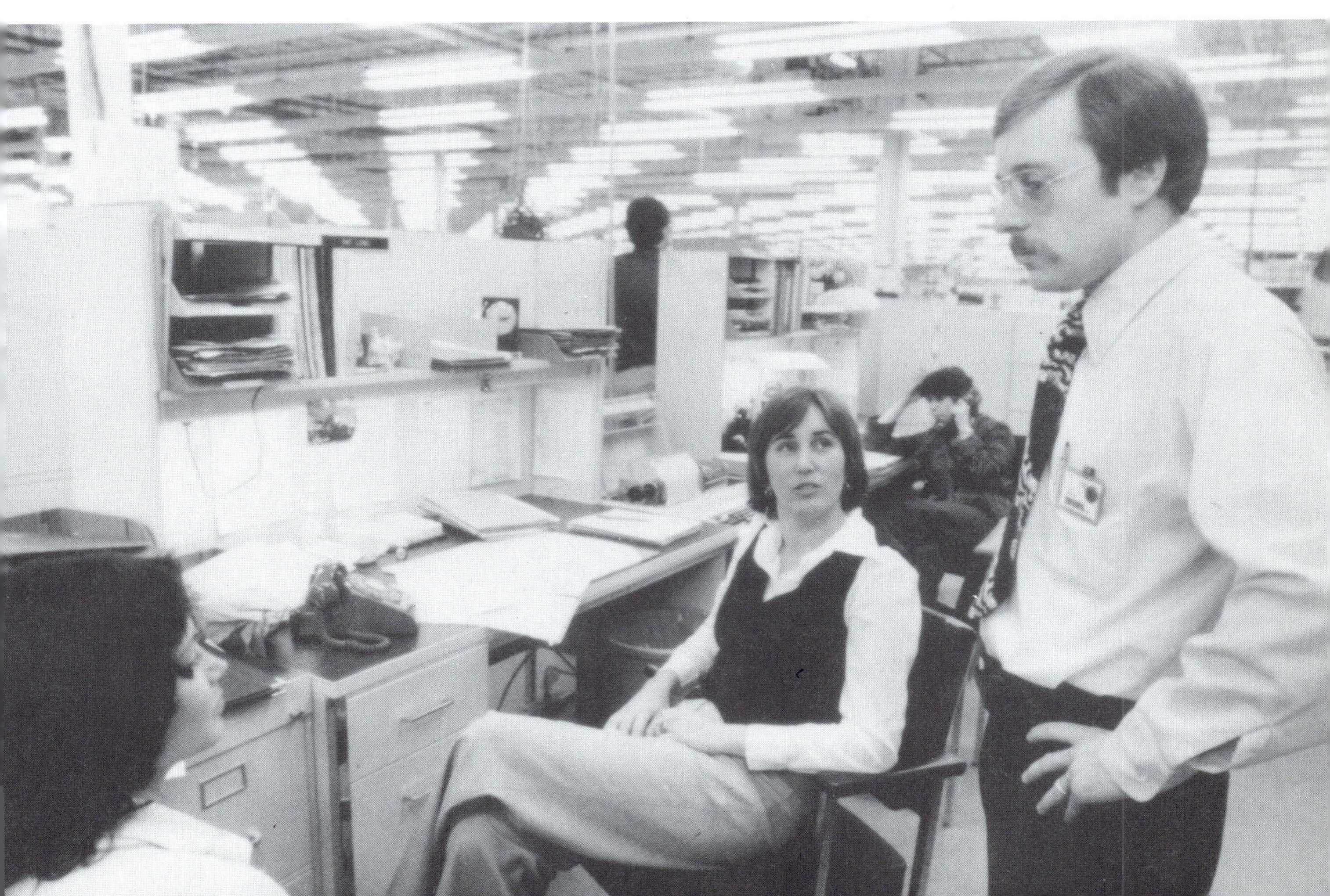

The "Star System" at Owens-Corning

Management Review,
September 1979

Owens-Corning Fiberglass Corporation's reinforcement plant in Amarillo, Texas, has a plant operating philosophy, "You're the Star," based on the concept that all employees play intricate roles in the plant's operation. Employees are encouraged to communicate with each other and with management to find new ways to develop teamwork and improve productivity. The plant's schedule also attempts to enhance the worklife of employees: They work 12-hour days for three days, and then have three days off.

Plant manager D. Bruce Salley said that Owens-Corning gave much thought to quality-of-worklife considerations even before the Amarillo plant opened. "We examined all possible influences on work environment and attempted to put the employee at center stage. Hence 'You're the Star.' " Key features of the program are:

- The plant's employee communications center, occupying a 40-foot wall near the workers' entrance and containing five separate information modules. The first, "Amarillo Views," offers a slide-screen area for conveying plant activities and for showing product information from corporate headquarters in Toledo, Ohio. The next module is an information board designed for communications in three key areas: safety, employee recreational and social activities, and the Focal (Fiberglas Open Communications Access Line) Point board. The latter is a 24-hour phone line hooked into a recorder so that employees may call anonymously, if they choose, and ask questions or make comments about working conditions. All responses to questions are placed on the Focal Point board.

  The third module is titled "People of Amarillo." It features a photograph of each worker with his or her name, grouped by the area of the plant where the person works. Workers wear ID cards on the job so they will learn one another's names. The fourth module in the group contains three sections: personnel information, employee trading post, and "Spotlight" featuring literature on products that Owens-Corning and its customers are manufacturing with fiberglass reinforcements. The last module of the communications center is called "Fiberglas in the News." Corporate headquarters prepares a monthly videotape spotlighting new uses for Fiberglas.
- The design of the plant itself. This, notes Salley, is another attempt to provide a stimulating work environment for employees. Graphics and colors enhance work and recreation areas. Wall-size murals are placed in certain areas and each work location is painted in its own distinctive color. This was done, Salley reports, to give employees the feeling that they are in a smaller area. They are said to become more productive in such an environment.
- The plant's training program. It is designed to maintain a steady supply of able production workers. New hourly employees are trained in an area of the plant set up to simulate actual production processes. Consequently, they are prepared to assume new jobs before vacancies actually occur.

Management in Practice,
Management Review, September
1979 (New York: AMACOM, a division of the American Management Association, 1979), pp. 41–42.

The "You're the Star" program is an excellent example of how companies can better motivate their employees. This chapter explains many of the factors affecting employee motivation and human relations in general.

When you get right down to it, the most important assets an organization has are its employees. Certainly organizational structure and management are related to a company's success or failure, and they have a heavy influence on employee behavior. But there are many other factors, many of them intangible, that affect employee behavior. A discussion of these intangibles is what this chapter is about.

The term **human relations** refers to how companies treat and manage their employees so as to increase worker and organizational effectiveness. In this chapter we explore several topics that are a part of human relations—motivation, leadership, and organizational development—and explain how managers should treat employees to enhance their effectiveness. Chapter 8 takes the discussion further, describing how companies organize themselves to manage their employees, or human resources.

Motivating Employees

What motivates people to work? What motivates working people to be more productive? The answers to these and similar questions are not known with certainty. However, since the early 1900s researchers have been trying to gain insights into what makes people work best. Researchers in the field of psychology have come to believe that indifferent or unfavorable treatment can reduce worker motivation and productivity. Furthermore, the more highly motivated the employee, the greater will be that individual's productivity. Thus managers must try to understand the behavioral and motivational consequences of their actions.

THE HAWTHORNE STUDIES

Until the 1930s, there was little recognition in business that human factors have a direct bearing on organizational performance and that how we do business affects worker behavior. One of the first major breakthroughs in this area resulted from Western Electric Company's experiments at their Hawthorne Works. These experiments, which are referred to as the **Hawthorne studies,** were originally conducted to determine the impact of work environment on employee productivity.

In an attempt to raise productivity, lighting in the factory was raised a little more every day. Productivity did indeed seem to increase in response. However, when the lighting was lowered, productivity continued to increase. The experimenters were at first puzzled but finally decided that employee productivity is not simply a function of the work environment but rather is a function of employee morale and how employees are managed. The employees in the Hawthorne studies had been separated from all other employees. They received special and constant attention from the experimenters. They came to see themselves as special, and this is presumably what raised their productivity.

Highlight Why Is Productivity So Important?

Why are businesses constantly trying to find ways to increase employee motivation? Because increased worker motivation eventually leads to increased productivity, which may be the only way for the United States to solve its problems of inflation, lagging exports, and unemployment.

From World War II to the mid-1960s, **productivity**—the relationship between the output of goods and services and the input of labor, material, and capital—grew at an annual rate of about 3 percent. Then it began a gradual decline. Although productivity increased by 3.5 percent in 1976 and 1.7 percent in 1977, it decreased by 1.1 percent in 1979.

Economic experts believe the only way to reverse this trend is to find a way to increase output without increasing the cost of the inputs. If we can do this, our standard of living may once again increase; inflation should decline, because we would be getting more output for the same costs; and unemployment might decrease, because companies would have more profits to reinvest in the business by hiring more workers.

What is the best way to increase productivity? All agree that increased worker motivation is the key.

THEORY X AND THEORY Y

The Hawthorne studies served as a catalyst for more research in the area of human relations and got businesspeople thinking about how they viewed and treated their employees. Probably the best description of the "traditional" management view appeared in Douglas McGregor's now-classic book, *The Human Side of Enterprise.* McGregor labeled the traditional view **Theory X** and outlined the assumptions behind it (see Exhibit 7.1). McGregor believed that an organization built around Theory X concepts would be characterized by close supervision and control over employees, centralization of authority, an impersonal attitude toward employees, and a dictatorial style of leadership.

Realizing that the Theory X approach did not take into consideration the human need for self-fulfillment, ego satisfaction, friendship, and group membership, McGregor posited a counterapproach—**Theory Y.** The assumptions behind Theory Y (see Exhibit 7.1) imply that management can have a more positive attitude toward employees, believing that they have the capacity and desire to exercise self-control and to take actions that are in the best interests of the organization. Implementation of Theory Y results in an organizational environment where employees have greater freedom of action and are more highly motivated to do a good job and where participative management is encouraged and rewarded.

THE FULFILLMENT OF NEEDS

McGregor, and other behavioral psychologists, believed that the key to organizational success is to properly motivate employees—to establish a relationship and climate that encourages them to take actions that are in the best interests of the organization. In order to motivate workers, it is important to identify and understand their needs, because it is the fulfillment of needs that motivates individuals to act in certain ways.

Psychologist Abraham Maslow devised what may be the most

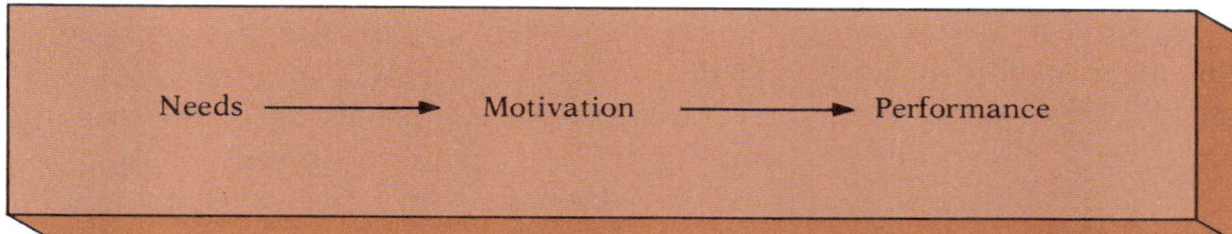

appealing approach for understanding motivation. In his **need hierarchy** theory, he defined the needs that individuals attempt to satisfy and arranged them in order of increasing importance, as indicated in Exhibit 7.2. The lowest-order needs, the primary needs common to all individuals, are physiological needs, security needs, and social needs. The physiological, or survival, needs represent the most basic requirements—food, shelter, sex, and survival. When these basic needs have been fulfilled, security needs become important. For workers concerned

EXHIBIT 7.1 The Assumptions behind Theory X and Theory Y

Theory X Assumptions

1. The average human being has an inherent dislike of work and will avoid if he can.
2. Because of this human characteristic of dislike of work, most people must be coerced, controlled, directed, threatened with punishment to get them to put forth adequate effort toward the achievement of organizational objectives.
3. The average human being prefers to be directed, wishes to avoid responsibility, has relatively little ambition, wants security above all.

Theory Y Assumptions

1. The expenditure of physical and mental effort in work is as natural as play or rest.
2. External control and the threat of punishment are not the only means for bringing about effort toward organizational objectives. Man will exercise self-direction and self-control in the service of objectives to which he is committed.
3. Commitment to objectives is a function of the rewards associated with their achievement.
4. The average human being learns, under proper conditions, not only to accept but to seek responsibility.
5. The capacity to exercise a relatively high degree of imagination, ingenuity, and creativity in the solution of organizational problems is widely, not narrowly, distributed in the population.
6. Under the conditions of modern industrial life, the intellectual potentialities of the average human being are only partially utilized.

Douglas McGregor, *The Human Side of Enterprise*, New York, McGraw-Hill Book Company, 1960.

with protection and safety, seniority systems, guaranteed wages, and pensions have been created. Once employees feel safe, their social needs emerge. That is, they need to have friends, to feel wanted and appreciated, and to have the opportunity to interact with others.

Finally, Maslow hypothesized that there are two sets of higher-order needs—the need for esteem (respect from others) and self-actualization (the desire to realize one's fullest potential, to become the best one can). Few people ever reach the advanced stages of self-realization, but it is the striving to satisfy this need that creates motivation.

Maslow's need hierarchy is important because it shows how management can motivate employees by providing an environment that allows them to satisfy their needs. It is interesting to note that people tend to satisfy their needs in the order of priority in Maslow's hierarchy. Therefore, from a motivational point of view, once a particular need is satisfied it no longer acts as a motivator.

MOTIVATIONAL THEORIES

There are several schools of thought in the behavioral sciences that suggest approaches to the motivation of individuals. Many of these theories are supported by research conducted in business organizations.

EXHIBIT 7.2 Maslow's Hierarchy of Needs

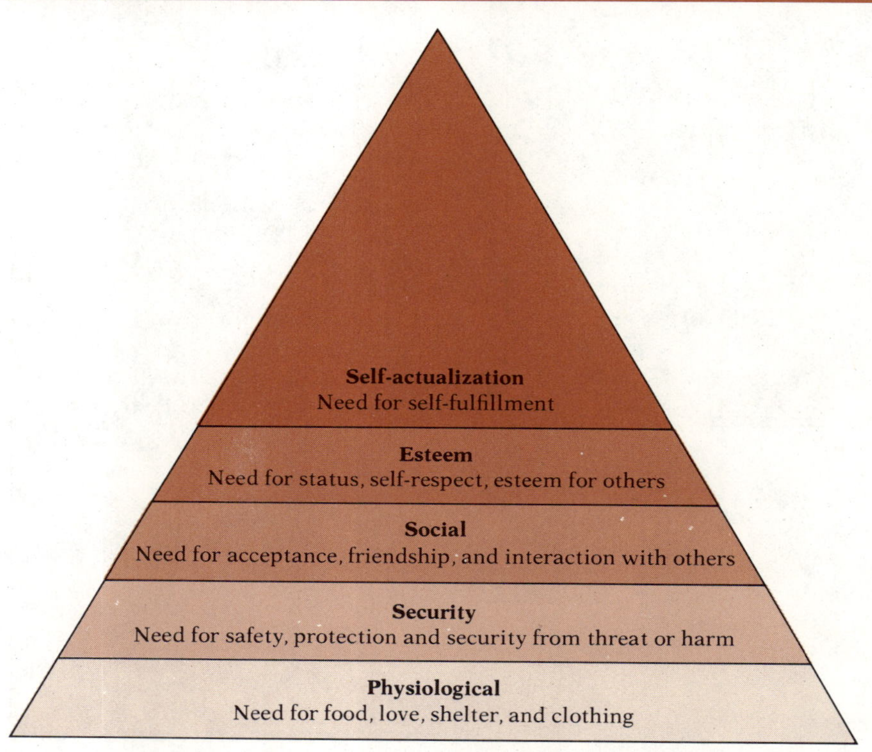

Source: Data (for diagram) based on Heirarchy of Needs in "A Theory of Human Motivation" in *Motivation and Personality,* 2d edition by Abraham H. Maslow, Copyright 1970 by Abraham H. Maslow. By permission of Harper & Row, Publishers, Inc.

Highlight "It's Not Just the Money"

Suppose you're a corporate executive earning $175,000 per year. Your firm supplies you with a luxury sedan, membership in an exclusive country club, and yearly bonuses of stock equal to half your salary. You've recently received a job offer from the government. The maximum salary is $50,000 per year. Would you accept?

Many executives do. They don't just accept government employment but also employment with other firms at salaries much, much lower than they've been earning. What prompts someone who has already climbed the corporate ladder to give up a huge salary and corporate perks for a lower-paid position?

In many cases it's the corporate ladder itself that initiates the decision to leave. Executives who have attained success and made it to the top may find little challenge there. Their jobs become routine, even dull. A new job offers a new challenge.

Most feel that salary is not the key issue. High salaries go hand-in-hand with high-pressure situations, and some executives want a less stressful job. Some seek positions of power, and others want to have some impact on society. These are the people who often succumb to the government's pleas for their expertise. For example, Robert McNamara left a high-level corporate position to become Secretary of Defense in the Kennedy and Johnson administrations.

They therefore have gained some degree of acceptance in the business world. The following is a brief description of four of the major approaches.

Participation theories are based on the premise that the more involved employees are in making decisions, the more highly motivated they will be to see the decisions executed properly. Thus these approaches follow logically from McGregor's Theory Y concept. Belief in the participative approach caused many large companies to decentralize in the 1960s.

Achievement theories are based on the assumption that some people have a greater need to achieve than others and that a person's "need to achieve" will motivate him or her. Overachievers are those who accomplish tasks beyond those normally expected from people with similar intellectual abilities; they are driven by a high need to achieve.

Expectation theories are based on the assumption that individuals are motivated to act in response to what they feel will happen to them if they take some action. For example, if you have to take an exam next week, your motivation to study (and how much to study) is contingent on what you expect will happen to you if you do not study. If you expect to get an A on the exam with little preparation, you will not be motivated to spend a great deal of time studying.

In a real sense, all theories of motivation are psychological in nature; participation, achievement, and expectation theories all start from psychological orientations. However, the approaches and perspectives labeled **psychological theories** focus on such elements as employees, jobs, attitudes, and occupations rather than studying organizational elements.

One of the most popular, and most criticized, psychological theories of motivation was developed by Frederick Herzberg in the

1950s. Herzberg studied job attitudes as the basis of the motivation to work. In one historic study he interviewed accountants and engineers, asking them to describe what made them feel good or bad about their work. From these interviews, he concluded that a distinction should be made between those factors that actually motivate employees and those essential to maintaining job satisfaction (see Exhibit 7.3). **Hygiene factors,** such as money and working conditions, do not motivate employees, although their absence or existence at unacceptable levels creates job dissatisfaction. In contrast, the presence of such **motivator factors** as recognition and achievement positively motivates employees. These factors are related to the job itself and must be considered in the design of jobs. Herzberg's work has been severely criticized over the years because of the sample he used and the way he collected his data. Nonetheless, his theory is widely used in business in designing jobs to motivate people.

Management Approaches for Increasing Employee Motivation

How does management put the theories of motivation into practice? In recent years, lots of practical techniques have been developed to implement these ideas. Two of them are management by objectives and job enrichment.

MANAGEMENT BY OBJECTIVES

One of the most popular tools of motivation is **management by by objectives (MBO).** It is used by thousands of organizations in both the private and not-for-profit sectors, from "mom and pop" shops to the federal government. It has been found to be particularly effective in motivating white-collar workers, those who work in areas outside of production.

According to one author who has written extensively on MBO, there

EXHIBIT 7.3 Herzberg's Theory of Factors

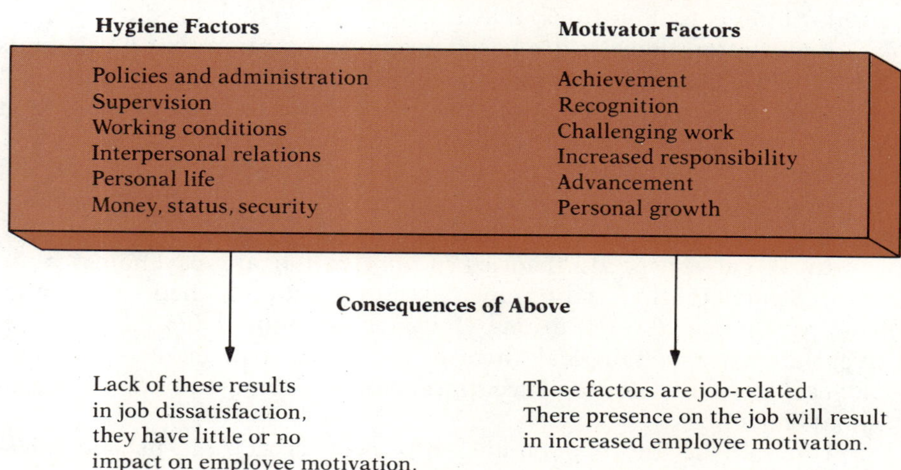

Hygiene Factors
Policies and administration
Supervision
Working conditions
Interpersonal relations
Personal life
Money, status, security
Motivator Factors
Achievement
Recognition
Challenging work
Increased responsibility
Advancement
Personal growth
Consequences of Above
Lack of these results in job dissatisfaction, they have little or no impact on employee motivation.
These factors are job-related. There presence on the job will result in increased employee motivation.

"Tell me, Cosgrove. Are any of my ideas seeping down to the people?"

are five primary steps in establishing an MBO program.* These steps, shown in Exhibit 7.4, are highly interactive. The first principle of MBO, referred to as work planning, includes steps 1 through 4. The second principle of an MBO program, feedback or work review, constitutes step 5.

For an example of how MBO works, let's look at the case of Joan Workhard. Joan sells computer products in five midwestern states. At the beginning of each year, she sits down with her boss, Amanda Jones, and establishes sales targets for the coming year. During these discussions, Joan and Amanda try to reach a consensus as to the sales amount

*Edgar F. Huse, *Organization Development and Change* (St. Paul, Minn.: West, 1975).

EXHIBIT 7.4 The Steps in Establishing an MBO Program

Step 1	Work group involvement	Members of the work group define goals and tasks for their group and for each member.
Step 2	Manager/employee goal setting	Manager and employee jointly establish the employee's job duties and responsibilities in accordance with the goals.
Step 3	Establishment of action plans	Manager and employee jointly develop action plans for achieving the goals.
Step 4	Establishment of criteria	Manager and employee jointly determine clear, understandable standards of performance and success.
Step 5	Review	Manager and employee (perhaps with other employees) review progress toward meeting the goals and replan and reformulate goals if necessary; manager provides counseling, coaching, and assistance as required.

Joan should generate during the year. Once these sales objectives have been established, they become standards of performance for Joan. If Joan meets or exceeds the targets, her performance will be considered good (all other things being equal). If she falls short of the targets, Amanda will want to know why. Joan could get an unfavorable performance review if good reasons are not forthcoming.

Why does MBO motivate Joan to do a better job? There are at least two reasons. First, she participates in establishing her own performance objectives and, as a result, is probably more committed to accomplishing them. Second, these objectives give her something to strive for, and she knows that if she achieves them, she will be rewarded with a good performance review.

As you might imagine, planning and executing a good MBO program is no easy task. It requires tremendous amounts of patience, work, and commitment on the part of both employees and managers. Because MBO programs are relatively new to the work world, their successes and weaknesses are still being determined. However, on the whole, they do seem to have some value as a motivating tool.

JOB ENRICHMENT

A second tool for increasing motivation is job enrichment, which is an outgrowth of Herzberg's theory. This technique is particularly useful in motivating production workers to do a better job. Basically, **job enrichment** means upgrading a job, usually by adding more responsibility and more meaningful work, providing more recognition to the employee, and developing greater opportunities for advancement. Specifically, job enrichment programs usually attempt to

- Give employees more freedom and more control over how they do their jobs
- Allow employees to complete whole pieces of a job rather than one small part
- Let employees know that the job they do has importance to others
- Encourage employees to develop additional skills that will allow them to vary the type of work they do

An excellent example of job enrichment exists in the Volvo Corporation, which has recently attempted to enrich the jobs of assembly workers. Instead of having one person put on hubcaps all day long, forty hours per week, a group of people build one car from the beginning to end. As a result, their jobs become more important to them, and their self-esteem increases. At Volvo, the program has increased employee motivation and productivity and has improved product quality. Similar programs have been established in many other companies, such as AT&T and General Foods, and have been found successful in motivating workers who previously had dull and repetitive jobs.

Highlight Leadership, Political Style

The stakes in the corporate boardroom seem inconsequential compared to the stakes in world affairs; a billion-dollar mistake is "peanuts" compared to a blunder in international politics, which could cost thousands of lives. So if ever there was a place to examine leadership qualities, it would be the political arena.

In March 1933 Franklin D. Roosevelt, former governor of New York, took office as President of the United States. The country was in the midst of financial chaos with little hope for immediate recovery. But Roosevelt had a vision he called the New Deal. To implement this plan, he gathered many bright people to his administration. Through his personal charisma and fortitude, Roosevelt was able to rally Americans to the task at hand. He gave them a focus and made them believe the Depression could be conquered.

The advent of World War II ended America's Depression and set the stage for Winston Churchill's finest hour—his leadership of war-torn Britain. Churchill, like Roosevelt, had great personal charisma. He, too, was able to rally his country against a common enemy. Following the disaster of Dunkirk and German bombings, Britons were demoralized. Churchill gave them courage to believe again in winning. At no time did he allow the population to think of defeat.

Churchill and Roosevelt had similar qualities that made them good leaders. True, they both were charismatic, but charisma is not enough. They both exhibited such other qualities as intelligence, managerial skills, and an ability to motivate others to some common end. Both formulated plans and developed strategies to accomplish them. They were able to choose and attract talented people to help in administering their plan. Churchill and Roosevelt knew the strengths and limitations of their subordinates as well as those they governed. Because of this, they were able to lead their countries in troubled times and realize impressive results against difficult odds.

Leadership Style

Managers are leaders in the sense that they have a responsibility for the direction of other people. But being a manager does not necessarily mean that someone is an effective leader. **Leadership** refers to a person's ability to direct others and to affect employee behavior positively. Thus leadership is very much a part of human relations.

LEADERSHIP TRAITS

Since the 1930s there have been a number of important studies conducted on leadership. One of the first approaches used in studying leadership was to identify the traits of recognized leaders. **Trait theory** was based on the assumption that certain physical and psychological traits differentiate a leader from the group. Some of the more frequently listed traits were intelligence, self-confidence, persuasiveness, and humor. However, further research has indicated that none of these qualities seem to be absolutely essential for leadership.

MANAGEMENT STYLE

Later studies in the area of leadership focused on the **management style** of the leader rather than on traits. For example, research conducted by Kurt Lewin, Ronald Lippitt, and Ralph White in the 1930s identified three basic leadership styles: autocratic, laissez-faire, and democratic

EXHIBIT 7.5 Management Styles

Autocratic Style

Leader

1. The individual is very conscious of his or her position.
2. He or she has little trust and faith in members of the group.
3. This leader believes that pay is a just reward for work and the only reward that will motivate workers.
4. Orders are issued to be carried out, with no questions allowed and no explanations given.

Group Members

1. No responsibility is assumed for performance, with people merely doing what they are told.
2. Production is good when the leader is present but poor in the leader's absence.

Laissez-faire Style

Leader

1. He or she has no confidence in his or her leadership ability.
2. This leader does not set goals for the group.

Group Members

1. Decisions are made by whomever in the group is willing to do it.
2. Productivity generally is low, and work is sloppy.
3. Individuals have little interest in their work.
4. Morale and teamwork generally are low.

Democratic Style

Leader

1. Decision making is shared between the leader and the group.
2. When the leader is required or forced to make a decision, his or her reasoning is explained to the group.
3. Criticism and praise are given objectively.

Group Members

1. New ideas and change are welcomed.
2. A feeling of responsibility is developed within the group.
3. Quality of work and productivity generally are high.
4. The group generally feels successful.

From Bradford, Leland B., and Ronald Lippitt, "Building a Democratic Work Group," *Personnel*, Vol. 22, No. 3, November, 1945 (New York: American Management Association, Inc., 1945).

(see Exhibit 7.5). These three styles differ mainly in the willingness of the leader to share involvement in the decision-making process.

Another popular method of classifying leadership style—the **managerial grid**—was developed by Robert Blake and Jane Mouton. As Exhibit 7.6 shows, there are five basic styles of management in this scheme, each characterized by a different combination of concern for production and for people. For example, a 9,1 manager shows maximum concern for production and minimum concern for people.

Another way to classify management style that has gotten a great deal of attention is based on research conducted by Rensis Likert at the University of Michigan in the 1950s and 1960s.* Likert found that there are four styles used by managers in organizations:

1. *Exploitive/authoritative* Manager attempts to exploit employees and rules with an iron hand.

*Rensis Likert, *New Patterns of Management* (New York: McGraw-Hill, 1961).

2. *Benevolent/authoritative* Manager rules with an iron hand but is paternalistic.
3. *Consultative* Manager solicits the assistance and participation of employees in decision making but reserves the right to make the final decision.

EXHIBIT 7.6 The Managerial Grid

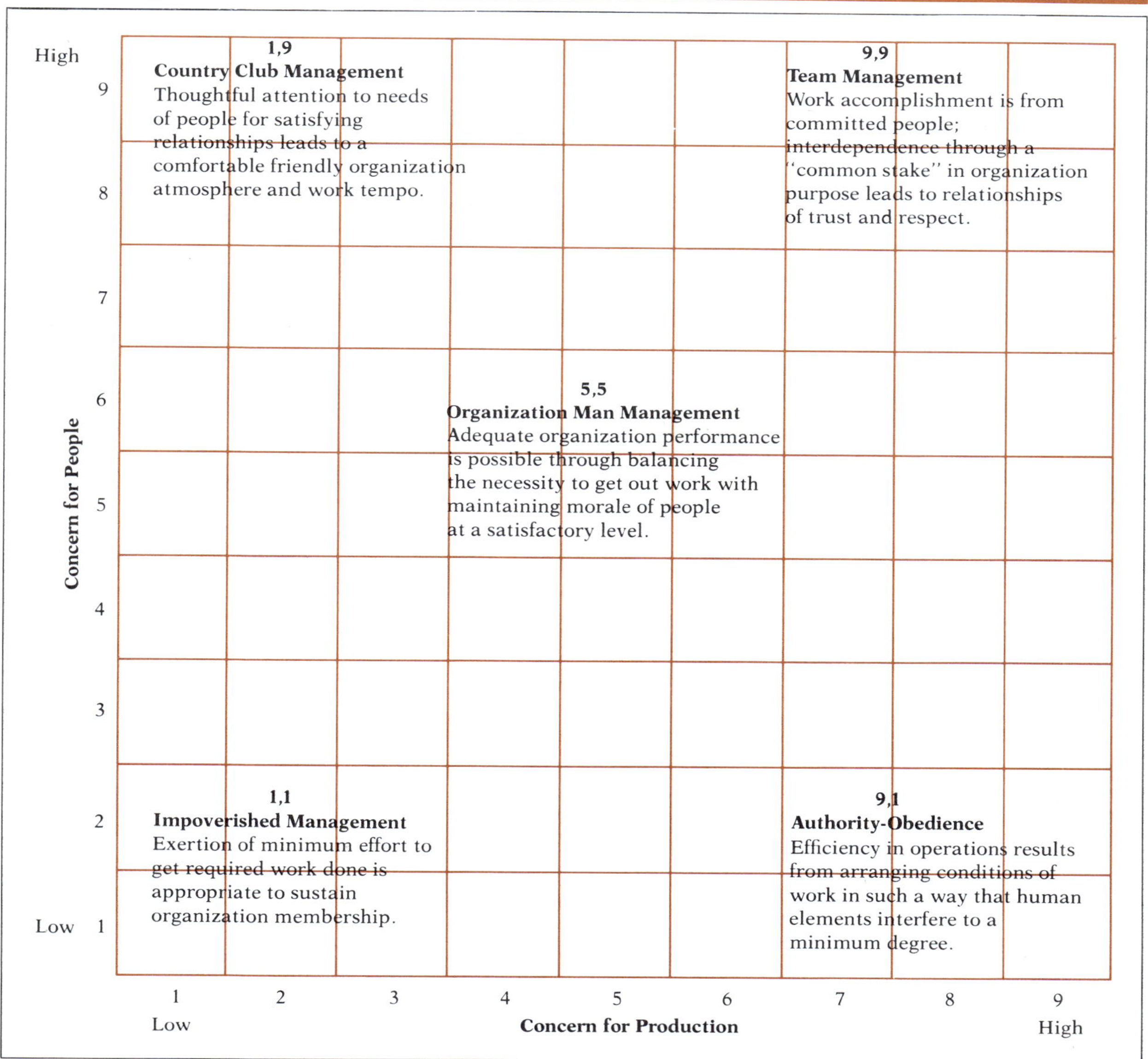
High
Low
Concern for People
9
8
7
6
5
4
3
2
1
1,9
Country Club Management
Thoughtful attention to needs of people for satisfying relationships leads to a comfortable friendly organization atmosphere and work tempo.
9,9
Team Management
Work accomplishment is from committed people; interdependence through a "common stake" in organization purpose leads to relationships of trust and respect.
5,5
Organization Man Management
Adequate organization performance is possible through balancing the necessity to get out work with maintaining morale of people at a satisfactory level.
1,1
Impoverished Management
Exertion of minimum effort to get required work done is appropriate to sustain organization membership.
9,1
Authority-Obedience
Efficiency in operations results from arranging conditions of work in such a way that human elements interfere to a minimum degree.
1 2 3 4 5 6 7 8 9
Low
Concern for Production
High

The Managerial Grid from *The New Managerial Grid,* by Robert R. Blake and Jane S. Mouton. Houston: Gulf Publishing Company, Copyright © 1978, p. 11. Reproduced by permission.

4. *Participative* Manager and employees work together in decision making, with the final decision being a consensus based on total participation.

From his research, Likert concluded that the participative approach was most effective, particularly in decentralized organizations, where delegation of authority and decision making is encouraged. This approach gives more employees an opportunity to participate in decision making and enhances worker motivation and job satisfaction.

CURRENT THINKING

More recent research suggests that management style is situational. That is, managers do not have one constant approach to managing but instead adopt whatever style is most consistent with the situation at hand. The forces influencing the choice of a style include the employees who are involved, the character of the manager, and the particular decision-making situation.

Organizational structure, leadership style, and employee motivation are very much interrelated. For example, a highly centralized organization may not be conducive to a participative management style, because decisions can be made by only a few people. In this environment, Likert's authoritative and consultative styles are likely to predominate. Whether these styles have a favorable or unfavorable impact on employee motivation depends on how the managers handle the situation. Normally, however, the participative style is more conducive to employee motivation.

A Word on Organizational Development

So far, most of this discussion has focused on how to motivate employees to do a better job. Our emphasis has been on individual employees based on the belief that by changing employee behavior, organizational effectiveness will improve. In recent years, however, businessleaders and researchers have been exploring an alternative approach to increasing organizational effectiveness.

Organizational development (OD), although it cannot be defined precisely, is a planned program of change initiated by a company's management to improve overall organizational effectiveness. Many of the techniques discussed in this chapter—MBO, job enrichment, and the managerial grid—are used in organizational development. The underlying objective of an OD program is to increase organizational effectiveness by improving the interpersonal relationships of employees.

An OD program is normally initiated in response to such problems as low profits, low employee morale, poor service, and high turnover. When these problems occur, management must either take action to correct them or jeopardize the success of the company. If it decides to take action, management first diagnoses the problems and their causes and then develops an action plan to correct the deficiencies.

Assume you own a well-managed, profitable business. Overall, you have good products and profits, an outstanding management team, and excellent employee productivity. However, one product line in a particular division seems to lose money year after year. Once you decide to do something about this situation, you discover that the division is poorly managed and overstructured and is run by a manager with an authoritative style. To overcome these problems, you develop an OD program that will make this division more like your other successful divisions. You and your staff decide to make the following changes over the next year:

- Decentralize operations and introduce participative management
- Streamline and simplify the operating procedures and policies used in the division
- Improve interpersonal relations and employee motivation by implementing MBO and job enrichment programs
- Improve communications by having "open door" meetings with employees

After implementing these procedures, you begin to see an improvement in the operations of the division: Profits increase, employees become more satisfied, and product quality improves. Thus your OD program not only helped improve motivation but also helped change the structure, climate, and performance of the entire division.

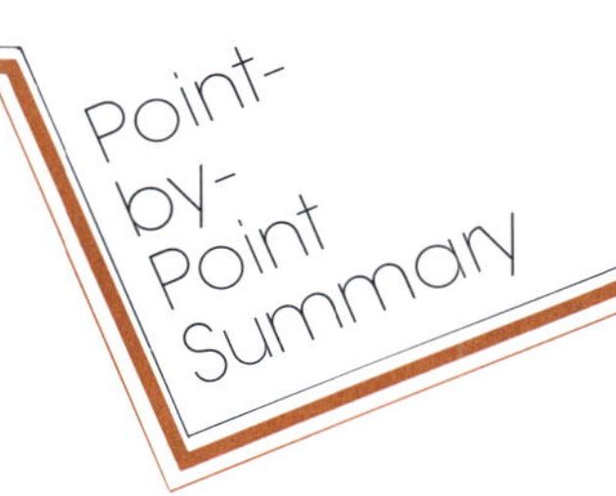

- Human relations is concerned with how companies treat and manage their employees. Business interest in human relations dates back to the Hawthorne studies in the 1930s.
- Douglas McGregor developed Theory X and Theory Y to represent opposing views of how organizations think about their employees. Theory X is the traditional approach; Theory Y gives employees credit for being able to think and feel.
- Abraham Maslow suggested that individuals attempt to satisfy a hierarchy of five basic needs: physiological, security, social, esteem, and self-actualization needs. Most researchers believe that motivation occurs when employees try to satisfy these needs.
- There are many theories that attempt to explain the motivation of employees, including participation, achievement, expectation, and psychological theories.

- Frederick Herzberg's theory suggested that there is a difference between job satisfaction and motivation. Hygiene factors are not motivators, but they do affect job satisfaction. Motivators are those factors that can positively or negatively effect motivation.
- Two of the most practical and widely used techniques to motivate employees are management by objectives and job enrichment. MBO programs are particularly appropriate for motivating white-collar workers; job enrichment works best in a production environment.
- Several theories exist to explain leadership, or management style, including trait theory, the managerial grid, and the four styles of leadership postulated by Rensis Likert.
- Organizational development (OD) is a program of change planned by management to increase the overall effectiveness of the organization.

1. How does Maslow's need hierarchy relate to the issue of motivation?
2. What is the difference between job satisfaction and motivation?
3. Are the four types of motivational theories discussed in this chapter mutually exclusive? That is, is one correct and all the others wrong?
4. What is management by objectives? What are its advantages and disadvantages?
5. Why is it that job enrichment programs are more applicable to production workers than to white-collar employees?
6. How did job enrichment grow out of Herzberg's theory?
7. Develop an overall approach to motivation using the concepts or theories developed by McGregor, Maslow, and Herzberg. How are they interrelated?
8. What leadership style do you feel you have? Explain.
9. How does organizational development relate to the topic of human relations?

APPLICATION

American Metal Treating Company

American Metal Treating Company (AMT), located in Cleveland, is not a corporate giant with hundreds of employees. In fact, in 1979 AMT had sales of a little over $1 million and employed twenty-six office and plant workers. The company is in business to provide a service—heat treating metal parts, particularly gears, that go into making all kinds of machinery.

A BRIEF HISTORY

AMT began operations in 1932 as a proprietorship under the auspices of Jesse L. Teegarden, uncle of the present owner. At that time the firm processed metal parts in furnaces. Herbert Summers, the present owner, joined the firm in 1937 as a furnace operator. Eight months later he became the sales representative, traveling throughout the Ohio area seeking new business.

By 1948 Summers was in charge of production, sales, and overall management. Teegarden was only marginally involved in operations, although he was still heavily involved in the decision-making process. Teegarden died in 1951, and the business was owned by his widow until 1958. When she died, ownership passed to her estate. Summers and two partners bought the estate in 1960 for approximately $100,000.

Summers bought new equipment in 1961 and 1962 to replace the original equipment, and in 1964 the company added induction and contour hardening processes to the business. In 1967 Summers bought out his partners and became the sole owner-manager of the company.

It is Summers's view that what differentiates his company from many others is the personal service it renders. He points out that approximately 20 percent of AMT's current customers have been with the firm for forty years, and he attributes this loyalty to his policy of providing advice, special services, and high-quality service. He also credits AMT's ability to provide a full range of heat treating, especially for parts that require more than one type of treatment. This saves customers the trouble and expense of transferring parts from company to company. In an effort to maintain old customers, he has driven up to 120,000 miles per year, at one time buying two identical cars so as not to seem ostentatious to the workers at the plant.

MANAGEMENT OF AMT

AMT has been a closely held family concern since its inception. Workers who have been with the firm since Teegarden's days describe him as fearsome, domineering, and controlling. Although he eventually delegated some of his day-to-day operating responsibilities, he maintained control over major decisions until he died. Summers has operated in a similar way until recently.

Human relations is particularly important to the success of AMT. With only twenty-six employees working in a close environment, any people problems could have serious consequences. The concepts of motivation, employee productivity, and morale are handled in a low-key, practical way.

Leadership Style

Summers has been owner-manager of his business for almost three decades. To properly manage his company and ensure its success, he had an authoritative style of management. Until recently, Summers made all key decisions and managed his business closely and firmly. Given the size of the firm, this was probably the only style he could have used. This approach was familiar to AMT employees, and no serious people problems existed.

In recent years, because of advancing age and the increased complexity of managing the company, Summers has delegated much of the responsibility for the management of daily operations to his son-in-law, Mr. Roenn, and nephew, Mr. Davis. Summers remains chairman of the board, and Davis and Roenn have become president and vice president of the company and minority owners. Thus Summers now has a more participative style, and Roenn's and Davis's motivation has increased. The change in style was not easy for someone who had been authoritative for so long, but the current situation dictated the change.

Relations with Workers

There are no other organizational or management levels below Summers, Davis, and Roenn. The plant and office staff work directly for these men. Wages and benefits are reasonable at AMT but not so high as at some larger firms. What the employees may be losing in terms of pay they are more than gaining in terms of how they are treated and the flexibility and freedom they have during working hours.

Employees are given turkeys at Thanksgiving and Christmas, they are given additional time off with pay when needed, they are treated with respect and are on a first-name basis with the three key members of the top management team. Because there is no elaborate management hierarchy, workers have the responsibility of doing their jobs without someone looking over their shoulders. They know their jobs are important to the success of the company, appreciate the fact that they are not closely supervised, and seem to work harder and care more for what they are doing. This has led to superior service, increased productivity, and a healthy organizational climate.

Recently the company has instituted a bonus system for a few key employees. These bonuses are based on the company's performance and an employee's contribution to the company. As time goes by and profits permit, this system will gradually be expanded to include other employees.

Employee turnover and absenteeism have never been a serious problem for AMT. Good workers are rewarded and made to feel as if they are an integral part of the team; poor workers are fired. Work standards are high and the work is difficult at times, but human relations seem to be good.

CAREER OPPORTUNITIES

Someone with a two-year degree could go to work at AMT as either a production worker or an office clerk. Production workers are trained on the company's induction equipment and given complete responsibility for running customers' jobs once they have been trained. Within a few years, they might be considered for the position of shift supervisor.

Office workers undertake some aspect of bookkeeping, with responsibility for such things as handling accounts payable, invoicing customers, or preparing financial statements. There is not much possibility for advancement in the office, because it is only staffed by three people. However, it might be possible in time to become office manager or to get more involved in customer sales.

FOR DISCUSSION

1. Do you feel management style is related to organizational size? Explain.
2. Was Mr. Summers's change in management style necessary? Explain your answer.
3. AMT's managers do not use, or even know about, many of the concepts and techniques presented in this chapter, yet they do a good job of managing their employees. How is this possible?

OBJECTIVES

- ☐ To explain the process of human resource management and its importance to companies
- ☐ To identify the major functions performed by human resource managers
- ☐ To understand how human resource managers perform their functions
- ☐ To identify the constraints on human resource managers and determine their influence
- ☐ To explain the importance of human beings to the organization

OUTLINE

KEY TERMS

AFFIRMATIVE ACTION

EQUAL EMPLOYMENT OPPORTUNITIES ACT (EEO)

EXECUTIVE "PERKS"

HUMAN RESOURCE MANAGEMENT

JOB ANALYSIS

JOB DESCRIPTION

JOB DESIGN

JOB ROTATION

JOB SPECIFICATION

OCCUPATIONAL SAFETY AND HEALTH ACT (OSHA)

PERFORMANCE APPRAISAL

PERFORMANCE STANDARDS

SUPPLEMENTARY BENEFITS

HUMAN RESOURCE MANAGEMENT

How Does the U.S. Treasury Reward Its Outstanding Workers? With Cash, of Course

Management Review, November 1979

The practice of recognizing outstanding job performance with a cash bonus, while common in business, is largely unknown in government agencies. But that may be changing. Early this year, the Treasury Department launched a pilot program that would be a harbinger of new performance appraisal and incentive bonus programs throughout the civil service.

According to Stephen Bashein, a program manager in Treasury's management analysis division, the program, called Work Planning/Performance Review, is tailored after employee appraisal and incentive-award systems common to many private corporations. The prime mover in introducing the program to the government sector was former Treasury Secretary W. Michael Blumenthal, who prior to his cabinet service was chairman of the Bendix Corporation.

Further impetus for the program came from a Treasury employee survey and a government-wide General Accounting Office survey. In the latter, more than a third of those surveyed reported that they received inadequate supervision as well as insufficient feedback.

Motivated by the survey results, Secretary Blumenthal named a management committee to come up with ways of improving the department's efficiency. The committee pinpointed several key areas where improvements in management practices could lead to significant improvements in employee performance. These areas included work planning, performance review, and use of incentives.

The department brought in a consulting firm with experience in servicing the nonprofit sector to assist in the design and implementation of the pilot program. More than 600 senior-level employees in the Office of the Secretary took part in the pilot program—less than one percent of the departmental workforce. Nearly ten percent of the participants earned cash awards totaling $150,000. Secretary Blumenthal stressed at the onset that performance would now be more closely linked to all forms of recognition.

The WP/PR procedure begins with a lengthy discussion between the employee and the supervisor. Together, they write down the tasks and responsibilities of the position and formulate an individual work plan that spells out the goals to be reached in the rating period, which was six months long in the pilot program. They agree on well-defined job standards against which the employee's performance can be measured. These standards should contain an appropriate mix of qualitative and quantitative criteria. If by the end of the rating period the employee has effectively met or exceeded the agreed-upon goals and performance levels, the supervisor will rate him or her as outstanding and recommend that a cash bonus be issued. Recommendations for cash bonuses are reviewed at each successive level of the chain of command. The final determination is made by a review committee chaired by the Secretary of the Treasury.

The procedure for the pilot program called for the use of three basic documents:

- *Work plan* At the start of the six-month rating period, the employee and supervisor collaborate in filling out the form that describes each major work assignment in terms of required job tasks, schedules, and objectives, and it delineates job standards against which performance will be measured.
- *Evaluation of job-related practices* This two-part form, completed at the end of the six-month rating period, requires the supervisor and employee to furnish inputs independently. The supervisor, on the first part of the form, rates the employee on attributes not immediately related to specific work assignments. These might include initiative, consistency, ability to work independently, and ability to develop good work relationships. The supervisor provides comments and specific recommendations for improvement. If the subordinate is also in a supervisory capacity, the rater must assess the supervisor's skills in assigning work, recognizing good performance, and dealing with subordinates.
- *Performance appraisal and overall achievement rating* At the end of the six-month period, the supervisor uses this form to summarize the employee's overall performance, making reference to the stipulations of the work plan. In effect, this form serves as the basis for determining whether performance merits recognition or needs improvement.

The pilot program's first rating period ended last June 30. While the overall pilot review is ongoing, Bashein notes some results already apparent: "The program initiated a process of supervisor-subordinate communication not happening before . . . employees were more aware of what was expected in terms of their performance."

Management in Practice, *Management Review*, November 1979 (New York: AMACOM, a division of American Management Association, 1979), p. 47.

Performance appraisals are just one of the many tasks performed by human resource managers. This chapter examines their other roles and how they manage the most important asset an organization has—its people.

Human resource management, or personnel management, is the management of people. According to some, this process is nothing more than a bunch of gimmicks inappropriately borrowed from manufacturing. Perhaps, but the management of people is complex and difficult at best. Human resource management seeks to control, direct, and motivate people in a way that best realizes the goals and objectives of the firm without sacrificing the needs of employees.

As you read this chapter, keep in mind that we can only touch on the tip of the iceberg. The world is much too complicated—and people are far too varied—for us to categorize every problem involved in human resource management.

Human Resource Management in Context

Personnel management involves planning, controlling, and coordinating the work force. Personnel managers are responsible for making sure that employees function to the best of their abilities and that the firm has the proper number and type of people to get the job done. As shown in Exhibit 8.1, human resource management follows every employee's career in a firm, beginning with job design and extending through employee recruitment, selection, hiring, compensation, training and development, performance appraisal, and finally retirement.

In today's society, human resource management is a complex task. Managers are responsible for more than just hiring and firing employees. They are also subject to various government regulations that control the hours employees can work, what they can do, and their working conditions. There are even laws that govern hiring and compensation practices. In addition, "social responsibility" is gaining greater attention and placing further constraints on management. The meaningfulness of the work experience, the hiring of minority workers, and the quality of life outside the work environment are now considered reasonable concerns of human resource managers. Managers are also expected to consider and sometimes to plan as well for the life of employees after they leave the firm.

A HISTORICAL PERSPECTIVE

Business owners have always had to manage, control, and oversee their employees. Until the industrial revolution, managers could even do this job with a whip in hand. Because one owner had only to manage a few employees, this autocratic style of management was quite effective, at least in the short run.

The industrial revolution brought about mechanization and subsequently the mass production of goods. With the increased demand for goods, the labor force had to expand. Hence, human beings became a more important and costly component of the production process.

As labor became more important managers became more interested in efficient management—reducing labor costs while increasing productivity. In the late 1800s, Frederick W. Taylor began to investigate the applicability of scientific method to human resource management. Taylor's primary emphasis was on planning and simplifying tasks, and to accomplish this he instituted the now-infamous time-and-motion studies. His goal was to reduce the time required to perform a task, in part by simplifying the process. Additionally, Taylor felt that encouraging cooperation between managers and workers was a crucial factor in the effective use of human resources.

In the early 1900s, beginning with the Hawthorne studies (refer to

EXHIBIT 8.1 The Scope of Human Resource Management

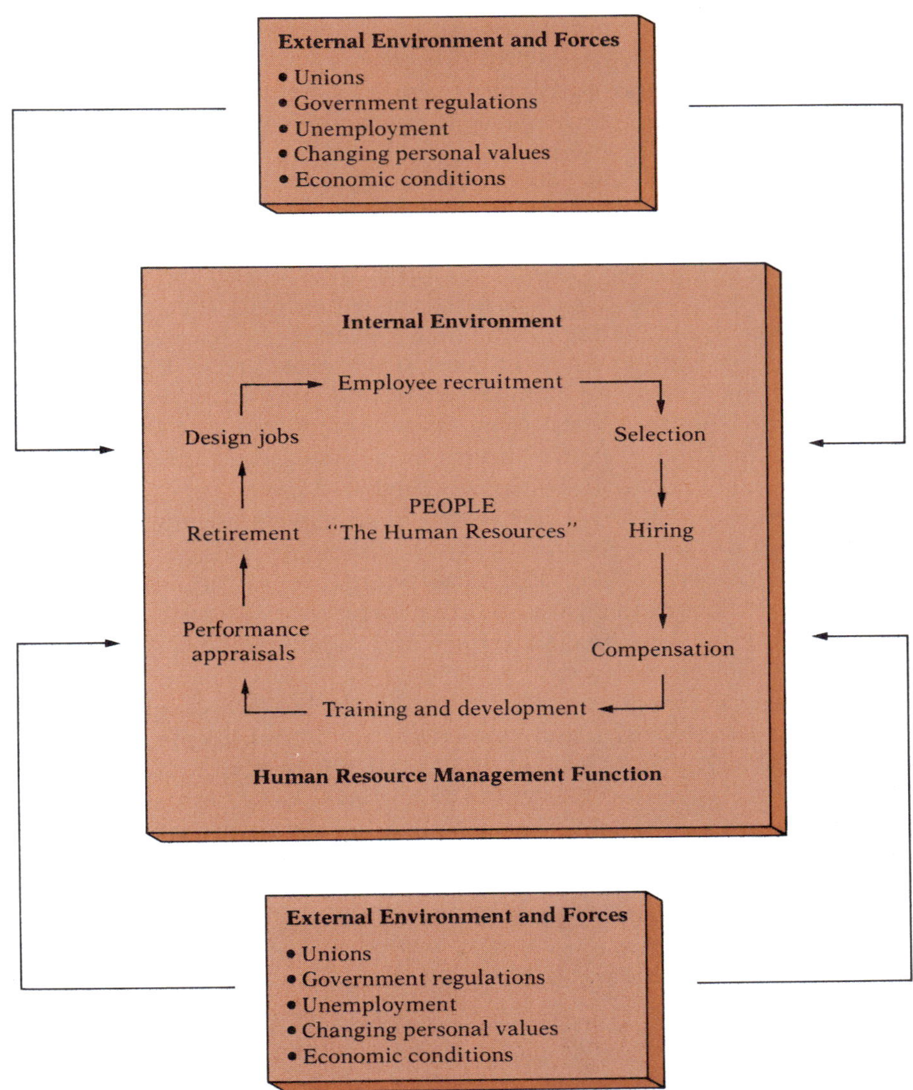

Chapter 7), the emphasis in human-resource research began to shift from efficient movement to employee motivation and morale. This change in focus has continued, with modern organizational-behavior theorists and industrial psychologists applying psychological theories to the study of human resource management. The focus is now on group behavior, attitudinal and motivational factors, effective ways of communicating with employees, leadership behavior, and job design. Organizational performance can be thought of as a function of many variables, including the extent to which management encourages employee effort, defines job direction and tasks, and analyzes and develops employees' abilities.

THE BUSINESS ENVIRONMENT

While researchers were studying productivity and the motivation of employees, unions and government agencies became concerned with the fairness of hiring and compensation practices and the treatment of employees. As a result of these concerns, human resource managers are now subject to many laws and regulations, some of which deserve mention. They directly affect the way managers behave toward employees.

Starting in the 1800s, laws prohibiting child labor, limiting the work day, establishing safety standards, and instituting minimum wages were passed in various parts of the country. By the early 1900s, the federal government began supporting such concerns, passing regulations like the Federal Child Labor Laws (1916), Social Security Act (1935), and the Fair Labor Standards Act (1938). In more recent years, regulations within the Civil Rights Act (1964) and the Age Discrimination in Employment Act (1967), have emphasized the rights of minorities (including women) and older workers.

One recent piece of legislation that has had a significant impact on human resource management is the Occupational Safety and Health Act (OSHA), passed in 1970. OSHA inspectors travel around the country inspecting work sites to ensure that they meet federal health and safety regulations. If not, employers are fined and required to bring the workplace up to federal standards.

Two federal programs that cause headaches for employers but greatly benefit minorities and women are the **Equal Employment Opportunity Act (EEO),** passed in 1972, and **affirmative action.*** Their purpose is to ensure that minorities and women have more of an equal chance at getting jobs. EEO was designed to help rectify past discrimination in hiring practices. When many employers failed to comply with the goals of EEO as quickly and as effectively as the government desired, affirmative action programs were created. Affirmative action forces employers to come up with a plan to comply with EEO. It sets goals and deadlines for employers in the area of hiring and in effect re-

*The original concept of equal employment opportunity was set-forth in Title VII of the Civil Rights Act. This Title was subsequently amended in 1972 resulting in the passage of the EEO Act.

quires that employers hire a certain number of minority employees by a certain date. This program has motivated many companies to actively recruit minorities.

HUMAN BEINGS AS A RESOURCE

All organizations use available resources in an effort to generate profits. Resources are, therefore, the tangible and intangible factors used to earn a profit, whether they are owned or merely used on a temporary basis. Even in today's highly mechanized, highly technical work environment, it is the brain and muscle of people that accomplish the day-to-day functions of any firm. Thus people are frequently the single most important resource in an organization.

Furthermore, human labor is often the most costly resource used by a firm. The typical investment in human resources, from the recruitment of potential employees through their retirement, is substantial. It is in the firm's interest, obviously, to achieve maximum productivity from this resource. The survival of the firm may very well depend on the effectiveness of its human resource management.

Before turning to the specifics of human resource management, we'd like to say a word about organizational goals. As with management of the other resources of a firm, such as cash and equipment, the first consideration must be to use employees to achieve the goals of the organization. Obviously, the ultimate goals are maximum profit and survival. Specification of the means by which to achieve these ends, however, is necessary in order to manage effectively the resources to be used to attain them. Nowhere is this more important than in managing human resources. Once the organizational goals have been specified, human resource managers can assure that the people necessary to accomplish these goals are available.

Staffing

Once organizational goals have been set, human resource managers can begin planning workforce needs and objectives. This process begins by determining the jobs to be done, specifying the qualifications of the people needed to fill those jobs, and recruiting and selecting people who fit those requirements.

JOB DESIGN

The purpose of **job design** is to divide all the tasks to be performed by an organization into distinct, manageable units. This can be done initially by a committee of managers who are familiar with the total operations of the firm. Although a vital part of this process is to differentiate between jobs, it is equally important to make sure that all jobs are integrated. That is, all parts of the organization must be coordinated so that the firm's total task can be completed in an orderly and efficient manner.

Once the jobs have been established and defined, managers need to describe the basic responsibilities and tasks of someone in that job—the **job description**—and to list the qualifications that are required—the **job specification.** The process of preparing these items is known as **job analysis.** (see Exhibit 8.2).

Knowing exactly what tasks are involved in a given job serves two purposes. First, it helps define the duties that an employee is expected to perform—role expectations—and how the company prescribes that the employee go about performing these tasks. Second, job descriptions help in determining what qualifications are needed to perform the required tasks. The sample job description in Exhibit 8.3 indicates that those who want to work in personnel should have a background in business administration with an emphasis in personnel administration.

It is important that job descriptions be accurate and readily understandable. If the description is imprecise or too vague, misunderstandings of expectations and performance levels can occur, resulting in poor employee performance or low morale. On the other hand, a job description that is too specific may discourage an employee from creative or productive problem-solving activities.

The primary reason for preparing a job description and job specification is to facilitate a match between the employee and the firm. Underqualified workers cannot fulfill the requirements of the job and are likely to become frustrated; overqualified workers are likely to experience dissatisfaction. Both lead to low morale and thereby inhibit productivity.

EXHIBIT 8.2 The Elements of Job Design

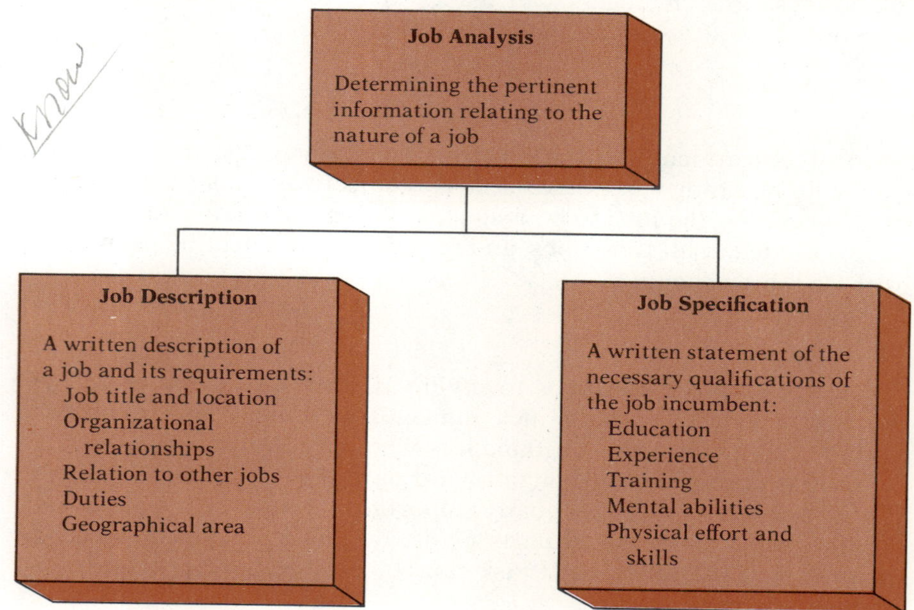

Job Analysis
Determining the pertinent information relating to the nature of a job
Job Description
A written description of a job and its requirements:
Job title and location
Organizational relationships
Relation to other jobs
Duties
Geographical area
Job Specification
A written statement of the necessary qualifications of the job incumbent:
Education
Experience
Training
Mental abilities
Physical effort and skills

EMPLOYEE RECRUITMENT

Once job descriptions and job specifications have been established, the hiring process can begin. It takes a determined effort to obtain the employees most suited to the job and to the organization. Remember that the future of the organization depends on the growth and development of its employees. Thus organizational success is frequently a function of selecting the proper people to do certain jobs.

There are two major pools of potential employees: current employees and new personnel. The labor pool already on hand should not be overlooked when positions need to be filled. This is often the best source of middle- and upper-management personnel. Many larger companies require that such positions be filled by current employees, if possible, because they have developed over the years an understanding of the needs and policies of their organization. Thus they can step into the new roles more quickly and efficiently than an outsider could.

If the position cannot be filled from within, the company must look outside for staffing. Sometimes management prefers to do this, in order to bring in "new blood" and new creative talent. However, because current employees sometimes resent outsiders, companies normally post any new vacancy and allow time for current employees to apply. Nevertheless, sooner or later hiring outside the firm becomes necessary. Common techniques for reaching outside sources include advertising in local or national newspapers, seeking help from academic or professional recruitment services, and on-campus recruiting. In addition, an efficient manager keeps a file on likely former applicants in the event that future positions develop for which they may be qualified.

EXHIBIT 8.3 A Sample Job Description

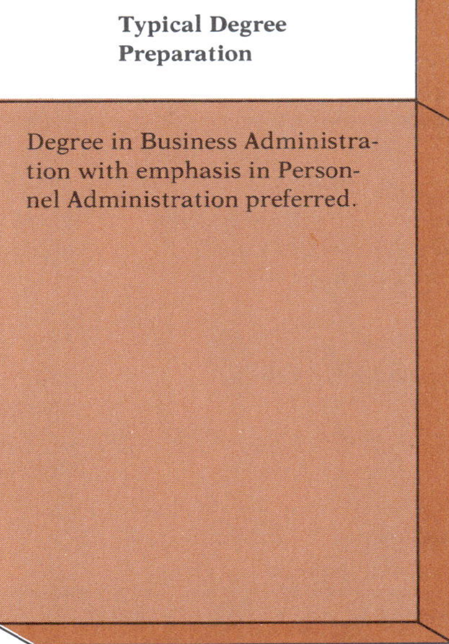

Department	Typical Degree Preparation	Job Description
PERSONNEL ADMINISTRATION	Degree in Business Administration with emphasis in Personnel Administration preferred.	Administer the industrial relations program of the company. Position includes staff forecasting, recruitment, interviewing, orientation, counselling, and employee relations. Specialized positions within any of these functional areas of the department may also be available.

Highlight Overqualified and Underemployed

During Memorial Day weekend in 1978, Hughes Aircraft chartered a plane to fly over Los Angeles beaches dragging a sign that read: "Hughes Needs Engineers: Call 648-3303." At the time, Hughes was in desperate need of 1,500 engineers to work on several government contracts it had recently received. The results of its efforts? Six walk-ins. During that summer, it was estimated that Southern California was in need of 30,000 engineers. Since then, recruiting for engineers has become even more competitive. It is not unusual for top engineering students to receive seven, eight, or ten job offers on graduation.

Yet engineers have not always had it so good. With the end of the Vietnam War, engineers glutted the market. Hardest hit was the aerospace industry. Employees with over ten years seniority, making up to $40,000 per year, suddenly found themselves without a job. The early 1970s abounded with horror stories of people with engineering doctorates driving taxis, waiting tables, and working as office clerks.

Underemployment occurs when an individual has qualifications that exceed those required for his or her job. Underemployment has become more prevalent since the 1950s as the work force has become more educated—in many cases, more educated than required for the jobs they are performing. Underemployment is a challenging and perplexing problem for human resource managers, who have to match qualifications with jobs.

SELECTION OF EMPLOYEES

The selection process, whether for internal or external applicants, is designed to determine applicants' abilities to perform effectively in the positions that are available. The selection process is both objective and subjective, the proportion depending on the level and type of position being filled. Exhibit 8.4 lists the stages that may be involved in the process; four of the most common devices are application forms, interviews, employment tests, and reference checks.

Application forms are often useful in the initial stages of employee selection. Information on previous work experience, education and

EXHIBIT 8.4 Stages in the Selection Process

Stages	Reasons for Elimination of Applicant
Preliminary screening from application, records data sheets, etc.	Lacks adequate education, experience, and performance
Preliminary interview	Expectations, qualifications and conduct indicate unsuitability for job
Employment tests	Fails to meet minimum standard
Background and reference checks	Unfavorable reports on past behavior and performance
Diagnostic interview	Lack necessary innate ability, ambition, or other qualities
Physical examination	Physically unfit for job
Personal judgment	
One applicant is extended an offer	

Adapted from Megginson, L. C., *Providing Management Talent for Small Business.* Baton Rouge. Division of Research, College of Business Administration, Louisiana State University, 1961, p. 108.

training, career goals, and expectations can be invaluable in eliminating unlikely prospects.

Personal contact with applicants is another valuable aid, especially in the search for middle- and upper-level managers. On the basis of an interview, managers can make a prediction (admittedly subjective) about most applicants' abilities to deal with and adapt to everyday working conditions. Furthermore, many managers judge applicants on such qualities as appearance, poise, and personality and consider these factors in making a final evaluation. It is important, however, to distinguish between liking and evaluating an applicant. An attractive personality may distort the interviewer's judgment of an applicant's ability and qualifications, a phenomenon known as the halo effect. Conversely, interviewers must avoid rejecting an applicant with the appropriate qualifications solely on the grounds of a personality conflict.

There are many types of tests available to personnel managers, including psychological and skill tests. Skill tests are especially helpful in filling such positions as those in secretarial or manufacturing fields. Psychological tests attempt to measure such intangible factors as motivation, mental suitability for the position, and intelligence. Although psychological tests have been used in some form since the late 1800s, they may be far more subjective than realized and therefore more subject to error or misuse. Furthermore, a controversy has recently developed over the accuracy with which achievement, aptitude, and psychological tests predict employee performance. The most controversial selection method now in use—polygraph, or lie-detecting, tests—are administered to determine whether potential employees are telling the

"Remember how steamed you were when I stole Harwick away from you? How would you like him back?"

Wall Street Journal, August 18, 1980. Reprinted by permission of the Wall Street Journal.

truth about their background and qualifications. Polygraph tests for employment purposes are banned in some states, but others continue to use them.

Although job candidates rarely provide references that they expect to be negative, prospective employers can nevertheless obtain valuable information from checking on past jobs and personal relationships. People occasionally claim work experience that they do not actually have. References can provide information on attendance records, reliability, desire, and ability to follow orders.

Employee Retention and Promotion

Once people have been selected to fill given positions, the company must make an effort to keep them working efficiently. It takes a sizable amount of money to find the right human resources and start them in a job. Training and development programs, performance appraisals, job enlargement programs, and compensation packages are all worthwhile means for protecting the company's investment.

TRAINING AND DEVELOPMENT

The effort to improve employees' skills and to help them make a career within the company occurs at various stages, in various forms. Formal training programs may take the form of seminars, specialized classes, orientation sessions, role playing, group interaction, and conferences and workshops. Frequently they are specific to a task or job assignment and have short-range objectives.

Programs intended to develop managers have a longer time frame. Ultimately, the aim is to provide employees with the intangible skills they may need to move up the management ladder. Seminars in such areas as listening skills, team building, and motivation techniques are designed to prepare potential managers for positions of responsibility.

Organizations have a variety of other methods at their disposal for developing potential managers. **Job rotation**—moving an employee through different positions within an organization—provides exposure to a broader range of operations and opportunities. Not only does this enhance the effective placement of employees, but it also enables employees to have a better understanding of the overall functions of the firm. Planned progression is similar to job rotation but has a longer time perspective. Employees spend time at corporate headquarters, at regional offices, in the field, and possibly overseas, in various jobs and managerial positions. Special, temporary, and "assistant to" positions are short in duration and have two main functions: They provide a special service to upper management and give participating employees exposure to specialized aspects of the firm's operations. Finally, continuing education programs send employees to attend formal courses at a local university, frequently for a degree. If these courses are required or encouraged by the company, they are generally paid for by the company.

PERFORMANCE APPRAISAL

Closely tied to the training process is the appraisal process. A key advantage of regular and well-conducted **performance appraisals** is the opportunity to teach employees through praise and constructive criticism (that is, with suggestions for improvement). All employees, including top managers, need positive reinforcement on a regular basis. Critical evaluation is also necessary, however, in order to provide employees with knowledge of how to improve. The appraisal process can be a difficult and uncomfortable experience for all parties, so it is important to emphasize its learning aspects. Evaluations are normally given on a fixed, periodic basis, at least every six months or when an employee is up for a promotion or salary increase. However, performance appraisal is an integral part of a manager's job and therefore an ongoing process.

Performance standards are the yardsticks by which managers and employees can judge their ability to do a job in a satisfactory manner. Most appraisal systems evaluate employees in the context of certain key characteristics, which may include reliability, congeniality, ability to get along with others, ability to follow orders, cooperativeness, positive attitudes, enthusiasm, dependability, work habits, and loyalty. Methods can be formal or informal, ranging from merit ratings, which rank employees along certain dimensions, to evaluation interviews and coaching. Regardless of the appraisal system used, it should seek answers to such questions as "Would I want to work with this employee again?" or "How far do I expect this employee to rise in the organization?" or "What are the major strengths and weaknesses of the employee?"

Whatever the system or criteria, it cannot be overemphasized that the appraisal should be treated as a positive part of the employee's career. There is probably no aspect of personnel management with a greater potential for positive or negative impact.

Appraisal systems are closely related to advancement opportunities. Efficient human resource management involves hiring competent, qualified employees as well as promoting them as they gain experience and maturity. By considering and planning for the future careers of employees, two costly mistakes can be avoided: promoting employees to positions they are not qualified for and failing to promote employees who could be more effective at a higher level. Furthermore, job satisfaction is frequently a function of understanding where the future lies, particularly for younger employees.

Compensation

Compensation is the total reward offered to an employee for the performance of a given task. It is the price charged for use of the human resource. Today, compensation packages often include more than the salary employees can expect to earn. The number of options has increased dramatically, as Exhibit 8.5 indicates.

Of course, employees are primarily concerned with wages. Govern-

Highlight My Boss? He Rates a 6.5

At General Telephone and Electronics, managers are learning how to do a better job of rating employees, and workers get a chance to rate their bosses. This new program is designed to increase communication and morale by getting both sides to share their perceptions.

GTE employs 220,000 people to produce lighting, electronics, communication, and primary materials. During the 1970s, GTE grew nearly sixfold by acquiring two dozen companies. Thus in a short period of time GTE had to assimilate myriad management interests, practices, principles, and appraisal techniques. To standardize management policies, GTE charged an outside consultant firm with designing and teaching new, uniform appraisal techniques. The consultants showed managers how performance appraisals can raise morale, increase employee performance, help achieve organizational strategy, and ultimately increase corporate profits.

GTE's new appraisal system is based on positive feedback and reinforcement of employee strengths. Managers learned to start by getting employees to discuss their strengths and then adding strengths that the employees may have missed. The same procedure is used to discuss employee weaknesses.

After their appraisals, employees are given a chance to rate their bosses on how well they communicated objectives, organized teamwork, and rewarded good performance. Rating the boss is a mild way of relieving the impulse to "tell him off." As an added benefit, it gives managers extra insight into their performance.

ment regulations, such as the minimum-wage law, establish base standards. If the company has a union, wages for union employees are established during collective bargaining. However, all wage packages are based in some way on

- Wage surveys (competitive salaries for a given job)
- The relative worth of jobs within the firm
- The productivity and qualifications of the individual
- The firm's ability to pay

To determine wages, management must essentially analyze the benefits that can be provided by a particular human resource and put a value on them.

The **supplementary benefits** provided in addition to the basic wage are becoming more important in business today. Some of these, such as worker's compensation insurance and unemployment insurance, are required by law. Others are provided at the option of the employer.

Some benefits exist because of society's increasing concern over organization's responsibility to employees. Such benefits as life, dental, health, accident, and hospitalization insurance are sometimes fully paid by the company; often the company and employee share the costs. Pension plans, intended to help employees after they reach retirement, are also important in the total compensation package. Vacation days, sick days, and holidays are offered to relieve employees of work pressures on a periodic basis.

Other benefits, such as profit-sharing and bonus arrangements, are intended to encourage employees to produce at their most efficient

EXHIBIT 8.5 Compensation Options

Accidental death, dismemberment insurance
Birthdays (vacation)
Bonus eligibility
Business and professional memberships
Cash profit sharing
Club memberships
Commissions
Company medical assistance
Company-provided automobile
Company-provided housing
Company-provided or subsidized travel
Day care centers
Deferred bonus
Deferred compensation plan
Deferred profit sharing
Dental and eye care insurance
Discount on company products
Education costs
Educational activities (time off)
Employment contract
Executive dining room
Free checking account
Free or subsidized lunches
Group automobile insurance
Group homeowners insurance
Group life insurance
Health maintenance organization fees
Holidays (extra)
Home health care
Hospital-surgical-medical insurance
Incentive growth fund
Interest-free loans
Layoff pay (S.U.B.)
Legal, estate-planning, and other professional assistance
Loans of company equipment
Long-term disability benefit
Matching educational donations
Nurseries
Nursing home care
Opportunity for travel
Outside medical services
Paid attendance at business, professional, and other outside meetings
Parking facilities
Pension
Personal accident insurance
Personal counseling
Personal credit cards
Personal expense accounts
Physical examinations
Political activities (time off)
Price discount plan
Private office
Professional activities
Psychiatric services
Recreation facilities
Resort facilities
Retirement gratuity
Sabbatical leaves
Salary
Salary continuation
Savings plan
Scholarships for dependents
Severance pay
Shorter or flexible work week
Sickness and accident insurance
Social security
Social service sabbaticals
Split-dollar life insurance
State disability plans
Stock appreciation rights
Stock bonus plan
Stock options plans (qualified, non-qualified, tandem)
Stock purchase plan
Survivors' benefits
Tax assistance
Title
Training programs
Vacations
Wages
Weekly indemnity insurance

From Thomsen, David J., "Introducing Cafeteria Compensation in Your Company," Reprinted with permission from *Personnel Journal*, Costa Mesa, CA copyright March 1977, p. 125.

levels. These are becoming more common. In addition, **executive "perks"** (or perquisites) are benefits available to employees who are moving up the management ladder. These can be of significant influence in motivating lower- and middle-level managers. Special recognition (perhaps a key to the executive washroom) and special privileges provide employees with symbols of status. For example, it is common for managers to receive bigger and more elaborate offices as they progress in the management hierarchy.

Retirement and Termination

With increased social concern for employee welfare has come increased concern for employees who are terminated or retire. Also, the way a company treats those who are leaving affects the morale and motivation of those who stay. The best way to handle termination or retirement is therefore to be as helpful and as sympathetic as possible.

Although employees are sometimes terminated for inadequate performance, many are terminated when their position is eliminated or

Highlight Perks Keep Executives Perking

Trying to live in today's economy is no easy task. Inflation, at the double-digit level in recent years, has increased faster than real wages. Federal income taxes are taking a larger portion of Americans' paychecks, resulting in smaller disposable incomes. In addition, as executives make more money, they are pushed into higher tax brackets. As a result, salary increases are less of a motivator than in the past.

Sensing the frustration of their executives, many corporations are attempting to help executives through the use of tax-free "perks." They increase the executive's status while supplying benefits that the executive would ordinarily have to spend salary on. In many cases, thousands of dollars' worth of perks are made available to an executive each year.

Some of the most common perks are personal use of company-supplied automobiles (often complete with chauffeur); limousine service; personal bodyguards; club memberships, including membership in exclusive country, professional, or athletic clubs; extensive medical, dental, health, psychiatric, and accident insurance; financial and legal counseling, including investment counseling, tax help, and estate planning; use of houses , apartments, and vacation lodging owned by the company; entertainment allowances that require no documentation of the money's use; and reimbursement for the expenses of the executive's spouse on a business trip.

when they can rise no further in the organization (an "up or out" company). More and more companies are responding to such situations by giving employees advance warning and allowing them to look for a position elsewhere while still employed. Personnel managers often help by making contacts with other employers, providing resume counseling, and even providing retraining programs. Such policies not only benefit the terminated employee but also help maintain morale among the other employees.

Companies now take an equally active role in the retirement process. The traditional response has been a gold watch and a handshake. Today, however, management is recognizing that someone who has spent forty years working may find it difficult to read books, watch soap operas, and go fishing for the remaining years of his or her life. Furthermore, people live longer now, and the cost of living rises rapidly, often preventing retired employees from maintaining their lifestyles. Thus companies begin training employees, frequently years ahead of time, to deal with the end of their work lives. Psychological preparation, leisure training, and encouragement of outside interests are all possible alternatives for the final phase of human resource management.

Highlight Getting Ready to Relax

Retirement may not be so easy as it appears. After spending twenty to fifty years working, many people have trouble adjusting to the so-called life of leisure. For some, retirement means that a life full of responsibility and purpose has ended.

To help with this problem, many companies are beginning to offer preretirement counseling. At IBM, for example, employees nearing retirement (and their spouses) are eligible to receive up to $2,500 each for courses designed to help develop postretirement careers or hobbies. The courses most often include TV-radio repair, real estate, carpentry, and interior decorating.

Kimberly-Clark offers a program called "Planning for Tomorrow" that is designed to help employees realize that retirement is a new career. For many people, the transition from fulltime work to fulltime leisure is frustrating, difficult, even boring. But participants of this program attend meetings that cover such topics as retirement benefits, financial planning, and the use of leisure time and thereby gain a sense of control over their future.

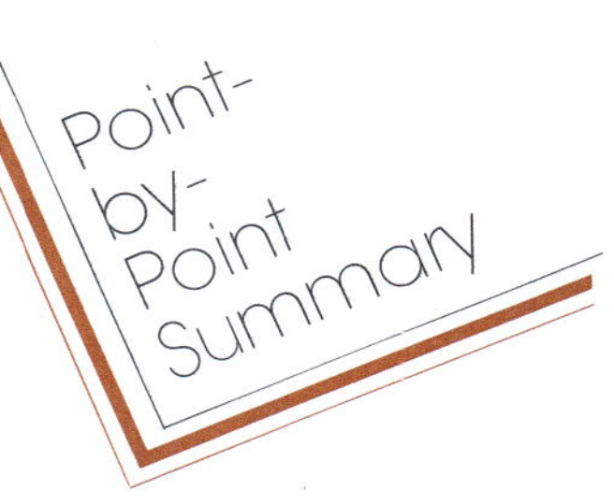

- Human resource management, which is the management of people, dates back to biblical times. The greatest advances in human resource management have occurred since the industrial revolution.
- The initial phase of human resource management is staffing, which begins with determination of the jobs to be done, specification of the requirements to fill those jobs, and recruitment of people with the necessary requirements.
- There are two major sources of potential employees: current employees and new personnel. The most-used tools in employee selection are applications, interviews, employment tests, and references.
- Once employees are on the job, human resource managers must be concerned with retaining and promoting them. Elements of this function are proper training and development, performance appraisals, and adequate and appropriate compensation.
- Human resource managers must be aware of the constraints imposed by government laws and regulations.
- Employee benefits vary according to the company and the job. In recent years, the types of compensation that are available to employees—beside wages—have become quite diversified. Managers often receive executive perks instead of larger salaries.
- Companies are becoming increasingly helpful in preparing employees for retirement and in assisting terminated workers in finding employment.

Questions for Review

1. What are the major functions performed by the human resource manager? How are these functions related to the process of human resource management?
2. What contribution has the scientific management approach, fathered by F. Taylor, made to the field of human resource management?
3. If you were hiring people for a mid-level managerial position, would you rather hire people from within the firm or from outside? Defend your answer.
4. What types of training programs are most effective for different positions?
5. How can performance appraisal systems be used to motivate employees?
6. Why is management of human resources so important to an organization?
7. What deficiencies would you anticipate in most job descriptions?
8. How might you avoid resentment in current employees when you want to hire from outside rather than promote from within?
9. Why are executive perks important to managers?
10. What was the importance of the Hawthorne studies to modern human resource management?
11. In what ways has government legislation affected the process of human resource management.

APPLICATION

Caterpillar Tractor Company

The year was 1904. The place was the fertile farmland of California's San Joaquin Valley. The problem: how to maneuver a twenty-ton steam-driven tractor through the valley's soft delta farmlands. The man with the answer was Benjamin Holt of Stockton. He developed a tractor with a circular track that laid down a continuous broad base as it moved, distributing the weight over a much greater area than was possible with wheels. This awkward giant was a far cry from today's powerful and sophisticated earth-moving machines, but Holt's idea was their forerunner.

GENESIS

During 1906, Holt began replacing the inefficient steam engines on his tractors with stronger, more efficient gasoline engines. Not only were these engines more powerful, but they were also smaller and lighter. More than a hundred of these new tractors were used to help build the Los Angeles aqueduct.

In 1909 Holt expanded his facilities by purchasing a former steam-tractor factory in East Peoria, Illinois. By 1915 the Holt factory had produced over 2,000 gas-powered tractors. In over twenty countries, people were finding that Holt tractors could do more than just plow farmland. These machines helped haul artillery and supply wagons for the United States in World War I. Many of the 10,000 Holt tractors built for use in World War I stayed in Europe afterwards , helping rebuild destroyed cities and farmland. The track-type tractor also inspired the British military and engineering personnel who invented the tank.

During this period, Holt became acquainted with C. L. Best, another manufacturer of crawler-type tractors. The Holt and Best tractor companies merged in 1925. Both men agreed that it was in their best interest to use Holt's well-known trademark, Caterpillar, as the company name. Their instincts proved correct. During their first year of business, sales rose to $13.8 million. By 1929, success had increased sales to $51.8 million. Only once in the years since then, in 1932, did the company fail to realize a profit.

Caterpillar tractors have literally helped change the shape of America. During the Depression, they created fire roads for the Civilian Conservation Corps and built roads and universities for the Work Projects Administration. Caterpillar engines, with a minimal amount of redesign, became the diesel engines of tanks used in World War II. And in the 1950s, Caterpillar tractors contributed to economic growth and industrial development around the world.

Today Caterpillar has twenty-six manufacturing plants in nine countries, including Brazil, France, Canada, Mexico, Belgium, and the United Kingdom. More than 266 independent Caterpillar dealers operate in 150 countries. With sales in 1979 of over $7.6 billion, Caterpillar is the largest manufacturer of earth-moving and materials-handling equipment. It is also a major manufacturer of diesel and natural gas engines.

HUMAN RESOURCE MANAGEMENT

Caterpillar employs approximately 90,000 people, some 55,000 in Illinois alone. With this many employees, it is essential that Caterpillar take the task of human resource management seriously. In a 1974 publication, "A Code of Worldwide Business Conduct,"

Caterpillar spelled out how it expects to relate with its employees.

As its general principle of conduct, Caterpillar states, "We aspire to a single, worldwide standard of fair treatment of employees." To accomplish this goal, Caterpillar has established broad policies applicable to all employees regardless of the country of employment:

We aspire to a single, worldwide standard of fair treatment of employees. Specifically, we intend:

1. To select and place employees on the basis of qualifications for the work to be performed—without discrimination in terms of race, religion, national origin, color, sex, age or handicap unrelated to the task at hand.
2. To protect the health and lives of employees. This includes maintaining a clean, safe work environment free from recognized health hazards.
3. To maintain uniform, reasonable work standards, worldwide, and strive to provide work that challenges the individual—so that he or she may feel a sense of satisfaction resulting from it.
4. To make employment stabilization a major factor in corporate decisions. We shall, among other things, attempt to provide continuous employment, and avoid capricious hiring practices.
5. To compensate people fairly, according to their contributions to the company, within the framework of national and local practices.
6. To foster self-development, and assist employees in improving and broadening their job skills.
7. To promote from within the organization—in the absence of factors that persuasively argue otherwise.
8. To encourage expression by individuals about their work, including ideas for improving the work result.
9. To inform employees about company matters affecting them.
10. To accept without prejudice the decision of employees on matters pertaining to union membership and union representation; and where a group of employees is lawfully represented by a union, to build a company-union relationship based upon mutual respect and trust.
11. To refrain from hiring persons closely related to members of the board of directors, administrative officers and department heads. If other employees' relatives are hired, this must be solely the result of their qualifications for jobs to be filled. No employee is to be placed in the direct line of authority of relatives. We believe that nepotism—or the appearance of nepotism—is neither fair to employees, nor in the long-term interests of the business.

Implementation of these objectives is the direct responsibility of each manager, regardless of level within the company or location. However, local managers have some authority to adapt these objectives to regional practices.

Although codes like these cannot directly be policed, review committees and auditors can help facilitate compliance—as is the case at Caterpillar. It is the responsibility of all department heads to determine annually whether employees in their areas of responsibility are following the guidelines. If present codes do not meet the needs of various managers, then it is their responsibility to say so. Finally, a corporate audit team reviews this process every year—and enforces the code and revises it when necessary. As stated by the company:

This code isn't an attempt to prescribe actions for every business encounter. It is an attempt to capture basic, general principles to be observed by Caterpillar people everywhere.

To the extent our actions match these high standards, such can be a source of pride. To the extent they don't (and we're by no means ready to claim perfection), these standards should be a challenge to each of us.

CAREER OPPORTUNITIES

It is unusual at Caterpillar for someone with a brand-new bachelor's degree to go directly into human resource management. The road to the employee relations department is quite interesting and usually quite long. Usually, new employees enter one of the company's training programs; depending on their backgrounds, they will likely be placed in manufacturing, marketing, engineering, or accounting. Developing a solid background and an understanding of the company is quite important in the early years of employment. Caterpillar wants its managers to know how the company operates and why. Furthermore, Caterpillar wants employee relations managers to be well-versed in corporate operations and policy. Thus many management trainees spend as much as one full year in training.

After training, management trainees assume entry-level positions. If they are successful, they may move through a series of assignments in different areas of the company. Once they have a solid and comprehensive background in the company, managers who want to may move into the employee relations department or related areas.

FOR DISCUSSION

1. Your company has a code similar to Caterpillar's, and your boss has informed you that the code of "relationships with employees" must be trimmed down to three items. Which three do you keep, and why?
2. If you were the vice president of employee relations at Caterpillar, how would you make sure that these codes were actually being used? How would you make sure that they were applicable to those who used them?

OBJECTIVES

☐ To define what labor unions are
☐ To discuss why unions are needed and why employees join them
☐ To describe the impact of unionism on employees, employers, and society
☐ To trace the history of the labor movement during the twentieth century
☐ To understand the basics of the collective bargaining process
☐ To evaluate the effect of the labor movement on companies and union members
☐ To understand how unions are structured and operated

OUTLINE

ARTICLE *High Wages Get Low Priority from the Rank and File*
WHY EMPLOYEES JOIN UNIONS
THE EVOLUTION OF UNIONS
Unions in the 1800s
Unions in the 1900s
Unions Today
UNION ORGANIZATION
Structure of the AFL-CIO
Union Security
THE COLLECTIVE BARGAINING PROCESS
Negotiation
Approval and Administration
THE FUTURE OF UNIONISM
Unemployment
New Areas of Union Activity
APPLICATION *Dow Chemical Company*

KEY TERMS

AGENCY SHOP
AMERICAN FEDERATION OF LABOR (AFL)
BARGAINING IN GOOD FAITH
BINDING ARBITRATION
CLAYTON ACT
CLOSED SHOP
COLLECTIVE BARGAINING
CONGRESS OF INDUSTRIAL ORGANIZATIONS (CIO)
GUILD
KNIGHTS OF LABOR
LANDRUM-GRIFFIN ACT
NATIONAL LABOR RELATIONS ACT
NATIONAL LABOR RELATIONS BOARD (NLRB)
OPEN SHOP
PREFERENTIAL SHOP
RIGHT-TO-WORK LAWS
TAFT-HARTLEY ACT
UNEMPLOYMENT
UNION SHOP

MANAGEMENT, LABOR, AND THE UNIONS

High Wages Get Low Priority from the Rank and File

Business Week,
April 2, 1979

For eight hours a day, Louis Vitolano buzzes around a freight yard in a specially designed truck tractor called a "jockey horse," moving trailers to and from loading docks. He pulls up up in front of a dock with a jaunty hiss of air brakes, jackknifes the rig and backs the 45-ft. trailer into place in one swing, then drives off to pick up another trailer. As a "yard jockey" at a Yellow Freight System Inc. terminal near Newburgh, N.Y., the 43-year-old Vitolano earns $19,500 a year. He could make quite a bit more than $30,000 on a Newburgh-to-Cleveland run, but Vitolano prefers regular hours and "a normal life" to the 70-hour week of a long-haul driver.

Vitolano is typical in one respect of most members of the International Brotherhood of Teamsters (IBT) in the trucking industry: They are relatively satisfied with their wages. Indeed, for workers whose union most probably will break the national wage guideline, rank-and-file teamsters are extraordinarily nonmilitant about wages. "Look, the money is sufficient," says Gene Fleszar, a 33-year-old city driver in Detroit who earns $22,000 a year. "It's tight with the cost-of-living payments we get, but a sufficient allowance would preserve our purchasing power. It's the benefits that are bad."

INCOME PROTECTION

The IBT is likely to exceed the guideline for reasons other than wages. But the rank and filers' moderate attitude about wages is important because it reflects changing perceptions about the economy, the future of the trucking industry, and personal lifestyles. Like unions in other major industries such as steel and autos, the IBT has had the bargaining power to keep its members ahead of inflation. Trucking wage rates increased 137 percent during the nine years ended in January, compared with an 81 percent rise in the consumer price index. But now teamsters are worried that fat wage boosts will only aggravate inflation and drive union carriers out of business.

As a result, trucking employees appear to be resigned to a slower growth in real wages, although they expect to keep abreast of the inflation rate. "Inflation's my biggest worry for the future," says Lonzo Sayset, 53, a local driver in Chicago,. "Who knows where it will end?" Sayset earned about $30,000 last year, working 55 to 65 hours a week. "I'm not bucking for an increase in wages," he says "What I would really like to see is a stabilization in the cost of living." Sayset, a large man with rough-hewn hands from driving and handling freight for 32 years, likes his job and is willing to work overtime to increase his income. He has put two sons through college and is proud of his 12-room, $91,000 home.

Now that Sayset has "made it," he wants to protect his income—and his job and his future—from the effects of inflation. And that means holding down wage demands, a common, though largely unnoticed, concern that develops even among unionists at times of high inflation. "I'm a teamster," Sayset says, "but I'm also a consumer and these big union contracts just make everything more expensive for everyone. We're just trading dollars around nowadays, but we're not really getting anywhere."

An increase in real wages ranked fifth in the rank and file's list of bargaining priorities, according to a poll conducted last year by the IBT. "Wages are so far down the line that [IBT leaders] won't be able to buy us with that in this contract," says Fleszar, who is a member of Teamsters for a Democratic Union, a dissident group that hopes to oust IBT President Frank E. Fitzsimmons in a 1981 election. Fleszar wants improved pensions and health-care benefits, and—like many of the younger, more militant teamsters—he wants the union to improve health and safety on the job and to resist company efforts to impose productivity standards.

Less militant teamsters are also stressing benefits rather than wages in this year's negotiations, partly because they see nonunion drivers—who work at lower wage rates—invading their territory. "The gypsies are hauling stuff dirt cheap and taking the bread out of our mouths," complains Richie Savachik, a 39-year-old driver at the Newburgh terminal. "We don't like them grabbing all the good gravy, and that's why the union doesn't want to milk our companies dry. We just want to keep up with inflation."

BETTER BENEFITS

The competition among truck operators has become so fierce in big trucking hubs, such as northern New Jersey, that many drivers fear for their jobs. In some cases, drivers at one company agree to "work under the pump"—at less than union scale—to enable their employer to cut freight rates and take work away from fellow unionists. Some drivers suspect the connivance of union officials in such deals, and they talk guardedly. "Hey, I could lose my job," says one driver, whose company has lost business in this manner. "You got to look out for the man who signs your paycheck," he adds, "because he can come to you and say, 'The world is running dry, fellas,' and then he puts the key in the door and you're out of a job."

In lieu of real wage increases, most drivers want better pensions and health and welfare benefits, the issues that topped the list in last year's poll. Workers covered by the National Master Freight Agreement can retire at a full pension at age 60 if they have 20 years of service; the maximum monthly pension for most of them is about $550. "Thirty-and-out would be beautiful," muses Lon Sayset, referring to pension plans that permit retirement with 30 years of service, regardless of age. Lou Vitolano, with 26 years on the job, says that even 30 years is too long to drive a truck. "I think pushing these things for 25 years is enough," he says. "I'd like to get out now and move south and spend my time boating."

Shorter hours of work also are a high-priority item for many teamsters, particularly over-the-road drivers. These drivers, who are paid on a mileage basis, earn much more than the average hourly rate of $9.40 for short-haul drivers, and their $30,000-plus earnings put them quite comfortably in the middle-income bracket. But many have to work 70 hours in eight days, the maximum allowed by federal law. For many of them, a middle-class lifestyle has become more important than big wage increases and long hours. Vitolano, for example, quit long-haul driving so he could spend more time with his wife and five children and sail his 22-ft. power cruiser. "I like to live a normal life," he says, "and being on the road constantly for 70 hours, you don't have too much of that."

Gene Fleszar also disliked road-hauling. "About 95 percent of the road haulers are not in good health when they retire," he says. "They get carbon monoxide, ruptured kidneys, hemorrhoids, and bad backs. I'd hate to see what time would do to me working under those conditions."

As this article indicates, the kinds of benefits unions are now seeking are different from those they sought in the past. Indeed, the role and objectives of unions have changed significantly since their creation in the seventeenth century. This chapter is a review of unionism in the United States—past and present.

There are two sides to every labor relations issue—management and labor. More often than not, management (the owner) takes this point of view: "Since I have put up all the money, since I take all the risks, since I live under the constant and unrelenting strains and pressures of running a business, you the worker have no right to tell me how much I must pay you!" In response to this argument, labor (the worker, or the union leadership) often replies, "Yes, you may do the planning, take some financial risks, and play the boss role, but I do all the work. You couldn't run this thing without me. All I ask is that you realize my importance, my right to have a decent life, and pay me a fair wage!"

In large part, the growth of labor unions and the labor movement is a response to workers' perceptions that working conditions, including compensation, are less than desirable. In this regard, modern unions are no different from their predecessors. But unlike the labor unions of forty years ago, today's labor movement is not confined to blue-collar workers. Unions serve, protect, and lobby for nurses, teachers, physicians, university professors, policeofficers, and even baseball players.

Does our society need unions? Not really. The primary reason unions exist and employees join them is because workers sometimes feel they are being mistreated by their employer. Through collective action, they can force their employer to treat them more fairly. If companies were fair and reasonable in the first place, unions probably would not be needed.

Most of the justification for the creation of unions in the United States stems from the improper way many companies treated their employees in the early years of industrialization. But for the most part, these abuses have been eliminated voluntarily by management, through the passage of legislation, and through unionism. In fact, many companies have shown that they want to provide their employees with adequate pay, working conditions, and job security. Some companies have begun trend-setting labor programs in an effort to provide for their employees or in an effort to keep unions out or to deunionize.

None of the above is meant to imply that the concept of unionism is bad or obsolete. No doubt there are still companies that mistreat their employees, and the existence of a union, or the threat of unionization, serves to minimize abuse and conflicts between management and labor. However, the primary purpose for unionism has changed in the last decade or two, as have the functions of unions and the rationale for creating them.

Why Employees Join Unions

Employees join unions for a number of reasons. Among them are the desires to increase wages and benefits and to make the working environment safer and healthier. Other reasons include:

1. *Job security* Within the collective bargaining process, unions attempt to achieve some form of job security for their members. At the very least, unions try to guarantee that layoffs occur in the fairest way possible (usually by some sort of seniority system).

Highlight Is No Union a Better Union?

Not too long ago it was a common sight to see a six-year-old child, hands mutilated by dangerous machines, working sixteen hours a day for 10 cents a day. Thus it isn't too hard to imagine why unions came about. But times have changed, and in large part, thanks to unions, so have working conditions. Some people are beginning to think that unions may not be meeting the needs of their constituents as effectively as they could.

One such individual is John Gerstenmaier, president of Goodyear Tire & Rubber Company. In a recent speech, Gerstenmaier asserted that although "unions are necessary and beneficial in a society such as ours, just as companies need competition to be effective and efficient, so do unions." Gerstenmaier contends that some unions have driven up production costs so much that certain plants and industries are no longer competitive. Gerstenmaier cites bicycle tires as an example. Today only one U.S. manufacturer has managed to stay competitive, in large part because it has a nonunion shop.

As we move from an economy based on manufacturing to a predominantly service economy, unionization may become less of a necessity. Many nonunion shops have been quite successful in providing their employees with a high standard of living and benefits. These workers are happy, productivity is up, and the plants are competitive in their industry.

2. *Socialization* People need to belong to a group. Unions bring together people who have similar interests and goals. Very often, unions help build strong personal bonds among workers through meetings, social events, projects, educational programs, and political action.
3. *Communication with management* Unions are a formal vehicle by which members can speak to management with one voice about problems in the workplace. Through the union, employees can express their dissatisfaction with management and with its policies and procedures. The union's "one voice" has more influence on management action than many individual voices do.

In short, a union's main function is to supply its members with the needs and wants that management has failed to supply.

The Evolution of Unions

The labor movement in the United States can be traced back to the origins of this country. As early as 1648, the coopers (wooden tub and barrel makers) and shoemakers of Boston formed an employee-employer **guild** to enforce manufacturing standards, thereby protecting their jobs from newly arrived immigrants.

It is important to point out that early American guilds were organized on a local basis to deal with local problems; thus their potential power was quite limited. Philadelphia, often referred to as the birthplace of the labor movement, was the site of an 1806 strike involving shoemakers. This was one of the first strikes attempted by anyone in the United States. The shoemakers were attempting to raise their wages, in part by creating a wage floor under which they would not work. Twelve jurors found the shoemakers guilty of an act of conspiracy, because their illegal coalition was inhibiting free trade. Although they lost their case, the shoemakers did encourage other guild members to use collective action.

By 1836 many different types of trade and craft unions had been established in New York, Baltimore, Boston, and Cincinnati. The objective of these early unions was to establish a forum for collective bargaining between employees and management. **Collective bargaining** occurs when a group of employees join together with the goal of establishing a dialogue between themselves and management. The resolution of any conflict applies to all employees, not just to those who represent the employees or to those who happen to like the resolution.

Time has proved that a group of employees can bargain with management for better wages and working conditions much more effectively than an individual can. If one employee quits or goes out on strike (withholds services to the company), very little work is lost to the company as a whole. However, if all the employees withhold services or perhaps slow down their work, production grinds to a halt and management loses money. Feeling abused by capitalists, early unions wanted to negotiate a contract for better wages and work conditions. They found that union leaders could negotiate a better contract for all employees than independent, nonunion individuals could negotiate for themselves.

UNIONS IN THE 1800s

Between 1836 and 1860, union activity was significantly curtailed. Court decisions worked against unionism, as did a depression and heavy immigration from Germany and Ireland. Many workers, fearing that a strike would put them permanently out of work, left their unions in search of any paying position that would keep them alive.

By 1861, the Civil War was working to change the environment for unions. Because thousands of workers were off fighting the war, northern industrialists had more jobs than workers to fill them. With demand high and the supply of labor low, workers began to organize again, banding together into craft unions to seek higher wages and better working conditions.

The Knights of Labor

Between 1865 and 1880, three important events took place that would shape the course of unionism for the next fifty years. The first was the industrial revolution in America; the second was the rise and fall of the Knights of Labor; and the third was the creation of the American Federation of Labor.

In the 1870s, the industrial revolution brought about advances in technology that quickly created hundreds of thousands of new jobs. Immigration increased again, but because of the increased demand for new workers, unionism began to flourish. Soon there was an abundance of unions. To help organize and centralize the needs and strengths of union membership, an overseeing organization called the **Knights of**

Labor, was conceived. Its goals were to coordinate the activities of over 200 individual unions and to offer membership to hundreds of thousands of workers not already unionized. The Knights of Labor sought to organize "good men of all callings," whether they were skilled craftworkers or not.

The Knights of Labor got off to a slow and shaky start, in part because of the economic depressions of the 1870s. But by the end of the decade, the Knights of Labor had roughly 70,000 members. In the mid-1880s the Knights voted to strike against the Wabash Railroad. Their success in one of America's first workers' strikes of any proportion led to phenomenal growth. Barely one year later, the Knights represented over 700,000 workers.

But growth brought its share of problems. Very simply, what was good for some workers in Baltimore was not always good for those in St. Louis. The leaders of the Knights were also ill-prepared to deal successfully with the conflicting interests of skilled plumbers and farmers in the same union. Hence the decline and fall of the Knights of Labor.

The American Federation of Labor

As the Knights of Labor declined, another labor organization began to grow in size and strength. Born in 1886, the **American Federation of Labor (AFL)** never sought to attract every worker. From the beginning, it considered itself a "highly realistic, no-nonsense union." It organized and worked only with skilled trade workers. The AFL also claimed to avoid aligning itself with political parties, maintained the autonomy of each national union within its ranks, and registered only one national union per skill or craft.

Following the election of Samuel Gompers of the cigar-makers' union as its president, the strike became a formidable weapon for the AFL, especially when negotiations with an employer broke down. Thus the AFL grew steadily but met with much violence along the way. Remember, even during the late 1880s, the courts still were not ruling in favor of unions. They were felt to inhibit free trade and the free-enterprise system. AFL members were frequently labeled socialists and/or communists, but the AFL continued to grow through economic depressions and a world war. By 1897 it had 447,000 members; 2 million by 1904; 4.2 million by 1919; and over 5 million by 1920.

UNIONS IN THE 1900s

The early 1900s brought about a resurgence of anti-union sentiment in the United States, although this new anti-unionism was more likely to be expressed in the courts and in Congress. The **Clayton Act** of 1914 attempted to break apart trusts and monopolies but did not include unions as a target. Nevertheless, by 1921 the Supreme Court had found that unions were not exempt from antitrust legislation and that injunctions against their activities could be issued. Barely two years later, the

Supreme Court struck down minimum-wage laws as violations of the liberty to contract with employers. With these stunning blows, the growth, prominence, and power of unions began to decline.

The Great Depression

From 1929 to 1933, during the greatest depression in the history of the United States, union membership declined by over 2 million. Unemployment rose from 3.2 percent to 24.9 percent of this country's work force, and the gross national product declined from $104 billion per year to just over $56 billion. The rest of the world was in the throes of a similar catastrophe.

The Great Depression did bring some good for the workers of this country—specifically, the legitimization of unionism in the United States. The **National Labor Relations Act** (also known as the Wagner Act) freed collective bargaining from judicial haranguing, marking a turning point for unionism. This dramatic change in public policy had many effects on individual workers. First, the act led the way to the end of child labor with the strict regulation and enforcement of child labor laws. It led to laws that lowered the work week from fifty-six to forty-eight hours, set a minimum wage for all fulltime employees in any industry, allowed workers to strike to gain better wages and working conditions, and set up a board—the **National Labor Relations Board (NLRB)**—to oversee the safe development of unionism in the United States. Most important, the NLRB became a guiding voice in the determination of what was fair or unfair in a union's attempt to organize employees or an employer's attempt to rebuff unionization. According to the act, employers had to abide by certain rules when trying to rebuff a union. If they did not, they would be committing an unfair labor practice and could be held liable. The NLRB became a forum for disputes and a tribunal for final arbitration between dissenting groups.

The Congress of Industrial Organizations

During this time, the AFL was organizing skilled craftworkers only, declining to represent the millions of industrial and semiskilled or unskilled workers. A new organization, the **Congress of Industrial Organizations (CIO),** arose in 1935 to fill the gap. Led by John L. Lewis of the United Mine Workers, the CIO sought membership in the AFL. After a series of bitter quarrels, the CIO was denied access to the AFL and decided to make it on its own.

Successful leadership helped move the CIO quickly into national prominence. By 1941, the CIO had 4.8 million members (the AFL had increased its membership from the 1933 level of 3 million to almost 5.4 million). After World II, union activities increased. By 1946, the number of union-sponsored work stoppages had increased to 4,985.

As the CIO's power grew, its rivalry with the AFL became more intense. There were strikes over who was the appropriate representative of workers, numerous walkouts over bargaining issues, refusal to negotiate with employers, and coercion of employees to become members of one union or another. Partly as a reaction to this labor strife, Congress amended the National Labor Relations Act in 1947 with the **Taft-Hartley Act.** Although many in the labor movement referred to it as the slave-labor act, the Taft-Hartley Act was meant only to restore some equality to negotiations between labor and management. Now unions could also be found guilty of unfair labor practices while attempting to organize employees.

Mergers and Rifts

By 1955 the power and prominence of the AFL and CIO were approximately equal. New leaders like Walter Reuther of the United Auto Workers and George Meany of the AFL inherited little of the animosity for one another that their predecessors had possessed. A change in union policies and philosophies soon led to a merger—the AFL-CIO.

Since then, unions have also split apart, causing bitter rivalries among those vying to speak for the workers of America. In 1957 the Teamsters, led by Jimmy Hoffa, were thrown out of the AFL-CIO for alledgedly corrupt practices. In fact, these practices encouraged Congress to pass the **Landrum-Griffin Act** (also known as the Labor-Management Reporting and Disclosure Act) in 1959. This act attempted to guarantee union members certain rights of participation in union affairs, helped to regulate union elections, and provided for financial accountability. However, bitter disputes over policy since 1968 have led the United Auto Workers, United Mine Workers, and other unions to walk out of the AFL-CIO.

EXHIBIT 9.1 Union Membership in the United States

	Union	Total Labor Force		Nonagricultural Employees	
Year	**Membership** *(in Thousands)*	*Number (in Thousands)*	*Percent Members*	*Number (in Thousands)*	*Percent Members*
1960	17,049	72,142	23.6	54,234	31.4
1962	16,586	73,442	22.6	55,596	29.8
1964	16,841	75,830	22.2	58,331	28.9
1966	17,940	78,893	22.7	63,955	28.1
1968	18.916	82,272	23.0	67,951	27.8
1970	19.381	85,903	22.6	70,920	27.3
1972	19,435	88,991	21.8	73,714	26.4
1974	20,199	93,240	21.7	78,413	25.8
1976	19,634	96,917	20.3	79,382	24.7
1978	20,238	102,537	19.7	85,762	23.6

Source: U.S. Department of Labor, Bureau of Labor Statistics, *News* (Washington, D.C.: Government Printing Office, September 3, 1979).

UNIONS TODAY

The state of the labor movement today is far different from conditions in either the 1870s or during the growth period from the 1930s to 1955. As indicated in Exhibit 9.1, union membership is currently on the decline, especially as a percentage of total workers in the labor force. Yet union membership has not declined across the board.

Over the past two decades there has also been a push to organize the previously independent government workers and professionals of America. Thus unionism is no longer a blue-collar phenomenon. As shown in Exhibit 9.2, unions attract up to 25 percent of all state and local government employees and have begun to make strong inroads into the ranks of college professors, nurses, and even doctors. Management can no longer ignore white-collar and professional unionism. Furthermore, unions are no longer just for men; over 21 percent of all union members are now women.

Union Organization

The 1955 merger of the AFL and the CIO brought about structural changes in both unions. The AFL-CIO strives to preserve the autonomy of local unions and leadership, and yet its committees and staff work for all of them (see Exhibit 9.3). In a sense, the AFL-CIO is organized along the same lines as government in the United States.

STRUCTURE OF THE AFL-CIO

The AFL-CIO has three major levels of operation. The national and international unions, which are analogous to the state governments, were established to direct unions with a particular function. For exam-

EXHIBIT 9.2 Unionization by Industry

Industry Classification by Degree of Unionization	
75 percent and over	**25 percent to 50 percent**
Ordnance	Printing, publishing
Transportation	Leather
Transportation equipment	Rubber
Contract construction	Furniture
50 percent to 75 percent	Machinery
Electrical machinery	Lumber
Food and kindred products	Chemicals
Primary metals	Electric, gas utilities
Mining	**Less than 25 percent**
Telephone and telegraph	Nonmanufacturing
Paper	Instruments
Petroleum	Textile mill products
Tobacco manufacturers	State government
Apparel	Local government
Fabricated metals	Service
Manufacturing	Trade
Stone, clay, & glass production	Agriculture, fisheries
Federal government	Finance

Source: U.S. Department of Labor, Bureau of Labor Statistics, *Directory of National Unions and Employee Associations*, 1975 (Washington, D.C.: Government Printing Office, 1977), pp. 70–71.

ple, the International Brotherhood of Electrical Workers (an international craft union) guides all local unions affiliated with it. Most national unions stage periodic delegate conventions to determine whether to affiliate with or withdraw from such labor federations as the AFL-CIO. National unions organize workers in unorganized areas and industries, assist in local bargaining sessions, render financial and strike assistance, and lobby for legislative reform.

Local unions, which are analogous to city governments, represent employees in a particular geographical area. Among the activities of a local union are negotiating and administering contracts, filing griev-

EXHIBIT 9.3 Organization of the AFL-CIO

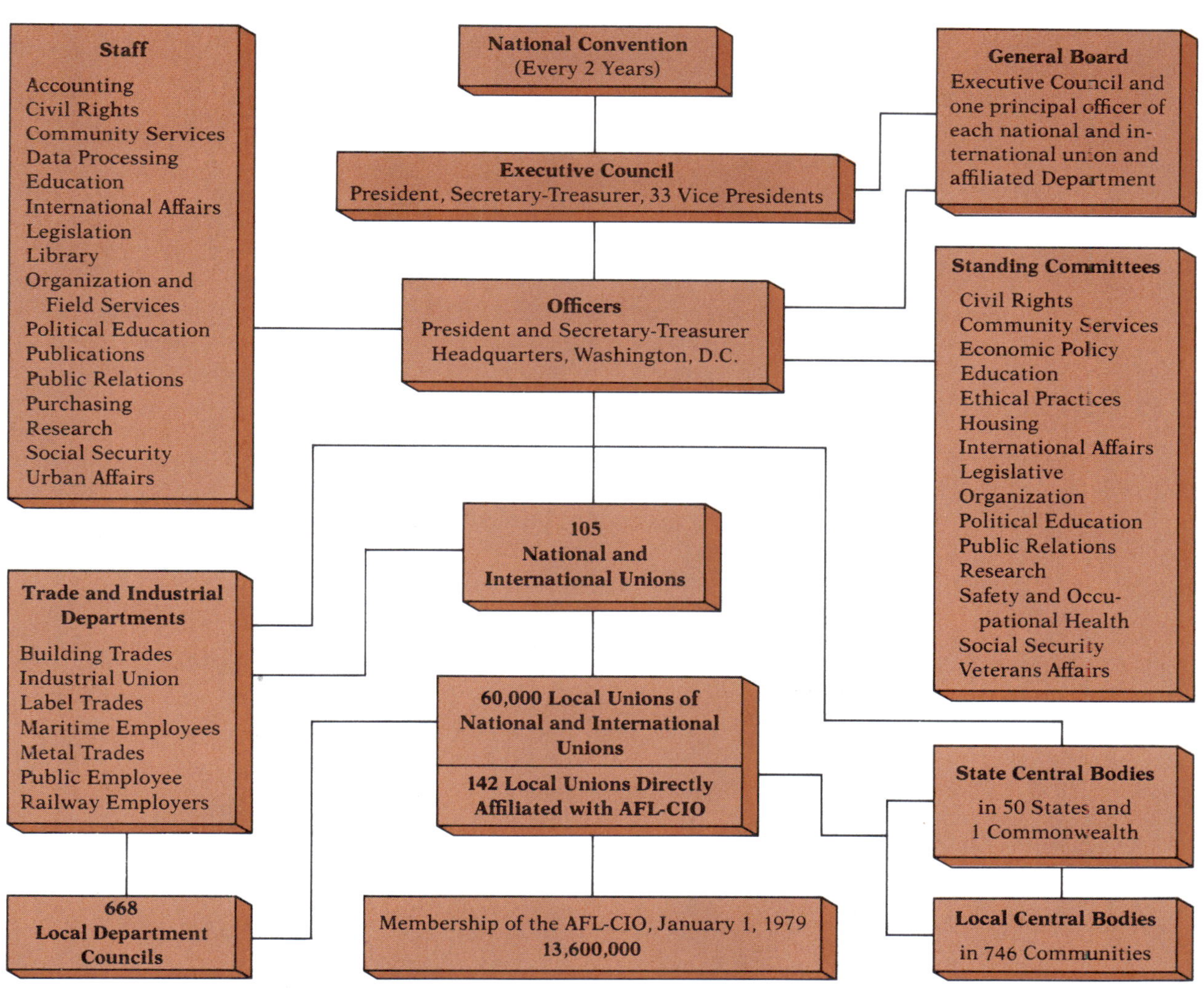

Source: *This is the AFL-CIO* (Washington, D.C.: AFL-CIO, 1979)

ances against companies, and organizing workers in a local area. However, national unions have the power to approve or reject all local bargaining settlements, to render strikes illegal or unauthorized, to require dues, to supervise local elections, and to review local discipline of members.

Labor federations are like the federal government. They are composed of national and international unions, local unions, state federations, independent city unions, and unaffiliated unions. For example, the AFL-CIO works on a national level for all its affiliates. Its activities include undertaking research and education, producing and distributing publications, lobbying legislatures, and resolving jurisdictional disputes of member unions. As shown in Exhibit 9.3, the AFL-CIO has staff departments and standing committees that work in legal, economic, and social areas for the unions, and the federation as a whole. Furthermore, the trade and industrial departments provide assistance to specific groups of unions, like metal or building trades. On the whole, the structure of the AFL-CIO works to preserve local autonomy while supplying needed support functions.

UNION SECURITY

Part of a union's function is to provide job security for its members. To do this, unions must attempt to provide security for themselves. If a union could force all employees of a unionized plant to join the union, even those who voted against the union or were newly hired, then they could increase membership and present a unified front to management. In contrast, management tends to prefer that employees not join unions, because if given the choice, management would rather not have to deal with unions.

Labor legislation has been passed in recent years to ensure that management does not go out of its way to dissuade employees from joining a union. This legislation also has provisions to make sure that unions do not force employees to join. As a result, different types of union "shops" have developed, each requiring a different degree of union participation.

A **union shop** requires all newly hired employees to join the company's union. Most labor-management contracts call for this type of contract. However, **right-to-work laws** (permitted by the Taft-Hartley Act) allow states to forbid union shops. In return, two people doing the same job must be paid the same wage, even if one is not a union member. Most right-to-work laws are in effect in southern and southwestern states, such as Georgia, Texas, Florida, and Arizona.

Anyone who is hired into a **closed shop** must already be a union member. This type of shop is illegal in its pure form, but modified closed shops do exist. For example, say that a welder is needed for one or two days on a construction site. The construction manager calls up a union hall and requests a welder. You can easily imagine that a nonunion member has little chance of being sent out to the construction site under these circumstances.

In an **open shop** employees are free to join a union if they so choose, management makes no effort to keep unions out nor do unions force employees to join their ranks.

In an **agency shop** all employees, whether they belong to the union or not, pay union dues. Since all employees receive the benefits of having a union, they must all pay for that benefit.

Finally, when a union is recognized, its members may be given some preferential treatment, especially in the area of initial hiring. However, such **preferential shops** are rare, because many of the advantages accruing to union members are currently illegal under provisions of the Taft-Hartley Act.

The Collective Bargaining Process

Collective bargaining serves both labor and management. The two parties negotiate, draft, administer, and later interpret a written contract. The contract, often referred to as a labor agreement, binds both parties to its provisions for a specified time period.

Before getting into a detailed discussion of contract negotiation, it might be helpful to outline briefly why the collective bargaining process came about and whom it serves. Unions evolved as a response to workers' needs for better working conditions and better wages. Workers found that if they bargained with management as a group, their collective strength (realized through the threat of strike, slowdown, and the like) generally got better results. Baseball players may have tremendous individual worth to an organization, but one out of 220,000 assembly workers probably does not. Collective bargaining also serves management. Bargaining with 220,000 individuals would be an awesome task. And very often, management prefers to set standardized wage rates for a given period of time, especially during times of high inflation.

Unions seek the following specific benefits for their members through collective bargaining:

- Higher wages
- Annual cost-of-living raises (very important when inflation is running at over 12 percent per year, as it is now)
- Greater fringe benefits (health and dental insurance, hospitalization and life insurance)
- Better working conditions to protect health and safety
- Job security via seniority rights (those with greater seniority are laid off last and rehired first)
- Job security via worksharing (instead of laying off workers, reducing everyone's hours by say, 10 percent)
- Union security, meaning that it becomes the sole bargaining agent of all workers at that particular plant
- Grievance procedures for settling disputes
- Binding arbitration to resolve stalemates (this is explained shortly)

Highlight Bailing Out the Boss

Traditionally, unions and management have existed in an adversarial environment: Unions have tried to bargain for as much compensation (wages, benefits, insurance, vacation time) as possible; management usually offers less than what unions want or think they're worth. What would happen if a union found out that a company was going bankrupt? Would it still demand as much in the way of wages and benefits?

Realizing the seriousness of automaker Chrysler's financial troubles, the United Auto Workers took a different attitude in its 1980 contract negotiations. The union felt that demanding large compensation increases would worsen Chrysler's financial troubles. Should these troubles get bad enough, thousands of union jobs could be lost.

To help get Chrysler back on its financial feet, the United Auto Workers agreed to minimal wage increases. Employees would receive only a 3-percent wage increase in 1980, 1981, and 1982, well below the current inflation rate. Additionally, employees would not receive any paid personal holidays during the three-year contract; they were scheduled to receive nine paid holidays in 1980 and eleven in 1981. Employees would also forgo their traditional December bonuses, usually equal to one day's pay.

In return, Chrysler would be obligated to give out $162 million in stock to employees over the next four years. Finally, Chrysler agreed to nominate United Auto Worker's president Douglas Fraser to its board of directors. This was an unprecedented move for an American automaker, although European union leaders have been on government and corporate boards for years.

- Greater pension benefits for retirement
- Longer vacations and more holidays
- Shorter work weeks

In return for these benefits, management generally seeks a number of items to balance the power of a union:

- A no-strike clause for the term of the contract, usually granted in return for binding arbitration
- Nonbinding arbitration
- A management-rights clause guaranteeing the right to hire and fire employees as management sees fit (for fair and justified reasons of course)
- The least costly wage and benefit package

NEGOTIATION

The first step in the collective bargaining process is negotiation, assuming that employees have already elected to be represented by a particular union. That union is the sole representative for all company employees represented by the union or for all employees in a certain segment of the company (such as all welders, whether they belong to the union or not). Negotiations over grievances generally start with lower-level management and move up the organizational ladder as necessary. Contract negotiations start out at a high level. Exhibit 9.4 illustrates the outcome of contract negotiations in the baseball industry.

A key concept during the negotiation process is **bargaining in good faith.** This phrase, taken from the National Labor Relations Act, describes the situation when both parties negotiate fairly and consistently in order to complete the negotiation process without resorting to strikes or work stoppages. Failure to negotiate in good faith can be a federal offense. Some of the instances in which management or unions can be accused of failure to bargain in good faith are the following:

- Managemant fails to meet with the union to negotiate its proposals.
- Management refuses to supply cost and other data about a group insurance plan.
- Management announces a wage increase without consulting with the union.
- The union refuses to negotiate with a legal representative of the employer.
- The union insists on a closed shop (made illegal by the Taft-Hartley Act) or discriminatory hiring practices.

If negotiations reach a stalemate, workers can go out on strike, management can lock employees out, or mediators or arbitrators can be brought in to help the negotiation process. Fortunately, this latter route is the most common. Mediators have no legal power but do attempt,

EXHIBIT 9.4 Baseball's 1980 Labor-Management Dispute

Issue	Owner's Position	Player's Position	Settlement
Present minimum salary for a major league baseball player is $21,000	Increase minimum salary to $30,000 in 1981 and $32,000 by 1982	Base salary of $40,000	Minimum salary of $30,000 per year
Current pension and benefits package worth $8.3 million	Increase benefits by 71 percent ($14.4 million)—a cost to each team of $550,000 per year	$16.5 million increase in benefits	Pension and benefits increased by $15.5 million
Free agents	A team losing a player to another team through the free-agent draft should be awarded a player of its choice from the roster of "unprotected" players (a team would "protect" fifteen players) of the team signing the free agent	No change in rules and a shortening of the time required (from six years to five years) for a player to elect to become a free agent	Current rules remain intact for one year. During this time, a study committee consisting of two player representatives and two owners will try to work out an acceptable compromise and report back to the negotiators by January 1981. If an agreement is not reached, the owners have the option of putting their plan into effect in February 1982, and the only recourse open to players is to strike (if they retain that option).

successfully in most cases, to get the parties talking and bargaining again.

If negotiations reach a stalemate, unions seek **binding arbitration.** The issue goes to a neutral third party who decides on a solution after hearing arguments from both sides. The decision of the arbitrator is final, and both sides must abide by it. A grievance procedure without binding arbitration is virtually worthless to a union, for management may disregard the opinions of the neutral party and do as it pleases.

APPROVAL AND ADMINISTRATION

Once management and the union come to terms on a fair contract, the contract must be approved by the union membership. If the members vote to accept the contract, it becomes law for the time specified, and both parties must abide by it. If the contract is not approved, union and management leaders continue discussions and try to negotiate a new contract. However, if an arbitrator has been brought in, his or her decision is usually binding, regardless of a union vote against the decision.

Once a contract has been drawn up and agreed on, it must be administered. Both sides watch to make sure the other abides by the agreement. Although basically a maintenance task, administration of the contract can be vital. If one side feels the other has violated provisions of the contract, it can take its claims to the NLRB for adjudication.

The Future of Unionism

As you learned in an earlier section, the structure and function of unions have been evolving throughout the years—in response to changes in society and in the business environment. No doubt they will continue to evolve. It is already possible to see at least two changes in progress: one a response to the age-old problem of unemployment and the other a response to the changing composition of the work force.

UNEMPLOYMENT

Unions have always sought to keep as many of their members working as possible. Management has always worked to keep profits high, even if that meant laying off workers because of declining sales. Of course, the result of such a policy is unemployment, a problem for society as well as the person who lacks work. Officially, **unemployment** is the number or percentage of people who are not working but are between the legal working ages of sixteen to sixty-five and are seeking employment. Unemployment statistics include people who are between jobs (waiting to start work at a new job), those on temporary layoff, those on seasonal layoff (a lifeguard in December, for example), but not those who are chronically unemployed, or who never even bother to look for jobs.

The solution to unemployment may seem simple: Create more jobs. However, the problem is far more complex. For one thing, reported unemployment is now running around 7 per cent of the total work force, which means that over 7 million people are unemployed. Who is going to hire 7 million people?

Another serious problem is that our system of unemployment compensation gives out-of-work employees 70 percent of the wage they were earning before they became unemployed. Why should someone who is paid $250 per week while not working bother to work in a job that pays only $270 per week? Why should a seasonal employee seek work in the off-season when he or she can collect enough money through unemployment insurance to live on? Why should someone who has temporarily been laid off seek a job, especially if having another job would jeopardize his or her chances of regaining the old job? And why should an employer hire someone who may quit as soon as the layoff is over? Finally, how can the chronically unemployed, seasonally unemployed, and temporarily unemployed be motivated to seek work? The chronically unemployed are usually unskilled and have a poor record of reliability. If they become unreliable at a new job, they are fired, which reinforces their feeling that no one wants to hire them and that it's pointless to look for a job.

A third problem is that unemployment statistics do not adequately account for those who are either overqualified or underqualified for most jobs. How can we create and finance enough programs to retrain, for example, overqualified aerospace engineers and underqualified janitors to work in an auto parts factory?

It is likely that unions will begin to take a more active role in dealing with these questions. By developing their own retraining programs, labor unions can help reduce unemployment. In addition, by promoting changes in unemployment compensation, they can help motivate those who are temporarily or seasonally laid off or chronically unemployed to rejoin the work force. If America is to combat unemployment, the labor unions must help.

NEW AREAS OF UNION ACTIVITY

As the proportion of industrial workers decreases, unions take a more active role in new areas. For example, they have recently begun to unionize athletes, health care professionals, and agricultural employees. The labor movement is also expanding into the federal government and, to a lesser extent, into state and local government. Although unions have made substantial inroads into new segments of the economy, most union leaders feel that much more progress is needed. In time it probably will come.

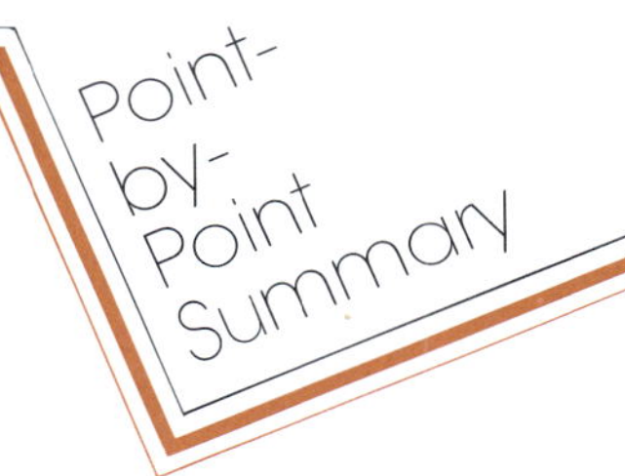

- Labor unions are formed in response to workers' perceptions that working conditions, including compensation, are less than desirable. The function of a labor union is to achieve better compensation and working conditions through collective bargaining, which offers a greater chance of success than individual effort. Employees also join unions for reasons related to job security, socialization, and communication.

- The labor movement was active in the United States as early as 1648. Yet until the Wagner Act of 1935, union activity was considered an inhibition to free trade.
- In 1947, sensing that labor unions had become too powerful, Congress passed the Taft-Hartley Act. Its provisions were meant to equalize the strength of labor and management at the bargaining table.
- National, local, and federated unions work closely together to satisfy members' needs. They operate in the context of several different kinds of shops, each requiring a different level of union participation—closed, open, agency, union, and preferential shops.
- There are three parts to the process of collective bargaining: negotiation of the contract, approval of the contract by union membership, and administration of the contract by both sides.
- The problem of unemployment is a complex issue involving seasonally, temporarily, and chronically unemployed individuals, as well as the undertrained and overtrained. Unemployment is a concern to both labor and management.
- Unionism is no longer a blue-collar phenomenon. Unions increasingly represent, serve, protect, and lobby for professionals in education, health care, sports, and federal, state, and local government.

1. Why might management favor the establishment of a union? Why might workers vote to keep a union out?
2. If there is now an overabundance of people who want jobs, why do unions keep negotiating for bigger and better contracts?
3. How can a union help in getting the seasonally, temporarily, or chronically unemployed back into the labor market?
4. In what way do unions hamper or restrict free trade?
5. Rank the items in the list of union preferences (on pages 213–214 in order of their importance to the average worker. Explain your choices. As management's representative, which of these items would you object to most strongly? Which would you give in to most easily?
6. Why might management vote for binding arbitration?
7. Why might management be glad to see more minorities and women joining unions?
8. What is the significance of the Taft-Hartley Act?
9. In your opinion, why was management unhappy with the passage of the Landrum-Griffin Act?
10. Identify the events that you feel are most significant in the growth of unionism in the United States.
11. How do you explain the fact that union membership is on the decline?

APPLICATION

Dow Chemical Company

In 1890 Herbert Dow arrived in Midland, Michigan with an idea, a process for extracting bromine from the area's plentiful brines. Unbeknownst to Dow, bromine (an inorganic chemical compound) was to become an essential ingredient in hundreds of Dow Chemical's future products. Herbert Dow's unyielding determination to develop his extraction process set a standard for chemical research and development and helped to make Dow Chemical the world's leading chemical company.

HOW DOW GREW

With the financial backing of J. H. Osborn, Herbert Dow established the Midland Chemical Company in 1891 to conduct chemical research and extract bromine. Four years later, Dow established the Process Company to undertake chlorine research and to make chlorine on an experimental basis. Finally at the age of thirty-one, Herbert Dow achieved financial success. During 1897, the Dow Chemical Company was organized the purpose of manufacturing chlorine bleach. With Herbert Dow serving as general manager, Dow Chemical recorded sales for the year ending December 1898 of $15,000.

The Dow Chemical Company grew quickly. In 1900 it merged with the Midland Chemical Company, which put Herbert Dow back into the bromine business. During the early 1900s, Dow Chemical helped to pioneer products like sulfur, chlorine, and aspirin. By 1925, a mere twenty-eight years after its origination, Dow Chemical was listed on the Cleveland Stock Exchange. Twelve years later Dow became one of the first chemical companies to be listed on the New York Stock Exchange.

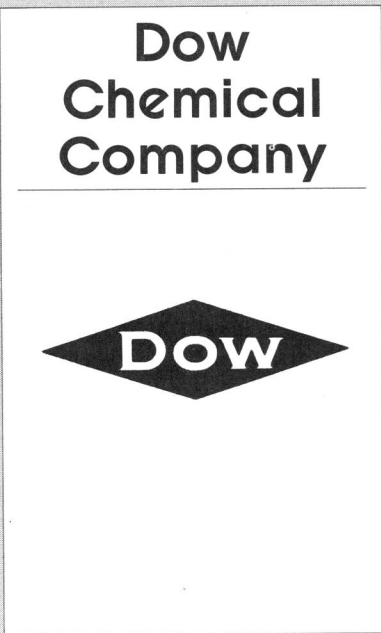

In 1938 Dow registered its trademark for the product STYRON. Today STYRON polystyrene is used in the manufacture of toys, appliance parts, container lids, cigarette packages, radio cabinets, heater ducts and many other products. Since the development of STYRON, The Dow Chemical Company became a leader in the chemical industry. It has secured trademarks for several other products including STYROFOAM plastic foam, HANDI-WRAP plastic film, SARAN WRAP plastic film, ZIPLOC plastic bags, DOW latexes (paint products), LIRUGEN one-shot measles vaccine, and BEXTON herbicide used in controlling corn and grain sorghum.

Today Dow earns more than any other chemical company in the world, with sales over $9 billion peryear. As an innovator and leader in chemical research, Dow is unmatched. It has received more than 10,000 patents. Dow Chemical's 2,200 products are manufactured by 53,000 people in twenty-nine countries. In the United States alone, Dow has twenty-one manufacturing locations in twelve states.

LABOR-MANAGEMENT RELATIONS

Although Dow employs over 50,000 people—from engineers and chemists to truck drivers and warehouseworkers—there are very few unions in the Dow organization. Instead, Dow offers employees "Salaried operations," "a method of operation designed to provide flexibility, efficiency, and economy to produce the maximum profit and growth for the company, the division or unit, *and each individual employee.*"

Basically, salaried operations provides for

Herbert Henry Dow
Founder of the Dow Chemical Co.

1. Individualized treatment of employees
2. Respect for the dignity of the individual, no matter what his or her position within the company
3. Elimination of artificial barriers between management and employees and a greater delegation of authority and responsibility to all (people are recognized for what they can do rather than for the authority of the position they hold)
4. Pay for performance
5. Broad job structuring, "a minimum number of job classifications of increasing degrees of skill and responsibility that are used to define and recognize expected contribution level" of the individual to Dow
6. Something for something (explained below)

Admittedly, these principles appear to be related more to human resource management than to labor relations. The point in mentioning them is that they are as vital to successful labor relations as they are to human relations management. Dow realizes that labor relations is more than just pay and benefits.

When Dow says it will provide something for something, it is referring to the traditional labor relations process. Dow feels it has a responsibility to provide good pay, good benefits, a safe place to work work, fair and well-trained supervisors, and honesty and integrity in all its dealings with employees. In return, Dow expects employees to show concern about their jobs and a sincere interest in improving them, to show concern and responsibility for safety, to attend and provide a fair day's work, to demonstrate loyalty to the company, and to show honesty and integrity in their dealings with other employees and management.

According to Dow, salaried operations provides four primary benefits to the company:

1. *Better use of employees' talents*
   Through elimination of strict jurisdictional lines, easy movement from one job to another, and greater consideration of merit and performance in promotion, employees are more likely to have broader, more challenging jobs and greater flexibility.
2. *Better employee morale*
   Through improved fringe benefits and pay, improved supervision, individual treatment, elimination of a double standard for treatment of managerial and other employees, pay for performance, and elimination of the adversary relationship between labor and management, employees win greater pride in their company and more interest in their jobs.
3. *Elimination of union costs*
   Strikes, arbitration, negotiation, union-mandated work practices, and negative attitudes toward the company and the job that often accompany unionization all increase the cost of doing business.
4. *Greater profit and growth potential*

In short, salaried operations has a beneficial effect on productivity and profit by increasing employee morale, enhancing the use of employee skills and resources, and helping to eliminate traditional problems brought about by unions and unionism. Salaried operations eliminates the threat of strikes, arbitration hearings and collective bargaining/negotiation procedures. Importantly, salaried operations helps to eliminate the polarization of thought and attitude often created between labor and management by unionization. Further, salaried operations helps eliminate negative employee attitudes toward the company and their jobs.

Salaried operations also provides many advantages for employees. Among the most important are superior fringe benefits and pay, better relationships among all employees, and a more enjoyable place to work.

CAREER OPPORTUNITIES

Nobody goes directly into Dow's Salaried Operations Department straight out of school. Normally, people striving for a job in this department must have a degree in some science-related field and approximately ten years of experience in production, employee relations, or labor relations, benefits administration, and salary administration. In addition, they should have skills in human relations and communications—both verbal and written—with the ability to communicate across the entire spectrum of management and labor.

FOR DISCUSSION

1. Has Dow's salaried operations concept eliminated the need for unions?
2. If you were a union leader, how would you persuade Dow employees to join your union?

OBJECTIVES

- ☐ To define and explain production management
- ☐ To describe the production processes used in different types of businesses
- ☐ To explain the planning and control functions of production management
- ☐ To identify the various ways products are made
- ☐ To discuss approaches to controlling product quality and cost

OUTLINE

ARTICLE *Robots Are Reaching for Assembly Jobs*

PRODUCTS AND PROCESSES

THE BASIC THREE
Sales Organizations
Service Organizations
Manufacturing Organizations
A Few Generalizations

MANAGING THE PRODUCTION PROCESS
Building and Designing the Plant
Forecasting Sales
Obtaining the Inputs
Setting up the Production Process

SETTING STANDARDS
Material Standards
Labor Standards
Using Standards for Planning and Control
Quality Control

APPLICATION *International Business Machines Corporation*

KEY TERMS

BILL OF MATERIALS
CONVERSION PROCESS
LABOR EFFICIENCY STANDARD
MASS PRODUCTION
MATERIAL PRICE STANDARD
MATERIAL QUANTITY STANDARD
PARALLEL-FLOW PRODUCTION
PRODUCT
PRODUCTION MANAGEMENT
PRODUCTION SCHEDULE
PRODUCTION STANDARD
PRODUCTIVE CAPACITY
PURCHASING FUNCTION
QUALITY CONTROL
SELECTIVE-FLOW PRODUCTION
SEQUENTIAL-FLOW PRODUCTION
STANDARD LABOR COST
STANDARD MATERIAL COST
WAGE-RATE STANDARD

PRODUCTION MANAGEMENT

Robots Are Reaching for Assembly Jobs

JOHN TERESKO
Reprinted from *Industry Week,* March 5, 1979

Upon hearing that the rights to AMF Inc.'s Versatran robot had been purchased by Prab Conveyors Inc., Kalamazoo, Mich., robot entrepreneur Larry Kamm looked relieved and pleased. Prab is extending its medium-technology line of robots with the more sophisticated Versatran. But Mr. Kamm is betting that the simplicity and low cost of modular machines, called Mobots, made by his Modular Machine Co., San Diego, will look better than ever.

He believes most U.S. robot-makers are in a race to anthropomorphize robots—endow them with human characteristics—at the expense of cost-effectiveness. "At a time when most of the equipment on the market represents technological overkill for the jobs they have to do, there is little point in adding more sophistication," he says.

Nonetheless, while Mr. Kamm is bootstrapping his way into low-technology robot applications, users such as General Motors Corp. and Westinghouse Electric Corp. are studying ways to add the senses of vision and touch to robots. "Those capabilities are important if robots are to move from 'put and place' tasks to the more complex assembly jobs of the future," says Donald E. Hart, head of the Computer Science Dept., General Motors Research Laboratories, Warren, Mich.

Line managers might agree more with Mr. Kamm.

One researcher reports that he proudly showed off a robot prototype with vision to a group of plant managers. Unimpressed, one of the plant managers responded that he had workers at his plant who could do the same task in a fraction of the time. The point—that a machine with a sense of vision could be developed—had been missed, the researcher notes.

He allows that today's applications of sensing robots may be unspectacular, but stresses that the technology being developed is important because it will enable future robots to do tasks that are unsafe or unappealing to workers.

One example of computer vision has been at work for almost two years at GM's Delco Electronics Div. in Kokomo, Ind. Called Sight-I, the system inspects integrated circuit chips and automatically positions electrical test probes—at a production rate of 3,000 parts per hour.

SEE IT NOW

The next step is to adapt such a computer-vision system to a robot, allowing it to work in a continually changing environment. The basic problem, says GM's Mr. Hart, is to find some way of limiting the amount of information the vision system's computer must handle. Early work used standard television cameras—which generated far too much data for an inexpensive minicomputer to digest and analyze.

More recently, work with a solid state digital camera reduced the amount of data by representing the field of vision with 100 rows of 100 columns, for a total of 10,000 light-sensitive elements, each capable of representing 63 shades from white to black. With the computer programmed to identify part edges, enough information can be generated to direct a robot to pick up a part.

Going further in reducing the amount of information a computer has to handle, GM has developed its Consight system. That system presumes the part to be grasped is moving along a conveyor line. As the part passes under a linear array camera, the part displaces a line of light projected onto the belt from a low angle. Thus the position of the part on the belt is represented by the absence of light. By scanning along this line only, the computer's job is reduced to handling a single line of light divided into 100 locations. The robot arm is downstream from the camera and light source; the computer calculates when the moving part will reach the robot and then issues the grasping command.

Something like the Consight system is probably what GM would like to eventually adapt to its Puma robots. (The acronym stands for Programmable Universal Machine for Assembly.) The Puma system combines robots, transfer devices, parts feeders, and employees in an assembly sequence.

GM's first Puma installation (at a Rochester, N.Y., plant of its Delco Products Div.) will be a relatively simple one where a hot part will be picked up, positioned, combined with another component, and placed on a track for further processing. Nine more will be installed this year at GM, and a complete Puma system which includes humans, mechanical support devices, and 13 robots is scheduled for installation in 1980, says Frank Daley, GM director of manufacturing development.

At Westinghouse's R&D Center, Pittsburgh, product assembly using robots is also being emphasized under a grant from the National Science Foundation (NSF). The goal is the development of a complete adaptable programmable assembly system (Apas) for batch manufacturing.

In an earlier NSF study, Westinghouse concluded that Apas could lead to a 3:1 productivity improvement for such products as outdoor lighting, compressors, and small motors.

Based on its current work with NSF, Westinghouse hopes to demonstrate by late 1981 an automatic motor assembly line similar to GM's Puma system, except that Westinghouse will use computer vision. Richard G. Abraham, manager of programmable automation at the R&D Center, says the system will include robot arms, equipment for presenting parts to the assembly area, fixtures and tools, transfer conveyors, vision and other sensory hardware, computer hardware and software—and people.

Whether humans or robots do the work, production remains the life blood of every organization. This chapter describes how products are made and how the production function is managed.

How does General Motors go about making a car? How does IBM make a computer or General Electric make a light bulb? Does the manufacturing process used by these companies differ significantly from those used by a law firm in settling a lawsuit or by a hospital in monitoring the health of a patient? This chapter focuses on how businesses go about producing their product, a process commonly known as **production management.** It describes how resources, or inputs, such as equipment, labor, and raw materials, can be converted into finished products. The nature of this process depends on the nature of the organization, its management, and its products.

Products and Processes

Products can be tangible or intangible. A tangible product, such as a car or appliance, has a form and substance. In contrast, an intangible product, or service, cannot be held or felt. For example, lawyers provide an intangible product in the form of legal services. Services do not have a physical form but still involve the conversion of scarce resources (the time expended by the legal staff) into a finished product (the settlement of a suit or the final resolution of some legal problem).

Products can possess many characteristics, and therefore the processes used to create them can be quite varied. In addition, the inputs

EXHIBIT 10.1 Inputs Needed for Production

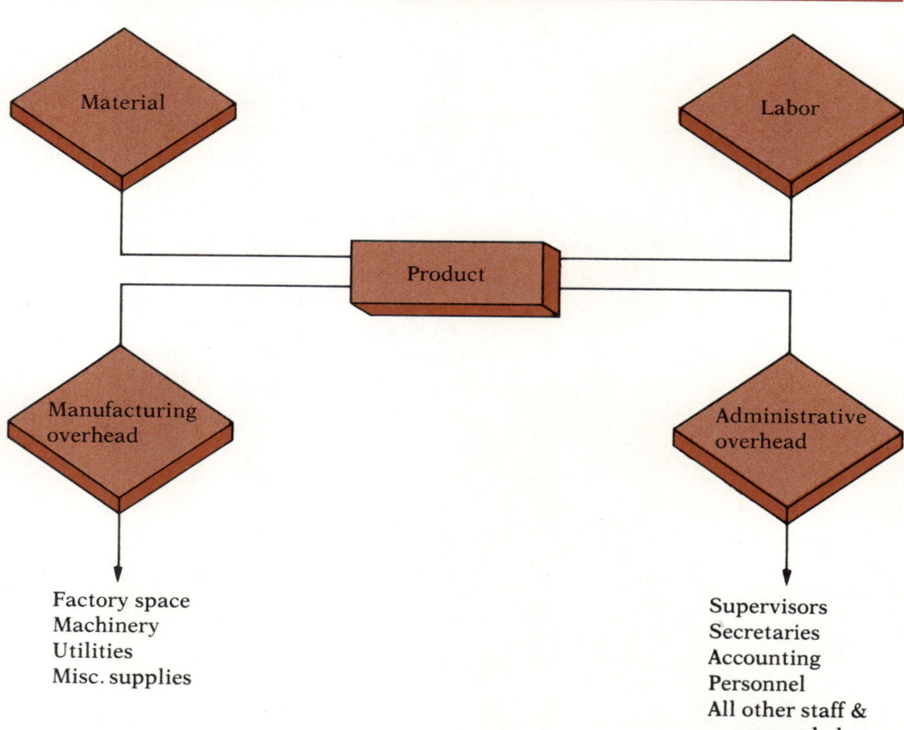

required to produce a product or service are diverse. Exhibit 10.1 shows the four basic inputs required to provide any product: labor, material, manufacturing overhead, and administrative overhead.

The Basic Three

The nature of the production process and the relative amount of each input that is used depend on the business. There are basically three types of businesses—sales, service, and manufacturing—and Exhibit 10.3 outlines the production process and the relative use of inputs in each type.

SALES ORGANIZATIONS

Companies whose main activity is selling products fall into two categories—retailers and wholesalers. Wholesalers purchase finished goods from producers and sell these products to retailers. A wholesaling network is particularly useful when there are a small number of producers and retailers in an industry. The basic inputs to the wholesaler are the finished goods purchased and the labor required to get these finished goods in the hands of the retailers. Overhead is generally low in a wholesaling company, with the primary costs related to sales, marketing, accounting, and the acquisition and delivery of goods.

The retailer's conversion process is similar to that of the wholesaler. The inputs are usually the finished products purchased from the wholesaler. These products are then sold to consumers with the assis-

EXHIBIT 10.2 Types of Business and the Production Process

Type of Business	Specific Example	Major Inputs used in Production	Nature of Conversion Process	End Product
SERVICE	Auto Repair Shop	• Labor • Materials	Skilled labor used to repair car is largest cost. Customer also pays for material.	Repaired Car
MANUFACTURING	Beer	• Materials • Mfg. overhead	Raw materials converted into a finished product (beer) through the use of mechanized production process.	A Six Pack of Beer
SALES/ WHOLESALER	Fruits and Vegetable Dealer	• Materials • Labor	Dealer purchases produce from the farmers and, in turn, sells it to the large grocery stores. Labor plays a significant role in process but overhead normally is low.	Fresh Vegetables and Fruits for Grocery Stores
SALES/RETAILER	Department Store	• Materials • Admin. Overhead • Labor	Store purchases finished goods from mfg. or wholesaler and, subsequently, sells these goods to customers at a higher price. Salespeople are required in the process as well as store space and admin. help.	Various Goods Purchased

tance of a labor force that consists primarily of sales personnel, buyers, and marketing experts. Therefore, material and labor costs in a typical retailing business are high. Overhead costs depend on the quality of the store and the image the retailer would like to communicate to buyers.

SERVICE ORGANIZATIONS

Service businesses offer diverse "products," ranging from hotel accommodations to income-tax preparation and automotive repair. However, there are some basic characteristics that set service companies apart:

- Most service companies specialize in a few services rather than a wide variety.
- The primary input in a service-oriented company is labor; the purchase and use of supplies is limited.
- The service is normally intangible, and the quality of service is the prime determinant of success.

Quite obviously, the production process in service businesses primarily revolves around the successful use of labor. Overhead and material costs are relatively low.

Because it costs so little to operate a service company as opposed to a sales or manufacturing company, there has been tremendous growth in this business sector in recent years. It is relatively easy for someone to begin this type of business. The initial investment is low, the production process is simple, (normally involving the use of people's talents), and overhead and materials costs are minimal.

MANUFACTURING ORGANIZATIONS

The production process is particularly important in manufacturing companies. A manufacturer purchases raw materials and converts them into finished goods with the use of labor and machinery. The time it takes to make this conversion, as well as the complexity of the production process, depends on the product. For example, in companies whose product is some type of natural resource, the production process—from locating the resource to extracting, refining, and delivering it to the customer—can take years to complete. It typically takes an oil company anywhere from two to nine years to find oil and finally get it to the pumps.

A FEW GENERALIZATIONS

Three broad generalizations can be made about the production process and the management of this process. First, the nature and complexity of the process depends on the product or service being provided. Second, the main inputs required to make a product or provide a service are labor, material, and overhead. Finally, the general framework of the production process is quite similar from company to company. In Exhibit 10.3, production is represented by the flow of inputs through various steps until these inputs are transformed into finished products.

At each step in this **conversion process,** value is added to the basic inputs and the utility of the ultimate product is enhanced.

Managing the Production Process

The survival of any organization is predicated on the fact that it has a viable product. Assuming that this is the case (subsequent chapters explore this assumption), let's investigate the procedure for managing production. The following discussion concentrates on manufacturing processes, but the general outline pertains equally to sales and service organizations.

BUILDING AND DESIGNING THE PLANT

Two of the most important decisions made during the planning stage relate to plant location and plant layout. These decisions are normally not part of the ongoing production process but are critical when a company opens a new production facility or when a new company is formed.

EXHIBIT 10.3 The Conversion Process

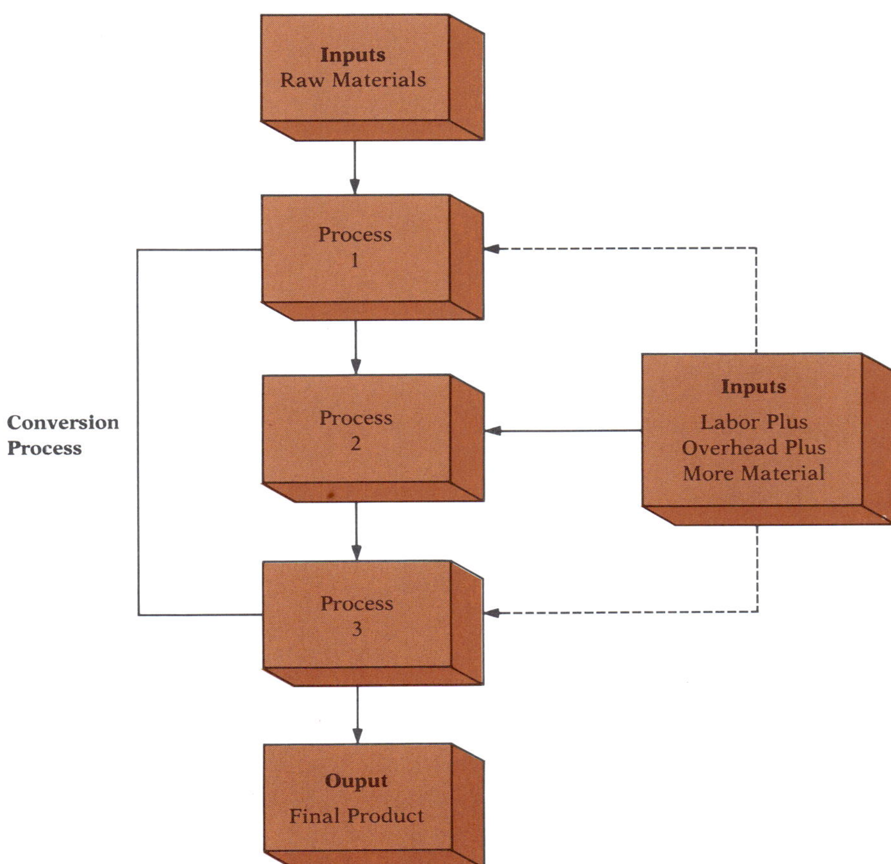

Highlight Wooing Manufacturing Companies

Not too long ago, Volkswagen of America announced that it was going to open a new production facility in the United States. Shortly thereafter, the company was besieged with invitations to visit several states and municipalities.

Whenever a company locates a plant, especially a large one, in a city or town, financial benefits are likely to accrue to the citizens, businesses, and government of that community. A plant opening results in more jobs, which means that more people will have more money and that they will probably spend that money in their place of residence. Other local businesses will benefit from the new funds circulating in the community. In addition, the company will probably spend money in its new home and might even be willing to invest in the community in the name of corporate social responsibility.

Thus attracting companies to a community is big business. Many cities provide such financial incentives as tax abatement (that is, a deferral of local taxes until the plant gets established), low-interest loans, low rent for facilities, and the like. These incentives, although costly, are likely to offer an attractive return to the community.

Why are these decisions so important? There are at least two good reasons. First, these decisions involve a significant investment of time and money. In many cases, a company's investment in its plant is the single largest it will ever make. A bad decision could cost the company thousands or even millions of dollars and quite possibly lead to financial ruin. The second reason these decisions are so important is that this investment represents a long-term commitment. Locating, designing, building, and setting up a plant normally takes years to accomplish; it is not done overnight. If it is not done carefully, problems will ultimately surface that could affect product cost and quality, the company's ability to compete, and its success.

Plant Location

In deciding where to locate a new plant, a company usually considers the following:

- Proximity to suppliers and customers
- Availability of supplies and materials
- Availability of an effective transportation system
- The costs of doing business in a particular area—taxes, utility and building costs, and the like

All of these factors are important to one degree or another. Their relative importance depends on what the company needs to support the production process.

In the early days of American manufacturing, most companies built their plants along waterways. Water was an energy source, and travel by water was the most efficient means of transportation. Today, however, air, rail, and highway transportation systems are more readily available. As a result, companies now locate plants in parts of the country that were previously considered unsuitable.

Many new plants are now opening in the South and Southwest. Because of heavy migration to the Sunbelt states, companies are finding a plentiful labor supply in these areas. In addition, unions are not so strong in the South as they are in the North. Thus companies expect to find lower labor costs in the South and Southwest.

Plant Layout

Once a plant site has been chosen, management must decide how to equip the plant and lay out the facilities. Basically, plant layout involves

- Deciding what equipment is needed and how it should be arranged
- Determining the proper work flow for materials, supplies, and paper
- Deciding where and how to store inventory and how to handle the receipt and shipment of goods
- Deciding how employees should do their work

Management's goal is to develop the most efficient production system possible.

To the extent possible, production managers want to make sure that space and equipment are used effectively. Idle space and equipment are costly. Employees' jobs should also be designed properly, so that productivity and morale are as high as possible. Finally, the production process should be designed to avoid bottlenecks and ensure the efficient movement of materials in and out of the plant. Later in this chapter we identify and discuss some of the product-flow systems most widely used in manufacturing. Suffice it to say for now that each of these systems would require a different type of plant layout.

Of course, it is never possible to design the ideal plant. However, if significant deficiencies are left in the production system, they will eventually surface and harm employee morale or the product.

FORECASTING SALES

Another fundamental issue confronting management is to try to determine how much of each product the company will sell during a specific time period. The answer to this question is the responsibility of the marketing and sales staff. These functions are so critical to the organization that all of Part Three is devoted to a detailed description of their responsibilities. For the time being, accept the fact that their sales estimate is one of the biggest factors in determining the amount and type of product to be produced.

Other factors that may affect the amount to be produced are

- Economic factors, particularly the state of the economy
- Availability of inputs, particularly capital and raw materials

- **Productive capacity**—whether the company has enough machinery, tools, personnel, and factory space to manufacture what is required

If management believes that the economy is heading downward, with a possible unfavorable impact on product demand, it will probably reduce production. Thus the company will not accumulate large inventories it cannot sell, and production costs will be kept to a minimum. The automobile industry, for example, must constantly adjust production for possible changes in the economy, shortages of capital needed to finance cars, and shortages of such raw materials as oil.

Once management has identified and evaluated the factors influencing product demand, it can establish production targets or quotas by product line and for specific time periods. Quotas are subsequently translated into a **production schedule,** a timetable indicating what products will be produced, when they will be produced, and what labor and materials are required by whom. The production schedule may be done on a daily basis, if necessary. It is the primary document implementing the production process.

"Faster!"

Highlight Excess Inventories Don't Come Cheap

Production managers often respond to projected sales by building up inventories of finished goods. When outside observers see inventories piled up in a warehouse, they often think of only one cost—the cost of storage, including air conditioning, security, lighting, perhaps even the mortgage payments on the warehouse. But in many cases, these costs are trivial compared to the cost of tying up money in inventories (or raw materials, for that matter) instead of some other investment.

Let's take a simple example. Say General Motors has a bad month and ends up with an unwanted inventory of 100,000 cars, with an average cost of production of $5,000. That comes to a cool $500 million in excess inventory for one month. Say that the going interest rate in the money markets is 12 percent, or 1 percent a month. If General Motors had invested the $500 million at 1 percent for one month instead of producing the cars, it could have made $5 million.

OBTAINING THE INPUTS

Once management has determined the production goals, it must ensure that the company either has or can acquire the inputs needed to meet those goals. We have already identified the main resources needed in production; now let's see how management goes about planning and controlling for them.

Productive Capacity

If the production quotas exceed the company's capacity to produce, management will have to decide either to expand capacity or to reduce its production goals. Either decision is critical. If management believes that product demand will continue to increase it will have to make large investments in new equipment and plant facilities. This capital investment will enable the company to expand sales and profitability. But if management errs in predicting continued growth of product demand, the decision to expand capacity could be disastrous, resulting in unused capacity, excess costs, and reduced profitability. A safer bet, if increased demand seems to be temporary, is to find other ways of meeting it—perhaps through implementing overtime, subcontracting work out, or rejecting sales.

Raw Materials

An important part of production planning is the **purchasing function**—determining when, from whom, and how to acquire raw materials. The purchasing department is responsible for acquiring raw materials at the least cost in time for production to continue in an orderly way. Many raw materials are in short supply, and capital is difficult and expensive to raise; hence the purchasing function is vital.

Some of the key issues related to purchasing:

1. A critical function of purchasing is to determine what specific raw materials will be required, based on production's estimates of how

much it is going to produce, when it will be produced, and how much raw materials are required to produce each unit of product. (More will be said on this latter point in a subsequent section related to setting standards.)

2. The amount of each type of raw material that the purchasing department orders often depends on the cost to order and store, inventory levels, anticipated need, availability of resources, and amount of time it takes to order and receive materials. For example, if a company is anticipating a shortage in a particular raw material, it might acquire more of that raw material than normal. However, there are costs and benefits to maintaining too small or too large an inventory of materials. (Specific problems related to inventory management are included in Chapter 16.)
3. The purchasing department must also decide from whom to purchase raw materials. Most large companies have multiple suppliers so that if a problem arises with one, the production process will not be disrupted. Factors influencing the choice of supplier include quality of service and product, cost, reliability, and general reputation.

Labor Pool

The proper mix of well-trained, skilled, and unskilled workers is particularly important in manufacturing. It is incumbent on management to ensure that people with the proper skills are available at each stage of the production process and that proper control is exercised. Lack of control or improper staffing will cause inefficiencies in manufacturing that may have an impact on the quality, quantity, or cost of the product. As in the case of raw materials, management can establish specific standards for how much of each type of labor should be used in production.

SETTING UP THE PRODUCTION PROCESS

An understanding of how products physically flow through manufacturing provides insight into the nature of the conversion process. Basically, there are two extreme approaches to the manufacturing of products—mass production and custom-made production. Between these two extremes there are a number of hybrid production systems tailored to the company's needs and the nature of the product.

Mass Production

Mass production is normally used when a company is producing a large number of homogeneous units. In such an environment, units are manufactured in a routine, standardized fashion. There are three common patterns of product flow associated with mass production.

In **sequential-flow production,** each product goes through the same set of operations in a similar sequence (see Exhibit 10.4a). Costs are transferred from one process to another as the product is transferred. Normally, a sequential product flow exists in companies making a single uniform product or products that get uniform processing, such as bread, refined ores and metals, sugar, beverages, cement, and many chemical products.

In **parallel-flow production,** two or more products go through two or more processes (see Exhibit 10.4b). These different processes may be carried on simultaneously, or one process may run for a while and then another started. When work is completed on the parallel processes, the products are normally brought together in a final process. The parallel-flow system is commonly used in the automotive industry. Subcomponents of a car—frame, engine, trim—are manufactured separately but brought together to complete the car.

Finally, in **selective-flow production,** manufactured items go through some but not necessarily all processing steps, depending on the nature of the product (see Exhibit 10.4c). For example, in meat processing, some of the butchered product goes directly to the packaging department for sale to consumers; some goes to the smoking department

EXHIBIT 10.4a Sequential-Flow Production

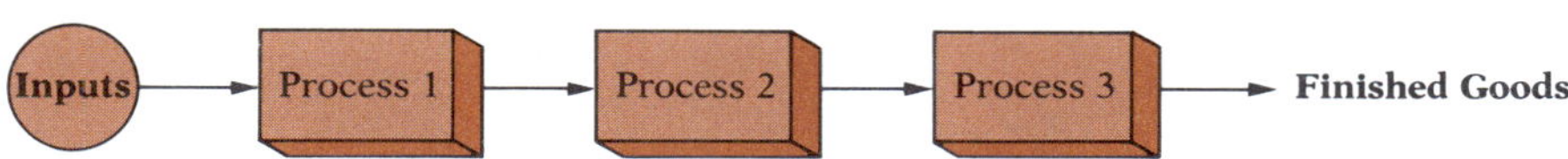

EXHIBIT 10.4b Parallel-Flow Production

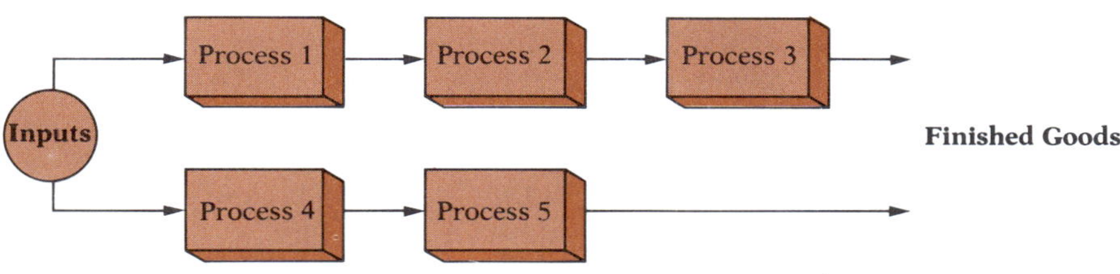

EXHIBIT 10.4c Selective-Flow Production

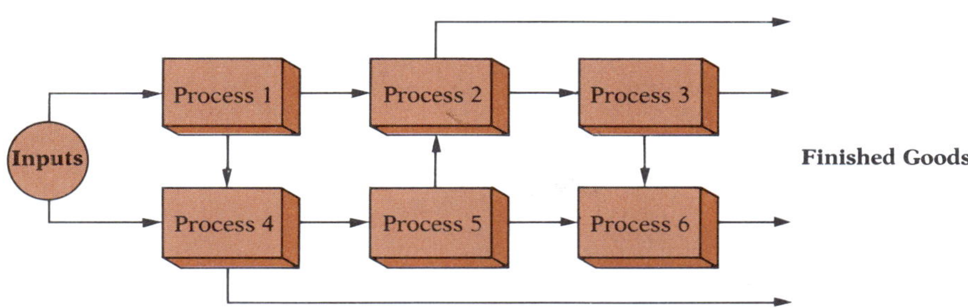

and then to the packaging department; some goes to the grinding department and then to the packaging department.

Custom-Made Production

The other end of the production spectrum exists in companies that make their products to suit individual customers. Custom-made production typically exists in service-oriented companies and in such manufacturing industries as publishing, construction, and tool-and-die making. Usually there is no standardized, routine production process; the steps in the production process and the types of inputs are dictated by the particular order.

Setting Standards

Most companies attempt to predetermine the amounts and kinds of labor skills and materials needed to manufacture a unit of product. These predetermined figures are commonly referred to as **production standards.** The development and use of these standards is complex, but once established, they are very helpful in planning and controlling the production process and in evaluating the performance of workers and departments.

MATERIAL STANDARDS

There are two kinds of material standards: those related to the quantity of raw materials to be used in making a product and those related to the price of the materials used. **Material quantity standards** indicate how much of each type of raw material should go into a finished product. These standards are initially established on the basis of the original engineering specifications. Of course, these standards may be modified on the basis of actual production experience or changes in the product or method of production. Exhibit 10.5a provides an example of the material quantity standards set in manufacturing a card table. Quantity standards often take the form of a **bill of materials,** which indicates how much of each raw material should go into making each finished product.

EXHIBIT 10.5a A Bill of Materials for a Folding Card Table

Part Identification	Description	Raw Material Required
A. Tubular steel legs	1 in. diameter × 30 in. long	9 ft.
B. Plywood top	1/2 in. × 41 in. diameter 1/2 in. × 3 sq. ft.	9 sq. ft.
C. Vinyl top	41 in. diameter 3 sq. ft.	9 sq. ft.
D. Assembly kit	1 in. flat steel edging, bolts, hinges, cardboard packing	1

The folding card table is a 36 in. square table and is 27 in. high.

EXHIBIT 10.5b Price Standards for a Folding Card Table

Materials	Quantity	Price	Standard Material Cost
A. Steel legs	9 ft.	$0.12	$1.08
B. Plywood top	9 sq. ft.	0.10	0.90
C. Vinyl top	9 sq. ft.	0.02	0.18
D. Assembly kit	1	1.00	1.00
		TOTAL	$3.16

Material price standards are normally based on vendor price quotations and experience. In Exhibit 10.5b, the standard price for each raw material specified in the bill of materials for the card table has been established. Note that multiplication of the quantity standard and the price standard yields the **standard material cost** of the product.

LABOR STANDARDS

The use of labor standards closely parallels the use of material standards. There are two types of labor standards: those based on the quantity and type of labor to be used (commonly referred to as efficiency standards) and those based on the wage rate of each type of worker. **Labor efficiency standards** are typically developed on the basis of time-and-motion studies, which time production workers as they manufacture the product. These measurements are used to determine how many products a worker can be expected to produce in a given time.

In contrast, **wage-rate standards** represent the expected wage per hour for each production worker. These standards are based on union contracts and on salary schedules established by personnel. As with materials, multiplication of the wage-rate standard and the efficiency standard yields the **standard labor cost** of each product. Note in Exhibit 10.6 that there are two types of labor functions performed on a folding card table—a machining function and an assembly function.

USING STANDARDS FOR PLANNING AND CONTROL

Once material and labor standards have been established, they can be used in production planning and control. For example, with the use of standards it is possible to convert production goals into specific needs for materials and labor and to plan for the proper acquisition of these inputs. If the manufacturer of card tables knew that it needed to make

EXHIBIT 10.6 Standard Labor Cost for a Folding Card Table

Direct Labor	Time per Table	Rate per Hour	Standard Labor Cost
For machining	9 min.	$6.00	$ .90
For assembly	12 min.	5.00	1.00
		TOTAL	$1.90

200 tables in the month of January, the production manager would need to have available the amounts of labor and raw materials specified in Exhibit 10.7. If these resources are available, the production manager should be able to meet the quota of 200 tables.

Production standards are as useful for control purposes as they are for planning. For example, at the end of January the production manager could compare how much labor and material were actually used with how much had been planned. If there were significant differences, the production manager would attempt to explain why they occurred. In the process of making these comparisons and finding explanations for differences, management is controlling the process and trying to isolate why and where their operations might have been inefficient.

The use of standards is equally important in nonmanufacturing companies as it is in manufacturing companies. Many service-oriented organizations, including banks, hospitals, and law firms, set and use standards in the same fundamental way.

QUALITY CONTROL

The other commonly used approach to production control is through **quality-control** inspections at various stages in the manufacturing process or at the end of the process. These inspections may indicate problems in the production cycle or product early enough so that something can be done before the product is completed and possibly ruined. Quality-control inspections increase the probability that the final product will meet quality standards.

It would be difficult and costly—and usually unnecessary—to inspect every single unit of product as it is produced. In most cases, production supervisors inspect a random sample of products. For example, they may inspect every hundredth unit and on that basis draw conclusions about whether there are any problems with the production process.

The idea of quality control has recently become more widely accepted in service-oriented businesses as well. For example, the account-

EXHIBIT 10.7 Production Standards for Folding Card Tables

Material	Amount Required per Table		Total Amount Needed in Month to Produce 200 Tables		
A	9 ft.		180		
B	9 sq. ft.		180		
C	9 sq. ft.		180		
D	1 kit		200		
Type of Labor	*Amount of Time Per Table*		*Total Tables to Be Produced*		*Total Time Required*
Machining	9 min.	×	200	=	1,800 min.
Assembly	12 min.	×	200	=	2,400 min.

Highlight Quality Control in the Garment Industry

When you think of all the clothing manufactured each year and all the people who handle each garment, the quality that is achieved is amazing. Do you ever wonder how this quality is maintained?

Quality control is a manufacturer's systematic inspection of products in order to maintain a consistent level of excellence. The garment industry usually inspects each item, often several times. First there is an inspection of the fabric, thread, and other supplies. There might be another inspection after the patterns are cut and a spot inspection of a garment during assembly. When the garment is completed, it is again inspected. If the garments exhibit fine workmanship, they are sent to retailers for sale. Many of these garments have a quality-control ticket reading "Inspected by . . ." tucked in a pocket or sleeve. The items that fail inspection are not resewn. They are bought by discount houses and sold to the public at considerably lower prices.

Why such an elaborate system of quality control? A manufacturer whose goods are consistently inferior will no longer be able to attract customers. Many firms charge higher prices for their clothing because they maintain high standards (Pierre Cardin, Bill Blass, Givenchy). If their quality suddenly became inferior, the public would refuse to pay more for products with their label.

ing profession has begun a "peer review" process in which one large accounting firm reviews the work of another. This inspection process has already enhanced the quality of work performed by accounting firms.

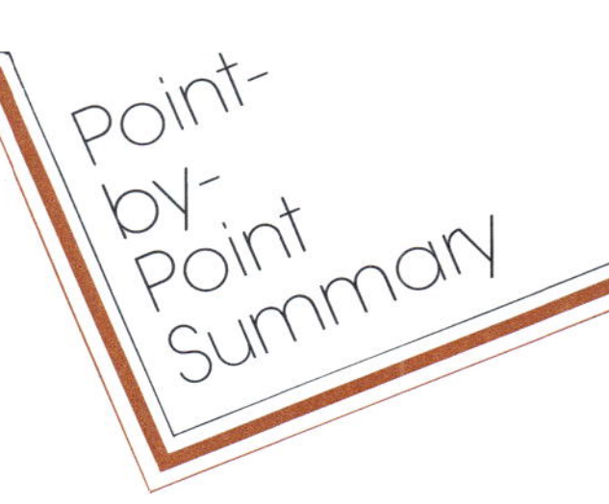

- Production management is the process by which an organization converts resources, or inputs, into a finished product or service.
- A product can be tangible or intangible, and the nature of the product affects the organization of the conversion process as well as the amounts and types of inputs required for production.
- The primary inputs in production are labor, materials, manufacturing overhead, and administrative overhead. The proportional amount of inputs used in producing a product or service is dependent on the nature of that product. In manufacturing companies, labor and material are often the most used inputs while in non-manufacturing companies material and overhead are the largest components of product cost.
- Production quotas are established primarily on the basis of the company's estimate of sales. However, production goals are also affected by other factors inside and outside the organization.
- Production planning revolves around the decision of what and how much to produce. Its major goal is to ensure that the required labor and material resources are available. The most critical decisions involved in production planning concern plant location and layout.
- Products can flow through the manufacturing process in many ways, but most organizations use mass production, which is geared to the

production of similar units. Custom-made production is used to accommodate customer specifications.

- The production schedule indicates what will be produced, when it will be produced, and who has responsibility for doing what.
- Labor and material standards are important in planning and controlling the production function. There are basically two types of standards—quantity and price—for both labor and materials.
- Quality-control inspections, another valuable way to control production, are normally performed on a random basis during various stages of the manufacturing process. They provide management with an opportunity to identify problems before the production process is complete.

1. Describe how the manufacturing process would differ for a law firm and a car manufacturer.
2. How does the type of business influence the amount and types of inputs used in production? Provide some examples.
3. What are the major steps involved in production management? Briefly describe what goes on during each phase.
4. What role do production standards have in production planning and control?
5. Discuss the role and importance of the purchasing function.
6. What are some of the characteristics of products made through mass production? What types of products tend to be custom-made?
7. What factors would you consider in establishing a quality-control program for a particular product?
8. Why is production management often considered to be the most important task performed by a company?
9. What type of plant layout would be required for each of the production processes described in this chapter?

APPLICATION

International Business Machines Corporation

In the 1880s, Herman Hollerith developed a mechanical method of processing census data for the U.S. Bureau of the Census. His method included two devices: one that coded population data as punched holes in cards and another that sensed the data. Their success led Hollerith to form a company in 1896 to manufacture and sell these devices. In 1911 the company became part of the Computing-Tabulating-Recording (CTR) Company, which manufactured commercial scales and tabulating and time-recording equipment. In 1924 CTR became the International Business Machines (IBM) Corporation.

Today IBM is the leader of the worldwide data-processing community, controlling over half of the industry's business. IBM's products include data-processing machines and systems, information processors, electric typewriters, copiers, dictation equipment, educational and testing materials, and related supplies and services. Most products can be either leased or purchased through IBM's worldwide marketing organizations.

IBM dominates two industries—electric typewriters and computers. IBM computers range from small but powerful minicomputers to high-performance computers for high-speed, large-scale scientific and commercial applications. The wide range of computer applications in scientific, industrial, and commercial areas requires machines of different sizes and capabilities. As a result, IBM custom-makes each computer to customer specifications.

THE PRODUCTION PROCESS

Production management is of great importance to IBM, because manufacturing a computer is a costly and complex process. Without proper planning and control, the company would have trouble staying ahead of the competition. A review of IBM's manufacturing process indicates that they have developed a truly comprehensive approach. And as might be expected from IBM, computers play a significant role in all phases of production, from initial planning to final testing and installation. Basically, IBM's production process consists of the seven events described below.

Planning

The production process normally begins with receipt of a customer's order at an IBM sales office. The sales office uses a centralized computer system to send the customer's order to the appropriate IBM plant. At the plant, another computer system creates an overall production schedule for all the parts, subassemblies, and subproducts that will go into the customer's computer. At the same time, the required manufacturing data—including parts specifications, quality requirements, and engineering testing data—are entered into a computerized control system that feeds this information to the production line and controls the manufacturing process.

Components

Thousands of parts are needed to build a complete computer. One of IBM's manufacturing computer systems makes sure these components are taken from stock or ordered from vendors or other IBM plants. They are scheduled to arrive on the manufacturing floor at the right time for assembly of the product. The idea is to minimize the level of inventory yet meet the manufacturing schedule of each product. The manufacturing computer system also controls the ordering, scheduling, stocking, and moving of parts to the manufacturing departments.

A bill of materials, or manufacturing parts list, describes the type and quantity of components needed to make each computer. This list is fed into another computer to generate orders to vendors and other IBM plants and also to send the lists to the production departments that will assemble the customer's computer.

Subproduct Assembly

The components and assemblies that make up subproducts are supplied according to the schedule and bill of materials provided by the manufacturing computer system. The next step is the assembly of component parts onto small plug-in circuit cards. The printed circuitry on each card interconnects the various components, forming a completed circuit package. These cards are plugged into printed circuit boards, which are then attached to gates, or frames, in the computer. Two different departments assemble and inspect these parts, then send their finished products to other departments for assembly into larger units.

The manufacturing control system supplies assembly and inspection instructions to the production line in the form of computer printouts and also displays instructions on computer terminal screens if required. Computers directly control some production machines, such as automatic wiring and testing, card testing, and board manufacturing.

In addition, employees use data-entry units to enter production information into a subproduct scheduling and tracking system, which monitors the steps of assembly and provides up-to-the-minute information on production status to inventory, production control, scheduling, and quality-control areas.

Subproduct Test

Test departments conduct functional tests on completed assemblies, and the results are communicated via computer to certain manufacturing support groups, such as Manufacturing Engineering/Quality Engineering and Quality Assurance.

Various automatic test machines, controlled by small satellite computers in the test department, test the completed subproduct assemblies. The test results are printed out on terminals or printers in the test department and also are fed back for analysis to assembly departments as well as to manufacturing support groups.

When testing has been completed successfully, the subproduct is sent either to unit assembly to be incorporated into the product or to other IBM locations.

Unit Assembly

All of the component parts, subproducts, and subassemblies come together in the unit assembly stage of the production process. The speciic features ordered by the customer are installed, and the unit takes final shape. At this stage, the production department is furnished with a description of the customer's computer.

Unit/System Test

The assembled computer is tested extensively as an individual unit and in a simulated operating environment before it is shipped to the customer. The test areas are linked directly to a computer that provides test specifications and test programs. Test results are collected automatically and fed back to production departments, manufacturing support organizations, and the engineering department for analysis and performance reporting.

When all the tests have been passed successfully, the side and top panels, in the colors selected by the customer, are installed. The new computer is ready for shipment.

Installation

The new unit is shipped to the customer's location, where it is connected to input/output devices to make a complete computer system. IBM customer engineers install these devices and test the total system before it is turned over to the customer for operation. According to prior instructions and scheduling, all input/output devices ordered from IBM are shipped from various plants of manufacture to arrive simultaneously. Installation data are returned to responsible plants for analysis and action where necessary, and quality monitoring continues at the customer's installation. In addition, a field control system maintains an up-to-date record of the system's performance throughout its life.

CAREER OPPORTUNITIES

A typical entry-level position in production management with IBM would require a bachelor's degree in industrial management (or the equivalent) and prior experience in sales, systems design, or programming. IBM's philosophy is that before people can work in production, they must have a basic understanding of the company's business. This can best be achieved by getting "hands-on" experience in sales or in some aspect of data processing.

The jobs available in production are quite varied but normally involve the employee with only one particular aspect of the production process. For example, it is possible to work in production planning, scheduling, or quality control. A manufacturing company as large as IBM, with all of its different products, has many opportunities available in the production area.

FOR DISCUSSION

1. How would you characterize IBM's system for manufacturing computers in terms of the production methods discussed in this chapter? Do you feel that the production process changes when IBM is producing typewriters instead of computers? If so, why and how would it change?
2. How can IBM justify conducting a quality-control inspection on every single computer?

RT III

MARY WELLS LAWRENCE

In 1950, Mary and Burt Wells moved from Ohio to New York City, and Mary joined the advertising department of Macy's department store. By thirty-five, Mary was divorced from Wells but a vice president of red-hot Doyle, Dane, Bernbach. Then she was lured to an elite problem-solving task force, Jack Tinker & Partners. But Mary grew impatient to run the show and left to set up her own agency. Wells, Rich, Green created an immediate sensation with its campaign for Braniff. Wells persuaded the airline's president, Harding Lawrence, to paint the entire fleet of planes in pastel colors and to outfit the stewardesses in Pucci designs. The industry snickered, but Braniff's ticket sales jumped 41 percent. Wells married Harding Lawrence in 1967 and replaced the Braniff account with an even-bigger TWA account.

Mary Wells Lawrence never pitched primarily for so-called women's accounts or tried to corner the female market; instead, she went after and won the most lucrative, male-dominated accounts. Her aggressive style drew inevitable flak from male competitors, who called her Bloody Mary. But by the early 1970s, she was earning more than any man in the business.

Marketing

OBJECTIVES

- ☐ To explain why it is advantageous for businesses to break the consumer population into smaller populations and to direct their attention to the appropriate market
- ☐ To explain how businesses determine what motivates a consumer to purchase a certain product and how the company learns about these preferences
- ☐ To understand how a consumer decides to purchase a certain product
- ☐ To describe, in brief, the methods used to forecast the sales of a product
- ☐ To evaluate the strategies that could be used to approach a market, depending on the type of product, its position in the product life cycle, the mix of products sold, and so on

OUTLINE

ARTICLE *A Matter of Taste*
KNOWING YOUR CUSTOMER
MARKET SEGMENTATION AND DIFFERENTIATION
Geographic Segmentation
Demographics
Family Life Cycle
THE HOW AND WHY OF PURCHASES
Need Fulfillment
Samples and Surveys
The Decision Model of Purchases
FORECASTING SALES
Time Series and Statistical Analysis
Surveys of Buyer Intentions
Test Marketing
PRODUCTS
Product Classification
Product Strategy
The Product Life Cycle
A MARKETING EXAMPLE
APPLICATION *The Procter & Gamble Company*

KEY TERMS

COMPETITIVE ADVANTAGE
CONCENTRATED PRODUCT STRATEGY
CONSUMER GOODS
CONVENIENCE GOODS
DEMOGRAPHICS
DIFFERENTIATED PRODUCT STRATEGY
EXTENSIVE PROBLEM SOLVING
FAMILY LIFE CYCLE
IMPULSE PURCHASE
LIMITED PROBLEM SOLVING
MARKET SEGMENT
PRODUCER'S GOODS
PRODUCT LIFE CYCLE
PRODUCT LINE
PRODUCT MIX
SAMPLE SURVEY
SHOPPING GOODS
SPECIALTY GOODS
STATISTICAL ANALYSIS
SURVEY OF BUYER INTENTIONS
TARGET MARKET
TEST MARKET
TIME SERIES STUDY
UNDIFFERENTIATED STRATEGY

CONSUMERS AND PRODUCTS

A Matter of Taste

LAWRENCE INGRASSIA
Wall Street Journal, February 26, 1980

Appleasy looked like a winner when it was whipped up in Pillsbury Co.'s test kitchen [in Minneapolis].

The new dessert—apples in cinnamon sauce with a crunchy streusel topping—was the product of three years of exhaustive research. It was cheap, easy to fix and fast.

There was just one problem: Not very many people liked it. There weren't enough apples, the cinnamon was overpowering and the topping was too sweet. "It was a magnificent flop," says one Pillsbury executive.

Appleasy went the way of most new food products—down the drain. The failure rate has always been enough to give food-company executives indigestion, and it is getting worse. More than 60% of all new grocery products introduced into test markets in 1977 failed, compared with about 50% in 1971, according to A.C. Nielsen Co. And the failure rate is well over eight in 10 counting all the products scrapped in the test kitchen before they are marketed.

TO LITTLE AVAIL

Batteries of tests and surveys are conducted to discern what shoppers want, to develop and refine recipes, to choose brand names and even to design packages for new products, but all these efforts have been to little avail. There still isn't a foolproof method of telling what will succeed. "If anybody really knew, the failure rate wouldn't be so high," says Edward Tauber, research director at the Dancer Fitzgerald Sample Inc. advertising agency.

A new food product needs a lot more going for it to succeed these days. Since grocery unit volume has been practically flat for several years, a new product has to bump something else off the supermarket shelf. And because of higher advertising costs, it is harder for a new product to pay for itself and turn a profit. But a real winner can mean millions of dollars in business for years—and more than pay for some losers.

With the success rates dropping and costs increasing, food companies have been more cautious in introducing new brands in the past couple of years. After topping 1,000 a year in the mid-1970s, the number of new-brand introductions slumped to 744 in 1978 and recovered only somewhat to 912 last year, according to A.C. Nielsen.

There have been some changes in strategy, too. Companies are dishing up more variations of old favorites. You now can buy Honey Nut Cheerios and Honey and Nut Corn Flakes, and there is Log Cabin Pancade Waffle Mix to go with Log Cabin Syrup. Companies are also taking fewer chances with long shots. "They're less likely to play the dartboard game—throwing out a product and seeing if it sticks," Mr. Tauber says.

SOLVING PROBLEMS

By and large, though, the way new products are developed hasn't changed. "You have to look at the consumer, find out what problems he's encountering and try to devise a new product which presents a better solution than the old product," says Marc C. Particelli, a vice president at the Booz, Allen & Hamilton management-consultant office in Chicago.

That isn't easy, though. New food products today have to combine quality and convenience without costing too much. A look at some products cooked up in Pillsbury's test kitchens in the past few years shows how difficult it is to get all the ingredients for success into a single product.

At Pillsbury, most ideas come from marketing or research-and-development executives. The vast majority of ideas are discarded early because they don't pass cost-analysis or technical-feasibility studies. Others are dropped after market studies and taste tests. Only a handful are made into products each year.

Unfortunately, this laborious process doesn't guarantee success on the supermarket shelf. "This isn't a science; almost anything can go wrong," says Edgar T. Mertz, until recently vice president of Pillsbury's consumer-products group. "Whenever we have something we think is going to set the world on fire, I have a drawer full of things to remind me of the losers."

Some food products fail because they simply don't taste good enough. No one sets out to make a bad product, of course. But in an effort to make a product convenient and inexpensive, too much quality can be sacrificed. That apparently was Appleasy's downfall.

Pillsbury began looking for an easy-to-prepare dessert in June 1975. Initial ideas ranged from instant yogurt to Boston cream pie to fudge sauce with a brownie topping. But a fruit dessert emerged as the favorite in "focus group" discussions with consumers.

Pillsbury chose apple because "the majority of consumers eat and perceive apples to be good; you know, 'An apple a day keeps the doctor away,' " explains Allen A. McCusker, a marketing executive who joined Pillsbury after Appleasy was developed. Pillsbury's test kitchen, which is a cross between a laboratory and a kitchen, came up with a recipe using freeze-dried apples. All you had to do was add boiling water, stir, wait five minutes and eat.

Consumer panels were interviewed to help pick a name. The early choice, Hot Apple 'n Crunch, was dropped because Appleasy conveyed the convenience image better. After consumer taste tests had been completed, however, Pillsbury began skimping on apples because the price of apples more than doubled. Appleasy was introduced in April 1978 and failed.

"The product became less Appleasy and more starch and sugar," Mr. McCusker says. He adds, "A lot of people tried it but didn't come back for seconds. There was no problem with convenience, but lots of problems with quality." Pillsbury won't say exactly how much it lost on Appleasy, but the figure was well over $1 million.

Some ideas sound good at the time but just misfire. One product the people at Green Giant would rather forget is vegetable yogurt. Green Giant, which was acquired by Pillsbury last year, went into a joint venture with Hawthorn Mellody Inc. in 1975 in an effort to cash in on the yogurt craze with something different. Different they were; the yogurt flavors were cucumber, beet, tomato and garden salad.

Vegetable yogurt was introduced in Cleveland to test consumer response. It bombed. "We lasted about six weeks before the supermarkets threw us out," recalls a Green Giant executive.

Even products that taste good may fail, often because market research doesn't measure consumer attitudes correctly. Green Giant executives thought they had a certain success in Oven Crock baked beans, which came already sweetened in the can. "We did a series of blind taste tests and had a significant winner over bland pork and beans by a 3-to-1 or 4-to-1 preference margin," says John M. Stafford, now an executive vice president at Pillsbury.

But Oven Crock was a disaster in a test market. Surveys later showed that people who ate heavily flavored baked beans added their own fixings to the bland variety and didn't want somebody to do it for them. "Our beans were terrific, but they were a solution to no known problem," Mr. Stafford says.

Because of high advertising costs, Pillsbury is trying harder than ever to weed out new products that show little promise in the grocery market. "Market research and product research is the cheapest part of the ritual," explains Mr. Mertz. Advertising is the most expensive. Pillsbury recently dropped plans to market a high-quality frozen croissant even though it got high scores in consumer taste tests.

"The problem was that people didn't know when to eat it," says Thomas R. McBurney, a Pillsbury vice president. "The reaction was, 'It sure tastes good, but I don't know what it is. Do I eat it for dinner or breakfast?' " Pillsbury deciced not to undertake the expense of trying to educate the public about croissant consumption.

In the food business, one big winner can make up for all the losers, and Pillsbury came up with one of its biggest ever in Totino's Crisp Crust Frozen Pizza. Like many successful new products, Crisp Crust Pizza satisfied a specific desire expressed by consumers. "Crisp Crust is a textbook story of how you ought to do things," says Kent C. Larson, vice president of frozen foods at Pillsbury.

In early 1976, Pillsbury held focus-group discussions around the U.S. and handed out 2,000 questionnaires to find out what consumers didn't like about frozen pizza. The response was overwhelming; about 60% hated the crust, which many said tasted like cardboard. "We knew we could be head and shoulders above everybody else with a good crust," Mr. Larson says. The problem was sent to the test kitchen.

Baking the crust, the conventional method of making it, was scrapped. Instead, Pillsbury decided to fry the crust, using an old family recipe of Rose Totino, a Pillsbury vice president. But what worked in her kitchen at home didn't work right away in Pillsbury's test kitchen. "The sudden heat from frying caused the dough to grow in every direction," says James R. Behnke, vice president of R&D. "They came out contorted and all puffed up. When you're running a commercial frozen-pizza operation, there's a carton at the end of the production line and the pizza has to fit into it."

It took several months to control the size (the process now is patented). Pillsbury took special precautions to keep the project a secret from competitors. When trial production runs were held, the frozen crusts were shredded into small pieces and dumped into a landfill.

Consumer taste tests convinced Pillsbury that it had a winner. "People liked it so much that they said, 'I don't believe it's frozen,' " Mr. Behnke says. In choosing an advertising strategy. Pillsbury decided to avoid the common mistake of promising the consumer too much. "Many advertising campaigns for frozen pizza said, 'We're as good as pizzeria,' " Mr. Larson says. "That promise is totally unbelievable to the consumer." Pillsbury's ad campaign was direct, saying that the Totino's frozen-pizza crust didn't taste like cardboard.

Crisp Crust pizza was introduced in August 1978, and Pillsbury hasn't been able to keep up with demand. Crisp Crust has made Totino's the best-selling frozen pizza, with a 30% market share, up from 18% with the old Totino's pizza. With about $700 million of frozen pizzas sold each year, the success of Crisp Crust pizza project means additional sales of about $60 million a year for Pillsbury.

Successful products are not necessarily those that have a high quality but those that consumers find acceptable in terms of quality, taste, price, and so on. This point and related concepts are treated in greater detail in this chapter.

Let's suppose you are in charge of product development for a major manufacturing company. You've always wanted to buy a light bulb shaped like a cheeseburger, and so you decide to have your development personnel invent one. They design one to your specifications, and you start a huge advertising campaign. At the end of the first year, the financial department gives you the results of your campaign:

Expenditures on research, development, production, and advertising	\$6 million
Sales revenues	\$2

The only reason you made \$2 is because you bought a cheeseburger light bulb for yourself.

Clearly, you weren't doing your job right. Nobody can develop a product without regard to the needs and desires of the intended buyers. Otherwise, there's a mismatch between consumer and product. In this chapter we're going to see how firms avoid such mismatches.

Knowing Your Customer

Businesses today need to be very much concerned with who their customers are. Knowing your customers, and knowing what they are looking for in a product, will give you a competitive edge. If you manufacture green cars but your potential customers prefer blue cars, you will soon go out of business if your competitor starts making them and you don't.

Back in the old days, surprisingly enough, businesses didn't seem so concerned with their customers. They felt that if they developed a quality product, it would sell itself—an approach called the product concept. That may have been a good approach when there were not many firms competing for customers. Now, however, there are so many firms producing so many products that customers can pick and choose among many different brands and styles. Competition is fierce.

A further complication is that in the modern-day business world, a manufacturer very rarely sells directly to customers. There are a lot of intermediate steps between the manufacture and final sale of a product. For instance, when you go to the hardware stores, the products there are from many different manufacturers. It becomes quite a problem, then, for a business to be able to determine who its customers really are and why they may be buying one product instead of another.

Market Segmentation and Differentiation

Let's look at a real product in the real world—ice skates. It is quite likely that not everybody buys ice skates. But who does? And why is it that some do and some do not? If it is your job to sell ice skates, the answer to these questions could mean the difference between buying a two-story house for your family and standing in line at the unemployment office.

The group of people who buy ice skates could be divided into many different **market segments.** First, you could consider the entire recreation market as a segment. Next, you could narrow this vision to the winter sports market. You could break down this last category even more to include the different games played with ice skates, such as ice skating and ice hockey. The purpose of delineating market segments is to give you a **target market** to focus on.

Once a manufacturer has deciced on a segment to focus on, it is necessary to show how its product differs from the existing substitutes in that segment. For example, Wendy's located an unserved segment in the fast-food industry and developed a product to take advantage of that segment. Wendy's has aimed for people twenty-four and older, whereas McDonald's has the twelve- to eighteen-year-olds.

GEOGRAPHIC SEGMENTATION

You are a resourceful businessperson, and you have noticed that the northern states have colder winters than the southern states. It strikes you that perhaps people up north will be buying more ice skates than those down south. Whether you realize it or not, you have just hit on a method of segmenting the potential market of ice skate buyers—on the basis of **geographic** regions. Now you know where to direct your promotional efforts. The problem of who will buy your product, however, still remains unsolved.

DEMOGRAPHICS

Do older women buy ice skates, or do young boys dicker with their parents for a pair at Christmas time? Are ice skates bought predominantly by poor people or by wealthy families? To what age group do ice skates have the greatest appeal? Trying to divide the market according to age, sex, income, occupation, education, religion, or nationality would be segmentation based on **demographics.**

If you find that ice skates are predominantly sold to girls between the ages of eight and twelve who are in families of moderate income, you have earned your pay for the month. Now the company knows whom to appeal to. Although the parents are the ones with the money, children are quite effective manipulators of their money. If a little girl doesn't like the style of skates, any attempt on the part of the mother or father to get her to accept them may only result in an embarrassing scene.

FAMILY LIFE CYCLE

Although you may not have recognized it, you coincidently segmented the ice skate market on the basis of the **family life cycle;** you discovered that ice skates might be sold to families with children between the ages of eight and twelve. This type of market segmentation attempts to predict the types of purchases a family might make on the basis of the stage of growth it's in. A family with one child in kindergarten has different needs than a family with four children, three of whom are in college.

If you are a good marketer, you might also point out to your boss that it would be a good idea to have adult skates to go along with the children's. After all, most parents have a little bit of the kid in them, and they may as well buy skates for themselves while they're buying skates for their children.

The How and Why of Purchases

Although any one of the above methods is useful in predicting who might be buying ice skates, none of them comes close to explaining why they buy or how they buy (unless you count trying to avoid embarrassment in the store). To try to picture the problems involved in discovering why or how someone buys, ask yourself these questions:

- Do you always buy the same brand of chewing gum?
- Why do you chew gum some days and not others?
- Do you always buy only one pack, or do you sometimes buy more than one?

If you have a hard time answering these questions, imagine how difficult it is for a business to try to find out why you are buying chewing gum.

"This may be your last chance to acquire a superpowered, oversized, hyper-polluting gas guzzler. Don't blow it."

NEED FULFILLMENT

Because so much money can be won or lost on efforts to meet consumer needs, a lot of research has been done on why or how consumers buy. Some researchers view all consumer purchases as an effort to fulfill one need or another. For example, once you feel a need to have a hamburger, you try as best you can to satisfy the need. You may go to a fast-food restaurant, cook your own, or if the need is not that strong, have something else instead. The stronger the need, the more likely it is that, in some way, you will guide your purchase decision to best satisfy that need.

A lot of things affect our needs and how we may go about trying to satisfy them with purchases. For one thing, most people simply can't afford to fulfill all their needs. For another, people from different cultures have different needs. Social class can also be a significant factor in the determination of needs. But perhaps the most obvious factor is the effect our friends have on our needs and purchases. It is quite likely that some people would not want to buy a fancy sports car unless a friend had taken them for a ride in one. The old expression "keeping up with the Joneses" is based more on fact than on fiction.

Even when they are from the same culture, social class, or perhaps the same group of friends, people still buy differently. Personal differences are the hardest for a business to study, but they offer the richest insights into consumer behavior. Your motivations, perceptions, education, attitudes, and personality all make you different from everyone else (thank goodness). Nevertheless, if you go out to buy a pair of ice skates, chances are you will find a pair that is really you. How can that happen?

SAMPLES AND SURVEYS

A business does not have to ask every potential consumer what he or she is looking for in a pair of ice skates. Chances are that at least several people will have similar tastes. Like everyone else, you've undoubtedly had the disappointing experience of finding the exact pair of slacks or shirt that you want—but only in the wrong size. Someone who wanted the same thing you wanted got there first.

To find out what products are most popular, businesses can take a **sample survey** of potential consumers in a particular market, like the one in Exhibit 11.1. If a business can discover which group in the market likes one particular aspect of the product, it can target its appeal to that group more easily than it can try to change the product according to different preferences.

THE DECISION MODEL OF PURCHASES

Did you ever "have to have" a piece of candy or a soft drink? You probably just stopped into the store and bought it. A quick purchase of this type, known as an **impulse purchase,** does not involve much thinking. On the other hand, when you go shopping for clothes, chances are you compare the offerings of several different stores before you finally buy something. You use a **limited problem-solving** approach to the pur-

EXHIBIT 11.1 Sample Consumer Survey

Which of the time periods listed below best describes how soon you plan to shop for a new car? ("X" one box.)

Within 6 months from now	☐
6–12 months from now	☐
1–2 years from now	☐
3–4 years from now	☐
More than 4 years from now	☐

Below are a number of car names. For each make of car, please "X" the box which indicates whether you plan to consider that make the next time you shop for a new car, or if you currently own a car of that make.

	Plan to Consider/ Own Already ("X" One Box)		
	Yes	**No**	**Own**
Audi-Fox	☐	☐	☐
Chevrolet Camero	☐	☐	☐
Chevrolet Chevette	☐	☐	☐
Chevrolet Citation	☐	☐	☐
Chevrolet Impala	☐	☐	☐
Chevrolet Nova	☐	☐	☐
Datsun 200-SX	☐	☐	☐
Datsun 210 or B210	☐	☐	☐
Datsun 310	☐	☐	☐
Datsun 510	☐	☐	☐
Dodge Challenger	☐	☐	☐
Dodge Omni	☐	☐	☐
Ford Escort	☐	☐	☐
Ford Fairmont	☐	☐	☐
Ford Fiesta	☐	☐	☐
Ford Mustang	☐	☐	☐
Ford Pinto	☐	☐	☐
Honda Accord	☐	☐	☐
Honda Civic	☐	☐	☐
Honda Prelude	☐	☐	☐
Mercury Capri	☐	☐	☐
Plymouth Horizon	☐	☐	☐
Plymouth Sapporo	☐	☐	☐
Pontiac Firebird	☐	☐	☐
Pontiac Sunbird	☐	☐	☐
Volkswagen Dasher	☐	☐	☐
Volkswagen Rabbit	☐	☐	☐
Make not listed			

Highlight Publishers Sample Too

Publishing textbooks may seem straightforward, but it is actually quite complicated. One of the most important decisions to a publisher is what to include in a textbook. We could have included at least a hundred additional topics, based on our own teaching experience. But what if we're oddballs, spending too much time on management and not enough on personnel, or spending too little time on accounting and too much on stocks and bonds?

One way to decide what to put in a textbook is to sample the audience. The audience is presumably the readers, but this is not strictly correct. It is actually your professor who determines which book to use. To be sure, if a professor consistently chooses a book that none of the students like, he or she will be forced to change. But usually professors choose a book that is most appropriate for their goals and for the ability and interest of their students.

Thus West Publishing Company conducted a teaching survey to guide us in our decision of what to include in this book. Some 2,000 surveys were mailed to professors around the country, 846 of them were returned. The results were collated by West's product marketing division, and then the editor of this book met with us to explain his perceptions of the market based on the results. Thus you are reading a compromise drawn between our desires for the book and the market's desires.

chase. That means you compare prices, styles, and colors and decide which you like best. If you ever buy a car or house, you will probably shop around even more, critically comparing different prices and characteristics. Because this is not an easy decision to make, you will most likely use **extensive problem solving.**

A model has been developed to explain what goes on in your head (in an abstract sense) when you buy. This model breaks the buying process into the five distinct phases shown in Exhibit 11.2. The first step is realizing a need. As we have already suggested, purchases are made to satisfy needs.

The next step involves gathering information about different products that might satisfy this need. If you just want some chewing gum, you will require very little information, but if you need shelter in the from of a house or apartment, you might have to gather a lot of information about what is available.

The third step in this model is the evaluation of alternatives. It could be, with things you purchase often, that there is only one brand you really like, and so you do not really consider alternatives. On the other hand, if you have never bought a car before, you may have to consider quite a number of alternatives—perhaps even a motorcycle. The more important the decision or the greater the amount of money involved, the more information you are likely to gather and evaluate.

At some point in this evaluation, you decide on an action. If your need is not strong enough to justify a purchase or if you are confused about which alternative to choose, you may decide to do nothing. Otherwise, you are likely to decide on a particular item to purchase and eventually to buy that product.

The final step of the model, very important to a business, is the postpurchase evaluation. You never know how good or bad your decision is until you buy the product and try it. Your evaluation of the product after you use it will determine whether you might buy it again, or try a different product the next time the need arises.

How is this model helpful to businesses? First of all, it helps a business decide how best to market a particular product. If you manufacture chewing gum and your research shows that most of your customers buy your product on impulse, you would try very hard to make the gum as visible as possible, in stores, drugstores, marketplaces, and candy machines. You would not sell much gum if the nearest store that offered it was twenty miles away.

On the other hand, a business could try to reduce the complexity of a decision involving an extensive amount of problem solving, like the purchase of a car. By offering numerous pamphlets on its cars, a car dealer can provide potential customers with reinforcing information about how a particular car will satisfy their need for transportation. Perhaps to reduce the number of alternatives and to encourage selection of their cars, dealers may offer a discount on the price or a loan service. Anything that can help reduce the complexity of the decision or the number of alternatives is good marketing strategy for a business selling expensive products.

Forecasting Sales

It is essential that any business have a good idea of potential sales. Say that you manufacture belts. The forecast of how many belts you might be able to sell can be used to determine how many to produce. Before you suggest that you simply produce as many as possible and then be

EXHIBIT 11.2 Decision Model of Purchases

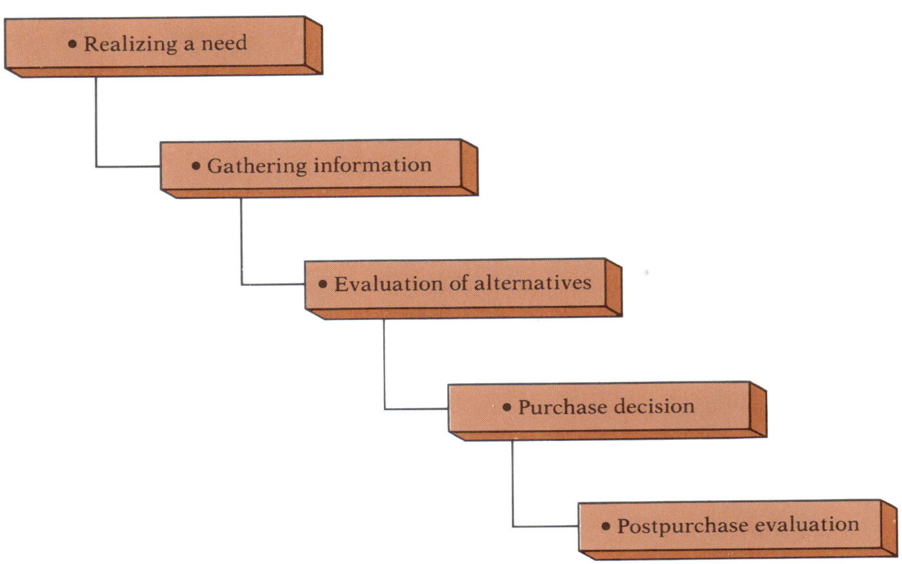

satisfied with what you can sell, consider how much it costs to produce belts. You have to buy the raw materials (leather, buckles), make sure you have enough machinery to manufacture them, and pay your labor force to produce them. If you do not sell all the belts you produce, you could go bankrupt. How will you pay your workers or cover the bills for the raw materials you used?

TIME SERIES AND STATISTICAL ANALYSIS

Businesses have developed a number of methods for forecasting how much they can expect to sell. The forecast is greatly simplified for products that have been selling for some time. By looking at the sales figures for the previous year or the year before, businesses can come up with a rough estimate of how much they might be able to sell in the current year. If sales have been going up from year to year, chances are that the firm will need to manufacture more (see Exhibit 11.3). A forecast that uses past sales data to predict future sales is called a **time series study.** If such a study indicates that sales may increase, the firm may have to make some adjustments—perhaps gearing up production, expanding, or contracting out to other businesses. It may also need to expand its sales force to handle the increasing demand.

Another method for predicting future sales—**statistical analysis**—tries to reduce the factors affecting the sales of a product to a mathematical form that is based on extensive and complicated studies. Using an overall, systems approach, statistical analysis may show how the price of the product, advertising expenditures, competition, and perhaps even the state of the economy affect sales. Naturally, since so much is included in this type of forecast, it involves enormous expense as well as a large number of assumptions. Nevertheless, if a good formula is developed, the firm may be able to predict quite accurately the sales potential for its product in the coming year.

EXHIBIT 11.3 Sample Sales Chart with Trend Projection

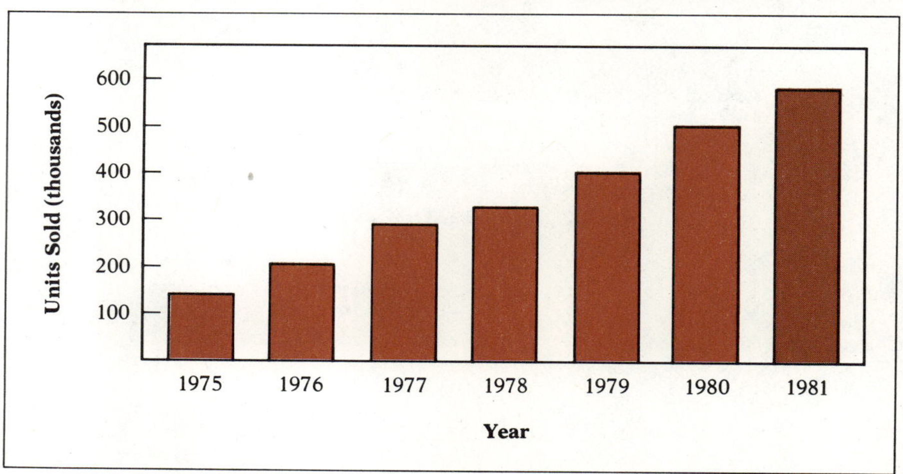

A business that is introducing a new product has a much more difficult time forecasting sales. However, a **survey of buyer intentions** allows a firm to test the acceptability of its product by polling a group of consumers in one of the markets that might be interested in the product. The survey can be quite useful in detecting flaws in product ideas as well as potential bonanzas. The bonus point with surveys is that their cost is quite low relative to the cost of a product failure.

SURVEYS OF BUYER INTENTIONS

Another way to predict sales on a new product is to select a sample group in the target market, offer the product for sale, and see what sort of response it gets—in other words, to conduct a **test market.** For instance, suppose you decided to offer wallets along with belts. You might offer a limited number of wallets for sale in two of the stores where you sell belts. On the basis of consumer response, you could decide whether to sell wallets in all your stores or to take the wallets off the market.

TEST MARKETING

Test marketing can be quite useful. First of all, it can save enormous expense. Instead of producing enough wallets for your entire market and risking failure, you can limit production and your initial expenses. Second, test marketing provides an opportunity to fine tune the product to consumer needs at minimum expense. You may find, if you contact some of those who bought your wallets, that you had an inferior card holder built into the wallet. Since that feature could easily be changed in the production process, you could modify your product early in its development, before too many of the inferior wallets were produced.

Products

Enormous expenses are involved in the development of a product, including expenses for test marketing and fine tuning the product. Therefore, failure to identify a market need correctly or to develop a product that meets a need may have disastrous consequences for a firm. It definitely pays to put time and effort into understanding the total market for a product, including what the target market is, the best way to reach that market, and what the competition is like.

PRODUCT CLASSIFICATION

Every product that is purchased is meant for eventual consumption, but the objective behind each purchase may be different. Purchases may be classified by objective as either consumer goods or producer's goods.

Products that are purchased for final consumption are called **consumer goods.** They can be classified in the following manner:

1. **Convenience goods** are those that normally are used quite regularly, such as soap. These goods are bought without any elaborate planning at home. As a result, they are often bought on impulse. Viewing such a product may suddenly create a want for it that has to be satisfied. The purchase of convenience goods is facilitated by strong

Highlight Direct Mail

Marketing experts have come up with highly refined methods to test markets, one of which is direct-mail advertising. Mailing lists are available from a variety of sources, at a price ranging from a fraction of a cent to several cents per name. The more highly specialized and categorized the mailing list, the more each name costs. For example, a mailing list for all homeowners would be a lot less expensive per name than a mailing list for homeowners in suburban areas with average family incomes in excess of $30,000 per year.

Direct-mail marketing experts suggest that the potential entrant in a new market buy only part of a mailing list—say only 5,000 random names, out of a total list of 30,000. Within the first seven days after the pieces of mail are received, about 15 percent should reply. On the basis of that response, the firm can make a prediction about total sales and evaluate the benefit of mailing to the whole list.

It costs anywhere from 20 cents to 35 cents per name to mail out a piece of advertising on a new product. That cost includes postage, printing, and the cost of the list.

identification with a favorite brand name; shoppers are unlikely to differentiate between the substitutes. Convenience goods are also those purchased in an emergency, (such as tires bought at a gas station 500 miles from home. In this case, price and quality are not so important, because the need for new tires is imperative.

2. **Shopping goods** are those that require a certain amount of time and effort on the part of the consumer. Shopping goods are sometimes homogeneous, or identical. For example, a shopper has to weigh the benefits of various television sets against their cost. Shopping goods may also be heterogeneous, with marked differences in quality or styling. In shopping for clothes, for instance, a consumer normally looks in a few shops before deciding what to purchase. Price may not be very important in this case, because the goods are different.
3. **Specialty goods** require extensive information gathering, evaluation of alternatives, and problem solving on the part of the buyers. In other words, customers are willing to make a special effort to fulfill their wants. Specialty goods are normally branded products (for example, drugs), and it is very unlikely that consumers will be satisfied with a good substitute.

Products that are purchased for use in the manufacture of other goods are called **producer's goods,** or industrial goods. Demand for these goods depends on the demand for the end product. For example, the demand for automobile accessories declined when the demand for automobiles declined in 1980.

These classifications help businesses meet their markets' needs. If you discover that the hand soap you produce is bought as a convenience good, you will concentrate your marketing efforts on establishing shelf space in stores with a lot of consumer traffic. But if you deal in specialty goods, like fine imported European wines, your marketing approach will be much different. First of all, your potential market is much smaller than the market for convenience goods. Second, although consumers may be able to appreciate your product, very few can pay for it. Thus, your efforts will be channeled into trying to locate your potential customers and to make them aware that a shop for fine wines is in the area. Finally, someone specializing in shopping goods, like clothes, might take a strategic approach. By establishing a store right next to another clothing store, a clothes retailer can give shoppers an opportunity to compare. Of course, the hope is that the products are either of such low cost or high quality that they can stand up to the competition.

PRODUCT STRATEGY

Knowing the marketplace is a great aid in focusing marketing and production efforts. A firm needs a battle plan in order to be effective: Is it going to try to complete with just one product, or will it offer several different products to different markets? The particular strategy is determined by choice of management and is often limited by financial constraints (there is just not enough money to produce more than one product), technological constraints (there are not enough qualified people to develop and manufacture the product), or even manufacturing constraints (the equipment cannot be modified to produce another product).

In determining the strategy it will use to approach the marketplace, a firm first looks inward and evaluates what it does best. This is its **competitive advantage,** the feature that will give it an edge in the marketplace. For example, if your business is limited to one small manufacturing plant, your competitive advantage over larger manufacturers in the field might be your ability to tailor your product to specific needs. Thus you would seek out customers that need your tailored products rather than the ones that can get by on standardized products.

The next step in determining strategy is to look outward. What is the particular market you want to appeal to? What are their needs? When there is little need to distinguish one buyer from another, a manufacturer would choose an **undifferentiated strategy.** This strategy, which is also known as mass marketing, is effective for marketing convenience goods like soap, soft drinks, and breakfast cereals.

A **differentiated product strategy** is used by businesses that see a better sales potential in offering a product that is tailored to meet specific market needs. For instance, a coat manufacturer may have a winter coat for sale in the North but market a parka in the Southeast, where the temperatures are warmer. Marketers often use the term **product line** in talking about the variations produced to meet different needs. In this instance, the general product is coats, and winter coats and parkas are two product lines.

A **concentrated product strategy**—specializing in one product—is akin to putting all of your eggs in one basket. By specializing in one product, a firm can develop expertise, a reputation, and a better understanding of its market's needs. This can be a very successful strategy, as Volkswagen proved with its Bug. Another example might be a ski manufacturer specializing in metal skis.

To further complicate matters, businesses determining their product strategy must consider their **product mix**—all the different product lines made by the firm. General Motors produces a mix of cars, trucks, and railroad engines; your store might sell a mix of wallets, belts, and perhaps purses and shoes. The point is that the products provide backup: If one is unsuccessful, the others can keep the business operating.

THE PRODUCT LIFE CYCLE

Businesses must continually monitor their products and their acceptance in the marketplace, because a business's concern with its products does not stop once a strategy has been decided on and a target market has been selected. Like people, goods have a **product life cycle,** starting with their introduction as a new product and ending when the need for the product declines beyond a profitable point (see Exhibit 11.4). At each point in this life cycle, different marketing strategies come into play.

A product in the introductory stage is relatively new to the market. A business selling a product in this stage should direct its marketing strategy to appeal to the particular group that would be most interested in it. For example, very few people are now buying home computers—only dedicated computer enthusiasts. Computer manufacturers are therefore seeking the enthusiasts and hoping that, over time, these users will influence others. The price for a product in the introductory stage may be somewhat high in order to recover the development costs.

EXHIBIT 11.4 Product Life Cycle

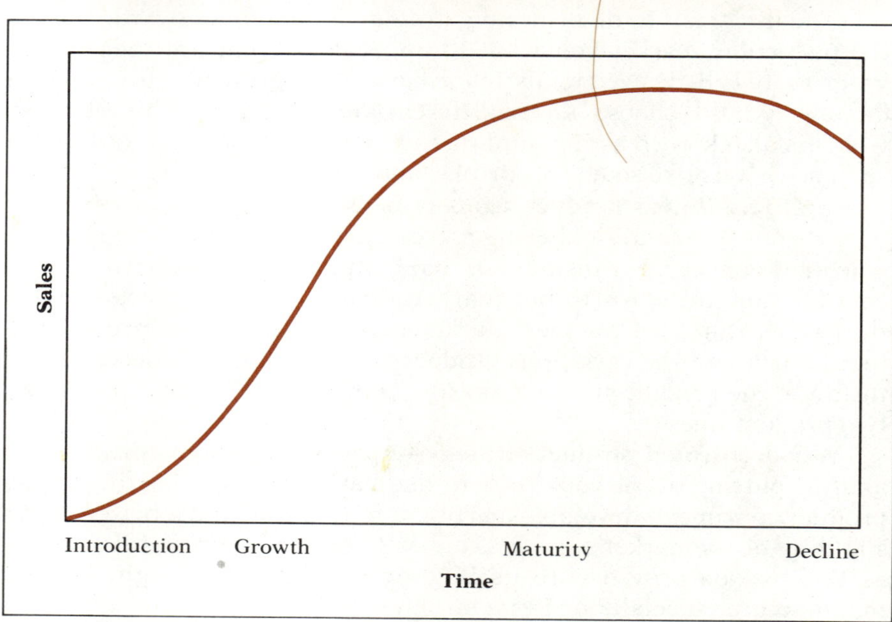

Highlight TSS Tragedy — A Shock for Procter and Gamble

As you will read in the Application of this chapter, Procter & Gamble has over the years become one of the world's most powerful marketing forces with sales of $10.8 billion in fiscal 1980. Procter & Gamble has built consumer confidence through aggressive marketing, quality products, and extensive consumer advertising. This consumer confidence was shaken to its very roots in September, 1980 when the Federal Food and Drug Administration linked tampon use, particularly Procter & Gamble's *Rely*, to increased risk of Toxic Shock Syndrome, a sometimes fatal illness. Within a week of this revelation, Procter & Gamble pulled *Rely* off store shelves. Days later Procter & Gamble offered consumers refunds and pledged to donate its research expertise to the Center for Disease Control to investigate TSS. Finally, P & G launched a massive multi-media advertising campaign warning women of the possible hazards of *Rely*. This decision could result in a write-off of $75 million.

Unlike previous controversies, including the Firestone 500 Tire and the Ford Pinto, in which the manufacturer of those products kept them on the market long after consumer groups, government agencies, and law suits had attacked them, Procter & Gamble in effect "demarketed" in a number of days a product that it spent sixteen years developing. This action could have major implications for future corporate liability and marketing strategies in the 1980s.

In spite of the strong and prompt action taken by Procter & Gamble, a number of law suits were filed stating that the product was unsafe and defective. While P & G's actions were hailed generally as a responsible move, nonetheless, the question remains . . .Why was *Rely* put on the market in the first place?

The growth stage of the product life cycle occurs as the product gains in market acceptance and awareness. As more people see home computers in their friends' houses and become aware of their advantages, more may be inclined to buy them. In the growth stage of a product, a firm is constantly increasing production facilities and marketing efforts in order to both stimulate and keep up with demand. However, competitors see the same potential for sales and come up with an alternative. Soon competition for customers drives down the price of the product as well as the profits.

Over time, the product matures, and a large portion of the potential market buys it. Thus a firm becomes interested in developing a market for repeat sales, replacement sales, or expanded sales. Sometime, most of the households interested in home computers will have bought one. As competition drives down the price, it may become possible for a family to have two computers. This is the case now with extension phones.

Finally, the product may decline because demand decreases. The rate at which the product declines could be influenced by a number of factors. For example, sudden technological development could render a product obsolete within a matter of months. The advent of pocket calculators drove slide rules from the market in less than a year.

The span of time between initial introduction and final decline is unique for each product. The hula hoop rose and fell in a very short time. But after decades, the automobile is still in the maturity stage. Black-and-white televisions are on the decline side of the product life cycle, but nylon has had its product life cycle extended several times as new applications have been discovered.

By maintaining a mix of products, each in a different stage of the life cycle, and by constantly attempting to introduce new and competitive offerings, businesses may be able to maintain their long-range success. If all their products are mature or entering the decline stage, they will eventually be driven out of business unless they take fast steps to develop and introduce new products.

A Marketing Example

Imagine that you are a young entrepreneur with a good engineering background. You have been working on a problem for quite some time: how to develop a television set that shows three-dimensional pictures. You feel that, given the vast number of television viewers in the marketplace, the introduction of three-dimensional television has enormous sales potential. You decide to take a survey of television users, to see whether they would be interested, and the response is beyond all reasonable expectation. If this survey is any indication of the true market, you could become a millionaire within three years.

Late one night, you achieve your technical breakthrough. Although your set only projects in black and white, you feel that will be no problem—considering its novelty. You quickly patent the processes required and contract out to a television manufacturing firm for the production of the new set, which you decide to call the three-dom set.

Who would be the first buyers for your new set? Your survey indicated they would have an annual salary of over $25,000 per year, probably one or more children, and in all likelihood a high degree of technical training. Since you know that it is important in the introductory stage to provide the target market with information, you take out ads in technical journals and popular magazines that engineers are most likely to buy, like *Popular Mechanics* and *Popular Science.*

You decide that your new company will initially follow a concentrated market strategy. First of all, the product is so new that it would be pointless to offer several different types. Besides, you realize that the expense involved in producing more than one type of three-dom set could bankrupt you. You hope to adopt a differentiated strategy and offer different models as the product gains in popularity.

You also realize that you do not yet have the production capacity to market to a large area, and so you decide to restrict your market to one or two large cities, where a few stores can serve a large number of new customers. As a specialty good, your new television would be sought after by those truly interested in buying it, and this allows you, initially at least, to take your own financial constraints into consideration.

Finally you have manufactured enough sets to start sales. The response is beyond belief! You instruct the manufacturer to work overtime to produce sets, but it still cannot keep up with demand. Soon word of your new set spreads to other cities, and you are swamped with orders.

You take out a loan from the bank in order to finance a large new manufacturing plant. Soon the plant is humming, and you are selling the three-dom sets like hotcakes. And now that the novelty of the set is wearing off, more customers are beginning to ask for different options, like remote control or variety in color and design. Soon you are marketing a line of three-dom sets, and everything is going smoothly.

Now that you are well on your way to becoming a millionaire, you buy yourself a home in Florida and hire enough people to take care of your business while you bask in the sun. You feel pretty good—even invincible—and lose touch with your customer.

But your competiton does not. One company has found that consumers have an overwhelming desire for color, and it has been working hard to develop a set that projects in color. Soon the breakthrough comes, and your competition begins to market the color set. The new technological innovation has the potential of driving you out of business altogether. Unless you awaken from your success-induced dream world, your competition will undermine your business. Your three-dom set may well be in the decline of its product life cycle.

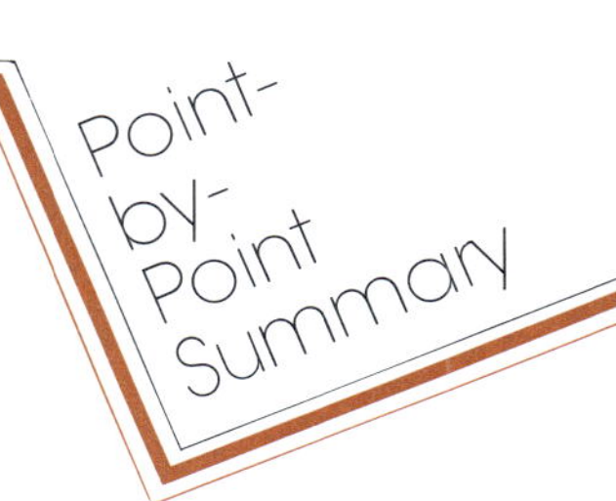

- Since modern businesses must produce on a large scale in order to survive, it is important for companies to try to determine whether their products can be sold.
- Companies like to identify specific segments of the population that they can aim their advertising to. The population can be segmented according to geographic location, demographic characteristics, and family life cycle.
- People purchase goods to fulfill their needs, which are dependent on station in life, upbringing, cultural background, and the like. These characteristics are identified through consumer surveys.
- A purchase may be made after careful consideration of its advantages and disadvantages or on an impulse. Marketers attempt to understand the decision-making process so that they can direct their appeals successfully.
- Since production takes place in anticipation of consumer demand, it is important to be able to forecast what sales can be expected to be. Such a forecast can be based on mathematical and statistical formulations or can involve a consumer survey or test marketing.
- Once it is determined that a product has a market, it must be properly classified and structured to meet consumer needs. As the product goes through its life cycle, the marketing process changes to reach the appropriate consumers.

1. Why is it so important to segment the market? Give two examples (not mentioned in the chapter) of a product being structured toward a specific segment of the market.
2. What factors do you think influence the consumer's choice of a product?
3. What kind of purchases is the average person likely to make on an impulse?
4. Why do most marketing experts prefer to use a test market to predict sales? What do you think should be an essential characteristic of such a test market?
5. What are the advantages of classifying products as convenience goods, shopping goods, or specialty goods? Give two examples of each type of goods.
6. You may have noticed how businesses come up with newer versions of old products. At which stage of the product life cycle do you think they do this?

APPLICATION

The story of Procter & Gamble is a story of the success achievable when consumer needs and product characteristics are both considered in determining a firm's final marketing strategy. Procter & Gamble combined the two from the very beginning.

The Procter & Gamble Company

PRODUCTS AND MARKETS

Procter & Gamble was founded in 1837 in Cincinnati, a bustling river port of 25,000 and home to James Gamble, soapmaker, and William Procter, candlemaker. There are several stories about how they decided to work together, but the most likely one involved Alexander Norris, father-in-law to both men. It was probably through his efforts that they formed a partnership. Norris was convinced that the business was a natural, since both men relied on common raw materials—fats and oils.

William Procter

Gamble and Procter proved to be a good team from the start. They were honest and willing to work. They shared the same heritage, both having immigrated to Cincinnati from the British Isles. James Gamble ran the factory, and William Procter ran the office or store. Early in the morning, Gamble would travel through Cincinnati collecting meat scraps and wood ashes to make the lye essential for soap and candles. He paid for them with barter in the form of small cakes of soap. As success made it necessary to collect more raw materials, kitchens throughout Hamilton and Butler counties, and even Indiana, were tapped for the meat scraps and wood ashes used in Procter & Gamble products.

At this time, grocers' shelves were practically the only advertising a product received, and the trademark might be the only advertising message. Many bulk products did not have a visible brand name at all. Procter & Gamble's soap was shipped in crates. To help them identify the boxes, wharf hands marked them with a simple X. This X was later embellished with a circle around it and eventually with a cluster of thirteen stars and a quarter moon, drawn as a human profile. This identification became the first standard trademark adopted by the company.

At first Procter and Gamble didn't realize the importance of

James Gamble

their trademark. In an attempt to simplify the design, they removed the man in the moon, but word soon arrived that a shipment of Procter & Gamble star candles had been rejected by a merchant for fear that they were imitations. The mark had come to mean quality, honesty, and integrity.

Although honesty and quality were important, the desire to meet consumer needs is what assured Procter and Gamble of their marketing success. Later products introduced by Procter & Gamble followed in this tradition. The introduction of Tide in 1947 was the result of over twenty years of research into how to make a better laundry soap—one that was insensitive to hard minerals in the water, did not generate "soap curd," and left clothes clean. Tide was an immediate and overwhelming success because Procter and Gamble had found a consumer need and satisfied it with a quality product at an affordable price. Other products introduced by Procter & Gamble with similar success include Crest toothpaste, Head & Shoulders shampoo, Pampers disposable diapers, Bounty paper towels, and Bounce antistatis laundry aids.

CAREER OPPORTUNITIES

Procter & Gamble pioneered the technique of brand management, in which market responsibility for each brand is placed in the hands of one manager, who then focuses all of his or her managerial and marketing skills on just that one brand. This allows products to be marketed independently from one another and assures that each brand is backed by the kind of single-minded drive it needs to succeed.

As a new employee in training for brand management, you would immediately be assigned broad responsibilities, including sales promotion or packaging, for a specific brand. You could monitor your brand's promotion budget, track the progress of a special test market, or develop sales promotion and display materials. As you developed your skills, you would move to one of Procter & Gamble's sales districts for three to five months, in order to get a broad understanding of how Procter & Gamble's products are merchandised.

After this training, you would return to the home office as an assistant brand manager of an entirely new product and face an entirely new set of challenges. If you showed the potential to assume the position of brand manager, you would be responsible for a total marketing effort. Success as a brand manager is determined by sales alone. Obviously, brand managers require creativity, intelligence, resourcefulness, leadership, and self-discipline, as well as confidence in their own ability. Those who are successful at Procter & Gamble get a unique feeling of personal achievement.

FOR DISCUSSION

1. Why is a brand name important? Would you purchase a no-brand product from the supermarket instead of a more expensive brand-name product? Give your reasons.
2. It is argued that marketing means not only meeting the needs of customers but also creating new needs. What do you think about this view?

12

OBJECTIVES

- ☐ To enumerate the factors that must be considered by manufacturers in setting the prices of their products
- ☐ To explain the role that manufacturing and other costs play in the pricing decision
- ☐ To explain how manufacturers price their products in order to compete effectively with competitors
- ☐ To explain how consumer demand can influence the pricing decision
- ☐ To predict the effect of the general economy on pricing strategy
- ☐ To determine how pricing strategies would differ for new and existing products

OUTLINE

ARTICLE *Where Does Your Money Go?*

THE COSTS OF PRODUCTION
Price, Volume, and Profitability
Fixed and Variable Costs
Total Costs
The Break-Even Point

SETTING PRICES
Demand-Oriented Pricing
Competitive Pricing
Product Line Pricing
New Products versus Established Products

PRICING CONSIDERATIONS
Economic Conditions
Special Prices
Psychological Pricing

NEGOTIATION AND COMPETITIVE BIDDING

APPLICATION *Bristol-Myers Company*

KEY TERMS

BREAK-EVEN POINT
CASH DISCOUNT
COMPETITIVE BIDDING
COMPLEMENTARY GOODS
COST-ORIENTED APPROACH
DEMAND-ORIENTED PRICING
FIXED COST
LIST PRICE
LOSS LEADER
MARKET PRICE
NEGOTIATED PRICE
ODD-FIGURE PRICING
PENETRATION STRATEGY
PRESTIGE PRICING
PRICE WAR
PROMOTIONAL PRICE
QUANTITY DISCOUNT
SKIMMING
TOTAL COST
TRADE DISCOUNT
VARIABLE COST

PRICING

Where Does Your Money Go?

MARK MEHLER
Country Music,
March 1980
Vol. 8; No. 6, p. 22-23.

A survey by a leading music industry trade magazine revealed that the average sale price of a current album ($7.98 list) is $5.90. The actual disc-shaped hunk of PVC (polyvinyl chloride) that the record is made of, and the jacket and sleeve that cover it, are worth a total of *under 65c*. Any record buyer being squeezed by the recent rash of record retail price hikes has a right to wonder what happens to the remainder of the $5.90 cash investment.

Ask a record company president (he's probably hoarse already from defending his pricing policies), and the answer you'll get is that the rest of the money goes to "merchandising," "marketing," "artist development," and "production." Ask what all that means, and you'll probably get another answer that will be even more nebulous. The following, then, is an attempt to put some sense into where the dollars and cents go in the $3 billion American record business.

The starting point for this discussion of high finance must be the artist himself (or herself). Let's consider an imaginary performer, Orange Blossom, a top country singer whose recent success on the pop charts has brought her into the world of big bucks. First, she has a "production deal" with Larry Lendo, a producer who has been credited with turning her career around. Every 12-18 months, when it's time to record a new Orange Blossom album, the two are given an "advance," or a "production allowance" by Blossom's record company. Out of that allowance of, say, $100,000, the artist and her producer must pay all their recording costs. These include studio rental averaging $150 to $200 per hour, union wages for studio musicians ("sessionmen"), raw equipment costs, mixing and remixing expenses, and hotel and food bills for the crew while recording sessions are underway.

Hopefully, out of that $100,000, the two will pay the excess out of their own pockets. (Since Orange is a superstar, the record label will pay the overrun).

Under terms of their deal with the record label, Orange and Lendo are to be paid an artist "royalty." This is figured as a percentage of the list price of every record sold over the counter. (A 10% 'container charge' is usually deducted off the top, mean-

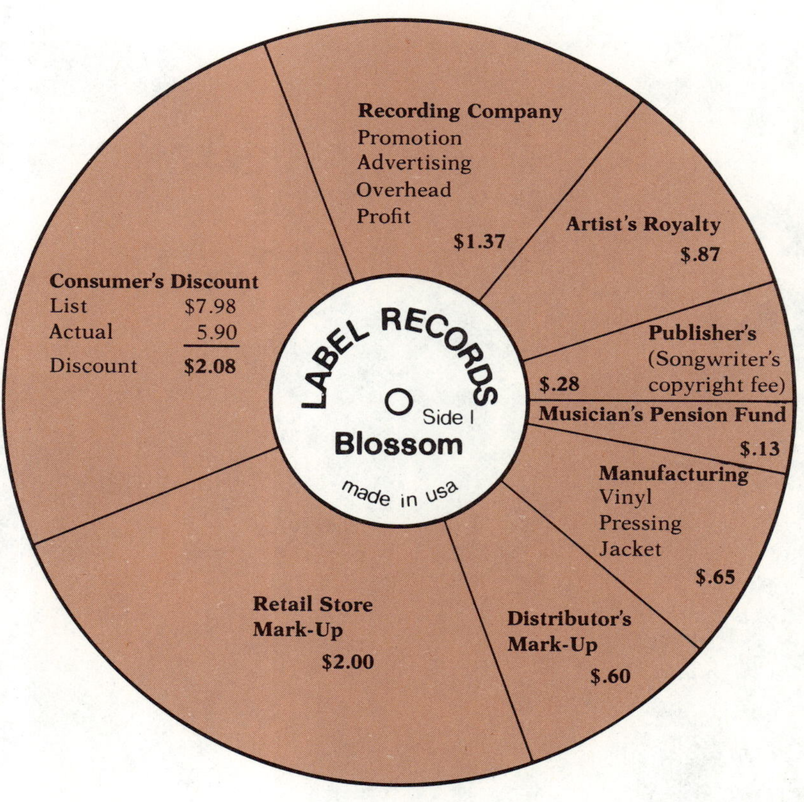

ing the $7.98 list price is actually computed at about $7.20). A superstar like Orange is getting 12% (8% for her, 4% for Lendo), or 87c for every record purchased.

There is, however, one snag. Orange and Lendo collect not one penny of that royalty until the $100,000 advance is repaid to the label. In other words, at 87c per copy, Orange Blossom must peddle about 115,000 LPs *before* reaping the fruits of superstardom. Of course, superstars generally sell 500,000 to 2,000,000 copies every time. If Orange's LP goes "gold" (500,000), she will net a total royalty of $334,500 (385,000 LPs × 87c).

Other royalties are also paid on every American album. The authors of the songs and their publishers are paid a legal rate of 2.75c per song (if Orange had written her own material, she could have supplemented her income nicely). Figuring an average of 10 songs per LP, about 28c in total writing royalties are distributed on every album. Finally, add about 13c in total royalties per LP for the pension funds of the musicians' unions.

All together, royalty payments on the Blossom disc amount to $1.28 (87c + 28c + 13c) of the $5.90.

Once the record has been mastered in the studio, it must be pressed into vinyl discs and stuffed into a sleeve (sometimes called "inner sleeve") and jacket. Prior to 1970, these factory costs amounted to less than 40c per disc. However, the three major raw material ingredients that go into the manufacture of a record have skyrocketed in cost. First, there's labor, then utilities to run the pressing machines (remember the Arabs?); second, there's the vinyl itself; and third, there's paper (cardboard) for the jackets and sleeves. Today, total manufacturing costs run about 65c per disc, and continue rising with the falling of each tree and the gushing of each oil well.

The next major cost of getting a record from the musician's mind to your stereo is the middleman's cost of distributing the LP from factory to store. The distributor generally works on a 15% profit markup. He will pay about $3.45 for the new Orange Blossom LP and sell it to a chain of record retail stores for about $3.90. Tiny "mom and pop" record stores will have to buy the Blossom album from a "one stop," a middleman who caters to low volume operations, and charges about $4.25 per disc. Assuming that you the consumer, purchase the Blossom LP from a large retailer, figure that 60c of your $5.90 goes to distribution expense. And assume that another $2 of your investment goes to the retailer's "gross profit" (the difference between the $5.90 retail price and $3.90 wholesale cost). A $2 profit may seem like a lot, but considering the high cost of the retail business today (salaries, rent, utilities, etc.) that 35% gross margin is just about enough to keep his store afloat.

So far, then, we've accounted for roughly $4.53 of the retail price. The rest of the $5.90, or about $1.37, goes to the father of it all, Blossom's record company. Out of that $1.37 comes funds for advertising (radio, TV, and print), promotion (the people who visit radio stations to get the records played), press parties, in-store merchandising tools (murals, posters), and a host of other in-house costs.

Perhaps, when all is said and done, the record company will realize a net profit-to-sales-margin of 10% (60c to 70c per disc). In the case of Orange Blossom, the money expended for advertising, promotion, and press parties will yield returns at the cash register. However, lesser lights who don't sell big numbers, will not even recoup the initial production costs. Clearly, at a unit profit of only about 60c an LP, the record company must rely on Orange Blossom and the rest of its "monster" sellers to balance the failures and make its corporate balance sheet read pleasantly at year end.

Already, industry executives and retailers are predicting a $1 increase in list price (and sale price) in the next year. They cite rising royalties, production costs, and advertising rates as the prime culprits. As these cost hikes are well documented, the buyer is better off pondering his own pockets than crying 'thief' at the record labels. If you, the buyer, decide that $5.90 or $6.90 is a reasonable price for a record, at least you'll know who's getting what.

Reprinted Courtesy Country Music Magazine

This chapter discusses some of the strategies used in determining the price of a product.

The price you are willing to pay for a product is a direct reflection of the value you place on it. In most circumstances, you will not buy a product unless you feel that the value you can get from its use is greater than its cost. As a consumer, you can either accept or reject the price of a product—by buying or not buying it.

The matter of prices is not so simple for businesses, however. Obviously they want to make some money, so their prices must reflect the costs of production. But if they charge too much, relatively few people will buy, especially if there is a lot of competition in the market. If they charge too little, they may encourage a lot of buyers, but they will not make enough money to cover costs. The pricing decision varies in importance with the type of product being sold, but it always has the potential of making or breaking a venture.

The Costs of Production

The price of a product is generally in line with the cost of producing it. A business that relies primarily on production costs as a basis for determining prices is using a **cost-oriented approach.** By focusing on costs, a business guarantees that—if nothing else—it will at least recover the costs of production.

PRICE, VOLUME, AND PROFITABILITY

Assume that your business sells one steel press a year at $100,000 and that it costs $95,000 to make. You are left with a profit of $5,000 per year. Now assume that you sell a different product, mousetraps at $1 each. They cost 95 cents to make, leaving a profit of 5 cents on each mousetrap sold. Which would you rather be selling?

At first glance, you might prefer to sell the steel press. But what if you can sell 100,000 mousetraps and only one steel press in a year? You would end up with the same profit—$5,000. Now which would you prefer? Perhaps it would take less work to sell one steel press a year, but you may have a better chance of increasing sales on the $1 product. In a good year you might be able to sell 200,000 mousetraps, at a profit of $10,000. Now which product would you rather produce?

In sum, the volume of sales can affect how much money a firm makes. Supermarkets use this principle, selling in large volume at a small profit margin. And oil companies make only about 3 to 5 cents on each gallon of gas, although they sell a lot of gas.

Naturally, the number of mousetraps you can sell depends to a great extent on the price you charge. The law of demand, introduced in Chapter 2, states that lower prices lead to higher sales. The problem is that lower prices mean lower profits—unless volume increases substantially. When volume increases, production costs per unit are likely to go down, which may allow prices to be lowered even further.

Highlight How Fixed Is Fixed?

People tend to think of fixed costs as being associated with fixed capital. When a machine is in place, particularly a big one, the possibility of moving it seems low. However, General Motors Corporation found differently.

In 1974, after the problems of gasoline availability arose, automobile manufacturers attempted to come up with smaller, gas-saving automobiles. General Motors wanted to put six-cylinder engines into most of its cars, but tooling up for a six-cylinder engine would have required about $15 million and two or three years. The immediate dilemma could not be solved in this manner.

However, GM had once owned an assembly line for manufacturing six-cylinder engines. In 1968 it sold the assembly line—considered fixed capital—to American Motors Corporation, which moved it and used it until late 1971.

GM bought back the six-cylinder production line from the Jeep Corporation, a subsidiary of AMC, for more than the $5 million that it had originally received. GM also incurred several million dollars' worth of additional expenses in moving, refurbishing, and changing the equipment to produce engines that conformed with new performance and pollution-control requirements. Nevertheless, buying and moving this "fixed" capital investment proved more economical than building one from scratch, particularly when the time factor was considered.

FIXED AND VARIABLE COSTS

Most businesses that own a production plant did not pay the full price for it in cash but rather took out a mortgage from the bank. They are paying the cost of the plant back to the bank over time. Say that it costs you $100,000 each month to repay the mortgage on your hypothetical plant. That $100,000 is a **fixed cost,** since it does not change. Whether you produce one steel press in your plant or 100,000 mousetraps, you will still face a monthly charge of $100,000.

Variable costs are those that vary with the number of units produced. The cost of raw materials would be one such cost. If you don't produce any mousetraps, you don't have to pay for any wood or steel springs. The more mousetraps you produce, however, the more wood and springs you have to buy, and so your variable costs increase. Another cost that increases with production is labor costs. The more the hours of production, the more money that must be paid to the workers who produce the product.

TOTAL COSTS

A firm's **total costs** of production are equal to its fixed costs plus its variable costs. A business that knows its total costs can more easily set a price for its product. Suppose that your firm has fixed costs of $100,000 per month. (The band across the bottom of Exhibit 12.1 represents these fixed costs. Variable costs, however, depend on the number of units you produce:

$$\text{Variable costs} = \text{Number of units sold} \times \text{Cost per unit}$$

If you produce 20,000 mousetraps, the variable costs would be 20,000 times 95 cents, or $19,000. (Exhibit 12.1 shows how these costs increase as production increases.) So the total cost for 20,000 mousetraps would be $100,000 plus $19,000, or $119,000.

THE BREAK-EVEN POINT

Once you know the total costs, you are very close to being able to determine how many units your firm has to produce or how much it has to charge per unit in order to stay in business. This is known as the **break-even point.** If analysis of the break-even point shows that a firm cannot possibly sell enough or charge a high enough price to cover its costs (and make a profit), it is best for the company to remove that product from the market—unless it feels that consumers will perceive the benefits of a particular product as being worth a higher price at a later date.

As an example of how the break-even point is calculated, let's reconsider your mousetrap business. If you charge $1 (the going market price) for every mousetrap you sell, you would have to sell 119,000 units to cover total costs of $119,000. Your total revenue would be the price ($1) times the quantity (which we are trying to figure out).

If you want to know how many mousetraps you would have to sell at the going price of $1 in order to cover all of your costs, you would have to use this formula:

$$\text{Total Revenue} = \text{Total Costs}$$

This translates into

$$\text{Price} \times \text{Quantity} = \text{Fixed costs} + \text{Variable costs}$$

Substituting the figures we know, we get

$$\$1 \times \text{Quantity} = \$119{,}000$$

Thus the quantity of mousetraps that your firm has to sell in order to stay in business is

EXHIBIT 12.1 Break-Even Point between Profit and Loss

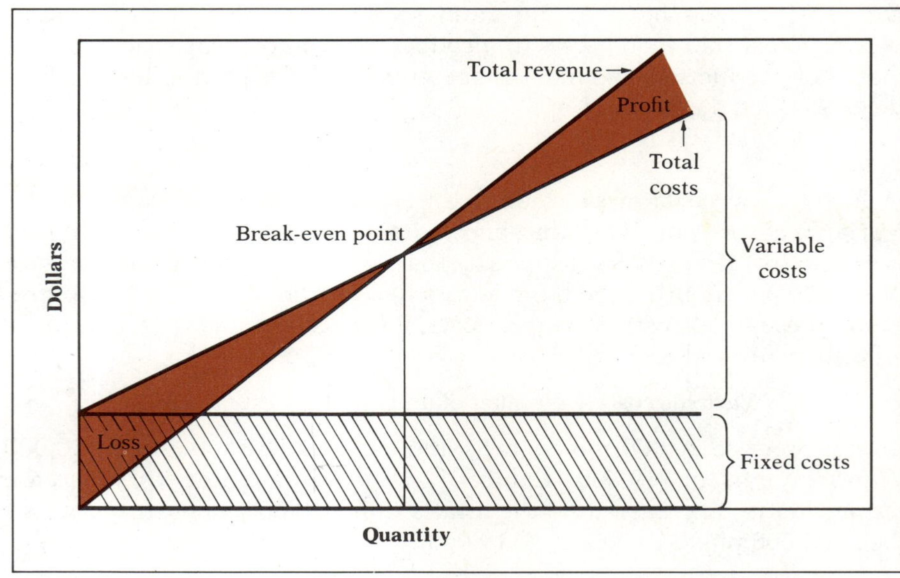

$$\text{Quantity} = \frac{\$119{,}000}{\$1} = 119{,}000$$

This is a fairly simple formula, but the expenses a real business faces are much harder to determine. In fact, it is often difficult to determine which costs are truly fixed or variable. Nevertheless, this formula can be quite helpful in determining the lowest acceptable volume of sales.

But how can you determine what price to charge using this formula? If sales projections indicate that you can sell 100,000 mousetraps, you could figure the price you would have to charge to stay in business as follows:

$$\text{Price} \times \text{Quantity} = \text{Total costs}$$
$$\text{Price} \times 100{,}000 = \$119{,}000$$
$$\text{Price} = \frac{\$119{,}000}{100{,}000} = \$1.19$$

Now you have a starting point for figuring a price.

Setting a Price

The final price for a product is set only after careful consideration of a number of interacting factors. For example, longstanding customer expectations may prevent price hikes. Lowering prices may instigate a price war, which can be costly to all the competitors. In the final analysis, a price is not just a magic number pulled out of a hat or an arbitrary figure set in the board room but rather the result of many interacting variables.

DEMAND-ORIENTED PRICING

The pricing method that takes into consideration the value that consumers place on your product is **demand-oriented pricing.** In its simplest form, demand-oriented pricing suggests that you charge a higher price when demand is high and a lower price when demand is low. This type of pricing is used by the telephone companies and electric companies, which raise their rates during periods of high use. This practice is an attempt to try to spread use over the entire day instead of concentrating it within only five or six hours. The higher price for peak use is an attempt to reflect the higher costs of providing the service to many users at once. Even then, demand-oriented pricing may not accurately assess the true costs. Hence it is not a purely cost-oriented approach to pricing.

COMPETITIVE PRICING

It is quite possible that a business that is trying to enter a market will have to face the existing price for a similar product. If that business is to compete at all, it will have to take its competitors' prices into account. This is not to suggest that charging the same price is the only option.

Depending on its market strategy, the new business may charge less or more than the going price.

Perhaps the strategy is to undercut the competition. This would mean producing and selling a competitive product at a lower price. However, if the price is set too low, the product may be burdened with an image of inferior quality. On the other hand, a price too close to competitors' may not be enough of a difference to sway consumers to the new product.

A higher price might be justified by a good reputation or special expertise, an approach called **prestige pricing.** Examples are Rolls-Royce automobiles and Curtis-Mathes television sets. Perhaps a firm's engineers have spent an inordinate amount of time developing a truly topnotch product. The costs of this development must be reflected in a higher price, otherwise the firm may not make any profit. Of course, the first step might be research to ascertain that there is a significant market segment willing to pay the higher price for a quality product.

Over time, a customary or traditional price may have been established for a particular type of product, as for the old nickel candy bar and 10-cent soda pop. Businesses often go to great lengths to keep the price constant; for example, Bic pens sold for 19 cents for nearly ten years. One way to do this is to revise production facilities in order to lower production costs. Another way is to gradually change the product, as candy manufacturers did by reducing the size of candy bars.

PRODUCT LINE PRICING

A firm should not set the price for any one of its products without considering the possible effects on its other products. Suppose you offer a line of washing machines, one the economy model and the other the deluxe model. If you raised the price on your economy model to cover increased production costs, the price difference between the two may not be big enough to make much of a difference to consumers. They may decide to spend a little more for the deluxe model, in which case sales of the economy model would decline—but of course sales of the deluxe model would increase.

Now suppose that, instead of two washing machines, you manufacture one washing machine and one dryer. These are **complementary goods.** Chances are that customers who buy a washer will buy a dryer too. If you raise your price on the washer, sales of both the washer and dryer may suffer. Exhibit 12.2 diagrams the relationship.

The price charged for a product may also affect consumers' willingness to substitute one product for a competitor's. For instance, if the price of butter gets too high, customers may switch to margarine (see Exhibit 12.2). Similarly, the price of gasoline may affect sales of cars and motorcycles (although in opposite ways). Of course, it is entirely possible that if you raised the price on your economy model of washer, customers may not consider any of your washers at all. The price on the economy model may be too high compared to the competition's, and the price of the deluxe model may be just out of reach. A competitor

EXHIBIT 12.2 Pricing of Complementary and Substitute Goods

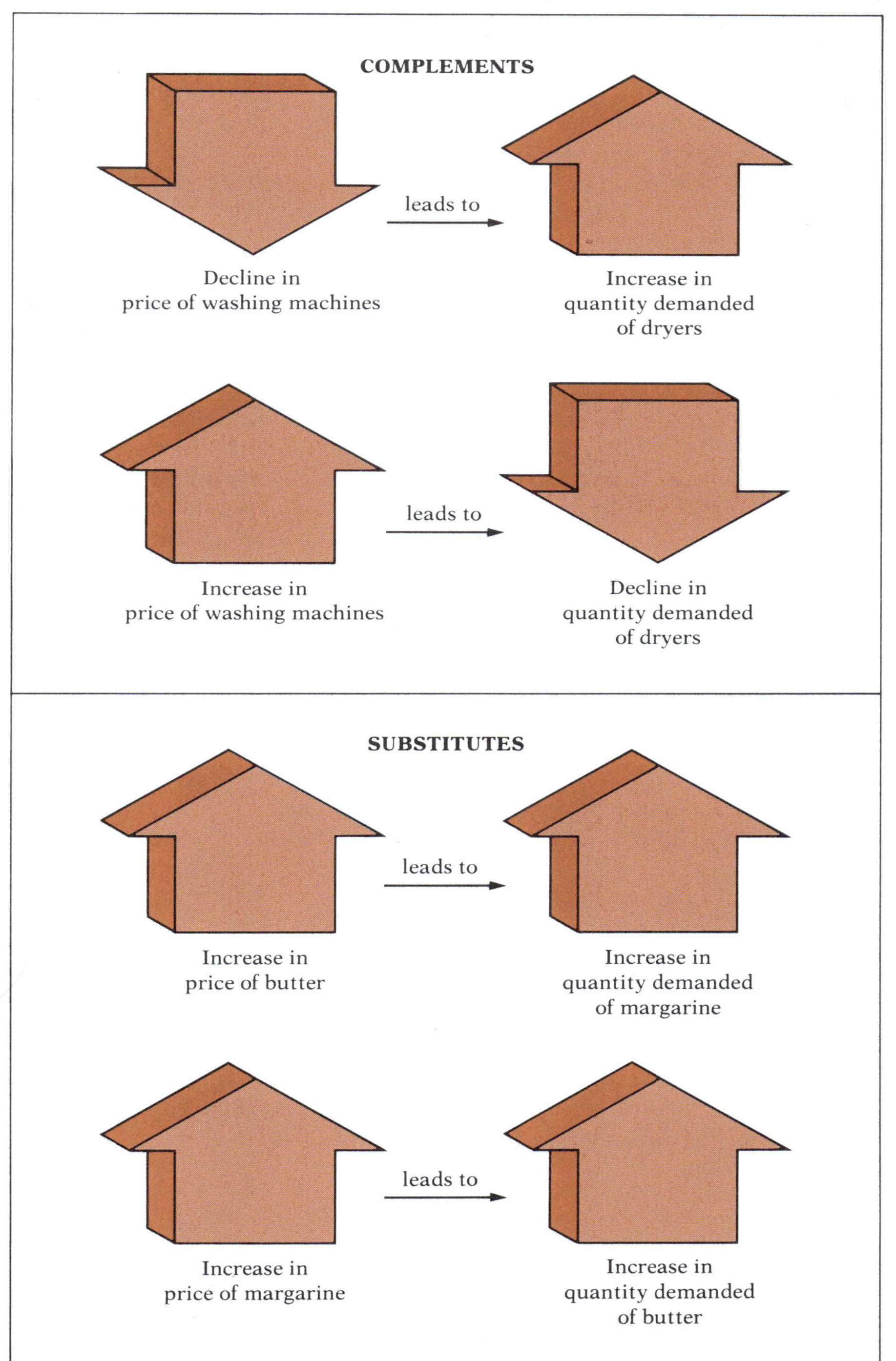

with a washer priced between these two may catch consumers who cannot decide which of yours to buy.

NEW PRODUCTS VERSUS ESTABLISHED PRODUCTS

Establishing an initial price for a new product is a tricky business, and it could well determine the long-range sales potential for the product. If potential customers think the price is too high, they may never look at the product again, even though the price may have been lowered. Prices put on established products, on the other hand, require fine tuning in response to changes in customer purchase habits, competition, product changes, and the environment.

The initial price a business sets on a new product depends on the strategy it wants to follow in gaining market acceptance. If a company has spent a lot of money on research and development of a new product, it may want to charge more at first to recover high development costs quickly, a strategy called **skimming.** Many people in the market may be willing to pay the higher price in order to be one of the first to own the product. When electronic calculators first came on the market, they cost around $200 each. Even so, enough people bought calculators to reduce the price rather quickly. Although skimming can be useful in developing high prestige, the high price encourages competition. Over time, as more competitors enter the market, the competition for customers drives the price down.

As an alternative, a firm may follow a **penetration strategy,** which affixes an initially low price to the product in order to gain quick market acceptance. In fact, sometimes new products are sold at a loss. If the type of product is relatively new, penetration pricing is very good at keeping competition out. If similar products are already offered by competitors, a penetration price can be quite effective in winning over some customers. Japanese automakers were accused of using this tactic in the United States during the 1980 recession. A problem with penetration pricing, however, is that as the price is raised to a more realistic level, a lot of former customers may rebel.

Pricing Considerations

Once a product has been established in the marketplace, several adjustments may still be required in the price. However, any price change should not be put into effect without careful consideration of the current economic environment and of the possible responses from competitors and consumers.

ECONOMIC CONDITIONS

The state of the economy may have an overall effect on the final prices that a company charges for its products. During a recession, a company may be less willing to initiate a price increase, however justified, for fear of alienating loyal customers and reducing sales. It may be better to

Highlight Do Business Firms Cause Inflation?

Consumers, labor leaders, government officials, and even business people often contend that business is responsible for our current bout with inflation, because it raises prices too fast. This is a theory of inflation, and since it is a theory, it should be subjected to empirical evidence. In other words, does it predict very well when we will and will not have inflation?

The answer is a resounding no. How can such a theory explain why we had no inflation in the 1950s, only a little bit in the early 1960s, but then quite a bit from the end of the 1960s into the 1980s? How does such a theory explain such periods in our history as the period prior to the end of the nineteenth century, when we had deflation—sustained drops in the average of all prices? The fact is that we are not dealing with a theory at all but rather an after-the-fact explanation, which may or may not be correct but which we can never disprove. If we were to tell you that rampant inflation was always caused by rising prices and that during times of little or no inflation businesses didn't raise their prices, you could not deny the validity of what we were saying.

So back to our initial question: Do businesses cause inflation? Yes, in the sense that inflation is defined as a time of rising prices. No, in the sense that we still don't have an accepted theory of why we have inflation in some years and not in other years.

suffer short-term losses in order to maintain the goodwill of the market, which is to any company's long-range advantage.

Even worse, a company's volume of sales may not be high enough during a severe downturn even to cover fixed costs. The choice is often to go out of business or cut prices. Fortunately, there is a good chance that cutting prices will allow the difference in profit to be made up, or at least covered, by increasing volume. Automobile manufacturers have used this device to increase sales during slump years, by offering factory rebates to customers who buy their cars. Very often the automobile dealers are overstocked with new cars and need to stimulate sales.

SPECIAL PRICES

A **price war** may break out when a business cuts prices to steal customers from the competition; the competition merely lowers prices even further. A price war can be quite costly if the low price persists over time. Because the competitors are selling at an artificially low price, they probably are not making much money. In fact, both might be losing money. Furthermore, customers may come to expect the low price. When the price war is over and prices return to their normal level, both competitors may experience serious declines in sales. For example, deregulation of the airline industry initially generated intense competition and reduced fares. However, such reductions could not be maintained for long, and fares have risen substantially since.

Even with these problems, small adjustments in the normal product price may be required. The **list price** is the price that a business quotes for its product; the **market price,** on the other hand, is the final price a consumer ends up paying. There are several options for lowering the market price, among them a **promotional price,** which is offered to increase sales on a particular item for a short period. Perhaps a new model of the product is coming out soon, or perhaps the product will spoil on the shelves if it is not sold. A retailing business might use a **loss leader,** a promotional price on one product that is meant to attract customers to the store to buy other products. A clothing store, for instance, may offer promotional prices on dress shirts in an effort to stimulate sales of ties, pants, wallets, or even shoes or a coat. The danger with promotional pricing is the same as with a price war or penetration pricing of a new product. Customers may come to link the lower price with the product and resist any attempts to change the price. Another danger is that customers may come into the store, buy the promotionally priced product, and leave. In this case, the reduced profit on the promotional item will not be made up with the sale of other products.

Industrial buyers tend to buy on credit instead of with cash. But because it may take a month or longer to receive the money for the sale, some companies offer **cash discounts,** percentage reductions in the list price, if a buyer pays its bill before a certain number of days have elapsed. This reduction in price is often justified by lower costs for billing and bad debts.

A manufacturer may also wish to offer **trade discounts** to wholesalers, if they assume part of the responsibility and added costs of storing the goods themselves. This trade discount often takes the form of a percentage off the list price, like a cash discount. Because they need not spend money on new storage buildings, manufacturers that use trade discounts may actually save in the long run.

Quantity discounts lower the per-unit cost in reverse proportion to the quantity bought; buying more means lower prices per unit. The rationale for these discounts is that sellers make more if they sell more. Quantity discounts can take one of two forms. A noncumulative discount is a one-time reduction in the list price of a product. For instance, for buying six boxes of fruit, a firm may give a 2-percent reduction in the list price. For twelve boxes, it may offer a 4-percent reduction. A cumulative discount is based on purchases over some period of time, usually a year. A business that has bought a certain number of products or paid at least a certain dollar amount is entitled to a refund. The cumulative discount is a very useful tool for encouraging patronage and repeat sales, since the more the customer buys, the more it saves in total costs.

PSYCHOLOGICAL PRICING

In retailing, prices are often adjusted to conform with consumers' images of products. As mentioned earlier, too low a price may convey an image of inferior quality, even though the product may be comparable to the competition's in all respects except price. With items like perfume, on the other hand, consumers often expect higher prices, since they connote high levels of quality and value. Psychological pricing attempts to reflect the expectations of consumers.

Odd-figure pricing is a particular form of psychological pricing. Re-

Highlight Cheap Product + High Price = Certain Profits?

Perhaps you have heard the story about a New York retailer who was having trouble unloading dollar bottles of perfume. He took them off the shelf for a month, put them back with a $10 price tag, and sold out immediately, making a killing. Sounds like an easy way to make a quick profit, doesn't it? Well, don't be so sure.

Presumably, the higher price of the product made it a prestige item. And its "snob" quality supposedly induced people to buy it at the higher price. But what did the retailer do to the quality of the product? Absolutely nothing. If, indeed, raising the price of the perfume caused more people to buy it, other retailers would buy exactly the same brand and set the price at, say, $9. Then some other retailer would set the price even lower. Eventually the price would go back down to $1.

The moral of the story is that you cannot create quality out of thin air. A prestige product is typically such because it offers certain quality characteristics that competing products do not. So the law of demand has not yet been refuted. At higher prices, all other things being equal, a lower quantity will be demanded. If you find something to the contrary, we would like to know about it, because that's the business we want to get into (and before anybody else finds out).

tailers feel that odd-numbered prices are more acceptable to consumers than even-numbered prices. You may consider $1 too much to pay for a toothbrush at one store but buy one at another store for 97 cents. Although odd-figure pricing is now a customary practice among stores handling consumer items, studies to test the effects of different prices have had conflicting results. In other words, changing the price to an unusual odd number may not really affect sales of a product.

Negotiation and Competitive Bidding

In such businesses as contracting or manufacturing large one-of-a-kind items, there may not be enough basis for comparison in the marketplace to set a price on the product. In fact, some of these businesses may not even produce the item unless they have specifically been requested to do so. For example, if you build houses, you may well build one-of-a-kind houses to meet people's particular needs. So how do you determine their price?

A **negotiated price** is one that buyer and seller agree on as a result of negotiations. A customer may agree to settle for only part of his or her dream house after you estimate how much it will cost. Eventually, you and the customer agree on a price and on what specific features you are to provide for that price.

Competitive bidding is used by companies and by governments to get cost estimates for projects they are proposing. They provide specifications, which describe the product or job to be performed, in order to help a firm determine potential costs. Once several firms have bid on the project, which could be the construction of a dam or the building of a warehouse, they usually select the lowest bid and give that firm the contract.

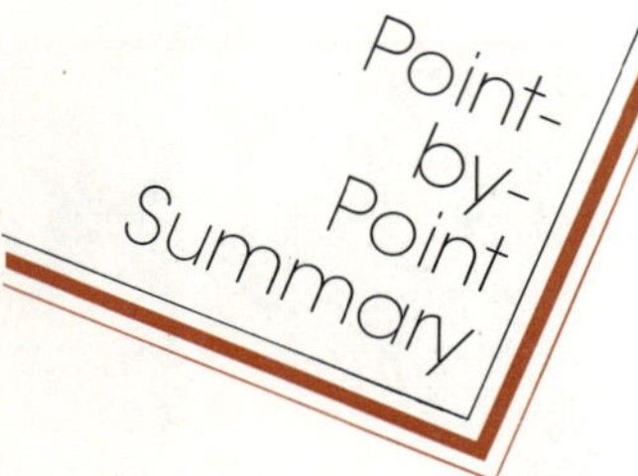

- The price you pay for a product is a reflection of the value you place on it. The correct price to charge for a product is determined by a number of factors, including production costs, customer demand, competition, the type of product, and economic conditions.
- A firm needs to charge a price that will, in the long run, cover production costs. Break-even analysis can be helpful in determining the volume that must be sold or the price that should be charged in order to cover costs.
- Customer demand for a product can be helpful in determining the price, since the greater the demand, the higher the value customers place on the product.
- Competitors' prices may affect the price of a product, because the seller can meet their price, undercut it to achieve market penetration, or charge a higher price to reflect greater value.
- The types of products offered by a firm affect its pricing policy, as the sales of complementary or substitute goods can be affected.
- The overall economic conditions faced by a firm may dictate pricing policy. Downturns in the economy may require lowering prices in order to sell enough to cover fixed costs. Or the need to maintain good customer relations may keep the price of a product constant, even though it should rise because of higher productions costs.
- New products' prices are set to coincide with the initial strategy the firm wants to use in gaining market acceptance. Skimming sets a high price initially, in order to recover research and development costs quickly. A penetration strategy sets a low price on the product when it is introduced, in order to gain quick market acceptance and to undercut competition.
- Established products' prices may need fine tuning over time. Promotional prices, cash discounts, trade discounts, quantity discounts, odd-figure pricing, negotiated prices, and competitive bidding are some of the methods that can be used.

1. Which costs should be considered in determining the price of a product?
2. Give one example of prestige pricing in the television-manufacturing and watch-making industries.
3. How do you think manufacturers would price their products in a recession, when demand for their products has fallen? What is the minimum that a manufacturer can charge in these circumstances?
4. Why is skimming not considered a long-term pricing strategy?
5. Do you believe that odd-figure pricing influences you when you go shopping? Are there some types of products for which this strategy can be more successful than others?

APPLICATION

Bristol-Myers Company

Bristol-Myers Company was founded in 1887 by William M. Bristol and John R. Myers. Their company was first named Clinton Pharmaceutical Company, but in 1900 the company became known by its present name. One of the first products successfully produced by Clinton Pharmaceutical Company was Clinton Salts, later renamed Sal Hepatica, stimulant laxative. In 1921 Ipana toothpaste was introduced, and by 1928 its profits exceeded those of Sal Hepatica. Advertising for these two products proclaimed, "Ipana for the smile of beauty, Sal Hepatica for the smile of health."

From 1930 on, Bristol-Myers distinguished itself by introducing Vitalis, Bufferin, Excedrin, and in the 1970s, Ultra Ban 5000, Tickle wide-ball antiperspirant, Clairesse (the first major development in hair coloring in seventeen years), Final Net, PreSun, Body-on-Tap, and Comtrex multisymptom cold remedy. One product pioneered by Bristol-Myers deserves special mention: Penicillin was first produced for the armed forces during World War II, by Bristol-Myers and other companies, but later it was manufactured by Bristol-Myers for public use. It is virtually indispensable today.

Although many of Bristol-Myers's products are consumer-oriented, the company is involved in two other major areas of research as well. In pharmaceuticals, Bristol-Myers expects to play a significant role in the 1980s in the production of prescription analgesics and in new products for cancer chemotherapy, hypertension and other cardiovascular diseases, and central nervous system disorders. In health care, Bristol-Myers is involved in medical equipment and devices, elderly nutrition, dental equipment, and infant formulas for supplemental nutrition and special nutritional problems.

William McLaren Bristol

John Ripley Myers

PRICES FOR PRODUCTS

With each new product, Bristol-Myers faces new pricing problems. The extensive amount of research that goes into the development of a new product, whether a new drug for consumer use or surgical tools for the operating room, makes the determination of a good price extremely difficult. The effects of potential competition and the state of the economy also influence the pricing decision.

Consider the attempt to recover high research costs using a skimming strategy. If the product is in a highly competitive market, the initially high price might alienate potential customers. Once they notice that the price on the new product is higher than the competition's, they may never compare prices again—even though the price becomes competitive after more of the product is sold. A penetration strategy may be just as risky. The lower price may guarantee initial market acceptance, but brand loyalty or consumer reluctance to try the new product may still inhibit sales volume. The result would be a loss on the product introduction.

Other considerations might affect the determination of a new product's price. When the new product faces no current competition, the price that is established must allow for potential profit in future sales but make the market as unattractive to new competition as possible. Another consideration might be the potential customer that the product is intended for. If you are marketing a nutritional supplement for the elderly, the price would necessarily have to reflect the lower buying potential of this fixed-income group. On the other hand, if the product is to be used for surgery, the final cost may not be so important as the long-term reliability of the product.

With each product, Bristol-Myers faces a different market, different competition, different users, and different product requirements. Nevertheless, Bristol-Myers has shown by its success that it can find the middle ground in the determination of prices. To give you an example of Bristol-Myers' pricing strategy, Exhibit 12.3 lists the prices of certain Bristol-Myers products and their competition, as displayed in a small drugstore in a midwestern town. The letters *B-M* indicate Bristol-Myers products, and the asterisks denote the product in each category that is selling best in that store.

CAREER OPPORTUNITIES

If you were to join Bristol-Myers as a new employee in the marketing department, you would most likely begin as an assistant product manager. You would be responsi-

EXHIBIT 12.3 Bristol-Myers' Competitive Pricing Strategy

Antiperspirants	
Ban Roll-on, 2.5 oz. (B-M)	$1.49
Secret Roll-on, 2.5 oz.	1.99*
Dry Idea Unscented	2.37
Pain Relievers	
Bufferin 100s (B-M)	$2.11
Excedrin 100s (B-M)	2.17*
Bayer Aspirin 100s	.99
Kitchen Aids	
Drano, 32 fl. oz. (B-M)	$1.24
Liquid Plumber, 32 fl. oz.	1.29*
Plunge, 32 fl. oz.	1.08
Shampoos	
Beer-enriched Body-on-Tap, 11 fl. oz. (B-M)	$1.97*
Head and Shoulders, 11 fl. oz.	2.67
Liquid Prell, 11 fl. oz.	1.69

ble for gathering information about new and existing products in order to help in the development of their marketing programs. You would be responsible for writing reports on any trends you observe from this research, as well as to maintain a familiarity with general market conditions.

In order to assist in the development of marketing programs, you would be responsible for interfacing with other departments besides marketing, such as finance, purchasing, graphics, promotion, market research, and sales. You would most likely be involved with others in the development, organization, coordination, and followup of these marketing assignments.

FOR DISCUSSION

1. Why do you think Bristol-Myers prices Excedrin at double the price of its competitor, Bayer aspirin?
2. Name some of the reasons why a manufacturer would disclose a reduction in price on the package.

OBJECTIVES

- ☐ To understand the need for some organization to mediate between the producer and the potential consumer
- ☐ To explain how wholesalers and retailers work together to make products readily available to consumers
- ☐ To suggest how a manufacturer could structure operations for efficiently moving the product closer to the consumer
- ☐ To explain the factors that would be involved in a manufacturer's decision to take over the role of middleman
- ☐ To evaluate how manufacturers would choose a marketing channel, depending on the nature of potential consumers

OUTLINE

ARTICLE *Japan: The Distribution Knot Strangling Consumers*

CHANNEL FUNCTIONS
Wholesaling
Retailing

PHYSICAL DISTRIBUTION
Transportation
Types of Transportation

VERTICAL INTEGRATION
Costs
Contractual Systems
Considerations in the Decision to Integrate

MARKETING CHANNEL STRATEGY

DISTRIBUTION STRATEGIES

APPLICATION *The Coca-Cola Company*

KEY TERMS

AGENT
AUCTION COMPANY
BROKER
CASH-AND-CARRY WHOLESALER
COMMISSION AGENT
COMMON CARRIER
COMPANY-OWNED WHOLESALER
CONTRACT CARRIERS
DROP SHIPPER
EXCLUSIVE DISTRIBUTION STRATEGY
FULL-SERVICE WHOLESALER
GENERAL-MERCHANDISE WHOLESALER
INTENSIVE DISTRIBUTION STRATEGY
LIMITED-FUNCTION WHOLESALER
LIST PRICE
MARKETING CHANNEL
NONSTORE RETAILING
PHYSICAL DISTRIBUTION
PRIVATE CARRIERS
RETAIL COOPERATIVE
SELECTIVE DISTRIBUTION STRATEGY
SINGLE-LINE WHOLESALER
SPECIALTY WHOLESALER
SUPERSTORE
TITLE
TRUCK JOBBER
VERTICAL INTEGRATION
WHOLESALER-SPONSORED VOLUNTARY CHAIN

MARKETING CHANNELS

Japan: The Distribution Knot Strangling Consumers

BUSINESS WEEK, September 18, 1978.

Japan's multi-tiered product distribution system not only confounds foreigners but also renders Japanese consumers among the world's wealthiest poor. To support multiple layers of overstaffed, often nepotistic middlemen, Japanese housewives pay 60¢ for a homegrown orange, $8.50 for a pound of discount beef (the regular price is $17 a lb.), and an incredible $36 for a fifth of Johnny Walker Black Label. For would-be exporters to Japan, the system—which employs some 8.6 million people—is an impenetrable web that frustrates efforts to deliver goods with a reasonable mark-up.

"We realize it is probably the worst in the world," concedes Takayuki Hazumi, Sumitomo Bank's senior economist. "But you can also argue that it is very necessary under present marketing conditions in Japan."

CASH AND TRADITION

Those conditions are uniquely complex. Because few of Japan's fiercely independent retailers have so far been edged out by supermarkets and department stores, wholesalers must provide rapid delivery of small quantities of goods, extend lengthy credit, stock a vast array of commodities tailored to Japanese tastes, and accept the risks of selling on consignment.

The sheer number of outlets is astonishing. With a gross national product last year that was one-third that of the U.S., and with only one-twenty-fifth the land area, Japan supports 1.61 million retail outlets, 6,000 more than in America. Average annual sales: $181,000 in Japan, $401,000 in the U.S. Serving the vast web of retailers are 340,000 wholesalers (vs. 370,000 in the U.S.), most employing fewer than 10 people.

Relationships along the chain of manufacturers, wholesalers, smaller wholesalers, and retailers are often like a family unit, with all levels interlocked not only by the cash nexus but by emotion and tradition. As one shocked foreign embassy official recalls: "A manufacturer told me recently that the recession forced him to cut off a distributor who had been handling his products for years. The man promptly killed himself. Understandably, the manufacturer is very hesitant about cutting off others. It's the Japanese way."

FOREIGN "LUXURIES"

Despite the difficulty the Japanese way imposes on foreign businessmen, some companies have managed to use existing channels via joint ventures or have set up their own networks. Among the more successful are Sears Roebuck, Olivetti of Japan, Estée Lauder, and Warner-Lambert Japan (Schick products). In some cases, a lean and hungry foreign distribution system has benefited Japanese consumers. With just 10% of the film market, Eastman Kodak's aggressive price-cutting earlier this summer—one of the first moves to pass along the gains of yen appreciation—forced rival Fuji Photo Film Co. and Konishiroku Photo Industry Co. to follow suit.

But imported goods still endure mark-ups that erase any price advantage. "Part of the problem," says a government official involved in stimulating imports, "is Japanese attitudes. They regard foreign goods as luxuries and give them as gifts. Retailers automatically mark them up because people don't want to give something cheap."

There are signs, though, that Japanese consumers might like to buy something cheap. In a rare display of militance on Aug. 23 Japanese housewives and labor unions began a petition campaign in Osaka demanding that importers pass along exchange profits. For the moment at least, they may as well have railed against the rising sun. Inefficient, and as overmanned as a bicycle built for 12, Japan's sprawling distribution system isn't about to be streamlined. Says one American executive in Tokyo: "If you expect to do business here, you get used to it. If you're a consumer, you'll pay the price for it in the market."

This article explains how Japan's distribution system complements the lifestyle and culture of its people. The following chapter describes the distribution system used in the United States.

Unlike their predecessors, modern businesses consider the entire country and possibly even the world as their market. It is good that they do so, because higher production costs force manufacturers to sell larger quantities of products in order to make a profit. But a larger market means more problems in getting products from manufacturer to consumer. Only rarely does a plant sell directly to consumers; usually products go through several hands before they are available for sale. The various paths that products may follow—**marketing channels**—are the subject of this chapter.

Channel Functions

Specialization over many years gave us businesses with different functions. Specialization of marketing channels occurred as well. Small businesses found they were not able to handle efficiently all of the tasks required to move products from the production site to the final consumers. Wholesaling in which a company acts as middleman between the manufacturer and retail store, developed as one specialization. Another was retailing which involves providing products for sale to consumers. Physical distribution has recently developed as a specialized marketing channel, as a result of high transportation costs and the potential for savings if efficient distribution methods are used.

WHOLESALING

How does a wholesaler help the overall distribution process? To answer that question, you need to take a look at the number of interactions that would be required of a group of manufacturers if no wholesaling function existed. If there are four manufacturers and four customers, as in Exhibit 13.1, each manufacturer would have to maintain contact with all four customers—a total of sixteen separate communication paths. But a wholesaler, a middleman, can buy from the four manufacturers and sell to the four customers. In other words, one wholesaler can represent four customers to one manufacturer and four manufacturers to one customer. Now only eight transactions are required. Imagine the savings in time and money if the number of plants were increased to 100 and the number of customers to 1,000. Wholesalers make the distribution of products much more efficient.

Wholesalers help in other ways, too. Manufacturing plants may not have much storage space. In fact, what storage space they do have they use to store the raw materials needed in order to produce a product. But wholesalers have little problem with storage. They can store products in their warehouses and take responsibility for their care until they are sold to retail stores. This saves manufacturers a lot of money; warehouses, like plants, represent a fixed expense.

Wholesalers are also very effective in breaking bulk. Suppose you are a retailer and you find that you are running low on a certain television set, say a portable model. If you had no wholesaler, you would have

Highlight Pity the Poor Middleman

As the name implies, a middleman participates in the middle of a transaction. Instead of selling directly to the consumer, a producer sells to a middleman. Despite the utility of this function, many people feel that anybody who profits from buying a product from a manufacturer and then selling it to a retailer is doing a disservice to society. In fact, many cooperative movements in the United States have attempted to eliminate the middleman's profits.

Believe it or not, middlemen may actually reduce the price of the products you want to buy. They stock the products of one or more suppliers in a warehouse and then sell them in smaller quantities to individual retailers. They set up a distribution system to service as many retailers as possible, providing those retailers with wholesale goods and information about those goods.

to order your portable TVs directly from the manufacturer. Would you be surprised when you found you could only order portable TVs in truckload quantities—and all you need is three! Fortunately, your wholesaler can order that truckload of portable TVs and deliver only three of them to you. When you consider that your retail store is likely to carry

EXHIBIT 13.1 Function of the Middleman

A. Before—Distribution from Producers to Consumers

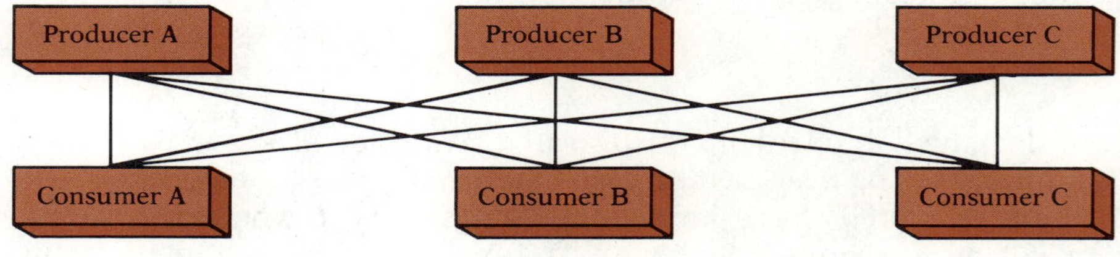

B. After—Distribution with a Marketing Intermediary Between Producers and Consumers

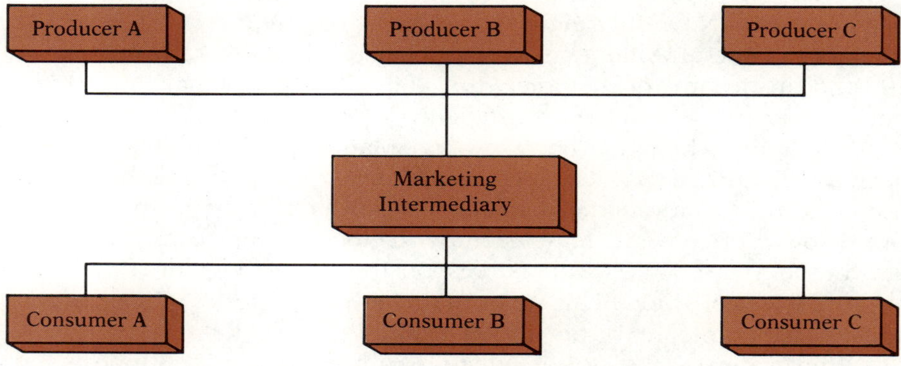

Adapted from Albert Wesley Frey, ed., *Marketing Handbook,* 2d ed. Copyright © 1965 The Ronald Press Company, New York.

many different types of television sets, you can really begin to appreciate the importance of the wholesaling activity. Instead of ordering from each separate manufacturer, all you have to do is order what you need on one form and send it to your wholesaler. Your wholesaler will select what you need, in the quantities you want, and ship the products to your store.

Types of Wholesalers

We have been talking of wholesalers as if there were only one type. However, in actual practice, there are several different types of wholesalers, although the differences are not substantial. Wholesalers can broadly be divided into full-service and limited-function wholesalers.

Full-service wholesalers provide all the important services mentioned previously as well as accept title to the goods. **Title** is a legal term meaning ownership. Once they receive goods from the manufacturer, full-service wholesalers accept ownership of them. The goods are then the property and responsibility of the wholesaler and not the manufacturer. There are several specific types of full-service wholesalers:

1. **General-merchandise wholesalers.** Handle a large assortment of nonperishable goods, such as drugs and cosmetics, and mainly serve drugstores, hardware stores, and the like
2. **Specialty wholesalers** Attempt to meet a specific demand and are willing to help retailers satisfy customers; normally deal in areas that require a certain technical or specialized knowledge; normally handle a limited range of related products—for example, mufflers and shock absorbers
3. **Single-line wholesalers** Restrict activities to only a few product lines—for example, paint or clothing

Limited-function wholesalers provide a limited variety of services. The important types are

1. **Cash-and-carry wholesalers** Handle the small retailers who cannot afford to pay for full services; do not deliver goods or grant any credit (all transactions are on a cash basis)
2. **Drop shippers** Collect orders from retailers and pass them on to manufacturers for direct shipment to retailers; have title to the goods but no physical contact with them
3. **Truck jobbers** Sell perishable goods in great demand—like candy—from a truck; normally serve small service stations and similar operations

Agents and Brokers

In contrast to wholesalers, **agents** and **brokers** do not take title to goods. They serve only to facilitate buying and selling and provide very few

Highlight "I Can Get It for You Wholesale"

You can't escape the jargon of the marketplace these days: *retail pricing, mark-up, wholesale pricing, factory-to-you savings*. Do these terms mean anything? Can you really save money by buying wholesale?

Most Americans buy primarily from retailers, those convenient "end-of-the-line" merchants. Naturally, retail customers pay full (retail) price. Why? Because retail pricing must not only cover the cost of the product but also the cost of overhead—staff, rent, floor displays, advertising, utilities—that the manufacturer or wholesaler does not pay. Although some wholesalers and manufacturers will not sell directly to the public, anyone who has the fortitude to penetrate the system can achieve considerable savings.

Consider the case of a customer in Ohio who wanted to reupholster a chair and found the ideal fabric in a sample book of fabrics. The retail cost of the fabric was $21.95 per yard. Hoping to save money, the customer contacted the fabric manufacturer in New York who told the customer that its textiles were sold only to wholesalers. The nearest wholesaler handling that particular fabric was in Philadelphia. But the wholesaler's story was the same—the company did not deal with the public, only retailers and occasionally interior designers. Undaunted, the customer located a local interior designer to act as intermediary and, after two months of persistence, was able to purchase 7½ yards of cloth. The wholesale price? $4.95 per yard. Just imagine what the manufacturer's price was.

Obviously, the more people involved in getting a product from the factory to the consumer, the greater the price. At each step in the production process, additional costs are incurred—and the consumer price is increased to absorb these costs.

services. Agents and brokers, who normally specialize in certain product lines, can be divided into the following categories:

1. **Auction companies** Provide a facility where buyers and sellers can meet to complete transactions, normally for such products as livestock and tobacco
2. **Commission agents** Normally situated in large cities and selling on behalf of agricultural producers at the best price over the stipulated minimum; remit the sales price less commission to the producers

Costs of Wholesaling

Of course, wholesalers do not perform these functions for free. When the manufacturer sells to a wholesaler, the wholesaler does not pay the **list price** (which the final consumer has to pay) but rather a lower figure. In other words, the wholesaler gets a trade discount when the wholesaler sells to the retailer, the price is still below the list price but is higher than the cost paid to the manufacturer. The difference is used to cover the wholesaler's expenses for storing, breaking bulk, and transportation, as well as for profit. The more functions a wholesaler performs, the more discount it will receive.

Retailing is by far the most visible of all marketing channels. Retailers like your neighborhood grocery store, drugstore, and department store offer products for final sale to consumers. As with wholesaling, the retailing function has evolved over time and includes several different types of outlets.

Types of Stores

Specialty stores offer a very select choice of products and normally concentrate on a particular product type and complementary goods. A fireplace store, for instance, specializes in all those products that are used in or around the fireplace—wood grilles, ash shovels, brooms, steel curtains, fireplace doors, perhaps even chimney flues. A lawn mower shop may carry only one manufacturer's lawn mowers or several competing brands. It might also carry complementary lawn-care equipment—shovels, spades, wheelbarrows, gloves, and the like. This particular store might even offer repair services for lawn mowers purchased there, in order to encourage purchases.

Department stores divide their products into several different departments, such as men's clothing, home furnishings, and stereo equipment. The purpose of this type of retailing is to provide consumers with a variety of "stores" under one roof so that they can satisfy most of their shopping needs in one place.

Supermarkets offer a variety of different types of food under one roof. Before the development of the supermarket, consumers were forced to do their food shopping at several different specialty stores. The supermarket, which brought produce, meat, breads, and so on under one roof, was an instant success. Instead of taking all morning to shop for food, consumers could get in and out of the store in a relatively short period of time.

The competitive advantage of convenience stores is location. By being near consumers and offering long store hours, they satisfy a number of shopping needs. They usually offer fast checkout and convenient parking for a small number of customers. Consumers may pay a premium price, but they gain convenience.

Discount houses offer products for sale at discount prices. They are able to sell their products more cheaply than some of their competition (namely, department stores), because they offer fewer customer services. Usually discount houses maintain a skeleton crew of cashiers and shelf-stockers, and the consumers are expected to serve themselves.

Superstores contain just about anything you could ever want or need, all under one roof. Somewhat like a department store, the superstore separates its different offerings, but it has more extensive product offerings in each department. Superstores basically try to provide consumers with all the items they purchase routinely, including supermarket items, fast foods, personal care products, alcohol, standard apparel, housewares, leisure goods, and lawn and garden materials.

Nonstore Retailing

Nonstore retailing is a form of retail sales—but without the use of stores. For example, door-to-door or house-to-house sales is grounded in the belief that consumers are more comfortable in their home and prefer to shop at home. By coming to consumers, house-to-house salespeople hope to get the jump on their competition. However, because some people feel unduly pressured by house-to-house salespeople, most states require a three-day "cooling-off" period for such sales. Exhibit 13.2 is a typical notice of cancellation to protect customers who decide within three days to cancel their orders.

Another type of nonstore retailing is mail-order sales. So-called "junk mail" is actually an effort to encourage sales by reaching consumers at home. Sometimes contests are organized, with prizes, to tempt customers to read the mailers. Since mail-order operations may not have the high overhead expense required to maintain a retail outlet, they may be able to offer their products at a reduced price. Also, companies like Sears augment their retail store sales with an extensive mail-order system.

A final type of nonstore retailing is the use of automatic vending machines. These machines, which can be put almost anywhere, bring the point of sale closer to consumers without incurring the expense of building a store and hiring clerks. However, the products offered by the vending machines are very often priced higher than they would be in a store, since a premium is associated with the convenience of having the product available nearby.

Physical Distribution

As the costs of transportation skyrocket, businesses give greater consideration to **physical distribution,** the movement of products from the producer to the final customer. New developments in all phases of physical distribution have made great cost savings possible. One example is the use of mathematical models to select the routes trucks are to take and the products they should take with them. The purpose is to minimize the number of trips and, hence, the costs.

Similar techniques help businesses locate their warehouses. The problem is to balance the fixed costs associated with each warehouse against the high variable costs of transportation. A business might decide to open new warehouses or to close some it already has in order to reduce overall warehousing expenses.

If a business has a number of warehouses and a large product mix, the costs of carrying inventory can be overwhelming. But if it carries too small an inventory, it may not be able to handle customers' orders. If it carries too great an inventory, it may suffer high "carrying" costs. Several mathematical models are available to help a business establish the best level of inventory for both serving customers and keeping carrying costs down.

The method used for handling and shipping orders can also greatly affect distribution costs. If one customer absolutely needs the shipment by next week and another expects a shipment in four weeks, it would be bad business to ship the second order ahead of the first. Although this example seems simple, the problem could be compounded greatly where 2,500 orders are processed in one week, with a choice among three different types of transportation (air freight, truck, train). Certain

EXHIBIT 13.2 Typical Notice of Cancellation

(enter date of transaction)

____
(date)

You may cancel this transaction, without any penalty or obligation, within 3 business days from the above date.

If you cancel, any property traded in, any payments made by you under the contract or sale, and any negotiable instrument executed by you will be returned within 10 business days following receipt by the seller of your cancellation notice, and any security interest arising out of the transaction will be canceled.

If you cancel, you must make available to the seller at your residence, in substantially as good condition as when received, any goods delivered to you under this contract or sale; or you may, if you wish, comply with the instructions of the seller regarding the return shipment of the goods at the seller's expense and risk.

If you do make the goods available to the seller and the seller does not pick them up within 20 days of the date of your notice of cancellation, you may retain or dispose of the goods without any further obligation. If you fail to make the goods available to the seller, or if you agree to return the goods to the seller and fail to do so, then you remain liable for performance of all obligations under the contract.

To cancel this transaction, mail or deliver a signed and dated copy of this cancellation notice or any other written notice, or send a telegram, to

____
(name of seller)

at ______________ not later than midnight of ______________________
(address of seller's place of business) (date)

I hereby cancel this transaction.

______________ ______________________
(date) (buyer's signature)

order-processing techniques can result in better customer service (always good for business) and lower costs (and better profits) to the firm.

TRANSPORTATION

Following commercial regulations, transportation companies are divided into three classifications:

1. Private Carriers
2. Contract Carriers
3. Common Carriers

A company that owns and operates its own transportation system for purposes of moving its own goods is categorized as a **private carrier.** These companies are not permitted to carry goods of another organization. Although the majority of private carriers use motor vehicles, other modes of transportation are frequently employed.

Contract carriers represent a group of companies that carry products on a selective basis for a limited number of customers. These companies enter into agreements with the companies for specific services. A contract carrier is not permitted to solicit business from the general public and does not maintain regular schedules or published rate structures.

The category most recognizable is the group of companies known as **common carriers** that offer their services to the general public. Government agencies and regulations carefully monitor and control the operation of these companies as their existence is often based upon government permission. Common carriers maintain regular service and form the backbone of business distribution.

TYPES OF TRANSPORTATION

Trains

Despite the continuing decline of the railroad industry in the United States, railroads still carry a greater percentage of goods than any other type of transportation. The reason for maintaining its leadership position is associated with the inherent flexibility of this mode. Although it may not offer the fastest delivery time or lowest cost per pound, the combination of its capabilities make railroad transportation the most frequent selection.

During the past ten years, the railroad industry has been working to modernize its freight capabilities. Containerization services, redesigned railcars, and high-speed loading and unloading equipment are examples of this committment. Innovation, not often associated with the Iron Horse, has displayed itself through railcars that can stack thirty autos vertically, air-cushioned cars that reduce breakage, and livestock carriers that minimize travel effects. A significant disadvantage is the need to ship in large quantities (60,000-100,000 pounds) to obtain optimum freight rates.

Business in Action

PORTFOLIO III: MARKETING

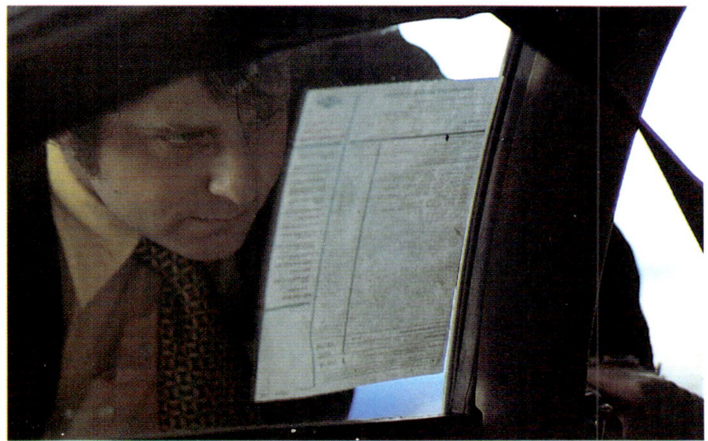

AN EXPANDING MARKET

Dodge
Omni
WHEN AMERICA NEEDS A BETTER IDEA
FORD
PUTS IT ON WHEELS
Ford

WILD COUNTRY

EVERY BODY NEEDS LEVI'S
MILK

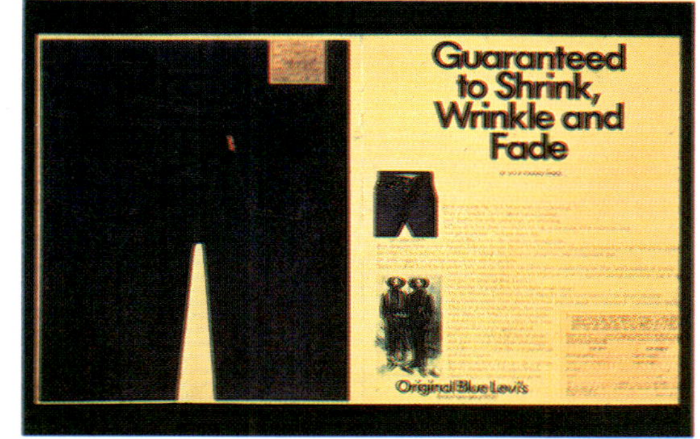
Guaranteed to Shrink, Wrinkle and Fade
Original Blue Levi's

Levi's

Old El Paso
68454

DELTA
DELTA
821

Trucks

The extensive highway network in the United States has made motor vehicle transportation an attractive alternative. Over 94% of the planned interstate system of 42,000 miles has been completed. Thus motor vehicles are able to transport goods to many more places than any other mode. This flexibility has accounted for the fact that nearly one-quarter of all freight traffic moves along the highways.

Motor carriers are most cost effective in short haul situations. Despite their comparatively high cost, they are able to provide service where it would otherwise prove impractical. However, since the principal components of motor vehicle expenses are associated with fuel costs and interest charges, it is conceivable that current economics will reduce reliance on highway carriers. The impact of bad weather on motor vehicles is one of the most critical disadvantages of this mode of transportation.

Airplanes

It has long been recognized that the fastest mode of transportation of goods has been air freight. Further, this speed advantage has continued to improve with the introduction of jumbo jet fleets designed for freight hauling. However, the growing importance of airlines in passenger travel has not been paralleled in freight transit. Airline carriers presently handle less than 5% of all freight, the least amount of traffic of any transportation mode.

There are two principle disadvantages associated with air freight: cost and inflexibility. The cost to utilize air freight is the most expensive of all modes. Further, because of their landing requirements, most jumbo jets are limited to carrying products to major cities. However, under certain circumstances such as perishable goods, high ticket small items, and small replacement parts, air transportation becomes the only viable alternative.

Boats

The least expensive mode of transportation, although the slowest, is seen on the inland waterways and oceans of the world. Slightly less than 20 percent of all goods are shipped via the water. However, the proportion rises dramatically when discussing international commerce. Special-purpose boats such as barges, tankers, auto carriers, and container ships carry the majority of the traffic with the freighter class being reduced in importance.

Obviously, shipping routes are limited by nature, thereby reducing the flexibility of water freight. The weather can become a dominant factor effecting boat transportation. Offshore pipelines and onboard computers are but two examples of modern technology being implemented to offset some of the inherent difficulties with the oldest mode of transportation. Bulky goods are the primary freight carried by boats underlining the relatively inexpensive nature of water transportation.

Pipelines

An often overlooked mode of transportation is the use of pipelines to carry liquids and gaseous products. Today more material is shipped via pipelines than by boats and airplanes combined. It is an extremely efficient transportation scheme. Therefore, once the enormous construction costs have been recovered, the incremental movement costs are negligible.

Attempts to move solid products by grinding the mixture into a slush have met with limited success. Pipelines by their nature are inflexible but not very succeptible to weather impact. The most famous pipeline recently constructed is the $9 billion Trans-Alaska covering nearly 800 miles across treacherous terrain. Tens of thousands of miles of pipeline exist in the United States principally carrying natural gas and crude oil.

Exhibit 13.3 shows how the costs associated with transporting goods, maintaining an inventory, and processing orders interact to affect a business's overall costs. Note that it is generally a bit more expensive to rely on transportation instead of warehouses.

Vertical Integration

Retailers, wholesalers, and manufacturers are in business to make profits. However, in order to remain competitive, a manufacturer may have to offer wholesalers and retailers discounts that greatly reduce the final profit it can make. After a while, it may decide that the lower prices it receives are not justified by the additional functions performed by the wholesalers and retailers. It may decide to establish its own wholesaling or retailing operation in order to save money. A company that chooses to handle more than one channel function is said to have chosen **vertical integration.**

COSTS

Suppose you are a manufacturer who sells a product to a merchant wholesaler. Your list price is $2.00, but you sell your product to the wholesaler at $1.10. Since the product costs 95 cents to make, you stand to get 15 cents for each one you sell. If you sold 10,000 in one year, you would make $1,500.

But how much did you lose by paying the wholesaler? Since the wholesaler is performing a number of necessary functions, you really do not lose any money unless you can do the job cheaper than the wholesaler. For instance, suppose the wholesaler sells your products to retailers for $1.50 each. Thus the wholesaler makes 40 cents ($1.50 minus $1.10) for each product it sells. If it sold 10,000, it would make $4,000 in revenue. Not all of that is profit, of course, since the wholesaler has to pay its expenses.

Let's suppose for a moment that you think you can perform the wholesaling job for less than $4,000. Should you do it? Many companies say yes because if they can, the price charged the customer can be reduced. Suppose it would cost you $3,000 to do your own wholesaling. If you can sell 10,000 units of the item per year, the wholesaling cost for each unit would be 30 cents. If it only costs you 30 cents per unit but the wholesaler charges 40 cents, you can lower the list price by 10 cents—to $1.90—without cutting into the retailers' profits at all.

A **company-owned wholesaler** is one that has been established and is run by a manufacturer. But sometimes retailers take on the wholesaling function themselves, hoping to save money and become more competitive. For example, stores like A & P and J. C. Penney are both wholesalers and retailers. But don't jump to the conclusion that wholesalers are always the bad guys. In fact, they may decide that retailers are not

EXHIBIT 13.3 Tradeoffs among Transportation, Inventory and Order-Processing Costs

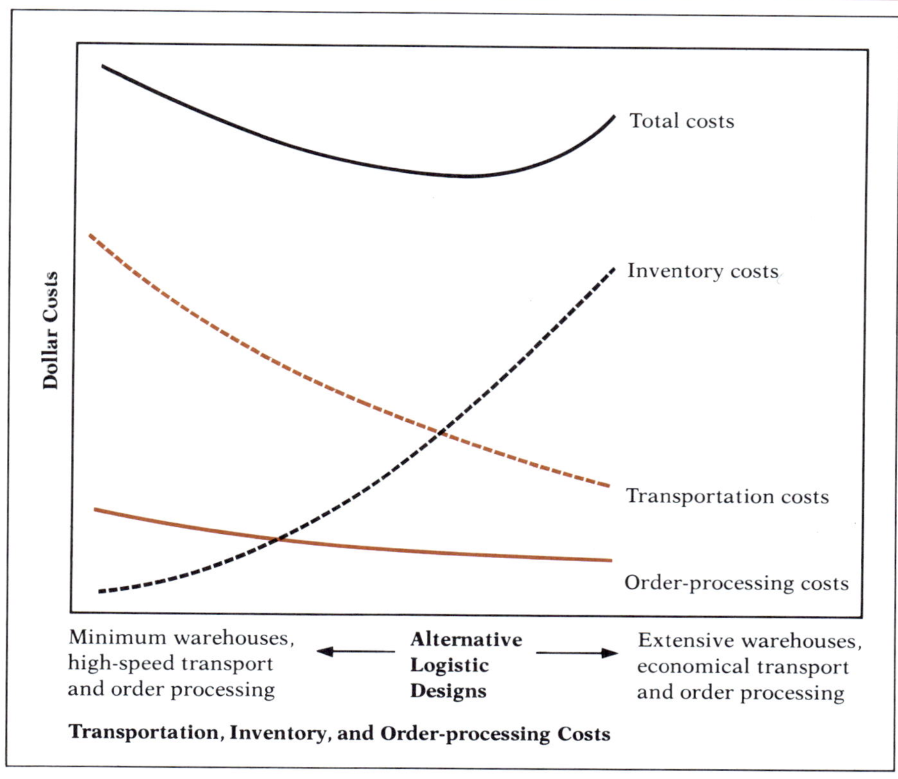

doing a good enough job selling the products they offer and attempt to take on part of the retailing responsibility. The point of this whole discussion is that there are a number of hybrid versions of marketing channels, all of which have developed in an effort to lower costs and increase competition.

CONTRACTUAL SYSTEMS

Instead of seeking to become vertically integrated, marketing channel members often enter into formal agreements with one another in an effort to reduce costs and become more competitive. For example, an independent wholesaler may seek independent retailers to market its products. Since the wholesaler can buy in bulk at lower costs, as well as develop a line of private brands, its affiliated retailers may then be able to compete more effectively against retail chain outlets. In return, the retailers agree to use a common name and to purchase products from the wholesaler. The common store name and similar product offerings result in lower costs to consumers. Advertisements that mention the name of the retail store promote sales at all outlets, which is an added benefit to the independent retailers. A good example of this type of **wholesaler-sponsored voluntary chain** is the IGA food stores.

Another variation in wholesaling is the **retail cooperative,** in which several retailers set up a wholesaling operation for themselves that allows them to compete more easily with the retail chains. As part of their agreement, they contract to purchase a certain percentage of their inventory from the wholesaling company they establish. Again, the development of a private brand name may help to reduce product costs.

The last variation is the franchise. Retail outlets agree to strict operating requirements and pay an operating fee in return for the use of a manufacturer's name and marketing, management, and other aids. Excellent examples of franchise operations are fast-food outlets like McDonald's and Kentucky Fried Chicken.

CONSIDERATIONS IN THE DECISION TO INTEGRATE

Complete vertical integration is achieved when a business has taken on responsibilities for manufacturing, wholesaling, and retailing. By assuming these functions, a business may be able not only to save costs but also to maintain better control over the product and the final price charged for it. The hope is that better customer relations and product quality will result.

However, decisions to integrate are not always successful. Part of the problem might be a lack of expertise. A manufacturer may be good at producing a product but know next to nothing about wholesaling. In fact, vertical integration may end up costing the manufacturer more. For instance, a wholesaler might have a fleet of trucks that can be used constantly—and therefore efficiently—to serve a large number of manufacturers and retailers. A manufacturer, on the other hand, may not use the trucks all the time. Idle trucks are a heavy expense, since they are not earning any money.

Exhibit 13.4 diagrams the relationships among the factors involved in the decision to integrate: the business environment, the competition, the expected consumers, the organization, and the product itself.

Marketing Channel Strategy

The type of marketing channels selected for a product depends on the type of customer being served. If your customers were predominantly industrial, chances are you would not be too concerned about retail outlets. You would, however, be concerned with finding a method of distribution that is reliable and inexpensive. If you cannot deliver on time, the delay in production you cause your industrial customers could very well eliminate you from future business. And since your product is being used as a part in another product, the lower your cost, the lower the final price can be.

If you sell to consumers, on the other hand, you would be concerned with determining which type of retailing method to use. Does your product have to be experienced firsthand, so that house-to-house sales are required? Is the product sold in such large numbers that extensive retail outlets are required? Is the product facing such intense competition in the marketplace that selling through discount houses, with their lower operating costs, would give you a more competitive price?

If you are concerned with maintaining control of product distribution, you may need to integrate your company into the channel functions. If, on the other hand, your strategy is to focus on manufacturing a quality product, you may want to be burdened with channel responsibilities. Naturally, financial limitations may limit your flexibility in choosing a channel.

EXHIBIT 13.4 Factors Affecting the Decision to Vertically Integrate

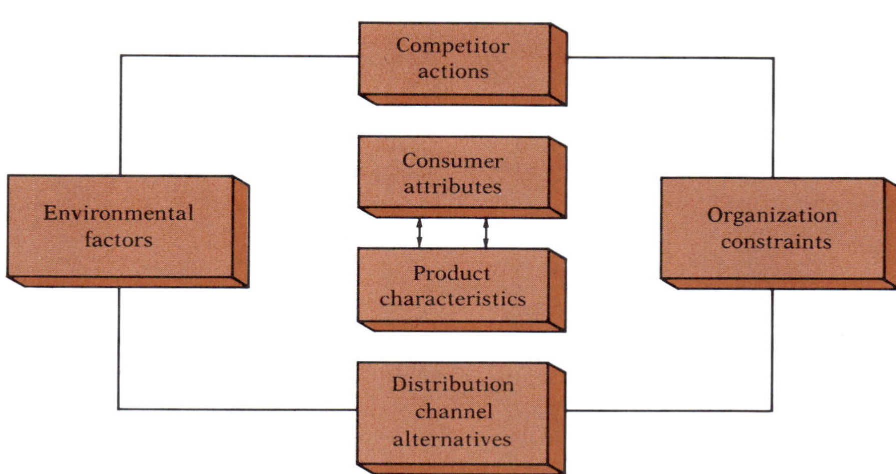

Distribution Strategies

The type of product you are offering for sale influences your choice of distribution channel. If you manufacture large, bulky items, you may be forced to transport by rail, regardless of needs for timely delivery. If your product is perishable, you will require fast truck transportation, even though it is more expensive. If you product requires immediate, timely delivery, you may need to use air freight, which may be the most reliable but is definitely the most expensive type of transportation. All of these considerations enter into your choice of a distribution strategy.

An **intensive distribution strategy** is used primarily by manufacturers of convenience goods. Since convenience goods are bought without much deliberation, they need to be readily available to consumers. This requires a large number of retail outlets and quite an extensive system of distribution. Since such large quantities of goods are involved, wholesaling is a very important function.

If the manufacturer wishes to limit the number of retailers allowed to sell the products, a **selective distribution strategy** is used. A selective strategy could result in lower overall marketing costs and better relations between the retailer and manufacturer. The manufacturer can also maintain better control over the product but still use the expertise of the retailer.

An **exclusive distribution strategy** is one in which the manufacturer grants exclusive rights to handle the product to a very limited number of retailers. A good example of an exclusive distribution strategy exists in the automobile industry, in the use of dealerships. Another example might be a fast-food chain granting the use of its name to a retail outlet. An exclusive strategy allows companies to maintain control over their products, which can be quite helpful in maintaining high levels of quality and prestige. On the other hand, exclusive distribution may drastically limit the number of retail outlets the business has and result in less market coverage.

As you can see, channel and distribution decisions, like pricing decisions, are numerous and complex. Each decision is affected by the type of product to be shipped, the nature of the competition, and the business's marketing strategy. The result of such complexity is specialization of the channel functions. But without the expertise and cooperation of all marketing channels, modern business would be tangled in a maze of communication, transportation, and storage problems.

- A manufacturer often has to use the services of wholesalers and retailers to make its product available to the final consumers.
- A wholesaler acts as a middleman between the manufacturer and the retailer. It offers to make a wide variety of goods available to retailers in the quantities demanded by them and offers storage facilities for the remainder.

- A retailer is the middleman between the wholesaler and the ultimate consumer. The retailer decides upon the medium to be used to make the product available and attractive to potential consumers. There are various types of retailers, ranging from the specialty stores to superstores.
- Since physical distribution costs are often heavy, manufacturers must find an optimal location for their warehouses and the most cost-effective method for getting their products from plant to warehouse.
- A manufacturer that wishes to avoid paying for a wholesaler's services may wish to consider the possibility of doing the wholesaler's job. The prime consideration is the effectiveness with which the manufacturer can usurp the wholesaler's role.
- There are five principle modes of transportation used in the distribution network: trains, trucks, airplanes, boats, and pipelines. Each has its special advantages and disadvantages.
- The choice of a marketing channel strategy depends on many factors, including the type of consumer, the type of product offered for sale, competitors, the business environment, and the organization itself.

1. Why would a manufacturer be willing to purchase the services of wholesalers and retailers? What services do wholesalers offer manufacturers? How do retailers benefit from the relationship between wholesalers and manufacturers?
2. How would you distinguish the types of products found in a specialty store and a supermarket?
3. What factors should be considered in deciding on the location of a warehouse?
4. What advantages are derived by the manufacturer from franchising its brand name?
5. What factors should be considered in deciding on the correct marketing strategy? The correct distribution strategy?

APPLICATION

Coca-Cola started in modest circumstances in Atlanta, Georgia in 1886. According to legend, Dr. John S. Pemberton, a pharmacist, produced the first syrup for Coca-Cola in a three-legged pot in his backyard; he sold the drink for 5 cents a glass at his soda fountain. Pemberton's partner, Frank M. Robinson, suggested Coca-Cola as a name and wrote it in the flowing script of the time. In the first year, sales of Coca-Cola averaged thirteen drinks per day, which was not a very big beginning. More than 245 million drinks of Coca-Cola are now sold each day.

The Coca-Cola Company

A BRIEF HISTORY

A few years after the initial mixing of Coca-Cola, Pemberton and his son Charles sold the rights to Coca-Cola to Asa G. Candler, a Georgian, for a sum estimated to be $2,300. Candler was a good marketer: By 1892, sales of Coca-Cola had increased nearly tenfold. Candler disposed of his drug business and devoted his fulltime attention to the soft drink with attorney John S. Candler, who was his brother, Frank Robinson, and two other friends. They formed a Georgia corporation to sell the syrup, The Coca-Cola Company, with capital stock of $100,000.

While Candler was concentrating on booming soda fountain sales, Joseph A. Biedenharn was installing machinery to bottle Coca-Cola in the rear of his store in Mississippi. Biedenharn took these bottles to plantations and lumber camps up and down the river.

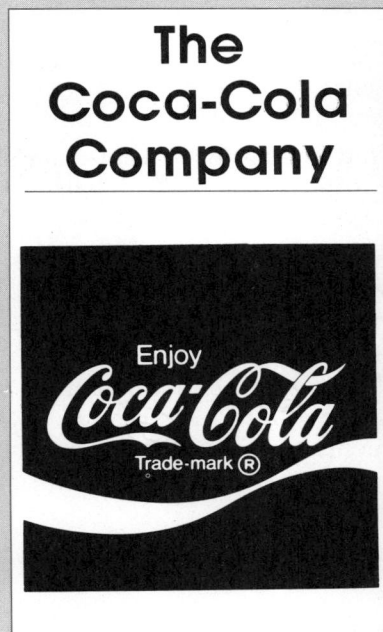

The large-scale bottling of Coca-Cola started in 1899, when Benjamin F. Thomas and Joseph B. Whitehead secured from Candler the exclusive rights to bottle and sell Coca-Cola in practically every state in the United States. Realizing their own inability to cover the country with bottling plants, they began to search for competent people in local communities to establish bottling operations. In return for their willingness to invest the necessary time and capital, Thomas and Whitehead gave them a defined geographic area in which to develop and sell Coca-Cola. This was the beginning of today's locally owned and operated Coca-Cola bottling industry, which is largely responsible for the widespread success of Coca-Cola.

THE COCA-COLA BOTTLERS

The locally owned and operated bottlers operate like a franchise system, in which a company grants a license to another business to sell its product and use its trademark. Basic to this arrangement is the existence of a standardized product, a set way of doing business, and an easily recognizable trade name. McDonald's is another good example of a franchised business.

The advantages of a franchise system are numerous. One is that the business granted the license is, in most cases, locally owned and operated. That keeps profits in the same geographical area as the business, helping to contribute to the growth of the community. Another advantage is that the product offered by the business has been proven successful. A local business would not have the money or expertise to embark on a testing campaign for a new product. A third advantage is that the franchised business has access to a lot of expertise on how to produce and sell its product from the company granting the

license. This allows the business to remain small but to maintain all of the advantages of a larger company.

The Coca-Cola Company does not sell the bottler anything but the syrups. It does, however, assist in locating and buying everything needed to bottle Coca-Cola, from machinery and equipment to the plant and personnel. The company also sets standards for these items and approves local suppliers who meet them. Company people work with the bottler's staff at every stage to ensure that production is of consistent quality. In the long run, this system provides all bottlers with the greatest edge for success—predictable high-quality products.

In each of the more than 135 countries around the world where Coca-Cola is bottled and sold, it is a local business. Bottlers of Coca-Cola are usually prominent in their communities. The main difference between Coca-Cola bottlers and most other entrepreneurs is the fact that the bottlers are linked through their franchise to a worldwide enterprise.

CAREER OPPORTUNITIES

The Coca-Cola Company offers entry-level jobs in the areas of finance, engineering, research and development, and sales and marketing. Those who take sales and marketing jobs might become fountain and bottle sales representatives or market researchers.

FOR DISCUSSION

1. What marketing channels has The Coca-Cola Company adopted? Could you suggest any new channels that it could use?
2. What method of physical distribution does Coca-Cola use to make Coke available all around the world?

OBJECTIVES

- ☐ To evaluate the effectiveness of advertising in informing, persuading, or reminding a potential customer
- ☐ To determine the applicability of different types of advertising media to different products
- ☐ To evaluate the extent to which financial resources, product characteristics, and other considerations go into the determination of which media should be used
- ☐ To speculate on the various strategies that could be used in a store to attract a consumer's attention
- ☐ To understand the role that salespeople, within the store or outside, play in educating a customer about the benefits of a certain product
- ☐ To outline the factors that a manufacturer must consider in formulating a promotional strategy

OUTLINE

KEY TERMS

CONTEST
COUPON
DEMONSTRATION
LOCAL SPOT
NATIONAL SPOT
NETWORK ADVERTISEMENT
PERCENTAGE-OF-SALES APPROACH
PERSONAL SELLING
POINT-OF-PURCHASE PROMOTION
PRESS RELEASE
PROMOTION
PUBLICITY
PUBLIC RELATIONS
PULL STRATEGY
PUSH STRATEGY
SALES PROMOTION
SAMPLE
SUGGESTION SELLING
SWEEPSTAKE

PROMOTION

Tobacco Marketers' Success Formula: Make Cigarets in Smoker's Own Image

JOHN KOTEN
Wall Street Journal, February 29, 1980

Thirty years ago, most cigaret smokers chose from among three brands: Camel, Chesterfield and Lucky Strike. Today, more than 160 brands adorn retail shelves.

"The market's become a darn mess," says a spokesman for R. J. Reynolds Industries Inc., the largest cigaret maker.

The reason is that to sell more cigarets, tobacco companies have been dividing the smoking public into relatively tiny sociological groups and then aiming one or more brands at each group. Vantage and Merit, for example, are aimed at young women, and Camel and Winston are aimed mostly at rural smokers.

Cigaret marketing success hinges on how effectively a company can design a brand to appeal to a particular type of smoker, and then how well it can reach that smoker with sharply focused packaging, product design and advertising. The strategy requires close attention to hundreds of details involving such things as typefaces used on the cigaret pack, the color of the filter paper and the kinds of models used in the ads.

PACKAGING AN IMAGE

"Smokers are self-image buyers," explains a spokesman for Lorillard Co., a subsidiary of Loews Corp. "They're attracted to a cigaret not because it contains a better grade of tobacco but because it conveys an image they like to identify with."

The package is a big part of the image. "A cigaret package is unique because the consumer carries it around with him all day," says John Digianni, a designer and vice president at Gianninoto Associates Inc., New York. "It's part of a smoker's clothing, and when he saunters into a bar and plunks it down, he makes a statement about himself."

As a result, cigaret companies are extremely cautious when they choose a new package. Brown & Williamson Tobacco Co., a subsidiary of B.A.T. Industries Ltd., ran market tests on 33 packages before deciding on the blue, gold and red design used for its Viceroy Rich Lights brands. And package colors are especially important.

"Red packs connote strong flavor, green packs connote coolness or menthol and white packs suggest that a cigaret is low-tar," says Mr. Digianni. "White means sanitary and safe. And if you put a low-tar cigaret in a red package, people say it tastes stronger than the same cigaret packaged in white."

Philip Morris, he says, heightened the appeal to the stylish of its Benson & Hedges brand by printing the company's Park Avenue address on the front and back of each pack. R. J. Reynolds gave its Now brand packages a "modern, chrome-and-glass look designed to appeal to up-scale city and suburban dwellers," Mr. Digianni adds.

Rodney McKnew, a creative director at Walter Landor Associates, New York, says the package his firm designed for Philip Morris' highly successful Merit cigarets is intended to connote a "flamboyant, young-in-spirit image—one that would offset the notion most people have that low-tar cigarets are dull." He says that the big yellow, brown and orange racing stripes on the merit pack give it "pizzazz."

Seemingly minor differences in design of the cigarets themselves also can influence a brand's appeal to a certain type of smoker.

FILTERS ARE A FACTOR

Philip Morris's Parliament and Lorillard's True cigarets, for instance, have been popular among women smokers because of their recessed filters. These filters, which work something like a built-in cigaret holder, supposedly lend a cleaner image to the brands and add to their style. A cork filter, by contrast, can make a cigaret seem powerful tasting.

Extra-long cigarets are designed to appeal to the fashion-conscious. Lorillard calls its Max cigarets a "cosmetic" product for women. "Max smokers like the way the cigaret looks on them," a Lorillard spokesman says. "They're the sort that care a lot about fashion. Maybe some are fat, but they'd at least be wearing the latest clothes."

R. J. Reynolds produces a long cigaret wrapped in brown paper called More, which is supposed to convey a "riverboat-gambler look"; it's aimed at big-city sophisticates.

Advertising also can make a big difference in a cigaret's appeal.

Liggett Group Inc. tailored its ads for Decade cigarets to appeal to young smokers with above-average educations, according to an account executive at Della Femina, Travisanno & Partners, the brand's advertising agency. The ads depict packages in surrealistic settings painted to catch the eye of college graduates, who presumably would best appreciate such artwork.

Researchers have discovered that people who choose low-tar cigarets tend to be better educated and wealthier than smokers of high-tar cigarets. Low-tar brands also are more likely to be smoked in urban than rural areas, and are more popular among women than men.

Thus, ads for low-tar Now cigarets have prompted the brand as a "satisfying decision" and used middle-aged models who pose as wealthy horse-breeders. Ads for 11-milligram Vantage, another low-tar brand from R. J. Reynolds, stressed how important it is to "think" when selecting a brand. Ads for high-tar cigarets, by contrast, have generally shunned the intellectual approach. As one model in a Winston ad succinctly puts it: "I smoke for taste."

The importance of an effective advertising campaign to final product sales is illustrated by the extensive research that cigarette companies conduct to develop their final promotional strategy. The factors that are important in the development of a successful promotional strategy are discussed in this chapter.

Once a manufacturer has decided on what product to sell, what price to charge, and through which marketing channel it should be distributed, potential consumers must be informed about the existence of the product. This last step is possibly the most important part of the marketing process, since a product's chances of success obviously depend on the potential consumer knowing that it exists.

A company's total effort to gain market awareness, eventual acceptance, and sales of its product is called **promotion.** As Exhibit 14.1 indicates, there are four major tools a company can use in its promotion efforts: advertising, personal selling, sales promotion, and publicity. These four tools may be used in various combinations to create a mix complementary to the company's marketing goals. For example, companies that sell consumer goods may be heavily dependent on advertising, whereas companies that sell industrial goods may rely on personal sales.

Advertising

If you are like most people, you see or hear hundreds of advertisements each day. But like most people, you probably don't remember everything that is flashed before your eyes on television, placed in the side columns in newspapers and magazines, or played over the radio. Why is it that people remember some ads and not others? This is a question of crucial interest to advertisers, as well as to scientists. Even more important is the question of what type of advertising works best to generate sales.

A COMMUNICATIONS MODEL

To help determine what makes advertising effective, a number of researchers have contributed to a model of the components and processes involved in the transmission of any advertising message.

EXHIBIT 14.1 Promotional Tools

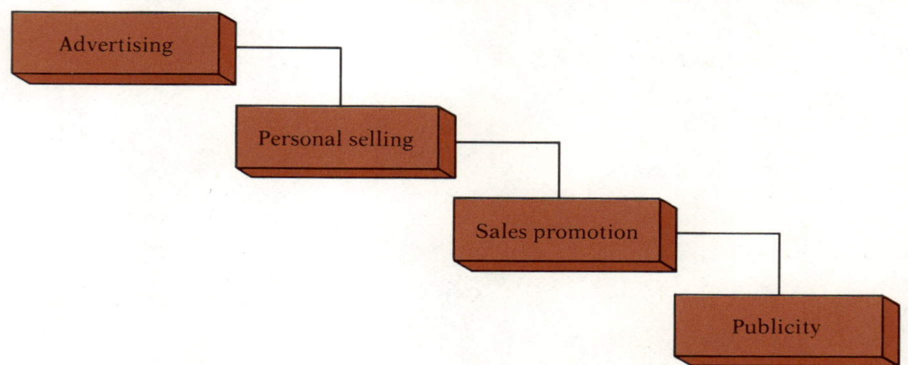

Attention

Scientists have done a lot of research to discover why people remember certain ads. Basically, they suggest that advertisements first must gain people's attention. That may not be easy. If you have been looking for a good set of golf clubs and you see an advertisement in the newspaper for a particular set of clubs, you may stop to read the ad. On the other hand, if you are looking for a new car, chances are you would pass right over the ad for golf clubs. Scientists explain this by saying that people have to be primed, or made ready, for a message in order to pay attention to it. In other words, an advertisement will get your attention if you are generally interested in the type of product or service offered in the ad.

Another way for an ad to get attention is to show something that catches people's eye or to make a noise that gets their attention (sometimes advertisements even use silence to get attention). People have an attention threshold, or level, that must be crossed if they are to pay attention. If an ad is catchy enough, people may pay attention whether they are primed for the message or not. However, there is no sure method for getting attention, and companies spend a lot of money trying to be one of the few that succeed.

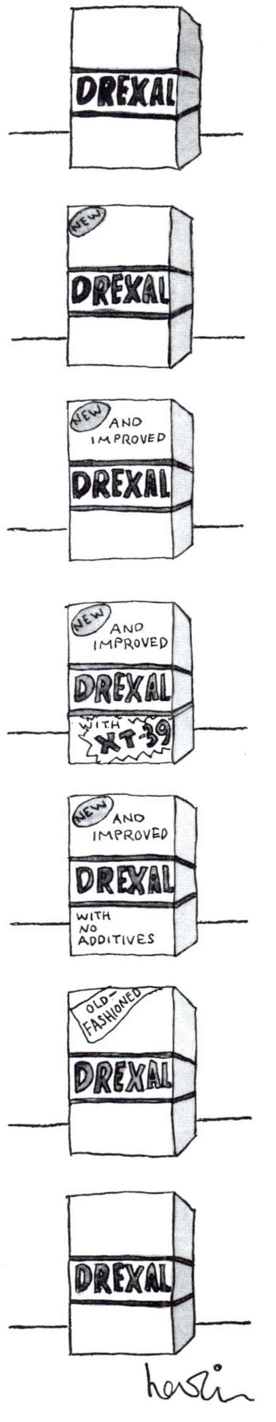

Drawing by Levin; © 1977 The New Yorker Magazine, Inc.

Message

Once an advertisement gets attention, it has to convey a message to do so, it needs to be clear, easy to understand, and easy to remember. An advertisement should also focus on the product—the characteristics and images that are most likely to appeal to the target market. Your product, for example, may be expensive or inexpensive. It may be dependable or disposable. Perhaps it is easily purchased, or perhaps it has to be ordered. It may appeal to all groups or just to the older generation. It may be for special occasions or for everyday use. Besides determining the product's characteristics, you may want to create a particular image for potential customers to associate with. A perfume manufacturer may not sell perfume but rather hope or sex appeal. A sports car may not represent transportation but excitement. The idea is to establish some sort of "pizzazz" or prestige for your product.

It should be apparent that developing a message for a product is not easy. When you realize that your ad will be one of hundreds and hundreds of advertisements that bombard consumers daily, you may well wonder if advertising is worth the expense and effort. Most businesses would agree, however, that advertising can be useful in three different areas: conveying information, persuading, and reminding.

If you are entering the market with a new product, advertising can be useful in making your potential customers aware that it exists and conveying information about its characteristics. Assuming that your market studies accurately evaluated market needs, your message will be noticed by those who are most interested in your type of product. Even if a consumer is not ready to buy the product right away, the information you provide in your advertisement may be quite useful in swaying him or her to your product when the time is ripe.

As your product gains in popularity, your advertisements can help persuade potential customers to buy it. The type of message put into these ads would therefore be less geared toward developing an awareness of the product, since you hope that you have already been successful in doing that. Persuasive ads might attempt to appeal to the emotions, perhaps by showing a handsome sports car driver wearing a leather jacket, cruising down a mountainside, hair blowing in the wind. Or you could provide factual data showing that your product outperforms the competition. The persuasive ad can be even more forceful if you specify that there is a particular deadline for taking advantage of a sale price or that supplies may be limited. Thus the potential customer is prodded to make the purchase decision soon.

Finally, as the product becomes successful, you may wish to provide reminder advertising, which aims to encourage repeat sales of your product and to keep its name in the front of the consumer's mind. Re-

EXHIBIT 14.2 Profiles of Major Advertising Media

Medium	Volume (in Billions)*	Example of Cost	Advantages	Disadvantages
Newspapers	14.58	$14,137, one page, weekday, *Chicago Tribune*	Wide coverage of target communities	Short life
Magazines	2.93	$36,160 one black & white page in *Newsweek*	Specialized target audience	Limited flexibility
Direct mail	6.65	$75 for names & addresses of chief executives of 500 largest manufacturers	Rapid action possible	Service
Television	10.12	$127,000 for 30 seconds of CBS network time	Broad dissemination	Cost
Radio	3.38	$125 for one minute of prime time in Nashville	Flexibility	Short message span
Outdoor	.53	$109,000 prime set of billboards, monthly, Los Angeles	Repetition creates needs	Visual pollution annoys consumers

*Data from *Advertising Age*, December 31, 1979, p. 52.

Highlight Try This, Join That, Etcetera

"Try the Uncola," "join the Pepsi generation," "things go better with Coke." Ads like these seem to impart little if any information. Consumers must be worse off because of such ads, right? Wrong, according to economist Phillip Nelson.* He claims that such ads are useful for consumers. They are related to what he calls "experience" goods, goods that consumers must try before they have any idea whether they will like the product.

A soft drink is a good example of an experience good. It would be useless for a soft-drink manufacturer to advertise all of the ingredients, because what is really important to most people is the taste (although some are worried about sugar content and food additives). But the taste can only be known after experiencing the product at least once. Hence, the only conceivable advertising for a product like this is one that simply states the name and maybe a little jingle.

Nelson's argument becomes even more interesting. He claims that heavily advertised experience goods are good buys. Advertising, particularly on a national level, requires tremendous sums of money, so manufacturers will only continue advertising if it pays. They know when advertising pays, because their sales continue to increase after an expensive advertising campaign. For experience goods, the only reason that sales will continue to improve is because there is a large segment of the buying population that likes the product. Thus, according to Nelson, a heavy advertising campaign for an experience good means that consumers who choose to buy it will be joining all of the other consumers who have proven to the advertiser that the good is indeed liked in the marketplace.

Nelson's suggestion: Buy heavily advertised experience goods rather than lightly advertised ones. That's how you'll get a good deal.

*Phillip Nelson, "Advertising as Information," *Journal of Political Economy* 82 (July/August 1974):729–754.

minder advertising can also be very helpful in the postpurchase evaluation of the product (see Chapter 11), as well as in reinforcement of the consumer's selection. By reminding consumers of the quality of your product, the price savings, or whatever message you have developed, owners of your product may feel better satisfied in their choice. This may result in repeat sales later on.

ADVERTISING MEDIA

There are many types of advertising media available to a company, including television, radio, newspapers, magazines, and direct mail. The one selected to promote a product depends on a number of factors, including the amount of money available for advertising, the type of product being sold, the market for the product, and the media being used by the competition. Exhibit 14.2 profiles some of these media.

Television

Television is the most pervasive medium in our society today. The marketing of televisions has been so successful that almost every family in America has at least one.

As an advertising medium, TV is well suited to products sold to undifferentiated, mass markets and sold in large quantities. Companies manufacturing products that appeal to a large audience—like soap, some types of perfumes, and perhaps beer—can reach a relatively large number of people with only one ad.

Television offers three different types of advertising time to businesses. A **network advertisement** is shown by all of a network's affiliated stations, thereby reaching a mass audience all at one time. A **national spot** is very similar to a network ad, but it may be shown by stations affiliated with different networks at different times during the day. By using spot advertising, a manufacturer can select the markets and stations that suit its marketing strategy. A **local spot** is advertising time purchased by a local store, usually in order to reach local customers.

Since TV programs are quite expensive to produce (a miniseries might cost up to $1 million per hour) and reach a very large audience, advertising rates often exceed $100,000 for a 30-second commercial in prime time (between 8 and 11 p.m.).

Radio

Although a radio does not provide a picture to go along with the sound, it does have advantages over television. For one, it can use the listener's imagination to create scenes that would be either too expensive or impossible on television. Radio is also immediate. Finally, it can provide advertising time at a much lower cost than television but still reach a potentially large audience.

Some stations, particularly in the FM band, specialize in a particular type of music—thus appealing to a particular market segment. Radio ads can therefore be directed to a highly differentiated, although fairly large, market.

Newspapers

Newspapers can provide intense coverage of a potential market, since most people in cities and towns subscribe to one newspaper or another. And since there are very few national newspapers, advertisements can be tailored to the local area. A distinct advantage of newspapers over either television or radio is the reader's ability to go back and look at ads again or to cut out coupons.

Magazines

There are literally hundreds of different types of magazines published in America. Most of them are geared toward a particular interest, hobby, or job specialty, which makes them very useful in trying to reach

Highlight Is "Puffing" the Product Duping the Consumer?

The Federal Trade Commission has the responsibility and power to control unfair or deceptive business practices. Advertising has received special attention by the agency during the last several years. Companies may be required to substantiate claims and show that their campaigns do not mislead potential consumers. "Puffing" is the practice of exaggerating the benefits within reasonable limits. However, when these bounds are exceeded, legal liability may result.

In GIZZI versus Texaco Inc. (437 F. 2d 308), the United States Court of Appeals stated:

"In support of their theory of liability (GIZZI) introduced evidence to show . . . that Texaco insignia and the slogan 'Trust your car to the man who wears the star' were prominently displayed. It was further established that Texaco engaged in substantial national advertising, the purpose of which was to convey the impression that Texaco dealers are skilled in automotive servicing, as well as to promote Texaco products, and that this advertising was not limited to certain service or products. . . ."

a highly select market. Their good quality of photographic reproduction can also be an advantage when clear, crisp, or colorful pictures are part of the selling effort.

Direct Mail

Advertising through the mails can be a successful technique for assuring that the market at least receives an advertisement. Direct mail can be used to reach everyone in a city or region or in the entire United States. The biggest problem is to maintain a mailing list of all the customers who might be interested in a certain product.

Mail lacks the immediacy of television or radio, but like newspapers and magazines, consumers can refer to the ad more than once. However, the cost of sending a letter to each household in a target market may be much greater than airing a similar ad on the radio or displaying it in the local newspapers.

MEDIA SELECTION

The final selection of a medium or mix of media for advertising a product involves a number of tradeoffs among the costs of the media, the type of product being sold, market characteristics, and the competition's advertising efforts. Because the selection of advertising media is not easy, it is often entrusted to an advertising agency. A lot of guesswork, some research, and careful consideration of the business, product, market, and competition is required. Even then, advertising offers no guarantee of success. As Chapter 11 explains, a number of factors work together to influence a customer in the selection of a product. Advertisements are only one small part of the chain of events leading to the purchase decision.

Highlight Ad Campaigns — Burger King's Way

MIAMI—Burger King Corp. is breaking a new advertising campaign in January (AA, Dec. 23) to replace its nearly two-year-old "Who's got the best darn burger in the whole wide world" pitch. Over the years, industry watchers have claimed that the nation's No. 2 fast-food chain has had some of the best darn advertising in the industry.

The company, founded in 1954, broke its first major campaign in 1955. Created by Hume, Smith, Mickelberry of Miami, the ads used the theme, "Burger King, the home of the Whopper."

"The Whopper was the one big differential Burger King had," HSM president David Hume told ADVERTISING AGE. "Approximately 40% of the business was coming from the Whopper. McDonald's coming out with the Big Mac was, in essence, one of its answers to the Whopper."

That campaign ran until 1968, when the account shifted to one of parent Pillsbury's shops, BBDO.

During the HSM stint, Burger King created the current setup in which each franchise allocates 4% of its sales to marketing and advertising and leaves control of the advertising solely in the hands of the corporate headquarters.

After the HSM days, the first campaign from BBDO for BK centered on the line, "It takes two hands to handle a Whopper." The double-fisted approach ran from '68 until 1973, when the famous "Have it your way" campaign began.

"Have it your way" was the first time Burger King really worked at setting itself apart from the pack of fast-food places, as it stressed that at a Burger King you were able to get burgers "exactly the way you want them," not the assembly line way. The jingle crooned, "Hold the pickle, hold the lettuce," and Burger King had found its niche. The company stuck with the campaign for three years, upgrading it with the addition of stars such as Vincent Price, decked out as the devil, and humorous Harlem Globetrotter Meadowlark Lemon, who stacked up burgers for a very big meal.

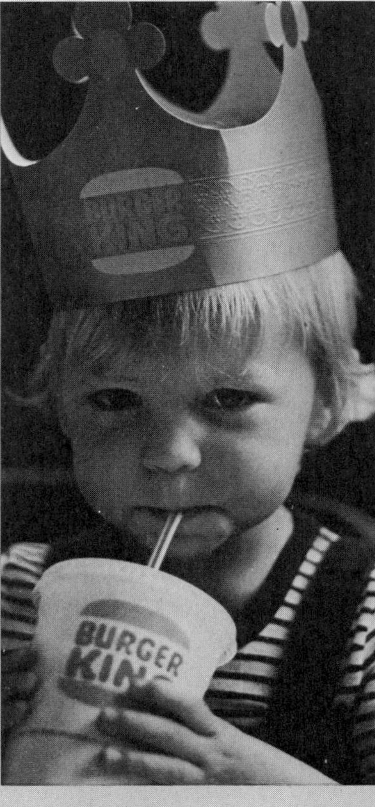

But in August, 1976, as fewer customers waited in long lines to get it their way, Burger King dropped BBDO, and picked J. Walter Thompson Co. to handle the account. Thompson came with fast-food expertise from Shakey's Pizza and the Red Barn systems.

JWT's first campaign for Burger King broke the following November and tapped the Bicentennial bonanza with, "America loves burgers and we're America's Burger King." That campaign ran, with some expansions, until the current "best darn burger" drive broke in February, 1978.

As in the early days, messages directed to children have played a special part in the Burger King strategy. In 1975, BBDO retired the early little King character and courted youngsters with live action ads that tapped the adult's "Have it your way" approach. In one spot, kids donned fake noses and glasses to stress their individuality and the special service they get at BK.

With Don Smith on board, the company began to shoot for the children's market with greater intensity when in the summer of 1977, it formally introduced the live Magic Burger King to the public. The subtheme of that first campaign was "Now you're old enough to enjoy Burger King." About the same time, the company made some subtle changes in its adult advertising to feature more children in its spots, munching along with their parents.

Financial Considerations

Most businesses have a limited amount of money to spend on advertising. This fact alone may drastically limit their selection of advertising media. Local newspapers are perhaps the cheapest media, but they lack the immediacy and attention-getting qualities of television or radio. Thus a business may decide that a good way of getting the most out of

EXHIBIT 14.3 Expenditures on Advertising by Several Large Corporations

BURGER KING restaurants
Pillsbury

	media dollars 1978	media dollars 1979
Magazines	$ 104,000	$ 77,000
Supps	—	—
Newspapers	15,000	(no data)
Network tv	20,447,000	21,403,000
Spot tv	15,726,000	22,202,000
Network radio	—	—
Spot radio	—	899,000
Outdoor	315,000	528,000
Total	$36,607,000	$45,109,000

McDONALD's
McDonald's Corp.

	media dollars 1978	media dollars 1979
Magazines	$ 468,000	$ 1,749,000
Supps	—	—
Newspapers	(no data)	(no data)
Network tv	48,547,000	62,456,000
Spot tv	66,320,000	75,334,000
Network radio	—	—
Spot radio	733,000	647,000
Outdoor	1,948,000	2,383,000
Total	$118,016,000	$142,569,000

PEPSI-COLA
PepsiCo

	media dollars 1978	media dollars 1979
Magazines	$ 31,000	$ 215,000
Supps	—	—
Newspapers	641,000	938,000
Network tv	11,655,000	18,561,000
Spot tv	27,679,000	33,329,000
Network radio	—	—
Spot radio	5,464,000	3,695,000
Outdoor	349,000	448,000
Totals	$45,819,000	$57,186,000

SEAGRAM'S liquors
Seagram

	media dollars 1978	media dollars 1979
Magazines	$36,690,000	$35,629,000
Supps	1,713,000	2,077,000
Newspapers	2,432,000	3,324,000
Network tv	—	—
Spot tv	—	—
Network radio	—	—
Spot radio	—	—
Outdoor	792,000	2,121,000
Total	$41,627,000	$43,151,000

KELLOGG'S products
Kellogg Co.

	media dollars 1978	media dollars 1979
Magazines	$ 1,923,000	$ 2,726,000
Supps	508,000	435,000
Newspapers	4,402,000	4,011,000
Network TV	40,479,000	53,198,000
Spot tv	18,633,000	18,478,000
Network radio	172,000	—
Spot radio	1,165,000	670,000
Outdoor	11,000	10,000
Total	$67,293,000	$79,528,000

WRIGLEY gum
Wm. Wrigley, Jr.

	media dollars 1978	media dollars 1979
Magazines	—	—
Supps	$ 135,000	$ 24,000
Newspapers	655,000	900,000
Network tv	6,578,000	16,494,000
Spot tv	26,438,000	22,952,000
Network radio	2,635,000	1,247,000
Spot radio	3,974,000	1,899,000
Outdoor	—	—
Total	$40,415,000	$43,516,000

Data from: *Marketing and Media Decisions*, July, 1980

its advertising money is to spend some on local television ads, some on radio, and the rest on a half-page spread in the local newspaper. The television ad could be devised to get the attention of potential customers (announcing a sale, for instance), and radio ads might carry a persuasive message. The newspaper could be used to show more detailed information: a picture of the product, its sale price, the location of the store, and even, perhaps, a redeemable coupon (to persuade potential customers to visit the store).

Of course, a larger business would have more to spend on advertising. (Exhibit 14.3 shows some examples.) The payoff is access to a larger market.

Type of Product

If a product is a specialty good, it should probably not be advertised nationally, unless it is supported by well-developed marketing channels and retail outlets. Even then, the percentage of potential customers reached via a national ad might be quite low compared to the percentage reached via magazine advertisements. Since most magazines appeal to specific markets, the particular people who would be interested in a specialty good can be reached in large numbers at a relatively low cost.

On the other hand, magazines such as *Time* and *Newsweek* cater to a very general market and can be used to advertise automobiles, cameras, cigarettes, liquor, and the like. Even though television may reach more people, these magazine advertisements could be more cost effective. Besides, a magazine ad is subject to repeat reading—for example, at a doctor's office.

Market Considerations

A product that would appeal to a highly undifferentiated, mass market could most effectively be advertised on television or radio. If the market is concentrated in a particular geographic area, local spots can be purchased on either television or radio, eliminating the expense of a national ad.

Mass media can also be used effectively if the market is highly differentiated but spread throughout the United States. For instance, the market for a Porsche sports car is highly differentiated, but the potential buyers of the car might live in all parts of the United States. National advertising on TV would be able to reach this small target market but might be unnecessarily expensive. Advertising in a mass-market magazine could also get the attention of prospective Porsche buyers—but at less expense.

Competition

The advertising media being used by the competition may offer insights into how best to counter their ads. It could very well be that the type of advertising best suited to one company's finances, product, and target market is the same one best suited to the competition. However, a business may also choose a medium that the competition is not using in order to keep potential customers from confusing the two products.

Personal Selling

Where advertising leaves off, **personal selling** begins. Advertising can make consumers aware, arouse interest, and perhaps even persuade them to come into a store. Once they are in a store, however, salespeople, the final link, become responsible for the final sale of the product.

RETAIL SALES

The sales force for a retail business should be concerned with four major things in their efforts to obtain a sale. First, they need to get the attention of the customer, much as an advertising message does. Next, they need to arouse the customer's interest. After that, they should attempt to create a desire for the product by explaining its good qualities. Finally, they should be concerned with motivating the customer toward action, which ideally means buying the product and not bolting out the side door.

It is interesting to notice the different styles of the salespeople in different stores. You could wait in one store for what might seem like hours before a salesperson would ever approach you. At another store, you may not get two steps into the door before someone asks if you need help. Discount stores, grocery stores, and some types of department stores follow the first type of routine. Small specialty stores might follow the second.

There is a reason behind the different strategies. As discussed in Chapter 13, discount stores can offer their products at lower prices by reducing the size of their sales force. They feel that the primary motivation for shopping at their store is to benefit from the lower prices—not to obtain good service. Specialty stores, on the other hand, use salespeople to arouse customers' interest, provide information about use of the product, and encourage the final sale.

Retail salespeople may also use **suggestion selling,** a technique in which they try to encourage the purchase of complementary items along with the original product. If you were to buy a tape recorder, for instance, the salesperson practicing suggestive selling might ask if you would like some tapes to go along with it. Suggestive selling can be quite helpful to the customer and lucrative to the store.

FIELD SALES

Salespeople "in the field" follow much the same procedure used by retail salespeople, but they are much more involved in identifying potential customers. Retail salespersons know that customers entering the store are probably interested in buying. Field salespeople, however, must seek out and approach potential customers, and this takes a lot of time and effort.

Companies usually offer incentives to their field salespersons to encourage the discovery of new customers and increased sales. These incentives can be monetary, in the form of commissions, or nonmonetary, such as sitting at the head of the table during a special dinner held for the year's top salespeople. Commissions are usually a percentage of the total sales made by the salesperson.

Field salespeople are also involved more with following up the sale, typically by asking customers whether they are satisfied with the product. They may discover product faults, which they can then relay to the manufacturer, or other concerns that could affect future sales. Postpurchase satisfaction is a very important factor in repeat sales.

Sales Promotion

Efforts to promote sales of a product by means other than advertising or personal selling might be called **sales promotion.** This category includes anything in the "bag of tricks" that a business feels can encourage sales.

Displays near the cash register in retail outlets are often successful in getting the customers' attention and generating impulse purchases. A **point-of-purchase promotion** may be part of a promotional strategy being used by the business, backed by local newspaper advertisements or television spots.

Another strategy is to give out free **samples** of the product. Much of the problem in encouraging sales is getting people to try the product. Customers who receive a sample for free might try it, like it, and buy more. However, giving something for nothing can be quite costly. Thus sampling is most effective for mass-marketed items of low unit cost. One example of effective sampling would be offering bits of cold meats to customers in a supermarket. Another example was the mailing of small bottles of Signal mouthwash when it was being introduced.

Some products require **demonstration** in order to stimulate potential customers' interest. Vacuum cleaner salespeople engaged in house-to-house retailing rely heavily on demonstrations to encourage sales. Many department stores offer product demonstrations, as do specialty stores, like stereo shops. Demonstrations may be quite effective in stimulating a desire for the product.

Contests and **sweepstakes,** which offer a chance at winning a substantial prize, are universally popular. Most people are willing to try their luck. Usually participation is limited to those who send in some proof of purchase of the manufacturer's product. Hence consumers are forced to sample the product. An example would be the sweepstakes

Highlight Field Sales: The Rewards Can Be High

Business students often have the attitude that sales or selling is an occupational hazard to be avoided at all costs. A typical response from a soon-to-be graduated business student: "I've had a great interview with XYZ Company. I'm going to travel a bit, but I won't have to sell." If everyone hates to sell, then who is out there selling?

The fact of the matter is that there are millions of field sales personnel, and they are out there selling all the time. Why? Some are natural salespersons; others, even though they lack the innate ability, like to sell; and, finally, the bulk of the field salespeople in America are out there selling because there can be significant monetary rewards for their troubles. Indeed, there are salespeople making over $100,000 a year. They make that much because they work hard and enjoy what they are doing.

The moral of our little story: Don't write off a sales job before you investigate its rewards.

organized by McDonald's every six months or so in which participants must get the entry form from the store.

Coupons guaranteeing a certain amount off the regular price of a product are useful to attract cost-conscious buyers whose preferences are not well-defined. An example would be the coupons or discounts on soft drinks that are found in supermarkets practically every week. The manufacturers are hoping that customers will purchase a certain soft drink because of the low price, like it, and remain faithful to the brand.

Publicity

Publicity is advertising that a firm receives from the media without paying for it, such as articles about the company or product comparisons by consumer groups. Good publicity can be quite helpful, since consumers have a tendency to believe unsolicited opinions presented in a neutral setting. However, some publicity is not good advertising. Consumer dissatisfaction, if publicized by local newspapers or carried on network news, can be devastating to a company's business.

Businesses often maintain publicity departments to publish **press releases** about the latest developments in the firm, new product offerings, or perhaps changes made in the old product line. These releases are then sent to local and national advertising media in hopes that the information will be used. Correct information can be important in countering rumors and unfair or untrue accusations published in the news media.

Publicity and press releases are part of the **public relations** function, which seeks to maintain the public image and prestige of the firm and to disseminate useful product and company information.

Promotional Strategy

With advertising, personal selling, sales promotion, and publicity all competing for a company's promotional budget, it is necessary to plan a promotional strategy. Which combination of methods will produce the "biggest bang for the buck"? Coming up with a strategy involves guesswork, intuition, and rational thinking about budget constraints, the characteristics of the product and the market, and the business philosophy of the organization.

PUSH AND PULL

There are basically two types of strategies a business can use to promote sales of a product. A business with a **push strategy** directs marketing efforts toward the marketing channels rather than the final consumers. It may offer incentives to warehouses or retailers in the form of added discounts for carrying its product or guarantee a certain amount of advertising to stimulate sales of the product. By encouraging channel members to carry the product, the business hopes to induce final sales to consumers.

A business with a **pull strategy** directs its promotional efforts toward the final consumer through advertising, personal selling, and sales promotion. The business hopes that consumer demand will encourage channel members to carry the product.

Usually, companies do not choose a pure push or pull strategy. The unique characteristics of the product, marketplace, and consumer may require a little of each. For example, stimulating consumer demand without giving channel members advance notice may result in lost sales and frustrated consumers. The most important thing is to coordinate all promotional efforts.

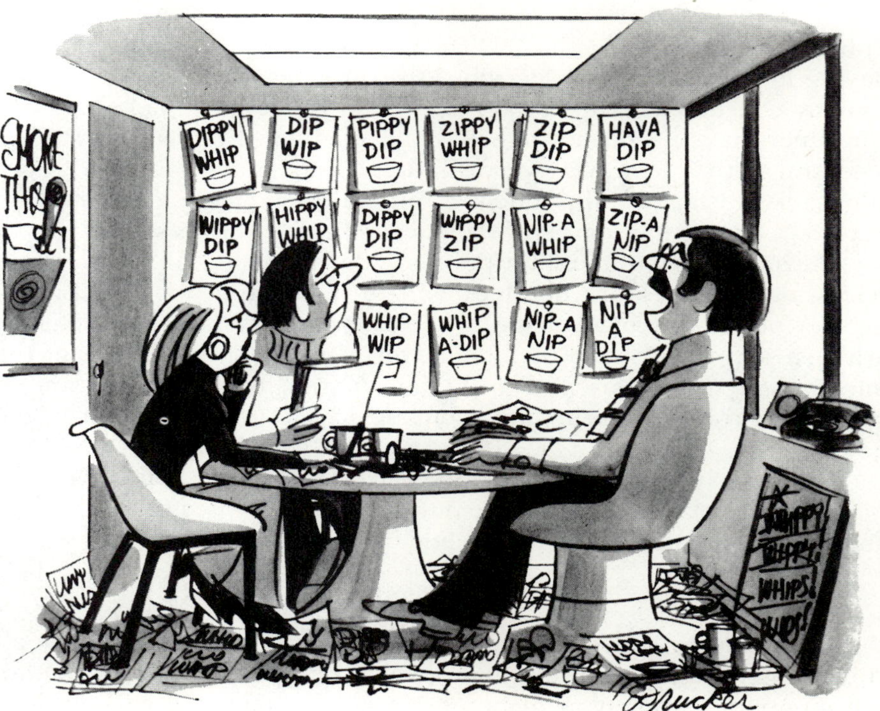

"On second thought, let's not take another crack at it."

SELECTING A PROMOTIONAL STRATEGY

A number of factors are involved in developing a successful promotional strategy for a business. The promotion budget, type of product, product life cycle, target market, and organizational philosophy all play important roles.

The Promotion Budget

Just as the size of a company's advertising budget can limit its selection of advertising media, the money available for promotion limits the mix of tools it can use to promote its product.

A company that emphasizes a push approach, encouraging channel acceptance of its product, will need to support a large sales force. The use of personal selling is especially important to a business selling to industrial rather than retail consumers, since the industrial buyer relies much more on rational detailed information in purchase decisions. Thus the sales force would be required to establish contacts, maintain and encourage sales, and provide information on the special sales promotion and advertisements planned for the products. On the other hand, if a company's strategy is to pull the product by stimulating consumer demand, its promotion budget may be directed toward advertising and sales promotion, with legitimate concerns focusing on the mix of media and the type of sales promotion to use. A company using a pull strategy would try to use its money to maximum efficiency by reaching as many potential customers as possible with the least expense.

Companies use a number of different methods to determine the optimal size of the promotion budget. One method is to spend as much money as the company can afford. Although this takes into consideration the financial limitations of the business, it may not match the promotional strategy of the firm. For instance, if the business is planning a large increase in sales and production, it may require outside financing in order to support the sales effort required to stimulate additional demand. By using only the money on hand, it may fail in its expansion efforts.

Another method is the **percentage-of-sales approach,** which earmarks a certain percentage of sales revenue for promotional expenses. Here again, budgeting promotion as a percentage of sales may not adequately consider all of the factors important to the firm's strategy. It could be that the competition is temporarily increasing its advertising level, in which case a percentage-of-sales budget may not allow the company to maintain its market share. Of course, a large sales volume subjected to the percentage-of-sales approach may provide more money than is required to the promotion effort, resulting in unnecessary expense.

Still another approach is for a company to match its promotion budget against the competition's. Although this may succeed in establishing a comparable level of effort, it does not take into consideration the company's own promotional strategy or product and market differences. It also requires that the company closely track its competitors' spending.

Finally, and perhaps more realistically, a promotion budget can be based on the promotional strategy for the coming year. Once the firm establishes its marketing plans—new product development, old product changes, and improvements in advertising—it seeks to determine how much money will be required to maintain that effort. Since this approach is most likely to take into account all of the marketing factors important to a firm, it can be the best approach to budgeting for promotion.

Type of Product

A company that manufactures and sells industrial products may wish to concentrate on personal selling instead of advertising in the mass media. However, trade journals circulated within the industry, as well as the types of magazines most likely to be read by industrial purchasing agents, may be an effective medium.

For retail consumer products, particularly specialty goods, highly select market groups are the target. Thus a company selling such products would use special-interest magazines or direct mail. For convenience goods distributed nationally, however, mass media would probably be more effective.

The particular image presented in advertisements depends to a great extent on the type of product being sold. If the product is bought on impulse, its seller may attempt an ad campaign that aims to keep the product name at the forefront of the consumer's mind. If there is a lot of emotion associated with the product, psychological appeals to the market may work best. Finally, if the product is highly specialized and sophisticated, rational information about its specifications and use may be most effective.

The Product Life Cycle

A new product may require a different promotional effort from one declining in sales volume. As Exhibit 14.4 indicates, promotional efforts for new products should be directed primarily toward providing information about the product and creating awareness in the potential market. As the product gains in acceptance, promotional efforts may be geared toward a push strategy, and discounts and advertising guarantees may be offered to channel members. If customer inquiries are strong enough, this approach may be successful in increasing sales of the product. As the product matures, reminder advertising will help promote repeat sales. Finally, as the product loses market acceptance and begins its decline, the company may wish either to reduce its promotional effort if the competitor's offering is superior (like slide rules compared to calculators) or to increase demand temporarily through increased promotion before the bottom drops out of the market.

The Target Market

The characteristics of a particular market may require a promotional strategy suited to its needs. For instance, if the target market is white-collar businesspeople in a large industrial city, a company may wish to use radio advertisements aired while they commute to work in the morning. Or it may wish to purchase local spots on television during the evening hours, when they are most likely to be watching. If the company hopes to appeal to young women, it may select women's magazines and daytime television to attract their attention and inform them of its product. Sales promotions involving point-of-purchase displays at stores frequented by young women might also be useful.

Organizational Philosophy

Finally, any promotional strategy used by a business must be consistent with corporate philosophy. If a company wishes to maintain a prestige image, it may spend more money on quality advertising for its products. A growth philosophy may dictate the use of mass advertising and a large promotional budget. And a selective production and distribution strategy may require careful use of media and sales promotion to get the attention of the target market and stimulate sales.

EXHIBIT 14.4 Advertising and the Product Life Cycle

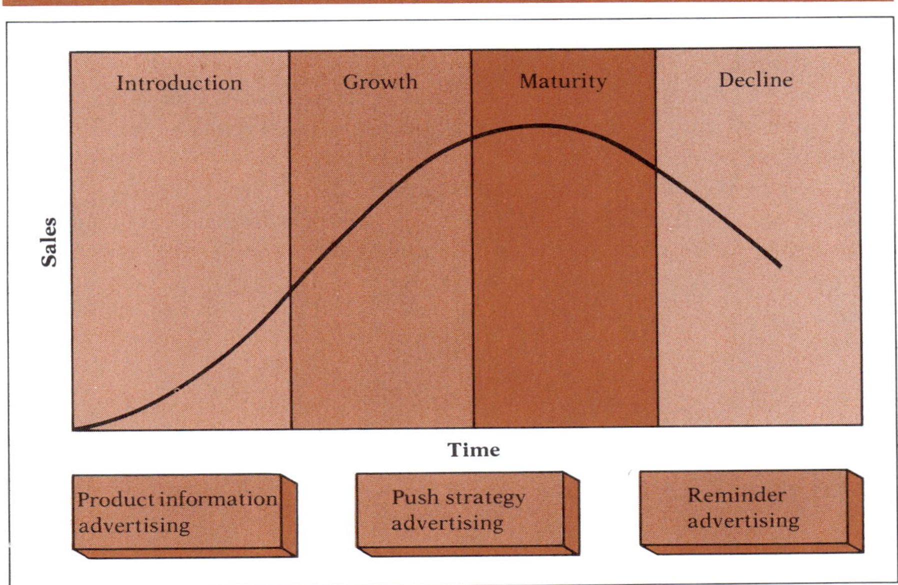

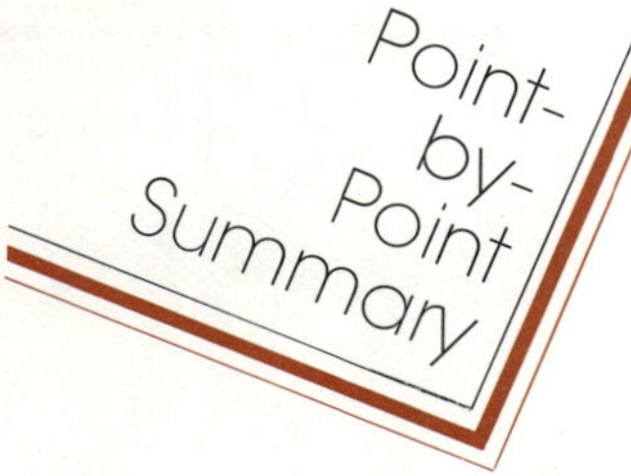

- Promotion is the application of advertising, personal selling, sales promotion, and publicity to gain market awareness and acceptance of products.
- Advertising must get the attention of the viewer or listener and send a message that best summarizes the advantages of the product. Advertising can be useful in providing information about the product, persuading a potential user to buy, and reminding users of the product's characteristics.
- There are five important types of advertising media that are readily available for use by a business: television, radio, newspapers, magazines, and direct mail.
- The selection of a particular advertising medium is based on financial, product, market, and competition considerations.
- Personal selling is conducted by salespeople who attempt to sell the firm's product directly to customers.
- Publicity is the unsolicited advertising received by a firm. Publicity can affect the firm's image and product acceptance by consumers.
- The promotional strategy used by a firm is determined by a number of factors, including budget size, type of product, stage of the product in its life cycle, target market, and organizational philosophy.

1. What are the characteristics of the TV advertisements that you remember? Does an advertisement have to be "artistic" to attract your attention?
2. What are the three purposes of an advertisement? Elaborate.
3. If you had manufactured a detergent for a mass market, what advertising media would you use?
4. What are the advantages of direct-mail advertising?
5. Why are certain products normally displayed near the checkout counter? What is that strategy meant to achieve?

APPLICATION

The Huntington National Bank of Columbus, Ohio and fourteen affiliate banks were recently consolidated into a statewide bank, Huntington Bancshares, Inc. The Huntington National Bank is a full-service bank providing specialized services in financing, lease financing, and real estate and investment management.

The Huntington was established in 1866 as P. W. Huntington & Co. By 1905 the bank was incorporated. It survived the money panic of 1907 because of its unusually liquid financial position, resulting from sound policies. It also survived the Depression era and has since grown as a result of successful mergers and branching out. Today Huntington and its affiliate banks rank among the 100 largest U.S. banks, with deposits of $1.94 billion and loans of $1.40 billion as of December 31, 1979.

PROMOTIONAL STRATEGY

Since 1976, the Huntington has been using as its advertising slogan "We're Never Satisfied Until You Are." In an effort to demonstrate its position as a consumer-oriented bank, Huntington has introduced many innovative services, such as both Master Card and VISA and simplified loan language. It was also the first bank in Columbus to offer simple-interest loans, and it pioneered a pay-by-phone system.

In March 1980, President Jimmy Carter imposed credit restrictions on the banking industry in an effort to curtail credit and lessen the inflationary spiral. As a result, most banks, including Huntington's competitors, levied an annual fee for handling credit card business. It was Huntington's strategy to let these banks notify their customers of these charges and then come out with advertisements announcing a $20 fee that would be waived for customers who maintained certain balances in their checking and savings accounts. The timing was of the greatest importance, because the advertisement was meant to influence customers who felt angry and frustrated with their banks.

The advertising began in mid-May with advertisements in newspapers and on TV and radio. TV carried the major thrust of the campaign, because it has the broadest reach and can deliver an effective appeal to the emotions.

You can see from Exhibit 14.5 that the programs selected for carrying Huntington's spots were either news programs (morning and evening) or prime-time programs. It was assumed that the decision makers that Huntington sought to influence would be out the entire day. The news programs were selected because they were thought to attract educated and sophisticated viewers who were sufficiently well-off to be interested in Huntington's pitch. Prime-time programs (8 to 11 p.m. Monday through Saturday and 7 to 11 p.m. Sunday) were selected because of their wide appeal to all audiences.

One of Huntington's newspaper advertisements is reproduced in Exhibit 14.6. These ads cost an average of about $2,500 per full page and were placed in the dailies of most of the large cities that Huntington operates in.

The total cost of this five-week campaign was estimated at $350,000, and Huntington believes that the investment paid off. In fact, the results exceeded all expectations, producing new credit card customers, new checking and savings accounts, and new certificates of deposit. As a bonus, many good current customers moved higher balances to the Huntington. Exhibit 14.7 summarizes the success of this campaign.

You may argue that new savings and checking accounts do not necessarily mean increased prosperity. But suppose a new customer brings her savings account balance of $500 to Huntington to obtain a credit card without a fee. With savings account interest of 5 percent, Huntington would pay yearly interest of $25. However, it could lend this money out at, say 11 percent and earn

EXHIBIT 14.5 Schedule for Huntington's TV Advertisements Week of May 12, 1980—Columbus, Ohio

#	Spot length	Program	Day/time	TV homes (000)	Total cost
WCMH-TV (NBC)					
3	:30	Today Show	M-F 7- 9:00 a.m.	15	$ 150
3	:30	Early News	M-F 6- 6:30 p.m.	168	750
3	:30	Late News	M-F 11-11:30 p.m.	186	750
	:30	F.D.R. Last Year	Th. 8-11:00 p.m.	73	1,000
	:30	Movie	Fri. 9-11:00 p.m.	57	700
	:30	Moviola	Sun. 9-11:00 p.m.	91	800
				659	$4,150
WTVN-TV (ABC)					
3	:30	Good Morning America	M-F 7- 9:00 a.m.	150	$ 300
2	:30	Early News	M-F 5:30-6:00 p.m.	132	600
3	:30	Late News	M-F 11-11:30 p.m.	141	900
	:30	Charlie's Angels	Wed. 8-10:00 p.m.	125	950
	:30	Barney Miller	Th. 10:00 p.m.	103	1,150
	:30	Love Boat	Sat. 8-10:00 p.m.	103	1,000
				754	$4,900
WBNS-TV (CBS)					
2	:30	Early News	M-F 6- 7:30 p.m.	280	$1,000
2	:30	Late News	M-F 11-11:30 p.m.	220	1,000
	:30	Late News	M-F 11-11:30 p.m.	110	650
	:30	M*A*S*H	Mon. 9:00 p.m.	160	1,200
	:30	Lou Grant	Mon. 10-11:00 p.m.	118	1,100
	:30	Dallas	Fri. 10:00 p.m.	143	1,500
	:30	60 Minutes	Sun. 7- 8:00 p.m.	153	1,300
	:30	Archie Bunker's Place	Sun. 8:00 p.m.	109	1,100
	:30	Trapper John	Sun. 10:00 p.m.	95	800
				1,388	$9,650
Weekly Totals		34 Spots		2,801	$18,700

Source: Arbitron Rating Service, Audience estimates in the market of Columbus, Ohio for the week ended May 12, 1980.

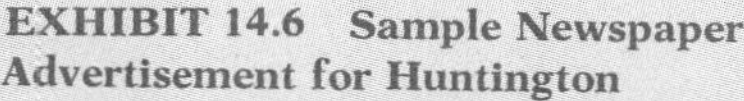

EXHIBIT 14.6 Sample Newspaper Advertisement for Huntington

Don't just get mad
at your bank for
charging you $20 for your
VISA or Master Charge.
Get a
new bank.
Huntington
Banks
We're never satisfied until you are.

$55 in a year. Even after figuring the costs of administering the credit card. Huntington stands to profit.

CAREER OPPORTUNITIES

Huntington employs new associates and graduates in business as management trainees. These management trainees are exposed to various departments—such as loans, data processing, customer service, internal auditing, economics, personnel, and marketing—depending on their educational background. Eventually, these management trainees are placed in departments that can best use their abilities and have existing vacancies.

FOR DISCUSSION

1. Why did Huntington use television for the bulk of its advertising?
2. Why was Huntington's TV advertising limited to the morning and evening time slots?

EXHIBIT 14.7 Business Trends following Huntington's Advertising Campaign

	Percentage change 1980 vs. 1979
New checking account activity:	
January to April	−6.5%
May	+37.8%
June	+29.4%
New savings accounts opened:	
January to April	−10.8%
May	+25.9%
June	+41.7%
New credit card activity:	
May	+30.2%
June	+77.0%

PART IV

AMADEO PETER GIANNINI

In true Horatio Alger fashion, Amadeo Peter Giannini began as a poor immigrant boy but formed the Bank of Italy in San Francisco by his early 30s. Giannini got a foothold in banking by encouraging small loans and picking up business from workers who had never used a bank before. Following the great earthquake of 1906, Giannini drove a vegetable cart through the streets with $2 million in gold and securities buried in a mound of produce. The next day the Bank of Italy went back into business, offering immediate loans to ruined businesses from a board across two barrels. This incident gave the Bank of Italy a reputation for stability.

The catastrophe led Giannini to believe that the only secure bank was a big bank. He began buying out small banks all around San Francisco, starting the nation's first major program of branch banking. Giannini formed the Bank of Italy Corporation in 1919 and the Transamerica Corporation in 1928. In the following year, he took over the Bank of America in New York and consolidated all his holdings into the Bank of America National Trust and Savings Association. This became the largest bank in the entire world.

Managing Financial Decisions

OBJECTIVES

- ☐ To define money and understand its three major functions
- ☐ To list the characteristics of money that allow it to perform its necessary functions
- ☐ To understand why checking account balances are considered money
- ☐ To outline the major elements of the U.S. banking system, including the relationship between the Federal Reserve and all other banks
- ☐ To distinguish among the three ways the money supply can be changed by the Federal Reserve
- ☐ To understand the other sources of loans that businesses have besides commercial banks
- ☐ To determine whether electronic money will lead to the cashless society

OUTLINE

KEY TERMS

BARTER
BILL OF EXCHANGE
CASHIER'S CHECK
CENTRAL BANK
CERTIFIED CHECK
CHECKING ACCOUNT BALANCE
COMMERCIAL BANK
CURRENCY
DEMAND DEPOSIT
DISCOUNT RATE
DRAFT
ELECTRONIC FUNDS TRANSFER SYSTEM (EFTS)
FIDUCIARY MONEY
FRACTIONAL RESERVE BANKING SYSTEM
LEGAL TENDER
LIQUID
MONEY
PROMISSORY NOTE
RESERVE REQUIREMENTS
TIME DEPOSIT
TRADE ACCEPTANCE
TRAVELER'S CHECK

MONEY AND BANKING

Who Uses All Those $100 Bills, Anyway?

DANIEL S. GREENBERG
Washington Post
Science & Government Report, Inc.

Let us examine the $100-bill explosion. Though little-known and poorly understood, this fiscal phenomenon suggests some important and peculiar goings on in American society.

While it is rare to encounter $100 bills in ordinary day-to-day dealings, this is not because they are rare. . . . According to the latest Currency and Coin Report of the U.S. Treasury, they already account for an astounding one-third of the total value of U.S. money in circulation, though they make up only about three per cent of all bank notes in current use.

Their prevalence simply reflects demand. The banks in the Federal Reserve System tell the Fed what they need to serve their customers, and the Fed places their orders with the Bureau of Engraving and Printing.

Thus, the national stock of $100 bills is growing because people want them. But why should this be happening at a time when extended use of checks and credit cards is supposedly creating a "cashless society"? And where are all those unseen $100s, of which nearly 290 million are in circulation? Who's doing what with the so-called century notes? . . . .

First, let there be no doubt about the trends and numbers. The $100 bill is the biggest growth item in the money business, outdistancing even the popular $20 in terms of increased dollar amounts ordered from the printers. Between 1960 and 1971, the value of money in $100 bills rose by 122 per cent, compared with 89.6 per cent of all money in circulation; at present, the figure is nearly 33 per cent. What's going on?

Inflation creates demands for the convenience of bigger denominations, but, then, some of that demand is countered by the ubiquity of credit-card systems. And, of course, organized crime, with its need for record-free transfers of large sums of cash, would rather tote one $100 than five $20s.

But among the few persons who have looked systematically at the $100-bill explosion, other possibilities are noted. For example, George E. Cruikshank, editor of the Morgan Guaranty Survey, thinks that part of the boom in $100s reflects a mattress-deposit mentality that, in turn, arises from widespread distrust of established financial institutions. A lot of people, he says, are tucking cash away at home because they worry about bank stability and also don't want anyone to know what they have. Anecdotal support for this assessment, he says, is to be found in reports from retail shops in strike-bound industrial towns. After the paychecks stop, idle workers start making purchases with big bills—presumably withdrawn from home storage.

A 1975 government-sponsored study by Arthur D. Little, Inc., estimated that in 1972, when $61 billion was in circulation, roughly $25 billion could be accounted for in business cash registers, banks and U.S. currency held abroad. The balance, at least $36 billion, works out to about $800 in cash on hand for the average family of four—a sum that is considerably at odds with the acknowledged cash-on-hand resources of most families of four. The report expressed doubt about any such evenness in currency distribution. It also stated that "it would appear that a significant fraction of cash either is immobilized or moves in other than normal channels."

Concerning the $13.2 billion in $100 bills at that time, the study added, "Most of these do not move actively in normal flows of cash; thus, perhaps 20 per cent of all cash in possession of individuals does not enter normal channels."

These findings raise interesting questions. If big bank notes play an important role in illicit dealings and a relatively minor one in normal commerce, why do we need big bank notes? Could the Mafia get along on $20s?

What economic consequences arise from the immobilization of billions in cash, which, after all, amounts to an interest-free loan for government and erosion-by-inflation for the home "depositor"?

Finally, anyone who claims we need $100 bills in the economy should first pass a severe test: Whose picture is on the big bank note?

The use of cash seems to be exploding in our economy. But after all, it wasn't until modern times that we had such a well-developed banking system in which checks were readily accepted. In this chapter, we will look at how the banking system is organized and the role it has in helping businesses operate.

When a business pays workers, the workers receive **currency** (bills and coins) or a check. If they are paid with a check and want to have currency, they generally go to a bank and cash the check, or they might exchange it with the seller of a product they wish to buy. The seller then deposits the check in the bank. In one way or another, most Americans deal with banks and with money in the form of currency and checks.

Money

The dictionary defines **money** as "anything customarily used as a medium of exchange and measure of value, such as sheep, wampum, gold dust, etc." Most Americans have a good idea of what money is in our society—bills, coins, and checks.

Money is useful because it facilitates transactions. Just think how society would be if people had to **barter** for everything—that is, exchange goods for goods. In economies based on a barter system, people spend tremendous amounts of time and effort making transactions. They waste much potential output by engaging in barter transactions instead of using money.

THE FUNCTIONS OF MONEY

There are three traditional functions of money. The one that most people are familiar with is that of serving as a *medium of exchange.* As a medium of exchange, money allows people to specialize in any area of endeavor in which they have a comparative advantage. Money payments for the fruits of their labor can then be exchanged for the fruits of other people's labor. The usefulness of money as a medium of exchange increases with the amount of trade and specialization in a society. Money would not be so important in a society composed of self-sufficient family units, for example, as it is in modern commercial economies.

Money is also a temporary *store of purchasing power,* or value. To understand what this means, consider the simple example of a fisherman who comes into port after two days of fishing. According to the going price of fish that day, he has $1,000 worth of fish on board his boat. But those fish are not a very good store of their own value. If the fisherman keeps them on board for any length of time (assuming he has no refrigeration system), they will probably rot and stink. If he attempts to barter them with other tradespeople, at least some of the fish may rot and stink before he gets the chance to barter the entire catch. On the other hand, if he sells the entire catch for money, he is storing the value of his catch in the money that he gets.

Money is the most **liquid** temporary store of purchasing power because it can immediately be exchanged for any goods and services at its face value. However, such is not the case with an antique vase, for example. Let's say that your boss pays you at the end of the month with an antique vase worth $1,000. You keep it for several weeks and then attempt to exchange it for goods and services that you want. But in order to do so, you would have to find people who know the value of the vase and who want to hold the vase as a store of purchasing power. The vase would clearly be very illiquid.

Finally, people need money as a *unit of accounting,* a way to measure value if they want to keep records of what is owed them, how much income they have made, how much income they have saved, and so on. It would be inconvenient to use, say, bushels of wheat as a unit of accounting and to express everything in terms of bushels of wheat, even though that could be done. Everything is measured in terms of dollars in the United States, in marks in Germany, in francs in France, and so on.

CHARACTERISTICS OF MONEY

To perform its necessary functions, money should have certain characteristics:

1. *Durability* Popcorn would be an inadequate type of money because it would get stale, crumble, mildew, disintegrate. We therefore use coins and paper currency, which wear out very slowly. A typical dollar bill can be folded over 4,000 times without falling apart.
2. *Difficulty in counterfeiting* The more easily money can be counterfeited, the less valuable it will be, because counterfeiters will increase the supply of money until no one wants to use it. Most countries go to immense lengths to prevent counterfeiting, using special silk threads in their paper and special plates in printing.
3. *Divisibility* If all we had in our money supply were hundred-dollar bills, that money wouldn't be very useful. Money must be divisible into small enough units so that it is conveniently matched to the size of the transactions in which we engage.
4. *Portability* If the typical piece of money we used was an iron anvil, it wouldn't be very useful. Individuals must be able to carry it around in order to use it.
5. *Predictability of purchasing power* If the purchasing power of a dollar bill is unpredictable, fewer people will want to hold it as a temporary store of value. Note that we talk about *predictability* as opposed to *stability* of purchasing power. Even in times of inflation, money still is used as a medium of exchange and a store of value; individuals still use money, even if its value is falling, as long as they can *predict* its future value.

TYPES OF MONEY

In the United States, the basic money supply consists of coins, paper bills, and checks. In recent years, several other types of money have also come into use.

Currency

Coins and bills are usually called currency. Coins include everything from pennies through Susan B. Anthony dollars. Whenever the value of

Different Types of Money That Have Been Used in the United States at Various Times

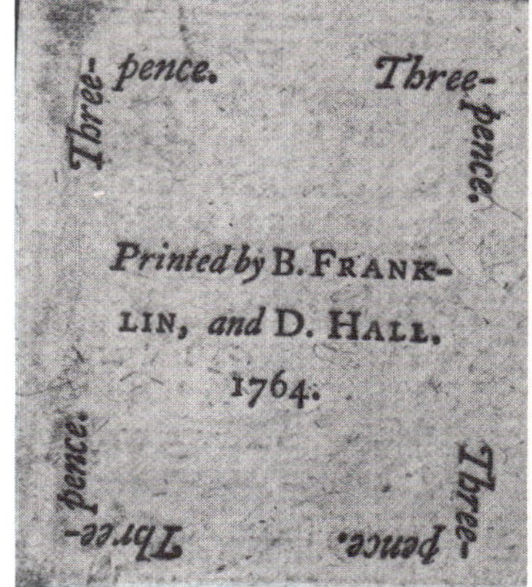

The President, Directors and Company of the Bank of North-America promise to pay to the Bearer, on demand, One Ninetieth of a Dollar. H
August 6, 1789.
Tench Francis, Cashier.
One Penny Specie.

Photos Courtesy of the Chase Manhattan Archives

the metal in a coin is greater than its face value, the coin risks being melted down. Even though this practice is illegal, it has occurred with such coins as pre-1965 quarters, half dollars, and dimes because the price of silver rose so high.

Paper money in the United States consists of one-dollar through hundred-dollar bills (although denominations up to hundred-thousand dollar bills have, on occasion, been used). Most of the bills in our money supply are Federal Reserve notes issued by Federal Reserve banks on the authorization of Congress. Americans have not always used Federal Reserve notes, however. They have, for example, used gold and silver as circulating currencies. Some societies have used other things.

Checking Accounts

In the United States, checks are also used as money. **Checking account balances** (also called **demand deposits**, because the owner of the deposit can demand payment at any time), on which people can write checks to pay for the things they buy, are considered a form of money because they serve all three purposes of money. About three-fourths of the entire money supply in the United States consists of these checking account balances.

"Almost" Checking Accounts

Since 1980, and passage of the historic Depository Institutions Deregulation and Monetary Control Act, all types of financial institutions have been allowed to issue checking accounts. Mutual savings banks, for example, have NOW accounts (*NOW* stands for *negotiable order of withdrawal*), which allow the owner of the account to earn interest on the balance and still write checks. Credit unions offer share draft accounts, which have a similar mode of operation. And owners can often write checks on money-market mutual funds (see Chapter 17). Today, to fully describe the nation's money supply, we would probably have to include all of the balances in NOW accounts, share draft accounts, money-market mutual funds that allow check writing, and others that will probably come into being in response to the new legislation.

Plastic Money

Many people believe that credit cards constitute an unlimited addition to the supply of money in the United States. At most, however, only the unused credit line available to owners of credit cards could be considered part of the money supply. Even so, several economists have found that credit cards add, at most only 1 percent to the stock of money in circulation. Presumably, recent restrictions on the issuance of credit cards will reduce this figure even lower.

Highlight What Backs the U.S. Dollar?

If you look at a dollar bill, most likely at the top of the face side it will say, "Federal Reserve Note." On the left it will say, "This note is legal tender for all debts, public and private." Nowhere is there any indication that the bill can be exchanged for a certain amount of gold or silver. It merely states that it is **legal tender.** This means that in the United States the bill has to be accepted in exchange for all debts owed. To summarize, *the dollar bill is not backed by anything. The only reason it is useful is that people have trust in it.* People have trust that a dollar's value—in terms of what it will buy—will not fluctuate dramatically. They also have trust that others will accept it in exchange for debts owed. In technical language, this is **fiduciary money**—money that people trust but that is not backed by any particular commodity.

The Development of Banks

Hundreds of years ago, rich moneylenders had strong vaults and tough guards. People who had valuables but no means of protection began to ask the moneylenders if they could leave their valuables with them for safekeeping. Undoubtedly the moneylenders charged a small fee for this service.

Finally it dawned on a few moneylenders that many of the people who were keeping valuables in their vaults usually kept the valuables there for fairly long periods. As the number of clients and the amounts deposited grew, the owners of the vaults realized that only a small fraction of clients would ask for their deposits at any one time. Thus the vault owners needed to keep only a relatively small fraction of the total deposits on reserve to meet the demands of those clients. They could lend the rest at interest and make additional income. This, theoretically, is the way our fractional **reserve banking system** grew up. All commercial banks (and most other banks) in the United States today operate on this principle.

Depositors as a whole will not demand more than a small percentage of any given bank's total deposits in any one day. The fact that it lends out the rest means there is more credit available in the economy.

That credit allows people to buy now and pay later, when they have more income.

COMMERCIAL BANKS

A major component of the money supply is demand deposits held in the 15,000 commercial banks in the United States. **A commercial** bank is a privately owned, profit-seeking institution. The most significant feature of a commercial bank is that it accepts demand deposits on which checks may be drawn.* Commercial banks can also transfer funds from one person's deposit to another's when told to do so by a customer's check. An additional function is to make loans to households and firms and to invest in government bonds.

Commercial banks also allow depositors to have **time deposits**—savings accounts and certificates of deposit. They are called time deposits because in principle the bank can require, say, thirty days' notice of the owner's intent to withdraw from such an account, although banks normally do not do so.

THE CENTRAL BANK

The commercial banks are the workhorses of the nation's banking system, but they do not completely determine the "work load"—the size and volume of demand deposits. Rather, at the head of our entire banking system, there is a **central bank.** In most countries, the central bank is either implicitly or explicitly owned and operated by the government. Also, a central bank is a bank dealing with other banks—a banker's bank. Commercial banks do business with both the central bank and the general public. Central banks regulate the commercial banking system and control the supply of money.

The Federal Reserve System

Our central bank was established by the Federal Reserve Act, signed on December 23, 1913, by President Woodrow Wilson. Basically, this act was an attempt to counter the periodic financial panics that had occurred in our country. The Federal Reserve System (also known as the Fed) was set up to aid and supervise banks and also to provide banking services for the U.S. Treasury.

ORGANIZATION OF THE FED

Exhibit 15.1 shows how the Federal Reserve System is organized. One component is the board of governors, which is composed of seven salaried, fulltime members appointed by the President with the approval of the Senate. There are twelve Federal Reserve banks, which have a total of twenty-five branches. Additionally, there is the very important Federal Open Market Committee (FOMC), which decides the monetary

*Since the passage of the Depository Institutions Deregulation and Monetary Control Act of 1980, the distinction between a commercial bank and all other financial institutions has been somewhat blurred. Virtually any other financial institution can now issue the equivalent of a checking account.

policy for the Fed in future days and weeks. This committee is composed of the members of the board of governors plus five representatives of the Federal Reserve banks, who are rotated periodically. The FOMC determines by its actions the future growth of the money supply and other important variables.

There are approximately 15,000 commercial banks in the United States. National banks receive their charter from the federal government; state banks receive their charter from the various state governments. All 4,700 national banks are required to be members of the Federal Reserve System. Although state banks are not required to join, about 1,000 of them have chosen to be members of the Federal Reserve System. Thus there are about 5,700 member banks. This is not the majority of all commercial banks, but still the bulk of deposits is held in Federal Reserve member banks.

REQUIRED RESERVES

The **reserve requirements** for member banks—the percentage of deposits that must be kept in Federal Reserve banks—are set by the board of governors of the Federal Reserve. These reserves provide some guarantee that unusual demands by depositors seeking to withdraw their money will not create havoc in the banking system. Since passage of the Depository Institutions Deregulation and Monetary Control Act, the majority of financial institutions must also keep a certain percentage of their deposits on reserve with Federal Reserve banks.

EXHIBIT 15.1 The Federal Reserve System

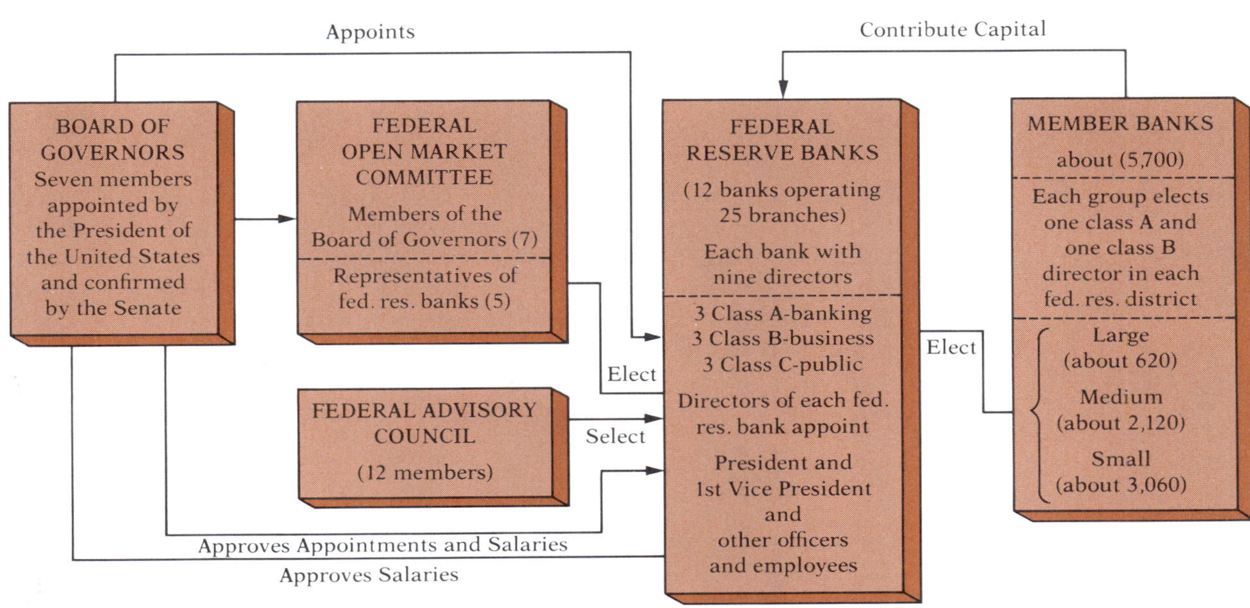

Source: Board of Governors of the Federal Reserve System

THE SUPPLY OF MONEY

The key function of the Federal Reserve is to control the amount of money in circulation in the United States in order to provide an adequate amount for the expanding needs of business in a growing economy. Another of its goals is to prevent an oversupply of money in circulation, which overheats the economy and causes inflation. The Federal Reserve can affect the amount of money in circulation in several ways.

Changing Reserve Requirements

One way the Federal Reserve can affect the money supply is by raising reserve requirements. Suppose a bank has $1 million in deposits and the reserve requirement is 20 percent. That bank can lend out $800,000. It must keep $200,000—the reserve requirement—on deposit with the Federal Reserve. Of course, when the $800,000 is loaned out, that money eventually finds its way into other banks. These banks can in turn lend out 80 percent of $800,000, or $640,000. The $640,000 will then find its way to other banks, which can lend out 80 percent of it, and so on down the line.

If the Federal Reserve raises reserve requirements to 40 percent, the bank with $1 million in deposits would have to have $400,000 on reserve. Thus it would have to call in $200,000 in loans, or at least not renew that amount as loans came due, in order to build up its reserve position to meet the legal requirement. Obviously, this would contract the amount of money in circulation in the economy, because not only would that bank lend less money but so too would all other banks.

In recent years, the reserve requirements have not been used often to change the money supply in the United States.

Changing the Discount Rate

If a bank does not have enough reserves to meet its reserve requirement, it has to borrow the portion needed, at least temporarily. One of the ways it may do this is by calling the Federal Reserve and asking for a loan. The Federal Reserve does not make this type of loan for free; it charges interest in the form of the **discount rate.** If the Federal Reserve raises its discount rate, it will discourage some member banks from borrowing reserves. Therefore, a change in the discount rate is also a way to affect the total money supply.

Affecting Reserves Directly

The most powerful and most-used means by which the Federal Reserve affects the supply of money in circulation is by changing reserves directly. It does this by buying and selling U.S. government bonds from and to the public or banks.

Suppose the Federal Reserve buys a $1,000 bond from a member bank. It credits $1,000 to the reserve deposit account of the bank from which it purchases the bond, so that the bank has one less bond and $1,000 more in reserves. Therefore, that bank can lend additional money.

When the Federal Reserve wants to decrease the money supply, it *sells* a bond to a member bank. The bank pays for the bond by having its reserve deposit account lowered by the amount of the bond. The bank then can lend less money.

Exhibit 15.2 shows all of the ways the money supply can be increased and decreased.

A CLEARINGHOUSE FOR CHECKS

The Federal Reserve System has greatly simplified the procedure for clearing checks—that is, for transferring a check that has been deposited in one bank to the bank on which it was written.

Suppose John Smith, who lives in Chicago, writes a check to Jill Jones, who lives in San Francisco. When Jill Jones receives the check in the mail, she deposits it in her bank. Her bank then deposits the check in the Federal Reserve Bank of San Francisco, which in turn sends the check to the Federal Reserve Bank of Chicago. The Federal Reserve Bank of Chicago then sends the check to John Smith's bank. There the amount of the check is deducted from John Smith's account. Exhibit 15.3 shows how this is done.

The Federal Deposit Insurance Corporation

The Federal Deposit Insurance Corporation (FDIC) was established in 1934, during the Depression. Its principal purpose was to insure commercial bank deposits against failure of the bank. At the beginning of the 1980s, each depositor is protected to an upper limit of $100,000 which applies to the total number of accounts a single depositor has under his or her name within a single bank. Thus if you had a $54,000 savings account and a $51,000 checking account, in one bank, you would

EXHIBIT 15.2 How the Money Supply Can Be Changed

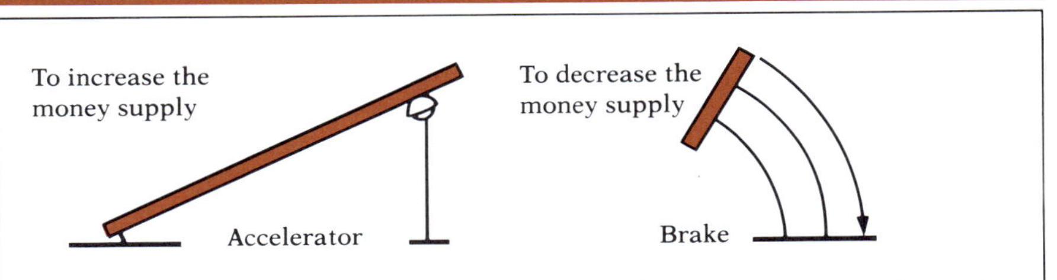

To increase the money supply	To decrease the money supply
1. Reduce member bank reserve requirements.	**1.** Increase reserve requirements.
2. Reduce discount rate that member banks must pay to borrow reserves.	**2.** Raise discount rate.
3. Buy bonds in the open market.	**3.** Sell bonds in the open market.

be insured only up to $100,000. Moreover, if you have accounts in the same name in a main office and in one or more branches of the insured bank, the accounts are added together to determine your insurance.

Lending Institutions

SAVINGS BANKS

There are numerous other financial institutions operating in the United States, including savings banks, savings and loan associations, credit unions, finance companies, and factoring companies.

Savings banks accept deposits and lend them out for long terms to reliable borrowers. They make a profit by lending the money at higher rates of interest than they had to pay the depositors who supplied the money. Such banks provide a safe place in which to invest savings. As with commercial bank deposits, savings bank deposits often require

EXHIBIT 15.3 How a Check Is Cleared

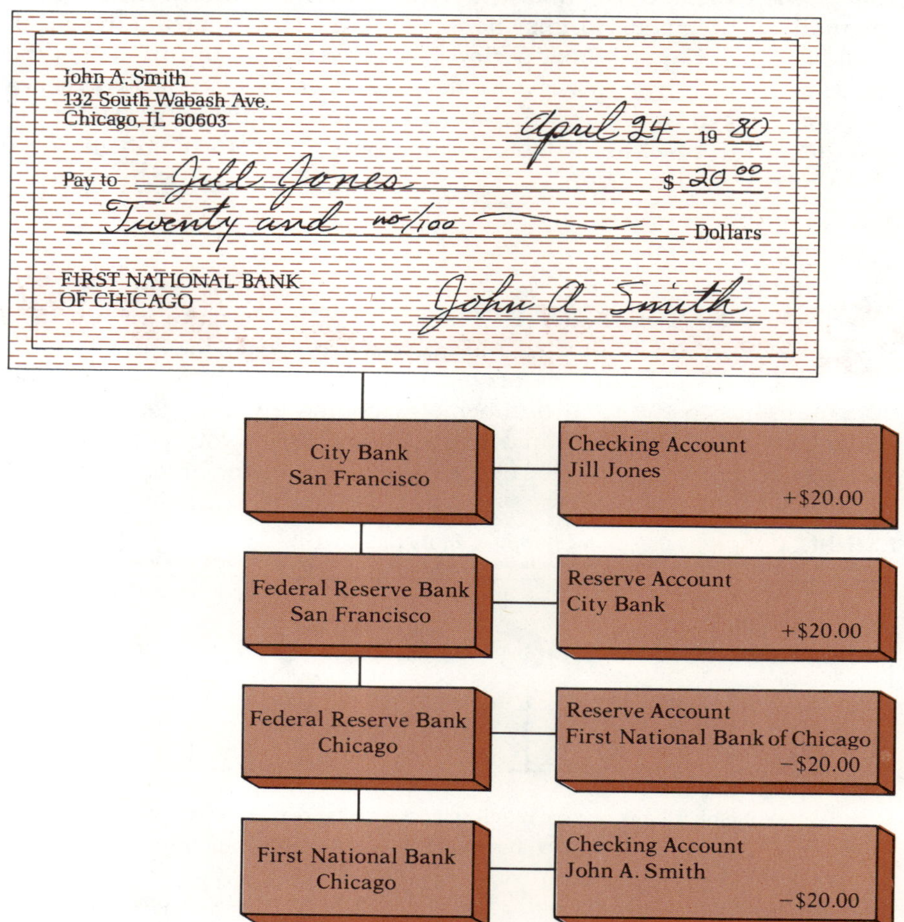

that notice be given before the money can be withdrawn. This provision is rarely put into effect, however. There are various types of savings banks, but the two main ones are stock and mutual banks.

Stock savings banks are organized and conducted for profit by the owners of their capital stock. The greatest number of stock savings banks are located in the midwestern United States. These banks are regulated by the state they are chartered in.

Mutual savings banks are owned by their depositors. In effect, the depositors pool their savings, which are invested by a board of trustees and a hired manager. Depositors are not paid a fixed rate of interest on their deposits; net earnings from the bank's investments are divided among the depositors in proportion to their deposits. Mutual savings banks are located primarily in the eastern United States, although there are a few in the Northwest. The total amount that a single individual can invest in a mutual savings bank is limited.

"My fellow-employees, it is my painful duty to tell you that discovery of a cash shortage was made this morning amounting to some eighteen million dollars."

SAVINGS AND LOAN ASSOCIATIONS

These so-called thrift organizations, of which there are some 5,400, are designed to assist present and future homeowners. The names by which these associations are known vary in different parts of the country. Some are called cooperative banks or building and loan associations.

Generally, when you put your money into a savings and loan association, you get a passbook that indicates you are a shareholder in that organization. As a member, you are entitled to receive interest on your deposits. Your deposits may be insured by the Federal Savings and Loan Insurance Corporation (FSLIC).

CREDIT UNIONS

One of the fastest-growing types of savings institutions is the credit union, which is owned by its members. Because a credit union typically is set up for a particular group—teachers in a certain city or state, members of a specific labor union, and so on—you must be part of such an organization in order to join. Credit unions have four purposes:

- To help their members save
- To enable their members to borrow money at lower-than-market interest rates
- To educate members in money management
- To provide opportunities for volunteer service

Members in a credit union usually buy shares, which are marked in a share booklet or passbook. In effect, credit unions are really cooperative small-loan banks that lend amounts to their members at "reasonable" rates of interest. Federal and state laws determine the maximum amount that may be loaned by a credit union.

Credit union deposits are usually insured by the National Credit Union Administration (NCUA), which supervises the national credit union shareholders' insurance fund.

FINANCE COMPANIES

People and companies that need short-term financing have an alternative to commercial banks, credit unions, and the like. Commercial, sales, and consumer finance companies serve the borrowing needs of specific groups.

Commercial Finance Companies

Commercial finance companies lend money to businesses through secured loans, which means that the debt is backed by such things as accounts receivable, heavy equipment, and inventories. Most firms that seek short-term loans from commercial finance companies are unable to obtain the loans from commercial banks.

Sales Finance Companies

Customers buying major items from businesses can go to sales finance companies, which finance installment credit on individual purchases of such things as refrigerators, freezers, and automobiles. An example of this type of finance company is General Motors Acceptance Corporation (GMAC). Some finance companies handle installment sales to businesses also.

In effect, sales finance companies buy installment credit from retail merchants. This way, retailers are able to transfer the risk involved in lending money.

Consumer Finance Companies

Consumer finance companies make small loans to consumers at relatively high rates of interest. These are the loan companies you hear advertised on radio and TV. They are the largest source of installment cash loans—that is, loans that consumers obtain for purposes other than the direct purchase of durable goods. There are perhaps 25,000 licensed consumer finance offices in America today. Some examples are Household Finance Corporation (HFC) and Beneficial Finance.

FACTORING COMPANIES

Factoring companies are similar to commercial finance companies, but they buy the accounts receivable from a business at a discount. For example, if XYZ Heavy Machinery Company has accounts receivable of $100,000, a factoring company may pay $90,000 for them. The customers pay their bills directly to the factoring company (or factor). If a customer does not pay his or her account, the factoring company takes the loss. Small firms find themselves using factoring companies more often than larger ones, because large companies usually can finance their credit needs through commercial banks at a lower cost.

Credit card companies are actually factoring companies. The retail establishment writes up a credit card slip when a purchase is made, say for $100. The businessperson then takes this piece of paper to the commercial bank holding his or her credit card accounts. The commercial bank may then deposit $96 in the business's account, charging a "discount" of $4. The bank repeats a similar transaction with the credit card company. The retail customer pays directly to the credit card company, which is really the factor.

TRUTH-IN-LENDING REGULATIONS

Consumer credit is heavily regulated. The most important piece of legislation regulating consumer credit is the Consumer Credit Protection Act, commonly known as the Truth-in-Lending Act. Under this law, sellers and lenders must disclose credit terms or loan terms so that a debtor can shop around for the best financing arrangement.

Disclosure

The disclosure requirements of the Truth-in-Lending Act apply to any installment sales contract in which payment is to be made in more than four installments. The following is a breakdown of the disclosure requirements as they would apply, for example, to the sale of a stereo on such an installment plan:

- The cash price of the stereo
- The down payment or trade-in allowance, if any
- The unpaid cash price (cash price minus the down payment)
- The finance charge, which includes interest, points, service charges, lender's fee, finder's fee, fee for investigation of credit, credit life insurance premium, accident insurance premium, and so on
- Charges not included as part of the finance charge
- The total amount to be financed
- The annual percentage rate of the finance charge
- The date that the finance charge begins to accrue
- The number, amounts, and due dates of payments
- The penalties in case of delinquency or other late-payment charges
- The security interest
- The prepayment penalty charge

Who Is Subject to the Act?

Only certain creditors or lenders and only certain types of transactions are subject to the Truth-in-Lending Act. It applies to persons who, in the ordinary course of their businesses, lend money or sell on credit or arrange for the extension of credit. For this reason, sales or loans between two consumers do not come under the act. Only debtors who are *natural* persons are protected by this law; corporations or other legal entities are not. Transactions covered by the act typically include retail and installment sales and installment loans, car loans, home improvement loans, and certain real estate loans—if the price is less than $25,000.

A creditor who fails to comply with the disclosure requirements may be liable to the consumer for twice the amount of the finance charge. In no event will that penalty be less than $100 or more than $1,000 for a violation against an individual consumer. The consumer has one year from the date of the violation to bring suit against a creditor who has failed to provide the disclosure statement or who has failed to correct an error in the disclosure statement.

Credit Instruments

Although they cannot always take the place of money, credit instruments—including drafts, promissory notes, trade acceptances, and special checks—are useful for documenting exchanges of money for goods and services. Exhibit 15.4 shows examples of the credit instruments described below.

A **draft** is sometimes called a **bill of exchange.** The party creating it orders another party to pay money to a third party.

When one person promises to pay a sum of money to another person at a definite time or on demand, a **promissory note** is used. Notes are used to extend credit in many kinds of businesses. For example, in real estate transactions, a buyer executes a promissory note for the unpaid balance on a house, secured by a mortgage on the property being purchased.

A **trade acceptance** is a special type of draft ordinarily used in the sale of goods. Essentially, the draft orders the buyer to pay a specified sum of money to the seller at a stated time in the future. Say that each fall Good Yard Company sells $50,000 of fabric to Lane Dresses on terms requiring payment to be made in ninety days. One year Good Yard needs quick cash, so it draws up a trade acceptance that orders Lane to pay $50,000 to the order of Good Yard Company ninety days hence. Lane accepts by signing the face of the paper, creating an enforceable promise to pay the installment when it comes due. Good Yard can turn around and sell this trade acceptance in the commercial money market more easily than it can assign the $50,000 account receivable. Thus trade acceptances are the standard credit instruments in sales transactions.

There are a number of types of special checks that can be issued. When a bank draws a check on itself, the check is called a **cashier's check.** In effect, the bank lends its credit to the purchaser of the check, thus making it available for immediate use in banking circles.

The **traveler's check,** like the cashier's check, is drawn by the issuer on itself. With traveler's checks, however, there is an additional requirement that the person receiving the money must provide an authorized signature in order for this transaction to occur.

When a person writes a check, it is assumed that he or she has money on deposit to cover the check when it is presented for payment. But sometimes the recipient wants to be sure the funds are on deposit. Thus the bank can issue a **certified check,** which prevents it from denying payment of the check. The usual method of certification is for the cashier or teller to write across the face of the check, over the signature, a statement that it is good when properly endorsed. This is a promise that sufficient funds *have been set aside* to cover the check.

EXHIBIT 15.4 Sample Credit Instruments

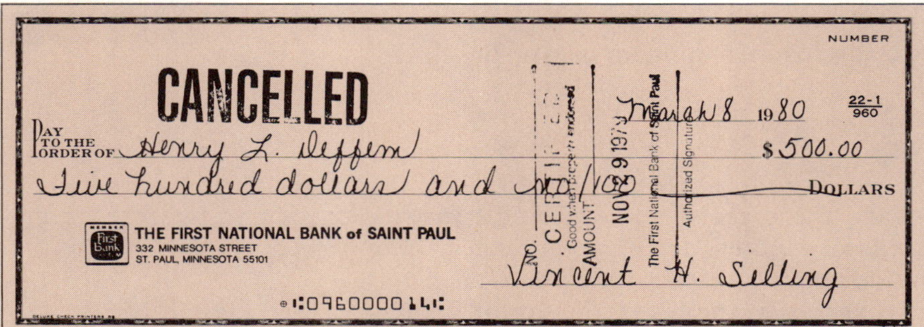
NUMBER

CANCELLED

March 8 1980 22-1/960

PAY TO THE ORDER OF Henry L. Deffem $500.00

Five hundred dollars and no/100 DOLLARS

THE FIRST NATIONAL BANK of SAINT PAUL
332 MINNESOTA STREET
ST. PAUL, MINNESOTA 55101

NO. CERTIFIED Good when properly endorsed AMOUNT NOV 29 1979 The First National Bank of Saint Paul Authorized Signature

Vincent H. Selling

⑆096000014⑆

Certified Check

Typical Promissory Note

$ ---3,000.00 ---- Saint Paul, Minnesota April 30, 19 80 Due 6/20/80

-------- Sixty days -- after date,

for value received, the undersigned jointly and severally promise to pay to the order of THE FIRST NATIONAL BANK OF SAINT PAUL at its office in Saint Paul, Minnesota, $ --- Three Thousand and no/100 Dollars with interest thereon from date hereof at the rate of -- 15 -- per cent per annum (computed on the basis of actual days and a year of 360 days) as indicated in No. 7 below.

7 INTEREST IS PAYABLE AT MATURITY
8 INTEREST IS PAID TO MATURITY
9 INTEREST IS PAYABLE ________ BEGINNING ON ________

CANCELLED

NO. 096-85-710
OFFICER Clark
BY RAD
ACCRUAL
☑ NEW ☐ REN'L
☑ SECURED ☐ UNSECURED

☑ SECURITIES ☐ INSURANCE ☐ SAVINGS ☐ OTHER
☐ SEC. AGREEMENT 1. INV. & ACCTS. 2. CONSUMER GOODS 3. EQUIP.

SIGNATURE Lawrence E. Roberts SIGNATURE Margaret P. Roberts

SIGNATURE ________ SIGNATURE ________

32-364 (8-71)

Typical Cashier's Check

F 537 M

THE FIRST NATIONAL BANK of SAINT PAUL NUMBER 644848
332 MINNESOTA STREET ST. PAUL MINNESOTA 55101

DATE February 27, 1980 22-1/960

PAY TO THE ORDER OF ------ Richard M... ---------------- $-- 500.00 --

CANCELLED

-------- Five hundred and no/100 --

CASHIER'S CHECK

Susan Walker CANCELLED

AN AUTHORIZED SIGNATURE

⑈644848⑈ ⑆096000014⑆ 01⑈00028⑈

Draft (Bill of Exchange)

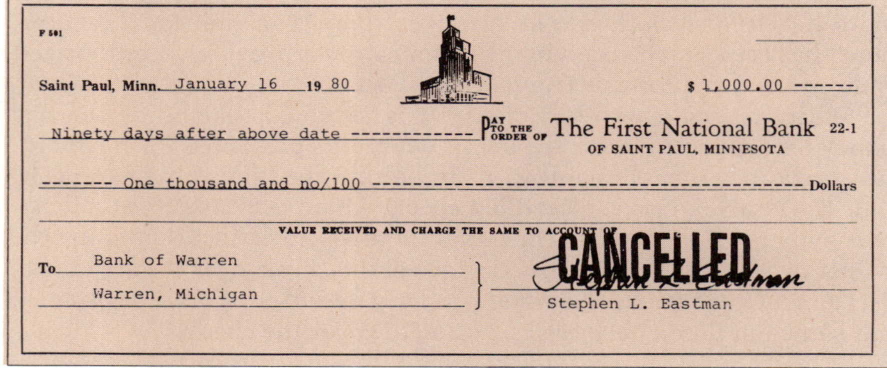
F 501

Saint Paul, Minn. January 16 19 80 $ 1,000.00 ------

Ninety days after above date ------------ PAY TO THE ORDER OF The First National Bank OF SAINT PAUL, MINNESOTA 22-1

------- One thousand and no/100 -- Dollars

VALUE RECEIVED AND CHARGE THE SAME TO ACCOUNT OF

CANCELLED

To Bank of Warren
Warren, Michigan

Stephen L. Eastman

The Cashless Society?

Money is defined by its roles: it serves as a medium of exchange, as a unit of accounting, and as a store of purchasing power. Since our receipts do not always match our expenditures, we generally keep some money in a checking account balance or in our wallets in order to meet expenditures when they occur. Recently, however, new developments in banking have led some people to proclaim the impending arrival of the cashless society. They predict more efficient means of handling money than the coins, bills, and checks we have become accustomed to.

ELECTRONIC BANKING

In some cities you no longer need to use paper currency and coins or checks in order to make purchases. You can have funds automatically transferred, by computer, from your checking account to a merchant. The official banking term for this is the **electronic funds transfer system (EFTS).** There are basically three parts to an EFTS: teller machines, point-of-sale systems, and automated clearinghouses.

Teller machines, also called customer bank communication terminals or remote service units, are located either on the bank's premises or in such stores as supermarkets and drugstores. Automated teller machines receive deposits, dispense funds from checking or savings accounts, make cash advances on credit card accounts, and receive payments. They are connected directly to the bank's computers.

Point-of-sale systems allow the consumer to transfer funds to merchants in order to make purchases. Computer terminals are located at checkout counters in certain stores. When making a purchase, the customer's bank card is inserted into the terminal, which reads the data encoded on it. The computer at the customer's bank verifies that the card and identification code are valid and that there is enough money in the customer's account. After the purchase is made, the customer's account is debited for the amount of the purchase.

Automated clearinghouses are similar to the ones banks now use to clear checks. The main difference is that the entries are in the form of electronic signals—there are no paper checks traveling between banks. Such systems are especially useful for recurrent business payments like payroll, Social Security, or pension fund plans that come up every week or every month.

MONEY STILL EXISTS

What do an EFTS and, in particular, a point-of-sale system do to the money supply? The answer is nothing. In a cashless, checkless society, you would still need a checking account balance on which to draw. You would have to deposit your salary checks into your account (or have it done by your employer) at the beginning of each month, just as you might do now. The basic advantage of a cashless, checkless society is that the costs associated with exchange could be reduced. It is estimated that the banking system now spends over $7 billion annually just to process 32 billion checks.

Will the cashless, checkless society make household budgeting more difficult? Not necessarily. Many monthly expenses are fixed, such as car and house payments. Paying them automatically will not alter your spending behavior. Moreover, you would get a statement detailing your transactions at the end of each month, just as you do now.

EFTS cannot alter the total amount of income that we spend. Nor will total money supply be affected by switching to EFTS. Money is here to stay, and no electronic funds transfer system can change that.

- The three functions of money are to serve as a medium of exchange, a store of purchasing power, and a unit of accounting. To perform these functions, money must be durable, difficult to counterfeit, divisible, and portable, and it must have a predictable purchasing power.
- The money supply consists of, at a minimum, currency (coins and bills) and checking account balances, also called demand deposits.
- The Federal Reserve System consists of twelve member banks with twenty-five branches. Since the Depository Institutions Deregulation and Monetary Control Act of 1980, virtually all banks, whether or not they are members, must keep reserves with the Federal Reserve System.
- The Federal Reserve can change the money supply by changing reserve requirements, changing the discount rate, and buying and selling U.S. government bonds.

- The Federal Deposit Insurance Corporation insures all deposits in its member banks up to $100,000.
- In addition to commercial banks, there are other financial institutions where businesspeople can go for loans. They include savings banks, savings and loan associations, credit unions, finance companies, and factoring companies.
- A draft, sometimes called a bill of exchange, is an unconditional written order to pay. A simple check is a draft. A promissory note is a promise to pay a sum of money to another person. A trade acceptance is a special type of draft that businesses use in the sale of goods. It orders the buyer to pay a specified sum of money to the seller at a stated time in the future. Finally, there are at least three types of special checks: cashier's, traveler's, and certified. All three are almost identical to cash in the sense that the acceptor can be certain they will not "bounce."
- Electronic banking will not eliminate cash in our society. It is simply a method of reducing the costs of making exchanges.

1. Why wouldn't popcorn be a good type of money?
2. Can you list the problems that might occur if gold became the circulating medium of exchange in the United States? What would be the benefits?
3. Could we have a system in which the medium of exchange was different from the unit of accounting? What would be the problems?
4. Can you distinguish between the predictability of purchasing power and the stability of purchasing power? Can you now explain why we still use dollar bills even though we have relatively high rates of inflation today?
5. Why is a checking account called a demand deposit?
6. We have a fiduciary system of currency. What does that mean?
7. Explain how the Federal Reserve's purchase of $1 million of government bonds from a commercial bank increases the money supply.
8. What is the difference between a credit card company and a factoring company?
9. If you had to ask for a special check in payment for a debt, would you prefer to have a cashier's check or a certified check? Explain your answer.
10. Can we ever get to the point where we have a truly cashless society? How would life be?

APPLICATION

In October 1904, a small neighborhood bank opened for business in a remodeled tavern in the North Beach area of San Francisco. Its assets at the end of 1904 were $285,000. Today, Bank of America has over $70 billion in assets, 1,100 branches throughout California, and 223 branches, affiliates, subsidiaries, and representative offices in seventy-eight countries abroad.

In the beginning, the founder of this bank, Amadeo Peter Giannini, had decided that small wage earners and small businesses should be offered the same banking services reserved for wealthy individuals and large companies. Giannini's Bank of Italy (so named until 1930) did well until the San Francisco earthquake of 1906. The bank was completely destroyed, but Giannini was able to load $80,000 in cash on wagons and move the money to his home for safekeeping. Before the larger banks could reopen, he was lending money from a plank-and-barrel counter at the waterfront. Surviving the bank-closing panic of 1907, by 1918 the Bank of Italy had twenty-four branches in California. Giannini was the leader in branch banking in spite of opposition from competitors and state officials.

During the Great Depression, management at the newly named BankAmerica considered breaking up the bank and salvaging its assets through contraction and liquidation. When Giannini heard about this, he got himself reelected chairman of the board at a special shareholders' meeting and again took active control of the bank that he had relinquished during several years of illness. His bank withstood the Great Depression in spite of the fact that 8,000 other banks either were liquidated, went bankrupt, or had to merge with other banks in order to stay afloat.

Bank of America

DEVELOPMENTS IN THE BANKING INDUSTRY

Bank of America has led the way to many new developments in the banking industry. For example, Timeplan® lending was an installment loan service that put the Bank of America first in the nation in the amount of money loaned. The Bank of America entered the electronics age in the mid-1950s with the development of ERMA, the first fully automated electronic accounting system in the banking industry. Later the bank issued its world-known BankAmericard, now called VISA.

On the international front, the Bank of America opened a branch in London during World War II. When the war came to an end, it expanded its overseas operations by opening branches in Manila, Tokyo, Yokohama, Kobi, Bangkok, Düsseldorf, Guam, and Osaka and by purchasing an interest in banks in Italy and Switzerland (thereby gaining entry into several African countries).

ORGANIZATION OF THE BANK

Bank of America is organized along traditional lines, with controllers, planners, and financial experts helping to manage the three major divisions—World Banking, California Banks, and Administration (see Exhibit 15.5).

Bank of America has attempted to increase its financial activities by the purchase of GAC Finance Corporation (now Finance-America Corporation), one of the nation's largest consumer finance companies. Bank of America has also become involved in computer leasing and financial data processing through its Decimus Corporation subsidiary. In addition, it deals in the following areas:

- *Investment and research services* BA Investment Management Corporation (BAIMCO)
- *Traveler's checks* BA Check Corporation
- *Venture capital investment* BA Capital Corporation
- *Real estate loans* BA Mortgage and International Realty Corporation (BAMIRCO)
- *Real estate investment trust* BA Realty Investors (BARI) and BankAmerica Realty Services, Inc. (BARSI)

Currently, Bank of America is struggling to assimilate the monumental Depository Institutions Deregulation and Monetary Control Act of 1980. As a result of this act, commercial banks like the Bank of America no longer have the exclusive right to offer checking accounts. All banking institutions will eventually be able to offer some type of checking account and many, if not most, will offer interest. The real question at Bank of America is whether it can cope with such changes and still maintain its position as the largest bank in the world.

CAREER OPPORTUNITIES

There are hundreds of career possibilities at the Bank of America, but we will concentrate on only two areas—operations and credit.

Operations Opportunities

These are the most complex jobs the Bank of America has to offer, because operations officers are responsible for the smooth functioning of branch offices. They schedule employees' hours, conduct performance appraisals, hire and promote, prepare the office budget, take care of upset customers, and work on business development plans. Even though they work under a branch manager, operations officers set their own work priorities. The preferred academic background for operations

EXHIBIT 15.5 Organization of the Bank of America

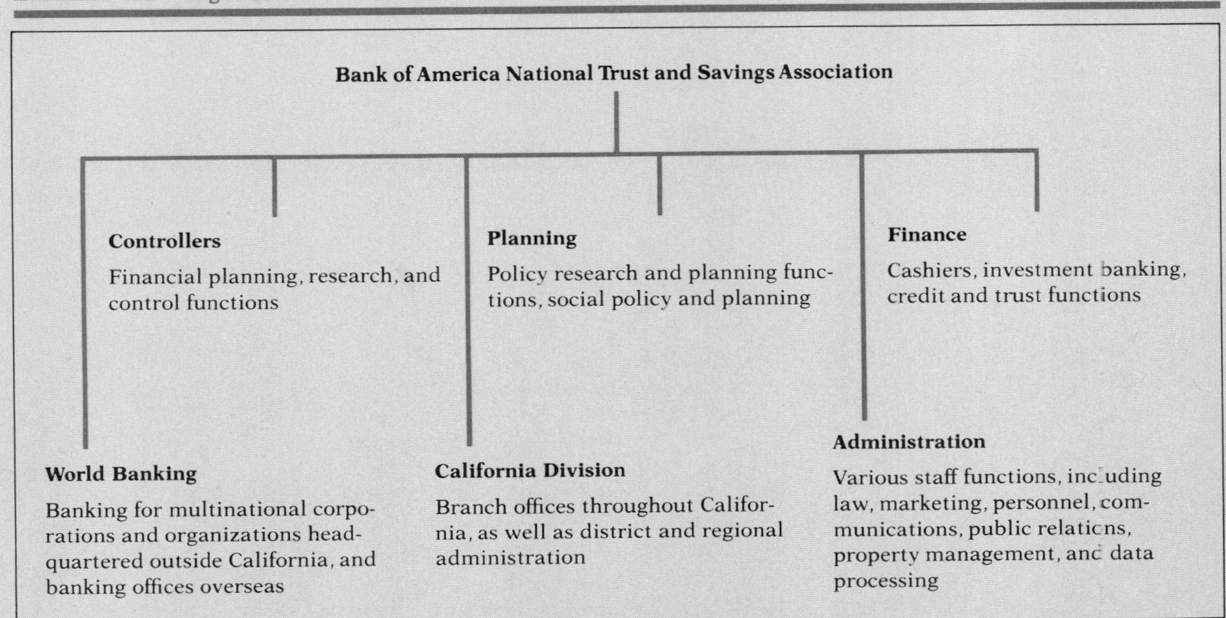

includes degrees in business administration and economics. Certainly experience in a branch office is useful.

An operations career starts with a self-paced management training program that lasts from seven to nine months. The training combines classroom work with self-study and job experience. During the training period, each participant is coached by an experienced operations officer.

After training, the new operations officer is immediately assigned to a branch. Advancement typically means moving to larger branches with more people and a broader mix of customers. Once an operations officer has reached the end of the line, there are several other options open: regional administration, credit training, and division or headquarters administration. Exhibit 15.6 shows a typical advancement pattern for operations professionals.

Credit Opportunities

The Bank of America makes loans. Making good loans is clearly of primary importance, so its effectiveness as an organization depends on its loan officers. Loan officers spend their time performing a number of tasks, including working directly with customers, developing financing plans, analyzing financial statements and applications, documenting loans, and developing and promoting new business. Again, the Bank of America prefers applicants with degrees in business administration or economics.

The typical new loan officer has responsibilities for arranging the financing of automobiles, mobile homes, and other consumer durables for dentists, physicians, and other professionals, who tend

EXHIBIT 15.6 Operations Career Path

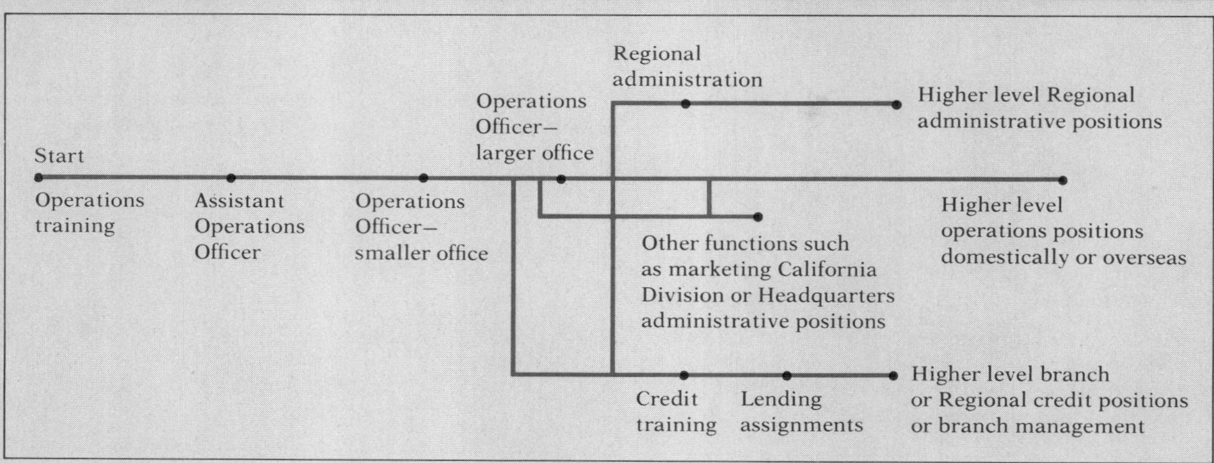

EXHIBIT 15.7 Credit Career Path

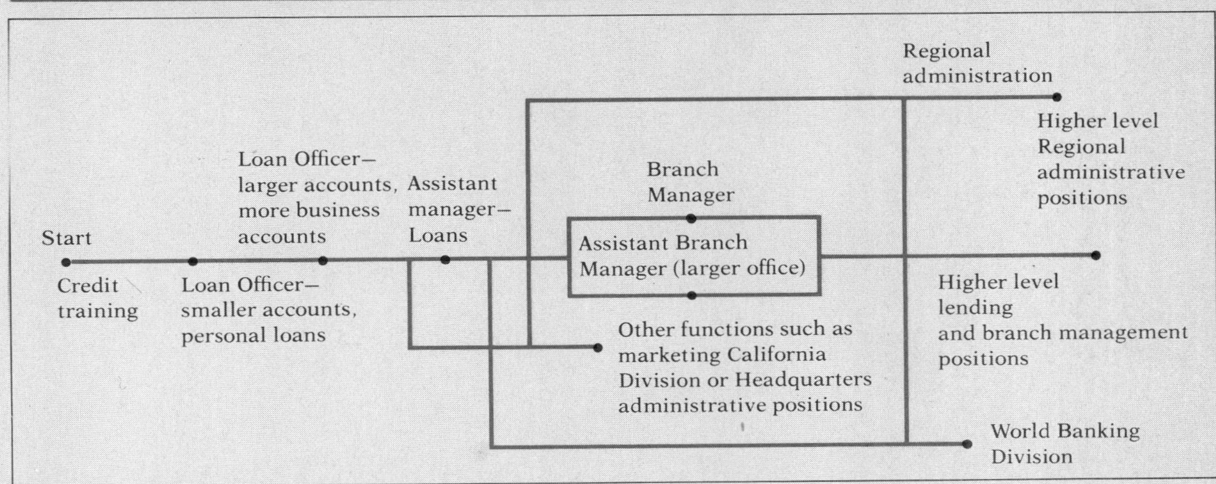

to present less risk of default. As loan officers advance, they begin lending to business, first to smaller companies, then to larger ones. Credit training may take as long as a year, although some people finish much sooner, particularly if they are well prepared in college. Again, after one has climbed the ladder in credit opportunities, regional and headquarter divisions may be the next step. The typical career path in credit is shown in Exhibit 15.7.

For those students terminating after two years of education in a community college, the Bank of America offers entry-level jobs as bank tellers with the possibility of advancement to teller management positions, and from there to other branches of the bank. Starting salaries for tellers with Associate of Arts or Associate of Science degrees are comparable to many entry-level positions in other industries where a four-year college degree is required.

FOR DISCUSSION

1. What has prevented the Bank of America from having branch offices in every state in the Union?
2. How do you think the Depository Institutions Deregulation and Monetary Control Act of 1980 will affect the profitability of Bank of America?

OBJECTIVES

- ☐ To explain the role and importance of a firm's financial manager
- ☐ To identify the goals of financial management
- ☐ To explain the problems encountered by financial managers
- ☐ To identify and describe the functions performed by the financial manager
- ☐ To identify and discuss the major sources and uses of funds

OUTLINE

ARTICLE *Slump Leads Firms to Lag in Paying Bills: Creditors Try Range of Strategies to Cope*

THE ROLE OF THE FINANCIAL MANAGER
The Goals of Financial Management
The Functions of Financial Management

USES OF MONEY
Current Assets
Fixed Assets

SOURCES OF FUNDS
Long-Term Financing
Intermediate-Term Financing
Short-Term Financing

MAKING THE FINANCIAL DECISION

NEW ROLES OF FINANCIAL MANAGERS

APPLICATION *Armco, Inc.*

KEY TERMS

ACCOUNT RECEIVABLE
ACQUISITION
ASSET
BALANCE SHEET
CAPITAL EXPENDITURE
CASH DISCOUNT
COLLECTION PERIOD
COMMERCIAL PAPER
CREDIT POLICY
CURRENT ASSET
DEBT FINANCING
DIVIDEND
EQUITY
EQUITY FINANCING
FINANCIAL MANAGER
FIXED ASSET
INTEREST
LEASING
LIABILITY
LIQUIDITY
MARKETABLE SECURITY
MERGER
TERM LOAN
TRADE CREDIT
WORKING CAPITAL

FINANCIAL MANAGEMENT

Slump Leads Firms to Lag in Paying Bills: Creditors Try Range of Strategies to Cope

MARK N. DODOSH
The Wall Street Journal, June 25, 1980

Richard H. Barrett does a lot of tightrope walking these days.

In trying to get his customers to pay their bills on time, he is walking a fine line between keeping them happy and alienating them.

Just a few months ago, prodding customers to pay their overdue accounts "took only about 10% of my time," says Mr. Barrett, president of Roberts Steel Co., a steel warehouse here. But now, with interest rates still relatively high and the recession deepening, more and more customers are delaying payments as long as they can, which means Roberts Steel winds up carrying these accounts' inventory costs.

The result: Keeping after these slow payers, including face-to-face meetings with some customers, "is probably at least 30% of my time today," Mr. Barrett sighs.

Many other companies are similarly struggling to keep a lid on their growing volume of accounts receivable. These businesses want, in effect, to avoid bankrolling their customers' purchases—and also to avoid the possibility that "slow pay" will become "no pay." For, as the recession takes its toll, more companies face financial difficulties, and ultimately bankruptcies, which can leave their suppliers in the lurch.

DELICATE DUNNING

Nonetheless, companies generally dread pressing customers to pay up, for fear customers will take their business elsewhere. Many top-management people, including some company presidents, therefore are helping to handle the delicate dunning of slow payers.

The extent of the current slow-pay problem is reflected in statistics from the Credit Research Foundation, an arm of the National Association of Credit Management. The foundation says the average age of all corporate receivables rose to 45 days in the first quarter. That is up from 43.4 days a year earlier and equals the record set during the 1969–70 recession. (The worst the problem got in the 1973–75 recession was 44 days.) Each day's increase means an additional $4.2 billion is tied up in receivables, a foundation spokesman says.

The approach executives are taking to alleviate the problem varies from company to company and even from account to account within a company. Some use tactful reminders. Others do a little arm-twisting. A few even try humor, such as the plumber in Indianapolis, Ind., who stamps "Pay the Piper" on his customers' overdue bills.

A few companies, however, refrain from nudging their customers to pay on time. "We're small in relation to our clients," says Thomas Ehrhart, chairman of Ehrhart-Babic Group, an Englewood Cliffs, N.J., marketing-research concern. "I'm not going to go to my clients and say I want my money and irritate them. There's nothing I can do" about slow-pay accounts, for fear of losing them.

CUSTOMER COMPLAINTS

Offending customers is indeed a hazard, especially in so personal a business as a restaurant operation, as Lee Comisar discovered. Mr. Comisar, owner of the Maisonette in Cincinnati, wrote to all 3,000 holders of the restaurant's no-interest charge card that the restaurant would start to "rigidly enforce" its policy of settling accounts within 30 days. The cards of violators would be canceled, the letter warned.

Despite an apology in the letter to prompt payers, a lot of them "unfortunately took the letter personally," Mr. Comisar says, and the mention of the letter in the local press was particularly embarrassing. "I'd like to forget the whole thing," he says.

Most companies, dealing with considerably larger sums, can't afford to take that attitude, so they try to collect firmly but politely. Many offer a small incentive, usually a 1% discount, to customers who pay up within 10 days of receiving an invoice. But when interest rates are high and business sluggish, the little discounts aren't very effective.

Roberts Steel raised its discount in January to 1% from 0.5%, and that brought about some increase in customers paying within 10 days. But Mr. Barrett, the president, says, "The ones that aren't paying wouldn't take the discount even if it were 2%. They don't have the money because they aren't getting it from their customers. Everything is backed up."

STICK OR CARROT?

Some companies prefer using a stick rather than a carrot. William E. Schultz, landlord of a commercial building in Twinsburg, Ohio, says he had several tenants who failed to pay their rent on time. So in four leases that came up for renewal in recent months, Mr. Schultz rewrote the terms. A tenant who was paying, say, $2,000 a month, now must pay $2,500—unless he pays by the fifth of the month, in which case the rent remains $2,000. "We don't have these problems [of slow pay] anymore," he says.

Companies tired of the old line that "the check is in the mail" are going around and picking up the checks in person. Mr. Barrett of Roberts Steel started doing that a few weeks ago and says that it so far hasn't seemed to alienate any customers.

Such visits to delinquent customers usually involve considerable diplomacy. "We don't like to start off saying, 'Hey, pay or no paint,' " says Ross E. Eyer, controller of Sherwin-Williams Co.'s stores division. A visit to a slow-paying paint purchaser typically is made by a Sherwin-Williams field supervisor and the store manager, Mr. Eyer says. They take the approach of "How can we work this out?" He says Sherwin-Williams will offer to help customers cut their costs and even go along with a customer to a bank to help obtain a loan.

HIGH-LEVEL AGENTS

Many companies send higher-level executives to visit major slow payers. "Rather than have a low-level collection guy dealing with an account that means $300,000 to $400,000 a year in continuing business, we'll send out division general managers to make sure that when they pick up the check, they also heal the wound," says the chairman of a New York consumer-goods manufacturer.

This company's chairman says he also has "put the people in our credit sections on the phone more" in recent weeks to cut the number of smaller accounts that are 60 days past due. His philosophy is, "Don't be embarrassed to call somebody who owes you money for two months, because somebody else is calling them, too."

Some collectors don't dun very heavily, especially when dealing with established customers. "Sometimes I hesitate to call," admits the office manager of a Midwestern air-cargo forwarder. When she does, "I kind of tell them that maybe the invoice is lost," she says. "Most say that it's just an oversight, and that they will take care of it." Even if a second phone call is necessary, her approach is hardly forceful. "I'll ask them, 'Is there any problem?' " she says, adding, "I think they appreciate that, rather than a 'pay-or-else' attitude."

In the last two months, the office manager says she has made "at least 10 calls a week" to slow-paying customers. Before, it was three calls a month. Hounding customers on the phone "is a little bit frustrating and takes some of the fun" out of her job, she says. It also takes time she normally would spend doing tax reports and bookkeeping.

SEEKING CONCESSIONS

Slow-paying customers of some concerns are seeking billing concessions. Harry W. Shaw, president of Huffy Corp., a bicycle maker, says he is devoting "two to three times" the attention he paid to receivables only a few months back because of pressure from retailers to extend Huffy's billing terms. But Huffy refuses to lengthen the payment period. Mr. Shaw says he must "spend a lot of my time on the telephone with some of our major customers trying to explain our position," as well as spending time with Huffy's own salesmen telling them to resist such pressure.

Huffy isn't stretching terms "because we've got the same problems as everyone else," says Stuart J. Northrup, Huffy's chairman. "If we've got to raise more cash" to cover customers' inventory costs, we've got to leverage our own company more," and Huffy doesn't want to do that, Mr. Northrup says. Besides, he adds, "the price either includes financing the sale or it doesn't, and the fact is, our price doesn't. Our margins just can't stand that type of thing."

A few retailers quit buying Huffy bicycles because of the company's stance, but Mr. Northrup says that they will come back. "They're moving from strong sources to weak sources of supply," Mr. Northrup asserts.

Other manufacturers that are extending terms to win business now can't do so for very long, Mr. Northrup says, because current industry pricing won't allow it.

One of the functions of a financial manager is to oversee the collection of bills from the company's customers to make sure that cash is not unnecessarily tied up. How well the financial manager performs this task, and others, has an impact on the financial success of a business. This chapter explores the job of the corporate financial manager.

All the decisions made by a company are essentially financial decisions. The purchase of equipment, the hiring of employees, or the remodeling of the office involve the use of one of the scarcest resources a company has—money. The acquisition and use of money is the responsibility of the financial manager.

The art of financial management is as old as money itself. However, it was not until the turn of the twentieth century and the emergence of large corporations that executives began to think seriously about the financial implications of their actions. Since that time, the field of financial management has grown rapidly, developing closer associations with the disciplines of economics and accounting. Financial management has become a critical element in any executive's repertoire of skills, whether that executive works in the federal government, at IBM, or at the Mayo Clinic.

In 1979 IBM Corporation decided it needed to raise money to finance expansion in the 1980s. Several fundamental questions were raised: How was the money to be used? How much money was needed? Where was the money to come from? IBM's financial executives were responsible for answering these questions. In the end, it was determined that the company needed $1 billion to finance the development of new products and manufacturing facilities, with the money being raised through the sale of bonds (which is a form of debt). Only time will tell whether IBM made the correct decision. However, without knowledge of the basic concepts of finance, these decisions might have been made in a haphazard manner.

The Role of the Financial Manager

A **financial manager** is any executive primarily concerned with the acquisition, investment, and management of money—or capital, in the parlance of financial executives. In smaller firms, the owner or president may be directly responsible for this function. In larger businesses, it is the responsibility of a vice president of finance, a treasurer, or a controller. Exhibit 16.1 summarizes the responsibilities of treasurers and controllers. As you can see, there is a very close relationship between the functions of these financial executives. That's why they both normally report to the vice president of finance.

In addition to these key executives, many companies also have teams of specialists who perform financial analyses in support of operating management or at the request of top management. An example of such a group is the capital planning and budgeting department at Burger King. It would not be uncommon for this group to be faced with a situation in which one store, with an estimated startup cost of $400,000 and first-year sales of $600,000, actually cost $800,000 and generated only $200,000 in sales. The group of financial specialists would determine the consequences of this situation and perhaps recommend a course of action to rectify the problem.

The finance function has become so important in many companies that corporate boards of directors also have finance committees, com-

EXHIBIT 16.1 Functions of Treasurers and Controllers

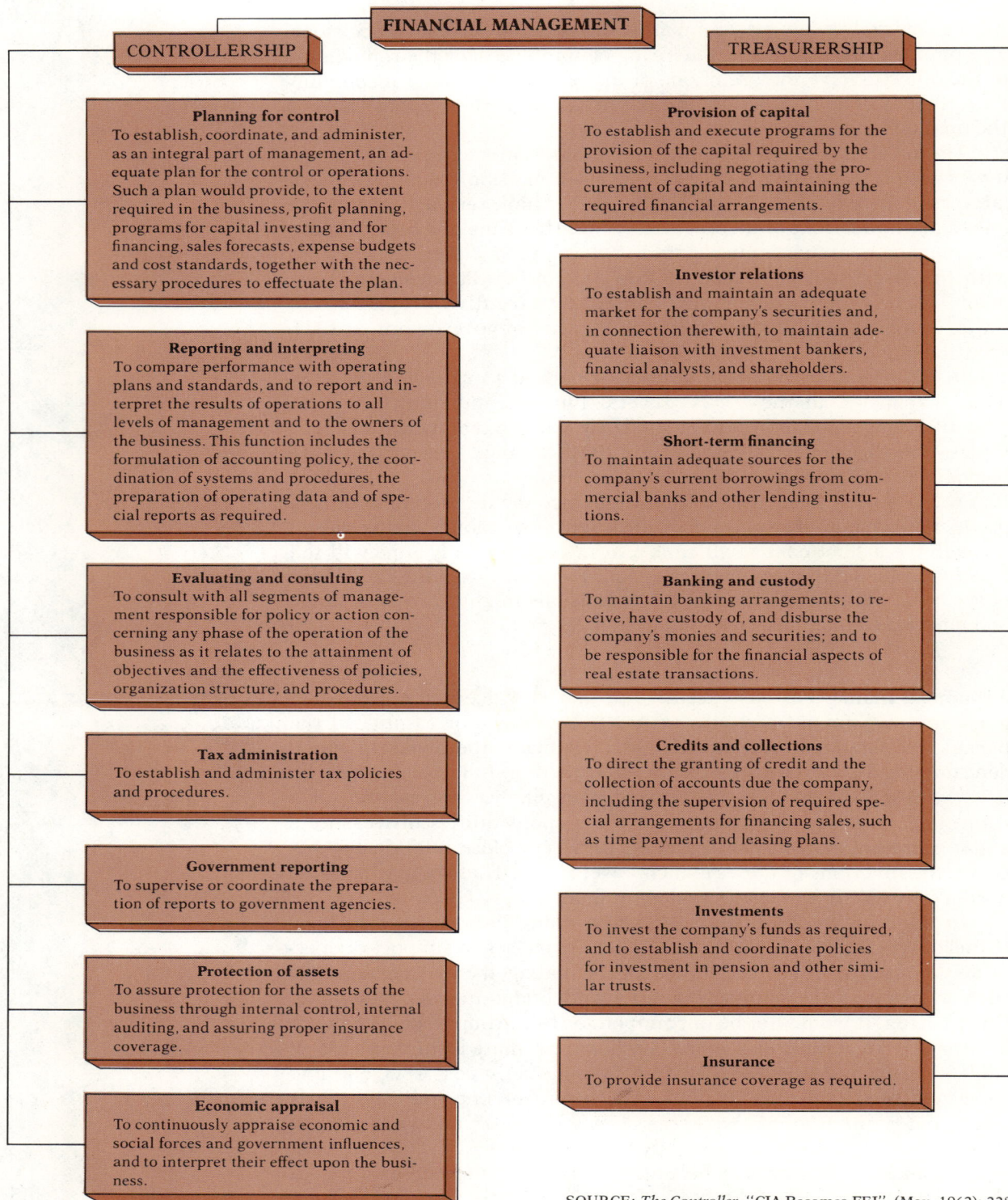

FINANCIAL MANAGEMENT

CONTROLLERSHIP

Planning for control
To establish, coordinate, and administer, as an integral part of management, an adequate plan for the control or operations. Such a plan would provide, to the extent required in the business, profit planning, programs for capital investing and for financing, sales forecasts, expense budgets and cost standards, together with the necessary procedures to effectuate the plan.

Reporting and interpreting
To compare performance with operating plans and standards, and to report and interpret the results of operations to all levels of management and to the owners of the business. This function includes the formulation of accounting policy, the coordination of systems and procedures, the preparation of operating data and of special reports as required.

Evaluating and consulting
To consult with all segments of management responsible for policy or action concerning any phase of the operation of the business as it relates to the attainment of objectives and the effectiveness of policies, organization structure, and procedures.

Tax administration
To establish and administer tax policies and procedures.

Government reporting
To supervise or coordinate the preparation of reports to government agencies.

Protection of assets
To assure protection for the assets of the business through internal control, internal auditing, and assuring proper insurance coverage.

Economic appraisal
To continuously appraise economic and social forces and government influences, and to interpret their effect upon the business.

TREASURERSHIP

Provision of capital
To establish and execute programs for the provision of the capital required by the business, including negotiating the procurement of capital and maintaining the required financial arrangements.

Investor relations
To establish and maintain an adequate market for the company's securities and, in connection therewith, to maintain adequate liaison with investment bankers, financial analysts, and shareholders.

Short-term financing
To maintain adequate sources for the company's current borrowings from commercial banks and other lending institutions.

Banking and custody
To maintain banking arrangements; to receive, have custody of, and disburse the company's monies and securities; and to be responsible for the financial aspects of real estate transactions.

Credits and collections
To direct the granting of credit and the collection of accounts due the company, including the supervision of required special arrangements for financing sales, such as time payment and leasing plans.

Investments
To invest the company's funds as required, and to establish and coordinate policies for investment in pension and other similar trusts.

Insurance
To provide insurance coverage as required.

SOURCE: *The Controller*, "CIA Becomes FEI", (May, 1962): 228

Highlight The Controller: Scorekeeper or Player?

Until the 1970s, most controllers were considered "bean counters" or "scorekeepers." Their primary functions were to keep track of how the organization was doing financially and to provide financial information to other managers to assist them in decision making. Controllers were not part of the top management team, nor was their function considered to be particularly challenging or critical to organizational success.

However, the increased inflation rate during the 1970s and its impact on the financial success of organizations have made controllers more visible. Managing companies in inflationary times requires a keen understanding of their financial structure and a creative approach to the management of financial resources. It appears that controllers are particularly equipped to be of assistance.

Controllers are still responsible for "keeping score," but they are now more involved in decision making. In fact, most of the people promoted to the presidency or chairmanship of large companies in the 1970s have a background in accounting—and many of them are former controllers. Maybe controllers really do know how to play the game.

posed of top executives from the various functional areas of the firm. The purpose of these committees is to oversee major capital expenditures and acquisitions to ensure that they are in the best interests of the firm in the short and long run.

THE GOALS OF FINANCIAL MANAGEMENT

The goal of the financial manager is to help the firm achieve its objectives. Organizational success is often measured in terms of survival and profits. To help achieve these basic objectives, financial managers pursue two basic goals.

The first goal is to maintain liquidity. To survive, a firm must be able to pay its bills when they become due. Therefore, one of the primary jobs of the financial manager is to ensure that the firm has enough cash on hand to pay outstanding obligations.

The second goal is to earn a satisfactory profit. The liquidity objective would present no difficulties if management could simply keep all the firm's cash in a savings account. However, owners expect a firm to earn more than they could earn in a savings account. Thus financial managers must attempt to use the money provided by owners to generate earnings in excess of what they would earn on their own.

Companies seek to maximize liquidity and profits within the confines of certain constraints. Some examples of factors that can limit a firm's ability to make money:

1. *Economic conditions* Such factors as inflation and government regulations often affect a firm's ability to maintain liquidity and increase profits. For example, in times of inflation it is often more difficult, and certainly more costly, for firms to raise needed capital for expansion and other purposes.
2. *Supply of needed resources* The supply of raw materials, labor, and capital is limited. Therefore, they may often cost more than a com-

Highlight John Q. Public, Financial Manager

There is little difference between the job of a financial manager and management of the family finances. The differences are in the complexity of the task—not in the concepts involved.

The family financial manager usually has fewer sources of income than the corporation does, with the majority of family income derived from salaries and wages. When money is in short supply, the family can borrow from local lenders or use savings. Such is also the case with large corporations that need money. The only real difference is that the family cannot sell shares of itself, whereas a corporation can.

There are even similarities in the use of available money for current needs and capital investments. Corporations use funds on hand to acquire inventory, pay bills, support working capital, and acquire long-term assets, such as a plant and equipment. Family financial managers use available funds to pay living expenses and to support the acquisition of such long-term assets as a house, boat, or car.

pany can afford. This point is particularly valid today, when shortages exist in many commodities, such as oil and gas. These shortages have had a significant impact on many companies.

3. *Social responsibilities* All companies have a responsibility to their employees, to the community, and to the environment. Yet it costs money to provide employees with benefits and the community with sustained levels of employment and still protect the environment from pollution and waste.

The constraints affecting the management of financial resources are increasing. Therefore, it may no longer be realistic to expect financial managers to maximize a firm's profits, and they may be forced to settle for a lower level of financial achievement.

THE FUNCTIONS OF FINANCIAL MANAGEMENT

Financial managers have two basic functions: using money and acquiring money. Appropriately enough, these two functions are reflected in the **balance sheet** (discussed in more detail in Chapter 19). A balance sheet presents a company's financial position at a particular point in time, normally at the end of a calendar year. The balance sheet indicates what the company owns (commonly referred to as **assets**), what it owes **(liabilities),** and the owners' investment in the business **(equity).** A balance sheet for a typical company is shown in Exhibit 16.2.

The primary uses of corporate money are to purchase and maintain assets, pay bills, reduce liabilities, and distribute company profits to owners through the payment of dividends. The money needed by the company can be acquired internally or externally. Internal sources of funds are generated by the areas of the business that make more money than they consume. Their profits can be used for whatever purposes management wants. If money is not available internally, companies have the option of going into debt to sources outside the company or of increasing owner's equity (selling more shares). Most companies use internal funds to finance operations, although external sources of funds

EXHIBIT 16.2 Sample Balance Sheet

XYZ Company
Balance sheet
As of December 31, 1980

Assets	
Current Assets	
Cash	$ 370.00
Marketable Securities	300.00
Accounts Receivable	1,700.00
Inventories	2,000.00
Total Current Assets	$4,370.00
Plant, Equipment and Other Properties	4,000.00
Total	$8,370.00
Liabilities and Equity	
Current Liabilities	$1,000.00
Intermediate Term Liabilities	700.00
Long Term Liabilities	1,300.00
Owners Equity	5,370.00
Total	$8,370.00

became more important in the 1970s. Exhibit 16.3 summarizes the sources and uses of funds.

There are many sources and uses of money, but the following discussion will assume that the primary use of money is to acquire and maintain assets (including cash). Likewise, the primary sources of money will be assumed to be owner's equity or borrowing from others.

Uses of Money

As we have just said, the primary use for a company's money is to acquire and maintain assets. **Current assets**—cash or assets that can readily be converted to cash—are also referred to as working capital. Fixed assets are the company's investment in facilities and equipment. They are expected to be the primary income producing assets of the firm in the long term. Different factors come into play in the management of these two kinds of assets.

EXHIBIT 16.3 Sources and Uses of Corporate Funds

Sources
- *Reduce Noncash Assets* Sell facilities and equipment
- *Increase Liabilities* Take out a loan; sell bonds
- *Increase Owner's Equity* Sell more stock; increase profits

Uses
- *Increase Assets* Facilities and equipment; inventory; accounts receivable
- *Decrease Liabilities* Pay off outstanding debts
- *Decrease Owner's Equity* Pay dividends; buy back stock

CURRENT ASSETS

The investment that a firm makes in cash, marketable securities, accounts receivable, and inventories constitutes its current assets, or **working capital.** Mismanagement of working capital could leave a company without enough cash to pay its bills or without enough inventory to satisfy customer needs. Thus the effective management of working capital is vital to the success and growth of a company.

The management of working capital is based on a precarious system of tradeoffs between risk and profitability. For example, one company may hold large cash balances because it is afraid it will lose money on investments. This strategy prohibits the company from investing in projects that could increase profitability. A perfect example of this situation occurred in the 1950s with Montgomery Ward. Shortly after World War II, Montgomery Ward, J. C. Penney, and Sears found themselves with large cash balances as a result of increased consumer spending. Ward's made the strategic decision not to use its excess cash, but Penney's and Sears used their money to expand facilities. Within a decade, Ward's, once the largest of the three, lost ground to Sears and Penney's. It was never able to regain that lead.

Another sort of tradeoff is for management to set higher credit standards for potential customers in an effort to reduce bad debts. This change in policy usually does reduce bad debts, but it also causes a reduction in sales and profitability, because the company loses sales to customers who might previously have qualified for credit.

A company might also reduce inventory levels in an effort to free up some working capital. However, it might wind up losing sales because it does not have products available when customers want them. For example, a friend of ours went to purchase a Mercedes from a local dealer. He wanted the car immediately. The dealer did not have the car he wanted in stock and, in fact, had very few cars available because of the high cost of maintaining an inventory of Mercedes. This strategy resulted in a lost sale of $36,000.

The management of working capital varies with each company, but usually working capital circulates in the manner shown in Exhibit 16.4. Financial managers work to maintain this flow through judicious management of cash, marketable securities, accounts receivable, and inventories.

Cash

There are generally three motives for holding cash on hand:

1. *Transactions motive* To pay for the goods and services necessary to run the business, including raw materials, labor (employee salaries), utility bills, and taxes
2. *Precautionary motive* To meet unexpected short-run expenses and seasonal increases in demand

3. *Speculative motive* To take advantage of money-making situations —for example, if a vendor offers a discount for paying the bill within a certain number of days

Yet there are costs and risks associated with holding cash. These include the implicit cost of foregoing other investment possibilities and the chance that reliance on cash will isolate the firm from outside financial markets and credit establishments.

Companies have several options for controlling the inflow and outflow of cash. One is to *control the patterns of collection.* For example, it normally takes several days for checks to arrive at and clear the bank. By expediting this process, a company can more quickly obtain access to thousands of dollars. Two specific ways to do this are to have customers pay banks in their area or to have them put checks in a special post office box that is emptied daily by the firm's bank.

Another option for cash management is to *control the patterns of cash disbursements.* This usually means slowing down cash payments, perhaps by paying bills on the last day due or issuing drafts (not payable until they are presented to the issuer's bank and covered).

A final option is to *set a minimum cash balance* that will meet the company's motives for holding cash. Excess cash can then be used for alternate investments.

Marketable Securities

Because of fluctuations in business activity, many firms often have excess cash available for short periods of time (less than one year). Rather than hold the cash, they can invest it in **marketable securities** that will

EXHIBIT 16.4 Flow of Working Capital

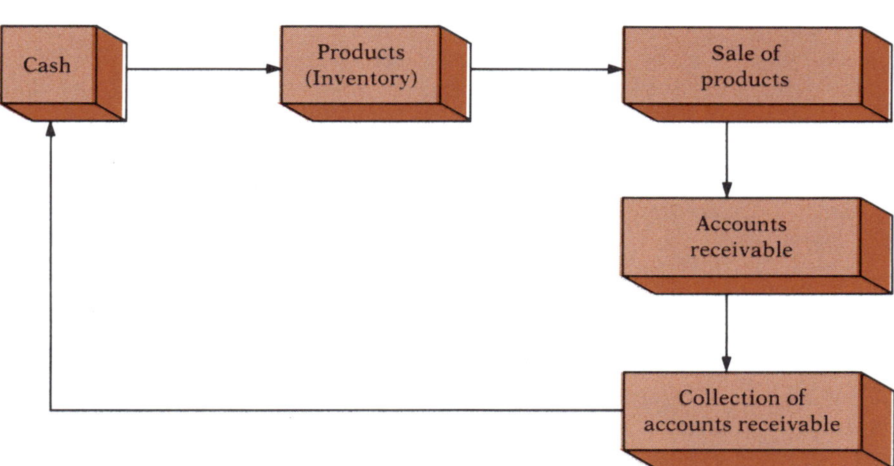

yield interest. Thus their idle money can make money. But the most important characteristic of these securities is that they can quickly be converted into cash when needed. For this reason, they are referred to as near-cash.

There are several types of marketable securities, with differing maturity levels and different interest yields. A few of the most common:

1. *Treasury securities* U.S. Treasury bills, notes, certificates, and bonds are considered the safest of all securities because they are fully guaranteed and backed by the U.S. Treasury. Yet they also yield the lowest interest rates. The yields on these securities change frequently, usually weekly, and fluctuate tremendously depending on economic conditions.
2. *Commercial paper* Short-term promissory notes are issued by large industrial firms, utilities, and finance companies. They generally have longer lives and higher interest rates than Treasury securities.
3. *Certificates of deposit* CDs are time deposits in a commercial bank or a savings and loan institution. Generally, their maturity periods and interest rates are somewhere between commercial paper and Treasury securities.

Accounts Receivable

Whenever a customer purchases a product or service from a company on credit, an **account receivable** arises. The amount of assets a firm has tied up in accounts receivable depends on two policy factors: collection and credit.

Generally, collection policies refer to the amount of time customers have to make payments. More specifically, collection policies involve what are called the terms of credit. One aspect of the terms of credit is the **collection period.** Sales generally increase as the time for making payments is lengthened, because purchasers realize that they have more time to meet their payments. Yet longer collection periods increase the company's investment in accounts receivable, which does not produce income.

Cash discounts, the other half of the terms of credit, are given to purchasers for paying their bills within a certain amount of time. For example, "2/10, net/30" indicates that if the bill is paid within ten days, a 2-percent discount will be given. If payment is not made within the discount period, the entire bill is due at the end of thirty days. Increasing these discounts normally motivates customers to pay their bills more quickly. However, the company also receives less per sale, and therefore its profits are less per sale.

A company's **credit policies** refer to the amount of trade credit a company will extend and to whom it will extend the credit. The more lenient the policy, generally, the greater the sales. However, these greater sales may be offset by the possibility of increased bad debts

Highlight Corporate Investor: Cooking Big Deals

I'm the firm's cash manager. It's my job to earn money by wisely investing the cash on hand in a variety of ways. Spend some time with me, and you'll see what wheeling and dealing is all about:

8:00 a.m. Read computer printout of company's balance in checking account. Balance: $5 million

8:15 a.m. Find out how much idle cash is on hand today. Have staff call all other banks where company maintains checking accounts.

8:30 a.m. Phone rings. It's the beginning of over forty phone calls from bankers and dealers, all logged in by the secretary.

8:35 a.m. Take phone call from money-market trader. Ask what's "good and short" (short-term investment with good financial return).

8:45 a.m. Take another call. "No, can't move anything yet. Don't have our cash figures in yet."

9:15 a.m. Speak to dealer in Treasury bills. Find out maturity date.

9:35 a.m. Cash figures in. Company has $15 million to invest today.

9:45 a.m. Action! Outgoing phone calls only.

11:15 a.m. Purchased for the day:

- $2 million in government securities (to be sold tomorrow)
- $5 million in Treasury bills (will mature in three days)
- $2 million in Federal Farm Credit System notes (mature in two months)
- $6 million in repurchase agreement

Total invested: $15 million.

11:20 a.m. For rest of the day, meet with bankers, return phone calls. Work on other administrative chores: forecasting company's future cash needs, checking for bank errors, and repaying company's long-term debt.

As you can see, I spend a lot of money each day. I must have realiable sources (dealers) and be able to move quickly into the money market. At the current 10-percent interest rates, I can earn $100,000 per year on an investment of $1 million. It would be foolish and possibly disastrous to let such large sums of money sit idle in a checking account (drawing no interest). The money I make can be used to build new plants, develop new products, or repay debts—without borrowing additional funds.

We did well today. The $15 million investment earned us $4,500. Just another average day.

because the company is allowing customers with questionable credit backgrounds to purchase goods.

Inventory

Companies that are in the business of selling a tangible product usually hold a certain amount of their product in anticipation of future sales. The products kept on hand for future use are known as inventory. Manufacturing companies normally keep three types of inventories:

- *Raw materials* Basic materials used in manufacturing a product
- *Work-in-process* Partially completed products still in the process of being manufactured
- *Finished goods* Products that are completed and available for sale

In contrast, retail companies normally have only a finished-goods inventory.

The proper management and control of inventory is of the utmost importance. Production people rely on the consistent supply of raw materials for production; salespeople rely on an adequate supply of finished goods to satisfy the demands of their customers. As with cash, however, tradeoffs exist. For example, a company that maintains large inventories of raw materials and finished goods may be in a good position to satisfy any unexpected increase in demand, but the money tied up in these excess inventories might better be invested in other income-producing assets or be used to decrease outstanding debt and reduce interest expenses. On the other hand, a company that minimizes its investment by maintaining low levels of inventory takes the risk of running out. This could result in lost sales and a loss of customer goodwill.

In recent years, companies have developed sophisticated techniques for controlling inventories, among them statistical modeling and coordinating production needs and timetables with inventory requirements. Whatever the method, all have the same objective: to determine the "ideal" amount of inventory that will meet foreseeable demand and minimize costs.

FIXED ASSETS

Capital expenditures are investments in fixed assets that have a useful life to the company of several years—specifically, expenditures for property, plant, and equipment. Capital expenditures can also be made for such things as a multiyear promotional campaign or long-term programs of research and development.

Capital expenditures may dramatically alter the financial position of a company. A few of the reasons:

1. *Large amounts of dollars* Capital expenditures normally involve large amounts of money, which may not be readily available. It takes careful planning to ensure the availability of adequate funds for a project without jeopardizing the financial stability of a company.
2. *Income-producing abilities* Normally, the fixed assets of a company are the primary source of income. Therefore, an ill-considered capital expenditure can affect the profits of the company for years.
3. *Long lives of assets* Income-producing assets are generally used for many years. This is further reason to evaluate carefully the potential productive capacity of an asset, its useful life, its service record, and the chances of its becoming obsolete.
4. *Competitive position* Most often, the purpose of purchasing new property or equipment is to enhance the competitive position of the company—that is, to get a "leg up" on the competition. Thus, a bad capital investment decision could seriously jeopardize a firm's ability to compete.

The evaluation of potential capital expenditures is an involved process and probably one of the most important functions performed by financial managers. An overview of this process appears in Exhibit 16.5. Basically, the decision involves determining the cost of the project (the amount the company will have to spend to acquire and maintain the needed piece of equipment), the amount of money that will be earned as a result of making the purchase, and the relationship between costs and benefits. If the benefits exceed the costs, the investment should normally be made.

Many mathematical techniques are available to help financial managers evaluate the costs and benefits of alternative investment projects. These techniques differ in complexity and sophistication, but all have the same end purpose—to pinpoint the profitability of potential projects and to assist managers in deciding how and where to invest corporate money.

EXHIBIT 16.5 Evaluation Process for Potential Capital Expenditures

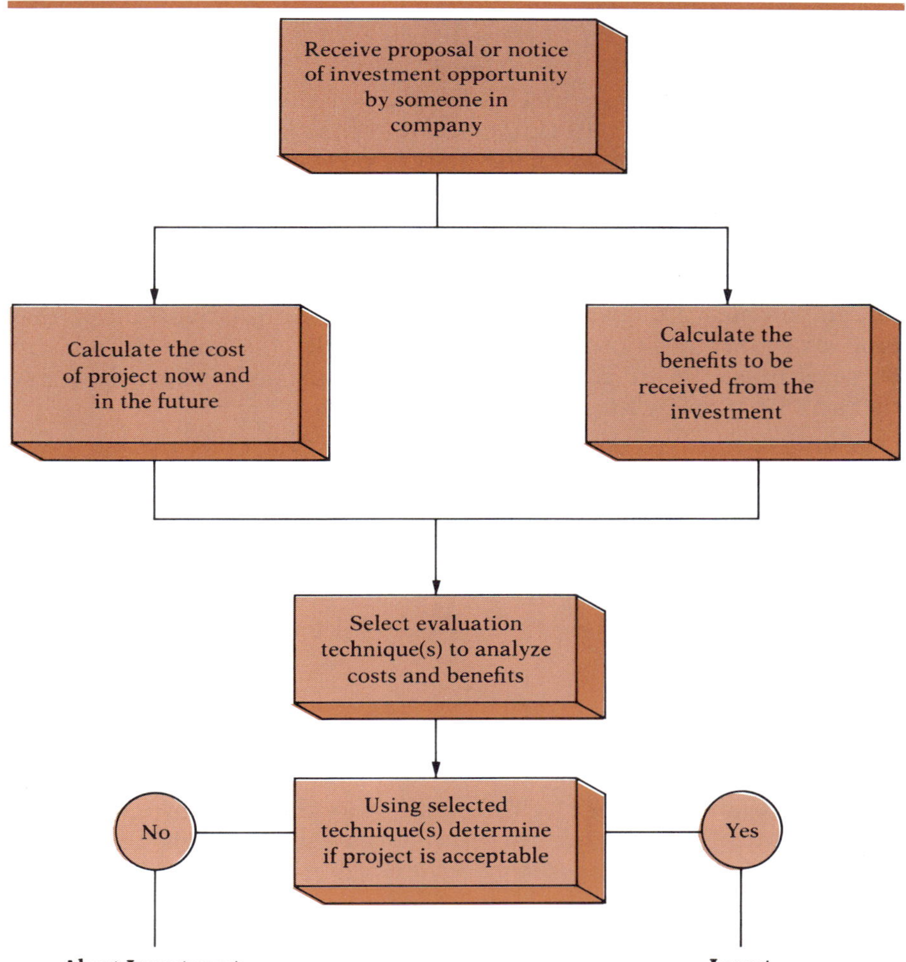

Highlight A Corporate Gamble

In the early days of American business, certain people are said to have literally risked all in business ventures. Some succeeded, some failed. Although we rarely hear of modern "winner take all" stories, the successful completion of the Alaska pipeline may be an exception.

In the early 1970s, the Standard Oil Company of Ohio (SOHIO) was a medium-size oil company, reasonably profitable, with a bright future. Maintaining this corporate status quo would have been quite acceptable to investors. But top management saw a golden opportunity—the chance to develop the Alaskan oil fields and transport the oil to the lower forty-eight states.

There was nothing small or short-term about this project. Before the decision was made to proceed, a capital budgeting analysis was completed. On paper, it appeared that the project could provide the company with attractive returns. Unfortunately, the analysis also showed that the project involved an expenditure of millions of dollars over a long period of time (ten to fifteen years) on a project judged to be quite risky. But SOHIO's management took the risk and put SOHIO's financial future on the line.

The story has a happy ending. The Alaska pipeline was successful and catapulted SOHIO to the fifth-largest oil-producing company in the nation within a decade.

Sources of Funds

Once a company has determined what types of investments it wants to make and how much it will take to finance these projects, the company must decide what types of financing best meet its needs. The options include long-term, intermediate, and short-term financing. In addition, it is quite possible to finance different parts of a project from different sources.

It is important to remember that the acquisition of funds is a critical and complex process. The type of funding acquired will affect the company's debt position, fixed costs (especially for interest), and of course earnings. In addition, these and other issues may affect the company's ability to raise funds in the future.

LONG-TERM FINANCING

There are basically two sources of long-term financing: equity and debt. The one common feature of these two sources is that the company has the use of these funds for a long period of time, usually for more than ten years. However, there are advantages and disadvantages peculiar to each, which are summarized in Exhibit 16.6. Chapter 17 also discusses these sources in depth.

Equity Financing

The issuance of stock—**equity financing**—has the effect of increasing the ownership of the company. In return for investment in the company, management sometimes pays stockholders a **dividend,** a distribution of the company's profits. Unlike interest on a loan, dividends need not be paid yearly. Dividends are paid only if management feels that the company made enough money during the year to pay out funds to stockholders without hurting the financial position of the company. By not paying a dividend, management can retain more money to reinvest in the business. Equity financing, therefore, provides great flexibility to management.

Yet there is a clear tradeoff here. If a company consistently fails to pay a dividend or if profits are inadequate, investors will not want to purchase the company's stock. This lack of enthusiasm may decrease the market price of the stock, which would not only be detrimental to current stockholders but could also make it more difficult to raise funds through a stock issuance in the future.

Debt Financing

The sale of bonds represents **debt financing.** A bond is simply a long-term promissory note to repay a loan from an individual or a company. Bonds, unlike stocks, are issued for a specific period of time, and they provide for interest to be paid during that period. **Interest** is the charge paid for the privilege of using someone else's money.

INTERMEDIATE-TERM FINANCING

Financing that has maturities in two to ten years and carries an interest charge is called intermediate-term financing. There are several types available, the most common being bank loans and lease financing. Intermediate-term financing is frequently used to purchase equipment. Again, the decision to use this type of financing is based on economic conditions and the company's needs.

Term loans are formal agreements between a bank and the company. They have a set maturity date and interest rate and usually need

EXHIBIT 16.6 Comparison of Debt and Equity Financing

	Advantages	Disadvantages
Debt Financing (Bonds)	• Less expensive to firm than equity financing • Owners don't share control • Interest payment is tax-deductible	• Company must pay interest, even if profits fluctuate • Fixed maturity date • Long-term commitment and, therefore, risk if economic climate changes • Creditors may impose operating restrictions • Too much debt financing makes firm appear more risky
Equity Financing (Stocks)	• Does not entail fixed payments; dividends are optional • No fixed maturity date • More easily sold than debt financing, as a hedge against inflation	• Extends voting rights and control to additional owners • Gives more owners the right to share in proffits • Dividends aren't tax-deductible

Highlight How to Recover $900 Million

Debt financing is a commonly used means of raising money. Most of us incur a debt when purchasing a home or car. We borrow money from the bank, and the home or car that we purchase serves as collateral for the loan. The bank risks little. It either gets a return on its loan through the monthly payments or takes possession of tangible property valued at the amount of the loan or more.

However mundane debt financing may seem, it played a starring role in the incredible case of the Hunt brothers of Dallas. When gold prices began to climb steadily upward at the end of 1979, many people made money by investing in it. When the price of silver also began to rise, the Hunts secured the necessary loans to buy up huge amounts of silver. Lending institutions considered the investment secure, because the value of silver was on the upswing and the Hunt brothers' silver holdings served as collateral.

But almost overnight silver went from $75 an ounce to $2 an ounce. The Hunts were left with $900 million in debt invested in silver worth far less than the amount of the loans. Nervous creditors began demanding other collateral to secure the loan. The Hunts were forced to mortgage most of their financial empire and to liquidate vast real estate and livestock holdings, as well as personal property (Mercedes-Benz automobiles, jewelry, coin collections).

What is the moral of this story? If you are going to borrow money, you'd better invest it in something that has more value than the loan itself.

to be backed up with some form of collateral (property or assets) in case of default. Term loans are generally smaller than the amounts raised through long-term bonds. The greatest disadvantage of term loans is that they are limited in length and in the amount that can be borrowed. Their distinct advantage is that the borrower must deal directly with the bank, which allows the loan to be tailored to the needs of the company.

Like commercial banks, insurance companies have become very active lenders of money. Their loans are competitive with those issued by banks but generally have slightly higher interest rates.

Leasing has become a very viable alternative to buying fixed assets. Equipment leases permit a company to use the equipment over an extended period of time, frequently at a lower cost than ownership. Leases can also provide for upgrading and maintaining the equipment. They are very advantageous in fields plagued by obsolescence, such as the computer industry. The choice between leasing and borrowing to buy an asset is based on their impact on cash flow and the opportunity costs associated with each. By leasing, a company avoids the risk of obsolescence and thereby achieves more flexibility. However, the total cost of leasing may be greater than buying, particularly if the investment can be expected to increase in value over time.

SHORT-TERM FINANCING

Generally, short-term debts are incurred to support the current assets of a company; the current assets are ultimately used to liquidate the corresponding short-term debt. Many types of arrangements can be made to deal with these short-term needs. The most frequently used are trade credit, commercial paper, and bank loans.

Trade credit consists of open accounts and notes payable to suppliers. With open accounts, suppliers ship goods to customers with an invoice (bill) allowing an extended period of time for repayment. Notes payable are more formal agreements—customers sign notes for the goods received and pledge repayment on a specified date. Trade credit is particularly desirable for companies whose business is highly seasonal, because they can forgo payment until their season is well under way.

Commercial paper is a short-term promissory note, or corporate IOU that is unsecured (not backed by any collateral). Typically, these notes are issued only by large companies, such as General Motors, with minimal risk of default. They are purchased by individuals or companies with excess or idle cash for a limited period of time—usually ninety days.

Bank loans are another source of short-term financing. Many short-term bank loans are unsecured, with no requirement that collateral be pledged against repayment of the loan. Instead, large institutions generally establish a line of credit, which allows them to borrow money from the bank at any time during the year, for whatever reason, up to the established credit limit. Lines of credit are reviewed and revised each year to match the projected short-term needs of customers.

Making the Financial Decision

There are nearly as many sources of money as there are needs for it. Thus financial managers must consider many factors in deciding how to finance a firm's operations.

1. *How the funds will be used* Generally, if the money is being used to finance short-term needs (working capital), short-term financing is

"I have before me, gentlemen, some figures that may shock you, as they did me."

Drawing by Modell; © 1977 The New Yorker Magazine, Inc.

best. The acquisition of long-term assets requires long- or intermediate-term financing.

2. *Corporate control* Whenever a company sells stock to raise capital (equity financing), it takes on more owners, which sometimes dilutes the power and control of the present owners. If companies fear increased ownership, they might be inclined to raise capital through debt financing instead.
3. *Debt position* The risks involved with each type of financing greatly influence the type that is chosen. Companies that already have a lot of debt have a higher risk of default and, therefore, tend to use equity rather than debt financing.
4. *Costs or interest rates* Each type of financing has a cost or interest rate associated with it. Companies with less collateral and poorer credit ratings have to pay higher interest rates for their financing. To avoid paying higher interest costs, these firms may try to raise money through the sale of stock.
5. *Economic conditions* Projected economic upswings, with lower interest rates, may lead companies to use more debt. They presume that they will repay creditors in future years with cheaper, inflated dollars.

New Roles of Financial Managers

In recent years, the role of financial managers has been expanded beyond the acquisition and use of money. They are now often involved in the decision process in such areas as mergers and acquisitions, reorganizations or liquidations, and international markets.

Financial managers are increasingly involved in determining whether horizontal and vertical growth is financially advisable. Vertical growth is usually accomplished through the purchase or **acquisition** of other companies that operate in a different stage of the production process. For example, U.S. Steel bought a fleet of ships to transport iron ore from its mines in Minnesota to its mills in Pittsburgh and Cleveland. Horizontal growth occurs when a larger company buys out smaller companies within the same industry. Thus the need for duplicate production facilities is reduced. **Mergers** are the joining of two or more companies in different industries into conglomerates with an enlarged asset and product base.

Businesses that continually lose money eventually face either reorganization or liquidation. Reorganization is the attempted rehabilitation of a company through the generation of additional operating funds and the elimination (or restructuring) of the operating and management procedures that caused the difficulty. Liquidation is the closing of a business and the selling of all its assets. In both situations, financial managers help to ensure the efficient execution of the process.

Finally, because much business is now conducted overseas, including the production and transportation of goods as well as the raising of money to finance investments, financial managers must often acquire a international outlook. Developing nations may represent a lucrative investment, and oil-producing countries are often a substantial source of funds. Meanwhile, European nations and Japan provide potential markets for American goods. The field of international finance also offers new opportunities for financial managers and the companies they work for.

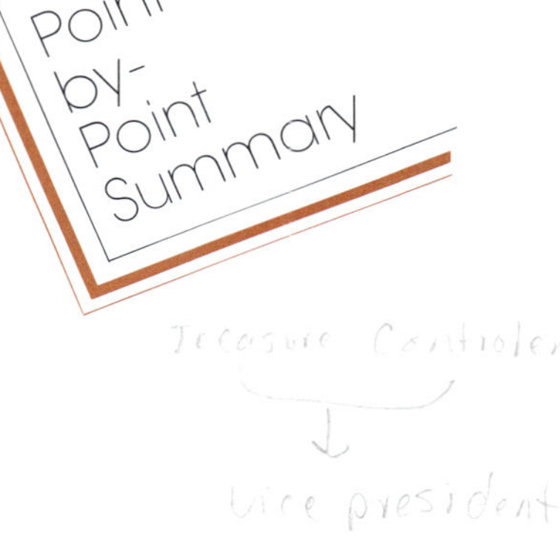

- Financial management involves the acquisition and use of money to achieve the corporate objectives of maintaining liquidity and increasing profitability.
- The key financial executives in a company are the treasurer, controller, and vice president of finance. There is a very close relationship between the functions of the treasurer and controller. That is why they normally both report to the same person in a company, usually the vice president of finance.
- The primary uses of capital in a company are investments in current assets and fixed assets. Money needed to finance these investments can be obtained through internal or external sources. The primary internal source of funds are profits while the primary external sources include debt and equity financing.
- Current assets, or working capital, consist of cash, marketable securities, inventory, and accounts receivable. In deciding how much of each type of working capital to maintain, financial managers must consider the costs and benefits of having too much or too little. Current assets are normally obtained with the use of short-term financing, e.g. trade credit, bank loans and commercial paper.
- The investment in fixed assets involves analysis of capital expenditures. In deciding whether to purchase a particular fixed asset, financial managers must consider the costs and benefits of various investments. They can use several different analytical techniques.
- The primary methods of long-term financing are debt financing (bonds) and equity financing (stocks). Intermediate-term financing, with maturities of two to ten years, usually consists of leases and loans from banks or insurance companies.
- The role of the financial manager has expanded rapidly in recent years to include involvement in mergers and acquisitions, corporate reorganizations and liquidations, and international finance.

1. What factors most influence the amounts and types of current assets that should be maintained?
2. Why has the role of the financial manager changed so significantly in the past forty years?
3. What are the differences and similarities between the functions of the treasurer and controller?
4. How do economic conditions affect the process of financial management?
5. How would you go about analyzing the decision to acquire a college degree as a capital expenditure?
6. Is there a relationship between the sources of funds and the uses of funds? If so, explain the relationship.
7. What is the primary difference between working capital and fixed assets? What is the significance of this difference?

APPLICATION

Armco, Inc.

In the late 1800s, a young man named George M. Verity, manager of a small roofing company, was looking for a reliable source of quality steel sheets. Since these sheets were not easy to find, Verity decided to become his own supplier. He organized the American Rolling Mill Company, the first to bring together all the equipment necessary to make steel, roll it into sheets, galvanize it, corrugate it, and fabricate the sheets into a finished product. Today Armco, Inc., headquartered in Ohio, is a highly diversified company that employs 52,000 people—a major producer of steel. In fact, it ranks third in the industry in assets, sales, and profits.

Armco's history falls into three distinct periods. From 1900 to 1925, Armco focused on expanding plant activity in the Midwest through acquisitions and internal growth. One of the company's most adventuresome business decisions during this period was the purchase of the Ashland Works. Ashland Works was located "at what seemed a fair piece away in Kentucky." In retrospect, this purchase, the first outside Ohio, was pivotal to the further success and growth of Armco.

The years 1926 to 1950 saw the company expand its operations to the East and Southwest, in largely metropolitan areas. Overseas business interests were also developed, particularly in England, Argentina, and Mexico. By 1950 Armco had established itself as one of the leading U.S. steelmakers as well as a major steel fabricator at home and overseas.

Since 1950, Armco has diversified. However, the company is quick to point out that diversification does not suggest a disinterest in steel but rather a belief "that a variety of business interests is better than sharing the ups and downs of a few major markets." As a result, Armco's business interests now include insurance, leasing, and oil-field equipment and production.

THE ROLE OF FINANCE

In a company as large and diverse as Armco (which had assets of $3.3 billion in 1979), the corporate financial function is critical. At Armco, this function is headed up by a vice president of finance, who is assisted by a treasurer, controller, and general auditor. The organizational chart in Exhibit 16.7 gives an overview of the functions performed in each of the major financial areas. In reality, most of the financial responsibilities discussed in this chapter are performed in the treasurer's office.

Ten goals provide direction for the activities performed by the treasurer's office. Five of these goals relate directly to topics discussed in this chapter:

- Assuring the liquidity of the company at all times at the least possible cost
- Obtaining the maximum return on excess cash and marketable securities
- Minimizing the long-term cost of financing for Armco's worldwide assets
- Determining future financing to assist the company in properly allocating resources
- Establishing criteria to evaluate the performance of existing assets and criteria, guidelines, and procedures for presenting, analyzing, and approving requests for new assets

EXHIBIT 16.7 Armco's Financial Organization

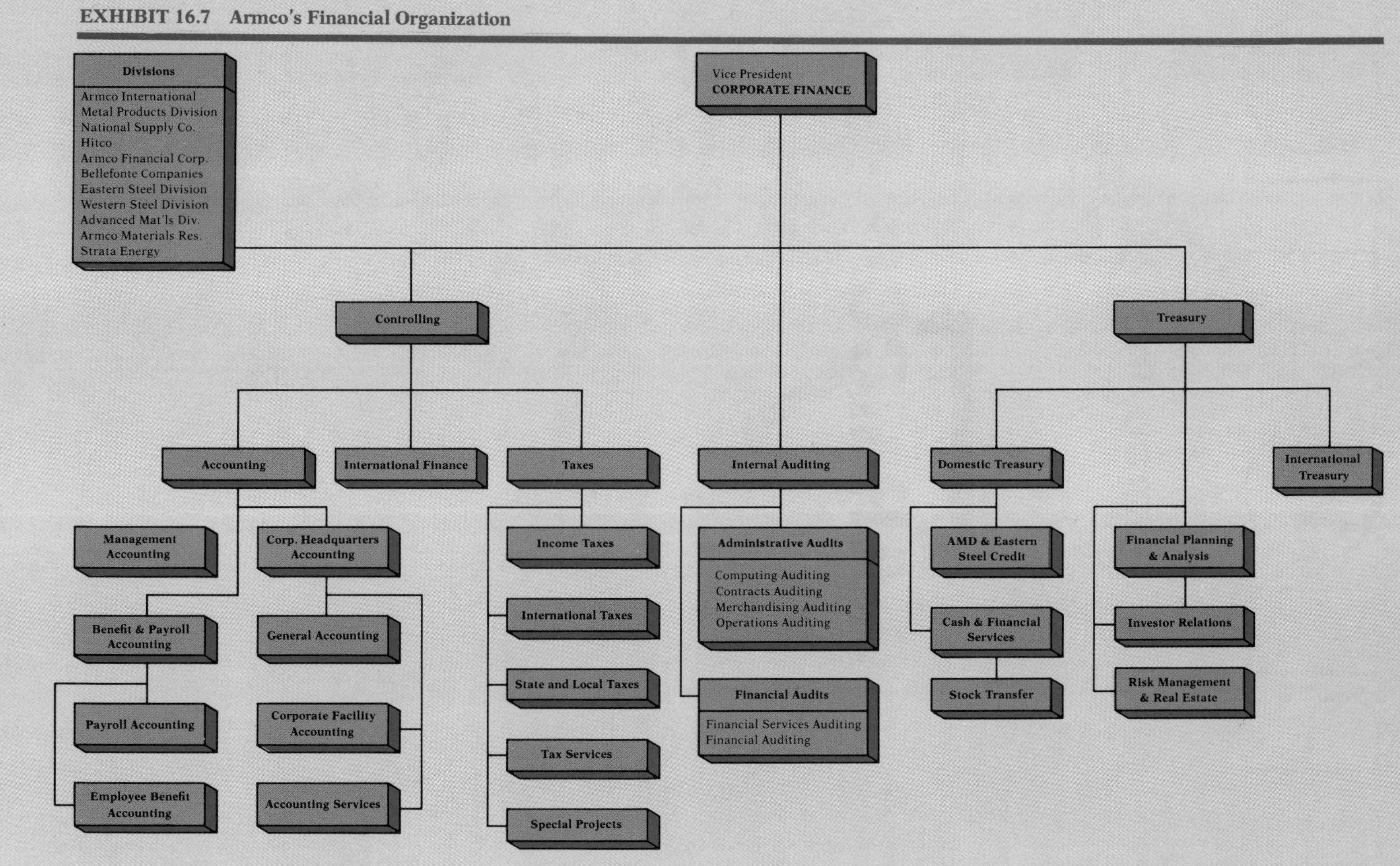

Divisions
Armco International
Metal Products Division
National Supply Co.
Hitco
Armco Financial Corp.
Bellefonte Companies
Eastern Steel Division
Western Steel Division
Advanced Mat'ls Div.
Armco Materials Res.
Strata Energy
Vice President
CORPORATE FINANCE
Controlling
Treasury
Accounting
International Finance
Taxes
Internal Auditing
Domestic Treasury
International Treasury
Management Accounting
Corp. Headquarters Accounting
Benefit & Payroll Accounting
General Accounting
Payroll Accounting
Corporate Facility Accounting
Employee Benefit Accounting
Accounting Services
Income Taxes
International Taxes
State and Local Taxes
Tax Services
Special Projects
Administrative Audits
Computing Auditing
Contracts Auditing
Merchandising Auditing
Operations Auditing
Financial Audits
Financial Services Auditing
Financial Auditing
AMD & Eastern Steel Credit
Cash & Financial Services
Stock Transfer
Financial Planning & Analysis
Investor Relations
Risk Management & Real Estate

It is interesting to note that the treasurer developed financial policies after these goals were established. Responsibility for achieving the goals was distributed to various departments within the treasurer's office. However, to ensure the effective overall management of working capital, Armco has developed a comprehensive approach.

Working capital at Armco is defined as current assets minus current liabilities that don't bear interst. The company has a goal of minimizing the investment in working capital and assuring corporate liquidity. To meet this goal, management attempts to keep the time between making the product and collecting payment for it (the working-capital cycle) as short as possible. The advantage of shortening this time period is that the company can minimize its investment in working capital and therefore have more cash available for alternative uses.

Armco shortens the working-capital cycle by

1. Reducing the time between receipt of raw materials and shipment of finished goods (minimizing corporate investment in inventory while ensuring enough inventory to satisfy customer needs)
2. Eliminating the deficiencies of the paperwork flow (making sure customers are billed on a timely basis and that the movement of cash is not delayed because the proper paperwork has not been done
3. Improving the terms for buying and selling goods and improving the process for receipt and disbursement of cash (making sure that customers pay their bills on time and that the company pays vendors on time)

A step-by-step checklist helps the operating units and the treasurer's office make sure that the movement of cash is not impeded at any phasé of the working-capital cycle.

Armco had working capital of approximately $705 million in 1979, spread throughout the corporation. Therefore, this particular aspect of financial management is critical. Armco's financial managers constantly monitor and evaluate the use of working capital and cooperate with various units in the company that have responsibility for managing working capital.

CAREER OPPORTUNITIES

A typical entry-level position in corporate finance at Armco would be financial analyst. Financial analysts normally have a bachelor's degree in finance. Working under the direction of the assistant treasurer for financial planning and analysis, these people might assist in the preparation of long-range financial projections, prepare quarterly reports comparing Armco's performance to that of other companies, consult with other divisions and corporate functions about financial matters, and prepare special studies related to financial matters, such as studies in financing alternatives or lease-versus-buy problems.

After this initial assignment, a financial employee might rotate to another staff position in the treasurer's or controller's office or get an assignment in the corporate finance area of an operating division. Eventually, this employee might move into some type of management position in finance, at either the divisional or corporate level.

FOR DISCUSSION

1. Discuss how Armco might go about minimizing its investment in each major component of working capital.
2. In 1979 Armco had a net investment in property, plant, and equipment of approximately $1.4 billion. Suggest ways Armco might measure the productivity of these assets.
3. Would corporate financial activity be different in a service-oriented company as opposed to a large manufacturer like Armco? If so, what would be the differences?

OBJECTIVES

- ☐ To explain the difference between a stock and a bond and the advantages and disadvantages of each for long-term financing
- ☐ To make the distinction between a preferred stock and a common stock
- ☐ To explain why the price of existing bonds fluctuates inversely with the market rate of interest
- ☐ To recognize the difference between public information (and its value to you as an investor) and inside information
- ☐ To relate the random walk theory of the stock market to the notion of getting rich quick
- ☐ To explain the workings of various stock markets and how stocks are bought and sold
- ☐ To read stock and bond quotations

OUTLINE

KEY TERMS

BOND
CALL
CAPITAL GAIN
CAPITAL LOSS
CASH ACCOUNT
COMMON STOCK
DEBENTURE
DIVIDEND
EQUITY CAPITAL
INSIDE INFORMATION
LIMIT ORDER
MARGIN ACCOUNT
MARKET ORDER
MORTGAGE BOND
MUTUAL FUND
OPTION
OVER-THE-COUNTER MARKET (OTC)
PAR VALUE
PREFERRED STOCK
PUT
RANDOM WALK
SECURITY
STOCK
STOP-LOSS ORDER
THIRD SECURITIES MARKET

STOCK AND BOND MARKETS

Throwing Darts: If a Monkey Can Pick Stocks This Way and Win, Why Not You?

ANDREW TOBIAS
Esquire Magazine

Even if this is a good time to buy stocks—even if they *are* cheap relative to other assets (and they are)—most people feel incompetent to choose the ones to buy. Either they pay through the nose to have someone else choose or they turn their attention to other, more palatable projects. But how highly trained must one really be to take the plunge? Not so highly as one might think.

A monkey throwing darts, it has frequently been said, can do about as well picking stocks as the average Wall Street professional. Or better. Invariably, when I make this claim—most recently on a spate of local talk shows—I get one of two reactions. From the Wall Street professionals: "---- you." From everyone else: "Where's the monkey?"

"The real problem," I say, warming to my shtick, "is finding a monkey that can throw darts."

"Where's the monkey?" the audience asks again.

"It is computer simulated," I admit. (Children are particularly disappointed by this.) "But it's true. A monkey is as good as a pro."

But *is* it true?

I recently had an opportunity to put my monkey where my mouth was, so to speak, using neither marmoset nor macaque (nor computer) but, rather, five obliging ladies from the studio audience of *The Bob Braun Show,* in Cincinnati.

Such experiments are not original with me. The editors of *Forbes,* in a now much celebrated bout of dart throwing, selected a portfolio twelve years ago that has consistently outperformed the bank trust departments, mutual funds, and popular stock averages. At last report, it was over 60 percent ahead of the Dow Jones.

But it is one thing to read it in *Forbes* and another to confirm it in fact. I will admit to having felt some trepidation as the darts began to fly. Perhaps I should have tested my hypothesis *before* proclaiming it on 112 talk shows.

My first thought had been to pin up the stock pages from an old *Wall Street Journal.* But the *Journal,* it seems, keeps its back issues on microfilm. The gals would have had to be sharpshooters indeed. Instead, we pinned up that morning's *Cincinnati Enquirer,* March 9, 1979. And from a distance of five feet, in front of an estimated 306,000 witnesses (the show is carried on six other television stations as well as ninety-seven cable systems), they threw. Each dart carried a hypothetical $1,000. One dart sailed over the backstop; several hit the government-bond and options tables and had to be rethrown. Eventually, we had holes in thirteen New York and American stock exchange common stocks. (One I eliminated be-

THE BOB BRAUN SHOW PORTFOLIO

NYSE	Now 3/9/79	Then 3/1/74	Growth of $1,000	Dividends Now	Dividends Then
1. Bendix Corp.	40	21*	$1,904	$2.56	$1.35*
2. Brockway Glass	16¾	9*	1,861	1.08	.56*
3. Integon Corp.	17	8⅞	1,915	.44	.28
4. Peoples Drug	10⅛	6⅝	1,528	.24	.20
5. Puritan Fashions	5¾	4⅜	1,314	—	.28
6. Talley Industries	11⅛	6¼	1,780	1.00	.60
7. Wrigley	64⅜	59	1,091	3.70	3.00
ASE					
8. Hampton Industries	5⅝	3¾	1,500	—	.32
9. La. Genl. Services	18½	7	2,643	.99	.62
10. Michigan Sugar	6¾	5*	1,350	.70	.43*
11. Richton Intl.	6½	1½	4,333	.44	—
12. Sysco Corp.	30½	19¼	1,584	.56	.20
			$22,803		
Dow Jones Average:	845	861			

*Adjusted for splits.

The professionals showed no gain over the past five years; the dart throwers were up 90 percent (plus dividends).

cause it had not been listed five years earlier.)

Herewith *The Bob Braun Show* portfolio (dart holes available for inspection on request): Bendix, Brockway Glass, Integon, Peoples Drug, Puritan Fashions, Talley Industries, and Wrigley (all on the New York Stock Exchange); Hampton Industries, Louisiana General Services, Michigan Sugar, Richton, and Sysco (on the American).

Of the dozen, I had never heard of eight.

I went home and pulled out the stock pages from March 1, 1974. On that day, the Dow Jones Industrial Average stood at 860.53. Five inflation-ravaged years later, as we threw darts, it stood at 844.85—slightly lower. Had you invested $12,000 in March of 1974 in the stocks that make up the Dow, your investment would have shrank slightly to $11,784 by the time we threw our darts. The same investment in the stocks that make up the Standard & Poor's average would have grown to $12,420. But if you had invested $1,000 in each of the twelve stocks that our ladies of *The Bob Braun Show* picked, your money would have grown to $22,803.

And you'd have earned some $3,000 in dividends on your investment to boot.

How could the monkey do so well? Is it possible he will continue to outstrip the pros? (The average money manager underperforms the popular averages because—unlike those averages—his results are diminished by commissions and fees.)

To begin with, it should be said that if you had bought this same dart-selected portfolio (or just about any stocks) in the late Sixties, you would have gotten killed. By any reasonable measures, the market was very high in the late Sixties, much less so in March 1974 or March 1979. It always helps to throw your darts when the market is low.

Low as it was, however, as 1974 progressed, the market went straight down. Had you sold out in despair—as so many did—you would have lost money. But monkeys do not sell out in despair. Nor do they change their minds. They do not generate brokerage commissions and incur taxes by selling one stock to buy another.

But the real advantage the monkey had in 1974 was in bucking what was known as the two-tier market. Back then, the top few hundred companies were accorded particularly wide premiums over the smaller, unknown, or uninteresting companies. Big companies tended to be overpriced; *most* companies were unfashionable—but cheap. While money managers concentrated on a few hundred overpriced stocks, darts landed at random among thousands of bargains.

Today, the relative valuations of big and little companies, glamorous and unglamorous ones, seem substantially more rational. So it is unlikely that dart throwers will do better over the next five years than professionals. But neither are they likely to do worse. Indeed, recognizing the difficulty of outperforming the averages, some billion-dollar money managers have turned (in desperation?) to "indexing," which is the practice of trying simply to match the averages by buying all the stocks *in* the averages (or at least a representative sample). To the extent that managers index their portfolios, they are making monkeys of themselves. They have given up trying to assess relative values—even though some stocks *are* better values than others—and just buy a little of everything. But even at that, they will do poorly because they will mindlessly stick to the large stocks that make up the averages, even at times when smaller stocks are better buys.

Of course, certain pros *will* consistently beat the averages. I do not believe this is impossible—just very difficult. But how do you find them? If you can spot the winning mutual fund, perhaps you can also spot winning stocks and save the fee.

I do not suggest that anyone seriously consider choosing stocks at random. However, it does seem wise to diversify (one dart won't do) and to ignore, as the darts ignore, whatever is the current fashion (this year: gambling stocks).

If the market is indeed low today (what else costs no more than it did fourteen years ago?), and if the world as we know it does not end (as after all it might not), then by choosing your own stocks, buying them through a discount broker, and sticking with them patiently, collecting dividends, you may not do spectacularly, but you are likely to do creditably well. Boring but true

Getting rich quick in the stock market is not an unusual goal. Whether you decide to throw darts as suggested here or become a technically savvy analyst, you'll still need to know the basics behind stocks and bonds. And that's what's ahead.

THE DOW JONES INDUSTRIAL AVERAGE JUMPS 23 POINTS
BOND PRICES PLUMMET AS INTEREST RATE RISES

For investors, business news about stocks and bonds is of the utmost importance, because it tells them whether they are doing well on their investments or doing poorly. For someone who is contemplating expanding an old business, starting a new one, or restructuring the financial arrangements of an existing one, news about stocks and bonds may indicate whether the timing for long-term financing is right and even whether additional projects should be considered and financed in public securities markets.

The Securities Market

Business firms and governments obtain long-term financing by selling securities to individuals and institutions. A **security** is the tangible evidence—a certificate—of an investment by individuals and institutions in the affairs of business firms and governments. Stocks and bonds are the two major types of securities.

STOCKS

A **stock** is a legal document giving its owner the right to a certain portion of the profits of the company that issued it. Suppose the woman who owns Naturall, a health food company worth $1 million, wants to raise $200,000 for expansion. To obtain the money, she would have to put 20,000 shares of Naturall stock on the market at $10 a share. If all of the stock were sold, she would get the money for expansion, and the people who bought stock would be part owners of the company. Assuming there were 100,000 shares of stock altogether, the new shareholders would collectively have a claim to one-fifth of whatever profits Naturall earned.

Stocks represent **equity capital** in a company. The concept of equity might best be understood in terms of the equity that homeowners have in their homes. If you own a house that has a market value (the price at which you could sell your house) of $100,000 and you owed $60,000 on your home mortgage, then you would have equity of $40,000 in your home.

Common Stocks

Most stock is **common stock,** usually called equity. Naturall offered common stock.

No firm can ensure that the market price per share of its common stock won't go down over time. Neither does the issuing firm guarantee a **dividend.** Indeed, some business firms never pay dividends. So why would an individual even consider investing in common stock? The

EXHIBIT 17.1 Sample Common Stock Certificate

MORE THAN 100 SHARES

NUMBER

SHARES

INCORPORATED UNDER THE LAWS OF THE STATE OF DELAWARE

MINNESOTA MINING AND MANUFACTURING COMPANY

THIS CERTIFICATE IS TRANSFERABLE IN NEW YORK, N.Y. OR IN ST. PAUL, MINNESOTA

See reverse for certain definitions

This Certifies that SPECIMEN *is the owner of*

CUSIP 604059 10 5

FULL PAID AND NON-ASSESSABLE SHARES OF THE COMMON STOCK WITHOUT PAR VALUE OF
MINNESOTA MINING AND MANUFACTURING COMPANY

Dated

Minnesota Mining and Manufacturing Company

SECRETARY

CHAIRMAN OF THE BOARD

REGISTERED: THE FIRST NATIONAL BANK OF SAINT PAUL, REGISTRAR

OR

REGISTERED: FIRST NATIONAL CITY BANK, REGISTRAR

COUNTERSIGNED: FIRST TRUST COMPANY OF SAINT PAUL, TRANSFER AGENT

OR

COUNTERSIGNED: MORGAN GUARANTY TRUST COMPANY OF NEW YORK, TRANSFER AGENT

answer is that each owner is entitled to a proportional share of the after-tax earnings of the corporation. If, for example, you own 100 shares (0.01 percent of a million shares outstanding) of a firm that earns $3 million after taxes, your proportional share is $300.

The earnings of a corporation are either paid out in the form of cash dividends to common stock shareholders or retained in the business to enhance future earnings. If the board of directors of your firm (and it is *your* firm if you're a common stock shareholder) declares a dividend of $1.20 per share, then you will receive $120 of your $300 earnings and the other $180 will be retained. Another benefit is the market price per share that you will receive when you sell part or all of your 100 common shares. But market price depends, among other things, on the recent earnings (and dividends) of the firm and, more importantly, on expectations for future earnings and dividends.

Common stock shareholders are last in line when it comes to receiving payment for their investment. Suppliers, employees, managers, bankers, governments, bondholders, and preferred stock shareholders must first be paid what is due them. Once those groups have been paid, however, common stock shareholders are entitled to *all* of the remaining earnings. This is the central feature of ownership in any business. The common stock owners occupy the riskiest position, but they can logically expect a greater return on their investment than that accruing to other groups.

Investors who own common stock have one vote per common share in elections of the firm's board of directors and in voting on any proposed changes in the ownership structure of the firm. For example, if you are a common stock shareholder in Naturall, you might be asked to vote on a decision about merging Naturall with Cosmos, a natural cosmetic company.

Certain common stocks have a value printed on them when they are issued. This is the stock's **par value.** In many states, this par value is the basis for state and corporation taxes. Because par value is strictly arbitrary, most common shares are issued today with no par value.

What is most important to the investor is the *market value* of a share of stock, that is, the value of the stock *in open trading.* The market value of stock in large companies can easily be found in the financial pages of a daily newspaper.

The **book value** of a company is simply its net worth (assets minus liabilities, including preferred stock). When the number of outstanding common shares is divided into the net worth, the book value per share is the result.

You may have read about major companies splitting shares of stock. A stock split is a procedure whereby a corporation doubles (or even triples) each share that a stock certificate represents. There are many reasons why companies split stocks, one being to increase the number of investors who can partake of ownership.

"See that chart? Don't you believe it!"

Preferred Stock

Unlike common stock shareholders, the owners of preferred shares of stock have no voting rights. **Preferred stock** is not included among the liabilities of a business, because there is no fixed maturity time when the preferred shares must be retired by the firm. Preferred stock shareholders get their investment back by selling their shares to another investor. Preferred stock shareholders may also receive periodic dividend payments, usually established as a fixed percentage of the face amount of each preferred share, but this is not a legal obligation on the part of the firm. However, preferred stock owners must be paid their dividends before common stock owners may be paid a dividend, and they have a superior claim on the assets of the corporation should the firm be liquidated.

One type of preferred stock is cumulative preferred stock. Any dividend payment for cumulative preferred stock not made in a given year must be made up in subsequent years before any dividends can be paid to the owners of common stock. Sometimes there are limits to how far back dividends have to be paid.

The owner of convertible preferred stock has the option of converting each share into a specified number of common shares. Sometimes convertible preferred stock can be exchanged for common stock in another company. In any event, the exchange ratio is determined when the convertible preferred shares of stock are issued. Hence, if there is an increase in the market value of the corporation's common stock, the market value of the convertible preferred stock also rises.

Redeemable, or callable, preferred stock is issued by a corporation with the explicit understanding that the corporation can, at some future time, buy back the shares of stock from the preferred stock owners. The terms of such a buy-back arrangement are specified when the preferred stock is issued. Corporations issue callable preferred stock so they can call in the higher-cost preferred stock and reissue lower-cost shares if interest rates fall in the future.

BONDS

A **bond** is basically an IOU or a promissory note from a corporation or government, usually issued in multiples of $1,000. The issuing company or government usually promises to pay the bondholder a specified amount of interest for a specified length of time and then to repay the loan (principal) on a specific *maturity date*. The bondholder is a creditor of the corporation or government and not a part owner, as is the common stock shareholder.

Bonds may be sold at face value or above or below face value. If they are sold above their face value, they are said to be sold at a *premium*. If they are sold below their face value, they are said to be sold at a *discount*.

Government Bonds

Government bonds are issued by the federal government, by various federal agencies, by states, and by municipal organizations. Bonds also are issued by foreign governments and municipalities.

The U.S. Treasury issues bills, certificates, notes, and bonds. Treasury bills, with maturities ranging from three months to one year, are sold through an auction process at a discount from their $10,000 face amount. No interest is paid. If you bought a six-month bill for $9,800, your dollar return would be $200 after a half year. Treasury certificates have a maturity of one full year, and buyers receive a single interest coupon that can be converted to cash. A 5-percent coupon on a $1,000 certificate would entitle you to a $50 interest payment. Treasury notes and bonds feature longer maturities and also have interest coupons attached. Income on all U.S. Treasury obligations is subject to federal income taxes but is exempt from state income taxes.

U.S. Treasury issues generally are considered the least risky of all securities, because the taxing power of the U.S. government stands behind them. Bonds issued by various agencies of the federal government are also considered safe investments. Differences in the yields for federal government and federal agency bonds are due largely to differences in maturities. Higher yields usually are associated with longer maturities. If you purchase federal government bonds, you might well require a higher return on a five-year bond than on a one-year certificate, simply because you must wait so much longer to get your money back.

State and municipal governments sell bonds to finance roads, schools, libraries, utilities, sewers, and fire and police stations. *Interest on municipal bonds is exempt from federal income taxes and, in some cases, from state taxes as well.* As a result, municipal bonds often are desirable securities for people in high tax brackets. But because the resources of state and local governments are not nearly so large as those of our federal government, there is greater risk associated with state and municipal bonds. Differences in yields among the bonds of state and local governments reflect differences in risk as well as varying maturities.

Corporate Bonds

Corporations sell both bonds and stocks. Corporate *bonds* are available with a wide range of expected returns, risks, and other characteristics. That's because corporations differ greatly in their abilities to generate the earnings and cash flow necessary to make interest payments and to repay the principal amount of the bonds at maturity. Furthermore, corporate bonds are only part of the total debt and overall financial structure of corporate business.

Because debt financing (issuing bonds) represents a legal obligation

Business in Action

PORTFOLIO IV: MANAGING FINANCIAL DECISIONS

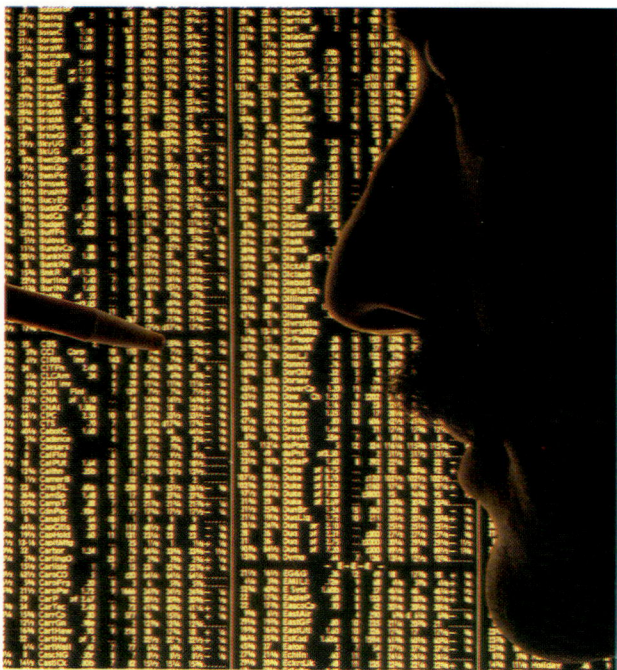

THE WALL STREET JOURNAL.
What's News—
Tax Report

EXHIBIT 17.2 Sample Corporate Bond

on the part of the corporation, the terms of a particular bond issue are specified in a lending agreement called a bond indenture. A corporate trustee, often a commercial bank trust department, ensures that the terms of the bond issue are met by the corporation. Most corporate bonds pay semiannually a coupon rate of interest on the $1,000 face amount of the bond. Thus if you owned a 6-percent corporate bond, you would receive $30 interest every six months. The indenture also indicates if any portion of the bond is to be retired each year in a series of so-called sinking fund payments. Any collateral for the bond issue, such as buildings or equipment, also is indicated. Additionally, the indenture indicates how you as a bondholder would fare—along with other creditors of the business firm—should the firm get into serious financial difficulty and not be able to meet all of its legal obligations.

There are several different types of corporate bonds. No specific assets of the corporation are pledged as backing for **debentures.** Rather, the general credit rating of the corporation is at stake, plus any assets that can be seized if the corporation allows the bonds to fall into default. **Mortgage bonds** are secured by a mortgage on all or part of the corporate-owned real property. The backing for equipment trust bonds is a specific piece of equipment. The title to the equipment is vested in a trustee, who holds it for the benefit of the owners of the bonds. Collateral trust bonds are secured by anything that is not real estate, such as shares of stock in another corporation or accounts receivable. Convertible bonds can be exchanged for a specified number of shares of common stock, when and if the bondholder so desires. The rate of conver-

Highlight The Fluctuating Interest Rate on Bonds

Interest rates on government and corporate bonds tend to fluctuate quite a bit. The *dollar* interest payment on a bond is fixed, but the actual yield, or rate of return, is not. Consider a simple example. You have just purchased a $1,000 bond that promises to pay you $100 a year forever. That means that your interest yield is $100 ÷ $1,000, or 10 percent. Suddenly everyone wants more bonds, so that the price of all bonds goes up. You find that you can now sell your bond for $2,000. It still yields only $100 a year, so the effective interest yield for the buyer of the bond goes down to $100 ÷ $2,000, or 5 percent.

The important point is this: *The market price of existing bonds is inversely related to the rate of interest prevailing in the economy.*

To drive this point home, look at the other side of the picture. Assume that the average yield on bonds is 5 percent. You decide to purchase a $1,000 bond that will pay you $50 a year forever, a 5-percent yield. But suppose something happens in the economy that allows you to obtain bonds that have effective yields of 10 percent. The market price of the old bond will fall. Why should anyone buy it from you, when a bond that costs only $500 would also yield $50 a year? An increase in the prevailing interest rate has caused the market value of your old bond to fall, once again proving that existing bond prices are inversely related to the prevailing interest rate.

sion is determined when the convertible bond is issued. Debentures or any other kind of bond may be callable, which means that the corporation can take the bond back and repay the principal whenever it wants to. The callable provision is put into the bond when it is issued.

STOCK VERSUS BONDS

A corporation can take two major roads for long-term financing—the sale of bonds or the sale of common stock. (To make the comparison easy, we'll ignore preferred stock.) Exhibit 17.3 outlines the pros and cons of each, which are detailed below.

EXHIBIT 17.3 Comparing Stocks and Bonds

Common Stocks	Bonds
1. Stocks represent ownership.	1. Bonds represent owed debt.
2. Stocks do not have a fixed dividend rate.	2. Interest on bonds must always be paid, whether or not any profit is earned.
3. Stockholders can elect a board of directors, which controls the corporation.	3. Bondholders usually have no voice in or control over management of the corporation.
4. Stocks do not have a maturity date; the corporation does not usually repay the stockholder.	4. Bonds have a maturity date when the bondholder is to be repaid the face value of the bond.
5. All corporations issue or offer to sell stocks. This is the usual definition of a corporation.	5. Corporations are not required to issue bonds.
6. Stockholders have a claim against the property and income of a corporation after all creditors' claims have been met.	6. Bondholders have a claim against the property and income of a corporation that must be met before the claims of stockholders.

Financing through the sale of common stock is riskless. There is no legal obligation to make dividend payments to common stock shareholders, and they do not have to be repaid at some future date. On the other hand, it is a relatively expensive way to finance a company. Any dividends are paid out after federal, and sometimes state, corporate income taxes have been paid. Additionally, whenever new common stock is sold, the original shares of stock are diluted. Thus initial stockholders' rights to future residual earnings are reduced.

Many financial managers of large corporations prefer to raise additional capital through the sale of long-term bonds. They are the cheapest way of financing, because bond interest is tax deductible to the corporation. Additionally, bondholders have no voice in management. The original bondholders' rights to residual earnings are also left untouched. The disadvantages of bonds are that they are highly risky. Holders of bonds have senior rights to the earnings of any company. If a company is unable to make interest payments, it may be forced into bankruptcy by its bondholders. Common stock owners cannot do this.

Why People Invest

Most investors have common stock as part of their portfolio of investments. Numerous studies on the stock market in the past have shown that, on average, one can expect to make 8 to 15 percent per year if all dividends are reinvested and no trading occurs over a long period of time. But look at Exhibit 17.4, which shows the Dow Jones Industrial Average (a leading indicator of stock prices) corrected for inflation and the amount of profits the companies pour back into themselves. It appears that an investor putting $100 in Dow Jones stocks in 1929 would still have only about $100 of real purchasing power if he or she sold them today.

And yet people continue to invest in stocks, as well as in bonds and other securities and investment outlets. We will briefly look at four reasons for this.

GROWTH OF PRINCIPAL

Stocks and bonds can go up and down in price. If you buy a stock at $10 and sell it at $15, you make a **capital gain** of $5 for every share. If the value of your stock falls and you sell it, you suffer a **capital loss.**

Some stocks pay dividends, but not all do. Normally, if you buy a stock that has never paid a dividend, you expect to make money on your investment by an increase in the value of the stock. That is, if the company is making profits but not giving out dividends, it must be reinvesting those profits. A reinvestment could pay off in the future by yielding higher profits. In that case, the value of the stock would be bid up in the market. Your profit would be in the form of a capital gain rather than dividend payments.

Investors who seek growth in their principal look for, among other things, shares of common stock in companies that never pay dividends but rather have a history of reinvestment in profitable ventures. It is

EXHIBIT 17.4 The Dow Jones Industrial Average, Corrected for Inflation and Retained Earnings

In this exhibit the Dow Jones has been corrected for inflation since 1930, using 1967 as the base. The averages also show correction for the 3 percent retained earnings that is the average for the economy. The figures given are the closing highs for each year. The corrected Dow Jones hit its peak back in 1965 and 1966, and has done little since then.

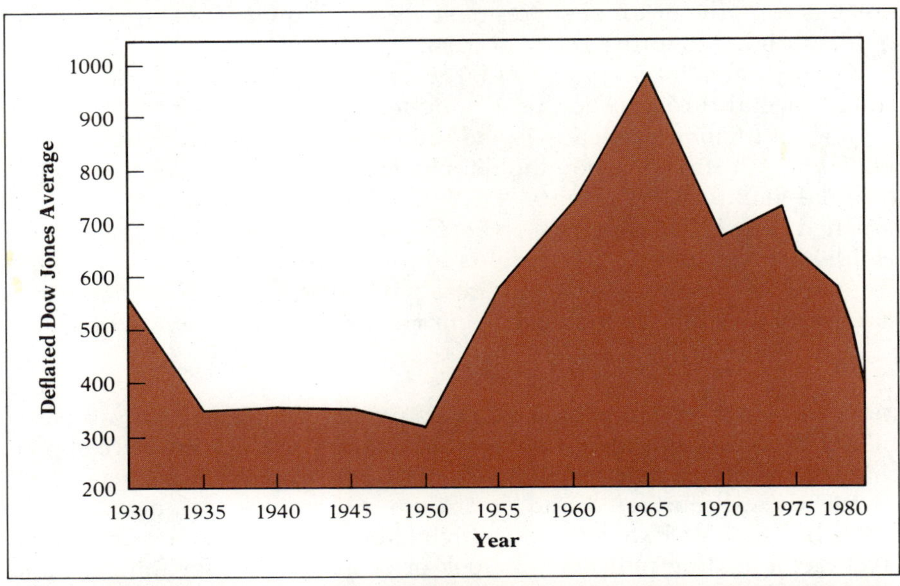

Source: *The Dow Jones Average, 1885-1970.* Annual High Closing Quotation. Dow Jones & Company, 1972; and Bureau of Labor Statistics.

also possible to invest in bonds whose price is expected to rise, particularly if they are sold at a heavy discount. However, most investors who are seeking only growth of principal buy more common stocks than bonds.

CURRENT INCOME

Investors who seek current income usually want to purchase preferred stocks in companies that have a history of paying all of their dividends on such stocks, common stocks in companies that have a history of paying dividends as opposed to reinvesting, and bonds that yield a fixed income.

Exhibit 17.5 shows the compounded effect of different yields on different investments. The investor who obtains, for example, only a 5-percent rate of return on a $100 investment will have only $265 at the end of twenty years. If that same investor were to receive a 12-percent return at the end of twenty years, the $100 will have grown to $965.

Some investors are interested in the safety of their investment. They lean toward bonds from companies that have an excellent reputation for paying off debts. Several rating services are available to tell the investor which bonds have the least risk. For example, Moody's Investors Service and *Standard & Poor's Register of Corporations* both provide ratings based on detailed studies of the government's or corporation's financial status.

SAFETY OF PRINCIPAL

People who "play the market" are pure speculators hoping to make quick profits on changes in stock prices (and also bond prices). These investors believe that they "have a feel for the market," a better understanding of how it works than other investors, or information that other people don't have.

PURE SPECULATION

Public Information

Information about a specific company rapidly becomes widely known. As soon as a company announces its profits or a new management team, literally thousands of people learn about it. Such information is not so readily available as the prices of listed stocks, but it flows quite freely within the American economy. The point is that by the time one investor reads about what a company, an industry, or for that matter, the national economy is going to do, most other investors have also read it. Public information cannot help much in a plan to get rich quick.

Suppose a company in your neighborhood has discovered a substitute for gasoline. You read about the discovery in the newspaper and decide that the company's stock would be an excellent purchase. But people who learned about the discovery before you have probably also realized that the company stands to make higher profits. Some will

EXHIBIT 17.5 Compounded Effect for Selected Returns on a $100 Investment

A savings account yielding 5 percent will produce $265 at the end of twenty years if $100 is invested. On the other hand, a stock yielding 12 percent will produce almost $1,000 after twenty years. If there is a 2 percent loss per year, the $100 will be reduced to only $67.

	Horizon—Number of Years				
Return	*1 year*	*2 years*	*5 years*	*10 years*	*20 years*
15%	$115	$132	$201	$405	$1,637
12%	112	125	176	311	965
8%	108	117	147	216	466
5%	105	110	128	163	265
− 2%	98	96	90	82	67
−12%	88	77	53	28	8

already have started to buy stock in the company. By the time you read about the discovery, competing investors will have already bid up the price of the stock.

Inside Information

The only useful information to a speculator is information that is not yet public. This information, known only to a small group of people, is called **inside information.** Literally millions of people go to great lengths and spend rather large sums to get information about organizations' future profitability.

Suppose a lawyer meets with an executive of the International Chemical and Drug Company in the executive's office. When the executive steps out of the office for a moment, the lawyer looks down in the wastebasket and sees a crumpled memo that reads, "Success! We've done it!" Recently, the lawyer has noticed several new items about a miracle drug the company is testing. Assuming that the company does not announce the discovery immediately, the lawyer has some very valuable information. If the lawyer were to buy as many shares of International Chemical and Drug Company as she could, she might be able to get rich quick. It is highly likely that the stock will be bid up when the inside information becomes public and investors anticipate higher company profits.

A Random Walk

If you have studied physics, you have probably heard about the Brownian motion of molecules. According to this theory, molecules jump at random. It is impossible to predict where a molecule might move next. Similarly, anything that follows a **random walk** takes directions that are totally unrelated to its past movements. No amount of information about its past is useful for predicting its future.

Because the stock market is so highly competitive and because information flows so freely, it follows a random walk. The market as a whole has trends, such as the general upward trend from its beginning, which reflects the growth in the American economy. The prices of specific stocks and the average of all stock prices, however, exhibit a random walk. Thus any examination of past stock prices will not yield useful information for predicting future prices. Years of academic research have left little doubt that the stock market follows a random walk.

Is There a Way to Get Rich Quick?

Will Rogers, although not known for his astute investments, did have some words of wisdom for potential investors in the stock market, a guaranteed scheme to get rich quick. We paraphrase:

"Take a bunch of stocks and buy them. Hold all of them for awhile. Sell every single stock that went up in price. Now, those stocks that went down in price? Don't buy them."

While it seldom works out to be that simple, many people think they *can* outsmart the stock market. Yet the facts are irrefutable. In the words of Nobel prize–winning economist Paul Samuelson: "Even the best investors seem to find it hard to do better than the comprehensive common-stock averages, or better on the average than random selection among stocks of comparable variability."*

Securities Exchanges

Securities—stock and bonds—are bought and sold at securities markets. A stock exchange is a physical entity where trading is limited to members of the exchange and a prescribed list of stocks. An organized bond exchange is similar, except that only bonds are traded. Memberships on securities exchanges are purchased. Most memberships belong to securities firms and other organizations in the business of providing information and other services to investors.

NEW YORK STOCK EXCHANGE

The largest organized exchange is the New York Stock Exchange (NYSE), commonly referred to as the "Big Board," which accounts for more than 70 percent of the total value of all stocks traded on organized exchanges. Common and preferred stocks of most of the largest companies are listed on the NYSE. To have its stock listed, a company must satisfy certain minimum financial requirements and also agree to keep the investing public informed about its affairs. A look at the *Wall Street Journal* or any other newspaper that prints information on the NYSE will show that AT&T, General Motors, Exxon, Texaco, Ford, Du Pont, Mobil, Sears, RCA, Xerox, and IBM are all listed. There are also some foreign stocks, including Sony from Japan and British Petroleum from the United Kingdom.

AMERICAN STOCK EXCHANGE

The second-largest stock exchange is the American Stock Exchange (AMEX). On average, the companies listed on AMEX are somewhat smaller than those listed on the New York Stock Exchange. Also, in general, the requirements for listing on AMEX are less stringent than for the NYSE. As with the NYSE, AMEX is located in New York. Such well-known companies as the *New York Times*, *Washington Post*, Braniff, Dunlop Tire, Gerber Foods, and U.S. Air are listed on AMEX.

*Paul Samuelson, *Bell Journal of Economics and Management Science* 4 (Autumn 1973): 369-374.

Highlight How to Get Your Firm Listed on the NYSE

To qualify for listing on the New York Stock Exchange, a corporation has to meet the following minimum standards:

- At least a million shares publicly held
- At least 2,000 investors who hold 100 shares or more
- Annual earnings of at least $2^1/_2$ million before taxes for the most recent year and at least $2 million for each of the preceding two years
- Net tangible assets worth at least $16 million
- A market value of at least $16 million for all outstanding common stock

Meeting these minimum requirements, however, does not automatically guarantee that your corporation will be listed. The governing board of the New York Stock Exchange looks at each applicant on a case-by-case basis.

REGIONAL AND LOCAL EXCHANGES

There are a number of regional exchanges, such as the Midwest (Chicago, Cincinnati), Pacific Coast (San Francisco, Los Angeles), and Philadelphia-Baltimore-Washington exchanges. Certain cities, such as Seattle, Spokane, Pittsburgh, Detroit, and Boston, have local exchanges.

Regional and local stock exchanges account for about only $6^1/_2$ percent of the annual volume on organized exchanges. Firms listed on regional exchanges are typically regional in nature, although a number of firms listed on the NYSE and AMEX are also listed on the regional exchanges.

THE OVER-THE-COUNTER MARKET

Stocks and bonds not listed on organized securities exchanges are bought and sold on what is called the **over-the-counter market (OTC).** This is really a complex communications network that transmits information about the prices at which securities firms scattered around the country are prepared to buy or sell securities for their customers. Price quotations currently go through a computer-based system known as NASDAQ. Most of the securities handled in the over-the-counter market are not listed on any organized stock exchanges, but those that are sometimes are referred to as the **third securities market.** Most government and corporate bonds are traded over-the-counter.

The over-the-counter market differs from the organized stock exchanges in how the market for a given security is made. On an organized exchange, a member firm establishes an auction market for each security. That firm is referred to as the *specialist* in that security. The specialist matches the buy and sell orders of broker firms, which represent the interests of the investing public, without actually owning securities. When necessary, the specialist also buys and sells the securities directly in order to maintain an orderly and continuous market. In contrast, the over-the-counter market consists of over 5,000 securities firms, acting both as brokers and dealers, in a decentralized, informal, negotiated market. No single member firm controls the consummation of transactions.

Buying and Selling Securities

TYPES OF BROKERAGE ACCOUNTS

Once an investor decides to trade particular stocks and bonds, he or she must implement the decision through a securities broker, sometimes called an account executive. Exhibit 17.6 shows the steps involved in the typical securities transaction.

An investor can have one of two types of accounts with a brokerage firm. A **cash account** is designed for investors who want to pay cash for securities. If you open a cash account, you may elect to hold the bonds or stock certificates yourself, preferably in a safe-deposit box. Or you may have the brokerage firm hold the bonds or stock certificates for you. Many investors prefer not to be bothered with physical possession of securities.

EXHIBIT 17.6 Steps in Buying Stocks and Bonds

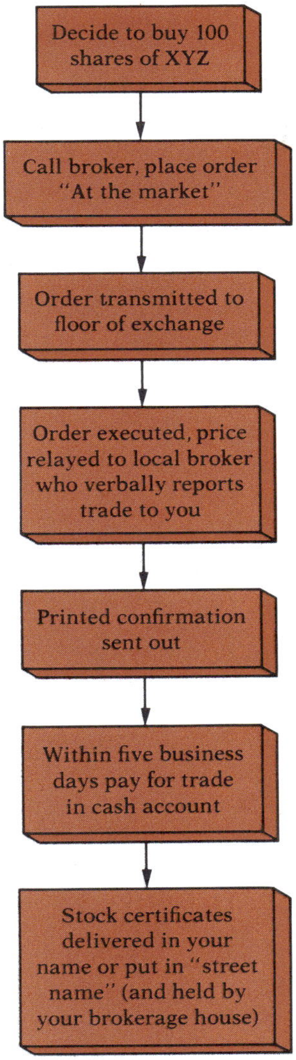

Decide to buy 100 shares of XYZ

↓

Call broker, place order "At the market"

↓

Order transmitted to floor of exchange

↓

Order executed, price relayed to local broker who verbally reports trade to you

↓

Printed confirmation sent out

↓

Within five business days pay for trade in cash account

↓

Stock certificates delivered in your name or put in "street name" (and held by your brokerage house)

Highlight Are You a Bull or a Bear?

Perhaps you've heard of "bulls" and "bears" on Wall Street. These expressions do not relate to a person's physical characteristics. Rather, bulls are investors who believe that the market is on an upswing or will be soon. Bears are those who are pessimistic. Bulls, then, think they should be buying; bears think they should be selling.

Cartoon by Martha Weston

A **margin account** is designed for investors who wish to borrow from their brokerage firm a portion of the funds necessary to purchase securities. The initial margin is the amount an investor must actually pay (typically 50 percent to 80 percent for stocks). The maintenance margin (say, 25 percent) is the point at which an investor must pay additional funds if the market price of the stocks begins to fall.

Suppose the initial margin were 50 percent and the maintenance margin were 25 percent. You would have to put up $2,000 to buy $4,000 worth of stocks. If the market price of those stocks fell to $2,500, your margin would be $500, which is only 20 percent of the market value of the stocks. You would receive a margin call asking for at least $125 to restore the 25-percent maintenance margin. Because margin calls during a depressed stock market are psychologically disturbing, most investors are advised to restrict their purchases of securities to a cash account.

In either case, a brokerage firm typically sends its customers a monthly statement of the securities they own as well as their present cash balance, which reflects interest and dividends earned by the securities. For a margin account, the cash balance also shows the funds borrowed plus interest owed to the brokerage firm for use of those funds. A positive cash balance does *not* earn interest, so any excess should either be invested in additional securities or sent to you. You probably won't be reminded to do so by the brokerage firm.

TYPES OF ORDERS

The simplest kind of order, a **market order,** instructs the broker to buy or sell securities for you at the existing market price. A **limit order** tells that broker to buy or sell only if the market price reaches a certain level. Limit orders can be used by investors to "ensure" that securities are sold for more than their purchase price. A **stop-loss order,** or stop order, is an order to sell stock when the market price hits or drops below a specified level. Presumably, a stop-loss order protects the investor against a rapid decline in a stock price.

COSTS OF BUYING AND SELLING SECURITIES

A broker's services are not free. There was once a fixed schedule of brokerage commissions, but since the mid-1970s, investors have been able to negotiate commissions (see Exhibit 17.7). Large institutions, whose transactions may involve thousands of shares, can bargain for commissions as much as 40 to 50 percent off any "fixed" schedule. In-

EXHIBIT 17.7 Cut-Rate Brokerage Fees

Only at Source. All these services at rates this low.

For nearly a decade, investors have been coming to Source to save money on commissions. Virtually all have stayed, not only because they saved money, but because they enjoyed quality service—and more service than you probably expect from a discount broker.

Services

- **Complete quote, execution, settlement and custody services** for all listed and OTC stocks, options, and fixed-income securities.
- **All types of accounts:** Individual, joint, corporate, partnership, estate, trust, pension, profit-sharing, and investment-club.
- **Premium interest** on cash balances through the nation's largest money fund.
- **All registered reps have direct voice communication** with exchange floors.
- **Each representative has personal CRT** for immediate account status retrieval.
- **Best price execution** on OTC stocks traded through NASDAQ.
- **Margin accounts** with maximum loan availability.
- **Prompt nationwide DVP service.**
- **Specialized trading service** for active traders and institutions.
- **Commission rebate for personal quote terminal.**
- **Complete commodities trading services.**
- **Members NYSE, NASD, SIPC.**
- **Worldwide clearing organization** with $500,000 securities protection coverage.

Comparative rates & savings

	100 shares @ $60	500 shares @ $25	1000 shares @ $15	15 options @ $3
Source Rates Base Rate	$30*	$112	$130	$92
At 25% Volume Discount	$30*	$84	$97	$69
Conventional Brokers' Rates**	$87	$227	$293	$161
Your Savings	65%	50% to 62%	55% to 66%	42% to 57%

*Minimum charge.
**Representative rates based on 1980 telephone survey.

To find out what you'll save on particular trades, or for more information on our services, mail the coupon or call toll free today, and ask to speak to one of our New Accounts Representatives.

Call free (800) 221-5338
In N.Y. State call collect **(212) 422-6000**

Source Securities Corporation
New Accounts Department
70 Pine Street, N.Y., N.Y. 10005
Please send me complete information about your commissions and services.

Name ____________
Address ____________
City ____________
State ____________ Zip ____________
Tel. (____) ____________

SOURCE
MEMBER NYSE, NASD, SIPC

dividuals usually cannot bargain so strongly, because their transactions are smaller. Furthermore, the brokerage fee for bond transactions is smaller than for stock transactions.

Before selecting a brokerage firm, you should find out exactly how much commission you will pay. Some brokerage firms attempt to attract customers by offering discounted fees on even smaller orders. But you probably shouldn't bypass a reputable and financially sound brokerage firm or a particular broker from whom you get useful advice and timely service just to save a few dollars.

Remember, when you sell securities, you may have to pay federal and state taxes on any capital gains that have accrued.

OTHER WAYS TO PLAY THE MARKET

Some investors "place orders short"—that is, they agree to sell shares of a stock that they do not yet own at a certain price. Short sellers obviously believe that the price will fall in the near future, so that they can purchase the stocks at a lower price than they can sell them for.

Another way to play the market is to trade in **options,** a method that has grown rapidly since 1973, when the Chicago Board Options Exchange opened for business. The listed options are basically **calls**—contracts giving their owners the right to buy 100 shares of the stock at a predetermined price at any time up to a predetermined maturity date. The Securities and Exchange Commission also permits trading in listed **puts**—the right to sell stocks at predetermined prices.

The buyer of a call aims to take advantage of a rise in the price of a stock above the price he or she agreed to pay. That is a valuable right, and buyers have to pay for it. Calls seem attractive to buyers because they get all of the action in the stock but put up only a fraction of its value. The maximum amount they can lose is the cost of the call. On average, options sell for about 5 to 15 percent of the price of the underlying stock.

Regulation of the Securities Markets

The days of market manipulation, stock swindles, deception, and the use of inside information by company personnel are basically over. The securities markets are heavily regulated today, at both the state and federal levels.

Congress has delegated to the Securities and Exchange Commission (SEC) the responsibility for administering all federal securities law. The SEC acts as an interpreter of federal statutes and investigates alleged infractions of the laws. The SEC has regulatory authority over brokers, dealers, and stock exchanges.

The Securities Act of 1933 was passed to avoid another stock market crash like the one of 1929. To that end, the act prohibits various forms of fraud and requires that all essential information concerning the issue of stocks be made available to the investing public through a registration statement (although it does nothing to guarantee that the offering is fair and equitable). The public sale of securities is generally accomplished with the aid of professional underwriters—investment bankers specializing in the sale and distribution of securities. Corporate management and the underwriters each retain a law firm specializing in securities law to assist them in complying with the law.

The Securities Exchange Act of 1934 provides for the regulation and registration of securities exchanges, brokers, dealers, and national securities associations and requires systematic disclosures from corporations with securities on the exchanges that have assets in excess of $1 million and 500 or more shareholders. One of the most important parts of the 1934 act relates to so-called insider trading. Because of their positions, corporate directors and officers often obtain advance information that can affect the future market value of corporate stock. Obviously, their positions can give them a trading advantage over the general public and shareholders. The 1934 act prohibits officers and directors from taking advantage of such information when they know it is unavailable to the person with whom they are dealing and requires them to turn over to the corporation all short-term profits realized on the purchase and sale of corporate stock.

Today, all states also have their own corporate securities laws. They are designed to prevent "speculative schemes which have no more basis than so many feet of blue sky."

Mutual Funds

Mutual funds pool the money of many investors and buy and sell large blocks of stocks; the investors get dividends or appreciation in their shares of the mutual fund. The mutual fund, then, is a company that invests in other companies but does not sell any product of its own. A study of mutual funds concluded that mutuals that did the least amount of trading made the highest profits, an expected result if one understands the competitive nature of the stock market.

A mutual fund, or investment trust, is one of two types. Shares in *closed-end mutual funds,* some of which are listed on the New York Stock Exchange, are readily transferable in the open market and are bought and sold like other shares. *Open-end mutual funds* sell their own shares to investors, stand ready to buy them back, and are *not* listed on any stock exchange.

The only commission you pay to buy closed-end mutual funds is the standard commission you would pay on the purchase of any stock. On the other hand, there are two types of open-end mutual funds, both of which may charge a yearly management fee. The *no-load mutual fund* does not charge you an additional amount to get into the fund; a **load mutual fund** imposes a setup or loading charge. The person who sells an open-end mutual fund with a loading charge usually keeps most of that charge as commission.

Reading the Financial News

In order to get information on specific stocks and bonds, you must be able to interpret the data provided in local newspapers and the *Wall Street Journal.* Exhibit 17.8 is a sample listing of New York Stock Exchange quotations. Below those quotations are explanations of each column. Exhibit 17.9 shows a typical set of quotations on bonds listed by the New York Bond Exchange.

Much of what we hear and read about the securities markets is actually information on the New York Stock Exchange as portrayed by one or more of the popular market averages. These averages differ in the number of stocks included and in how the averages are constructed. The New York Stock Exchange Index includes all of its listed stocks, Standard & Poor's Composite Index includes 500 stocks, and the Dow Jones Industrial Average (DJIA) includes only 30. The DJIA is an unweighted average of the market prices of its stocks, whereas the other two indexes weight each stock price by the number of outstanding shares. The DJIA is the average mentioned most often in the financial news, but it is considered to be less representative of the total stock market because of its smaller sample.

EXHIBIT 17.8 Sample New York Stock Exchange Quotations

A	B	C	D	E	F	G	H	I	J	K
High	Low	Stocks	Div.	Yld %	P-E Ratio	Sales by 100s	High	Low	Close	Net Change
46 1/8	37 1/4	Interco	2	4.6	8	2	43 7/8	43 7/8	43 7/8	...
20 1/2	7	IntDiv	8.11e	...	9	27	17 3/4	16 3/4	17 3/4	+1 1/4
34 1/2	24 5/8	Intrlk	2.20	7.8	11	60	28 1/2	27 1/4	28 3/8	+ 3/4
23 1/2	12 3/4	IntAlum	1	4.5	8	122	22 7/8	22	22	− 5/8
275 1/2	234 3/4	IBM	11.52	4.3	14	2125	267 5/8	265	266	−1 1/4
25	18 3/4	IntFlav	.56	2.3	19	521	24 7/8	24 5/8	24 7/8	...
37 5/8	26	IntHarv	2.10	6.2	5	1612	34 1/2	32 1/8	34	+1 1/4
44	35 1/4	IntMin	2.60	6.0	7	212	43 1/2	43	43 1/8	...
25 1/4	18 1/8	IntMulti	1	4.0	9	335	25 1/4	24 3/4	25 1/4	+ 1/2
58	35 1/8	IntPaper	2	4.6	8	589	44 3/4	43 7/8	43 7/8	− 3/8

The above stocks and prices are excerpted from a page in the *Wall Street Journal.* Below you will find definitions of the abbreviations used and explanations of the columns.

A. High: This is the highest price paid for the stock to date this year.
B. Low: This is the lowest price paid for the stock to date this year.
C. Stocks: This is the name of the company, usually abbreviated.
D. Div.: This is the most recent annual dividend for each share.
E. Yld%: The percentage of market price yielded by the dividend.
F. P-E Ratio: This is the ratio of the current selling price to the earnings per share.
G. Sales in 100s: This is the number of round lots (100 shares each) sold that day. The odd lots, which are less than 100 shares each, are not listed.
H. High: This is the highest price paid for the stock the day it is listed.
I. Low: This is the lowest price paid for the stock the day it is listed.
J. Close: This is the price of the stock at the end of the trading day.
K. Net Change: This is the difference between the closing price of the stock the day it is listed and the closing price of the stock at the end of the previous trading day.

EXHIBIT 17.9 Sample New York Bond Exchange Quotations

A	B	C	D	E	F	G	H
Bonds		**Cur Yld**	**Vol**	**High**	**Low**	**Close**	**Net Chg**
WillR		cv	5	70	70	70	$-1\frac{3}{8}$
Wms		9.7	25	$106\frac{1}{8}$	$105\frac{5}{8}$	$105\frac{5}{8}$	$-\frac{1}{2}$
WiscTl		8.1	3	$98\frac{3}{4}$	$98\frac{5}{8}$	$98\frac{3}{4}$	$+2\frac{1}{4}$
Witco		cv	1	73	73	73	-1
Womt		cv	6	$84\frac{3}{4}$	$84\frac{5}{8}$	$84\frac{5}{8}$	$-\frac{1}{8}$
Woolw		8.9	10	$101\frac{1}{8}$	$101\frac{1}{8}$	$101\frac{1}{8}$	...
WldAwy		10.	55	98	98	98	$+\frac{1}{8}$
Wyly		cv	50	$24\frac{3}{4}$	$24\frac{3}{8}$	$24\frac{1}{2}$	...
Xerox		cv	33	$92\frac{1}{2}$	92	92	$-\frac{1}{2}$

A. Name of the company.
B. Coupon or nominal interest rate of the bond and its due or maturity date.
C. Current yield, or the coupon rate divided by the current selling price, where "cv" appears. (This indicates that the bond is convertible into the company's stock. The price of the conversion is not given, however. Rather, a *Standard and Poor's* or a *Moody's Bond Book* or the financial statement of the corporation will give such information.)
D. Volume of sales in lots of 100.
E. Highest selling price of the bond that trading day. (Bonds are quoted in $\frac{1}{8}$ points. A bond selling at $106\frac{1}{8}$ has a price of $1061.25.)
F. Lowest price paid for that bond that trading day.
G. Closing price.
H. Net change from the previous trading day's closing price.

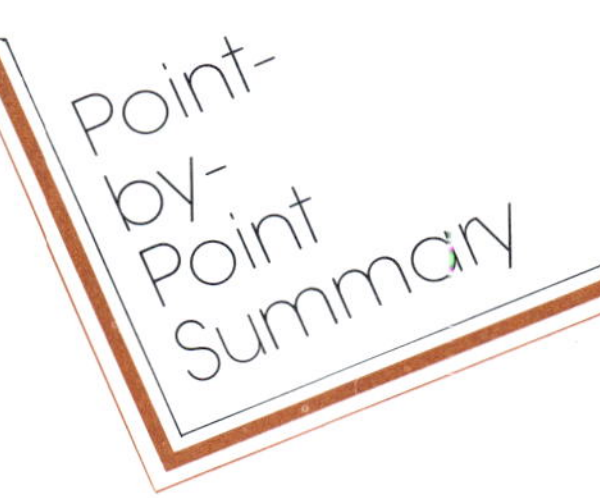

- Stocks may be common or preferred; the latter are a type of bond.
- When firms don't pay out all of their after-tax profits to stockholders, they keep what are called retained earnings. Such retained earnings presumably are used to increase the value of the corporation. Hence, the market price of that corporation's stock should rise.
- Bonds are issued by the U.S. government, state and municipal governments, and private corporations. A bond issued by the U.S. Treasury is considered the least risky of all securities since it is backed by the taxing power of the U.S. government. Bonds issued by state and municipal governments are more risky.
- There are many types of corporate bonds, including debentures, mortgage, collateral trusts, equipment trusts, convertible, and callable.
- Of the numerous organized exchanges for stocks and bonds, the most well-known are the New York and American Stock and Bond exchanges.

- It is difficult, if not impossible, to make a killing quickly in the stock or bond market, unless one has inside information. This is because securities markets are highly competitive.
- There are two types of brokerage accounts—the cash account and the margin account. With both of them, investors receive a monthly statement from their brokerage house.
- The two types of orders are market and limit. The latter supposedly ensures investors of a gain, or at least not too much of a loss.
- In short selling, shares of stocks are sold before they are owned. Short sellers trust that the price will fall before they have to buy the stocks to satisfy their sale.
- Options can be either calls or puts. The former is the right to buy at a predetermined price, and the latter is the right to sell at a predetermined price.
- Mutual funds can be closed-end or open-end. The latter, which are more popular, sell their own new shares to investors and stand ready to buy back their old shares. They are not listed on any exchanges.

1. Some observers claim that a preferred stock is just like a bond. Are they right? Why or why not?
2. What does it mean to say that common stock shareholders get "the residual"?
3. Would it bother you to own a share of stock that had no par value? Would that mean that it was worthless?
4. What is the difference between a corporate bond and a government bond? Which one would you prefer to hold?
5. List some of the ways it is possible to make a higher-than-normal rate of return by investing in the stock market. How long is your list?
6. What does the notion of a random walk have to do with investing in the stock market?
7. Do you think it is truly possible to use a limit order to ensure making money in the stock market? Do you think it is possible to use a stop-loss order to ensure yourself of not losing money in the stock market?
8. Go the the *Wall Street Journal.* Find some of the stocks listed in Exhibit 17.8. Compare the prices today with the old prices. What has happened to dividends and yields?
9. Compare the bond quotations in Exhibit 17.9 with the corresponding quotations in the *Wall Street Journal.*

APPLICATION

Merrill Lynch is almost synonymous with the stock market. At the beginning of the 1980s, this corporation had revenues well in excess of $2 billion, with total assets of around $11 billion. A company with 55,000 shareholders and 27,000 employees, it is a formidable entity in the investment community. But it wasn't always that way.

WAY BACK WHEN

Before incorporation, the company was known as Merrill Lynch, Pierce, Fenner & Smith, a partnership. At least forty-nine firms are known to have merged into what became Merrill Lynch. Another eighteen firms contributed parts of themselves to the company, and historians in the company believe that there were hundreds of other firms whose identities, as well as records, might be in some forgotten warehouse. One of the earliest known predecessor firms was W. W. Gwathmey & Company, founded in Richmond, Virginia, in 1820. That company opened for business as "Ship Chandlers and General Commission Merchants." Shortly after the Civil War, the son of the original Mr. Gwathmey moved to New York and continued the business there, mostly selling cotton. The Gwathmeys were commission brokers in various fields, except the securities business, until they merged with a New York Stock Exchange firm, A. A. Houseman & Company.

Merrill Lynch & Company, Inc.

Merrill Lynch Pierce Fenner & Smith Inc.

In 1914, a twenty-nine-year-old bond seller, Charles E. Merrill, started his own brokerage company. Another bond seller, Edmund C. Lynch, became his partner. Their firm sold blocks of existing stock at retail and underwrote new capital ventures. A year later, Winthrop H. Smith joined the company as a runner and office boy. In 1929, he was admitted as a partner. Merrill Lynch was one of the few brokerage firms that started telling its customers a year before the October 1929 market crash to get out of stocks. In 1930, Merrill Lynch joined forces with E. A. Pierce & Company, which traced its lineage to W. W. Gwathmey & Company.

Over the years, another name, Fenner, was added. And then someone named Cassatt, whose name disappeared for a while, and then someone named Beane, whose name also disappeared. Finally, in 1971, the partnership of Merrill Lynch, Pierce, Fenner & Smith became a publicly owned corporation. In 1973, it changed its name to Merrill Lynch & Company, Inc., becoming the first securities firm to announce a holding company structure.

STRUCTURE OF THE COMPANY

Merrill Lynch has not remained simply a stock brokerage firm. It now consists of a number of divisions.

Merrill Lynch, Pierce, Fenner & Smith

Keeping the old name of the partnership, this division is the largest securities firm in the United States. It offers services as broker in securities options, commodity futures contracts, and mutual funds. It is also an investment banker and dealer in corporate and municipal securities, and through associated agencies, it sells life insurance and annuity products.

This division has business in Canada through a wholly owned subsidiary, Merrill Lynch, Royal Securities, which also deals in Canadian government securities. MLPF&S makes a market in amost

700 common stocks traded in over-the-counter markets. Finally, MLPF&S is active in mergers and acquisitions.

Merrill Lynch Government Securities, Inc.

This division is a primary dealer in obligations issued by the U.S. government and federal agencies. It also deals in money-market securities, such as certificates of deposit and commercial paper.

Merrill Lynch, Hubbard

This division is an outgrowth of the 1968 acquisition of Hubbard, Westervelt & Mottelay. It is engaged in real estate financing, banking in government-backed mortgages, and real estate asset management.

Merrill Lynch Realty Management

This division acts as a broker in the sale and lease of real property and provides real estate asset management and services.

Other Divisions

Merrill Lynch Leasing, Merrill Lynch Relocation Management, Merrill Lynch Realty Associates, Merrill Lynch Wood Markets, Merrill Lynch Asset Management, and Family Life Insurance are all additional divisions of this financial conglomerate. Finally, Merrill Lynch has a subsidiary, Merrill Lynch Economics, that provides economic consulting services to corporate clients.

CAREER OPPORTUNITIES

An organization of this size is bound to have a tremendous number of professional opportunities for the business-trained student. Indeed, Merrill Lynch's recruiting literature lists the following:

- Finance, accounting, and planning
- Accounting
- Financial and credit analysis
- Budgets and planning
- Treasury functions
- Internal auditors
- Investment banking and financing
- Trading
- Law and compliance
- Securities research
- Operations

As an example, we will describe an entry-level position as account executive, servicing securities accounts. Merrill Lynch has a training school, which was started in 1945. Since then, over 15,000 account executives have been graduated. The company spends many thousands of dollars to train each account executive.

The first twelve weeks of training are spent in the branch office

Merrill Lynch—A Breed Apart

for which one has been hired. A course of program instruction introduces the new employee to the entire business, and he or she gets on-the-job experience working with the office manager and other account executives. Trainees are periodically tested to make sure they are progressing satisfactorily.

Starting in the thirteenth week, trainees spend five weeks at the company's headquarters in New York. The first week is spent in intensive review for the general securities examination that one must pass in order to become a registered representative. The following four weeks are spent learning how to prospect for clients and sharpening selling skills (this is, after all, a selling job). Trainees work in small groups, using role playing and other learning techniques. At the end of the five weeks, trainees return to the office where they started.

Some people are more interested in selling commodities or commodity futures than securities. They are hired as commodity account executives. The training is different but runs along the same lines. Trainees have to study for a national commodity futures exam, which must be passed to become registered as a commodity account executive. They spend a month in New York attending classes and finally return to a branch office.

The job picture at Merrill Lynch for the graduate with an A.A. or an A.S. degree is encouraging. Although a four-year college degree is preferred, there are numerous account executives working today who do not have a bachelor's degree. A lot, of course, depends on how tight the job market is at the time you choose to seek a career as an account executive. If the stock market is booming with a large volume of sales, many companies such as Merrill Lynch will gladly accept graduates of community colleges, provided they have sufficient training and high enough grades. Some experience in the real world in business is, of course, always preferred.

FOR DISCUSSION

1. A number of years ago, the commissions charges for the buying and selling of stocks on the national stock exchanges were fixed by the Securities and Exchange Commission. Many consumers argued that these rates should be competitive to reduce the cost to the consumer of buying and selling shares of stock. The majority of stock brokerage firms opposed competitive rates. Merrill Lynch, however, was extremely aggressive in arguing in favor of competitive negotiated rates. Why do you think Merrill Lynch, among all of the brokerage firms, was so much in favor of competitive brokerage commissions?
2. For a long time, Merrill Lynch was a partnership. It became a corporation after the law changed to allow the incorporation of brokerage firms. What do you think the advantages were to Merrill Lynch to its incorporation?

OBJECTIVES

- ☐ To explain the meaning and nature of risk
- ☐ To describe how risk affects the operation of a business
- ☐ To show how risk can be managed in the business environment
- ☐ To explain the importance of insurance to business managers and to individuals
- ☐ To list and describe the essential elements of all insurance policies
- ☐ To list and describe the different types of insurance policies available
- ☐ To describe how the insurance industry is organized and how insurance is marketed

OUTLINE

ARTICLE *Fire for Hire*

RISK AND THE BUSINESS ENVIRONMENT
Risk Management
Types of Unexpected Loss
Consequences of Unexpected Loss
Risk, Probability, and Expected Loss

INSURANCE FUNDAMENTALS
The Law of Large Numbers
Elements of Property Insurance

INSURANCE COMPANIES
Stock Companies
Mutual Companies

TYPES OF INSURANCE
Property and Casualty Insurance
Life Insurance

INSURANCE MARKETING

APPLICATION *Xerox Corporation*

KEY TERMS

ACTUARY
CASUALTY INSURANCE
COINSURANCE
CREDIT INSURANCE
DEDUCTIBLE
EXPECTED LOSS
FIDELITY BOND
FIRE INSURANCE
INSURABLE INTEREST
LAW OF LARGE NUMBERS
LIABILITY INSURANCE
LIFE INSURANCE
MARINE INSURANCE
MUTUAL COMPANY
OPPORTUNITY COST
PREMIUM
PROBABILITY
RISK MANAGEMENT
SELF-INSURANCE
STOCK COMPANY
SURETY BOND
TERM INSURANCE
TITLE INSURANCE
WHOLE LIFE INSURANCE
WORKER'S COMPENSATION

RISK AND INSURANCE

Fire for Hire

RICHARD GREENE
Forbes, September 3, 1979

Morrie Klein was a smooth-talking Pittsburgh businessman with a ready supply of expensive suits and cars and even a private airplane. Klein differed from thousands of other prosperous entrepreneurs in only one respect. His business was arson. In just 15 felonious years, according to the Federal Strike Force Against Organized Crime, Klein sucked an astonishing sum, some $45 million, from insurance companies for himself and his clients.

Klein had a simple formula: Approach desperate businessmen ("Business Opportunities" ads in the *Wall Street Journal* were a productive source of leads) with the possibility of ready cash to turn their firms around. After a few months, he would bring them the sad news: There was no financing available. But there was an alternative—arson.

Klein could provide a package deal, all the way from arranging for a dishonest insurance adjuster to providing a professional arsonist (a "torch") to burn the place down. His fee varied widely but was often 20% of the insurance payment, plus kickbacks from his referrals.

Klein would probably still be at it, were it not for three years of arduous lead-following by attorney Carl LoPresti of the Federal Strike Force and others. Klein finally turned state's evidence and provided LoPresti with material to catch up with 32 of his associates. Klein now resides in Terminal Island federal prison.

Although Morrie Klein was a master at his chosen trade, he was not unique. His colleagues range from juvenile delinquents who will throw a match into a gasoline can for $100 to the expert, professional torch who charges thousands of dollars to reduce a building to ashes.

Accurate, comprehensive statistics are scarce, but experts sifting estimates are convinced that arson-for-profit has reached epidemic proportions in the U.S.

Back in 1968, for example, it was estimated that insurance companies paid off under $500 million in arson-related fires. By last year that had more than tripled. According to experts cited in Senate hearings on the arson problem, the incidence of the crime is growing at about 25% a year. The number of arson-related fires last year was put at over 250,000—with more than 1,000 lives lost.

Of course, many deliberately set fires are the result of passion (a jealous boyfriend getting even) or of madness (demented thrill seeking). And there is a long history of businessmen, desperate for ready cash, turning to an eager torch instead of a reluctant bank. Back in 1974, with the U.S. in its deepest recession in 40 years, the incidence of arson rose sharply. But, alarmingly, the linkage between hard times and arson appears to have broken down.. . . Although recessions increase the incidence of arson, it is a lucrative, growing crime in good times and bad. After the 1974 recession, the growth of arson did not stop. Today, according to John Barracato . . ., retired deputy chief fire marshal of New York City and now in charge of Aetna Life & Casualty's major antiarson program, upwards of 40% of all arson is profit motivated.

No authority sees much hope for a substantial reduction in arson-for-profit anytime soon. On the contrary, the present economic slowdown can only fuel an increase. John Barracato will even name a time for a new surge."Arsons will be increasing at an alarming rate by about the 15th of September," he says. "Certain seasonal businesses will realize in late August that they can't make it. So a portion of them will burn their buildings for the insurance money."

Many arson experts, including Clifford Karchmer of the Battelle Institute in Seattle, agree that certain businesses are particularly vulnerable: restaurants, hotels, bars, beauty parlors and women's wear factories, to name a few. A business that survives on discretionary income, especially one in a resort area, is more likely to burn than others.

Automobile arson also seems likely to grow. Explains Major John Regan of the Massachusetts State Police Arson Strike Force: "With the price of gas going up, people know they have to get into a small car. They go to the car dealer and find that the car they bought last year for $9,000 is worth much less now. So, we're going to see a lot of big expensive cars going up in smoke."

But automobile arson and even the guy who lights up his own little restaurant are trivial compared to the complex, highly orchestrated scams that make up the ghastliest cases of arson-for-profit.

Slum apartment houses, for example, lend themselves to easy scams. You buy a building for, say, $10,000. Then you sell the building back and forth among a few friends, inflating the price each time. No money need actually change hands. You then insure it for the final sale price, burn it down and collect.

Such amoral enterprise puts insurance companies in a quandary. If they insure no more than the market value, these schemes work well for the arsonists. If they insure replacement value, they still wind up paying unrealistic amounts for old, expensive to rebuild, structures.

A rare but especially ugly arson-for-profit ploy is one used by bank loan officers desperate to keep their records clean. Ernest Garneau, project director of the Urban Educational Systems in Boston, a research concern devoted to the study of arson, explains how it works: Imagine that a loan officer has given out a $100,000 mortgage on an apartment house that goes under. Rather than take over the building or take a big loss, the loan officer might instead turn to a so-called speculative real estate operator and give him the building and the mortgage for almost no money down. In addition, the bank might throw in another $10,000 loan to fix up the place.

Too often to explain by coincidence alone, such buildings have a way of burning down only months later. The bank gets its money from the insurance company and the building's buyer gets some, if not all, of the improvement-loan money. After all, receipts can be faked, and it's nearly impossible to check on improvements in a pile of ashes. Says Garneau, "Even if they prove arson, they also have to prove that the bank was implicated or they have to pay off anyway. It hardly pays even to investigate."

The loan officer gets no money out of the deal, but he protects his record.

The victim of these planned fires, obviously, is everyone else directly or indirectly paying a fire insurance premium—in effect, all of us. Less obvious, but affecting all of us, too, is fire's impact on big cities' tax bases. In addition to all its other woes, according to the New York City Fire Marshal's Office, some $25 million in taxable real estate in the Big Apple was wiped out by fire in 1978.

It has taken a long time for arson to be viewed as something other than a victimless crime in which only the insurance company is hurt. "I know of cases where people wink at each other when they talk about so-and-so's fire," says John Connell, owner of the largest arson investigation company in the country, which bears his name. "It is the only felony people wink at. Nobody winks at rape or robbery." But that incredible nonchalance seems to be giving way, forcing insurance companies to do more than they have done. They needed some prodding. After all, an insurance company can simply jack up rates to cover increased payouts. And the higher the premiums, the more assets the companies have to invest.

Some companies—Aetna Life & Casualty notable among them with a basic investment of over $5 million this year alone—have been pouring money into antiarson programs. They are not just sponsoring fire prevention weeks. Now, more of them are trying cases in court that previously would have been paid off.

Urban areas—like New Haven, Seattle and Boston—are also investing time and money in finding solutions. New Haven, for example, has set up a special strike force composed of both policemen and firefighters to examine every suspicious fire and identify arson when they can.

Arson is widely assumed to be nearly impossible to prove. You must see the arsonist holding a match, the myth goes, to convict him. Present conviction rates support that. Less than 1% of all suspected cases of arson result in a conviction. The fact is, arson is not that tough to spot—by trained eyes. Such factors as point of origin and the type of accelerant used can tell much about a fire. Barracato: "The fire talks to you if you just know how to listen. You can describe a fire to me over the phone: 'I had a fire in the back room.' Back room tells me burglar, right away. 'All the file drawers were open.' It doesn't tell me burglar, it tells me the guy is under investigation and is trying to destroy his records . . ."

The problem is, there aren't enough skilled men. Training them is expensive, prosecuting on their findings more so. Despite serious efforts by insurance companies and government, whose programs tend to be long term, there is little reason to hope the fire-for-hire business is headed for a recession soon.

This article demonstrates how the legitimate function of insurance can be violated by unscrupulous persons. This chapter, on the other hand, points out the importance of the concepts of risk and insurance in modern life.

Many centuries ago, Chinese merchants would make periodic journeys into the heartland of China in order to secure goods to be sold on the coast. On the return trip, dangerous rapids in the Yangtze River would occasionally capsize one of the cargo vessels, causing financial ruin for the owner. Eventually, the merchants learned to reduce this risk by meeting above the rapids and redistributing the cargo so that each ship carried a portion of each merchant's merchandise. Thus if any one ship in the fleet capsized, no one merchant would suffer a complete loss.

Today's business environment is, of course, far removed from that of the ancient Chinese merchants. The hazards of today are quite different, and the techniques used to surmount these hazards are much more sophisticated. Yet in many ways, business is as risky a proposition now as it was in days of old. This chapter discusses business risks and ways to manage them in the contemporary business climate.

Risk and the Business Environment

Risk—the chance of incurring a loss—is an unavoidable element in any business enterprise. A fire or flood may damage or destroy the physical assets of the firm. Humans are a source of loss through theft, fraud, and vandalism. A firm also faces the threat of loss through the normal course of business. Inventory may have to be sold at less than cost, advertising dollars may be wasted or misused, investments may prove to be worthless. Yet, in spite of all these threatening forces, new businesses continue to form and old businesses continue to operate. It is the successful control and management of risk that allows businesses to survive and prosper.

Normal business risks are those inherent in day-to-day operations. Businesses buy inventory, acquire such assets as property, buildings, and equipment, and incur such costs as wages and salaries in hopes of turning a profit. Yet the risk of loss from these transactions is always present. However, businesspeople trust that gains or profits will exceed losses, at least in the long run. If losses exceed gains, the business will fail. Thus management of normal business risk is essential in order to ensure the existence of a firm.

RISK MANAGEMENT

Sound general management is the key to controlling normal business risk. **Risk management,** however, is specifically concerned with casualties—situations in which potential loss is coupled with no chance of gain. A businessperson buys inventory with the hope of selling the inventory at a profit before it becomes obsolete. Obsolescence is a gradual process and constitutes a normal business risk. Risk management, however, would seek to protect the firm from the sudden loss of the inventory, as in the event of fire or theft.

In general, risk management deals with risk in four different ways:

- Avoid the risk
- Reduce the risk

- Assume the risk
- Shift the risk to another party

These methods are not mutually exclusive and, in fact, are often used in combination.

Risk *avoidance* is seemingly the easiest of the policies to implement. A firm simply avoids the potential loss-producing situation. The risk of loss from flood, for instance, may be avoided by locating the business on high ground. Risk avoidance can lead to other complications, however. Locating a business away from a floodplain may lead to transportation problems, for instance, or to a loss of business due to inconveniences for potential customers.

Although risks cannot usually be avoided totally, they can be *reduced* or mitigated. For instance, fire-proof buildings can be constructed, sprinkler and/or fire alarm systems can be installed, and "no smoking" rules can be enforced. The possibility of loss is still present, but this possibility has been reduced. However, preventive measures have a cost associated with them. Good risk management sees to it that the cost of preventive measures is outweighed by the benefits of reduced potential for loss.

A firm is said to *assume* a risk when management decides to absorb internally any potential losses. For instance, a firm may tolerate a certain amount of shoplifting as part of normal business risk. In other cases, a firm may set aside a reserve of funds in order to handle losses, a practice known as **self-insurance.** A firm with a large fleet of vehicles may set aside funds to replace vehicles lost through accidents. A major problem with self-insurance, however, is that it cannot usually cover a large loss. Thus self-assumption of risk may be a suitable technique only when potential losses are small in relation to the size of the firm.

The final method in the risk-management arsenal is *shifting* the risk. Most commonly this involves the use of insurance. The insuring company agrees to bear a specified risk in return for a fee. The business benefits from this arrangement in that a known and relatively small loss, the cost of the insurance policy, is substituted for an unknown and potentially large loss. But insurance is not the only means of shifting risk. For example, a business usually has the option of buying or leasing equipment and buildings. Although the purchase price of such assets is generally less than the total lease price, the leasing agent often bears most of the risk for damage to or loss of the leased property. Transferring the possibility of loss to others for a fee is one of the most important methods of risk management.

TYPES OF UNEXPECTED LOSS

Losses subject to risk management fall into two general categories. The first category is physical damage—economic loss to the firm's physical assets. Property may be destroyed or damaged by fire, storms, theft, vandalism, and so on. The loss to the firm from such events is twofold. First, there is the actual loss of the asset. Second, there is usually a loss associated with the business interruption. For instance, a business may be obligated to continue paying employee salaries even though the workplace no longer exists. Another associated business loss is the **opportunity cost** of the damage—profits that can no longer be earned because the income-producing asset has been lost.

Legal liability may be another source of unexpected loss. If a business or an agent of the business, such as an employee, performs an "unreasonable" act that causes harm to another business or individual, the business becomes liable for the second party's loss. For example, a business that knowingly or unknowingly sells an unsafe product may then be responsible for any bodily harm suffered by users of that product. Or an employee may operate a vehicle in a reckless manner while performing duties for the firm. Damages caused by that employee would be the responsibility of the firm. Unfortunately, it is not usually easy to determine what constitutes "unreasonable" behavior. In many cases, legal action is necessary to resolve the issue.

CONSEQUENCES OF UNEXPECTED LOSS

The least harmful consequence of improper risk management is *financial embarrassment.* In other words, the firm becomes unable to pay its debts on time because of a shortage of cash. As a consequence, trade credit may become restricted, and the firm may have a difficult time securing the inventory or other assets it needs to continue operations. Furthermore, the firm may be forced to pay high rates of interest in order to obtain the loans it needs to pay its debts.

A more serious situation is *partial insolvency.* In this case, creditors may institute legal action to force payment on debts. A court may force the firm to sell its assets to meet the creditors' demands. Unfortunately, forced sales often mean that the assets have to be sold for a loss. In such circumstances, the future earning ability of the firm is seriously impaired, and prospects for additional financing would be bleak.

Business failure is the ultimate consequence of improper risk management. A business has failed when the business cannot satisfy creditors' demands by any means. Usually a business in this position is totally insolvent. That is, total liabilities, or creditors' demands, exceed the firm's total assets. The firm is bankrupt and generally cannot continue to operate.

The causes of business failure, whether complete or partial, are many. However, improper risk management is certainly a prime contributor to any business downfall. Perhaps large amounts of inventory were allowed to become obsolete. Perhaps the business extended credit to other parties who suffered business failure. Although, these are examples of the mismanagement of ordinary business risks, they still have the effect of making the business illiquid. Of course, if the firm suffers large-scale physical damage or is hit with a large lawsuit stemming from a legal liability, liquidity and solvency will also be impaired. Cash will be needed to restore the damaged asset or to satisfy the legal suit, and if proper provision has not been made to secure this cash, the firm will be unable to cover both the unexpected loss and normal business obligations.

RISK, PROBABILITY, AND EXPECTED LOSS

Other important factors in risk management are the probability of a certain loss occurring and the size of the loss. **Probability** is a statistical concept; it means the odds or chances of some specified event occurring. If a normal coin is flipped into the air, the probability of it landing heads up is 0.5. In other words, half of the tosses should result in heads. Similarly, the probability that a washer in a shipment of washers will be defective might be 0.01. Therefore, in a shipment of 10,000 washers, 100 will probably be defective.

It is not sufficient to know the probability of an undesired event occurring; business managers must know what the cost will be if the event occurs. Multiplying the probability of the event occurring times the cost yields the **expected loss.** Assume that any shipment of 10,000 washers has 100 defective washers, a probability of 0.01. Say that the cost of those washers is only 1 cent apiece or $100 for the whole load. Thus the expected loss involved in a shipment of 10,000 washers is only $1. Clearly, it would not pay to try to ship 10,000 perfect washers all the time. The company will accept a small expected loss because the cost of trying to reduce that expected loss would not be worth the effort.

A drug manufacturer, however, would probably not be able to tolerate a 0.01 defective rate, especially if the defective drug could lead to the injury or death of the drug user. The possible loss from a lawsuit in this case is much more severe than the possible loss in the washer case. Thus the same probability of a defective unit presents a much riskier situation for the drug manufacturer.

Risk management, then, involves identifying the sources of risk, identifying the consequences of risk, and quantifying the risk in terms of the cost of losses and the probabilities of losses occurring. Finally, the risk manager must decide on a course of action to handle the risk. Each possible action—avoidance, reduction, assumption, and shifting—carries its own benefits and its own costs. Unfortunately, the costs, benefits, and probability figures needed to evaluate alternatives are not always readily available. Furthermore, one's subjective view of a certain risk situation may differ greatly from the objective or actual risk involved. For example, the probabilities of certain types of airplanes crashing are well documented; in fact, plane travel is one of the safest forms of transportation. Yet some people refuse to fly because the subjective risk, or the risk as they perceive it, is much greater than the actual probability of an accident. A successful risk manager is one who can be quite objective in evaluating risk situations.

Insurance Fundamentals

To avoid the risk of large unexpected losses, businesses insure. Voluntary insurance allows people and businesses to share losses by spreading them over a group. The insurer, usually an insurance company, agrees to bear the specific risk in exchange for a periodic payment called a **premium.** Out of the fees—the premiums—compensation is paid to those who suffer losses. This pooling of risk does not necessarily reduce the total losses. Rather, it spreads them over the insurees. Basically, then, insurance converts each party's risk of a possible large loss into the certainty of a small loss—the payment of the premium.

THE LAW OF LARGE NUMBERS

The probability of a certain event occurring and the expected losses can usually be determined with a great deal of certainty. For example, in a given area it may be known that an average 0.02 percent of the homes will be destroyed by fire every year. Therefore, in a community of 5,000 homes, one home (on the average) will be destroyed by fire every year. However, the odds are different for the individual homeowner—either 0 percent or 100 percent that his or her home will burn. In fact, for 4,999 homeowners the odds of a fire are 0 percent; one homeowner will have odds of 100 percent. The problem is that nobody knows ahead of time who falls into the group of 4,999 and who falls into the group of 1 (assuming the fires are not intentionally set). Since the loss of one's home is extremely costly, most of the people in the community will obtain fire insurance to protect themselves.

Although the risk of losing a home by fire is either 0 or 100 percent for homeowners, it remains at a fairly constant 0.02 percent for the insuring agent or agents. The **law of large numbers** accounts for this phenomenon. In fact, as the area in question is increased to include more houses and as the time frame is increased to include more years, the insurance company's probability of loss becomes more and more stable. The law of large numbers implies that in the long run the probability of an event occurring becomes the expected probability of the event. The more homes that become insured, the more likely the insurance company will actually experience the same number of fire claims as the expected average. Of course, if some fires are being set intentionally, the probabilities are reversed: The individual homeowner would know for sure when the loss would occur, but the insurance company's probability factor would no longer be meaningful. This is why insurance companies will not reimburse the policyholders when an intentional loss can be proven.

The law of large numbers, or the law of averages as it is sometimes called, is used to determine the rates charged by insurance companies. In our example, the average value of the homes in the coverage area would be determined. From this figure, the expected annual loss from fire could be computed and, from that, the insurance rates. If, for instance, the average value of the homes in the coverage area was $50,000 and the probability of destruction by fire was 0.02 percent, the expected annual fire loss would be $10 per home per year (0.0002 × $50,000).

The actual premium paid by the homeowner would be higher than this amount—for several reasons. First, fire insurance not only covers complete destruction of a home but also partial damage. Thus the annual fire loss in the area would be greater than $50,000. Second, the insurance company must add its operating expenses and its desired profit margin to the rate base. Finally, all the homes in the area may not purchase fire insurance, and this may affect the rates. In short, rate setting is a complicated process, although expected losses play the major part in rate determination.

ELEMENTS OF PROPERTY INSURANCE

There are many different kinds of insurance, as you will discover later in the chapter. However, insurance against damage to or loss of property is perhaps the most important general type available to businesses with a large investment in assets. Therefore, our discussion of the typical elements in an insurance policy focuses on property insurance.

Deductible Clauses

As you now know, individuals and businesses purchase insurance policies in order to substitute a relatively small known cost for a relatively large and unknown loss. An insurance company, for its part, must set its rates to cover its expected losses as well as its operating expenses and profit. A problem for insurance companies, however, is the disproportionately high cost of handling small claims. It may cost the insurer as much to service a $200 insurance claim as a $2,000 insurance claim. Therefore, a typical insurance policy contains a **deductible** clause, which allows the insurance company to deduct a certain amount from the final payment on a claim. If an insurance policy contains a $200 deductible, the insurer will pay $1,800 on a $2,000 claim. Insurees usually have the resources to handle such small losses.

The advantage of deductibles for the insurance company is that it can avoid the disproportionately high cost of paying small claims. The advantage of deductibles for the insured party is that insurance rates can be lowered. In essence, the insured party is agreeing to use the coverage only for large, serious losses.

Insurable Interest

Businesspeople can basically insure anything they own that has a determinable value, except land. In other words, most insurance companies will insure any property that if damaged, lost, or stolen will cause financial loss for the insured party. Thus you cannot insure your best friend's car—even if you drive it occasionally—because you have no monetary interest in the property.

If you could insure other people's property, you would have an incentive to let their property be damaged or destroyed, because you would always be paid. Or imagine that you own a building and have full-coverage insurance on it. You may sell the building but forget to cancel your insurance policy. If the building is detroyed by fire, the insurance company will not pay you, because you no longer have **insurable interest** in the property. You suffer no economic loss from the building's destruction.

One can have an insurable interest in individuals as well as property. Clearly, you have an insurable interest in your own life, and marriage and blood relationships also can create an insurable interest. From a business point of view, perhaps the most important insurable interest involves co-called *key people.* Men and women in management positions are very valuable to a business, particularly if they have a tremendous amount of knowledge that no one else in the business has. The death or incapacitation of a key individual can place a great financial burden on the firm. Thus insurance companies issue policies on highly paid executives. Similar policies are available for partners in a partnership. And, finally, businesses can obtain life insurance policies on people who owe the business a lot of money. The size of the insurance policy, however, is limited to the extent of the debt.

Coinsurance Clauses

Many property insurance contracts require that the policyholder buy insurance equal in amount to a certain percentage of the replacement value of the property. Policyholders who comply with this requirement will be reimbursed for all losses, dollar for dollar, up to the policy limit. But if they do not carry a minimum amount of insurance, they do not receive full payment for losses. Such a **coinsurance** clause is aimed at discouraging people from underinsuring their property in the hope of collecting full market value if the property is destroyed. (Of course, too much insurance can be as costly as too little.) Usually, real property—buildings, in particular—must be insured for 80 percent of their replacement value in order to collect full replacement costs rather than the depreciated value.

Let's consider a simple example. The ten-year-old roof on your business is damaged in a fire. It costs you $2,500 to replace it. If you have at least 80-percent coverage on the entire structure, your insurance company must pay you the full amount of the roof damage. If, on the other hand, your business structure is covered for less than 80 percent of replacement value, you will not get the full $2,500. You will be paid only a portion of the loss, as indicated in this equation:

$$\text{Proportion of loss covered} = \frac{\text{Face value of policy}}{80\text{ percent} \times \text{Full market value of property}}$$

Imagine that your business structure has a replacement value of $50,000. Assume, though, that you only have insurance coverage equal to $30,000. To find out what your insurance company would pay on the $2,500 loss of the roof, first find the proportion of loss covered:

$$\text{Proportion of loss covered} = \frac{\$30{,}000}{0.8 \times \$50{,}000} = 0.75$$

Thus for your $2,500 roof loss, you will receive

$$\$2{,}500 \times 0.75 = \$1{,}875$$

If you had had at least $40,000 worth of coverage, you would have recovered the full $2,500.

"Other Insurance" Clauses

Suppose that you have medical insurance on your automobile policy and health insurance offered by your employer. You are injured in a car accident, and your total medical bills amount to $2,000. But you cannot be reimbursed simultaneously by your health insurance policy and your automobile insurance policy. Why? Because most insurance policies have an "other insurance" clause stating that any person with more than one insurance policy on property or health cannot collect more than the total financial loss sustained.

Here's another example. You take out fire insurance on your $50,000 house from two different companies, each policy having a face value of $50,000. But should the house burn down, you won't be paid $100,000. Each insurance company will pay you its share of the loss— in this case, 50 percent.

Insurance Companies

Many different types of companies offer insurance coverage in this country, but the two main types of firms are mutual companies and stock companies. This classification refers to how the ownership of the insurance company is organized. Stock companies represent the most prevalent form of organization, as Exhibit 18.1 indicates.

STOCK COMPANIES

A **stock company** sells insurance for a profit and is therefore operated like any other for-profit venture. Stock companies sell stock, or ownership shares, to the general public. The stockholders vote to elect the board of directors of the firm. The board of directors selects the main corporate officers, who are responsible for the day-to-day operations of the company. Stock companies are regulated by state and federal insurance commissions that determine, within certain limits, the rates the companies can charge, the types of insurance they can sell, and the amount of funds they must maintain in order to satisfy potential claims.

MUTUAL COMPANIES

Mutual companies, unlike stock companies, are organized as nonprofit organizations. The policyholders own mutual companies. Thus purchase of a policy with a mutual company is purchase of a portion of the business.

Like the stock companies, a board of directors, elected by the owners, is responsible for general company policy. The mutuals are regulated by state insurance laws. Profits earned by the mutuals, however, are returned to policyholders through either the payment of dividends or the reduction of premiums. Losses must also be borne by policyholders, and many mutuals have the right to assess policyholders for any business losses incurred—usually because of excessive payouts. (In the stock companies, the stockholders must absorb any business losses.)

Some types of mutuals are set up for a specific class of customers. For example, there are farm mutuals and factory mutuals.

EXHIBIT 18.1 Life Insurance Companies Operating in the United States

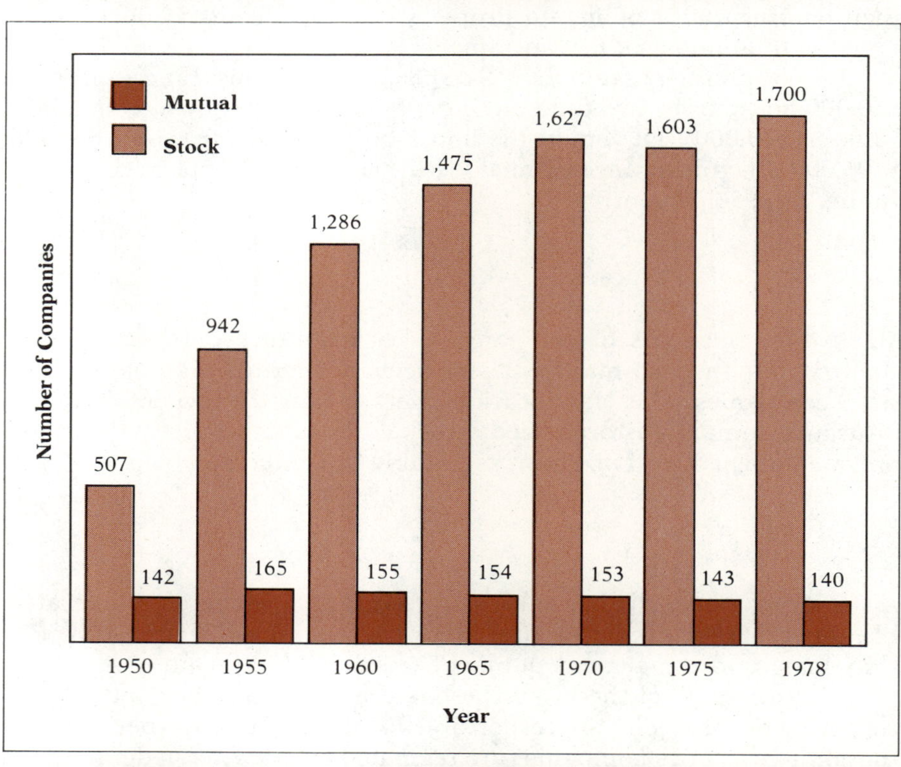

FROM: *1980 Life Insurance Fact Book,* American Council of Life Insurance, 1850 K Street N.W., Washington, DC 20006

Types of Insurance

PROPERTY AND CASUALTY INSURANCE

There are hundreds of types of insurance policies that businesses and individuals can purchase. In the insurance industry, they are divided into two categories: property and casualty insurance, which encompasses a great many subtypes, and life insurance.

As the name implies, property and casualty insurance covers losses of property.

Every 13½ seconds, a fire starts somewhere in the United States. This year, $4 billion in property will be destroyed or severely damaged because of fire. Not surprisingly, **fire insurance** is one type that most businesses carry. A fire insurance policy generally pays off on all damages due to fire, including water and smoke damage. The policy usually covers a specified building and its contents. Premiums for fire insurance depend on such factors as the type of construction used in the building and the quality of fire protection in the area. Most fire insurance policies have coinsurance clauses to discourage property owners from underinsuring their property.

Casualty insurance covers any unexpected accident or occurrence—theft, storm, or fire—resulting in loss to a specified property. Thus casualty insurance is said to provide *multiperil* coverage. Casualty insurance is most frequently purchased for motor vehicles, with provisions to cover certain types of risks. Property damage coverage pays off in the event that a motor vehicle damages another vehicle or property. Public liability insurance covers bodily injury to persons outside the vehicle. Collision insurance covers damages to the vehicle itself. Finally, comprehensive insurance covers such events as loss from theft, fire, or storm damage. People and firms can usually tailor motor vehicle casualty insurance to meet their own needs, but state laws usually mandate a minimum amount of coverage for vehicles licensed in that state.

Motor vehicle insurance usually includes public liability insurance, but public **liability insurance** may be purchased for other situations as well. Firms may want to be covered for bodily injury suffered by the general public while on the firm's premises. Furthermore, the firm may want to be covered for injuries caused by the firm's products. Professionals such as doctors and lawyers, whose "product" is a service, may buy malpractice insurance to protect themselves against claims that they misperformed their professional duties.

A firm may also want to protect itself against claims arising out of job-related injuries to its employees. Insurance coverage of this type, called **worker's compensation,** pays an employee or family for any loss suffered due to injury, disease, or death arising out of work-related conditions. It usually covers medical expenses and, to some extent, lost wages. Premiums for coverage depend on how hazardous the work is. A company engaged in mining, for example, would pay higher rates than a company whose workers are primarily engaged in performing clerical duties. Worker's compensation coverage is mandatory in most states and is, in fact, generally administered by state governments.

Two more types of insurance policies of interest to many firms are

Highlight Writing Insurance in the Old Drury Ale House

Some historians believe that the first recorded life insurance policy was written in June 1536 in London's Old Drury Ale House. A group of marine underwriters agreed to insure the life of William Gybbons for the grand sum of $2,000 for an $80 premium. Unfortunately for the underwriters, Gybbons died a few days before the policy was to expire. And so it was that life insurance became a sideline for marine underwriters.

In 1692, the Society for the Equitable Assurance of Lives and Survivorship began issuing policies covering people for their lifetimes. Old Equitable, as it became known, exists today.

In North America, the first corporation to insure lives was the Presbyterian Ministers' Fund, started in Philadelphia in 1759. But by 1800, there were still only 160 life insurance policies in force in the United States. After the Civil War, however, the industry began to flourish.

fidelity and surety bonds, both of which insure against failure to perform agreed on duties. **Fidelity bonds** insure against dishonesty by an employee. They would be purchased by a firm to cover an employee who handles large sums of the firm's funds. The firm would be paid in the event of theft or embezzlement by the bonded individual. **Surety bonds** insure against the failure of a firm to meet its contractual agreements. A construction company, for instance, may agree to construct a building. At some stage of construction, however, it may find that it cannot complete the job—due, perhaps, to a lack of funds or a failure to obtain needed materials. The surety bond would cover any claims arising out of the firm's failure to fulfill its contract.

There are many other types of policies to meet specialized needs. **Credit insurance** covers losses arising out of debts owed to the firm. **Title insurance** protects owners of buildings and land against the claims of previous owners. Owners of shipping companies may buy **marine insurance** to protect themselves from the perils of the sea. In short, wherever a business risk exists, there is usually a policy available to cover it.

LIFE INSURANCE

The second general category of insurance is **life insurance,** but it is usually more important to individuals than to firms. Life insurance policies come in a wide variety of forms. **Term insurance,** one of the two major types, covers the insuree for a specified period of time, usually five to fifteen years. Term policies are generally renewable up to the age of sixty-five, although usually at higher rates as time goes by. Payment is made to the beneficiary named in the policy if the insured dies while coverage is in effect. The size of the premium is based primarily on the age of the insured, although his or her health is also a factor. Basically, insurance companies use the law of large numbers to determine how much to charge for their policies. **Actuaries,** or statisticians employed by the insurance industry, construct mortality tables like the one in Exhibit 18.2. The actuaries use such tables to compute expected payments and premium levels needed to meet these payouts.

EXHIBIT 18.2 Sample Mortality Table for United States Total Population in 1980

Age	Deaths Per 1,000	Expectation of Life (Years)	Age	Deaths Per 1,000	Expectation of Life (Years)
0	20.02	70.75	50	7.38	25.93
1	1.25	71.19	51	8.04	25.12
2	.86	70.28	52	8.76	24.32
3	.69	69.34	53	9.57	23.53
4	.57	68.39	54	10.43	22.75
5	.51	67.43	55	11.36	21.99
6	.46	66.46	56	12.36	21.23
7	.43	65.49	57	13.41	20.49
8	.39	64.52	58	14.52	19.76
9	.34	63.54	59	15.70	19.05
10	.31	62.57	60	16.95	18.34
11	.30	61.58	61	18.29	17.65
12	.35	60.60	62	19.74	16.97
13	.46	59.62	63	21.33	16.30
14	.63	58.65	64	23.06	15.65
15	.82	57.69	65	24.95	15.00
16	1.01	56.73	66	26.99	14.38
17	1.17	55.79	67	29.18	13.76
18	1.28	54.86	68	31.52	13.16
19	1.34	53.93	69	34.00	12.57
20	1.40	53.00	70	36.61	12.00
21	1.47	52.07	71	39.43	11.43
22	1.52	51.15	72	42.66	10.88
23	1.53	50.22	73	46.44	10.34
24	1.51	49.30	74	50.75	9.82
25	1.47	48.37	75	55.52	9.32
26	1.43	47.44	76	60.60	8.84
27	1.42	46.51	77	65.96	8.38
28	1.44	45.58	78	71.53	7.93
29	1.49	44.64	79	77.41	7.51
30	1.55	43.71	80	83.94	7.10
31	1.63	42.77	81	91.22	6.70
32	1.72	41.84	82	98.92	6.32
33	1.83	40.92	83	106.95	5.96
34	1.95	39.99	84	115.48	5.62
35	2.09	39.07	85	125.61	5.28
36	2.25	38.15	86	137.48	4.97
37	2.44	37.23	87	149.79	4.68
38	2.66	36.32	88	161.58	4.42
39	2.90	35.42	89	172.92	4.18
40	3.14	34.52	90	185.02	3.94
41	3.41	33.63	91	198.88	3.73
42	3.70	32.74	92	213.63	3.53
43	4.04	31.86	93	228.70	3.35
44	4.43	30.99	94	243.36	3.19
45	4.84	30.12	95	257.45	3.06
46	5.28	29.27	96	269.59	2.95
47	5.74	28.42	97	280.24	2.85
48	6.24	27.58	98	289.77	2.76
49	6.78	26.75	99	298.69	2.69

From: *1980 Life Insurance Fact Book*, American Council of Life Insurance, 1850 K Street, N.W., Washington, DC 20006

Whole life insurance, or straight life insurance, is the second major type of life insurance. It too will pay the face value of the policy if the insured dies while the policy is in effect. However, whole life differs from term life in several important respects. First, the whole life insurance policy is generally in force for a longer period of time, and during this time, premiums remain at a fixed level. Second, if the insured is still alive when the policy expires, the insured receives the face value of the policy at the expiration date. Also, the insured can always borrow the amount paid into the policy, which is called the cash value of the policy. Any borrowings that are not repaid are deducted from the final payment. Finally, whole life premiums are much higher than term insurance premiums for a given face value.

EXHIBIT 18.3 Relative Importance of Term and Whole Life Insurance in the United States

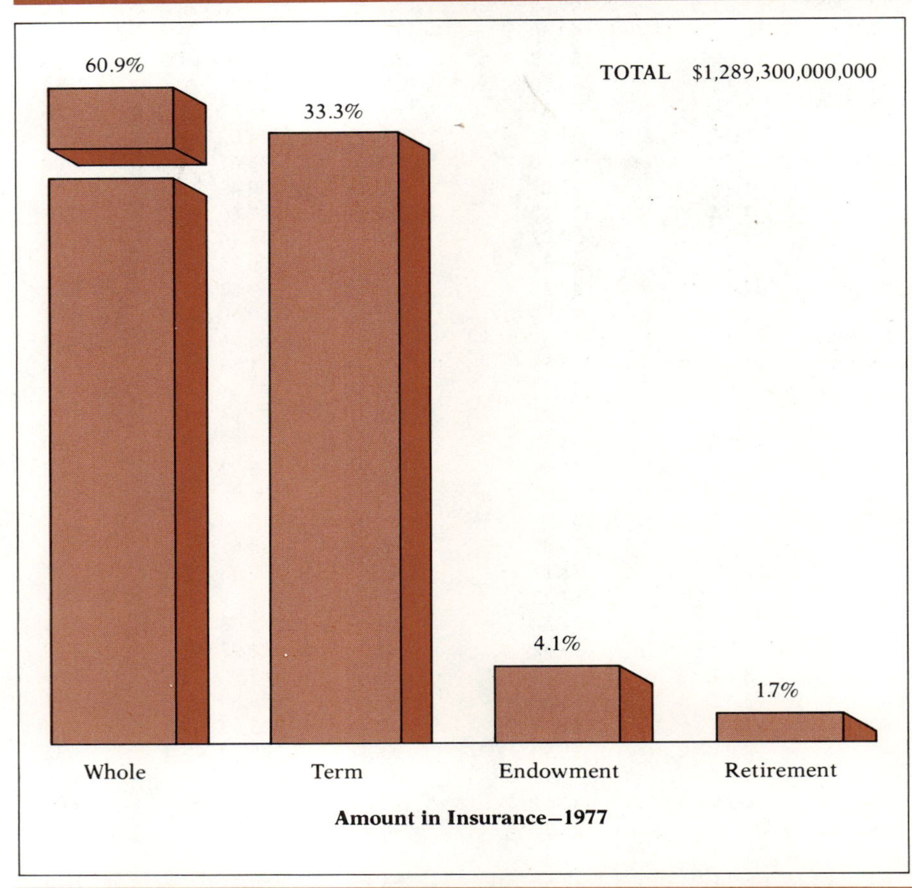

Data from: *1980 Life Insurance Fact Book,* American Council of Life Insurance, 1850 K Street, N.W., Washington, DC 20006

The primary advantage of term insurance is that it allows people to insure their lives for the benefit of their heirs over a relatively short period of time at relatively low rates. Wage earners, for instance, may desire term life coverage until their children are self-sufficient. On the other hand, whole life insurance is, in effect, a form of forced savings that includes an element of term life insurance. The beneficiaries of the insured are covered while the insured is working. On retirement, however, the insured becomes the beneficiary of the face value of the policy. The price for this type of coverage is higher premiums over the life of the policy. Variations in both types of life insurance coverage include the possibilities of a double or triple payoff in the event of an accidental death and, usually, no payoff or only a fractional payoff in the event of a suicide. Exhibit 18.3 shows the relative importance of term and whole life insurance in the United States.

A business can use life insurance in two ways. First, it might buy a policy on the life of a key employee, with the business itself as beneficiary. Second, it may pay for, partially or in full, life insurance policies for most or all employees. In this case, the employees can name their own beneficiaries. The premium payment is considered a part of the compensation package. Employees benefit from this practice in several ways. The cost of the insurance is lower, because the employer can get group rates. Also, the employee does not pay income taxes on this benefit. Finally, some employees not normally eligible for coverage on an individual basis would be insurable on a group basis. Employers may also buy health insurance for employees for many of the same reasons.

Insurance Marketing

Insurance companies sell their product to consumers in a variety of ways. One way is to use a general agent, who contacts potential consumers directly. General agents usually represent one company and are paid on a commission basis. Each general agent may hire other agents. Policies that are sold become the property of the home insurance office, which takes responsibility for servicing the insurance contract. All premiums go to the home office, and payouts originate there as well. Life insurance policies are generally marketed through this direct approach.

The other primary form of marketing and distributing insurance policies is through an indirect channel. This approach also uses general agents but here they have much more authority to adjust premiums and control coverage clauses. Furthermore, they usually represent more than one insurance company. In this situation, general agents deal with local independent agents who deal directly with consumers. These independent agents represent many insurers and work on a commission basis. The advantage of dealing with an independent agent is the ability to compare competing policies for a given coverage. Property insurance is usually sold through such indirect lines.

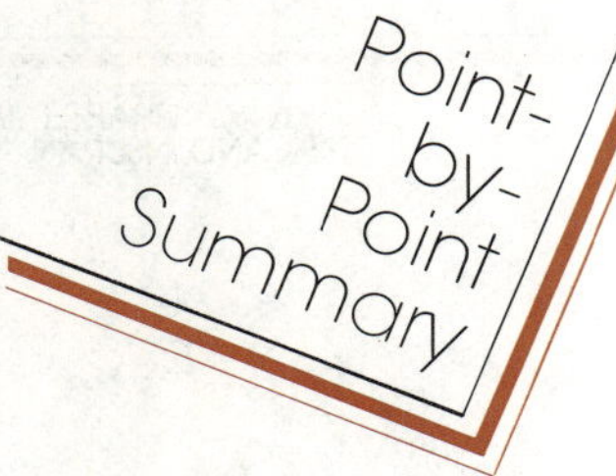

- Risk is related to both the probability of a specific event occurring and the effect of that event on an individual or organization. Business risk refers to normal, everyday risks involved in running a business. A casualty is a major unexpected occurrence that leads to a large loss.
- Risk management deals with controlling risk. Risk is handled through avoidance, reduction, assumption, or shifting the risk to another party. Improper risk management can have dire consequences for a firm. It can lead to insolvency or complete business failure.
- The use of insurance is an important technique for risk management. By shifting risk to an insurance company, the business can substitute known costs (premiums) for unknown losses. The law of large numbers allows insurance companies to predict losses for a large population with a great degree of certainty.
- All insurance policies contain certain common elements. An insurable interest and the possibility of loss must exist before property or person can be insured.
- Coinsurance clauses exist to discourage property owners from underinsuring their property. The property owner and the insurance company become coinsurers under certain conditions when a coinsurance clause is in effect.
- The insurance industry comprises mutual companies, wherein policyholders become shareholders in the firm, and stock companies, which are organized like conventional corporations.
- Fire, liability, and casualty insurance and worker's compensation are some of the types of insurance policies of interest to most firms. Insurance can be purchased to cover one risk or several specified risks (multiperil).
- Life insurance is of interest primarily to individuals. Term life insurance covers a specific time period; whole life insurance generally covers a lifetime.

1. What is the law of large numbers? How does the insurance industry use this law to set insurance rates?
2. Discuss some of the ways firms and individuals can handle risk. What are the advantages and disadvantages of each of these methods?
3. What is a deductible? How does the use of deductibles benefit both the insurer and the insured?
4. What are the advantages of whole life insurance? What are the advantages of term life insurance?
5. How is a casualty different from normal business risk?
6. Is buying insurance the same as gambling? Why or why not?

APPLICATION

Xerox Corporation

XEROX

A special type of risk incurred by manufacturing firms is the risk associated with the development of new products. In the annals of American industry, few companies have endured the risk of product development as great as that incurred by a small firm known as The Haloid Company. The product was xerography, or dry document reproduction. Quite literally, the entire existence of the firm depended on the success of that one product—even though it was doubtful at the time that anyone would ever buy the end result.

Today The Haloid Company is known as Xerox Corporation, one of the nation's largest firms and the leader in sales of office copiers. Indeed, *Xerox* is synonymous with document copying, or reprography. In 1979, Xerox reported total revenues of $7 billion, of which $5.3 billion came from the lease or sale of reprographic equipment and services. Xerox is also becoming entrenched in the area of word processing, which refers to the use of microcomputerized devices to store, edit, and print textual material. Finally, Xerox is now developing the Xerox Telecommunications Network, which will allow offices to transmit and receive data from affiliates around the world through the use of a communications satellite.

FROM RISK TO RICHES

The story of Xerox's success is really the story of two men—a businessperson and an inventor. In the 1940s, Joseph C. Wilson was president of The Haloid Company, a firm started by his father in Rochester, New York in 1906. Haloid was founded to produce and sell photographic paper and supplies to the fledgling photography industry. Haloid grew throughout the 1920s and 1930s, but it was never more than marginally successful. By the 1940s, increased competition had greatly cut into Haloid's market. Thus Wilson was on the lookout for a new product or service to make his firm unique.

Meanwhile, Chester Carlson had what he considered to be a unique idea, but he could not find a firm interested in developing it. Carlson, who had majored in physics and chemistry as an undergraduate, was a patent lawyer in New York City. In his patent office, Carlson noticed that there never seemed to be enough copies of documents. Of course, carbon copies could be prepared when a document was initially typed, but a problem existed if additional copies were needed afterward.

Working at night in his own laboratory, Carlson tackled the problem of document reproduction. Instead of using chemicals to copy an image, as in photography, Carlson directed his research toward the problem of dry reproduction. Previous work had been done in the area, but no one had developed a practical way to make the procedure work. Carlson used an electrically charged, sulfur-coated sheet of metal. Carlson placed a glass slide bearing an inscription on top of the metal sheet. When a beam of light was shone on the setup, the electrical charge in the sulfur was reversed—everywhere except underneath the inscription. When a powder was sprinkled on the metal plate, it would stick wherever the opaque inscription had blocked the light's rays. Through the use of heat, this powdery image could be transferred to waxed paper.

As crude as this process now seems, it was a revolutionary breakthrough in reprography—at least in the mind of Chester Carlson. Finally, in 1944, Carlson

was able to persuade the Battelle Memorial Institute, a nonprofit research laboratory, to develop his process. Although many people at the Institute thought that the idea was little more than a novelty, Battelle researchers continued to improve and refine the process. In 1947 the Haloid Company, under the direction of Wilson, bought a license to produce and sell the technique.

For Haloid, the struggle had just begun. Xerography (Greek for "dry writing") was still in the very early stages of development. The concept was feasible, but the process was still slow, dirty, and relatively expensive. Furthermore, Haloid did not really have the resources to refine the process to a salable point. However, Wilson was unable to persuade any large firm to share development costs. So the decision was made in the early 1950s that the little firm would put all the resources it had, and some that it did not have, into the development of xerography. To compound the risk, several new methods of office copying were on the market.

Clearly, the odds of success were formidable. If xerography could not be refined adequately to make it acceptable for general office use, the company would be unable to survive. Yet Wilson risked everything he had. Of course, the gamble paid off, even though it was 1959 before Haloid Xerox (as it was then known) put its first copier on the market. In the twenty years since then, Xerox has achieved an extraordinary return on an extraordinary risk. Perseverance was the key: It took Chester Carlson ten years to sell his idea, and it took Wilson and Haloid another ten years and $12.5 million to make even one cent on the product.

CAREER OPPORTUNITIES

At Xerox, as at most companies, sales and marketing play an important role in corporate growth. Consequently, Xerox is continually seeking qualified business graduates to serve as sales representatives. Xerox sales representatives are responsible for selling one of Xerox's several lines of products, such as copiers and duplicators, computer peripherals, or computer services. A sales representative calls on customers within his or her own sales territory, which could lie almost anywhere in the United States.

Xerox trains its sales representatives with a variety of methods. The initial training consists of a rigorous two-week self-study program at the Xerox branch office where the job candidate will eventually work. During this time, the candidate will also accompany an experienced sales representative during actual calls on customers. Subsequently, training for the prospective employee shifts to Leesburg,

Virginia, where Xerox maintains its International Center for Training and Management Development. Here, a variety of training courses are taught by experienced Xerox personnel in a collegiate setting. One highlight of this two-week training course is the videotaping of a simulated sales presentation by the trainee. This tape is then analyzed by class members and instructors.

Eventually, the trainee becomes a full-fledged Xerox sales representative and is given his or her own sales territory. Xerox sales representatives operate on a very independent basis, being responsible for their own budget, travel arrangements, and sales coverage. After several years in the position, the sales representative has several career alternatives. He or she may be given one or more large national accounts to manage or become a regional or branch manager with responsibility for supervising several sales territories. A transfer into the marketing department is also a possibility.

Whatever the career decision, selling for Xerox is a very demanding job. Visibility is high, and performance levels are made known to co-workers and supervisors. Fortunately, however, the rewards are also high, in both financial and personal satisfaction.

FOR DISCUSSION

1. How can the concepts of risk management be applied to new-product development?
2. Can you think of any firms that have failed because of the failure of a new product they were trying to develop? What lessons does Xerox's success hold for other firms trying to develop new products?

PART V

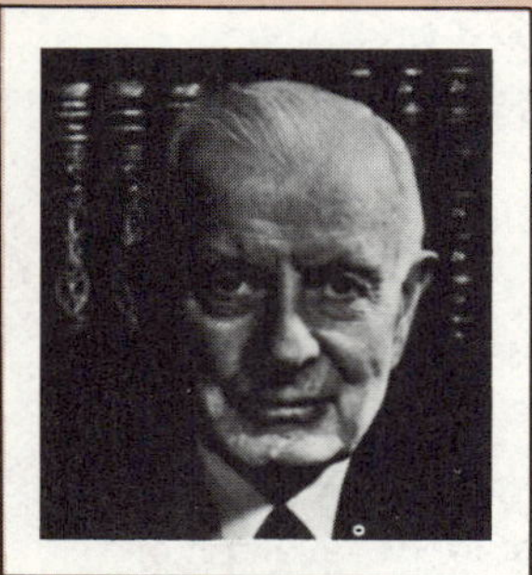

THOMAS J. WATSON

In 1914 Thomas J. Watson took over the small, debt-ridden Computing, Tabulating, Recording Company of New York City. His immediate goal was to boost sales and to expand CTR's line of time clocks, scales, and office machines. But Watson was constantly alert for new markets and needs in the area of business accounting, and an early line of electric business machines was developed as a result. By 1924, CTR had plants in the United States, Canada, and Europe, prompting Watson to rename the firm International Business Machines Corporation.

When the Great Depression withered IBM's markets, Watson responded by doubling the sales force and maintaining production levels. Because of its ample inventory, the federal government turned to IBM for tabulators to implement the Social Security system. At the onset of World War II, IBM's momentum, reliability, and record for prompt delivery brought major government contracts for more computing machines, bookkeeping systems, and the like. As Watson's presidency drew to a close, in 1952, the research and development department he had established when he joined the firm was designing the prototype electronic computers—IBM's ultimate triumph.

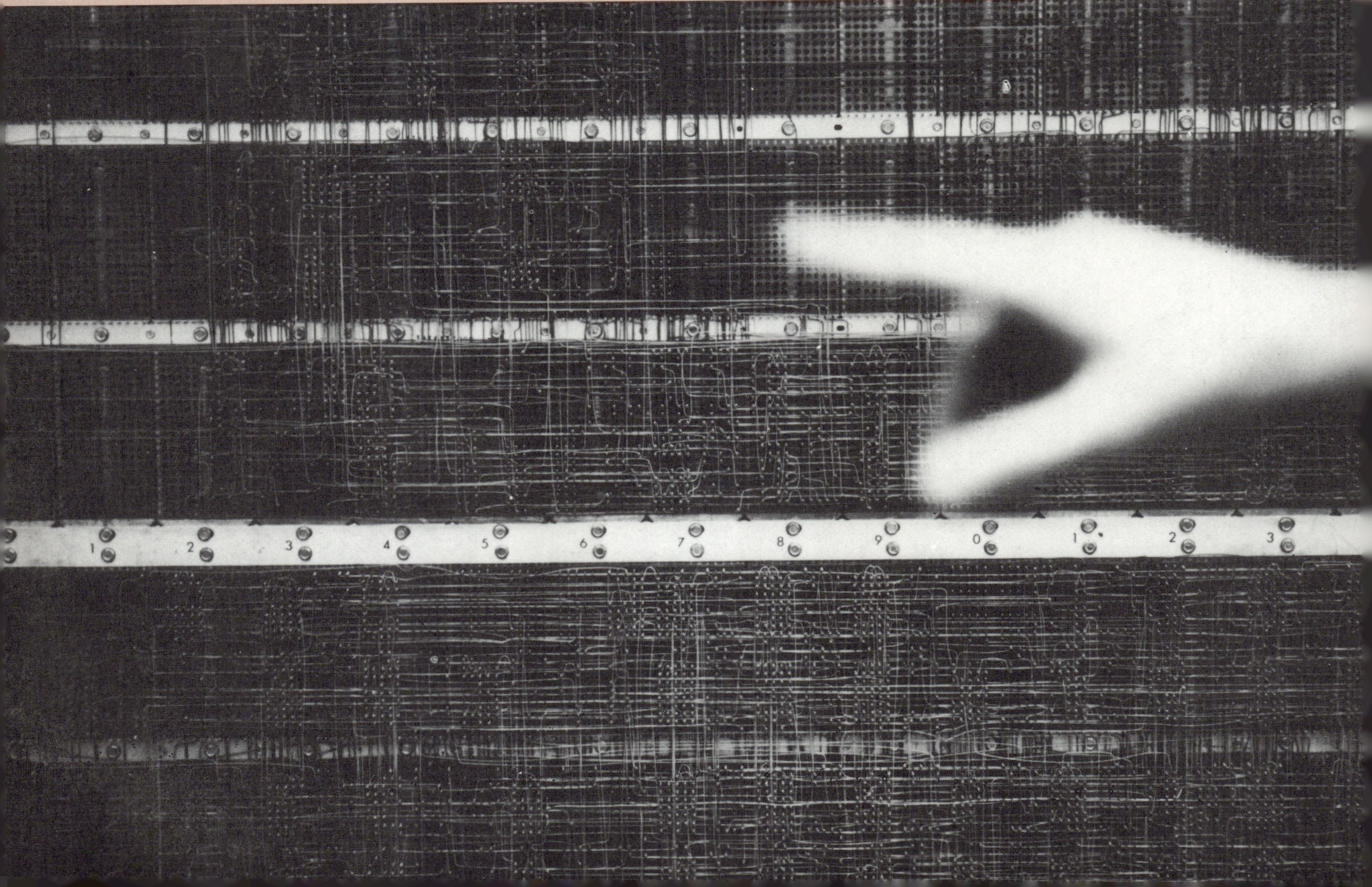

Quantitative Decision Making

OBJECTIVES

- ☐ To define accounting and explain its role as a form of business communication
- ☐ To identify the primary users of financial statements
- ☐ To distinguish financial accounting from management accounting
- ☐ To describe the purpose, content, and format of financial statements
- ☐ To describe how financial statements can be analyzed through the use of ratios

OUTLINE

ARTICLE *Putting Pizzaz in Our Profession*

THE NATURE OF ACCOUNTING

FINANCIAL ACCOUNTING

Income Statements

Balance Sheets

Annual Reports

Financial Statement Analysis

MANAGEMENT ACCOUNTING

APPLICATION *Marathon Oil Company*

KEY TERMS

ACCOUNTING

ACTIVITY RATIOS

ANNUAL REPORT

AUDITOR'S OPINION

BUDGET

CONSTANT DOLLAR ACCOUNTING

DEPRECIATION

EXPENSE

FINANCIAL ACCOUNTING

FINANCIAL STATEMENT

GENERALLY ACCEPTED ACCOUNTING PRINCIPLES (GAAP)

INCOME STATEMENT

LEVERAGE

LEVERAGE RATIO

LIQUIDITY RATIO

LOSS

MANAGEMENT ACCOUNTING

PROFIT

PROFITABILITY RATIO

RATIO ANALYSIS

REVENUE

ACCOUNTING

Putting Pizzaz in Our Profession

ROGER F. PICKERING
Wisconsin CPA, December 1974

Dear Mr. Editor:

In his recent report, Elmer Otte, our public relations consultant, states that we need more contact with the press, educators, and the general public. His conclusions should come as no surprise to the profession. The generally accepted version of the accountant is almost classic; unimaginative, flinthearted, pot-bellied and penurious, but a whiz at figures!!

The prototype is, of course, Ebenezer Scrooge, the surviving partner of the Counting House of Scrooge and Marley, whose image was scarcely redeemed by his turnabout on Christmas morning. The Scrooge image of the CPA has been nourished ever since Dickens, by countless authors and playwrights who find it convenient, if not derigueur, to use an accountant when they need a character that is, well—a clod.

When it comes to PR, other professions back accountants right off the map. On TV, for example, you can hardly turn on your set without finding a show based on medicine or law. What we need is a TV series in which a CPA is the central figure, a la Marcus Welby, M.D. or Owen Marshall.

In the show I envision, our hero, a CPA, would be presented a difficult situation and in 60 minutes, with time out for commercials, would carry the day. A typical plot would have our man (probably played by Paul Newman) saving a company treasurer from divorce, alcoholism and the axe by reorganizing the accounting department and chopping out 17 jobs. In the closing scene, the President, Treasurer and our Star toast the New Year with *lemonade* at the office Christmas party as dismissal notices are passed out to the displaced employees.

If this surefire concept could not be sold in prime time, perhaps a more modest start could be made on daytime TV, with a soap opera format and a CPA firm setting. The typical sequence would have Ms. Peabody, a junior, and the managing partner, Mr. Winkle, falling in love while amortizing good will. Mr. Winkle is about to leave his wife for Ms. Peabody when she turns up pregnant.

But, wait a minute, Mrs. Winkle has been seeing the tax man, Mr. Keystone (hint, hint) and it looks like the old switcheroo is coming up. Then Keystone splits for New Zealand and . . .

You get the idea.

Space does not permit a discourse on other image building ploys, such as adding Golf as a fifth part to the CPA exam. (In case you haven't noticed, our golf outings are an encyclopedia of shanks, slices, duck hooks and other public displays of ineptness.) If we put our minds to it, surely we can raise the status of our profession to a point where at least some of our members can evoke such remarks as "Isn't that what's-his-name, the CPA?"

Reprinted with permission from the *Wisconsin CPA,* December 1974 issue.

Accountants are often characterized as being dull and uninteresting, and some people consider their profession one of the most conservative. However, as this chapter indicates, accountants play a vital role in helping managers and investors to make decisions and to understand how the organization is doing financially.

Accounting which may have originated as far back as 4000 BC, is often referred to as the language of business. This language has been used by all kinds of organizations—from private, profit-oriented businesses to churches, universities, hospitals, and government units—to describe in financial terms their operations. Like any other form of communication, accounting has its own specialized vocabulary, principles, and concepts.

In general, **accounting** is the process of providing financial information to those who must control and manage scarce resources—labor, materials, and capital. The "art" of accounting has evolved rapidly in the twentieth century to meet the needs of our growing economic system. As our economic and business operations became more complex, accounting became more sophisticated to better communicate the financial impact and results of these operations.

The Nature of Accounting

The accounting process begins when an event occurs that affects the financial position of an organization. The financial impact of that event is analyzed and systematically recorded in the organization's financial records according to a predetermined set of principles and concepts. In the process of recording financial events, they are classified into similar groups. On a periodic basis (perhaps monthly), the entries made in the financial records are summarized and reported in **financial statements** that are made available to management and other interested parties. These statements summarize in a few pages the financial position of an organization and the progress it has made during a certain period of time.

There are two primary groups who use financial statements: those inside the organization (management and owners) and those outside the organization (investors, government agencies, special interest groups, and the public). Exhibit 19.1 summarizes their needs. Because these two user groups have different needs, accounting has two kinds of reporting functions. The first function, which meets the needs of external users, is broadly known as financial accounting; the second function, which satisfies the needs of internal users, is referred to as management accounting.

Financial accounting is concerned with developing a set of financial statements (described later) that provide a historical account of what has occurred financially in a company during a given period of time. Because the information contained in these statements is not always consistent with the information requirements of a company's management, another accounting function has developed. **Management accounting** serves to bridge the gap between the needs of internal management and the information provided by the firm's financial accounting system. This is not meant to imply that financial accounting and management accounting bear no relationship. In practice, one area has often had an effect on the other.

The methods for accumulating and reporting information for financial accounting have remained virtually unchanged for years and years. On the other hand, management accounting has had to change to reflect the increased complexity of management decision making. Thus management accounting now accompanies economics, financial budgeting, operations research, and behavioral science techniques in management's arsenal.

Financial accounting is performed in accordance with **generally accepted accounting principles (GAAP),** which specify what financial information should be reported in financial statements and how it should be reported. In the absence of these guidelines, individuals who rely on financial statements for the information they need to make decisions would face a bewildering variety of formats. The responsibility for establishing GAAP lies primarily with the Financial Accounting Standards Board, a private nonprofit organization, and the Securities and Exchange Commission, a federal government agency. Management accounting is not bound by any such set of formal principles. This is not to imply that GAAP have no impact on this process; rather, the connection between them is indirect and informal. Management accounting is performed in whatever manner best serves internal management.

Many financial accounting procedures have evolved to satisfy legal requirements established by such regulatory agencies as the Securities and Exchange Commission and the Internal Revenue Service. In contrast, there are no legal requirements that make it mandatory for a business to do management accounting. However, if a firm is to be successful, it must engage in financial analyses that go beyond what is legally required.

Financial Accounting

The end result of financial accounting is the preparation of two key financial statements—the balance sheet and the income statement.

The balance sheet summarizes the financial position of an organization at a given moment, it is a "snapshot" of the firm. The balance sheet reflects the status of the organization's assets (the economic resources owned by the organization), liabilities (the debts owed to creditors), and equity (the owners' investment in the organization). As its

EXHIBIT 19.1 Primary Accounting Concerns of Various Groups

User	Primary concerns
Owners	How much money will I earn on my investment? How risky is the investment?
Creditors (banks, vendors)	Is the company capable of repaying me the money they owe?
Management	How efficiently and effectively am I running the business?
Government Agencies	Is the company violating any legal or regulatory requirements?
Public	Is the company making a contribution to society? How are its operations affecting us?

Highlight Is a Management Accountant Really an Accountant?

Yes, I am an accountant, even though you don't see me auditing financial statements, working in a public accounting firm, or preparing tax returns. As a management accountant, I usually work in a private company, the government, or some type of not-for-profit organization, such as a hospital or university. I am not really concerned with developing the organization's financial statements or with "keeping the books." I am more interested in using the financial information that other people develop to help managers evaluate the financial performance of the organization and to make decisions.

As a management accountant, I get involved in all kinds of decisions. For example, last year I worked on a study to determine the cost and market price of one of our new products, I developed a budget process for one of our major divisions, and I worked on a task force exploring the possibility of opening a new plant.

I have a certificate in management accounting (CMA), which is every bit as important to my profession as the CPA certificate is to someone in public accounting.

name implies, the balance sheet should indicate that these elements are in balance.

$$\text{Assets} = \text{Liabilities} + \text{Equity}$$

This fundamental relationship must always exist, because the assets represent the things owned by the organization and the liabilities and equity indicate how much was supplied by both creditors and owners.

In contrast to the balance sheet, the **income statement** shows the organization's financial progress over a given period of time. The income statement also is based on an equation:

$$\text{Revenues} - \text{Expenses} = \text{Profit (or loss)}$$

Revenues are the resources, primarily cash, coming into the organization as a result of goods sold or services rendered. **Expenses** are the resources used by the organization to provide goods or services. If revenues are greater than expenses, the business has realized a **profit.** If expenses exceed revenue, the business has realized a **loss** from operations.

As you read the following detailed descriptions of balance sheets and income statements, keep in mind that there is a direct and important relationship between the two. The profit (or loss) realized by a business over a period of time affects the amount of equity. Equity in a business comes from two sources: direct investment by the owners and profits from business operations. Therefore, the bridge between the income statement and the balance sheet is in the relationship between equity and profit or loss.

INCOME STATEMENTS

Exhibit 19.2 is the income statement for HYPO, Inc. for the period from January 1 to December 31, 1980. It shows that HYPO had *revenues* from two sources:

EXHIBIT 19.2 Sample Income Statement

HYPO, Inc.
Income Statement
For Year Ending December 31, 1980

Revenues:		
Net sales	$3,787,248	
Other income	42,579	
Total Revenues		$3,829,827
Expenses:		
Cost of goods sold	$2,796,459	
Administrative and selling expenses	637,509	
Interest expenses	47,516	
Other expenses	22,061	
Total Expenses		$3,503,545
Earnings before Income Taxes		$ 326,282
Income Taxes		152,039
Net Earnings		**$ 174,243**

1. *Net sales* All resources earned by the company from the sale of its products and services
2. *Other income* Generally resources from such sources as interest on bank accounts, cash dividends from investments in other companies, and interest on bonds

The following *expenses* are subtracted from revenues:

1. *Cost of goods sold* All the expenses incurred in making the products sold during the period, including the cost of materials, labor, and factory overhead (rent, utilities, and maintenance)
2. *Administrative and selling expenses* The costs of running and promoting the business, including the president's salary, the salaries of all management personnel, advertising costs, and sales commissions
3. *Interest expenses* The interest that HYPO paid during the year on money that it borrowed
4. *Other expenses* This would include any other unusual expenses incurred by HYPO to run the business not otherwise accounted for above, e.g. research and development expenses, and organizational costs.

Expenses are subtracted from revenues to yield a figure that indicates HYPO's earnings, but this figure still does not reflect HYPO's profit. During 1980. HYPO paid over 46-percent of its earnings to the Internal Revenue Service as taxes. Thus its net earnings, or the amount of profit the company earned in 1980, is $172,243.

BALANCE SHEETS

Exhibit 19.4 is the balance sheet for HYPO, Inc. as of December 31, 1980. The first component is assets—current and fixed. *Current assets,* as Chapter 16 explains, are those the business expects to turn into cash

Highlight Inflation Accounting

Inflation has a severe impact on the finances of many companies. To make sure that investors (as well as managers!) know what is really happening to a company, the Financial Accounting Standards Board issued a statement in 1979 that requires major companies to report on the impact of inflation using an experimental approach referred to as **constant dollar accounting.** This approach measures the approximate effect of general inflation as reported by the Consumer Price Index. Exhibit 19.3 shows a simple example taken out of the 1979 annual report of Bethlehem Steel. Note the tremendous reduction in the net income per share—from $6.31 to $1.24. The cost of goods sold was adjusted for the effects of price changes, and depreciation was adjusted to take account of the inflated replacement costs of the machines and buildings that Bethlehem uses.

The moral: In times of inflation, simple dollar figures don't tell the full story.

EXHIBIT 19.3 Sample of Constant Dollar Accounting

Bethlehem Steel Corporation Income Statement Adjusted for Changing Prices For Year Ending December 31, 1979 (dollars in millions, except per-share data)	**As reported on Historical Cost Basis**	**Adjusted for General Inflation (Constant Dollars)**
Net sales and other income	$7,219	$7,219
Cost of goods sold	6,077	6,102
Depreciation	351	548
Selling, administrative, and general expense	316	316
Interest and other debt charges	80	80
Provision for taxes on income	119	119
Income	$ 276	$ 54
Net income per share	$ 6.31	$ 1.24

during the next year. The cash generated from current assets is used to pay expenses and repay liabilities. Current assets include

1. *Cash*
2. *Marketable securities* Temporary investments (generally ninety days) of excess or idle cash; listed at cost, or market value, since they are converted in to cash within one year
3. *Accounts receivable* Money owed to the company by debtors, generally for the purchase of goods and services
4. *Inventories* The value of products that have been completed and are in storage waiting to be sold (finished goods), products that have partially been completed (work in process), and raw materials
5. *Prepaid expenses* The value of items that the company has paid for in advance, such as insurance premiums

Fixed assets are things of value that will provide benefits to the company for one or more years. Fixed assets are reported in three categories—land, buildings, and machinery and equipment. Fixed assets are recorded on the balance sheet at the cost to purchase or acquire the asset minus the depreciation accumulated on the assets since the time of purchase. **Depreciation** is the estimated decline in the useful value of an asset due to gradual wear and tear. Since this decline is value can not be estimated with certainty, accountants use various standard methods to approximate it.

The second major section in a balance sheet is devoted to liabilities. *Current liabilities* are the debts that a company must pay off within the coming year:

1. *Notes payable* Money owed to banks or other lending institutions; generally short-term loans (up to one year) used to finance short-term needs
2. *Accounts payable* Money owed to vendors for the purchase of goods and services
3. *Payrolls and other accruables* Money owed to people or institutions that have performed services, including salaries owed to employees, salaries owed to employees on vacation, attorney fees, insurance premiums, and pension benefits owed to pension funds
4. *Income taxes* Money owed to the Internal Revenue Service; may sometimes be deferred and paid later but must always be paid

EXHIBIT 19.4 Sample Balance Sheet

HYPO, Inc. Balance Sheet
December 31, 1980
(dollars in thousands)

Assets	
Current Assets:	
Cash	$ 59,770
Marketable securities	87,466
Accounts receivable	559,144
Inventories	618,120
Prepaid expenses	49,986
Total Current Assets	$1,374,486
Fixed Assets:	
Land	$ 25,807
Buildings	716,076
Machinery and equipment	1,010,770
	$1,752,653
Less allowances for depreciation	800,103
Total Fixed Assets	952,550
TOTAL ASSETS	$2,327,036
Liabilities	
Current Liabilities:	
Notes payable	$ 48,563
Trade accounts payable	207,887
Payrolls and other accruables	411,362
Income taxes	124,684
Total Current Liabilities	$ 792,496
Long-Term Liabilities	431,350
Total Liabilities	$1,223,846
Shareholders' equity	1,103,190
TOTAL LIABILITIES AND EQUITY	$2,327,036

Highlight The Balance Sheet: What's Missing?

The balance sheet is a financial statement that indicates an organization's financial status at a particular moment in time. But does it really tell the complete story? No, say many accountants. In fact, the balance sheet fails to mention, much less account for, the most important asset an organization has—its human resources.

Since the 1960s, there has been a movement in accounting to incorporate in the traditional financial statements information relating to the value of an organization's human resources. This movement is commonly referred to as human resource accounting (HRA). Proponents of HRA believe that an organization's human assets are very similar to the other fixed assets an organization may own.

The costs incurred to acquire land, buildings, and machinery and equipment are shown on the balance sheet, and their value is gradually decreased through the process of depreciation. Why not use a similar approach in accounting for human assets? The cost of developing these assets would include such things as the money spent to recruit, hire, train, develop, and maintain employees. Once this value has been determined, it can be shown as an asset on the balance sheet and gradually be depreciated over the life of the employee.

Unfortunately, although the concept sounds attractive, it is difficult to implement in practice because accountants have difficulty determining the value and useful life of human assets. Therefore, even though human resources are the most valuable asset an organization has, they remain off the balance sheet.

Long-term liabilities are obligations, usually loans, that are due to be paid not in the current year but in some future period. The amount specified in the balance sheet is equal to the total amount borrowed.

The final major section, the *equity* section, summarizes the owners' investment in the business. Individuals and institutions become owners of a company by purchasing shares of the company's stock. Equity increases as more people purchase stock and as the company retains increased profits.

ANNUAL REPORTS

By law, certain types of companies must prepare and issue to their investors an **annual report** that provides an overview of company progress during the past year. Because the annual report is the primary medium of communication between the company and its investors, management makes every effort to disclose and explain information—financial and nonfinancial—that will help investors determine how well the company is doing. Annual reports are normally divided into at least four main parts.

The *president's letter to shareholders* summarizes in two to three pages the accomplishments of the company during the past year and corporate plans for the future. In addition, the president briefly reviews the financial results of the past year and highlights the most important problem areas or accomplishments.

The *operations review* provides a segment-by-segment analysis of operations—by product, operating division, or geographical territory, depending on how the company is organized. This section provides an overview of how each segment performed during the past year, how the past year's performance compares to prior years, and the future outlook for the segment.

The operations review is usually followed by the company's *financial statements and auditor's opinion.* The financial statements include the income statement, balance sheet, and any other statements that are required by law or that more fully describe how the company performed during the past year. An integral part of these financial statements are the accompanying financial footnotes, which explain in more detail many of the items appearing in the financial statements. The **auditor's opinion,** which follows the financial statements and footnotes, indicates that an independent accounting firm has reviewed the company's statements. It evaluates the accuracy and fairness of the financial information.

The last major section of an annual report is the *statistical summary,* which normally provides five to ten years of key financial information. These data provide a historical perspective on how the company has done financially and is an invaluable tool in evaluating the performance of the company and its management.

"That's the gist of what I want to say. Now get me some statistics to base it on."

FINANCIAL STATEMENT ANALYSIS

Financial statements may appear to be dry collections of numbers, but they are actually quite revealing. The trick is to know how to evaluate them. One of the most commonly used tools of financial analysis—known as **ratio analysis**—involves comparing certain types of financial information to come up with ratios. Four families of ratios are particularly useful in providing an additional perspective on the financial health of an organization.

Profitability Ratios

The most basic of all financial ratios are those that determine the profitability of a company in relation to its assets and sales. **Profitability ratios** indicate how successful a company really is and how effective management is in operating the business. The three most common profitability ratios are return on assets, profit margin, and return on equity.

Return on assets (ROA) tells how much money the company earned on each dollar it invested. It is a measure of overall company earning power or profitability. If you refer back to Exhibits 19.2 and 19.4, you can see that HYPO had an ROA of 7.5 percent in 1980:

$$\text{ROA} = \frac{\text{Net earnings}}{\text{Total assets}} = \frac{\$174}{\$2{,}327} = 7.5 \text{ percent}$$

Profitability Ratios

This means that for every dollar invested in assets, the company is earning 7.5 cents of income.

Profit margin is a ratio that shows the relationship between net earnings and net sales. It indicates how much profit the company is earning on each dollar of sales. Using the figures for HYPO:

$$\text{Profit margin} = \frac{\text{Net earnings}}{\text{Net sales}} = \frac{\$174}{\$3{,}787} = 4.6 \text{ percent}$$

This means that HYPO made a profit of 4.6 cents for every dollar in sales.

Return on equity (ROE) indicates the amount of net earnings per dollar of equity. Shareholders are particularly interested in this ratio, because it shows them how much they are earning on each dollar of investment.

$$\text{ROE} = \frac{\text{Net earnings}}{\text{Shareholder's investment}} = \frac{\$174}{\$1{,}103} = 15.8 \text{ percent}$$

Thus HYPO's owners are earning 15.8 cents for every dollar they invest.

Liquidity Ratios

Liquidity ratios measure the short-run solvency of a company—its ability to meet current debts. These ratios tell managers whether they have enough cash on hand, or assets that can quickly be converted to cash (such as accounts receivable), to pay current bills. The two ratios used to measure liquidity are the current ratio and the quick ratio.

The *current ratio* indicates whether there are enough current assets to meet current liabilities. The current ratio should be 1.0 or greater; that is, the company should have more current assets than current liabilities. For HYPO:

$$\text{Current ratio} = \frac{\text{Current assets}}{\text{Current liabilities}} = \frac{\$1{,}374}{\$792} = 1.73$$

It would appear that HYPO is solvent.

The *quick ratio* is a variation of the current ratio, calculated as follows:

$$\text{Quick ratio} = \frac{\text{Current assets} - \text{Inventories}}{\text{Current liabilities}} = \frac{\$756}{\$792} = 0.95$$

By this measure, assuming a standard of 1, HYPO appears to be having some trouble. The quick ratio is considered a more accurate measure of liquidity, because it excludes inventories from current assets. Inventories are probably the least liquid of current assets.

Leverage Ratios

Leverage ratios measure how much debt the firm uses to finance its assets. The more debt a firm has, the more **leverage** it has. The primary ratio of this type is the *debt ratio:*

$$\text{Debt ratio} = \frac{\text{Notes payable} + \text{Long-term liabilities}}{\text{Total assets}} = \frac{\$480}{\$2{,}327} = 20.6 \text{ percent}$$

In other terms, approximately one-fifth of HYPO's assets are financed by debt.

A variation of the debt ratio that is commonly used in practice is the *debt-to-equity ratio*. This ratio is calculated as follows:

$$\text{Debt-to-equity} = \frac{\text{Notes payables} + \text{Long-term liabilities}}{\text{Shareholders' investment}}$$
$$= \frac{\$480}{\$1{,}103} = .43$$

This ratio indicates that for every \$1 of shareholder equity the firm has \$.43 of borrowed debt.

Activity Ratios

Activity ratios indicate how efficiently the company is using its resources. They measure the consumption of goods, such as inventory, and the speed with which accounts receivable are collected. The primary activity ratios are total asset turnover, inventory turnover and the accounts receivable collection period.

The *total asset turnover ratio* indicates how much sales dollars the company earns for each dollar invested in assets. The ratio is calculated as follows:

$$\text{Total asset turnover} = \frac{\text{Net sales}}{\text{Total assets}} = \frac{\$3{,}787}{\$2{,}327} = 1.6$$

Hypo is generating a $1.60 in sales for every $1.00 invested in assets. In practice, the total asset turnover measures how efficiently management utilizes its assets. Normally the higher this ratio the better.

Inventory turnover tells how many times during the year the inventory turned over—that is, how many times the entire stock was sold. This ratio helps management determine how much inventory the company should have on hand at a given time.

$$\text{Inventory turnover} = \frac{\text{Cost of goods sold}}{\text{Inventories}} = \frac{\$2{,}796}{\$618} = 4.5$$

In HYPO's case, the inventory turns over four and a half times a year, or about every three months.

The *accounts receivable collection period* indicates how often the company collects its accounts receivable. This figure must be evaluated in light of the firm's collection policy and the experience of similar companies.

$$\text{Collection period} = \frac{\text{Accounts receivable}}{\text{Net sales} \div \text{Days}} = \frac{\$559}{\$3{,}787 \div 365} = 54 \text{ days}$$

It takes HYPO an average of fifty-four days to collect an accounts receivable.

Using Ratios

Once these ratios have been calculated, the business can be evaluated by observing how they changed over time or by comparing one firm's ratios to those similar firms. Some of the most-used sources of comparative ratios are shown in Exhibit 19.5; Exhibit 19.6 shows the average ratios for several different industries.

EXHIBIT 19.5 Sources of Comparative Ratios

- Dun & Bradstreet, *Fourteen Key Business Ratios*, published annually—ratios for 125 types of business activity, based on companies' financial statements
- Robert Morris Associates (an association of bank loan officers), *Statement Studies*, published annually—eleven ratios calculated for 156 types of business activity, based on the financial statements of firms that the banks deal with.
- Government agencies, such as the Federal Trade Commission's, *Quarterly Financial Report for Manufacturing Corporations*
- Trade associations

Regardless of the method of interpretation, ratios must be interpreted with caution. They are intended only to assist statement users in evaluating the financial position and solvency of a company—not to provide definitive answers. To truly determine how well a company is doing, one must assess the company over time, assess the relative state of the company at the time of analysis, assess the position of the company with respect to other companies in the industry, and assess the maturity of the business (product life cycle). Only then is it possible to form an accurate picture of the company's financial position.

Management Accounting

Management accounting provides information to assist an organization's management in decision making. It is difficult to generalize about management accounting, because systems differ so much from firm to firm. Unlike financial accounting, which is a fairly structured process that leads to a discernible end result, management accounting systems are tailored to satisfy the information needs of specific companies. However, just about any important decision that management makes will have a financial impact on the organization. Thus management accountants get involved in all aspects of managerial decision making that may have financial impact.

The planning function involves management in deciding what the company will be doing in the future. During the planning phase, management is concerned with answering such questions as

- What products or services should we provide?
- How big should we be?
- Where do we want to be financially one to five years from now?
- What effect does increased volume have on profitability?

EXHIBIT 19.6 Key Ratios for Various Industries

Industry	Total Asset Turnover *Sales / Total Assets*	Profit Margin *Profit* / Sales*	Return on Equity *Profit* / Net Worth*	Debt-to-Equity *Debt / Net Worth*
• Grocery and meat retailers	5.84	1.4%	20.3%	1.5
• Auto retailers—new and used	4.59	1.5%	21.6%	2.1
• Motels, hotels, and tourist courts	.71	6.7%	11.4%	3.7
• Water utilities	.22	18.2%	9.1%	1.5
• Detective agencies	3.43	2.8%	20.4%	3.8
• Aircraft manufacturers	1.36	4.7%	20.2%	1.6

*Before-tax profit.
Source: Robert Morris Associates

The budgeting process, in particular, is where management accounting and planning overlap.

A **budget** is a formal dollar-quantified statement of expected performance.* Budgets indicate what resources—people and dollars—are required to implement the plans that management develops. Since businesses operate in a world of unlimited needs but limited resources, the budgeting process forces managers to identify their objectives, clarify their priorities, and allocate resources accordingly.

The complexity of the budgeting process depends on the size and nature of the organization. Larger organizations with many different product lines, like General Motors or IBM, tend to have more sophisticated and formal budgeting systems. Their budgets are used not only as planning tools but also as a way of integrating the operations of diverse organizational units. The end result of their budgeting process is usually a detailed set of budgets covering all operations of the organization. In reality, however, their budgeting is not entirely unlike household budgeting.

Once budgets have been developed, actual results and budgeted results can be compared periodically (say, monthly). Any significant differences indicate that the organization is not operating as originally planned. There could be any number of reasons for these differences, among them inefficient operations, a poor job of budgeting, a poor job of planning, and changes in economic or business conditions. Budgeting lets managers know if they are on target and if not, where they might be going wrong—a crucial tool for their control function.

In addition to providing assistance in the planning and control functions, management accounting aids in other ways. For instance, management accountants can design systems to identify and measure the costs incurred in making a product or providing a service. This cost information is essential in assessing the efficiency of operations and in establishing product prices. Management is also concerned with evaluating the profitability of operations—products, plants, sales territories, salespeople, and so on. This type of evaluation is also possible through management accounting.

*In some cases, budgets are presented in terms of machine or labor hours. In any case, the budget is still a *quantified* plan.

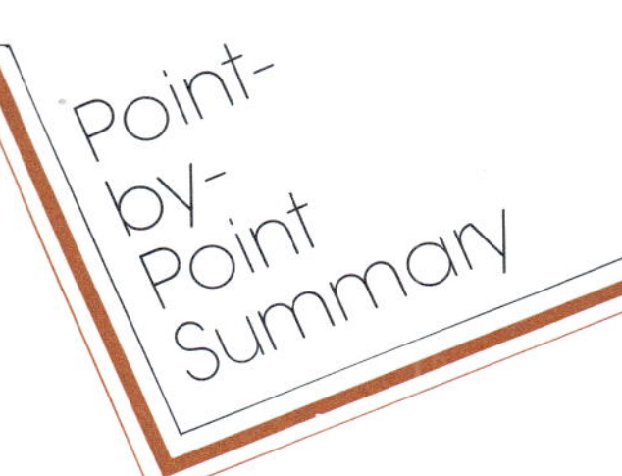

- Accounting is concerned with collecting, measuring, recording, classifying, reporting, and interpreting financial information to assist people inside and outside the organization in making decisions. The primary users of accounting information are owners, managers, creditors, special interest groups, the government, and the public.
- Financial accounting is concerned with providing information to people outside the organization; management accounting focuses on

the information needs of people within the company. The primary differences between financial and management accounting are in the orientation of the data gathered and used, the approach to data gathering, the guiding principles, the legal requirements, and the end product.

- The two key financial statements are the balance sheet and the income statement. The balance sheet indicates the status of the company's assets, liabilities, and equity at a given moment in time. The income statement shows the changes in revenues, expenses, and profit or loss during a given period of time.
- The annual report is the primary medium of communication between a company and outsiders. The most important sections of the annual report are the president's letter to shareholders, the operations review, the financial statements and auditor's opinion, and the statistical summary.
- Ratio analysis is often used as a tool to analyze financial statements. The most commonly used types of ratios are the profitability, liquidity, leverage, and activity ratios. These ratios take on meaning when they are analyzed over time for the same company or compared with the ratios of similar companies.
- Management accounting assists managers in performing the planning and control functions. Budgeting, in particular, is an invaluable accounting tool that facilitates planning and control.

1. What are the primary differences between financial and management accounting?
2. What is the purpose of an income statement? A balance sheet?
3. What is the purpose of an annual report, and how is this report useful to investors and creditors?
4. Using your own finances as an example, explain assets, liabilities, and equity. Distinguish between current and fixed assets and between current and long-term liabilities.
5. What do the terms *planning* and *control* mean? How does accounting help managers perform these functions?
6. Prepare a personal budget for yourself for the next month. What implications does it have for your own planning and control?
7. If you had to analyze the financial ratios of a company, how would you go about interpreting them?
8. Why is accounting "the language of business"?

APPLICATION

Marathon Oil Company, with general offices in Findlay, Ohio, engages in exploration, production, transportation, and marketing of crude oil and natural gas, as well as refining, transportation, and marketing of petroleum products. The pursuit of these activities has led to significant operations on six continents, involving over 13,000 employees. With revenues of almost $5 billion, Marathon is ranked among the fifty largest industrial corporations in the United States.

Marathon Oil Company

ANALYZING MARATHON'S FINANCIAL STATUS

Before Marathon's financial statements can be analyzed, it is important to point out that the business Marathon is engaged in is quite different from the manufacturing business run by HYPO Company, the company whose financial statements are discussed in this chapter.

This Is the Oil Business

Companies involved in oil and natural gas are permitted, at present, to use either of two methods—successful-efforts or full-costing—to account for certain costs relevant only to this business. The method of accounting employed by Marathon and most other large oil companies, the successful-efforts method, initially considers as assets all the costs of acquiring leases and of drilling. However, if a site is determined to be unsuccessful, these costs are then charged off as an expense. As a result, only the costs of successful wells are allowed to remain as assets. In contrast, most independent oil producers use the full-costing method. It, too, initially considers all acquisition and drilling costs as assets. However, it retains those costs as assets, even for the unsuccessful ventures.

The financial statements of Marathon Oil disclose another item that needs clarification—depletion and depreciation. In addition to owning depreciable assets such as property, plant, and equipment, Marathon also owns oil and natural gas wells. These assets were developed after spending substantial sums on drilling and other costs that are considered assets. In this case, it is not possible to write off the total cost over the estimated useful life, as for depreciation, because the estimated life varies according to how much oil or gas is extracted each year. Hence depletion measures the cost of the oil or gas extracted each year by dividing the total drilling and other costs by the total reserves available.

Say that $1 million was spent to develop an oil lease that is expected to have reserves of 10 million barrels of crude oil. (The $1 million is initially considered an asset, because it was spent to acquire something of future value.) If 2 million barrels are extracted in the first year, one-fifth of the value of the oil well has been depleted. Therefore, one-fifth of the cost, or $200,000, should be written off as an expense instead of an asset. This write-off of $200,000 is called depletion.

Marathon's Income Statement

The income statement in Exhibit 19.7 shows that Marathon's sales and other operating revenues increased from about $4.6 billion in 1977 to about $4.9 billion in 1978, an increase of 6 percent. However, in a company that, like

Marathon, has more than one activity, it is useful to check on the sales mix (see Exhibit 19.8).

Although refined products and merchandise remained the biggest source of revenue in both years, sales of crude oil increased substantially in 1978.

Once sales have been analyzed, it is logical to focus on how sales dollars were spent. Except for minor variations, Marathon's expenses have maintained substantially the same relationship to revenue in 1977 and 1978. In absolute terms, the only expense that changed substantially was lease impairment, which increased from $12.6 million to $34.5 million. This increase was mainly caused by the writeoff of the acquisition cost of an exploratory lease, which proved disappointing, to 50 percent of its cost.

It is interesting to note that Marathon's net income increased in 1978 by about $28 million. However, much of this gain was the result of an "extraordinary credit," a one-time reduction in West German taxes. This figure is shown separately because the net income figures would be distorted if it was considered as net income. Therefore, in reality, Marathon's net income increased by only about $100,000 between 1977 and 1978.

Now let's compute the profit margin for both years:

$$1977: \frac{\text{Net earnings}}{\text{Net sales}} = \frac{\$196{,}959}{\$4{,}656{,}940} = 4.2 \text{ percent}$$

$$1978: \frac{\text{Net earnings (excluding tax relief)}}{\text{Net sales}} = \frac{\$197{,}067}{\$4{,}954{,}710} = 4.0 \text{ percent}$$

EXHIBIT 19.7 Marathon's Income Statement

	Year Ended December 31 1978	1977
INCOME		
Revenues		
Sales and other operating revenues	$4,904,688,000	$4,634,492,000
Investment and other income	50,022,000	22,448,000
TOTAL REVENUES	4,954,710,000	4,656,940,000
Costs and Expenses		
Purchased crude oil, petroleum products and merchandise	2,764,161,000	2,605,098,000
Operating, selling and general expenses	583,444,000	505,118,000
Taxes, including income taxes—.	1,024,396,000	1,014,609,000
Depletion and depreciation	166,769,000	158,548,000
Exploration, lease rentals and nonproductive well costs	87,342,000	76,347,000
Lease impairment	34,539,000	12,626,000
Interest and debt expense	96,992,000	87,635,000
TOTAL COSTS AND EXPENSES	4,757,643,000	4,459,981,000
INCOME BEFORE EXTRAORDINARY CREDIT	197,067,000	196,959,000
Reduction of West German taxes resulting from utilization of net operating loss carry forwards—.	28,102,000	—
NET INCOME	$ 225,169,000	$ 196,959,000
NET INCOME PER SHARE—*based on average shares outstanding*		
Income before extraordinary credit	$6.52	$6.54
Reduction of West German taxes resulting from utilization of net operating loss carry forwards	.93	—
NET INCOME	$7.45	$6.54
RETAINED EARNINGS		
Balance at beginning of year	$1,089,568,000	$ 958,852,000
Net income for the year	225,169,000	196,959,000
Cash dividends paid per share—$2.20 in each year	(66,456,000)	(66,243,000)
Balance at end of year	$1,248,281,000	$1,089,568,000

SOURCE: Marathon Oil Company 1978 Annual Report, p. 35.

EXHIBIT 19.8 Marathon's Sales Mix

	1977			1978
		(Amounts in millions)		
Refined products and merchandise	$3,676,447	81.5%	$3,216,725	75.7%
Crude oil and natural gas liquids	581,037	12.9%	796,551	18.7%
Natural gas	209,772	4.7%	200,038	4.7%
Transportation revenue	41,136	0.9%	37,756	0.9%
All other	,998	—	958	—
	$4,509,390	100.0%	$4,252,028	100.0%
Excise taxes	395,298		382,464	
	$4,904,688		$4,634,492	

Hence, in terms of profitability, Marathon earned less per dollar of sales in 1978 as compared to 1977.

It might also be instructive to compute the return on assets employed in the business (refer to the balance sheet in Exh bit 19.9):

$$1977\text{: } \frac{\text{Net earnings}}{\text{Total assets}} = \frac{\$196,959}{\$3,445,626} = 5.7 \text{ percent}$$

EXHIBIT 19.9 Marathon's Balance Sheet

	December 31 1978	1977
ASSETS		
Current Assets		
Cash	$ 169,689,000	$ 115,849,000
Time deposits and short-term investments	10,017,000	—
Accounts receivable	411,328,000	417,456,000
Inventories:		
Crude oil and natural gas liquids	120,040,000	142,272,000
Refined products and merchandise	170,082,000	169,995,000
Materials and supplies	88,133,000	79,404,000
	378,255,000	391,671,000
Prepaid expenses and other current assets	20,757,000	20,743,000
TOTAL CURRENT ASSETS	990,046,000	945,719,000
Investments and Other Assets		
Investments and advances—affiliated companies	90,111,000	85,229,000
Other assets	16,901,000	14,056,000
TOTAL INVESTMENTS AND OTHER ASSETS	107,012,000	99,285,000
Property, Plant, and Equipment—Note C		
Oil lands and leases, plants and equipment, pipelines and other properties—at cost	4,216,466,000	3,809,609,000
Less allowances for depletion, depreciation and lease impairment	1,583,195,000	1,428,841,000
TOTAL PROPERTY, PLANT AND EQUIPMENT	2,633,271,000	2,380,768,000
Deferred Charges	27,833,000	19,854,000
TOTAL ASSETS	$3,758,162,000	$3,445,626,000
LIABILITIES AND SHAREHOLDERS' EQUITY		
Current Liabilities		
Notes payable, including commercial paper	$ 59,615,000	$98,005,000
Accounts payable	657,048,000	611,650,000
Accrued taxes, including income taxes	179,062,000	161,497,000
Current maturities of long-term obligations	7,256,000	3,823,000
TOTAL CURRENT LIABILITIES	902,981,000	874,975,000
Long-Term Debt— Note D	1,011,564,000	975,739,000
Other Liabilities and Deferred Credits		
Proceeds from gas production agreements—Note E	115,230,000	108,195,000
Deferred income taxes	240,584,000	167,780,000
Capitalized lease obligations	40,271,000	32,214,000
TOTAL OTHER LIABILITIES AND DEFERRED CREDITS	396,085,000	308,189,000
Shareholders' Equity		
Preferred shares, without par value:		
Authorized 5,000,000 shares—none issued	—	—
Common shares, without par value—Notes G and H:		
Authorized 50,000,000 shares		
Outstanding: 1978—30,242,734 shares; 1977—30,190,505 shares (excluding shares in treasury: 1978—451,133;1977—481,892)	199,251,000	197,155,000
Retained earnings	1,248,281,000	1,089,568,000
TOTAL SHAREHOLDERS' EQUITY	1,447,532,000	1,286,723,000
TOTAL LIABILITIES AND SHAREHOLDERS' EQUITY	$3,758,162,000	$3,445,626,000

$$1978: \frac{\text{Net earnings (excluding tax relief)}}{\text{Total assets}} = \frac{\$197,067}{\$3,758,162} = 5.2 \text{ percent}$$

By this measure, too, Marathon did better in 1977 than in 1978. In both years, however, Marathon earned less than 6 percent on its investments (after taxes). If all the funds that stockholders invested in Marathon had been used to purchase U.S. and municipal bonds, which are practically risk-free by contrast, they would perhaps have earned a comparable amount of net income.

CAREER OPPORTUNITIES

Marathon Oil, a progressive organization with substantial growth potential, offers many opportunities to high-potential candidates with bachelor's and master's degrees. Many of these opportunities are available in the controller's office and auditing division, which actively recruit graduates from such major areas as accounting, finance, computer science, and engineering (the latter, of course, supported by adequate business courses).

For example, employees in the auditing division have a fine mix of backgrounds—from college graduates in their first major positions to professionals with experience in CPA firms or other industrial companies. The main purpose of the auditing division is to evaluate the reliability of accounting data being produced by the corporation and to review and appraise the administrative and accounting controls. Auditors also work to verify the assets and liabilities of the corporation and to evaluate companies being considered for acquisition. Typically, an auditor is assigned to corporate headquarters but travels about 40 to 45 percent of the time. It is expected that a variety of audit engagements will broaden an individual's experience and knowledge and could lead to promotions within the auditing division or in other divisions of the corporation.

FOR DISCUSSION

1. How does Marathon's financial performance in 1978 compare to 1977?
2. Do you think that Marathon's performance is comparable to, say, Exxon's? In general, do you think Marathon's profits are exorbitant—and hence exploitive?

OBJECTIVES

- ☐ To understand the basic functions and limitations of computers
- ☐ To trace the evolution of computers
- ☐ To outline recent developments in computer technology
- ☐ To explain how computers receive data and process it
- ☐ To describe the levels of programming languages that are used to instruct computers
- ☐ To outline the development of information systems
- ☐ To understand the growing importance of management information systems and the problems associated with their development

OUTLINE

KEY TERMS

ARITHMETIC/LOGIC UNIT (ALU)
ASSEMBLY LANGUAGE
AUTOMATIC DATA PROCESSING
BIT
CATHODE-RAY TUBE (CRT)
CENTRAL PROCESSING UNIT (CPU)
CONTROL UNIT
ELECTRONIC DATA PROCESSING (EDP)
FIRST-GENERATION COMPUTER
HARDWARE
HIGHER-LEVEL LANGUAGE
INPUT
LIGHT PEN
MACHINE LANGUAGE
MAGNETIC INK
MANAGEMENT INFORMATION SYSTEM (MIS)
MICROPROCESSOR
OPTICAL CHARACTER RECOGNITION (OCR)
OUTPUT
PRIMARY STORAGE UNIT
PROGRAM
SECOND-GENERATION COMPUTER
SOFTWARE
THIRD-GENERATION COMPUTER
UNIVERSAL PRODUCT CODE (UPC)

COMPUTERS AND DATA PROCESSING

Plugging in Everyman

Time, September 5, 1977

Michael Mastrangelo, 40, a Manhattan audiovisual consultant, has a servant who keeps the temperature and humidity in his home at just the levels he demands, puts his favorite music on the stereo as he pulls into the driveway, and phones him at the office in case of fire or burgulary. If Mastrangelo wanted, his majordomo could also wake him in the morning, make him a cup of tea, brief him on the day's business appointments as he has breakfast, remind him that the car needs an oil change and, after he drives off, water the lawn and roast a turkey dinner for twelve.

Where did Mastrangelo get help like that these days? The answer: from a custom-built household computer and some auxiliary gadgets. The computer cost him $11,000 six years ago, but with advances in technology the same hardware today would be only $4000, and some new models are as compact and inexpensive as a good color TV set. The age of the home computer (or microcomputer, as it is often called) is at hand.

Since Micro Instrumentation & Telemetry Systems Inc. of Albuquerque 2½ years ago introduced its Altair 8800, a 250,000-calculations-per-second computer that retails for $1070, some 30 other manufacturers have begun producing similar equipment. . . . "Some day soon every home will have a computer," says Byron Kirkwood, a Dallas microcomputer retailer. "It will be as standard as a toilet."

A slight exaggeration, perhaps. But already some 50,000 microcomputers have been sold, largely for home use, and industry analysts predict sales of three times that many in the next year alone. Some 500 retail outlets have opened in the past couple of years to sell and service microcomputers—and serve as hangouts for the growing legions of home-computer nuts, or "hackers," as they call themselves. For further companionship, hackers have formed at least 150 computer clubs across the country and launched a dozen home-computer magazines. Says Theodor Nelson, author of a book called *Computer Lib:* "The lid is off. There's going to be an avalanche as there was with hi-fi, calculators, and CB radio."

Like their big brothers in business and government, microcomputers have a central processing unit to do the thinking, an input/output device (typically an electric typewriter connected to a video-display screen) for giving instructions and receiving answers, and a memory for storing information. A microcomputer can easily perform such sedentary chores as keeping track of an investment portfolio, maintaining an up-to-date Christmas card list, collating menus, or entertaining the kids with a vast Olympiad of electric games, from TV tennis to Star Trek (destroy the Klingons before they capture the starship *Enterprise).* Other tasks—reporting on water seepage in the basement, watering the lawn when it reaches a given aridity, locking the front door at night—require the addition of various switches, sensors, and motors that can send a house-proud hacker's outlay soaring. Says James Warren, a California microcomputer consultant: "You keep adding components until you exceed your yearly income."

So far the hardware is more easily available than the software, or ready-made programs telling the computer what to do. But addicts nevertheless manage to find plenty of applications for their new toys. Robert Goodyear, 62, a Framingham, Mass., physicist, uses his computer to tap out and edit personal correspondence. Manhattan physician Joseph J. Sanger cross-indexes his medical journals to provide him with instant, tailor-made refresher courses on any disease he asks for. Ham radio operator Irving Osser of Beverly Hills has programmed his computer to keep a log of the people he talks to on his radio and to translate Morse code into a typewritten message. Boston pediatrician Lawrence Reiner uses his machine to relax by playing TV games with his children. Robert Phillips, president of Gimix Inc., a Chicago firm that computerizes entire households, has installed terminals in every room of his Chicago apartment. He uses them to dim and brighten his lights, tune his stereo, turn his television on and off, even to open and close his drapes.

For many household operations, however, microcomputers are clearly inferior to simpler and less expensive devices. Like fingers. Michael Mastrangelo finds it easier to make his own tea than program a computer for the task. Says David Korman, who has an IMSAI 8080 in his Belmont, Mass., apartment: "I tried doing my checkbook on it. It's a lot faster by hand." And even though prices have dropped, microcomputers remain complicated devices that require long hours of study to use properly. When Robert Phillips let his sister give a party in his computerized Chicago apartment, he dutifully left a long list of instructions. Not long enough. Someone accidentally hit a button that killed all the power, reducing the puzzled guests to carrying candles. "The hard part," says Phillips, "is making the computer compatible with people."

Computer powers and costs have changed dramatically over the last thirty years. This chapter traces the computer's evolution, explains some of its functions, and describes new applications that continue to expand its role in society.

The computer has become a dominant force in our society. Corporations, government agencies, nonprofit organizations, and small businesses depend on the computer to process data and to make information available for use in decision making. As the costs for computer equipment continue to go down, computers will become an even more integral part of our daily lives. It is therefore essential that people gain a basic understanding of computers—their capabilities, limitations, and applications.

The Nature of Computers

Many people envision electronic marvels with mystical powers when they think of computers. In reality, a computer's capabilities are quite limited and directly related to the imagination of people. A computer possesses no independent intelligence; it cannot perform any tasks that a person has not predetermined. Therefore, a computer's IQ is zero!

The number of different instructions that a computer can follow is quite limited—often fewer than 100. These instructions are built into the electronic circuitry of the machine. By manipulating this small set of instructions, people can harness the computer's power to achieve desired results.

COMPUTER POWERS

Computers derive most of their power from three features: speed, accuracy, and memory. Modern computers are capable of performing up to 100 million calculations per second and are quickly approaching the limitation of the speed of light. A nanosecond (a billionth of a second) is a time slice so short that it is almost beyond comprehension. Light which moves at a speed of 186,300 miles per second, travels eight inches in a nanosecond. A picosecond (a trillionth of a second) is to one second as one second is to thirty years. And yet IBM has recently been developing a circuit that will operate in thirteen picoseconds.

Error-free computation is for all practical purposes a reality due to internal, self-checking electronic features of modern computers. However, this accuracy relates to internal operations; it does not imply that what comes out of the computer is correct regardless of what is put into the computer. *Garbage in, garbage out* (GIGO) is a phrase used to describe the effects of incorrect input. The GIGO concept is fundamental to understanding computer "mistakes."

The ability of a computer to store and recall information is almost unlimited. In fact, the storage capacity is increasing, even though physical size of data storage devices is continually shrinking. In addition, the time required to retrieve stored information is decreasing.

COMPUTER PROCESSING

All computer processing follows the same basic flow pattern (see Exhibit 20.1). Data must first be collected and translated into a machine-readable form that can be used as input. The computer then transforms (or processes) the input through arithmetic and logical operations. The end result is output. Obviously, then, input and output requirements shape the computer instructions necessary for the transformation.

This same basic flow is common to all data processing, whether a computer or a human processes the information. However, when a computer is used, the processing depends directly on the capabilities of the instructions given to the computer. Therefore, the transformation must be both objective and mathematical. Human processing, in contrast, is often subjective and intuitive.

A HISTORICAL REVIEW

Today the terms *data processing* and *computer processing* are almost synonymous. However, the first use of written language could be considered the beginning of data processing. Humans have always used some method of keeping track of information. Most early records were kept by religious leaders or merchants; merchants kept records of sales and prices.

As time progressed, so did data processing. The portable printing press greatly increased the volume of data; the development of mass media enabled that data to be disseminated to a large number of people. Computer data processing followed logically as a means to simplify and increase the processing of data. The development of the computer extended over several centuries, although many of the most dramatic advances are recent.

In the past, manual techniques of collecting and manipulating data were known as data processing. As technology developed, however, the term **automatic data processing** came into use for manual techniques. Today, an electronic computer can achieve many of the results formerly accomplished by humans and machines, a fact that gave rise to the term **electronic data processing (EDP).**

The Adding Machine

Automatic data processing began in 1642 with Blaise Pascal's adding machine, which used gears with teeth to store digits (see Exhibit 20.2). When a gear rotated past the tooth representing the digit 9, the next gear to the left shifted one tooth, or digit. This concept was expanded by Gottfried Leibnitz, who constructed a machine to add, subtract, multiply, divide, and calculate square roots.

EXHIBIT 20.1 Data Flow in Computer Processing

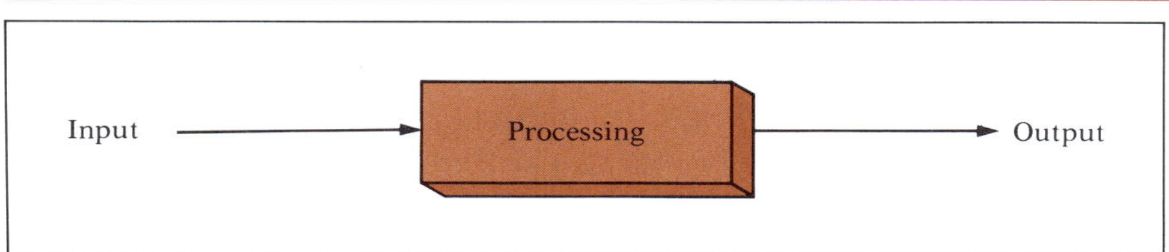

EXHIBIT 20.2 Pascal's Adding Machine

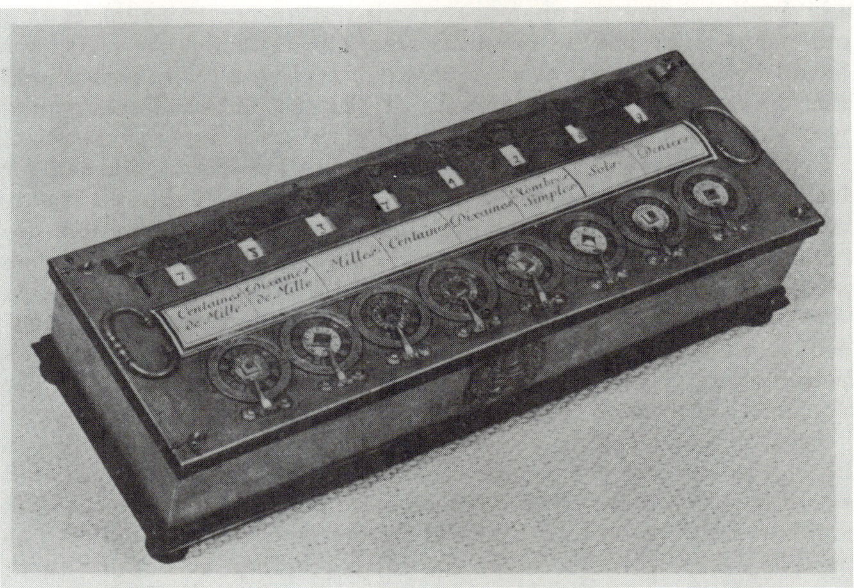

The Difference Engine

In 1822 Charles Babbage developed the concept for a machine that could execute complex computations and print results without human intervention. Using this idea, Babbage built a machine called the difference engine (see Exhibit 20.3), which could compute mathematical tables to five significant digits. But when Babbage tried to build a larger model, he found that accurate parts could not be produced.

Babbage did not give up, however. In 1883, he developed the idea of an analytical engine. This machine was to be capable of addition, subtraction, multiplication, division, and storage of intermediate results in a memory unit. Unfortunately, the analytical engine was too advanced for its time, and parts could not be manufactured for it. It was Babbage's concept of the analytical engine, however, that led to development of the computer more than 100 years later.

The First Real Computers

In the 1880s, Dr. Herman Hollerith developed a device to code data for the U.S. Bureau of the Census (see Exhibit 20.4). By using punched cards with census data on them and a machine to do the sorting, 250 cards could be sorted in one minute. This reduced the time needed to process the 1890 census data from 7½ years to 2½ years.

In the late 1930s and early 1940s, the first automatic calculator was introduced—the Mark I. The Mark I was controlled by punched cards and paper tapes and could multiply ten-digit numbers in three seconds. Then, in the mid-1940s, the ENIAC (Electronic Numerical Integrator and Calculator) was developed. It was a thirty-ton, 1,500-square-foot machine. The ENIAC did not have a memory capable of holding instructions; rather, it was programmed by a combination of switches. Even so, its multiplication abilities far exceeded those of the Mark I: The ENIAC could handle 300 numbers per second. These first two calculators were experimental and not available for practical use.

The U.S. Bureau of the Census became the first organization to make real use of a computer—in 1951 with a UNIVAC I produced by Sperry Rand. In 1954, IBM installed its first commercial computer, an IBM 650, in Boston, Massachusetts. These **first-generation computers** were expensive and at times unreliable. They were also quite bulky, because they had vacuum-tube memory and circuitry. However, the storage of both instructions and data in the computer removed the need to wire or read in the instructions for each job.

EXHIBIT 20.3 Babbage's Difference Engine

EXHIBIT 20.4 Hollerith's Census Tabulator

Enter Solid State

In 1958 and 1959, transistors became available for commercial installations, and they soon replaced vacuum tubes. The use of transistors greatly reduced the heat generated by the machines, as well as their bulk. With this new development, **second-generation computers** were born. The computer's speed increased, and its cost decreased.

Third-generation computers introduced solid-state technology and integrated circuits, improving memory and communication ability. These computers could be applied to both business and scientific processing, whereas the first- and second-generation computers had been geared specifically to one or the other (see Exhibit 20.5).

Technology has now advanced to the point where components can be put on circuit chips less than 1/8-inch square, a process that gives still faster processing at a lower price. The future promises further miniaturization, increased speed, greater versatility, and greater storage capacity.

COMPUTER HARDWARE

It is not necessary to acquire a working knowledge of the internal electronic circuitry of a computer in order to obtain valid output from it. However, a basic understanding of computer technology—or **hardware**—is essential. The most important thing to realize is that a computer is a system composed of devices for communicating with the computer as well as a machine that processes information.

Input/Output Devices

Input is the way a computer receives the instructions and data needed to solve a problem; **output** is the method the computer uses for communicating results to people. Input to and output from a computer can take many forms—magnetic tape, keys on a terminal keyboard, punched cards, printed lines, graphic displays, and voice response. Terminal entry is fast replacing punched cards as the most common method of data entry. Output is normally a printed document generated by the computer.

Central Processing Unit

The **central processing unit (CPU),** also known as the main frame, is the heart of the computer system. It is composed of three units: the control

EXHIBIT 20.5 First-, Second-, and Third-Generation Components

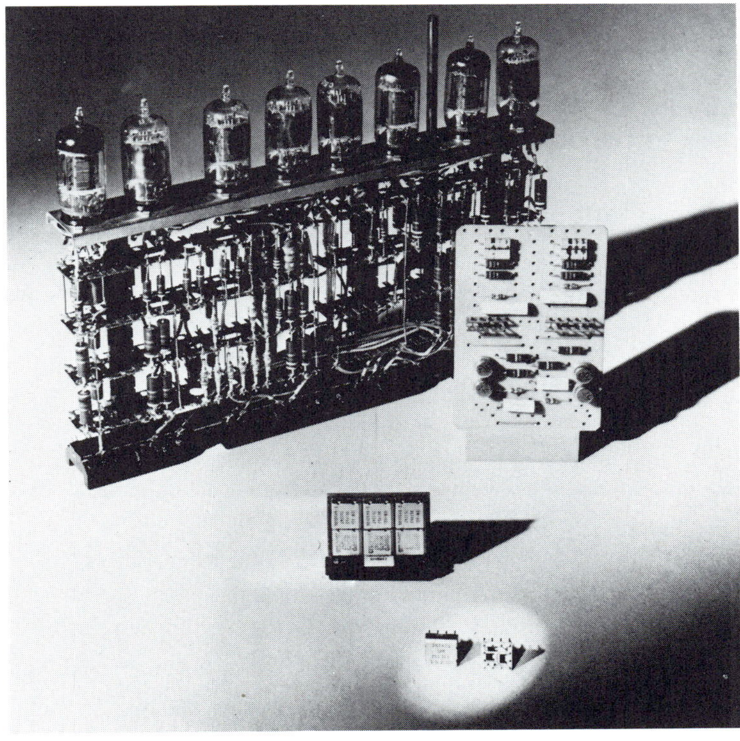

unit, the arithmetic/logic unit, and the primary storage unit. Each unit has its own function.

The **control unit,** as its name implies, maintains order and controls what is happening in the CPU. It does not process or store data. Rather, it directs the sequence of operations. The control unit interprets the instructions in storage and signals the circuits to execute the instructions. It also communicates with the input device and initiates the transfer of results from storage to the output device.

The **arithmetic/logic unit (ALU)** executes all arithmetic computations and logical operations. Since the bulk of internal processing involves calculations or comparisons, the capabilities of a computer often depend on the design and capabilities of the ALU. The arithmetic/logic unit does not store data; it merely performs the necessary manipulations.

The **primary storage unit** (internal memory) holds all the instructions and data necessary for processing. Data are transferred from the input device to the primary storage unit, where they are held until they are needed for processing. Data that are being processed and intermediate results from ALU calculations are also held in primary storage. After all computations and manipulations have been completed, the final results remain in memory. The control unit directs them to be transferred to an output device.

NEW DEVELOPMENTS

Recent technological innovations have significantly expanded the techniques available for submitting input to and receiving output from computers. These new methods increase the versatility of computers and expand their applications.

Magnetic Ink

One of the more interesting new input methods was **magnetic ink,** which was introduced in the late 1950s. Magnetic-ink characters have the advantage of being readable to both machines and humans. Exhibit 20.6 shows the standard fourteen-character set.

EXHIBIT 20.6 Magnetic-Ink Character Set

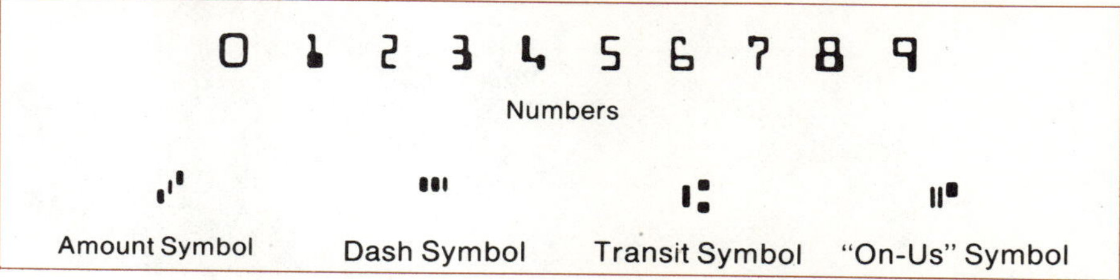

The banking industry has found magnetic ink very useful in check processing. Magnetized particles of iron oxide appear in the form of numbers along the bottom edge of each check (see Exhibit 20.7). These numbers identify the bank (an aid in routing the check through the Federal Reserve System) and the customer's checking account. A clerk manually inserts the amount of the check after the check has been written and received at the bank. A magnetic-ink character reader (MICR) reads and sorts checks as they are fed into it. Between 750 and 1,000 checks per minute can be read and sorted by an MICR.

Optical Character Recognition

There are now electronic scanners that can read a wider variety of numbers, letters, and other characters. Exhibit 20.8 shows a document prepared for **optical character recognition (OCR).** The documents are fed into a reader, and each optical image is converted into an electrical signal, which is used as input to the computer. Specialized OCR devices can even recognize hand-printed characters that meet certain standard requirements. OCR is especially valuable for high-volume standardized processing operations. For example, sales slips with credit card information can be read directly into a computer system. Other applications include scoring tests, sorting mail, and processing utility bills. Through

EXHIBIT 20.7 Magnetic-Ink Characters on a Check

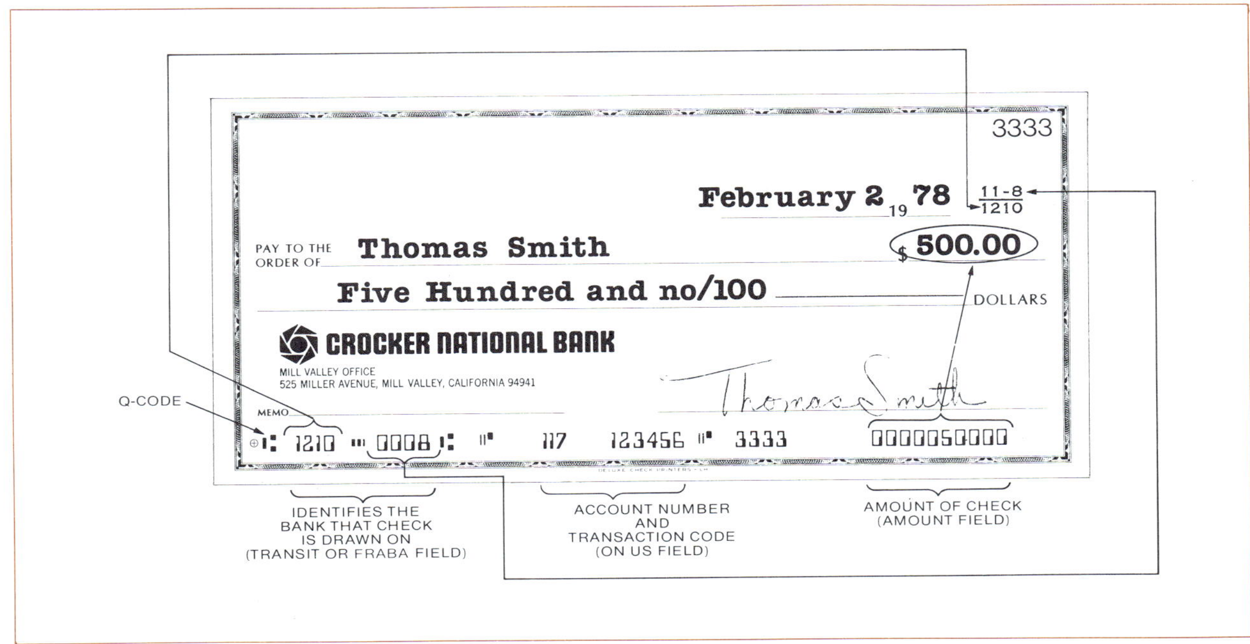

the use of automated entry, the likelihood of human error is greatly reduced.

Another form of OCR is direct sensing, a technique that allows data to be entered directly into the computer. The best example of this is the **universal product code (UPC)** carried on many grocery items. The combination of lines is read by a laser beam in the input unit, and an impulse is sent from the cash register to the computer. The price of the item is then flashed on the screen of the cash register. The receipt that is given to the customer includes not only the price but also the name of each item. The computer retains in its memory data about the specific items sold.

Light Pens

Another way to enter data directly into a computer is with a **light pen,** a pen-shaped mechanism with a light-emitting cell at its end (see Exhibit 20.9). Lines can be drawn on a visual display screen by indicating the ends of the lines with the light pen, a quick way to alter graphs and line drawings. The light from the pen is detected by the screen, and electrical impulses are transferred through the system to the computer. It is possible to achieve the same result with one's finger if the screen is heat-sensitive.

EXHIBIT 20.8 Optical Character Recognition

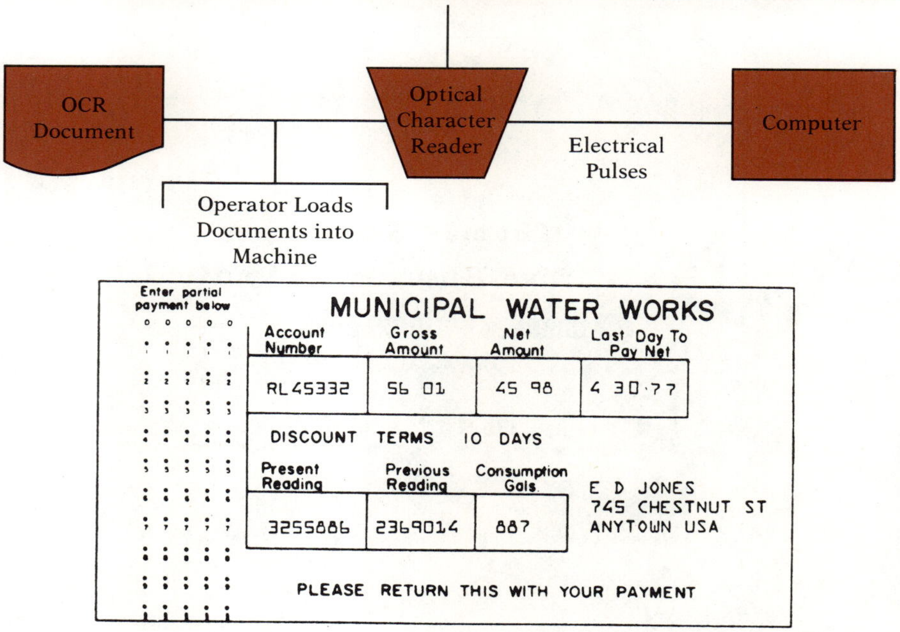

Enter partial payment below

MUNICIPAL WATER WORKS

Account Number	Gross Amount	Net Amount	Last Day To Pay Net
RL45332	56 01	45 98	4 30·77

DISCOUNT TERMS 10 DAYS

Present Reading	Previous Reading	Consumption Gals
3255886	2369014	887

E D JONES
745 CHESTNUT ST
ANYTOWN USA

PLEASE RETURN THIS WITH YOUR PAYMENT

Cathode Ray Tubes and Talking Computers

Methods of providing output have also advanced. Visual display devices use a **cathode-ray tube** (CRT) to provide an image like that on a television screen. A typical display screen can hold twenty four lines, each containing eighty characters. If the images shown on the screen need to be preserved, equipment that makes photographs of the screen pictures can be added to the system.

Some computers have a vocabulary made up of half-second recordings of voice sounds. By arranging the recordings in a particular order, the computer system can respond vocally. This approach is used in the banking industry to report on customer account balances. It is well suited for low-volume, highly formal messages.

The ability to synthesize speech is currently receiving a great deal of attention in laboratories. The results of such investigations could produce significant breakthroughs in audio response by computers. Other techniques, like voice input, are in the experimental stages or, like com-

EXHIBIT 20.9 Visual Display Unit with Light Pen

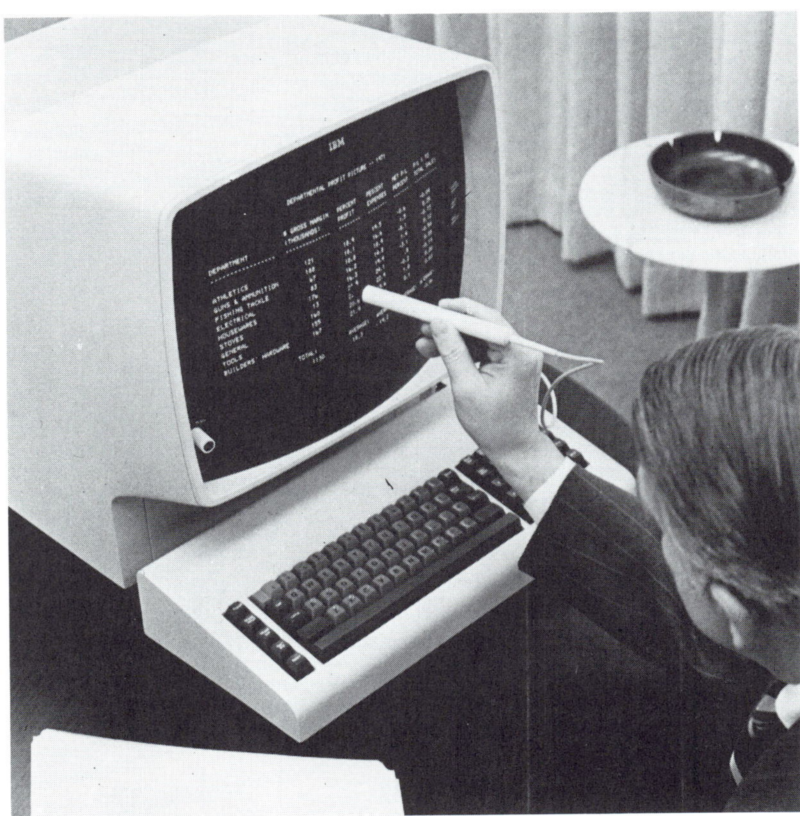

puter graphics, have recently been accepted in the commercial world. The variety of input/output methods indicates that the principal limitation to advancement is the imagination of designers.

Processing Advancements

New developments have not been limited to input and output; changes have been occurring in all areas of data processing. In 1980, IBM released information on a new line of computer circuits. The new circuits, called current injection logic, operate at temperatures so cold that metals lose resistance to electrical current. The less the resistance, the faster the current flows; thus the faster the computer operates. The new circuits operate in thirteen picoseconds, which is much faster than the nanoseconds of today's circuits. Faster computing will expand the application of computers into more complex problems, such as weather prediction, which requires millions of calculations.

"As of September 1st, I'm sorry to say, you will all be replaced by a tiny chip of silicon."

Highlight The Super Computer

Seymour Cray has recently released a new "super computer" through his own company. The new computer, called the Cray I, performs 100 million calculations per second and is currently selling for $8 million. Because of the high cost and large size of these computers, they have only been used where there is an enormous demand for high-volume, timely processing. For example, these computers have been used in U.S. weapons-research laboratories, the European Centre for Medium Range Weather Forecasts in England, and the National Center for Atmospheric Research in Boulder, Colorado.

The super computer draws its name from its ability to process data 20 to 100 times faster than most general-purpose computers. But a super computer is not simply a very large computer. Unlike other machines, whose purpose is to keep track of facts, it is designed strictly to solve problems. One way it accomplishes this is through the simulation of complex events, such as a nuclear explosion, space flight, or weather forecast.

Cray has predicted that computers in the future will be capable of performing anywhere from 500 million to a trillion calculations per second.

New developments have also appeared in silicon chips, the type that operate hand-held calculators. Someday all the circuits of a large computer will be compressed onto a chip the size of a match head. Even now, hand-held calculators can perform functions once limited to large-scale computers. If progress continues at its present pace, one chip will be able to store about 250,000 **bits,** or basic units of computer information, in a few years. In ten years, it is estimated, one chip will be capable of holding a million bits of information. This could eventually lead to a desk-top computer with the capabilities of a large-scale computer.

New Applications

Where will all these new developments lead us? The possibilities are endless! **Microprocessors,** small computers on a silicon chip, are already finding applications in products such as cars and sewing machines. And Texas Instruments has marketed several new consumer products that contain microprocessors. For example, Speak and Spell is designed to teach children how to spell and pronounce new words. The child selects a word, Speak and Spell pronounces it, and then the child gets a chance to spell it. If the spelling is incorrect, Speak and Spell repronounces the word and spells it correctly. This technology has been put to similar use in hand-held foreign language translators.

Other applications involve the use of microprocessors for personal computing. Personal computers can be programmed to do almost anything. Businesses can use them to control inventories, maintain tax records, and estimate costs. Teachers can compute grades and devise exams. These computers can also be used at home for maintaining Christmas card lists, developing menus based on what is in the refrigerator and the recipes stored in the computer, and playing electronic games such as baseball and backgammon. With sensors, motors, and switches added, home computers can automatically water or mow the lawn, regulate the heating system in a house, and control alarms. There are now well over 200,000 microprocessors in American homes and small businesses. This market was first exploited in 1975, when MITS introduced the Altair 8800 for less than $500. Radio Shack has recently developed the TSR 80 microcomputer for about $600 to $700, and other companies have entered the home computer market.

Computer Programs

When a problem is to be solved with the assistance of a computer, certain procedures must be followed. Despite the apparent complexity and power of computers, they have a limited ability to communicate with humans. Therefore, they must receive step-by-step instructions that provide the problem solution. This series of instructions is known as a **program.** There are two basic types of programs: application programs that solve user problems and system programs that coordinate the operation of all computer circuitry. The term **software** is used to describe all computer programs.

System programs are provided by computer manufacturers or by specialized programming firms. They are designed to facilitate the use of the hardware and to help the computer system run quickly and efficiently. System programs are initially written to meet all possible requirements that a computer facility may have to handle; they can be modified later to meet an organization's specific needs.

Application programs, on the other hand, solve problems facing management. They are generally developed within an organization, although some can be purchased. The job of the application programmer is to use the capabilities of the computer to solve a specific problem. Typical examples of application programs are those in inventory control and accounting. For instance, application programmers working for banks write programs to update customer accounts. These types of programs can be written without an in-depth knowledge of the computer.

Programming Languages

Programmers use a specific set of instructions to communicate with and control computers. As computers have developed in complexity, so have computer languages. Today there are three language groups—machine languages, assembly languages, and higher-level languages.

Machine languages are as old as the computer itself. Machine language, a combination of 0s and 1s, is the only language a computer can execute directly. Machine language, therefore, can be called the language of the computer. Each instruction must specify not only what operation is to be done but also where the items to be operated on are stored. Programming is therefore extremely complex, tedious, and time-consuming. A machine-language program has no obvious meaning to people who are not skilled in deciphering the 0 and 1 combinations. In fact, the machine language of one brand of computer (i.e., IBM) cannot be understood by another competitor computer (i.e., DEC).

Because machine-language programming is so difficult, other languages have been developed. **Assembly language** is close to machine language but one step closer to human understanding. As with machine language, programmers using assembly languages must designate data storage locations as well as operations to be performed. Instead of the 0 and 1 groupings of machine language, however, convenient symbols and abbreviations are used in writing programs. For instance, STO may stand for *store* and TRA for *transfer*. Even with these conveniences, programming in assembly language is cumbersome, although it is not so difficult as machine-language programming.

Higher-level languages are designed so that the programmer can concentrate on solving a problem rather than figuring out how the computer operates. Whereas one assembly-language instruction is generally equivalent to one machine-language instruction, one statement in a higher-level language can accomplish the same result as a half dozen or more machine-language instructions. The main reason for this is that the addresses for many of the storage locations do not need to be specified; they are handled automatically. Many higher-level languages are like English, and they allow the use of common mathematical terms and symbols, making programs easier to correct or modify. Machine-language and assembly-language programs are written for a particular computer and cannot generally be executed on another computer. Programs in higher-level languages, however, can usually be transferred from one computer to another with little change. Many higher-level languages have been developed, including FORTRAN, COBOL, PL/1, BASIC, APL, and RPG. Each has its own advantages, disadvantages, and applications.

Information Systems

Every organization has a method for transferring information from one person to another, whether by memo, telephone, or computer printout. A system is a set of interrelated parts—equipment, procedures, and personnel—that work together to achieve an overall objective. An *information system* is an integrated network designed to satisfy the information requirements of management. Some information systems are computerized, and some are manual. Some work well, and some don't.

There are several reasons why management may want to review its present information system:

- The system is not functioning properly.
- A new aspect has been added, such as a new product or procedure.
- A new development in system technology has been proposed.
- The organization wants to update the entire system.

As this list indicates, even a good information system may eventually outgrow its usefulness. When that happens, a new one can be developed through the logical sequence of phases outlined in Exhibit 20.10.

SYSTEM ANALYSIS

The first phase in developing a new information system is an investigation process, or system analysis. An analyst conducts preliminary interviews with users of the system to determine what information they need, when they need it, and how they will use it. These requirements are the core for a statement of objectives.

A detailed study of the processes the organization uses to manipulate its data is the next step. Some of the considerations:

- Is the input to the system obtained and processed as efficiently and inexpensively as possible?
- Is the information provided by the system in a form suitable for decision making?
- Is the information ready when users need it?
- Is there information overload?

By examining the present system, the analyst can determine whether it needs to be altered, restructured, or replaced. If the system is adequate, the analysis ends. But if the study shows that changes are in order, the investigation continues.

A system analyst acts as an interface between users of the information system, such as managers, and technical persons, such as computer programmers and operators. Thus the analyst needs a background in organizational operations and a knowledge of computer technology.

EXHIBIT 20.10 Developing an Information System

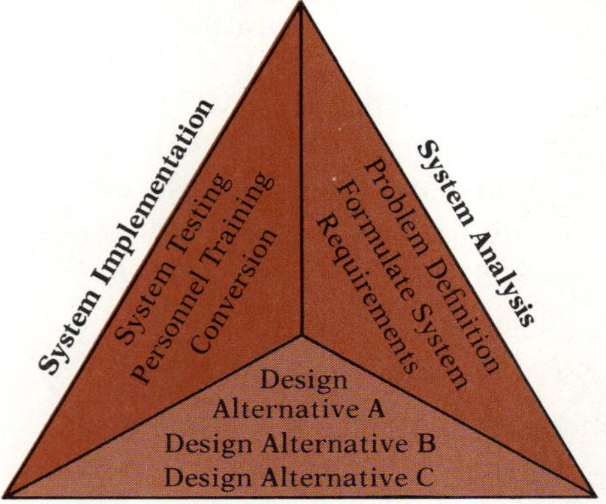

SYSTEM DESIGN

After the analysis has been completed, system design begins. Now the information system analyst has the task of translating information requirements into a feasible and detailed plan. This involves developing alternative designs, building formal models of these designs, determining the cost-effectiveness of the alternatives, and then making recommendations.

When considering alternative designs, the analyst must be aware of conflicting objectives that may be present in the organization. For example, the sales department may want as many models of a product as possible, but the production department may want to limit the varieties to a minimum. The problems of each functional area should be resolved according to the overall goals of the organization.

In designing alternatives, the analyst becomes involved in structuring forms and reports, determining computer program specifications, creating a data base, organizing clerical procedures, and instituting control measures. He or she must determine the costs of the alternatives in terms of money, personnel, time, and facilities, because the value of an information system must exceed the cost associated with it. In analyzing and designing these alternatives, the analyst must use such quantitative methods as sampling and model simulation as well as judgment, common sense, and experience.

SYSTEM IMPLEMENTATION

Next the chosen alternative is developed, installed, and tested. This phase is often the most involved phase for the organization. When the design includes a computer, the computer system must be programmed, installed, and checked to remove any bugs. Computer personnel must be trained to use the new system. Similar training must be provided for managers, because their involvement is critical to the success of the system. While testing the system, the analyst must be on the alert for significant oversights or omissions carried forward from earlier phases.

Even after the new system has been implemented, there is a continual need for system maintenance and audit. The analyst must be prepared to explain various aspects of the system and to identify system malfunctions. He or she should monitor the system throughout its operating life, constantly looking for ways to improve performance and to keep the system responsive to user needs.

MANAGEMENT INFORMATION SYSTEMS

When an organization first acquires a computer facility, it frequently produces an overabundance of statistics—many of which are confusing and unnecessary. Computers are a definite asset in producing things like payroll reports and bank statements. This use of computer power is a faster way of producing the same kinds of reports as were once prepared manually. A new concept has been introduced that extends computer use beyond routine reporting and into the area of management decision-making. This approach is known as a **management information system (MIS).** An MIS is a formal network using computer capabilities to provide management with the information necessary for decision making. The goal of an MIS is to get the most useful and correct information to the appropriate manager at the right time. It is also important to set up an MIS that can be expanded as the need arises.

Typically, a management information system can generate four kinds of output:

- *Scheduled listings* Received at regular time intervals; constitutes the majority of output
- *Exception reports* Monitor performance and indicate deviations from expected results; action-oriented management reports
- *Predictive reports* Allows organizations to project future results on the basis of models; used for planning
- *Demand reports* Produced only on request

An MIS is an effective tool, but it cannot guarantee decision-making success. One problem that frequently arises is determining what information management needs. Frequently, a manager requests everything the computer can provide. The result is an overload of information. Instead of assisting the manager, information overload makes it necessary to distinguish what is relevant from what is irrelevant, a job the computer can be programmed to do. Many MIS installations get around this problem by allowing managers to interact directly with the computer. This approach is particularly effective in aiding decisions that affect an organization's current operations.

Of course, there may be problems with an MIS. For one thing, managers do not always feel as though the change is beneficial. Often this feeling arises because the people who must use the system were not involved in the analysis and design of it. Another problem is that management frequently expects totally automatic decisions after implementation of an MIS, failing to realize that only routine decisions can be programmed (such as ordering purchases when inventory stock goes below a certain point or scheduling production). Decisions that depend on nonquantitative data require human involvement, because a computer system has no capability for intuition and experience. Finally, as routine decisions are taken over by the computer, managers may become resistant to future changes, either because their responsibility for decision making is reduced or becasue individual managers fear that the computer may make their positions obsolete.

In a very real sense, then, the success of an MIS depends on user involvement. Furthermore, an MIS is most apt to be successful when it is implemented by an organization that is not seeking a miracle.

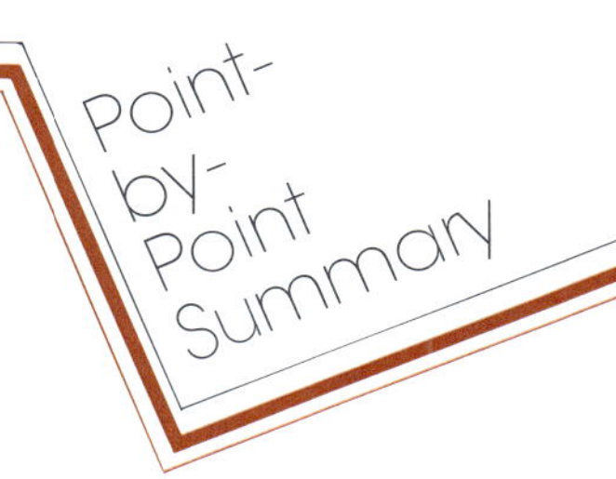

- A computer is a general-purpose machine that derives its power from speed, accuracy, and memory. The basic flow of all computer work is input, processing, and output.
- Data processing has existed since the beginning of written language and was greatly expanded by the portable printing press and mass media techniques.
- The first generation of computers used vacuum-tube memory and circuitry. The second generation replaced vacuum tubes with transistors. The third generation introduced solid-state technology and integrated circuits.
- New methods of input and output have expanded the use of the computer: Magnetic ink has aided check processing in the banking industry; optical character recognition devices are especially valuable for high-volume standardized operations; direct sensing devices are used to record and process the universal product codes on grocery items; and the light pen can be used to alter and clarify graphs and line drawings on a visual display screen.
- The central processing unit (CPU), the heart of the computer, is composed of three units: the primary storage unit, the arithmetic/logic unit (ALU), and the control unit. The control unit maintains order and controls what is happening in the CPU; the ALU handles the execution of all arithmetic and logical operations; and the primary storage unit holds all data and instructions for processing.
- A program is a set of step-by-step instructions for solving a problem. Application programs solve user problems; system programs coordinate the operation of all computer circuitry.
- There are three language groups: Machine language, a combination of 0s and 1s, is the only language the computer can execute directly; assembly language provides convenient symbols and abbreviations for writing programs; and higher-level languages are like English and can easily be transferred from one type of machine to another.
- Development of an information system consists of three principal phases: system analysis, system design, and system implementation. The analysis phase defines the problem, studies the current system, and identifies information requirements. In the second phase, the analyst develops alternative designs, builds formal models of these designs, and determines the cost-effectiveness of the alternatives. The implementation phase includes converting to the new system, testing the new system thoroughly, and training the people who are to use it.
- A management information system (MIS) is a formal network using computer capabilities to provide management with the information necessary for decision making. The goal of an MIS is to get the most useful and correct information to the appropriate manager at the right time.

1. Why are computers indispensable to modern businesses and other institutions?
2. What important features distinguish first-, second-, and third-generation computers?
3. Name three products not mentioned in this chapter that use small computers on a silicon chip (microprocessors).
4. What are the various parts of a central processing unit (CPU)? Which of these parts directs the operation of the computer?
5. Why is it necessary to program a computer? Don't all computers have the same instructions built into them by their manufacturers?
6. How would you distinguish an assembly language from a higher-level language? What is the advantage of a higher-level language?
7. Why would management wish to review its present information system? Should system analysis always result in one or more new alternative designs?

APPLICATION

Leisure time is an integral part of society today. People everywhere find time for amusement and recreation. Among the most unique entertainment experiences of the past two decades are "theme parks," a concept created by Walt Disney in his imaginative reworking of the old-time amusement parks. These parks enchant visitors by surrounding them with a whole new world, shutting out reality and allowing them to "leave today and enter the world of yesterday, tomorrow, and fantasy."

There are now nearly fifty major theme parks across the nation. But the grandfather of these parks, and still the leader of the industry, is Disneyland. Opened at Anaheim, California in 1955, Disneyland is visited by more people each year than all professional football and basketball games of the year combined. It draws more than twice the combined annual attendance at the Yosmite, Yellowstone, and Great Smokies national parks.

From Anaheim, the Disney imagination spread across the United States to Lake Buena Vista, Florida, where Walt Disney World opened in 1971 after an investment of more than $700 million. Walt Disney World is now the number-one vacation destination in the world. Disneyland and Disney World's annual revenues of $411,238,000 account for about 40 percent of the theme-park industry total.

Walt Disney Productions

COMPUTERS, FANTASY, AND REALITY

Computers play an integral part in the operation of the Disney theme parks. They are used to control entertainment facilities as well as to monitor and control the parks' operations. For example, the lifelike animated figures in numerous attractions are controlled by computers. A system of seven computers controls the Peoplemover transportation system at Walt Disney World. The Space Mountain double roller coaster is also computer-controlled. The roller coasters run next to each other on two almost identical courses, inside a huge six-story concrete planetarium. For safety, the cars on each roller coaster must stay at least eighteen seconds apart. This safety feature is controlled by a computer. If a car begins to gain on the one ahead of it, the tailgater is slowed down. Computers also release the blast-off roar in the final tunnel of the ride and control the forty projectors in Space Mountain that recreate the Milky Way, meteors, and stars.

In the major hotels adjoining Disneyland, data-entry terminals are used for guest reservations, registrations, and checkouts. For example, as guests prepare to leave, a clerk in the lobby punches their room numbers into one of several terminal keyboards. The terminals print itemized statements for payment at the cashier's window.

At Walt Disney World, a computerized system checks the operating conditions of everything from fire alarms to golf course sprinklers. If an equipment malfunction or a fire occurs, the system identifies the problem by flashing coded messages on visual display terminals located at two fire stations and two security locations and on the maintenance console in the main service area.

Audio-Animatronics, a patented invention, is one of Disney's most important and popular contributions to the entertainment world. The system is also known as the Digital Animation Control (DAC) System. Voices, music, and sound effects are electronically combined and synchronized with lifelike movements of three-dimensional objects, ranging from birds and flowers to humans. Eight major attractions at Walt Disney World use Audio-Animatronics—the Mickey Mouse Revue, the thirty-seven presidents in Liberty Square's Hall of Presidents, Country Bear Jamboree, Haunted Mansion, Enchanted Tiki Birds, Mission to Mars, Pirates of the Caribbean, Jungle River Ride, and Carousel of Progress.

A much-simplified diagram of the Audio-Animatronic system is shown in Exhibit 20.11. The equipment in the show area is used both to move the Audio-Animatronics (AA) figures and to allow the animator to communicate with the figures via the computer.

EXHIBIT 20.11 Simplified Audio-Animatronic Control System

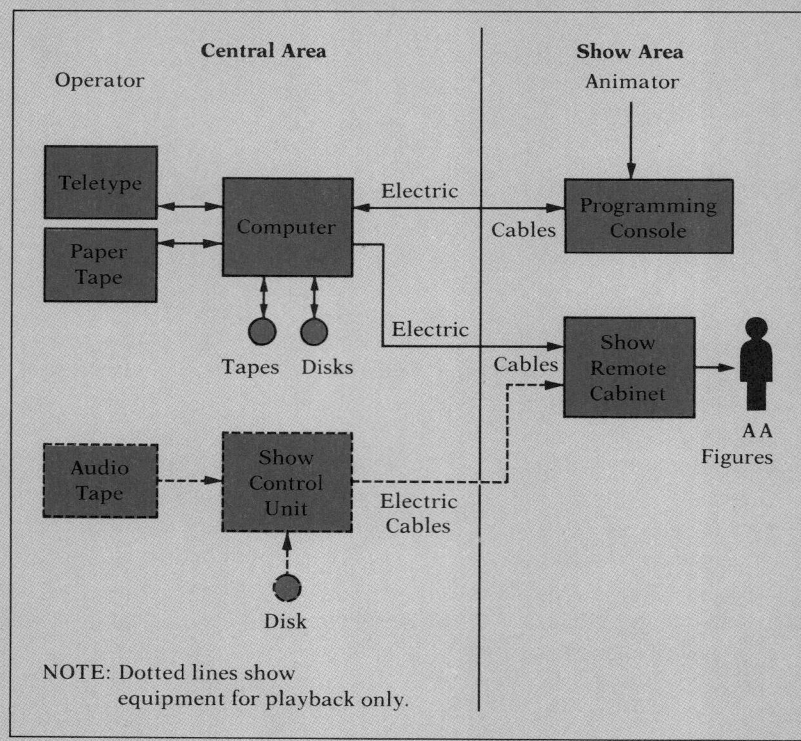

CAREER OPPORTUNITIES

Entry-level programmers at Walt Disney Productions are assigned to a small staff that creates computer programs for the new attractions, outdoor entertainment projects, and transportation systems at Disneyland, Walt Disney World, and Tokyo Disneyland. They need three years' hands-on experience with minicomputers manufactured by Data General, Intel, and General Automation and should be comfortable with languages such as Assembly, FORTRAN, and PL/1. There is hope for advancement to senior programmer, project manager, and other supervisory positions.

FOR DISCUSSION

1. Do you think that Walt Disney Productions could use the same computer programs in all its theme parks? Elaborate.
2. Are there any other entertainment industries that widely use computers? Elaborate.

OBJECTIVES

- ☐ To discuss the importance of quantitative analysis in managerial decision making and problem solving
- ☐ To identify the steps in the decision-making process
- ☐ To explain the difference between internal and external sources of data
- ☐ To explain some basic uses of statistics
- ☐ To describe decision theory and its applications

OUTLINE

KEY TERMS

ATTITUDINAL SURVEY
CENSUS
DECISION THEORY
DECISION TREE
DESCRIPTIVE STATISTICS
DIRECT OBSERVATION
HYPOTHESIS
INFERENTIAL STATISTICS
MEAN
MEDIAN
MODE
MODEL
OPERATIONS RESEARCH
PROBABILITY
QUANTITATIVE ANALYSIS
RANDOM SAMPLE
SAMPLE
STATISTICS
SURVEY

QUANTITATIVE METHODS

The Ratings Everyone Ignores

ROBERT MUSEL, Reprinted with permission from *TV Guide* ® Magazine.

Scene: a darkened screening room somewhere in London. Two British television executives are watching the pilot episode of a new series. As the video tape ends, one executive turns to the other and exclaims, "They're going to love this, J.B. People are going to love it!"

"I don't care whether they love it or hate it," growls J.B. "As long as they watch it."

That may sound callous, but our hypothetical TV executive is only being realistic. He knows that, just as in the United States, what makes a show a success—and draws in advertising dollars—is the number of viewers who watch it. Naturally, England has a ratings system for determining just how many people are watching any given show: it's called JICTAR and it's followed every bit as greedily as America's Nielsens.

But—and here is where England differs from the U.S. at present—England also has a secondary ratings system. This one measures not *how many* people are watching, but *how well* they like what they see: quality rather than quantity. Known as the Audience Reaction Assessment (AURA for short), it is a weekly survey put out by Britain's Independent Broadcasting Authority (IBA). But despite the fact that people in the television industry receive a copy of the survey every week, most of them react just the way the aforementioned J.B. would: they pay not the slightest attention to it.

So why, when they know that no one cares about the answer, does IBA bother to ask the audience how it liked what it saw on the screen that week?

"It's not a case of whether we want to do it. We've got to do it," said Dr. Ian Haldane, head of research for the IBA and the father of AURA. He explained that the decree to set up a qualitative ratings system came from Parliament 12 years ago. The IBA hastened to oblige, since Parliament is, in effect, its boss. Parliament originally created the IBA to supervise commercial television and specifically directed it to make arrangements "for ascertaining the state of public opinion concerning the programs and for encouraging the making of useful comments and suggestions by members of the public."

Now, depending on their mood, Haldane and his staff either can look back proudly on 12 years of achievement in setting up a complex sampling system, or they can regard them as 12 years of unmitigated frustration. After all, no one pays them much attention.

Don't assume that Haldane and his crew are naive about the financial realities of the television industry. "If you're running a commercial network and all you want to do is make money, then all you need to know are the quantitative ratings," Haldane says. Peter Dannheisser, senior research officer, agrees. "The advertisers are interested in the most-watched programs, not the most-loved programs," he says. But their hope is that someday commercial television will be so financially—and emotionally—secure that it will want to devote more time to improving programs. Then, they hope, AURA will make a difference.

Meanwhile, they keep their sophisticated polling system humming. Different regions of the country are covered separately. In London, for example, about 1000 viewers participate at any one time, and they are chosen by interviewers who work for an associated research group. The viewers are not told that the research is being conducted by the IBA because that might prejudice their answers. Those few panelists who happen to find out the purpose of the poll are quietly dropped. Every two weeks the 1000 viewers are sent diaries listing the programs for that period on both the independent commercial network and the BBC, which is noncommercial. The viewers note the shows they watch and rate each one according to how much or how little they enjoyed it. They also indicate their age, sex and occupation. AURA needs only about 500 responses a week for a firm statistical base.

When all the replies are processed, Haldane and his staff can arrive at an Appreciation Index (AI) for each show. Theoretically, the AI can range from 0 to 100, or, as Haldane puts it, "from rock bottom to sheer and utter perfection. But in point of fact, it doesn't work out that way. You get a range that goes roughly between 40 and 85. If the thing is awful, people switch it off and you never hear about it." Sometimes, though, some real surprises emerge. For example, you'd think that the shows with the highest numerical ratings would also score the highest enjoyment ratings. It ain't necessarily so.

"I can tell you there is no necessary relationship between enjoyment of a show and the size of an audience," Haldane says. "You can get programs of very small numerical ratings that are being very highly enjoyed. You can get programs of very high numerical ratings that are not enjoyed. Size of the audience alone is not always an indication of the enjoyment of the show. Size of the audience can depend on the day of the week, or the time of the day, whether it's snowing, what's opposite on the other channels, anything."

In a recent week in the action adventure-show category, for example, *Danger UXB,* a British series about a bomb squad, received the highest Appreciation Index: 86. By comparison, *Vega$* scored an Appreciation Index of 75, and *Petrocelli* 72. But *Charlie's Angels* and *Starsky & Hutch* both trailed with AIs of only 63—and yet almost as many viewers watched those shows as watched *Danger UXB.* People were tuned in, but apparently *not* turned on.

Children's programs are not listed in the adult diaries because there is a separate panel of children that reports every two months on programs for the young. Dannheisser, who organized the simplified diaries supplied to children aged 4 to 12, was told at the outset by skeptics that his task was impossible. Children, according to these naysayers, would be unable to make up their minds without help, and the assistance of their parents would influence their attitudes. Their memories are unreliable and their tastes are capricious. Luckily, Dannheisser found all these fears without basis.

"We found a terrific ability among children not only to give opinions, but to hold quite dramatically polarized opinions, too," he said. "The range of scores given by children is much wider than that given by adults. Children are willing to say when they hate something and when they love something."

Dannheisser, like Haldane, is disappointed that AURA's voice is so faint in the halls of power, but he considers it valuable nonetheless "as a contribution to the ongoing debate on improving programs." This is a growing American concern as well. Not long ago, the Markle Foundation, a group that specializes in the issues of mass communications, staged a symposium in New York to discuss organizing a system of quality rating for TV in the United States. The National Citizens Committee for Broadcasting said it is trying to raise money for viewer panels to sample the quality of American TV fare in the fall. Whether American producers will pay more heed to the quality ratings than the British will have to be seen.

Meanwhile, Haldane continues to study the quality of British programming, with "cajolery and persuasion" as his only weapons against offenders.

"If a series was made and it was very low in appreciation, we would not hesitate to point this out quite firmly to the program company and try to discourage them from putting the series on again. But," he adds, "I can't give you a specific instance of anything being shifted on the schedule or taken off the air because of AURA. I can't put my hand on my heart and say it has made any difference."

J.B. wouldn't argue with that.

TV ratings are only one form of quantitative analysis. In fact, the quantitative approach to management is widely used in business and government today, in all kinds of situations. This chapter describes some of the more common varieties and explains how they are used in managerial decision making.

The quantitative approach to management involves the use of mathematical techniques in the decision-making process. Although businesspeople have always considered such numerical factors as profits in their decisions about what goods to sell, this approach really got going during the late 1800s, when Frederick W. Taylor first applied the scientific method to management (see Chapter 5). The quantitative approach has become more and more appropriate as our environment has become more complex. And with the increased availability of computers, managers are more capable than ever of using sophisticated quantitative techniques for summarizing and analyzing data.

Quantitative Analysis

All too often, important organizational decisions are "seat of the pants" or "gut" decisions that rely on personal experience, mental state, and intuitive feel for a problem. In contrast, **quantitative analysis** encourages decision makers to identify all relevant data—objective and subjective—and then to express problems in mathematical or graphical form. This information, when combined with expertise and subjective judgment, helps managers reach sound decisions.

A BRIEF HISTORY

Although Taylor can probably be considered the father of scientific management, a contemporary, Henry L. Gantt, had a broader influence on the quantitative approach to management. Specifically, Gantt advocated the application of scientific research principles to managerial decision making. His work eventually led to the field of **operations research.** A discipline that uses quantitative analysis in decision making and an interdisciplinary, team approach to solving business problems.

The quantitative approach and scientific analysis of management problems gained a great deal of attention during World Wars I and II. In 1914 and 1915, F. W. Lanchester in England tested a model of battlefield decision making against current battle problems. The model proved helpful in planning battles and in determining how such factors as number of troops and terrain would affect the outcome of a particular encounter. This technique was applied again during World War II.

During World War II, increased production needs encouraged the development of the quantitative approach. The military continued to use such methods after the war. As a result, industry tended to use these more sophisticated techniques as well. It was readily apparent that wartime was not the only time they could be useful.

THE ROLE OF QUANTITATIVE ANALYSIS

It should be noted that subjective factors are not eliminated when a quantitative technique is applied. Quantitative techniques merely help measure the possible impact of all factors that can be quantified—subjective and objective. For example, say that you want to buy a car. Your peers drive Volkswagens, and you'd like to surpass them. On the other hand, your funds are somewhat limited, and small, gas-efficient cars are

Business in Action

PORTFOLIO V: QUANTITATIVE DECISION MAKING

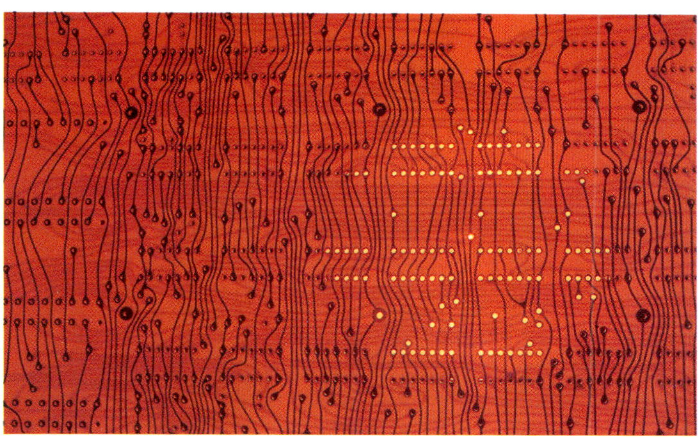

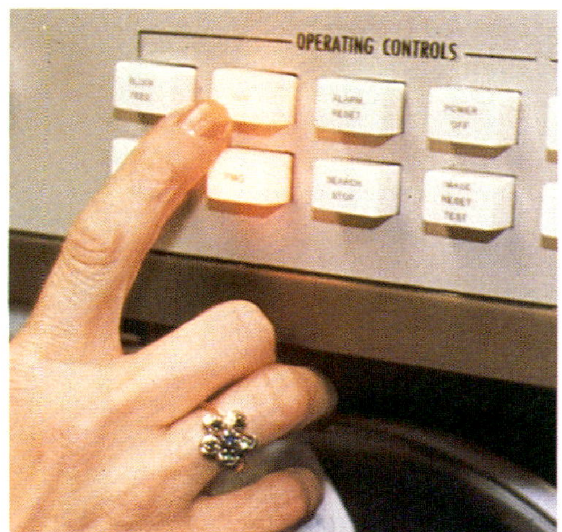
OPERATING CONTROLS
ALARM RESET
POWER OFF
SEARCH STOP

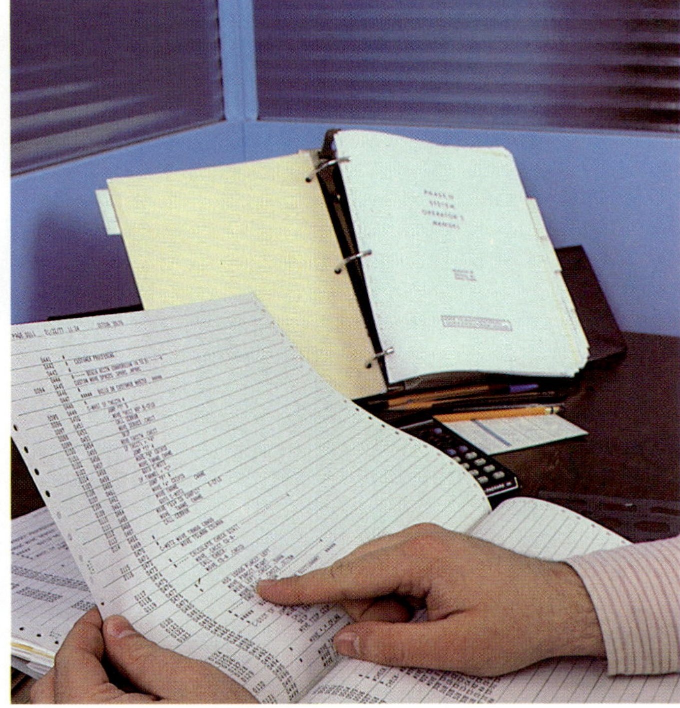
PHASE II
SYSTEM
OPERATOR'S
MANUAL

popular. You spend six weekends in a row driving cars—everything from the Dodge Omni to the Datsun 280ZX to the Buick Riviera. The decision is tough, but you prefer the Datsun. After all, it's small, so it probably saves gas. And it's a sports model, so you're going to feel great driving it. The question is, Is this an economically feasible decision?

Consider the following somewhat hypothetical figures on the costs of the three cars you're most interested in (the per mile estimates include gas, maintenance, and the like):

	Estimated Purchase Price	**Estimated Cost per Mile**
Dodge Omni	$ 5,580	18¢
Datsun 280ZX	$15,120	36¢
Buick Riviera	$10,080	24¢

Clearly, the Datsun 280ZX is more expensive to buy and to drive than the Omni or Buick. Now you can judge how much the subjective factors—like driving pleasure and status—are actually worth.

The same situation arises in business management. Decisions about inventory policy, credit policy, and alternative financing sources, for example, can obviously be approached from a quantitative perspective. But sometimes financial managers decide that the good relationship they have had over the years with one bank offsets the lower interest rate they might obtain elsewhere. The point of quantitative analysis, however, is that they can evaluate the worth of such issues in a more objective fashion.

MANAGEMENT DECISION MAKING

Why should quantitative analysis be gaining in popularity? Perhaps because it is becoming more and more difficult to deal with all the factors in a business problem. It has become necessary to summarize, weed out, analyze and quantify data to be used in decisions relating to inventory control, resource allocation, information system design, product mix determinations, new product analysis, manpower planning, credit policy decisions, investment analysis, and make-or-buy decisions. Exhibit 21.1 outlines the decision-making process and shows where quantitative analysis enters the process.

Quantitative techniques save money by providing a standardized way of making decisions that must be made repeatedly. By establishing set procedures for ordering inventory, for example, management can spend more time on the long-range, nonrepetitive decisions.

Quantitative analysis is also helpful when a problem involves large sums of money, in which case managers want to be certain that they have considered all relevant factors. For example, before making any large capital expenditures, it is important to estimate and quantify the costs and benefits associated with all options. It is then possible to use some type of analytical model to determine whether a given investment is worthwhile.

In essence, the quantitative approach forces managers to identify and quantify the factors that are likely to have an impact on a decision. Furthermore, such analysis helps managers defend their conclusions to superiors, particularly in areas that are new to the managers. If they have no past experience in an area, it can be difficult to make or defend a decision.

EXHIBIT 21.1 Overview of the Decision-Making Process

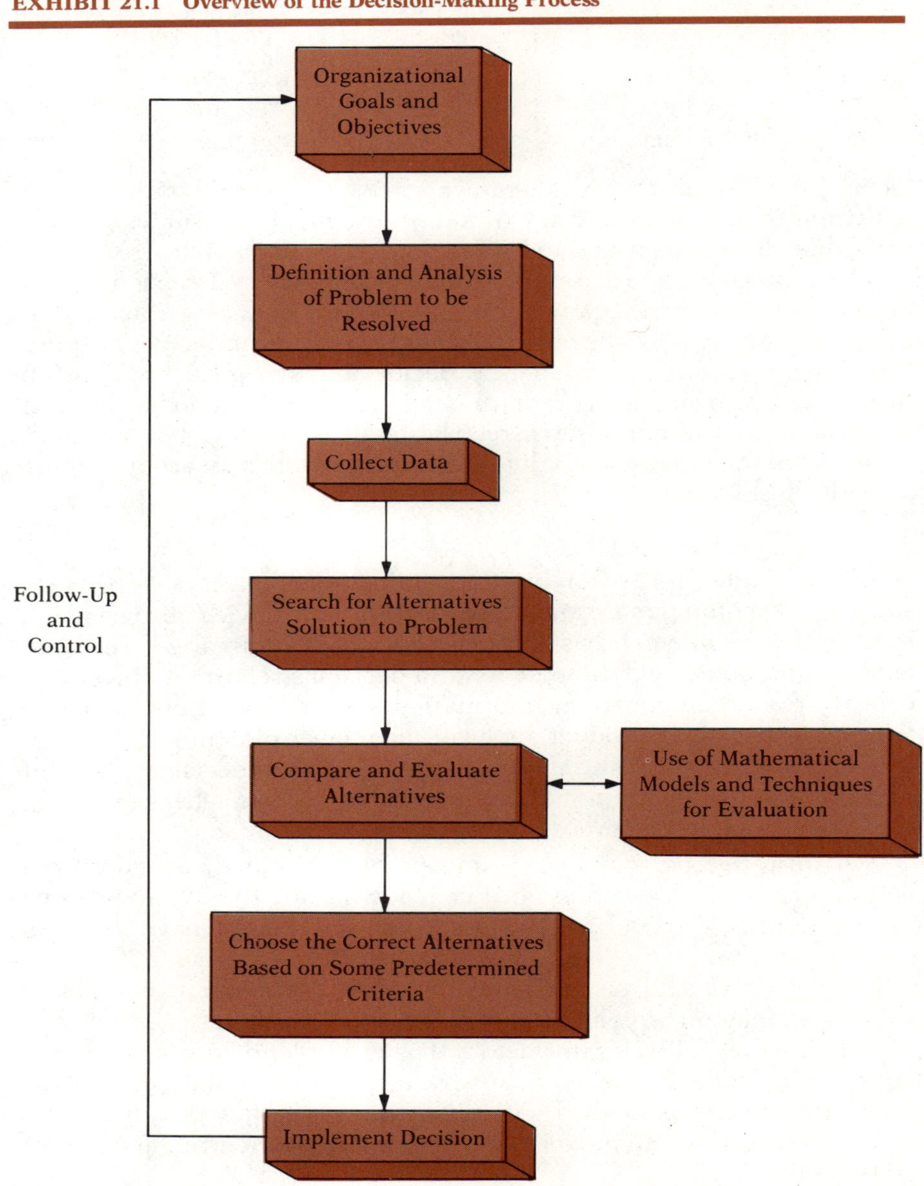

It should be noted that quantitative methods are not all elaborate, incomprehensible, frightening, and overwhelming. For example, the financial statements discussed Chapter 19 are forms of quantitative analysis. Simple ratio calculations based on these statements are another form of quantitative analysis. Even more mathematical techniques need not be unnerving. Many can be applied with rather simple computer programs, and many others are actually rather simple once one reaches a basic level of understanding.

The Scientific Method in Management

As we mentioned earlier, Henry Gantt was one of the first businesspeople to formally apply the principles of scientific research to the solution of management problems. The scientific method, as you may recall from science class, is a series of steps for the objective analysis of problems and possible solutions. Management decision making follows a similar series of steps.

STEPS IN SCIENTIFIC DECISION MAKING

Exhibit 21.2 compares the steps involved in scientific research and in scientific management. The three main phases of both approaches are (1) identifying and specifying the problem, (2) finding possible courses of action, and (3) choosing among alternative courses of action. The idea is to accumulate facts and then to formulate a theory about the significance of the information. The theory is often modified to correspond with reality.

Problem Identification

The purpose of the first stage is to find the problems that deserve the attention of managers. It is also important to specify the form the solution should be in and the nature of the expected solution. For example, a music store manager may have noticed that she can never keep in stock enough albums by a particular singer. This is indeed a problem, but it indicates an even greater problem: she is probably losing business to the store on the next block.

EXHIBIT 21.2 Steps in Scientific Decision Making

Scientific Method	Scientific Management
1 Observation	Problem identification
2 Definition of problem	Analysis of problem
3 Formulation of hypothesis	Construction of model
4 Experimentation	Solution and qualification of model
5 Verification	Application of model

Analysis of the Problem

If it appears that further analysis is beneficial, the manager should determine what key factors are likely to influence the decision. For example, are people going to the competing music store primarily to buy the particular singer's albums? If so, is the demand for this singer's albums only temporary, or is it part of a trend? Would former patrons return if more of this singer's albums were in stock? What are the costs and benefits of keeping more of these albums in stock? The music store manager must calculate the amount of lost business, the cost of purchasing more of this singer's albums, and the amount of storage space needed to stock the additional albums.

As you can see, this is a clarification stage—specifying the limits of the investigation, the approach to be followed, and the assumptions to be made. This stage should be as specific and detailed as possible to avoid time-consuming and possibly costly redundancies or omissions of information.

Construction of a Model

In the third stage, the manager should establish the parameters of the solution. In other words, what are the expected results of the possible solution? This sort of "if . . . then" statement is a **hypothesis** in scientific terminology. In scientific management, the hypothesis is represented by a **model**—a mathematical or graphical representation of a real-world situation. Construction of a model enables a manager to test the factors that have an effect on the solution.

A model does not have to be an extensive or elaborate construct. The basic accounting equation—Assets = Liabilities + Equity—is a model of the financial condition of a company. The income equation—Revenue − Expenses = Profit—is also a model.

The music store manager might make the decision to stock the additional albums if the benefits of doing so exceeded the costs. Thus, her simple decision model would be to stock the albums if the difference between benefits minus costs is positive.

Formulation of the model is probably the most crucial stage in scientific decision making. If assumptions are ignored or misstated, the model will fail to represent the real world accurately. Thus the solution or decision will be flawed.

Solution and Qualification of the Model

The next step is to test the model to see if it accounts for all the factors and to see whether the solutions appear reasonable. The music store manager would plug her data into the model and check to see whether it came out negative (indicating that the costs outweighed the benefits) or positive.

Highlight Predicting the Outcome of Battle

If you're going to fight a war, don't use volunteers. This would seem to be the rule suggested by a study recently conducted by the Historical Evaluation and Research Organization (HERO) in Dunn Loring, Virginia. Through the use of computerized mathematical models, it was determined that the top Allied fighting unit in World War II (the 88th Infantry Division) was made up entirely of draftees. Furthermore, draftee units outperformed not only all-volunteer Army units but also National Guard units.

The original intent of HERO's computerized model was to predict mathematically the outcome of certain battles that occurred during World War II. The model also allowed researchers to rank the combat effectiveness of certain American, British, and German military units. Using such measurable factors as weapons, number of troops, weather and estimates of training, motivation, and the like, the model allowed researchers to predict which unit should have won each battle. The model's predictions were correct 85 to 95 percent of the time.

It is tempting to draw conclusions from this model about what factors are important in war and about the apparent effectiveness of nonvolunteers, but remember that HERO's model is historical and may not really imply any cause-and-effect relationships. To make it useful for prediction and planning, much more information must be gathered, quantified, and analyzed.

The test may indicate that additional assumptions or limitations have to be specified. It is also necessary at this stage to specify under what conditions the model is relevant and under what conditions the model will *not* work.

Application of the Model

The final step in scientific decision making is to apply the model to the real-world situation. The music store manager, for example, might buy a certain number of additional albums and would watch for increased sales. A few refinements may still be necessary, but if the previous steps were performed properly, the decision should at least be acceptable. This stage may also show that further adjustments to the model are necessary.

A COMPREHENSIVE EXAMPLE

Let's return to the question of buying a car to see how the scientific method might be applied to decision making. First, the problem may be identified in a number of ways. Perhaps the old car died on the freeway and was taken away for burial. Perhaps you have a standard policy to buy a new car every two years. Perhaps your peers have purchased new cars, and you are feeling pressure to do so. In any case, you determine that you want to solve the problem by purchasing a new car. You could analyze all the cars on the market, but you decide that the costs of such analysis are too great for the benefits—so you will analyze only the Dodge Omni, the Datsun 280ZX, and the Buick Riviera.

Highlight Why Managers Make Bad Decisions

In recent years, a number of studies have indicated that managers make bad decisions because of incompetence, or an inability to properly organize the decision-making process. The most common sources of problems:

- Not having a clear idea of what the problem is
- Not knowing what information is relevant to a particular decision under review
- Having incomplete information or, in some cases, having too much
- Not knowing how to organize information once it is obtained
- Relying solely on a subjective evaluation of alternatives, without using quantitative techniques
- Not implementing the decision once it is made

Successful decision makers are not born; they acquire their skill through experience, an application of common sense, and the use of whatever techniques—quantitative or otherwise—can assist them in decision making.

In analyzing the problem, you determine that the key factors influencing your decision are cost, mileage, and personal gratification. You assume that all cars will be available to you.

To build the model, you simply formulate the problem by stating that the purchase decision is a function of the quantifiable factors of price and mileage: Purchase = *f*(Price, Mileage). You can further state that the optimal solution is the one that results in the lowest monthly cost based on a three-year life (assuming the car has no value at the end of this period) and 1,000 miles per month of driving. For example, if the Omni's price is \$5,580 and the cost per mile is 18 cents, the monthly cost is

$$C_O = \frac{\$5{,}580}{36 \text{ months}} + (\$0.18 \times 1{,}000 \text{ miles}) = \$155 + \$180 = \$335 \text{ per month}$$

The Datsun's monthly cost would be

$$C_D = \$420 + \$360 = \$780$$

The Buick Riviera's monthly cost would be

$$C_B = \$280 + \$240 = \$520$$

You can solve the problem by comparing the monthly costs. If your only criterion was cost per month, you would choose the Omni. However, personal gratification is also a factor. Now that you have information on what you are paying for this subjective factor, you are free to choose either of the other two cars.

To apply the model, you might actually purchase the Datsun. You would then have an opportunity to verify your cost estimates and to evaluate the subjective factor that caused you to buy it. You might also have an opportunity to check the estimates on the Omni and the Buick. If you are satisfied with the results, you could use the same model for a future car purchase. Or perhaps you will find that you left out important data or that you included a factor that is not really important to you.

Data Gathering

Data gathering is an important part of quantitative analysis. It involves assembling information from one or more sources—internal and/or external. In essence, this data is grist for the quantitative mill.

The internal sources of data include accounting records, customer records, personnel records, and so forth. External sources include information published by government agencies or private organizations as well as information that can be gathered by the business or a consulting group. Census, business, and economic data are available from many government agencies; private publications of potential value are Dunn & Bradstreet's compilations of financial and marketing data, Moody's manuals, the *Fortune* directory, and many others. The internal and published data are usually the most accessible and probably the least costly. They merely need to be summarized and presented in some usable manner.

Although it is expensive and time-consuming, gathering original data often provides the most relevant information. The two chief sources of original data are direct observation of behavior and surveys. **Direct observation** involves measuring and recording the behavior of people or activities. This sort of investigation was used in the famous time-and-motion studies to determine the most efficient methods of production.

"Damn it, you guys are simply not living up to the printout!"

Surveys are useful when the number of people to be studied is too large for direct observation or when their opinions, ideas, or particular characteristics are needed. The **census** conducted every ten years by the federal government is a survey of all the people in the United States. Most **surveys,** however, collect data from only a select group of people—a **sample**—rather than from all the people in the population. The answers provided by this smaller group can be used to determine what the entire group is thinking. This approach is widely used in predicting political races, rating television shows, and determining what the public feels about a particular issue. Sample surveys that give everyone in the population an equal chance of being selected for the survey are considered **random sample** surveys.

Surveys may be conducted through the mail, over the telephone, and by personal interview. For example, in the process of deciding which car to buy, you might send letters to current owners of each model, asking for a history of problems or benefits. You might then telephone selected owners to obtain the same information and personally interview friends and neighbors. In general, the mail questionnaire can generally be sent to larger numbers of people than can be interviewed on the telephone or in person, but people often do not respond to mail surveys. Telephone interviews are effective because there is direct contact, but they must be kept short. Personal interviews are the most effective, because they offer opportunities for clarifying questions and introducing new questions, but they are more time-consuming and costly.

Basic Quantitative Approaches

STATISTICS

Once data have been gathered, they must be assembled in useful form. Decision making can proceed only if data have been organized in logical categories or sequences. Two of the most common methods for organizing data are the use of statistics and the use of decision theory. Managers often use both methods simultaneously.

The first step in simplifying masses of data into some understandable form is commonly the compilation of **statistics**—the presentation of information in numerical form.

Descriptive statistics are data organized, summarized, and presented in a form that a manager may find useful for decision making. The numbers in a firm's balance sheet and income statement are descriptive statistics. The test scores and grade-point averages used in college admittance procedures are descriptive statistics. Such statistics enable managers to compare and contrast groups, individuals, products, or companies.

There are three basic statistics used to describe subpopulations. They are the mean, the median, and the mode—the three Ms of statistics. The **mean** is simply the arithmetic average. Do you want to find the mean profit in some industry you want to enter? Just add up the profits of all the companies in the industry and divide by the number of companies. The **median** is the middle score in a set of numbers. If your company has the median rate of profitability, half of the other compa-

Highlight Monitoring the Trends, Surveying the Market

In the late 1950s, the Ford Motor Company wished to market an "affordable" luxury car. Its market researchers had done surveys on the acceptability of such a car, and the results were favorable. Thus Ford retooled for the production of "the car of the future"—the Edsel.

But the Edsel failed miserably from the beginning. What went wrong? Hadn't market research done its job? Unfortunately, because the public's attitudes change rapidly, this market information about the Edsel's acceptability was good, at best, for three to four months. In the eighteen months between the survey report and Ford's decision to produce the Edsel, the public had gone from being enamored with chrome rocketships and space travel to being caught up in the "Pepsi generation." Americans were clamoring for "young-looking" sports cars just when the futuristic Edsels were rolling off the assembly line. The result was one of the biggest disasters in auto history.

Shortly thereafter, in an effort to recoup its losses and its lost markets. Ford responded to more current market surveys. This time, it gave America the car it wanted—the industry's most successful car ever—the Ford Mustang.

nies in your industry have less profitability and the other half have higher profitability. Finally, the **mode** is the most frequent value in a set of numbers. Say that the following rates of profitability were observed in your industry: 4 percent, 3 percent, 1 percent, 10 percent, 6 percent, 11 percent, 7 percent, 6 percent. The mode would be 6 percent.

Inferential statistics are data drawn from some information base, but they do not include all possible information. They allow the user to infer a conclusion about an entire group without having to take the time or spend the money to survey or test the entire group. Market research and political predictions often involve the use of inferential statistics. Inferential statistics are also frequently used for decision making under uncertain conditions. When all the facts cannot be known—possibly because the number of people or factors are too great or because the relevant information concerns the future—inferential statistics can be used to make forecasts.

It is frequently helpful to present statistical summaries in some visual form. Line charts, bar charts, and pie charts (like those in Exhibit 21.3) often help managers gain fresh insights into the relationships among statistics.

DECISION THEORY

Sometimes there are a number of alternatives for a manager to choose from, and the future is uncertain or risky. In such cases, **decision theory** can be used to determine the most effective strategy to follow. For example, when considering how many bathing suits to stock for a given summer season, a manager knows neither the demand for the bathing suits (because it is in the future) nor the weather conditions that will prevail. Other areas where decision theory is appropriate are decisions about production volume, the size of a computer system, the scope of distribution for a product (whether local or national), the distribution of an advertising budget among different media, and the like.

EXHIBIT 21.3 Formats for Statistical Presentation

Pie Chart

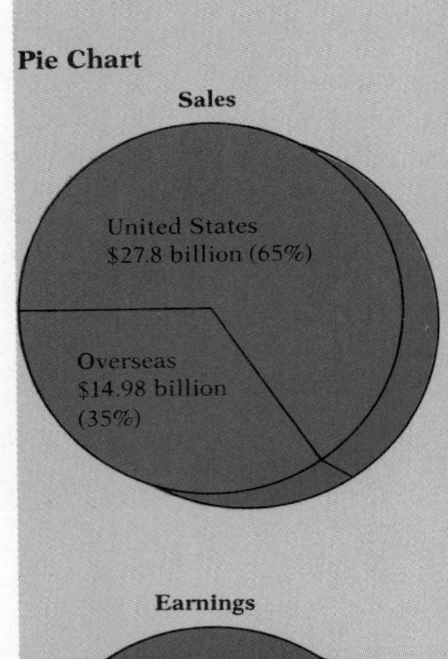

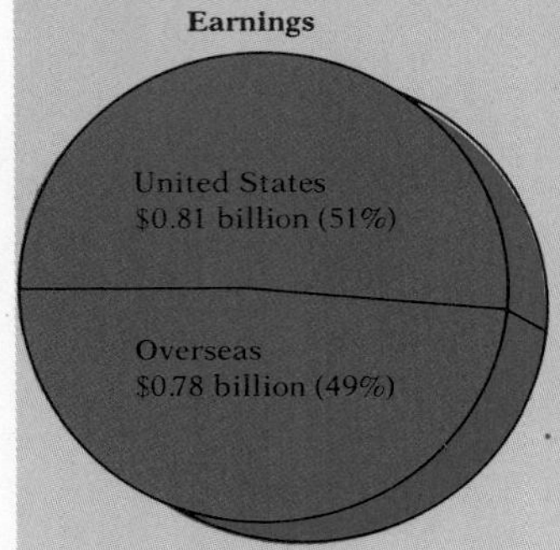

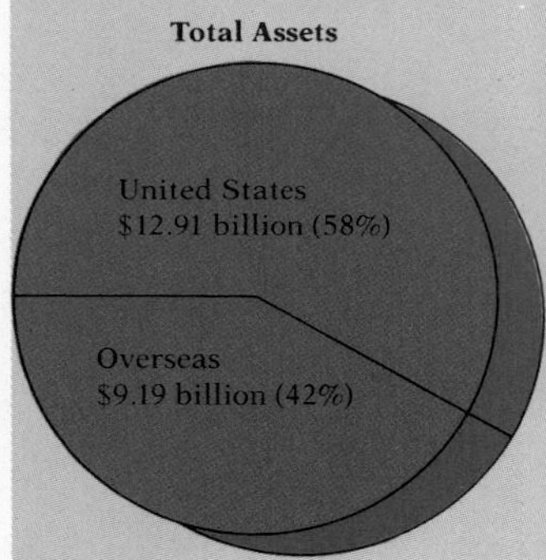

Bar Chart

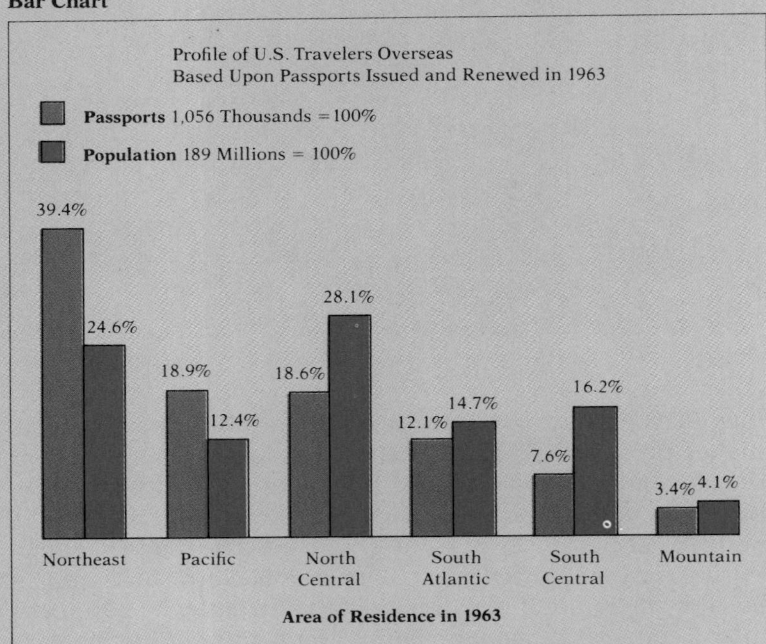

Line Chart

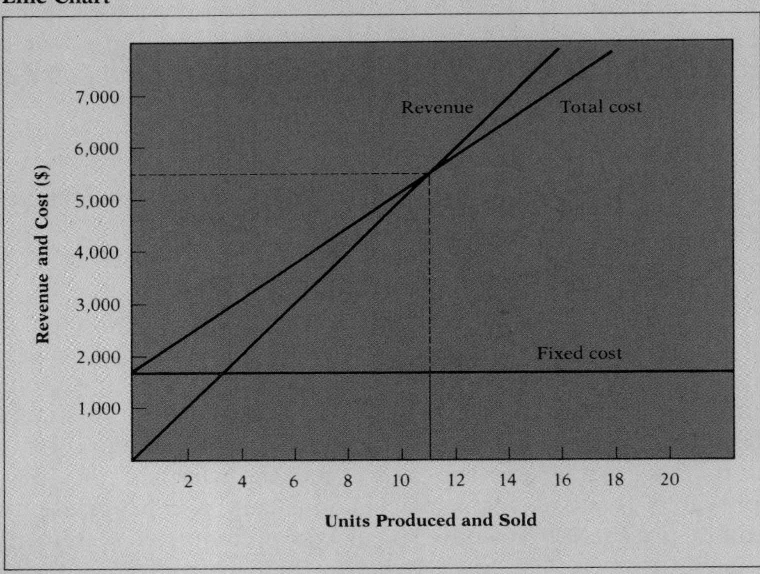

Highlight Evaluating TV Shows

The well-known Nielsen ratings tell TV executives which television programs are being watched and are therefore likely to stay on the air. But what determines which programs get on the air in the first place?

Attitudinal surveys are used to determine what people think about a program and whether they will watch a program if it is put on the air. Questionnaires, telephone surveys, and preliminary showings of prospective programs are all used to determine what people like, what they don't like, and what they want to see on television.

Such surveys are hazardous. Unlike Nielsen's surveys, which simply record what is being watched, attitudinal surveys run up against the respondents' self-image. People may actually watch a show about two girls and a guy living together, but they may tell survey researchers that they want more documentaries and more educational television. Furthermore, attitudinal surveys, by looking for common ground, seldom encourage originality and creativity. *All in the Family* failed dismally when it was originally pretested.

So why is time, money, and effort spent on such research? Television executives report that it may assist in borderline cases and may guide the development of currently popular shows. Most probably, however, it is used to reinforce their hunches, judgments, and opinions: "Give me some facts to support what I'm going to do anyway."

The basic procedure in decision theory is to list all possible alternative decisions. The second step is to list all possible conditions that will affect the decision, such as high demand for the product or no demand for it. If possible, managers should assign probabilities to each of these conditions. The term **probability** refers to the likelihood that a future event will take place. Probabilities are usually stated on a percentage basis. For example, the probability of tossing a heads on the flip of a coin is 50 percent. By making a series of calculations and judgments, managers can then determine the "best" decision. "Optimal" solutions are generally unlikely, because the conditions impinging on a problem are infinite. It would be unreasonable to expect anyone to be able to consider them all.

One common form of analysis is the **decision tree,** which is a methodical presentation of conditions and alternatives for coping with each condition. If constructed properly, a decision tree can be of assistance in leading one to a "good" decision. Exhibit 21.4 is an example of a decision tree.

Quantitative Methods in Perspective

Quantitative methods are tools to assist managers in decision making. They are not designed to replace managers or their experience. In fact, managers play a crucial role by keeping the decision and the limitations of the model in perspective. For example, studies have indicated that the money spent to encourage motorcycle riders to wear helmets has saved numerous lives. Other studies have shown that the enormous amounts spent on cancer research have not saved so many lives. But it would clearly be fallacious to conclude that funds should be withdrawn from cancer research and channeled into advertising for motorcycle safety equipment. Managers must continue to rely on their judgment

EXHIBIT 21.4 Sample Decision Tree

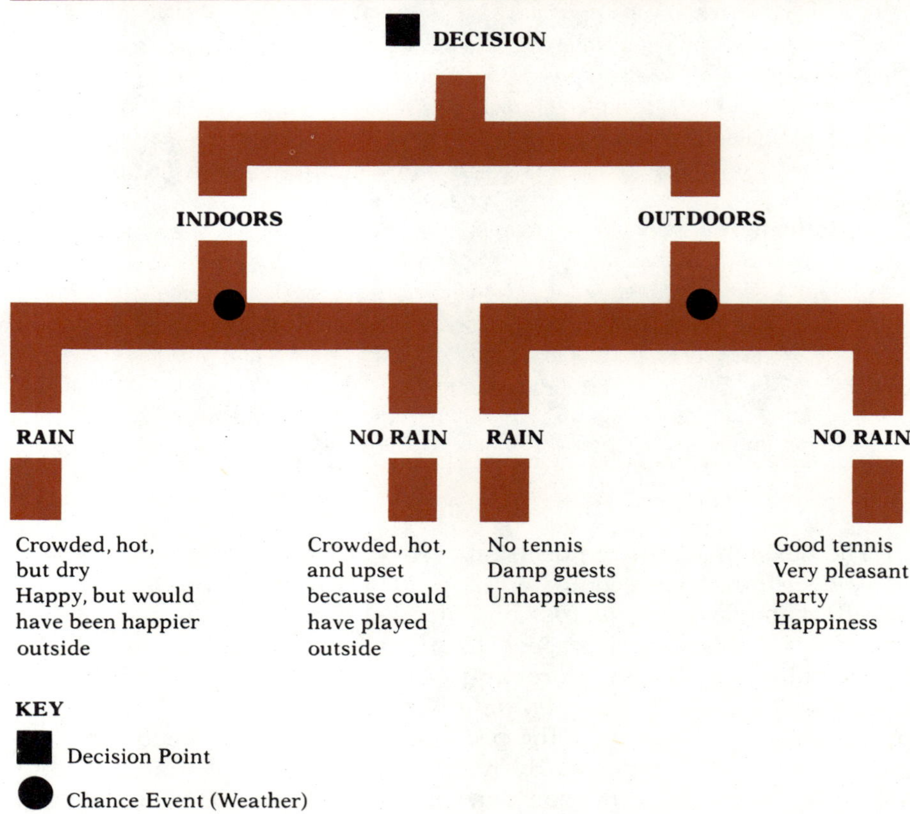

for those factors that cannot be quantified into a mathematical model.

Another warning: Managers must unquestionably be aware of the "garbage in, garbage out" syndrome in quantitative analysis (refer to Chapter 20). The assumptions, limitations, and alternatives of any quantitative analysis are prepared by human beings and therefore subject to all the error and ill use accompanying human invention. Faulty methods or data cannot produce a good decision. In short, there is no substitute for sound judgment and realistic analysis.

- Since their introduction in the late 1800s and their expanded use during World War II, the techniques of quantitative analysis have gained widespread acceptance as an aid to managerial decision making.
- Quantitative analysis helps decision makers specify the objective aspects of a particular problem situation, standardize their decision making process, and become make systematic in decision making.

- As problems become more complex and as the costs decrease for making routine decisions with a computer or some standardized form, quantitative techniques can be expected to become more popular. These techniques are widely used in the private and public sectors to solve diverse types of management problems.
- The application of the scientific method to managerial decision making has assisted managers in clarifying their problems, their alternatives, and their decisions. The five basic steps of scientific analysis are identifying the problem, analyzing the problem, building a model, solving and qualifying the model, and applying the model.
- The basic quantitative techniques available to managers include statistics and decision theory. Statistics—descriptive and inferential—are particularly helpful to managers in organizing and analyzing masses of data while decision theory provides guidance for managers on the process of decision making.
- There are many sources of data—internal and external—available to firm. Internal sources are the most readily available and least expensive to acquire. However, external sources—in particular survey's and interviews—may be more appropriate if original data is required.
- Managers must be careful to treat quantitative techniques as tools. Quantitative analysis cannot replace judgement and consideration of subjective factors.

1. What are quantitative techniques of analysis? Why are they useful to managers?
2. How would you apply scientific analysis to the decision of whether to rent or buy a home? What subjective factors might influence such a decision?
3. What statistics might affect your decision to invest in a particular company?
4. What statistics would you find useful if you were considering opening a short-order hamburger stand?
5. How would you apply a decision-tree analysis to the question of how large a computer system your company needs?
6. What techniques do you think would be useful in determining the share of the frozen-food market that your company might have next year?
7. Compare a census to a sample. What are the pros and cons of each as a method of collecting data?
8. How might statistics such as test scores and grade-point averages be misleading? What other factors might be important in deciding which students to admit to college?

APPLICATION

Gulf Oil Corporation

Spindletop, the most famous oil well in the world, roared in on January 10, 1901; it established Texas as a major oil source. The well was financed with $300,000 borrowed from a Mellon-controlled Pittsburgh bank. In May, Andrew W. and Richard B. Mellon organized the J. M. Guffey Petroleum Company and acquired the assets of the partnership that had drilled Spindletop (Mr. Guffey being one of them). The Gulf Refining Company was chartered by the Mellons on November 10, and construction began on a Texas-based refinery to manufacture and market Spindletop oil. Crude oil production was 670,000 barrels in that first year.

Today, Gulf Oil Corporation produces approximately 650 million barrels of oil per year. It employs some 58,000 people all over the world and has assets of $15 billion. In addition, Gulf has become a "total energy" company: It finds and produces crude oil and natural gas, refines crude oil, processes gas and gas liquids, mines coal and uranium, produces synthetic fuels made from coal, and manufactures chemicals and petrochemicals.

SPECIALIZATION

For three-quarters of a century, Gulf Oil Corporation was vertically integrated: A single organization managed all operations from wellhead to pump. Faced with problems in operating a centralized organization of its size and complexity, Gulf adopted a new system for doing business in 1975. Now seven functional companies exist each operating under the Gulf corporate umbrella. These companies include the: Gulf Oil Exploration and Production, Gulf Mineral Resources, Gulf Refining and Marketing, Gulf Trading and Transportation, Gulf Oil Chemicals, Gulf Service and Technology and Gulf Canada.

The Gulf Science and Technology Company, for example, was formed to provide complete technical support to all Gulf companies—from research and development to ongoing technical services, to the development of technical and managerial skills for people throughout the corporation. Part of this company, the Gulf Management Science Group, provides "assistance to the Gulf Companies and Corporate Departments in the application of Management Science techniques to the solution of problems and decisions facing management." The term *management science* refers to the use of quantitative techniques in managerial decision making. As you can see, Gulf has placed great importance on using analytical and quantitative approaches to decision making and problem solving.

Spindletop—January 10, 1901

THE MANAGEMENT SCIENCE GROUP

The people working in this group are highly trained in the application of quantitative methods and operations research and have years of experience with Gulf Corporation. Each professional in the group tends to specialize in one or more types of problems or in the use of a particular quantitative method. Some of these specialties:

- Mathematical models: unit and plant scheduling and planning; crude oil or feedstock evaluation; gasoline blending; refining, supply, distribution, and marketing; optimum distribution and warehousing; site evaluation)
- Energy forecasting
- Financial models
- Risk analysis studies
- Decision analysis
- Product forecasting
- Budgeting techniques and procedures
- Evaluation of information requirements
- Statistical studies
- Assistance in establishing planning procedures

The Gulf Management Science Group provides its services to others in the corporation on a consulting basis. Thus the nature of the problems and projects its members face is ever-changing. The following is a brief description of a few of the projects conducted by the group:

1. *U.S. energy model* Specifies the energy requirements, raw material sources, and conversion and distribution facilities in the United States by geographic region. This model can be used in making strategic decisions about resource acquisition, research and development priorities, development of conversion processes, and marketing of products.
2. *Service station site evaluation model* Used to estimate the volume of gasoline that could be sold at a given location, based on its traffic volume, its position relative to the traffic flow, and the number of pumps. This model pinpoints the most critical physical characteristics of the location and the station.
3. *Crude oil evaluation model* Used to determine the least costly method of refining oil in different types of refineries. It is also used in determining the impact, in financial and quality terms, of using a given crude oil alone or in conjunction with other crudes.
4. *Capital expenditure analysis* Involves an analysis of the potential risks and rewards associated with alternative investment opportunities. Several quantitative techniques can be used to compute the expected returns and risks of a project.

CAREER OPPORTUNITIES

Normally people who join the Gulf Management Science Group have an advanced degree or experience in the petroleum industry. Degrees are usually in Petroleum, Chemical, or Industrial Engineering; Operations Research; Economics; or Statistics. Depending on the employee's experience and expertise, initial assignments may involve working on a task force composed of other group members and operating personnel to solve a particular problem, to analyze a situation independently, or to develop a quantitative technique or a model that will be used by operating personnel.

FOR DISCUSSION

1. How might Gulf gather the data it needs to analyze potential locations for a service station? What specific data do you feel are needed?
2. How does the quantitative approach differ when doing a capital expenditure analysis as compared to developing a crude-oil refining model?

PART VI

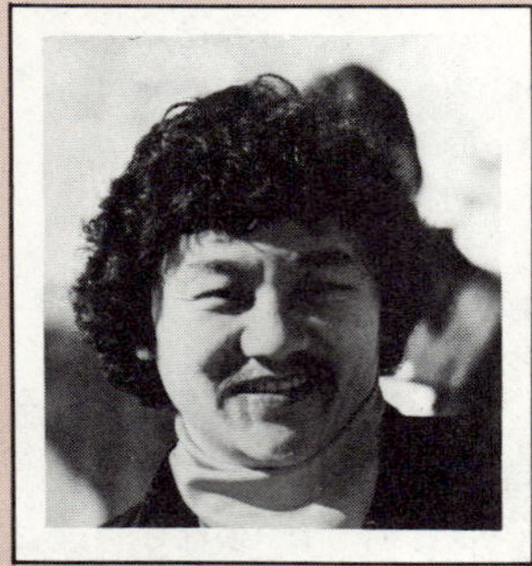

ROCKY AOKI

His name was Hiroaki, and he came to the United States in 1959 on a college wrestling tour. He liked New York and stayed, going to City College and working as a dishwasher, parking lot attendant, and ice cream man. By graduation in 1963, Rocky Aoki, his Americanization proclaimed in his new name, had opened a small restaurant on Manhattan's West Side.

Aoki worked eighteen hours a day to get Benihana of Tokyo going. Against all odds, he sat strangers together at large tables. He made it work by turning meals into "entertainment," dispatching a cook to prepare meals on a grill right at the table. Soon Benihana East, appeared, followed by a larger Benihana Palace. Throughout the late 1960s, Aoki opened new restaurants. When the chain grew beyond his immediate administrative capabilities, he launched a separate franchise operation. Rocky says, "The money is really here in America. In Japan, no one moves to top until someone dies off."

SR. COST ANALYST

re a strong local mfr with excellent history of rapid notions? Suburban firm is ing individual with 3+ yrs exp to work in close coop- on with their Upper MW plants. MBA almost a must. ry to $28,000. Job #1279.

CONTROLLER (Service Co)

you a take-charge person hands-on systems (EDP) Our client is ready to make cision before New Years. A company bkgd with an essive flair for getting s done is required. Salary o High Twenties. Job #1301.

ROBERT HALF

2236 IDS Center
Minneapolis, MN 55402
Chuck Squires, CPC
(612) 339-9001

7901 Xerxes Ave South
Bloomington, MN 55431
arb Hammerberg, CPC

ACCOUNTANT

COST ACCOUNTANT

To assume cost accounting duties with a medium size manufacturing firm. A minimum of one year cost accounting experience in a manufacturing setting is required. Excellent salary and benefits. Contact: Tonmy Sworsky

TRANSPORTATION EQUIPMENT CORP.

900 6th Ave SE
Mpls. Mn 55414
378-1100
Equal Opp. Employer M/F

ACCOUNTANT

CPA or equiv w/2-4 yrs audit and tax exper wanted immed. Exc opportunity for advancement with a quality-oriented, fast-growing CPA firm. Salary commensurate w/exper. Please send resumes to: Fredrickson and Kolquist, CPA's, 700 First National Bank Bldg, Duluth, MN 55802 or call (218)727-8030. All inquiries kept confidential.

ACCOUNTANT-Degreed accountant w/2-4 yrs exp. To assume comptroller position in lg Mpls non-profit organization. Relaxed atmosphere, exc. benefits, salary negotiable. 871-4555.

ACCOUNTANT

Mid America Dairymen Inc., 2424 Territorial Rd. Midway area, St. Paul, needs individual with accounting degree for supervisor of accounts payable & accounts receivable. Would also work into the general accounting area. 1-3 yrs. mfg experience, preferably in dairy industry.

from IA/MN border. Call or write today.

AGRIcareers, Inc.

515-394-3145
NEW HAMPTON, IA 50659

AGRI-BUSINESS

PLANT ENGINEER

Needed for Mn. grain processing plant. Need ME or ChE degree & 2+ yrs. related exper. in grain, chemical or food industry. Upper $20s. Job#376

SALES PROJECT ENG.

To recommend new dairy & food processing equip., present quotes, supervise installation & start-up. Need degree & exper. w/ultra filtration & reverse osmosis equip. Definite plus to $32K. 3 Wi. & Maine locations. Job#379

FEED SALES/MANAGEMENT

Our client feed companies currently have openings in Mn., Ia. & Neb. Previous feed or related sales exper. & degree preferred. $15-$24K base, car, comm., exp. & benefits. Job#332

AG RETAIL MANAGER

Needed by specialized farm equip. distributor in So. Wisc. Req. 3+ yrs. ag equip. retail mgmt. exp. Ag degree pref. Salary $25-$40K, benefits, etc. Job#395.

MANAGEMENT TRAINEE

Supervisory exper. & food or

needs A/V tech. Responsibilities include new equipt check-out, in-house & field service, installations throughout USA, etc. Call 835-5787 for details.

AUDIT

INTERNAL AUDIT MANAGER

The Internal Audit Manager will be charged with setting up & directing the internal audit function. The applicant must be degreed with 2-4 yrs. public accounting or internal audit experience. Communication skills & an interest or experience in the aviation industry will be a plus.
Travel will be approximately 50% including trips to most major U.S. cities & some international cities.
Position is with a publicly traded, $100 dillion distributor & reports to the V.P. Finance. Competitive salary & benefits.
Send your resume to:
V. P. Finance, P. O. Box 1898, St. Paul, MN 55111

AUDITOR

Audit & hotel experience pref. Hrs 10pm-6am. For info, please contact the Granada Royale at 884-4811, ask for Mike.

AUDITOR-NIGHTS

F&B. Full time. Must have good figure aptitude. Sun-Thurs. 11-7am.

HOTEL AUDITOR

Full time. Must have good figure aptitude. Sun.-Thurs. 11-7am
Apply at security

L'Hotel de France

494 & Hwy. 100
Bloomington, Minn.

perform secretaria the Vice President We offer an attracti venient downtown o more about this op calling Jan Dick at 3

Knutson Mortg Financial Corp

Equal Opp. Emplo

banking

MORTGAGE COU

Our Mortgage Dept. other person to pr mortgage loans from cation stage up to t closing. Would like who has 6 mos. to 1 y ience in the mortgag ure aptitude & mini skills. This position p house training as a c exposure to many asp mortgage field.
For more info call Nelson at 371-3700.

FIRST FEDERAL SA

Equal Opportunity E

Banking

SAVINGS OFFIC

Responsible for the g ministration, direction vision of branch offic operations. Must po years supervisory exp a Bank, Savings & Credit Union. Please sume listing qualificati ary requirements to H sources, Northern

Your Future in Business

OBJECTIVES

- ☐ To define small business
- ☐ To understand why and how small businesses are created
- ☐ To describe the different kinds of small businesses and the characteristics of each
- ☐ To understand how the application of management principles and practices differs between small firms and their larger counterparts
- ☐ To identify the major sources of financial and managerial assistance to small businesses

OUTLINE

KEY TERMS

ENTREPRENEUR
FRANCHISE
SMALL BUSINESS
SMALL BUSINESS ADMINISTRATION (SBA)

THE ENTREPRENEUR AND SMALL BUSINESS

Testing the Entrepreneurial You

Your psychological makeup can play a strong role in making your business a success or a failure. Here are some questions based on ideas supplied by Richard Boyatzis and David Winter, two psychologists who have studied the entrepreneurial character. The questions are designed to reveal whether you have entrepreneurial attitudes. Even if no answer fits your feelings precisely, choose the one that comes closest. The answers are below.

1. If you had a free evening, would you most likely a) watch TV b) visit a friend c) work on a hobby?
2. In your daydreams, would you most likely appear as a) a millionaire floating on a yacht b) a detective who has solved a difficult case c) a politician giving an election night victory speech?
3. To exercise, would you rather a) join an athletic club b) join a neighborhood team c) do some jogging at your own pace?
4. When asked to work with others on a team, which would you anticipate with most pleasure: a) other people coming up with good ideas b) cooperating with others c) getting other people to do what you want?
5. Which game would you rather play a) Monopoly b) roulette c) bingo?
6. Your employer asks you to take over a company project that is failing. Would you tell him that you will a) take it b) won't take it because you're up to your gills in work c) give him an answer in a couple of days when you have more information?
7. In school, were you more likely to choose courses emphasizing a) fieldwork b) papers c) exams?
8. In buying a refrigerator would you a) stay with an established, well-known brand b) ask your friends what they bought c) compare thoroughly the advantages of different brands?
9. While on a business trip in Europe you are late for an appointment with a client in a neighboring town. Your train has been delayed indefinitely. Would you a) rent a car to get there b) wait for the next scheduled train c) reschedule the appointment?
10. Do you believe that people you know who have succeeded in business a) have connections b) are cleverer than you c) are about the same as you but maybe work a little harder?
11. An employee who is your friend is not doing his job. Would you a) take him out for a drink, hint broadly that things aren't going right and hope he gets the message b) leave him alone and hope he straightens out c) give him a strong warning and fire him if he doesn't shape up?
12. You come home to spend a relaxing evening and find that your toilet has just overflowed. Would you a) study your home-repair book to see if you can fix it yourself b) persuade a handy friend to fix it for you c) call a plumber?
13. Do you enjoy playing cards most when you a) play with good friends b) play with people who challenge you c) play for high stakes?
14. You operate a small office-cleaning business. A close friend and competitor suddenly dies of a heart attack. Would you a) reassure his wife that you will never try to take away any customers b) propose a merger c) go to your former competitor's customers and offer them a better deal?

QUIZ ANSWERS

1. c; **2.** b; **3.** c; **4.** a; **5.** a; **6.** c; **7.** a; **8.** c; **9.** a; **10.** c; **11.** c; **12.** a; **13.** b; **14.** c.

Score one point for each correct answer. Questions 1, 2, 3, 7, 9 and 12 suggest whether you are a realistic problem solver who can run a business without constant help from others. Questions 5, 6 and 8 probe whether you take calculated risks and seek information before you act. Questions 4, 10, 13 and 14 show whether you, like the classic entrepreneur, find other people most satisfying when they help fulfill your need to win. Question 11 reveals whether you take responsibility for your destiny—and your business. If you score between 11 and 14 points, you could have a good chance to succeed. If you score from seven to 10 points, you'd better have a superb business idea or a lot of money to help you out. If you score seven or less, stay where you are.

Are you an entrepreneur? If not, you may not want to run your own business. This chapter identifies some of the perils of operating a small business and addresses other factors related to business success.

Although they are not so visible as the corporate giants, small businesses are critical to the growth of the U.S. economy. In 1980 there were over 500,000 new business incorporations, more than three times the number in the early 1960s. Of the 12 million firms in the United States at the beginning of this decade, approximately 8.5 million were considered small businesses. Of these, over 50 percent had annual sales of less than $100,000 and employed fewer than ten people. About a third of all paid employment in the United States is provided by firms employing fewer than fifty people. Small business is equally important to the sustained health of larger businesses. For example, it takes an average of 500 small suppliers and 3,000 retailers to support every large manufacturing company in this country.

In previous chapters we have explored numerous aspects of business in our society, including management, marketing, and financial decision making and the quantitative tools for making these decisions. These issues are no less applicable or crucial to a small business. Although individual talent and creativity are the keystones of the smaller enterprise, they are not enough to sustain such a firm. In fact, failure to adapt and to recognize the need for good management have contributed to the downfall of many small firms.

How Big Is Small?

There are many definitions of small business—some relating to the number of employees, others to sales volume or amount of assets. Generally, a **small business** is one that has sales of less than $25 million, employs between one and a hundred people, and has assets of less than $10 million. These numbers may appear large, but compared to figures for a company like IBM—with sales of over $21 billion, assets of over $20 billion, and over 300,000 employees—they are quite small.

In addition to having a certain level of sales, employees, and assets, small businesses usually have the following characteristics:

- Ownership is closely held; managers and owners are frequently the same.
- Capital is supplied by one individual or by a small group.
- Relative size, in terms of market share in a given industry, is small.
- There is a lack of personnel to provide the full range of management expertise.

Of these characteristics, the one relating to market share may be the most misleading. For example, the government considers American Motors a small firm, because compared to General Motors and Ford Motor Company, it has a relatively small share of the market. The most important of the preceding characteristics may be lack of management expertise, because it is a major cause of most small-business failures.

However it is defined, small business is generally subject to more constraints than are large companies, because of its environment, lack of funding, and inability to survive bad decision making. A large organization can affort to make occasional risky (possibly bad) decisions, but such actions can destroy the smaller company.

Types of Small Businesses

Small business enterprises exist in all phases of the economy. However, like larger companies they can be classified broadly as service, manufacturing, or sales companies (see Chapter 10). The operations of such firms tend to be similar to those of their larger counterparts, but they serve narrower markets and fewer customers.

The *service* sector of American business is characterized by its diversity and phenomenal growth. There are as many types of special services as there are individuals with special talents. Owners of small businesses do everything from running hotels and restaurants to servicing automobiles to providing tax or legal counseling. Generally there is easy entry into these markets (no large capital investment), and small service businesses rely primarily on human ability for their product. Thus the opportunities for exploiting individual uniqueness are greater. A large number of small firms are in the business of providing services.

The small *manufacturer* converts raw materials and labor into a usable product needed by customers. Frequently, the product is also unique, something that would be unprofitable for a larger enterprise to mass produce. Production and marketing management are particularly important in this type of business. Many small manufacturing companies are in the printing and clothing industries.

Wholesale and retail sales companies are those that sell finished products. The wholesaler sells the product to a retailer; the retailer in turn offers the product to consumers. Such companies are common in all areas of the economy, and they market a wide range of products, including drugs, groceries, clothing, appliances, shoes, and arts and crafts. Market studies, pricing policies, and inventory control tend to be crucial factors in the decisions these types of businesses make.

Entrepreneurs

One of the biggest advantages for small firms is their relationship with **entrepreneurs.** Such individuals have the type of creative business mentality that functions best in an unstructured, opportunistic environment. Entrepreneurs are generally more concerned with originality of thought and personal fulfillment of a vision than with a particular organization. Thus they fit more comfortably into the close, personal environment of small organizations. Being caught in a research department of a large institution, giving ideas for others either to reject or to implement, is not the entrepreneur's style. Entrepreneurs need to see their projects through from beginning to end. Coca-Cola Company was initiated by a druggist who discovered a syrup that tasted good; McDonald's Restaurants was started by a man with a better hamburger.

The relationship between the entrepreneur and the small firm is, therefore, one of mutual benefit. The entrepreneur provides the inno-

Highlight Do You Have the Personality to Own Your Own Business?

So you want to be a millionaire and run your own business. You want independence and excitement. Exciting it may be, but successful entrepreneurship requires a special person. Let's look at some critical qualities.

Are you a worrier? Starting a small business is a risky venture. Failure is a real possibility. Earnings may be uncertain or irregular, particularly in the early years, and perhaps less than if you had stayed with your old company as an employee. If you are a worrier, you probably are unsuited to the task.

Are you a hard worker? Small-businessowners normally work harder than any employee in their company. They must not be discouraged easily and must manage their time and energy effectively. Small-businessowners work much more than the typical 9-to-5, forty-hour work week.

Are you a planner? Have you saved money, investigated business contacts, estimated the income that can reasonably be expected? Anticipation of needs, planning for contingencies, and good organization are musts for the small business.

Are you qualified? Have you had training or experience in your proposed business? Have you analyzed the special requirements to be successful and taken special courses or other steps to improve qualities that are weak?

Starting a small business is exciting, challenging, and potentially lucrative. But success takes a combination of hard work, planning, creativity, and luck. The person suited to the typical uncertainties and crises is rare indeed.

vative products or services; the small firm provides the vehicle for the ideas. It is important, however, to remember that pitfalls exist as well. The entrepreneur is not by nature inclined to consider survival of the organization. It is the implementation of his or her idea that is fullfilling. Accordingly, management expertise generally must come from others. An entrepreneur must recognize this reality and welcome partners with the talents he or she lacks.

Getting into Small Business

Entry into the small-business sector can be accomplished in a number of ways, including franchising, buying an existing business, or starting a business from scratch. Regardless of the method that is chosen, initial investigation and planning are crucial. Franchising and purchasing an existing business may at first require more capital, but they suffer less uncertainty; starting from scratch can be done on a shoestring, but the risk of failure is frequently greater.

FRANCHISES

A **franchise** operation like Wendy's, McDonald's, or Pizza Hut is a system for distributing goods or services under a known name even though the business is operated by a small, independent owner. The franchise owner keeps the profits and runs the risks of operation but pays the franchisor for the right to use the name and for the know-how.

This form of business operation is not new but has become more popular in recent years; 90 percent of today's franchise companies were started in the early 1950s. Fast-food chains, which market anything from hamburgers and pies to tacos and steak dinners, are among the most common franchises. However, franchising has spread to other industries, including real estate, drugs, and convenience stores.

Generally, the parent company (franchisor) provides a brand name, a known product, know-how, and if necessary, financial assistance. The franchisee runs the business and pays the parent company royalties plus an initial fee. Thus franchising normally involves a substantial capital outlay. Furthermore, the franchisor's control over the product and claim on part of the profits often are areas of difficulty for the franchisee.

EXISTING BUSINESSES

Buying an existing business can be an effective way of getting into business for someone who has adequate investment capital and the expertise to operate the business. Such buy-outs are common in service industries when the originator of a business decides to retire. An existing business provides an exceptionally good opportunity if present operations have been poorly managed or undercapitalized. But this way of entering the small-business market can be expensive, because the initial capital outlay must reimburse current owners for their investment.

NEW BUSINESSES

Starting a new business is, of course, the most risky method of entering the small-business market. If the product is a service, the new business can be started with minimal capital outlay and financial risk. Wholesaling or retailing can also involve a rather small capital investment, but manufacturing can be quite expensive.

A new business allows the owner to have complete control over the operation and to conduct business with anyone in any way. The lack of an established organization (present when buying an existing business) and the lack of managerial and financial assistance (which exist in a franchising operation) can be overcome through careful planning and, perhaps, a little luck.

ADVANTAGES AND DISADVANTAGES OF SMALL BUSINESS

In addition to being the key vehicle for the entrepreneur, the small firm has a number of advantages over larger firms that may be overlooked and underused. For one thing, it has greater flexibility and offers more opportunities to reach customers through personal service. For another, small firms can sometimes attract more competent employees, because many people are now recognizing the advantages of being close to the boss. The ability to satisfy unusual demands for high-quality, custom-made products is another constant source of opportunity. Other advantages include

Highlight A Chicken Lays a Golden Egg

In six years, Ted Giannoulas pushed his salary from $2 an hour to $5,000 or more a day—and became a folk hero in the process.

As a journalism student at San Diego State University in 1974, Giannoulas accepted a week's assignment from San Diego radio station KGB to don a chicken costume and distribute free candy at the San Diego Zoo.

An enterprising young man, Giannoulas convinced the station that the chicken gimmick should be introduced to games of the San Diego Padres. What he saw as merely a free ticket to the baseball games, however, became a career for himself and a fad nationwide.

Over the next few years, Giannoulas improved his act, got a new costume, and increased his salary to $6.40 an hour. The public responded, and mascots in flashy costumes were soon doing their bit to entertain fans between pitches at many other ball parks. But none of them matched the success of the Chicken.

This fact was noted by Ted Turner, eccentric owner of the Atlantic Braves, who offered Giannoulas $100,000 a year in 1978 to move his act to Georgia.

Not about to let a good thing go, the station countered by raising Giannoulas' salary to $900 a week. Suddenly, the Chicken was making more than many of the station executives and they began to take special interest in him.

Big money meant major arguments, and in the spring of 1979, the radio station fired Giannoulas and got a court order enjoining him from wearing a chicken costume.

The matter was finally settled to everyone's satisfaction, and Giannoulas returned to the Padres. San Diego's biggest crowd of 1979 roared its welcome as the Chicken emerged from a styrofoam egg ten feet high.

The turmoil and its resultant publicity only increased the public's enthusiasm for Giannoulas, who now makes personal appearances at baseball parks around the country. In the spring of 1980, he toured 40 cities in 41 days, earning $5,000 or more at each show.

- Faster response time in making changes (not so much red tape involved)
- Better ability to give personal attention to customers
- Closer contact with all personnel
- Greater ability to make decisions based on direct, personal knowledge
- Faster decision-making capabilities

Offsetting the advantages of owning a small business are difficulties in obtaining financing without relinquishing control, problems of promoting a new product and a new company, and lack of management skills to properly manage the company. These factors reduce the small company's ability to grow and adapt to changing conditions. Because of difficulties like these, managers of small firms may tend toward conservatism, with too little willingness to take the risks that may be necessary for growth. Furthermore, the consequences of a bad decision can be far more detrimental to the survival of the small firm than the large firm.

The Management of Small Business

Although small businesses are a viable and growing part of our economy, the failure rate is high. Nearly 1,000 small businesses fail each day, over half of them less than five years old. The causes of failure are varied, but the major cause in most cases is managerial incompetence.

Some of the specific reasons a small business may not succeed:

- Failure to plan properly for capital needs
- Failure to evaluate adequately market and inventory needs
- General lack of planning
- Failure to promote the product or service effectively
- Failure to control expenses
- Failure to collect receivables
- Haphazard expansion
- Inadequate compensation for key employees
- Uninformed pricing policies

All of these factors arise when the management techniques discussed in previous chapters are not adapted to the operations of a small business.

MANAGEMENT PRINCIPLES AND PRACTICES

Owners and managers of small businesses often try to run all aspects of the business, but they seldom have the training to do so. Even when they try to adopt effective management techniques, they may simply copy those used by larger firms. When they do seek assistance, they often hire people only to carry out orders. Thus a crucial first step is to hire, train, and adequately compensate expert managers. Of course, it is also necessary to give these managers the authority to carry out the programs they develop.

Planning

The one indispensable factor for all businesses is the planning process. Before a company is even set up, someone should investigate the demand for the product or service and how other firms in the industry operate. Only then is it possible to determine whether the company can generate profits. During the life of the business, proper planning enables management to foresee difficulties and to anticipate management, financing, and marketing needs.

Planning in small businesses is frequently inadequate because the managers are preoccupied with day-to-day operations, to the exclusion of matters that have no immediate payoff. Thus the first step in developing a more effective operation is to undertake long-range planning. All phases of operations—including merchandising, production design, pricing, personnel, profits, promotion, the legal form of organization, and cost control—must be considered. When necessary, outside consulting or marketing companies should be brought in to help.

Highlight Whose Fault Is It?

"It's not my fault" would seem to be the common lament of managers of failed small businesses. In one recent survey, over 70 percent of the owners of defunct small companies blamed external factors for their failure. The most prominent scrapegoats were bad economic and business conditions as well as an inability to raise needed capital.

In contrast, nearly 60 percent of the creditors who had loaned money to failed companies believed that the primary cause of trouble was inefficient management. Although both owners and creditors considered competition, poor location, and financing factors, there remains a difference in perception.

What happened to other small businesses that began or were operated during the same period as the ones that failed? Were they not subject to the same general business conditions? Are not most new companies subject to the pitfalls of competition and poor location? All owners of failed small companies must consider the possibility that their initial planning and/or subsequent management was faulty. A good or original idea simply is not enough. Careful analysis of location, financing needs, and competitive outlook can frequently prevent failure simply by preventing the initiation of a project that is doomed to fail.

The basic element of any plan is a specific set of goals and objectives for the company. Each stage of the planning process must follow and support these objectives. It is important to note that a set of objectives is of little value if the company's progress toward meeting them cannot be measured or evaluated somehow.

In addition to a set of objectives, the long-range plan should include

- Projections of assets and financing needs
- A timetable for results
- The delegation of specific responsibilities for implementing the plan
- Projections of personnel and management needs

Although flexibility is a key advantage of small firms, emphasizing flexibility to the detriment of planning can mean the death of a company. By preparing for contingencies, by specifying the direction to move in, and by raising the proper questions, managers of small firms can enhance their chances of survival.

Organizational Development

In the planning process, managers should keep in mind the gradual development of the organization. At the beginning, a company is likely to be a one-person show, but if it is successful, that one person will rapidly become overworked. For that person's and the company's sake, there should be a plan for coping with growth.

Generally, a business goes through four stages in its life cycle—birth, growth, maturation, and possible decline (see Exhibit 22.1). Each stage in the life cycle is characterized by a different level of growth and prosperity. Thus each stage requires a different approach to management. There are various sources of assistance during these stages. A knowledgeable board of directors can provide much expertise while the small company is in the birth and growth stages. A company's bankers and accountants are also an excellent source of assistance in financial planning, cost control, and design of information systems. As the company expands, however, management should begin to look for staff to take over these functions. The first two areas needing additional attention are generally production and sales. However, marketing, financial management, and information processing are not far behind. As the organization develops, management must create detailed job descriptions and project personnel needs. This may be a painful process for the original managers, so it is important that they delegate authority for this task to those with more specialized expertise.

Human Resource Management

Even with proper planning for personnel needs, small firms sometimes cannot attract the necessary expertise. Larger organizations offer many advantages. However, small firms have many advantages of their own, and they should be emphasized in the recruitment process. Some of those advantages are the satisfaction provided by working closely with

EXHIBIT 22.1 Life Cycle of a Business

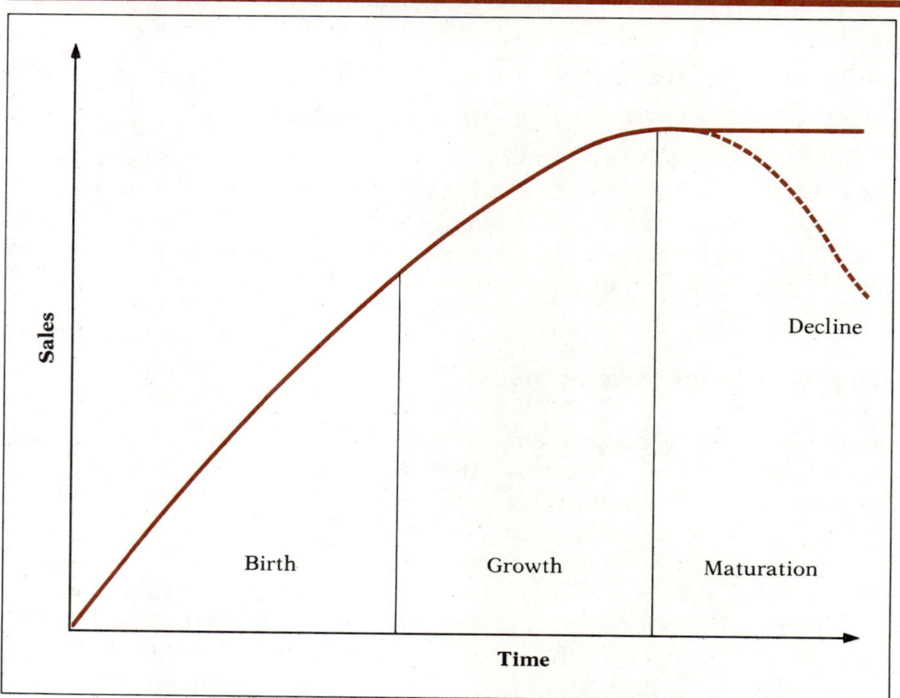

the others in the company, the opportunities for rapid professional growth, and the close, family-type atmosphere.

The major difficulty in competing with larger organizations for employees has been the inadequate compensation packages offered by smaller businesses. Managers of small companies are often extremely cost-conscious and attempt to bring in employees at the lowest possible wage. As you can image, small organizations consequently have trouble attracting top personnel. Furthermore, even if a company can hire the people it needs, it may lose them to higher-paying positions in the future. So when developing compensation packages, managers of small companies should consider the costs of recruiting, training, and developing new employees and the costs of failing to have adequate expertise available.

A possible source of experienced labor for small businesses is the older employee. These people obviously will not remain with the company for many years, but the expertise they have acquired from working with other firms can be invaluable.

Once a small firm has the necessary personnel, it is important for management to maintain the close working relationships that may have attracted the employees from the outset. As with larger firms, regular and positive performance reviews are crucial. Tying compensation to productivity may also be beneficial. In any case, staff members should be aware of the goals of their positions and of their role in the success of the firm. One of the major benefits a small firm can offer an employee is close identification with the fortunes of the organization.

Production Management

The key aspect of production management is generally control of costs. Initially, the owners and managers of small firms have a close relationship with the cost factors and therefore have the ability to control them. However, problems can develop as firms grow. Inventories and product and cost controls can soon expand beyond the capacity of the original management to oversee them. Thus production operations should be investigated carefully in the planning stages, and specialized personnel needs in this area should be anticipated. For a small company, perpetual inventories of materials and products may be essential. The responsibility for controlling such items should be assigned to someone who is closely involved with the production process.

MARKETING

The factors affecting demand for a firm's product or service are often the most misunderstood of all areas in small business. Information about changing customer needs and environmental patterns is frequently inadequate or comes too late. Thus price and inventory adjustments in a small business often do not correspond to market needs.

One of the first steps in the marketing process is to develop a technique for judging customer needs for a particular product. This can be done by producing limited quantities of the product and evaluating its success, by commissioning outside market studies, or by personally investigating customer needs. One of the key advantages of small firms is their ability to shift gears in response to customer demand and unique opportunities. But all too often management loses track of the customers and the market and continues to provide the same product or service, at inappropriate prices, after customer needs and desires have changed. Thus it is necessary to keep a constant eye on developments in the marketplace.

In planning what products to offer, small companies should usually concentrate on providing something a little bit different from what is generally available. Radical innovations are in order only when there is no other choice. In addition, it is important for small companies to maintain superiority in some manner, so they should concentrate on one or two items rather than an entire line. Improvements in these items can help maintain a company's reputation for unique products.

It is hard to design and market unique products and services, but many important developments in our economy (Polaroid cameras, Xerox copiers) have resulted from the efforts of small groups of people with limited resources. As with other areas, the crucial factor is the adequacy of the planning process.

FINANCIAL MANAGEMENT

Although inadequate management can be blamed for many failures of small organizations, inadequate financing is certainly a contributing factor. New businesses are usually financed primarily through owner investments, so the capital base may be small. Working capital needs are often ignored or underestimated, and financing opportunities are often overlooked. Of course, inadequate financing is frequently a function of inadequate management.

At the outset of a business venture, entrepreneurs must prepare a schedule of financial needs and determine methods for satisfying those needs. Since working capital is often a problem, they should establish a close relationship with a bank that would be willing to help out in a cash crunch. Much financing of this nature is on a personal level, so managers of small businesses should be careful to cultivate their contacts in the banking community. They should also cultivate their trade suppliers, who can often extend payment terms or hold shipments to assist in times of tight money.

To avoid cash-flow difficulties, managers of small firms should attempt to commit the least possible amount to fixed assets. Building and equipment leases allow greater flexibility in financing and relieve small firms of the problems of possible obsolescence. If it is more desirable to purchase equipment, managers should investigate used equipment and try to get the most extended purchase terms possible.

Highlight Going Public

The joys of success! The small business that grows large, expands, and becomes a big business eventually reaches a decision point: Should the owners offer shares to the general public?

In a growing company, the decision to "go public" involves many tradeoffs. The reasons for selling shares commonly involve financing needs—for investment and operating funds. However, there may be personal reasons as well, including the owners' desire to diversify, to minimize estate-tax problems, or to resolve personal cash-flow difficulties.

The immediate result of going public is primarily the loss of control. Not only will there be a large number of new owners, but the company will also have to conform to regulatory guidelines applicable to publicly-held companies (established by the Securities and Exchange Commission). Ironically, as the company continues to expand, this loss of control will continue.

The final consideration in going public is whether the attempt will be successful: Will the public invest in this company? Two criteria for success seem dominant. First, the company should have a higher growth rate than its competitors to attract the necessary investors. Second, the owners and managers must be able to make the necessary adjustments to new interests and new scrutiny so that all may enjoy a profitable relationship.

In no case should permanent needs be financed with short-term debt. Trying to repay debt before the financed assets are returning adequate profits places severe cash strains on the company. Remember that many current assets, such as inventory, are actually held over long periods. Because some inventory must always be kept on hand to meet customer demands, inventory tends to grow as the company grows. Financing inventory with short-term debt can therefore disrupt cash flow.

SOURCES OF ASSISTANCE

There are many sources of financial and managerial assistance available to managers of small firms. These are particularly important in the initial stages. For example, the federal government supports small business in this country by providing numerous free services, including management advice, help with financing, and help in obtaining government contracts. One of the major sources of government assistance is the **Small Business Administration (SBA).** The SBA has financial resources for making loans and can guarantee loans with local lending institutions. It also has numerous management-assistance services that are available to help train and assist entrepreneurs in organizing a business.

A small company's local bank and accountants may be able to provide managerial expertise as well as financial support when seeking financing. The small-business manager should remember that a banking institution's flexibility and willingness to provide support during periods of crisis may be more important than interest rates.

For a small company that is contemplating "going public," the Securities and Exchange Commission (SEC) can be helpful. It has reduced the cost and complexities of the process of offering shares and has made it more attractive for small businesses.

Other organizations that may be able to provide financial or managerial assistance include

- Business resource centers (BRGs)
- Minority enterprise small-business investment companies (MESBICs)
- The Inter-racial Council for Business Opportunity (ICBO)
- Small-business investment companies (SBICs)
- Local chambers of commerce
- The Service Corps of Retired Executives (SCORE)
- The Active Corps of Executives (ACE)
- The National Federation of Independent Business
- The National Small Business Association
- The Small Business Legislative Council

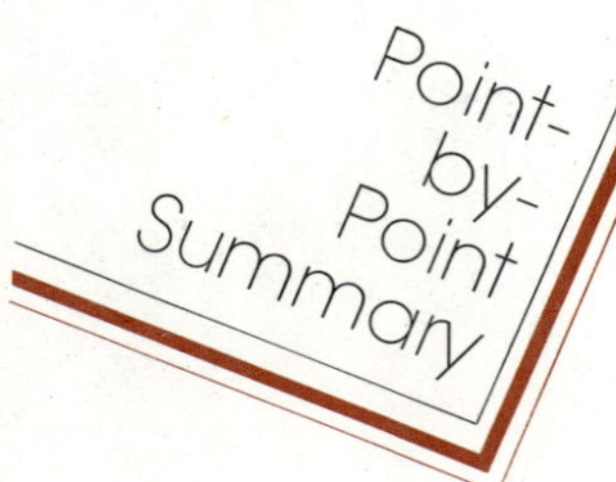

- Small business is vital to a healthy economy, and the small-business environment is probably crucial for the continued functioning of the entrepreneur in our society. Small businesses have many advantages over large businesses, including more flexibility, closer customer contact, and more opportunities for personal satisfaction and growth.
- The small-business sector can be entered through franchising, purchasing an existing business, or starting a business from scratch.
- One of the major reasons for small-business failure is inadequate or incompetent management. The crucial deficiency of most small-business managers is poor or nonexistent planning ability. As the organization develops, there is an even greater need for managerial expertise and delegation of authority.
- Small businesses can attract top-quality personnel by establishing competitive hiring practices and by emphasizing the personal fulfillment to be gained from working in a small organization.
- Although cost control is one of the initial advantages of a small enterprise, this can become a problem area as the company grows. Management personnel should be hired to supervise the production function.

- Introducing a new product and firm to the marketplace can be one of the most difficult problem areas for a new firm. Careful planning can help determine the needs and desires of consumers, an appropriate price, and ways to adapt to changing market conditions.
- Financing is a vital aspect of planning for the small firm. Failure to adequately anticipate financing needs is one of the major causes of small-business failure.
- Small businesses often fail in the first five years of existence. Over 90 percent of the time, they fail because of managerial incompetence. Managers of small businesses should therefore take advantage of the expertise and advice available from other organizations.

Questions for Review

1. What is a small business? Why is small business important to the proper functioning of the economy of the United States? What are the key advantages of a small firm? Why would large businesses support the continued existence of small firms?
2. How do entrepreneurs fit into small enterprises? Large enterprises?
3. In what ways do the management practices of large businesses differ from those of small businesses? What aspects of financial management in a small business are likely to be different from those in a large business?
4. In what ways does the U.S. government support small businesses?
5. What are the first steps that should be taken by someone contemplating starting a new business? Compare purchasing an existing business to starting a business from scratch.
6. How can the common errors made by small-business managers be avoided?
7. What advantages might you cite to someone you were trying to hire for your small firm?
8. How might management of the production process change as a company grows?
9. What amount of dividends would you expect a small company to pay in the first five years of existence? Why?
10. What marketing information might be useful to the manager of a new small business? A growing small business?
11. What are the advantages of buying and operating a franchise? The disadvantages?

APPLICATION

Hewlett-Packard Company

David Packard and William R. Hewlett started their electronics business about forty years ago, with an initial investment of $538. In their first year, sales were about $5,000. By 1979 sales had grown to $2.4 billion, with profits of $203 million, and their company employed 52,000 people. Four decades of growth obviously is accompanied by many changes. To its credit, Hewlett-Packard managed change gracefully. It provides an example of how a small company can grow into a big one and still retain some of the qualities that made it successful in the first place.

HOW IT ALL STARTED

Packard and Hewlett first met in the fall of 1931, when they were Stanford University sophomores. They soon found they had a mutual interest—electronics. By the time they graduated in 1934, they had become close friends and were seriously contemplating going into business together.

In 1938 they did, setting up shop in the one-car garage behind the Packards' rented home in Palo Alto, California. Their first product was a new type of audio oscillator, an electronic instrument used to test sound equipment. Hewlett had designed the circuitry as a thesis subject while working toward his electrical engineering degree. Late in 1938, Hewlett presented the oscillator at a convention of radio engineers on the West Coast. The model attracted a lot of attention because it offered new performance standards at less cost than competitive oscillators on the market at that time.

Because of this initial interest, Hewlett and Packard decided that the oscillator would be a good product to market, and they devoted the remainder of the year to manufacturing their first instruments. The two men also sent information about the oscillator (designated Model 200A) to prospective customers. Among their first orders was a particularly important one from Walt Disney Studios. The studio asked the young engineers if they could build an oscillator with somewhat different capabilities from Model 200A. Model 200B was developed shortly thereafter, and Disney purchased eight to help develop the unique sound system for the classic film *Fantasia*.

Hewlett and Packard formally organized their partnership in 1939. In 1940 the company moved out of the garage into a small building nearby. The first employees were hired that same year. The company moved into its first company-designed and -owned building in 1942. By 1943, the work force had grown to about 100 people, and sales were approaching $1 million annually.

Other measuring instruments followed the 200A and 200B, including a vacuum tube voltmeter designed by Packard that gained wide acceptance in the growing electronics industry and a microwave signal generator introduced after World War II.

By 1950 Hewlett-Packard had 200 employees, seventy products, and $2 million in sales. Although Hewlett-Packard had grown modestly during the war and immediately thereafter, it began a period of sustained and substantial growth in the 1950s, fueled by a strong research and development effort that significantly broadened its family of electronic test and measurement instruments. After making several additions to its original plant, Hewlett-Packard broke ground for a new engineering and manufacturing complex in 1956. This facility in nearby Stanford Industrial Park also became the company's administrative headquarters.

GROWTH MEANS CHANGES

The first significant change in the company's profile began to emerge in the late 1950s and extended into the mid-1960s. In part, this resulted from Hewlett-Packard's acquisitions of several smaller firms, which took it into new and promising markets. In 1958 Hewlett-Packard acquired a California-based producer of high-quality graphic recorders. Two acquisitions in the early 1960s also proved to be particularly important. One was the Sanborn Company, a pioneer in electrocardiography and a prime supplier of other recording instruments. The other was a manufacturer of gas chromatographs. These acquisitions enabled Hewlett-Packard to apply its expertise in electronics technology to the fields of medicine and analytical chemistry.

Another factor in Hewlett-Packard's changing profile was the establishment of company operations overseas. In 1959 it created a European marketing organization in Switzerland and established its first manufacturing plant overseas, in West Germany. A second overseas plant was built in the United Kingdom in 1961, and two years later, Hewlett-Packard entered into a joint business venture with a Japanese company in Tokyo.

During this period, the company continued to expand in the United States, establishing an instrument manufacturing operation in Colorado and forming an organization in Palo Alto to develop high-quality solid-state components. It also was in the early 1960s that Hewlett-Packard acquired a number of the independent sales companies that had been marketing its products in the United States. These firms formed the base for today's regional sales organization.

In 1966 the company introduced its first computer. It was designed specifically to work with Hewlett-Packard instruments; in fact, it was called an instrumentation computer. Two years later, Hewlett-Packard announced the development of an electronic desktop calculator, also for engineering and scientific applications. In 1972 the company

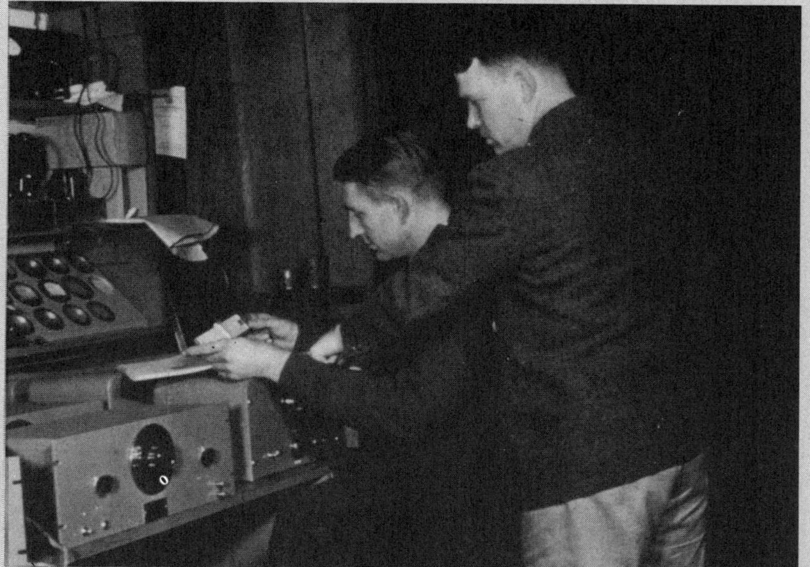

David Packard and William R. Hewlett began their electronics business in 1939 in a one-car garage (shown here: circa 1940), with a $538 investment and a single product. Today, Hewlett-Packard has more than 4,000 products, over 40 manufacturing plants in 23 cities in the U.S. and eight countries overseas, about 60,000 employees, and annual sales approaching $3 billion.

introduced the HP-35, the world's first handheld scientific calculator. Many other computational products have been developed for business, industrial, and educational markets in the years since. To keep pace with this expanding data-products business, Hewlett-Packard has built new plants in France, Singapore, Malaysia, and Brazil and has formed new divisions in California, Colorado, Idaho, Oregon, and Washington.

Today the company's data-products activity represents over 40 percent of the company's total business. Moreover, its achievements in computer technology, especially in the area of integrated circuitry, have extended the capabilities of the company's other products. Many have built-in computer memories and integrated circuitry to increase speed and versatility. And most can be connected with external computers and calculators to form automatic instrumentation systems.

FROM SMALL COMPANY TO BIG COMPANY

Hewlett-Packard's continuing growth and entry into new markets, plus the fact that many product organizations were being established away from Palo Alto, brought about a need to restructure. Beginning in 1960, divisions were formed along product lines. Each division was organized to operate much like a separate business; each had its own research and development, manufacturing, marketing, and support operations, as well as its own distinct family of products.

Continuing diversification led to the establishment of a group structure in 1968. This structure was refined to its present form in 1974, when divisions with related products were combined into six major categories—electronic test and measuring instruments, computers and computer-based system, calculators, medical electronic products, solid-state components, and electronic instrumentation for chemical analysis. Group management staffs were formed to coordinate activities for their respective divisions.

Changes in top management have also occurred. In 1977 John A. Young succeeded Hewlett as president of the company, and the following year Young was elected chief executive officer. Hewlett now serves as chairman of the Hewlett-Packard executive committee and as a member of the company's board of directors. Packard is chairman of the Hewlett-Packard board.

Despite these changes, the management philosophy and concepts originally formulated by Hewlett and Packard in 1938 to shape the company and guide its growth remain unchanged. These concepts, in the form of a set of corporate objectives, were first put into writing in 1957. They have been modified periodically to reflect the changing nature of the company's business and the environment in which Hewlett-Packard operates. Even so, the essence and intent of today's objectives remain remarkably similar to the original versions. A summary of these objectives:

1. *Profit* To achieve sufficient profit to finance our company growth and to provide the resources we need to achieve our other corporate objectives
2. *Customers* To provide products and services of the greatest possible value to our customers, thereby gaining and holding their respect and loyalty
3. *Fields of interest* To enter new fields only when the ideas we have, together with our technical, manufacturing, and marketing skills, assure that we can make a needed and profitable contribution to the field
4. *Growth* To let our growth be limited only by our profits and our ability to develop and produce technical products that satisfy real customer needs
5. *Our people* To help our people share in the company's success, which they make possible; to provide job security based on their performance; to recognize their individual achievements; and to help them

gain a sense of satisfaction and accomplishment from their work

6. *Management* To foster initiative and creativity by allowing individuals great freedom of action in attaining well-defined objectives
7. *Citizenship* To honor our obligations to society by being an economic, intellectual, and social asset to each nation and each community in which we operate

CAREER OPPORTUNITIES

Hewlett-Packard normally hires college students with a bachelor's degree in engineering or one of the sciences or with a master's degree in business administration. In addition, the company hires students with a two-year technical degree, especially in the field of electronics. Once employed, these students are given an opportunity to acquire a four-year degree, or if they choose, they may continue as technicians.

New employees are given initial job assignments in their area of interest and expertise at either the corporate staff level or within an operating division. During their first few years with the company, employees rotate jobs within their area and between the operating units and corporate staff, getting broad exposure to the organization. Eventually, employees are put in more permanent positions in their particular area of interest.

FOR DISCUSSION

1. What characterized the primary stages of growth in Hewlett-Packard's history?
2. What are the most important factors in Hewlett-Packard's success?

OBJECTIVES

- ☐ To explain the theory of comparative advantage, which shows how international trade benefits all
- ☐ To evaluate the arguments and policies that have been adopted to restrict international trade
- ☐ To discuss the factors that a corporation would have to consider before deciding to invest in a foreign country
- ☐ To list the avenues through which international trade can be carried out
- ☐ To describe multinational corporations and the advantages and disadvantages they offer to the host country
- ☐ To analyze U.S. trade relations
- ☐ To explain how international debt was and is now settled

OUTLINE

ARTICLE *Daniel Ludwig's Floating Factory*
THE THEORY OF COMPARATIVE ADVANTAGE
The Benefits of Trade
Applying the Theory Today
FREE TRADE: BLESSING OR CURSE?
Some Arguments against Free Trade
Restrictions on Trade
Factors Affecting International Trade
FORMS OF INTERNATIONAL TRADE
Exporting
Branch Operations
Licensing
Foreign Manufacturing
Multinational Corporations
U.S. TRADE WITH THE WORLD
ACCOUNTING FOR INTERNATIONAL TRADE
The Gold Standard
The Bretton Woods System
Floating Exchange Rates
APPLICATION *Ford Motor Company*

KEY TERMS

BALANCE OF PAYMENTS
BALANCE OF TRADE
EMBARGO
EXPORTING
FLOATING EXCHANGE RATE
FREE TRADE
INTERNATIONAL MONETARY FUND (IMF)
LICENSE
MULTINATIONAL CORPORATION (MNC)
PROTECTIVE TARIFF
QUOTA
REVENUE TARIFF
TARIFF
THEORY OF COMPARATIVE ADVANTAGE

INTERNATIONAL BUSINESS

Daniel Ludwig's Floating Factory

Time, June 19, 1978

Longer than two football fields, taller than a 16-story building, the off-white structure floating up the Amazon looked like a jungle apparition. In fact, it was a huge paper factory that Daniel K. Ludwig, the secretive shipping, mining and real estate industrialist whose net worth is estimated to be as high as $3 billion, intends to use in exploiting 500,000 acres of timberland that he owns in the Brazilian wilderness.

The barge-borne plant was towed by tugboat through the Indian and Atlantic oceans on a 15,000-mile, 93-day voyage from Kure, Japan, where it had been built by Ishikawajima-Harima Heavy Industries (I.H.I.). In Brazil, it was taken to a docking area that had been constructed by 2,500 workers on the Jari River, an Amazon tributary 250 miles inland. The factory and its separate 55,000-kw power plant were floated into position over 4,000 submerged pilings last month. Then water under the pilings was drained, and Brazil's Mungulu district, which before Ludwig was little more than a swatch of forest, got a new industrial enterprise. Why was the plant towed halfway round the globe instead of being built on the site? Says an I.H.I. spokesman: "It would have taken far more time to build so sophisticated a project there, with inadequate roads and cargo-handling facilities."

The $250 million plant will go into operation next year and by 1981 will turn out 750 metric tons of bleached kraft pulp a day, enough to make a single strand of toilet paper stretching more than 6 1/2 times around the world. (The pulp will be used for other products as well.)

Brazilian environmentalists worry over the long-range impact of Ludwig's deforestation. To feed the mill's appetite, Ludwig's crews have cleared nearly 250,000 acres of jungle so far and planted 81 million fast-growing trees; the raw wood will be hauled to the plant on 150 miles of Ludwig-built railroad.

Ludwig is a restless recluse at 80 and, some employees suggest, is seeking to build a pyramid to himself, a monument to his ten-year quest to tame a stretch of jungle almost the size of Connecticut and make it productive. Says an associate, Luis Antonio Oliveira: "Mr. Ludwig is nearing the end of his life, and he is more interested in undertaking something of great socioeconomic significance than in earning quick profits." Still, Ludwig is betting that a worldwide paper shortage is coming by 1985 and will make his gamble pay off.

Photo courtesy of Manchete/Pictorial Parade

If Ludwig's floating paper mill is any indication of the path that civilization is about to venture on, the possibilities are endless. The ingenuity being used to expand international business is an indicator of the future.

Today we drive cars made in Japan and West Germany, use gas extracted in the Middle East and often refined in Europe, watch our favorite television programs on Japanese-made TV sets, and wear clothes made in Taiwan or Hong Kong. Similarly, foreign countries enjoy the benefits of our technology, our made-in-Hollywood movies and TV shows, our soft drinks. International trade allows the inhabitants of one country to enjoy the fruits of the labor of people in another country.

Countries trade for the same reason that people living in the same country trade with one another. Unlike Robinson Crusoe, they are not living on a desert island and hence do not have to produce everything needed for their survival. A country that shunned trade with other countries would be unable to survive—unless it had the natural and financial resources to produce all the articles that its population needed. However, such a fortunate situation is very rare indeed, and so each country specializes in the goods and services that it can produce efficiently. It can then exchange the excess for the other goods and services it needs for its survival.

The Theory of Comparative Advantage

David Ricardo, a nineteenth-century economist, formulated a **theory of comparative advantage** for international trade on the basis of these simple truths. This theory ignored money as the medium of exchange and picked a more stable medium: All outputs were measured in terms of labor hours used. He also rather simplistically assumed that there were only two regions involved at any one time (say the United States and Europe) and that only two products were produced (say food and cloth).

In order to understand the theory, let's assume that the labor hours needed to produce one unit each of food and cloth, in the United States and in Europe, are the following:

	United States	Europe
Food	1	3
Cloth	2	4

Clearly, the United States can produce both food and cloth with fewer labor hours per unit than Europe can. However, the production of food takes a third of the effort, whereas the production of cloth takes half the effort. In this case, the United States would specialize in the production of food, because it is relatively more efficient at that task than at producing cloth; it has a comparative advantage in the production of food. Europe, although absolutely inefficient in the production of both food and cloth, has a comparative advantage in cloth.

THE BENEFITS OF TRADE

The preceding figures indicate that the United States can produce either one unit of food or half a unit of cloth with one labor hour. Therefore, if it could get more than half a unit of cloth in exchange for one unit of food, it would benefit. Similarly, Europe produces one unit of cloth and three-fourths of a unit of food using the same amount of labor hours. Therefore, if Europe can get more than three-fourths of a unit of food for one unit of cloth, it would gain from trade. The productivity equations for the two regions can be summarized as follows:

United States: 1 unit food = 1/2 unit cloth
Europe: 3/4 unit food = 1 unit cloth

Say that the United States and Europe agree on an exchange rate of one unit of food for one unit of cloth. For the United States, this trade will be beneficial: For every unit of cloth it produced, it would have to give up production of two units of food; hence, exchanging one for one is definitely profitable. Europe. too, would benefit from the exchange, because the labor hours it would spend to produce three-fourths of a unit of food can more efficiently be spent producing one unit of cloth to trade for a full unit of food.

APPLYING THE THEORY TODAY

Assume that a Japanese steel company develops a method of producing steel that would reduce the cost per ton by half. In addition to using the process in its own factories, the Japanese company decides to license it in such foreign countries as the United States and Germany. This decision to license would permit the cost of research to be recovered sooner, through royalty payments from the users, and would benefit Japanese consumers by making the steel they use less expensive. In addition, the Japanese company would make good profits, distribute high dividends, increase wages, and pay a larger share in taxes. It may be argued that the Japanese company would be losing its comparative advantage, since its competitors would be using the same process. But this argument ignores the fact that innovation is a continuing process, and with early recovery of its research costs, the Japanese company could reinvest in additional research and thereby keep one step ahead of its competition.

This licensing agreement would benefit the receiving countries, too. U.S. steel companies would be spared huge research costs and the risks of research and get a packaged product ready for use at a lower price. A U.S. steel company would only purchase the license if the cost of the new method (including royalty payments) would be less than the cost of the old method. But, if the U.S. steel mills wanted to compete with Japanese steel, they would have to reduce the price of steel to consumers. The money left in consumers' pockets would either be invested in some new venture or be spent on consumption, which would also encourage new ventures. Hence the licensing agreement with Japan would help the U.S. economy. This scenario is not too far from reality: The United States, which helped Japan rebuild its steel industry after World War II, is now willing to adopt advanced steel-making technology from Japan. For example, U.S. Steel signed a technology agreement with Nippon Steel in 1980 for help in modernizing its old steel mills.

Free Trade: Blessing or Curse?

It may seem apparent from the discussion of comparative advantage that **free trade** benefits the countries that engage in it. However, many countries do not consider the issue of international trade to be quite so simple. They perceive many problems with free trade and have developed several ways to restrict it. And even without legal restrictions, trade may be limited by other socioeconomic factors.

SOME ARGUMENTS AGAINST FREE TRADE

Here are some of the arguments and counterarguments on the issue of free trade.

Unemployment

Some people believe that when free trade is allowed to flourish, efficient foreign companies may outsell the local competition, forcing the local competition out of business. The result is unemployment in the receiving country.

Let's assume that you wish to purchase a color TV set. After considering several, you narrow your choice to two sets, which are equally good in your opinion. One is Japanese-made, costing $300, and the other is U.S.-made, costing $400. If Japanese sets were not allowed to enter the United States, your decision would be simple: You would purchase the American set for $400. However, if you have the choice of buying the Japanese set, you can save $100. Say that you decide to buy the American set anyway. That $100 difference becomes a gift that you are granting for safeguarding employment in the United States. Now perhaps you can understand why American companies that are losing ground to foreign competition are so eager to pressue Congress for restrictions on trade.

Proponents of free trade argue that the $100 you save by purchasing the Japanese TV set could be invested or consumed. If it is invested, it would help make funds available for future businesses, which would create jobs and add to the national wealth. If it is used for consumption, it would encourage production and employment in some sector. Therefore, it can be argued that the loss of jobs due to foreign competition would be made up by increases in jobs in other sectors of the economy.

Infant Industry

The government in developing countries is often pressured to protect its industries against more established foreign competition. As in the case of the unemployment issue, the consumers in developing countries indirectly subsidize growing industries by paying higher prices.

One unpleasant fact of protective arrangements between government and developing industries is that there is a great temptation for

Highlight Eisenhower's Strategic Oil Decision

In 1954 and 1955, a first voluntary and then obligatory oil-import quota system was instituted in the United States. Under this system, American oil refineries could import only a specified amount of relatively cheap crude oil. One of the arguments given by President Dwight Eisenhower was strategic: We must be worried about our supply of oil during times of war (the Korean conflict was in progress).

Critics of the program questioned the strange reasoning of Eisenhower and his advisers. How do we preserve more oil for wartime by importing less? Don't we use up more domestically?

the industries to find excuses to keep the protection as long as possible. Therefore, even if the infant-industry argument is accepted, government protection should be a short-term measure.

Military Preparedness

Possibly the most convincing argument in favor of trade restrictions concerns military preparedness. This argument states that all essential military equipment must be manufactured in the country, even if similar equipment can be purchased cheaper elsewhere, because military supplies may be cut off if there is an altercation. For example, in 1979 the United States cut off military supplies to Iran in retaliation against imprisonment of American embassy personnel. To prevent such problems, the Soviet Union has apparently spent most of its resources on military equipment, depending on the West for providing everything else, including food and technology.

Strategic Considerations

An extension of the military-preparedness argument states that it is in the nation's best interest to be self-sufficient for essentials. The U.S. Congress, fearing that oil imports from the Middle East may either be curtailed for political reasons (as in 1973) or priced very high, introduced a bill in 1979 that will provide about $250 billion over the next ten years to develop alternative energy sources.

Unfair Competition

Often a country will restrict trade with another if it believes that it is being subjected to unfair competition. Such a charge has been brought by the U.S. steel industry against its Japanese counterparts. It is claimed that Japanese steel manufacturers can reduce their selling price because they get subsidies from their government. Although it is difficult to verify this charge, because information from Japanese manufacturers is not available, it is easy for a government to subsidize the production of a certain product.

If the U.S. government wanted to help some industry compete favorably with foreigners, it could reduce the tax on that industry's profits from about 50 percent to, say, 10 percent. Then the industry could lower the price to consumers and still make the same profit. To see how this works, study the following table (all figures are for one unit of the product):

	Tax at 50 Percent	Tax at 10 Percent
Selling price	$66	$50
Total cost	− 30	− 30
Profit before tax	$36	$20
Tax	− 18	− 2
Profit after tax	$18	$18

As you can imagine, the product that sells for $50 is far more likely to be bought by consumers than the one that sells for $66. Thus a government that is willing to manipulate tax policy can make its industries very competitive—perhaps unfairly so.

RESTRICTIONS ON TRADE

Governments use a variety of methods to restrict international trade. When a government taxes imported goods on their value, it is imposing **tariffs.** Tariffs are normally used for two purposes: to raise revenue and to protect home industry from foreign competition. A **revenue tariff** is levied mainly on expensive luxury items that are used only by the wealthy. For example, a refrigerator imported into a developing country such as Brazil or Argentina would very likely be taxed at rates exceeding 100 percent of its value. **Protective tariffs** are introduced to make imports expensive in relation to the local product. If you have a choice between a shirt made in the United States that costs $15 and one made in Hong Kong that costs $10, you are likely to purchase the shirt made in Hong Kong. But if the U.S. textile industry could persuade Congress to approve a 100-percent protective tariff, so that the shirt made in Hong Kong costs $20, you would purchase the shirt made in the United States.

Words of Wisdom from Mark Twain

"Free traders win all the arguments; protectionists win all the votes."

A government may also place a restriction on the amount of certain goods that can be imported, in order to protect the home industry and its jobs. The U.S. government has used **quotas** in the past for imports of sugar, cattle, and the like. More recently, President Jimmy Carter stated that the United States would not import more than a certain quantity of oil, mainly to enable the home industry to expand exploration and to force Americans to conserve. Similarly, the steel, automobile, and television industries are pressuring Congress to put a limit on competing imports, mainly from Japan.

An **embargo** is a more general restriction of trade between countries, mainly for political reasons. Some historians believe that the U.S. embargo on shipments of steel, fuel, and so on to Japan was partly responsible for the bombing of Pearl Harbor. More recently, the Arab oil-producing countries imposed an oil embargo against supporters of Israel, and the United States cut off shipments of technology and grain to the Soviet Union in retaliation against the Soviet invasion of Afghanistan.

There are may ways to restrict foreign competition. Tariffs, quotas, and embargoes do the job, but there is also a much more subtle way: defining "quality" in such a way that foreign products don't meet the minimum standards. Such is the case with Mexican tomatoes.

In the past, the United States has put size restrictions on imported tomatoes, knowing full well that many Mexican tomatoes are smaller than their American counterparts. This action has effectively restricted tomato imports into the United States and has protected tomato growers, particularly in California and Florida.

Do consumers mind if the tomato is too small? That depends on the price. At the "appropriate" price, American consumers will buy smaller Mexican tomatoes.

FACTORS AFFECTING INTERNATIONAL TRADE

In general, companies like to trade where they are welcome and where their assets and rights are safeguarded. This preference obviously precludes countries where governments change in fast progression, either through democratic means or through coups. Such a prejudice is understandable, since many new governments have refused to honor promises made to foreign interests by their predecessors. A good example is the takeover of American oil interests in Libya after Colonel Moammar Khadafy assumed power.

Other factors, alone or in combination, determine the existence and scope of trade relationships.

Demographics

Such factors as level of prosperity, size of the population, age levels, and level of education affect a country's imports. A rough measure of prosperity, for example, would be per-capital income. A TV manufacturer would have a greater chance of success shipping TV sets to France, which has a per-capita income of over $5,000, than to Nigeria, which has a per-capita income of about $200. Similarly, it would not be smart to ship books to a country that is undeveloped and largely illiterate.

Economic Stability

Just as most companies would like to trade with a country that is politically stable, they would also like to trade with a country that is economically stable. However, political and economic stability are not necessarily linked: Some people may consider the United Kingdom politically stable but economically unstable, whereas Chile might be considered politically unstable but economically stable.

Economic stability depends on such factors as the rate of inflation, the general attitude toward foreign businesses, the strength of the labor unions, and the amount of tax relief offered to businesses that invest in the country.

Exchange Rates

Currency exchange rates play a very important role in international trade. Assume, for example, that the exchange rate between the United States and Japan is $1 = 300 yen. If the exchange rate moves in favor of Japan—say to $1 = 200 yen—then the U.S. dollar would be cheaper for the Japanese. Furthermore, an article imported from Japan that cost Americans $1.00 at the rate of $1 = 300 yen would cost $1.50 at the rate of $1 = 200 yen. In other words, a favorable exchange rate encourages imports but discourages exports. A recent example is the temporary decline in American sales of Japanese autos in 1978 and 1979. When the Japanese yen gained strength against the dollar, Japanese autos became more expensive in relation to American autos.

Tariffs and Transportation Costs

Tariffs and transportation costs influence the price at which a product can be sold in a foreign country. They are also important factors in a company's decision whether to ship products from its home country or to set up a manufacturing plant in the foreign country. Since foreign countries have control over the tariffs they can levy, tariffs can be used to entice foreign companies. New plants are a good way to employ excess labor.

An example would clearly illustrate this point. Say that an American company wishes to ship refrigerators to Saudi Arabia by sea. Each refrigerator costs $200, and the tariffs and transportation costs for each are expected to total $120. Obviously, that company should ship the refrigerators only if they cannot be manufactured in Saudi Arabia for less than $320. A real-life example is Ford Motor Company, which manufactures its Fiesta car in Europe and then ships it to the United States. The production costs in Europe are less than in the United States, so much so that even after adding transportation costs and a token 5-percent tariff, Fiestas can compete with American-made cars.

Cultural Differences

Because people in different countries have different religions, different philosophies toward life, different idiosyncrasies, it is very important for a company to analyze the culture before it begins to trade with a country. For example, McDonald's hamburgers would most likely be a flop in India, where most people do not eat meat because their religion prohibits it or because they are too poor to afford it. Nor would a discotheque do well in modern Iran.

One particular cultural difference deserves attention: Most developing countries cannot affort to pay their civil servants enough to prevent them from asking for bribes. Thus most foreign companies have to grease the palms of a few government officials. This habit is now frowned on by Congress, which has enacted the Foreign Corrupt Practices Act of 1978, making it illegal to give bribes to foreign officials. Unfortunately, this high-minded legislation puts U.S. companies at a disadvantage, because foreign competitors remain unhindered in their efforts to get business abroad.

Production Costs

Developing countries normally have lower pay scales than developed countries, mainly beacause competition for scarce jobs brings wages down. In addition, many developing countries are not so concerned about environmental issues as the United States is and do not require their companies to install expensive equipment for reducing pollution. These factors keep production costs low in many developing countries. Thus U.S. manufacturers find it possible, for example, to have certain electronic equipment assembled in Taiwan, because even after considering two-way transportation costs and labor costs in Taiwan, it is still less expensive than having the equipment assembled in the United States.

Forms of International Trade

Once a company decides to trade with another country, it must decide the level of involvement that would be most appropriate. The company must consider not only its own needs for workers, raw materials, and a distribution or transportation system but also the needs of the country it will be dealing with. Several alternatives have developed for structuring the relationship between a company and a foreign government.

EXPORTING

Exporting is normally used when a company wishes to penetrate the market of a foreign country without making a major investment. Companies that go this route engage agents in the foreign country and pay them commissions on the basis of the number of units sold. Agents are expected to represent the manufacturer and to look out for its interests in the foreign country.

BRANCH OPERATIONS

Once a company has penetrated a foreign market, it might consider setting up a branch in that country. Setting up a branch is usually more expensive than engaging an agent, but branch operation bestows certain advantages. For example, the employees of a branch office or plant could help analyze the local political situation, make useful government contacts, and use the home company's sales and marketing expertise to further penetrate the foreign market.

LICENSING

A company may **license** its name or technology to a local group, which would permit that group on payment of royalties, to produce the company's product. An excellent example of this is The Coca-Cola Company, which licenses bottlers all over the world. However, the company keeps a certain amount of control by manufacturing the syrup in the United States; its secret ingredients are known to only a few people.

Licensing is suitable when a company finds it uneconomical to ship the products, because they can be produced at less cost in the foreign country, or when it does not believe investment in a branch in that country would be profitable. Most developing countries should encourage licensing, because they get foreign technology that gives employment to their workers and satisfies the wants of consumers. However, some countries do not quite see licensing this way. For example, India

"ou est Burger King?"

asked The Coca-Cola Company to leave when it refused to divulge the secret formula; now Indian businesspeople are trying to find a substitute for Coke to fulfill market needs.

FOREIGN MANUFACTURING

As an alternative to licensing, a company may prefer to get into foreign manufacturing—especially if it seems that the return on its investment will exceed the return on some other investment. Ford and General Motors, for example, have manufacturing plants in Europe, and Volkswagen manufactures in Pennsylvania. Japanese auto manufacturers were pressured by American labor unions to open plants in the United States or face restrictions in the form of quotas; Honda apparently agreed to open a plant in Ohio to appease the labor unions and to meet the U.S. demand for its autos.

Some countries require that local inhabitants or the government be part owner of a foreign-owned plant. Examples are India and the United Arab Emirates. However, IBM left India rather than share ownership of its Indian operations.

MULTINATIONAL CORPORATIONS

A **multinational corporation (MNC)** is one that has its headquarters in one country but whose operations are worldwide. MNCs may combine one or more of the forms of international trade discussed so far. Examples of MNCs are The Coca-Cola Company, International Business Machines (IBM) Corporation, and Ford Motor Company (all based in the United States) and Nestle, Volkswagen, and Siemens (based in Europe).

Benefits of Multinational Corporations

Multinational corporations offer benefits of free trade to the home and host countries alike. The *home country* may derive the following important advantages:

1. *Exploitation of existing technology* Since MNCs have already spent a fixed sum of research dollars to develop technology, it is in the best interests of the MNC to broaden the market for that technology. Examples would be the oil-drilling technology developed by oil companies or the advanced drug and pharmaceutical technology developed by U.S. drug manufacturers. Of course, the more revenues an MNC can generate the more it can return to its country in the form of profits and dividends to stockholders.
2. *Improvement in the standard of living* When additional foreign profits are earned, they are normally divided between the government, stockholders, laborers (in the form of higher wages), and the MNC. This inflow of profits into the home country increases the demand for consumer goods, production, jobs, and so on.

Highlight The World Car

The international basis of the Ford Motor Company is emphasized both in its design and marketing of the Escort model. Called the World Car, the Escort, incorporates technological advances made at company engineering facilities throughout the world.

Ford of Germany worked on refinements to the basic engine design and Ford of Britain handled performance development, while Ford's U.S. engine engineering operations ensured that design, development, durability, and feasibility objectives were met for the North American market. The result of this worldwide effort is the smallest and most efficient engine in the history of Ford U.S.

Ford's $3-billion Escort development program also produced a sister line of cars for Europe that carry the same nameplate. With minor differences, the interior dimensions of both Escorts are the same, while the exteriors are tailored to individual market tastes.

Prior to its unveiling, the Escort was pictured in print and television ads draped in a cover made from the flags of several different countries. Although Ford says that 95 percent of the Escort's parts are made and assembled in the United States and Canada, the tenor of its advertising is to lessen the identification of Ford as strictly an American car.

3. *Increased profitability for local manufacturers* When an MNC sets up a capital-intensive operation in a foreign country, it is likely to give the contract for building the machinery to a supplier in the home country whose quality it is confident about. For example, the machinery for most oil rigs in the world was manufactured in America.
4. *Cheaper products imported into the home country* Most often, MNCs do business in countries where the costs of production, whether for raw materials or labor, are substantially lower than those in the home country. This enables them to produce cheaper goods, and these goods are often exported back to the home country. For example, clothing and TV sets manufactured in Taiwan are relatively inexpensive in the United States.

The MNC and the home country are not the only parties to benefit. There are also a few important advantages to the *host country:*

1. *Transfer of proven technology* The host country benefits from an inflow of technology that it has no resources to develop. For example, it would have taken West Germany and Japan much longer to develop economically after World War II without American technology. And the Middle Eastern oil-producing countries would not be so prosperous today without the aid of American technology.
2. *Creation of employment* When an MNC starts a plant in a host country, it must hire a work force. It offers employment to many who would otherwise have no jobs and would therefore have to depend on welfare or starve to death.
3. *Increase in national wealth* When an MNC makes a profit in a foreign country, it has earned more revenue than it has incurred in the form of expenses. This prosperity is shared by the host government (taxes sometimes amount to 60 to 70 percent of profits), local work-

ers, and the MNC. The government can then spend more on social programs to help its citizens.

4. *Provision of good but inexpensive products to consumers* MNCs usually introduce sophisticated technology to a host country, which results in inexpensive products in the place of expensive products manufactured by antiquated technology. Its citizens can therefore buy better products and save some money as well.

Problems with Multinational Corporations

In view of all these advantages it may appear that MNCs are an unmixed blessing. However, that view is not shared by many host countries, for the following reasons:

1. *Influence on the government* Some governments fear the power of MNCs to influence the direction in which the host country is heading. However, an MNC often has to protect its investment, often from the whim of a despotic dictator. An extreme example of this interference was the role of International Telephone & Telegraph Corporation in the downfall of the Chile's Marxist government in 1970.
2. *Exploitation of the host country* The most common complaint against MNCs is that they earn exorbitant profits and thereby exploit the local government and its people. This argument is unfortunately unresolvable, because what is exorbitant is a matter of opinion. However, many countries, such as Iran, have used this excuse to expropriate MNCs' interests.
3. *Imposition of foreign culture and practices* Some countries disapprove when MNCs behave as they would in their home countries. For example, local employees in MNC operations are usually expected to follow the dress and other standards of the MNC's home country.
4. *Introduction of superfluous products* Many developing countries do not like to waste valuable foreign exchange by sharing MNC's profits and paying royalties on such presumably superfluous luxury products as cosmetics, soft drinks, and the like. Thus most host countries issue licenses only for those products that they believe are useful for their development.
5. *Exploitation of cheap labor* Many MNCs have been criticized, often by their executives, for offering much lower wages to workers in developing countries than they would offer to workers in the home country. However, in defense of the MNCs, it must be stated that their laborers are generally paid more than other workers in the host country.
6. *Transfer of inappropriate technology* Most of the technology exported by MNCs is related to labor-saving devices, whereas most developing countries have an abundance of cheap labor and hence would prefer labor-intensive technolgoy. For example, the Indian

Highlight Does Direct Investment Do Harm?

If an American company went into France and gained a monopoly in the production of transistors, France would undoubtedly suffer from distortion in prices and quantities. But France has no more reason to fear an American monopoly than a French monopoly: Both would have exactly the same effect on prices and quantities. French, German, Spanish, Japanese, Italian, and other countries' antitrust laws could be enforced against MNCs just as easily as against national corporations. The entrance of American MNCs into a foreign country should therefore be no cause for alarm—at least not because of the possibility of a monopoly.

What about the possibility that an American MNC would take all its profits out of France? Certainly, that possibility exists. But so what? When Americans take profits out of France they take them in the form of French francs. Those francs are only useful if Americans somehow spend them in France. Thus any profits that are taken out of France will ultimately come back to France in exchange for French goods. There is really little chance that American MNCs could somehow "bleed" a foreign country of its resources.

government under the premiership of Mr. M. Desai reintroduced the spinning wheel as a means of employing more workers.

7. *Dominance of foreign nationals* Because most developing countries were colonies in the nineteenth and twentieth centuries, they are deeply sensitive to the fact that almost all the high-level jobs in MNCs' operations are held by foreign nationals. Some people argue that these foreign nationals are not uniquely qualified managers but just long-time employees who are given a brief stint in a top position before they retire.

U.S. Trade with the World

Given all the possible forms of international trade and the vitality of American business, it should come as no surprise that the United States has considerable trade with other countries. Exhibit 23.1 shows one measure of U.S. trade in 1973 and 1978. Note that the United States purchased (or imported) more than it sold (or exported). The result was a deficit in both years. The 1973 deficit was attributed mainly to the Vietnam conflict; productive resources were diverted to producing guns and munitions. The 1978 deficit was due primarily to the quadrupling of crude-oil prices by the Organization of Petroleum Exporting. Coun-

EXHIBIT 23.1 U.S. Trade with the World in 1973 and 1978

	1973 (in million of dollars)	1978	Increase (in percentages)
Exports	49,676	143,660	189
Imports	55,555	172,952	211
Deficit	5,879	29,292	

NOTE: From Statistical Abstract of the United States, U.S. Department of Commerce, Bureau of the Census, 1979.

tries (OPEC). Nevertheless, U.S. trade increased dramatically between 1973 and 1978.

Exhibit 23.2 shows U.S. *exports* by commodity for 1973 and 1978. As you can see, the mix of exports has not changed substantially. In absolute terms, however, exports of machinery increased from $13.5 billion in 1973 to $38.1 billion in 1978.

Exhibit 23.3 shows the mix of *imports* in the two years. Even though the share of transport equipment decreased from 17.1 percent in 1973 to 13.3 percent in 1978, the value of these imports increased from $9.5 billion in 1973 to $22.9 billion in 1978. However, the greatest change in the mix of imports is the increase in crude-oil purchases from $4.8 billion in 1973 to $42.1 billion in 1978, which was the primary cause for trade deficits in 1978.

Now consider which countries the United States traded with. Ex-

EXHIBIT 23.2 U.S. Exports in 1973 and 1978 by Commodity

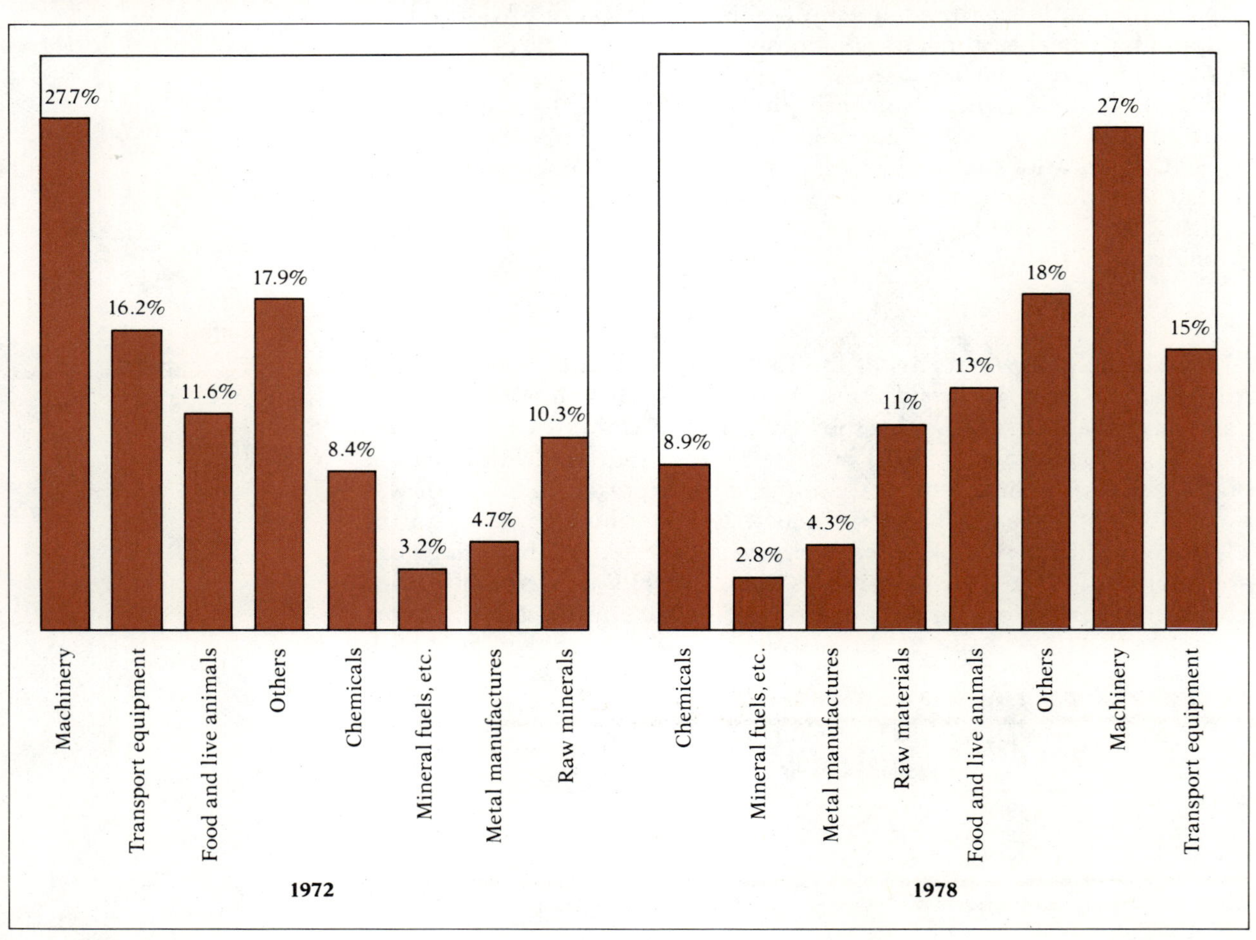

hibit 23.4 shows U.S. exports and imports in 1978 by region and country. Europe, for example, took 30.5 percent of our exports but sent only 22 percent of our imports; in this case, the United States is a net exporter. However, Japan had a trade surplus with the United States of $11.5 billion, mainly because of heavy U.S. imports of automobiles, TV sets, and steel. Africa's trade surplus is mainly the result of oil purchases from Nigeria and Libya, which had surpluses of $3.8 billion and $3.3 billion, respectively.

Accounting for International Trade

U.S. trade deficits are continuing in the 1980s. Let's examine how those trade deficits are settled by nations and how those settlements lead to inflation, loss of jobs, and other economic problems. But first, let's differentiate between balance of trade and balance of payments. **Balance of trade** is the difference between the exports and imports of a country. **Balance of payments** is the difference between the amounts earned and

EXHIBIT 23.3 U.S. Imports in 1973 and 1978 by Commodity

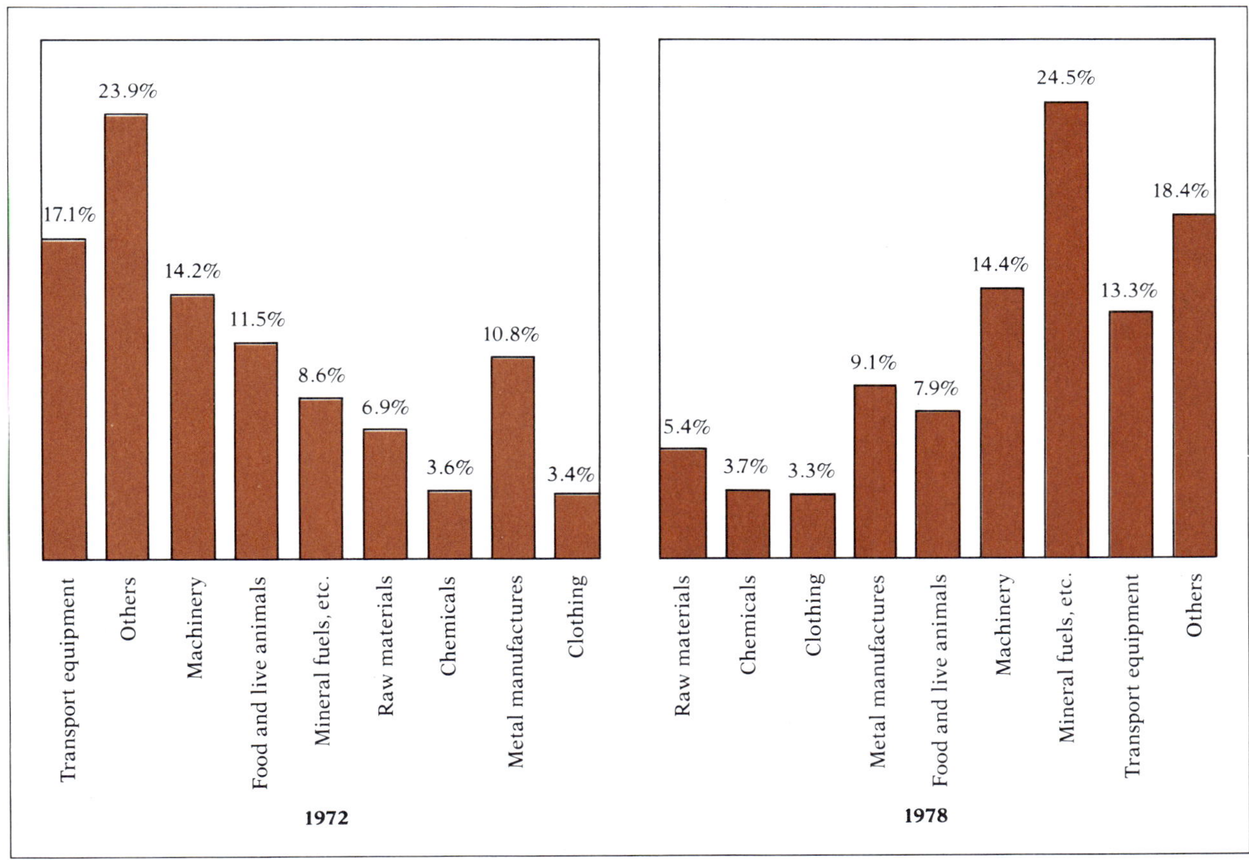

owed by a country. These amounts would include payments and receipts for commodities traded but would also include fund transfers for services such as banking, insurance, and investment.

THE GOLD STANDARD

Until the early twentieth century, gold was the crucial medium of exchange in national and international trade. A nation's volume of currency, whether of cheaper metal or paper, was based on the volume of gold that it owned. When one country, say England, had a trade deficit with the United States, it would transfer gold and thereby reduce the volume of its currency in circulation. As a result, England would undergo a minor economic transformation that would cause prices to fall. Simultaneously, the United States would have to increase the currency in circulation to account for the inflow of gold, leading to higher prices. Obviously, in a case like this, England would be the country to buy in and the United States would be the country to sell in. But eventually

EXHIBIT 23.4 U.S. Exports and Imports in 1978 by Country

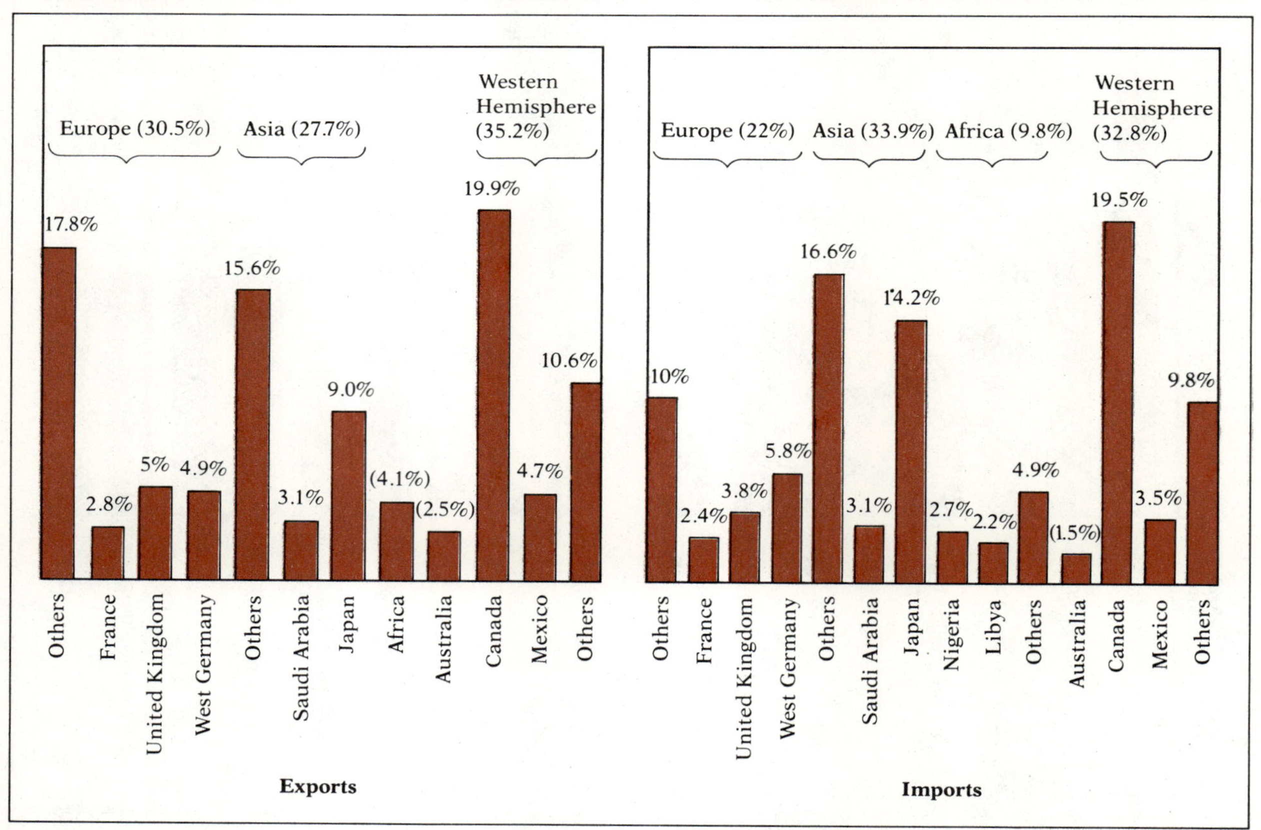

England would have the trade surplus and win back at least part of the gold it had shipped to the United States.

The gold standard therefore kept exchange rates stable at the expense of economic stability in the trading countries. Attempting to avoid disruptions, many countries refused to increase or decrease the volume of currency as their situation demanded. Use of the gold standard ended when countries refused to settle their debts in gold.

THE BRETTON WOODS SYSTEM

After World War II, most of the industrialized nations came together at Bretton Woods, New Hampshire to work out a substitute for the gold standard. It was decided that trade debts could be paid in the local currency of the debtor. However, only a few countries, like the United States, still converted their currencies into gold on demand. Thus other countries could easily be tempted to pay their debts by printing extra currency. The International Monetary Fund was formed to prevent this problem.

The duty of the **International Monetary Fund (IMF)** was to watch out for countries with continuous trade deficits that were printing up notes to pay for them. The IMF was expected to ask such a country to pay in gold or to reduce its exchange rate in comparison to other currencies.

By the 1960s, the United States was having balance of payments problems, due to heavy investments all over the world and unproductive expenditures during the Vietnam conflict. For some time, the United States paid off its deficits in gold, but when gold became quite scarce, it gave other countries IOUs, convertible into gold. This policy of "benign neglect" suited the United States, because all it had to give for imported goods was a piece of paper printed with a promise. However, the other countries soon caught on and began demanding gold for the IOUs. Since the United States no longer had enough gold, it had to abandon convertibility of the dollar into gold in 1978. The IMF lost influence then, because it had apparently been unable to control the United States.

FLOATING EXCHANGE RATES

The collapse of the gold standard and the Bretton Woods system indicated that no system could avoid daily fluctuations in the exchange rates. Hence **floating exchange rates,** based on demand for the supply of a currency, came into play. If a country exports some commodity from the United States, it must buy the dollars to pay for the commodity from some country that has earned dollars in trade with the United States.

Say that there is $1 billion floating around in Europe and that Europe needs $100 million to pay for its imports from the United States. Since the supply of American dollars is much greater than the demand, the dollar would come cheaply in exchange for a currency such as the German mark. This fall in the value of the dollar should make U.S. exports cheaper and imports into the U.S. more expensive and thereby restore equilibrium.

Unfortunately, the United States has certain domestic problems, such as inflation and low productivity, that suppress the value of the dollar, and so it pays for imports by printing more dollars. One of our country's oil suppliers, Saudi Arabia, warned in 1979 that it would have to increase its oil prices to make up for the decreasing value of the dollar.

- International trade forces local businesses to compete with foreign businesses, thereby allowing customers to choose the cheapest and best product.
- The theory of comparative advantage is that each country or region should concentrate on producing those commodities that it can produce more efficiently than other countries. The theory is based on the concept of specialization, which means that Brazil produces coffee, Cuba produces sugar, the Middle East produces crude oil, and so on.
- Free trade between countries is often restricted, for several reasons. Some believe that free trade transfers unemployment to the host country and hurts local industries that are attempting to develop. It is also argued that no country should depend on another for strategic weapons and materials. Lastly, host countries are often upset by the subsidies granted to foreign businesses by their home governments to make them more competitive; many host countries have instituted laws that prevent foreign businesses from selling at less cost than at home.
- Governments have often restricted trade by stopping all imports into the country to protect developing industries or by taxing imports to make them uncompetitive with local products. Sometimes governments have set quotas for imports. They have even stopped all trade with foreign countries for political reasons.
- Before a company decides to trade in a foreign market, it should evaluate the political and economic situation in the host country, including the level of prosperity, the level of education, the culture, and economic stability, which is often reflected in inflation and exchange rates. Besides these general considerations, a company that wants to do business in a foreign country should consider the availabilty of raw materials, cheap labor, tariffs, and transportation costs.

- A company can trade in a foreign market through various channels. It can export its merchandise to an agent or set up a branch office in the host country. Or it could license its technology, as The Coca-Cola Company does, or set up manufacturing plants in that country.
- Multinational corporations are those whose operations cross international borders. Some countries have welcomed the MNCs as harbingers of prosperity, whereas other countries have accused them of exploiting developing nations.
- In the 1950s, the United States had a favorable trade balance. But the Vietnam conflict in the late 1960s and the quadrupling of oil prices in 1973 have turned the surplus into a deficit.
- Trade surpluses and deficits were originally settled by a transfer of gold. After World War II, paper currency was used to settle debts, with the International Monetary Fund acting as an overseeing authority. After 1972, the IMF lost its importance in the monetary world, and debts were settled by purchasing in the open market the foreign currencies needed for trade.

1. Explain the rationale behind the theory of comparative advantage.
2. What are the popular reasons for restricting trade?
3. Say that you are the vice president in charge of foreign operations for a multinational corporation: Outline your considerations in establishing trade with Argentina.
4. Under what circumstances would a corporation prefer to license its technology rather than set up a manufacturing unit?
5. Evaluate the arguments against MNC operations in the developing countries. Do you disagree with the arguments presented in the chapter? Why or why not?
6. Name and describe three American MNCs that operate in at least six other countries.

APPLICATION

Ford Motor Company, with sales of over $40 billion and earnings of over $1 billion, is the second-largest automobile corporation in the world. It has manufacturing, assembly, and sales facilities in 30 countries, and its products are sold in 200 countries. It has over 500,000 employees worldwide and over 300,000 stockholders.

Ford Motor Company

A BRIEF HISTORY

Ford Motor Company was started by Henry Ford in 1903, with ten employees in a small converted factory in Detroit, Michigan. Its first car, the Model A, sold for less than $1,000. The company really took off with the introduction of the legendary Model T in 1908. The Model T was the embodiment of Ford's dream of manufacturing low-cost reliable transportation, and it sold for less than $400. Although 10,000 Model Ts were produced in the first year, demand was much greater. After experimenting for three years, Ford introduced an assembly line for automobiles that allowed production to increase dramatically. In 1914, Ford again surprised the world by offering $5 to employees for an eight-hour day, which was double the existing rate for a nine-hour day.

By 1927, when the Model T was discontinued because it could no longer compete with the vast variety of autos on the market, Ford had sold 1.5 million units and was on its way to becoming a giant industrial complex that spanned the globe. However, this growth suffered during World War II, when Ford was involved in the production of bombers, aircraft engines, and other war materials. In 1945, when Henry Ford II became president, the company was losing several million dollars a month. He rebuilt the company by adding twenty-four manufacturing and thirteen assembly plants in the United States. Ford regained its leading position in the automobile industry.

Today Ford produces not only cars, trucks, and tractors but also steel, glass, vinyl, and paint. It also produces sophisticated electronic components for use in communications, space exploration, and national defense.

INTERNATIONAL OPERATIONS

Ford's venture into the international market started when a Model A was shipped to a Canadian distributor in 1903. By 1915, Ford had built assembly plants in Canada, England, and France, and by the 1920s, it had assembly plants in other parts of Europe, Mexico, Latin America, and Japan. However, these assembly plants used components shipped primarily from plants in the United States. Sensing the growing frustration of the host countries with this arrangement, Ford instructed its overseas managers in 1924 to purchase more components locally as long as the local cost was less than the U.S. cost plus freight, insurance, and tariffs.

As its operations grew and Ford realized the need for more overseas manufacturing and assembly plants, Ford encouraged cooperation between its overseas operations. As a result, manufacturing plants in, say, Europe shipped the components they specialized in to assembly plants all over Europe. This practice reduced tooling and production costs due to economies of scale. For example, Pinto engines and components are produced in Europe and assembled in the United States and Canada.

The importance of Ford's overseas operations can be judged from the charts in Exhibit 23.5. The charts indicate that Ford earned almost 49 percent of its net income by investing 44 percent of its total assets overseas (i.e., outside the U.S.). In other words, Ford made better use of its resources overseas than at home. For each dollar invested, Ford earned 10 cents overseas and only 6.9 cents at home. Similarly, Ford earned 49 percent of its net income on 35 percent of total sales. This means that the overseas profit margin was better. For every dollar of sales, Ford earned 5.3 cents overseas and 2.9 cents at home.

NEW REALITIES

Ford and other U.S. automakers have realized that they can no longer sell large quantities of highly profitable cars because of high oil prices and oil scarcity. Ford's global strategy for survival in the 1980s therefore depends on (1) avoiding direct competition with General Motors Corporation in the United States and (2) making optimum use of its facilities all over the world.

Because Ford does not want to trade punches with General Motors in attempting to reach the same market segment, Ford's cars are expected to be slotted between General Motors cars in size and price. An example would be Ford's new Escort, which is slotted between GM's Chevette and Citation.

Ford intends to make optimum use of the facilities it has already invested in by producing a new "world car" and by "upsizing" its smaller cars. The rationale behind a world car is to be able to produce components in large quantities but to put them together to suit different customer preferences in different countries. For example, Europeans prefer powerful cars and would probably be dissatisfied with U.S.-made cars, which lose power because of emission-control requirements. The Escort and the Lynx is Ford's world car, and Ford plans a variation on the basic model every six months in North America. Ford expects to start out by producing 500,000 of these cars in North America annually but expects to reach the profitable plateau of 1 million cars a year.

As for "upsizing," Ford believes that it can put some luxuries that people want—like air conditioning—into its basic small car and sell it for a good profit. This concept is in contrast to GM's strategy of "downsizing" its large cars by shortening and lightening them but charging the same price. Ford's concept of upsizing is

EXHIBIT 23.5 Ford's Overseas Operations for 1978

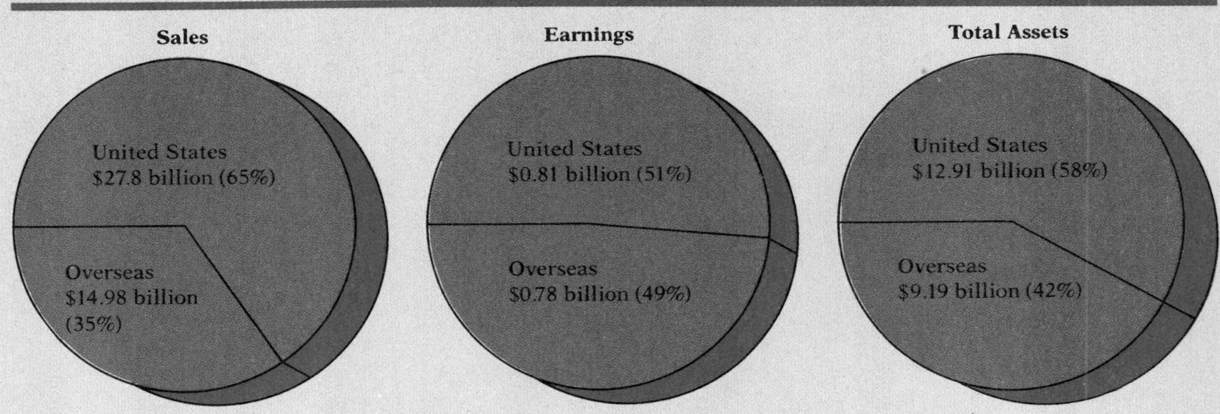

meant to reach people who would have ignored the small car with its regular features.

These strategies were designed to help Ford compete effectively at home, but Ford expects its international operations to contribute and benefit as well. Since Europe represents about 60 percent of Ford's total overseas sales, it has developed specific plans for its European operations. First, to use its American capacity more efficiently, Ford introduced the U.S.-made Mustang to Europe, which has received it warmly. If this trend develops, Ford could replace the German-made Capri with the Mustang. This would free the European facilities for production of the Escort.

This strategy could be affected by the European proposal to limit the work week to thirty-five hours. A shorter work week would waste existing capacity and increase the production costs of all European manufacturers, making their cars uncompetitive with U.S.- and Japanese-made cars. In fact, Ford is already facing underutilization of its Spanish plant. The union's refusal to allow work on Saturdays had limited production to 450,000 Fiestas yearly, although more could be produced and sold.

Many European auto companies have started collaborating on production, and even sharing assembly plants, to make better use of facilities. An example is the joint venture between Volvo, Peugeot, and Renault to build engines in France. But a similar venture between GM and Ford would very likely be prevented in the United States, due to antitrust laws. U.S. law also penalizes U.S. auto producers by demanding more stringent pollution standards than other countries do.

Besides attempting to better utilize its capacity, Ford is forced to compete with Europe-based automakers that are either partly or fully owned by the host government—for example, British Leyland in the United Kingdom and Renault in France. These companies are not allowed to go bankrupt because of the jobs that would be lost. Therefore, the government set prices at an artificially high level which has the effect of increasing profits for Ford.

Another area of concern to Ford is the rising labor costs in West Germany, which makes German-made cars more costly to produce. Besides, the strength of the German mark in relation to other currencies means that German-made cars are more expensive. German manufacturers such as Mercedes Benz, and to a limited extent, Volkswagen have gotten around this problem by aiming their cars at the high-price segment—where price does not matter too much. Ford, however, does not presently appear to have any car that it could aim at that exclusive segment.

Ford's future in Europe depends on the success of its world car and its ability to achieve optimum use of its facilities.

CAREER OPPORTUNITIES

Although entry-level positions in Ford Motor Company's overseas operations are usually restricted to local people, many of Ford's top managers have served stints overseas while climbing the corporate ladder.

Ford offers entry-level positions in this country for graduates in business administration, engineering, science, and other related fields. New employees can join such areas as product planning, product engineering, manufacturing and plant engineering, sales and marketing, supply, industrial relations, and finance systems.

Let's look more closely at one of these areas—say product planning, which involves the development and design of cars. A recently hired graduate would probably start as an analyst, working as a part of a small project team. Participation would involve cost-benefit studies, optional-equipment evaluation, pricing determinations, and the like. With experience and proven performance, an employee could advance to more responsible management positions in Ford's worldwide operations.

FOR DISCUSSION

1. Why is the concept of a "world car" so attractive to Ford? What specific advantage does it offer?
2. What specific factors are preventing Ford from efficiently using its capacity in Europe?

OBJECTIVES

- ☐ To describe advances in technology that will affect the business environment in the world of tomorrow
- ☐ To show how the management function will change
- ☐ To describe some of the most recent computer developments in the workplace
- ☐ To describe what it will be like to work in an automated office
- ☐ To describe the security problems inherent in a computerized workplace and methods of coping with computerized crime
- ☐ To describe how the use of computers by organizations can affect individual privacy

OUTLINE

KEY TERMS

CATHODE-RAY TUBE (CRT)
COMPUTER GRAPHICS
COMPUTER MODELING
ELECTRONIC MAIL
ENCRYPTION
INFORMATION OVERLOAD
MANAGEMENT WORK STATION
PRIVACY ACT OF 1974
SATELLITE-BASED COMMUNICATIONS NETWORK
TELECONFERENCING

BUSINESS IN THE WORLD OF TOMORROW

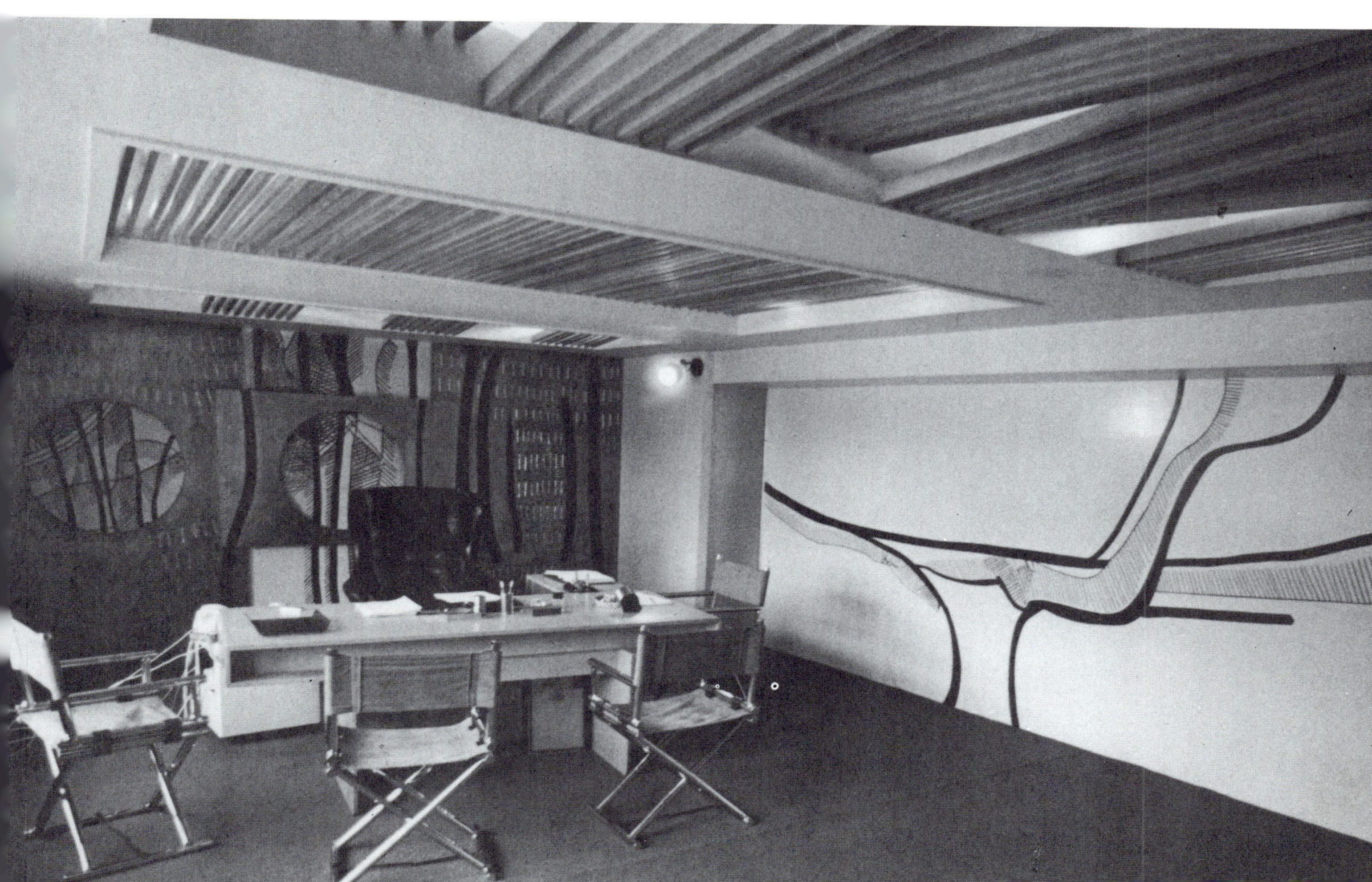

The Future of Work

DAVID CLUTTERBUCK
International Management, August 1979

The explosive growth of automation predicted during the remaining years of the 20th century could produce a push-button, drudgery-free work environment in industry. Or it could prove a dire threat to economic, social and even political stability. No-one, least of all the experts, is prepared to predict which scenario will emerge from the current revolution in the partnership between man and machine.

But a few clues are becoming apparent, even to the most sceptical of crystal-ball gazers. Job, and even career, mobility, for example, will become commonplace in the future. Computerized information processing could wipe out the jobs of many middle managers or change them so much as to make them unrecognizable. The distinction between blue-collar and white-collar workers is almost certain to narrow and perhaps disappear altogether. The giant manufacturing plants of today, with thousands of workers on a single site, will become museum-pieces.

Overlying all this will be a dramatic reduction in the need for labour, at least in the manufacturing sector. Thomas Stonier, professor of the school of science and society at Bradford University in the UK, predicts that the manufacturing sector will shrink from its present 50% of the total work-force in most industrialized countries to only 10% by the end of the century. Other experts put the figure at closer to 30%. Although it is generally agreed that most people in developed countries will have some kind of job in the year 2000, this reduction, whatever its size, implies a major switch of labour resources from production industries to the service sector.

Adrian Norman, a UK-based consultant with US firm Arthur D. Little Inc., borrows a concept from nuclear physics to dramatize the rate at which technology is swallowing up jobs. He suggests that the "half-life" of jobs, that is, the period of time in which the market demand for a particular type of job is halved, has been falling for the past 180 years. That is virtually ever since the Industrial Revolution created the modern concept of work.

"People entering the work-force in 1920 could expect their jobs to have half-lives of 30 years," says Norman. "Now we are down to 20 or even 15 years. So there is an even chance that everyone will change his career twice in a life-time. In ten years' time, though, people may have to change careers three or four times."

Few workers at any level, however, have the wide range of skills needed to make such transitions. In part, this reflects current corporate attitudes. "Companies tend to train and qualify their staffs in a way oriented to their own fields of business," explains a spokesman for the Commission of the nine-nation Common Market. "This creates a qualified staff for individual firms, but a national labour force that is segmented by businesses."

Some firms are attempting to meet this problem. Royal Dutch/Shell Group, for example, holds self-development seminars for employees. The one-week courses teach personnel from all levels to understand their obejctives in life and how to seek career goals, inside or outside Shell, that will meet them.

Like a number of other firms, Shell is also encouraging small firms to set up around its plants to soak up the labour that technology is forcing it to make redundant.

It has also been suggested that companies should carefully vet technical innovations that will displace workers to make sure they are truly cost-effective. Barry Sherman, research officer of the UK's Association of Scientific, Technical & Managerial Staffs (ASTMS), for example, proposes that companies appoint independent "technology stewards." Explains Sherman: "They would be informed by a company of its future intentions regarding technological change and the likely direct and indirect effects. They would ensure that trade unions had time to come to terms with the changes and look at the retraining opportunities and alternative market possibilities."

The effectiveness of corporate training schemes may well be a key factor in determining market success in the future. Industries that adopted the new technologies quickly have grown and taken on more labour. Those that have been slow have shrunk and shed employees.

In fact, claims Dr. Thomas Sommerlatter of Arthur D. Little's West German office, some sectors of industry are already running into trouble because they cannot train their employees fast enough to cope with technological advances. "Many telephone companies, for example, are slowing down the introduction of new technology because so many of their employees are unfamiliar with micro-electronics," he says.

Philip Sadler, principal of Ashridge Management College in the UK, sees training and education as a major growth industry in the future. He forecasts that continuous education will become a commonplace of industry in the future, especially for top managers.

However, for this training to be effective, the quality of corporate education will have to be vastly improved, says Sadler. "Any other activity with as low a productivity increment as education would have gone out of business years ago," he says.

Retrained or not, however, middle managers face a depressing future, if they have one at all. Academic Stonier predicts that middle managers will gradually be phased out as their function becomes obsolete. Sir Charles Handy, warden of St. George's House conference centre in the UK, agrees. "The whole of middle management is information processing," he says. "That can almost all be done by computer. Middle managers' only function will be to produce reports on exceptions to general rules."

UK consultant Norman believes that every level of management will become less interesting, but at the same time more demanding. The instant information available from a desk-top terminal will cut out much of the rewarding personal contacts and relationships that managers today enjoy. The manager of the future will be faced with a rapid succession of raw data upon which, in virtual isolation, he must take decisions.

The shrinking need for middle managers will be accompanied by a narrowing of the distinction between blue-collar and white-collar employees. The difference between a shop-floor operator programming a machine tool at a keyboard and a clerical worker at a visual display unit will not be great, except that the shop-floor employee will probably have a greater knowledge of the working of his machine. For many jobs in manufacturing, the manual content will consist largely of monitoring automatic equipment and making occasional adjustments.

The effects of these changes on job satisfaction are wide open to speculation. Whether future patterns of work will create more interesting jobs or condemn large numbers of workers and managers to mindless machine minding is a contentious issue.

Arthur D. Little's Sommerlatter believes job satisfaction will improve in the future. Social and technological changes, he says, will create more jobs, particularly in electronics, rather than more unemployment. In many of the new jobs, he maintains, people will have increased scope for using their own creativity.

Other experts agree, arguing that new technologies could be used to open up previously "closed" professions such as medicine. Computer-controlled diagnostic equipment could provide new careers in the medical profession for employees with currently unacceptable qualifications.

On the other hand, it is widely admitted that advanced technology frequently lowers job satisfaction, as is the case with managers. A study by UK bank Williams & Glynn Ltd. into the effect of new technology on work and recruitment highlighted this.

The study started on the basis that the bank might need proportionately more people of higher skill to handle advanced technological systems. In fact, the study indicated the reverse. It revealed that the amount of work requiring the attention of highly qualified staff would increase much more slowly than the volume of routine work.

Much of this down-grading of jobs is connected with the physical reorganization of industry that is likely to take place. It is generally agreed that the large-scale manufacturing plant will disappear. "It no longer seems necessary to bring all the people in a firm together in one place to do a job," says UK conference organizer Handy. "In fact, it is stupid to do so. It allows them to increase their bargaining power.

"In the future, companies will keep their units very small. They will dismantle the hierarchy and spread out the work. This will make them more flexible. Some functions will be kept at the centre. But there will be a lot fewer people there. The centre will simply co-ordinate things, with much of the rest of the work being contracted out."

This decentralization of industry will coincide with, and reinforce, the social movement of people away from declining inner city areas into more prosperous and pleasant medium-sized towns. This trend could produce its own social and possible political problems, however. It has been suggested, for example, that it could lead to a divided industrial work-force. The fortunate, well-paid, probably highly skilled workers will be dispersed into service and light manufacturing industries away from the cities. Behind them they will leave a reservoir of less well paid, less skilled workers dependent on failing heavy industries.

Another aspect of this problem is expanded by Dr. Mario Unnia of Italian management consultants Prospecta SARL. Unnia has been looking into future work trends for the state-owned ENI group of companies.

The rapid automation of the early 1980s, he suggests, will lead to a growth in the number of part-time workers in manufacturing industries. By the end of the 1980s, only 80% of the labour force in an industrial plant will be full-time. By the mid-1990s, this could be less than 50%.

The major problem companies will face will be how to deal with what amounts to two completely different work-forces. The full-time employees will include managers and a small nucleus of essential staff. But the rest of the work-force, such as salesmen, maintenance engineers and production workers, could all be part-time. "We will have to work out how to compensate these two groups of people," says Unnia. "Companies will have to design completely new personnel and industrial relations policies."

Part-time workers are less likely to feel company loyalty, he points out. At the same time, though, they are more difficult for unions to organize effectively.

In addition, Unnia claims, the growth of part-time work will have consequences for training and job satisfaction. Companies will be less willing to train their part-time workers. "And if a high proportion of people choose to work part-time," he says, "many jobs will stay as basic piece-work activities. It is easier to put part-time workers in simple, repetitive jobs than in complicated work."

As more and more people leave the full-time labour market, companies will have to face up to changes in the definitions and interrelationships of work and leisure.

They will have to decide how far they want to become involved in preparing employees for greater leisure. Some experts, for example, suggest that there could be special company training programmes on the lines of the now widespread pre-retirement courses.

John Hughes, former deputy chairman of the recently disbanded Price Commission in the UK, thinks that companies should encourage under-utilized workers to take time off for voluntary community service. The Post Office Engineering Union in the UK has already suggested that its members should install telephones in elderly people's homes in their spare time, with the state-run Post Office providing the equipment.

Sadler, of the UK's Ashridge Management College, suggests that while companies are helping employees identify career paths towards which training and education should be directed, they should also seek out talents that are unrelated to particular jobs. An employee may have an undeveloped talent as a singer, for example, or as a craftsman.

"The whole development of leisure is yet to come," says Sadler. "In the end, it will spill over into the commercial world because talent and skill always find a market. We will have to drop the distinction between amateur and professional. It's a hindrance to the development of talent. So too is the distinction between work and leisure."

The applications for automation are growing, and so is its effect on the labor force. This chapter discusses the various uses for automation in the form of computerization, in the workplace of the future.

The world of tomorrow will be filled with electronic gadgetry. Picture phones and satellite communications systems will enable executives around the world to hold meetings as if they all worked in the same building. Typewriters outfitted with logic chips will become powerful word processors. Businesses, banks, and homes will be linked through computer-controlled communications networks, thus greatly reducing the need for cash. Unfortunately, some people will discover that the computer can be used just as easily outside of the law as within, and a new breed of computerized criminals will be spawned. The computer will also cause the disruption of many current jobs. The computer, therefore, will bring both desirable and undesirable changes into the world of tomorrow.

The Computer and the Manager

One of the nicest things about computer-controlled machines is that they will assume much of the drudgery of the workplace. Not only are we likely to have robots on the assembly line, however; computers and other advanced technologies will increasingly become critical to managers. The hope is that managers will be able to cope with these changes and to use them to enhance the quality of life for workers, customers, and society as a whole.

TOOLS FOR COMMUNICATIONS

Perhaps the greatest management role for computers and other technologies will be in the area of communication. This has been, after all, one of management's main functions. In the future, however, managers' powers to communicate—with workers, customers, and other organizations—will be boosted by some very efficient machines and systems. A few of them are described here.

Teleconferencing

Imagine that four regional sales managers for a large firm are discussing among themselves marketing strategies for the upcoming year. Meetings like this are carried on every day throughout the country. What makes this particular meeting unusual, however, is that the four sales managers are in Los Angeles, New York, London, and Sydney.The four managers are **teleconferencing,** or using computers and satellite communications networks to hear, see, and talk to their counterparts—and to make regional reports instantly available to all conference members.

The advantages of teleconferencing are fairly obvious. The main advantage to executives is that a communications network is being substituted for a transportation network. The data can be transmitted much quicker through electricity than through physical distribution systems. Thus executives can put their time to better use.

A question that remains, however, is whether data can be transmitted more cheaply through teleconferencing. Although the costs of transmitting a given amount of data are quite small, a major obstacle to most firms is the high initial fixed cost of setting up the system. Thus, for the present, a full-scale teleconferencing system is beyond the financial reach of all but the largest firms.

Satellite-Based Communications Networks

At the heart of a teleconferencing system, or any large-scale communications system of the future, will be a satellite communications link. At present, most computerized data is transmitted over conventional telephone lines. Yet a telephone-based system is relatively slow and expensive and has a limited capactiy. Furthermore, the sound quality of telephone transmission can be quite unreliable. A computer hooked into any communications system will not function if it does not "hear" what it is programmed to hear.

A **satellite based communications network** will overcome these dificiencies. Such a system could transmit nearly a million characters of data per second, a rate sixty times faster than most telephone-based systems. The capacity would be increased similarly: It has been estimated that such a system could transmit the equivalent of a truckload of printed material in just half an hour. Furthermore, costs would be much lower (on a unit basis), and reliability is much higher with the satellite-based systems.

Several different types of systems have been proposed. In one, a user company could lease space on a satellite for transmission purposes. That firm would install a ground-to-satellite communications station at as many of its own sites as it would like to include in the network. Communications to and from the satellite would take place with a rooftop "dish" antenna. Communications between sites would be possible by bouncing transmissions off the satellite.

Another type of system would have only one ground-to-satellite station per metropolitan area. This station would be operated by a service company. Subscribers to the service would transmit electronic messages to the station, which would in turn be transmitted, via the satellite, to a similar station in another city. The service company there would transmit the message to the customer on the receiving end. The advantage of this system would be that the initial costs of setting up the earth stations could be spread over many users. The service company would also be better able to maintain the system. The primary disadvantage would be that only large cities could support such a system.

There are substantial costs and technical problems inherent in implementing large-scale communications networks, and government regulations could also hinder their development. Congress has allowed telephone companies a monopoly in certain areas—so that telephone companies can recover their high fixed costs and so that all areas of the country will be guaranteed access to telephone services. The pertinent legal question is whether satellite-based systems will infringe on the legislated rights of the telephone companies. Furthermore, the Federal Communications Commission is concerned that satellite systems will use publicly owned broadcasting frequencies.

Electronic Mail

Both voices and data can be communicated over satellite communications systems. Actually, however, voice communications are translated into numbers representing all the characteristics of speech; the numbers are then transmitted. On the receiving end, the numbers are reassembled as human speech. Thus voice and data communications via satellite are really the same thing.

Printed material can also be transmitted through an **electronic mail** system. A letter or any other document can be typed on a keyboard controlled by a computer and linked to a communications system. Instead of mailing the letter, it can be electronically transmitted and recontructed on the receiving end. Thus the recipient gets a facsimile of the original correspondence. The participants in the teleconference described earlier could use facsimile transmission to share reports, data, graphics, and any other documents needed to conduct business—instantly. Obviously, such a system would be much quicker than using conventional mailings. A firm could also program its computer to mass mail automatically such information as price changes. The computer would draw on a mailing list in its memory in order to send the right information to the right parties.

Computer Modeling

In the world of tomorrow, mathematical modeling through a computer will play an important role in managerial decision making. In **computer modeling,** a complex formula with many variables is evaluated by a high-speed computer for the optimal solution to current problems. For instance, a manager may have to make a decision on a site for a new plant. Almost an infinite number of solutions (sites) exist for the problem. To arrive at the best decision, many factors have to be considered. What are the cost and availability of such items as labor, capital, energy, and transportation for each site? How will the supply of these items change over the next several decades? What are, and what will be, the rules, regulations, and tax laws at the various sites? Computer models would evaluate and weigh these and other factors according to a predetermined equation and would rank the alternatives according to their desirability.

Before any computing on such a model can take place, values must be found for the variables in the equation. Thus accurate and reliable data must quickly be obtained for each of the alternatives. Fortunately, wherever there is a demand, there is usually a supply. In the future, a company will be able to buy data on any subject under the sun—or beyond the sun, for that matter. Meteorological, geological, and astrophysical data bases will quantify the conditions of the weather, the earth, and the stars. The latest financial and accounting data will be made available for the major firms in the world. Biographical data for important world figures will also be provided. Local and national laws, as well as important court cases, will all be available in a computer-readable format.

This sort of information will be available in several formats. Users will be able to buy tapes on certain topics to use with their own computers and with their own models. Other users will tap into the service agency's own data files. They may use the data directly, or they may choose to let the service agency construct the model. Firms providing economic models for future conditions are already in heavy demand.

Another type of firm will also arise in the field of information services. Since many firms will probably specialize in one type of data, information "retailers" will buy information from many specialists so they can provide a general package to interested users. This information will not be cheap, but the cost will be small when compared to the multimillion-dollar decisions that will be based on the data.

Computer Graphics

Information overload, or information pollution, is a hazard that could exist in the business world of tomorrow. The exponential proliferation of words and numbers made possible by technological advances will tend to overwhelm unwary executives. Ironically, too much information can lead to the same results as too little information. It will be a challenge to find ways to help users call only the relevant information.

Computer graphics is one way to present large amounts of data in an easily digestible form. Thousands of numbers on reams or paper can be condensed into one picture through graphical techniques. For example, population densities can be presented in many columns and rows of tiny numbers, telephone-book style, or they can be presented in three-dimensional, colored graphics, as in Exhibit 24.1. Computer graphics like this might help a harried sales manager quickly find the relationships he or she is looking for.

Computer graphics will also be of interest to such professionals as architects, engineers, and physicians. For architects, computer graphics may someday supplant the traditional drawing table and T-square. Computers can be programmed to draw straight lines or any other type of line that would be needed. Rough sketches made by a drawing implement linked to a computer can be transformed electronically into finished products. Changes in blueprints can be incorporated quickly. Engineers will use graphics capabilities in a similar fashion. The computer can also be used to test a design for its ability to handle loads and stress, for instance. Doctors will use computers to generate maps of patients that will be used to diagnose certain illnesses. In all likelihood, the potentially dangerous use of X-rays will be eliminated, and computer systems will take over the task of looking into the human body and showing its condition.

Computer graphics should also help free executives and professionals from any drudgery associated with their jobs. The value of the architect, for instance, does not lie in his or her ability to draw straight lines. Computers should expand rather than hinder the capabilities of their users, and they will enable decision makers to make quicker decisions—an important consideration, whether one is a doctor trying to save lives or an executive trying to save money.

EXHIBIT 24.1 Sample Computer Graphic (U.S. Population Density, 1979)

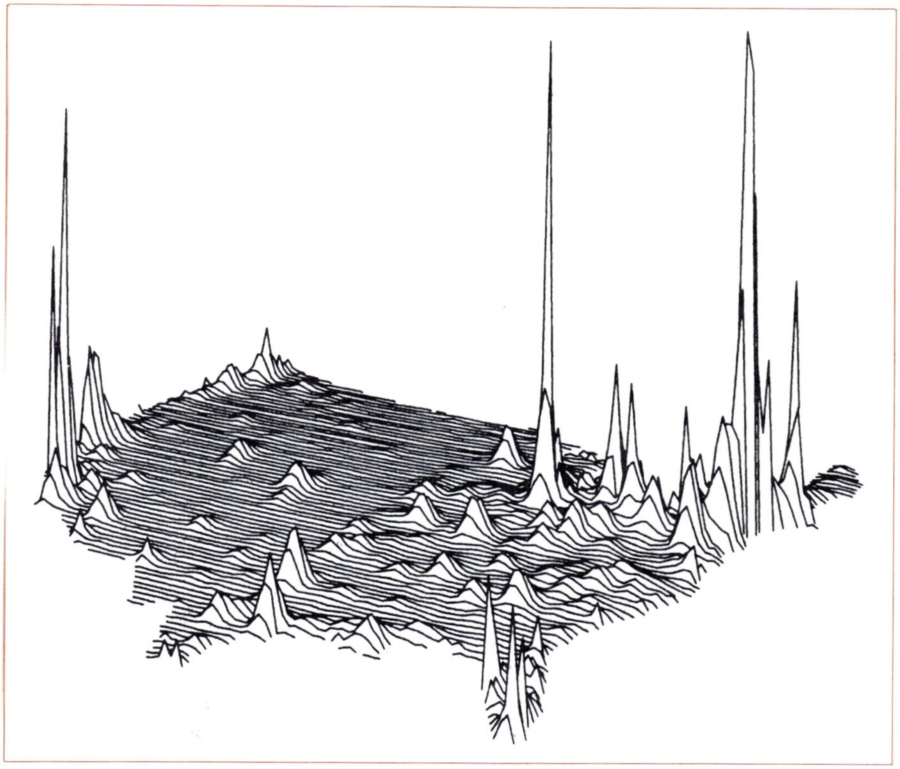

Harvard Laboratory for Computer Graphics and Spatial Analysis. Used by permission.

THE MANAGEMENT WORK STATION

Managers of the future will have all the electronic apparatus needed to perform their duties at one place, called a **management work station.** The management work station would be built around a **cathode-ray tube (CRT),** basically a small television set with a typewriter-like keyboard connecting it to the firm's computer system (see Exhibit 24.2). Since a CRT produces soft copy, as opposed to hard copy (namely paper), the management work station would be largely paperless, although printers could be available to produce copies.

The first thing managers of the future might do in the morning is check to see whether they got any electronic mail overnight. Electronic correspondence could arrive at the firm at any time and be stored on a magnetic tape or disk until the manager is ready to peruse it. A push of a button or two would cause the electronic letters and reports to be displayed on the CRT screen. Not only would managers be freed from the paper blizzard that seems to be raging in most offices, but they would also have access to up-to-the-minute data at the push of a button. When not needed, the electronic messages could be filed away neatly and securely in the computer's memory.

"Plugged-in" managers will also have access to other company data through links to their firm's data base. Information on inventory levels, customer accounts, cash balances, and the like will all be instantly available. Furthermore, managers can request the computer to perform projections. What will sales be like next month, next year, or in five years? What are projected expenses over the next twelve months, and

EXHIBIT 24.2 Management Work Station

what will be the effect on cash needs? The computer can be programmed to provide this data on the basis of information stored in its memory.

Of course, managers can use the CRT to communicate with other managers. Hence the work station is at once a calculator, a filing system, a mail system, and a phone system. Furthermore, it can be on duty twenty-four hours a day, seven days a week, if need be. And unlike a phone system, any messages sent to a specific work station can be held until the manager is ready to receive them.

TOMORROW'S SECRETARY

Many of the typing and filing duties of today's secretaries will be curtailed or eliminated in the automated office of the future, primarily because the amount of paperwork will be reduced greatly. Electronic documents will, of course, be filed automatically by the computer. The need for expert typing skills will be reduced, since documents will be composed on a CRT, and the electronic brain will take care of such tasks as editing and laying them out. It is also quite possible that the machine will eventually be able to correct spelling and grammatical errors. Frequently used form letters will be stored in the computer's memeory, ready for instant recall. And many managers will take to composing their own letters and memorandums, since the computer's assistance will make this task as easy as writing or dictating the document. Ultimately, voice recognition devices will eliminate almost completely the need for a keyboard. Machines will translate spoken words into electronic data.

Thus secretaries will probably become more corporate representatives with many managerial duties. Instead of performing routine clerical work, they will have to call up from the computer's memory the programs necessary to perform the tasks at hand. One such secretary will be able to do what many secretaries do now. He or she will be trained technically to operate a computer-controlled, automated office.

The Computer and the Criminal

The computer will certainly become an important and useful tool for the manager of tomorrow, but it will also become a valuable tool for the criminal of tomorrow. In fact, the speed and power of the computer will augment the criminal's capabilities so as to make crime possible on a gigantic scale. Thus a major challenge to tomorrow's manager will be to counter the activities of computerized criminals.

TYPES OF COMPUTER CRIME

Computerized crime may take many different forms. For example, the computers have the ability to miniaturize data. Large amounts of data can be stored in a relatively small amount of space. A firm could possibly put all its accounts receivable records on a single, easily stolen reel of magnetic tape. Moreover, a small magnet could quickly erase or garble the contents of the tape.

Programmers pose another potentially serious threat to the integrity of a computer system. Computer programs are written in a code that is not readily comprehensible to the average manager. Thus it is difficult for managers to determine what a computer program is actually doing. Programs could easily be written with extra routines that would cause the computer to perform unauthorized procedures. For example, "skimming" is a particularly insidiuous programming scheme. Banks use computers to calculate interest earned by customers' accounts. A programmer could instruct the computer to deposit a small amount of the interest from each customer's account into an account controlled by the programmer or a confederate. This scheme often goes undetected, since the bank is not losing any money and each customer is losing very little. But the ultimate loss to the bank is the faith and confidence of its clientele, a very severe loss indeed.

Many other avenues are open to the potential computer criminal. Input to the computer can be altered to produce a desired result. Phony timecards can be processed to make the computer write checks for "phantom" employees. Similarly, faked invoices can be entered into the input stream to program payment for nonexistent debts.

Telecommunications systems are also vulnerable to attack. Computer communications can be copied, altered, or misrouted—all to benefit the criminal. As the lines of communication lengthen, so does the security threat. For example, a construction company used a computerized communications network to transmit bids for major construction jobs from its field office in Alaska to its home office in Texas. A rival firm eavesdropped on the transmissions. Consequently, the bids of the second firm were always slightly lower than the bids of the first firm.

COPING WITH COMPUTER CRIME

Firms can take several mechanical steps to cope with computer crime. First, the firm can protect against the loss of data tapes by making multiple copies of the tapes and storing them at different locations. Security can also be enhanced by keeping all computer components away from areas of high traffic. All too often, firms locate their computer operations in an area of high visibility in order to showcase the electronic gadgetry. Firms with telecommunications networks can use **encryption,** or secret codes, to thwart attempts at eavesdropping.

However, the key is the realization that computer security is a "people problem." Indeed, far more computer crimes have been perpetrated by insiders at corporations than by outsiders. Perhaps the best solution is therefore to reduce the opportunity for criminal activities by separating "incompatible" functions. Programmers, for example, should not be allowed to operate the computer or to run "live," or actual, data through the system. A separate group of employees should be responsible for bringing input to the machine and for distributing out-

Highlight What Constitutes Property?

As societies have grown more complex, the definition of property that is subject to criminal statutes of larceny has been expanded. The legal definition of *larceny* is "the wrongful or fraudulent taking and carrying away by any person of the personal property of another." Today, stealing computer programs constitutes larceny, even though they consist of magnetic impulses. Stealing the use of telephone wires by a device known as a "blue box" is also subject to larceny statutes.

put. Finally, an independent team of auditors should have the responsibility of ensuring that the system is operating as intended.

Several trends in data processing will serve to minimize the effectiveness of the foregoing procedures. For instance, the trend toward automating the data flow tends to reduce human contact with the data. Humans, however, are a natural checkpoint for assessing the reasonableness of the data. Another trend is toward smaller computers situated close to the origin of the data. The small computers, however, are more vulnerable than large ones. Furthermore, a system of many small computers provides less of a chance to segregate the various computer functions. Finally, the multiple sites complicate the auditing process.

Perhaps the best solution to the security problem is for the firm to hire quality employees and maintain good relations with them. Persons unsuitable for sensitive positions must be identified and screened at the outset, and those with positions of great responsibility should be compensated fairly. Ethical behavior must be encouraged, and upper-level management must set the example. Lines of responsibility should be delineated, and all employees should be trained in security matters.

Finally, violations of security should be punished. Too frequently, victimized firms fail to prosecute computer criminals. One reason is the fear of negative publicity. Another reason is that computer crime is a white-collar crime—crime performed in broad daylight by educated, middle-class criminals. Only when firms begin to take a hard line toward computer criminals will this type of activity cease to be attractive.

The Computer and the Individual

People in our society spend a goodly amount of time filling out forms. From the time their birth certificates are prepared to the time their death certificates are filed, a whole host of organizations, both public and private, ask for and collect information about individuals. Tax bureaus collect financial information, as do private businesses that grant credit to individuals. Employers, schools, and social agencies collect condensed life histories. Draft boards, driver licensing bureaus, and insurance agencies are repositories for the vital statistics that summarize a person's existence. The list is seemingly endless.

In the past, all these files posed little threat to the privacy of the individual. Each organization held only a fragment of the individual's life history. Furthermore, most of the files were poorly maintained, because the sheer volume of paperwork made it difficult to keep each file up to date. However, the advent of computers and the trend toward centralized data banks has now made it technologically possible to tie together all of these disparate files. Hence the most intimate details of a person's life—some erroneous—could become part of the public domain.

The **Privacy Act of 1974** was enacted by Congress in an attempt to curtail an Orwellian scenario. Basically, this act attempts to take the secrecy out of information collection. Individuals were given the right to see their own data files being held by federal agencies. They were given the right to correct any inaccuracies that might exist in such files. Furthermore, the act stated that such information is to be used only for the original purposed for which it was collected. The Civil Service Commission could not, of instance, check records of the Internal Revenue Service for purposes of making personnel decisions. Finally, federal agencies are charged by law to take reasonable steps to protect the integrity and veracity of data files in their custody.

The Privacy Act is a laudable effort to protect individual rights, but it is not without cost. Restrictions against sharing data mean that several agencies will have to collect, maintain, and store essentially the same data. There is also a cost involved in maintaining security for data files. And additional resources will be needed to handle individual requests about files. These costs, of course, will ultimately be borne by the taxpayer.

One shortcoming of the Privacy Act is that it applies only to federal agencies. Yet much information about individuals is being stored in the private sector, by businesses and private organizations. Records of, say, fund transfers could be used to trace someone's movements throughout life. Businesses also may take a cavalier attitude toward data files. Too frequently, unauthorized individuals can browse through the files at will.

Another related issue is the selling of data files. State automobile licensing agencies frequently sell the names and addresses of automobile owners to vendors of automobile accessories. The issue here is who owns the names and addresses and whether they can be sold like other forms of merchandise.

Legislation will probably be forthcoming to regulate the use of individual data in the private sector. Business groups will lobby against the proposed rules because of the additional cost and inconvenience. They could, of course, take the initiative to self-regulate the use of data files. Unfortunately, however, it is often the actions of only a few firms that lead to statutory regulation of all firms. Thus the manager of the future must be aware of the rights and privileges of employees and customers and of his or her responsibility to protect those rights. Only by protecting the rights of others can our own individual rights be preserved.

Point-by-Point Summary

- Satellite communications systems and advanced computer-controlled hardware, such as the cathode-ray tube, will enable the manager of tomorrow to participate in teleconferencing. Teleconferencing will allow managers around the world to engage in common meetings.
- Many conventions in today's society will be altered or reduced in importance in tomorrow's world. Ordinary items such as mail and currency may be obsolete in the future.
- The manager of tomorrow will rely heavily on computer power to help make decisions. Managers will be equipped with electronic work stations to aid them in their duties. Computer graphics and information utilities will play an important role in the manager's work life.
- Many jobs in the future will be changed. Secretaries, for example, will manage computers, which will perform much of the actual office work.
- Computer crime will become a serious problem in the world of tomorrow. Highly trained individuals will use the power of the computer for criminal activities.
- Managers will be called on to provide creative answers to the problem of computer crime. Firms must, however, show more willingness to prosecute white-collar criminals.
- The computer poses many threats to individual privacy. With the computer's assistance, a detailed dossier of every citizen's life could be assembled. Legislation like the Privacy Act of 1974 will be required to protect individual rights and freedom.

Questions for Review

1. This chapter mentions a new type of industry that is developing to provide firms with information. What other new types of industries will appear in the world of tomorrow? What present industries might become obsolete?
2. What are some of the problems inherent in teleconferencing? Would a worldwide communications network lead to a common global culture and language? Why or why not?
3. Is the legislative process keeping pace with advances in technology? What new laws will be needed in the future? What present laws should be repealed or altered?

4. Does computerized crime pay? That is, does the punishment meted out really outweigh the potential rewards? What can be done to make the general public more concerned about white-collar criminals?
5. George Orwell in his novel *1984,* presented a society wherein the government controlled the people through the use of electronic spying devices. Will Orwell's prophecy come true? Why or why not?

APPLICATION

Digital Equipment Corporation

In the late 1950s, a technological revolution was taking place in the infant computer industry: The transistor was beginning to replace the vacuum tube in the logic circuits of computers. In contrast to the vacuum tube, the transistor was smaller, faster, more reliable, and less expensive to buy and to operate. Nevertheless, initial industry reaction to transistor technology was mixed. Industry leaders, like IBM and RCA, saw in the transistor the means to make their big computers more powerful than ever before. Other firms and individuals, particularly those on the fringe of the computer industry, were not convinced that bigger was necessarily better. They felt that computers could better serve many of their users if they were reduced in size and capacity and distributed to the sites where the data originates.

SERVING A NEW MARKET

One of the first individuals to formulate this concept was Kenneth H. Olsen a researcher in the field of electronics at Massachusetts Institute of Technology. Instead of batch processing, in which data and instructions are loaded into a centralized computer and processed while the user waits, Olsen proposed interactive computing, in which the user is in contact with the computer while processing takes place.

Unfortunately, Olsen could not interest any of the established computer powers in his idea of small computers. So in 1958, Olsen left MIT to found his own firm, Digital Equipment Corporation (DEC). In an old textile mill, just down the road from MIT, the minicomputer industry got its start. In 1970, DEC's first machine, the PDP-1, was introduced to the marketplace. What was extraordinary about the PDP-1 was that it sold for $120,000—about one-tenth the price of its nearest competitor.

In the beginning, DEC focused its sales efforts on two separate markets. DEC sold equipment to research and development laboratories, which used the machines in scientific and engineering applications. DEC's second market was original-equipment manufacturers (OEMs), who used the DEC equipment as components for other products or services. For example, some OEMs would use DEC minicomputers as parts of oil and gas drilling rigs and flight simulators. Other firms purchased DEC products for use in "turn-key" business systems—complete systems that a customer could operate without further development, at the turn of a key. In short, DEC's initial marketing strategy was to concentrate on sophisticated users. DEC provided the hardware, and the customer provided the programming, or software. Using this strategy, DEC was able to funnel its meager resources into the production end of the business without having to worry about costly software development.

DEC was moderately successful through the early 1960s, but the development of a solid-state technology in the mid-1960s provided a tremendous boost to the small firm's sales. Solid-state electronics, wherein microscopic circuits are etched on thin metallic wafers called semiconductors, brought improvements in speed, accuracy, cost, size, and reliability. In 1965, DEC brought out the PDP-8, its first solid-state machine and probably the first true minicomputer. In 1966, when DEC lowered the price of the PDP-8 to $10,000, the firm started making serious inroads into the small-computer market. DEC eventually produced a scaled-down version of this machine that is primarily used as a controlling device in many manufacturing processes.

Today, DEC produces a wide variety of products and services. DEC entered the microprocessor market with a computer on a chip of silicon. At the other end of the scale, DEC has a machine capable of storing and processing up to 4 billion characters. DEC has also developed DEC net, a computer system that allows the products of DEC and other manufacturers to be interconnected through telecommunication links. DEC is also involved in the manufacture and distribution of such devices as keyboard terminals and cathode-ray tubes.

Obviously, DEC has come a long way. DEC still occupies the mill, but it now owns some seventy-five other manufacturing facilities worldwide. DEC is the acknowledged leader in the minicomputer field, with nearly 40 percent of the market. In fact, DEC is the second-leading manufacturer in the entire computer industry (second only to IBM), with sales in 1979 in excess of $1.8 billion. DEC's products are used throughout the globe is areas as diverse as health care, law enforcement, architecture, and farming. And it started with a man who had the idea that, at least as far as computers are concerned, bigger is not necessarily better.

CAREER OPPORTUNITIES

With its high growth rate, DEC is always searching for qualified personnel. A sales position within the firm is especially challenging. The salesperson must not only have an aptitude for selling but must also be qualified technically to sell complex products to sophisticated users. Members of DEC's sales force must work closely with customers to develop and upgrade their systems. In addition, the salesperson must work with the marketing group to prepare long-range sales forecasts and to assist in developing new products as well as new applications for existing products.

Of course, continuing education is a must for participants in this fast-changing environment. DEC provides for personnel development by operating its own 5,000-student university in nearby Burlington, Massachusetts. At DEC's school, customers and employees can choose from over 250 courses—in everything from such basic skills as typing to such Ph.D.-level courses as advanced computer architecture. DEC is a firm believer in the philosophy that future growth can be assured by obtaining and training competent and dedicated employees.

FOR DISCUSSION

1. DEC's initial marketing strategy was to deal with sophisticated customers who would find their own uses for DEC products. Do you agree with this strategy? What problems could it cause for a manufacturing firm?
2. What will the computer industry be like in the future? Do you think there will be many small firms or a few large firms? From which end of the scale will the technological advances originate?

OBJECTIVES

☐ To understand how the Systems Interactive Guidance Information computer program works
☐ To know how to prepare your credentials file to maximize your chances for a good job
☐ To know where to go for specific information on business-related jobs
☐ To know how to prepare a winning resume
☐ To prepare yourself to be interviewed

OUTLINE

ARTICLE *Does College Really Matter Anymore?*
FINDING YOUR GOALS AND VALUES
PREPARING YOUR CREDENTIALS FILE
CHOOSING AN OCCUPATION
Career Clusters
Information on Specific Jobs
PREPARING A WINNING RESUME
Presentation
Format
BEING INTERVIEWED
SOME FINAL POINTERS ON JOB HUNTING
APPLICATION *Rockwell International Corporation*

KEY TERMS

CAREER CLUSTER
CREDENTIALS FILE
ENTRY-LEVEL JOB
RESUME

CAREERS IN BUSINESS

Does College Really Matter Anymore?

Changing Times, November 1979.

The college degree has lost some of its aura. The magic carpet to higher-paying, successful careers is dumping many passengers short of that destination.

From the heyday of the 60s, when a sheepskin was almost sure to open the way to a professional job or managerial position, we've come to this prediction from the Bureau of Labor Statistics: There's a one-in-four chance that students earning degrees between now and 1985 will wind up in blue-collar or clerical jobs or other occupations that traditionally haven't been filled by college-educated workers.

The change (some call it a collapse) in the college job market is neither new—it has been confronting grads for several years—nor difficult to explain. It's primarily the result of the bulge in the number of Americans who carry college credentials. During the 1960s an average of half a million students received bachelor's degrees each year; now the figure is close to one million and expected to hover around that mark for a few more years before beginning to decline. The supply of college grads is simply outstripping the number of jobs requiring them. Harvard economist Richard Freeman, who examines the shifting economic status of college graduates in his book *The Overeducated American,* concludes that "knowledge is power only if most people do not have it."

Today's plentiful supply of graduates means increasing competition for jobs, disappointment for many in terms of pay or type of work and, for some, no job at all. Tales of college graduates toiling in jobs once considered beneath them or carrying their expensive degrees along to the unemployment line have made a lot of people wonder whether it's still worth it to go to college.

COST-BENEFIT ANALYSIS

College is expensive and growing more so every year. The basic average cost per student at public universities is now estimated at $3,258. (That's 22% more than those in the class of '79 paid for their freshman year.) Estimates of the nation's investment in higher education have run as high as 85 billion dollars annually, a figure that includes earnings students passed up by sitting in a classroom rather than working at a job.

Would going to college be worth the cost for you? To answer from a purely financial standpoint, you must gauge how much more money you could hope to earn with a college degree than without one and compare that with the cost of four or more years of college. This is a tricky business because, among other things, it depends on the type of degree and work you get and requires making and projecting assumptions for a 40- to 50-year working life.

Many attempts have been made to put a dollar value on a college diploma. Several years ago Census Bureau figures provided this precise calculation for men: Getting a degree would add $231,695 to their lifetime earnings. One researcher found that each additional year of schooling after high school added an average of more than $800 to annual salaries. However, a recent BLS assessment of the payoff cited such variables as inflation and offered this conclusion: "How much more money does a college graduate make? Maybe a little, maybe a lot."

One thing is certain: While the cost of college keeps going up, the earnings advantage bestowed by a degree is slipping. Median income of college alumni has been running more than 30% higher than that of high school grads; ten years back the premium was about 50%. The narrowing gap reflects both better pay for high school grads and the growing number of degree holders in jobs that don't demand a college education.

DON't JUMP TO CONCLUSIONS

Although a degree has lost some of its financial clout, the economic advantages for those who go to college are still significant. The following table compares the median annual incomes of college graduates with those of workers who didn't go beyond high school. These are 1977 figures, the most current available.

Education	Income Men	Women
High school	$15,434	$ 8,894
Four or more years of college	20,625	12,656

A college degree may not guarantee you a good job—it never could—but the lack of one can bar you from even being considered for certain positions. The BLS believes that by 1985, 18.1% of all jobs will be reserved for college graduates. And although the surging supply of graduates may deflate the economic value of their credentials, it can make things tougher for those without a degree. Other things being equal, many employers will choose a college grad over an applicant who didn't go beyond high school.

Higher education does carry protection against unemployment. In early 1976, for example, the jobless rate among young college graduates ages 20 through 24 was 6.1%; for high school grads of the same ages it was 14.1%. At that time the national unemployment rate was 7.5%, more than triple the 2.4% rate among all college graduates. Certainly, college graduates are spilling over into job areas that used to be the province of nongraduates. But they're often getting those jobs at the expense of less-educated workers, outbidding them rather than being left unemployed.

Another advantage, although difficult to measure in dollars, is that a college education may enhance your ability to adapt to changes in the job market and other economic conditions. In his book *Investment in Learning,* Howard Bowen, professor of economics and education at Claremont Graduate School, writes that "education has the effect of keeping lifetime options open. If a person stops his education short of college, he may cut off access to further education, to many jobs and to other lifetime opportunities and satisfactions."

THERE'S MORE TO IT THAN MONEY

Judging the value of higher education only on its financial return would be a big mistake. Bowen, who argues that the monetary return is sufficient to cover the cost of college, says other benefits—including "personal development and life enrichment"—are more significant.

We asked Freeman, whose *The Overeducated American* was taken by some as a broadside attack on the value of college, his advice for students wondering whether they should continue their education. "I think most people should still go to college, but not for the economic payoff," he responded. "You have to weigh the fact that a college degree doesn't guarantee a good job or high pay the way it used to against the obvious fact that it's going to widen your horizons to an extent few other experiences do."

How do you measure those other benefits? Grand concepts like the "whole person" or "educated man" are intangible and can't be tallied up like salaries. But that doesn't diminish their value.

College will introduce you to different people and new ideas and ways of thinking, and it can lead to what Loren Pope, director of the College Placement Bureau, calls "intellectual flexibility." The theme of self-discovery is woven through much of the commentary on the goals of higher education.

A great deal of research has been done to pinpoint the nonmonetary effects of higher education. Here's a collection of some of the findings:

- College graduates are, in general, more satisfied with their jobs than are less-educated workers. (This varies according to the job, however. A recent survey found that among secretaries the most dissatisfied were women with college degrees.)
- College grads are more likely to vote and to participate in political and civic organizations.
- They own and read more books than high school graduates and watch less television. College alumni also attend more motion pictures and are more likely to take advantage of adult education programs.
- When freshmen are asked why they decided to go to college, the number one response is "to get a better job." By the time they graduate, though, they put more emphasis on getting a general education and less on vocation.
- College graduates are less likely to consider life routine or dull than are nongraduates.
- They save a higher percentage of their income than others do.
- The more education one has, the more tolerant and understanding of others he or she is likely to be. Bowen reports that most alumni say "getting along with people is one of the most significant results of their college education."
- Women who have been to college are more likely to be in the labor force, and college graduates in general are more likely to approve of women working.
- Husbands who have been to college are more likely to help around the house, and college-educated parents devote more time and money to their children. The effects of college on family life, Bowen concludes, may be among its most significant outcomes.
- College graduates are probably better able to cope with the growing complexities that confront Americans these days.
- Alumni are likely to work longer hours. One study found that each extra year of school added about one hour to the average workweek.
- College graduates enjoy better health and, on the average, live longer than nongraduates.

There's no assurance that going to college would affect you in any of these ways. In fact, it's impossible to conclude that college alone is responsible for the differences that have been cited.

MAKING YOUR DECISION

So how do you decide whether you should go to college? As with any important and expensive decision, it's not easy. Academic ability and motivation are critical; so is the ability to meet the mounting bills you'll face if you pursue a degree. Relatives and friends may influence you, too.

If you have a certain career in mind—as a physician or a physicist, for example—you know college is essential. Being uncertain of what you want to do, however, doesn't mean you shouldn't go on in school. Somewhere between one-third and two-thirds of all students change their major fields of study or career plans during their college years, a fact that supports the view of college as an opportunity to broaden your outlook and make decisions about your future.

Don't be scared off by the knowledge that the financial promise of a degree, though still great, is diminishing. The demand for graduates depends mightily on their field. Currently, for example, the market for new engineering grads is booming while that for graduates with liberal arts degrees is in a slump.

Freeman sees an advantage in the declining "get ahead" appeal of college. He says people who aren't academically oriented and don't want to go to college aren't under so much pressure to do so for fear of "turning down the future." The growing emphasis on adult education means those who don't go directly from high school to college have opportunities to return to the classroom later, either to delve into a subject to satisfy intellectual curiosity or to specialize with an eye to entering a new profession. Remember, too, that college doesn't hold a monopoly on exposure to new ideas.

There are appealing jobs available that don't require a college education. For some occupations, such as skilled trades and some technical fields, special training can give you better credentials than a bachelor's degree in liberal arts. There are high-paying jobs that don't require college and positions that demand degree holders but don't offer hefty salaries. Last year, for instance, the average starting salary for a college graduate in the humanities was just over $10,000; a journeyman plumber could easily earn twice that amount or more.

There's no reason, of course, that a plumber or an electrician or a computer technician shouldn't have a college education or that a college grad should spurn these fields. In *Investment in Learning* Bowen challenges the "widespread but obsolete assumption that blue-collar work is in some sense inappropriate for educated men and women. This assumption is a carry-over from an aristocratic conception of both work and higher education."

As you weigh the question of whether you should go to college, consider all your options but don't overplay the financial factors at the expense of other results of higher education. Remember that the much-talked-about concepts of being "over-educated" or "underemployed" relate only to the 40 or so hours each week that a person devotes to earning a living. Many argue that even if college had no impact on that part of your life, it would still be a good investment.

Consider these remarks by an Oxford professor, as reported by a student who was to become Britain's prime minister, Harold Macmillan: "Except for [those who will become teachers], nothing that you will learn in the course of your studies will be of the slightest possible use to you in later life—save only this—that if you work hard and intelligently, you should be able to detect when a man is talking rot, and that, in my view is the main, if not the sole purpose of education."

This article was written in 1979. Since then, the only thing that has changed is starting salaries. You've already made the decision to pursue a college education. Now you have to determine what to do with it. And that's where this chapter comes in.

The choice of a career will determine to a large extent not only your future income but also your future happiness. What determines the occupation you choose is your aptitudes and values, as well as the income you want to make. The best way to determine what is important to you is to seek help from your college or university guidance center.

Finding Your Goals and Values

One thing the career guidance center may ask you to do is to participate in a nationwide computer program called Systems Interactive Guidance Information (SIGI). SIGI asks you to rate ten values, including variety, leisure, and income security, and then to compare your ratings with those of various job possibilities. Suppose that you pick *variety* as an important value. You might find that 90 percent of the jobs you have chosen are very low in variety.

If your guidance center does not offer SIGI, you should try on your own to determine what job conditions are important to you.

Preparing Your Credentials File

One of the first things your guidance counselor will ask for is a **credentials file.** Anyone who might be interested in hiring you will glean that very important first impression from your file.

Every placement center assembles a different credentials file, although most of them require the following:

1. Complete transcripts of your academic work to date. (Be sure to obtain transcripts from other schools that you have attended.)
2. Information on yourself, such as health, marital status, where you have lived, your current address, and so on.
3. Letters of recommendation from, for example, professors who know you best, former employers (those you impressed!), and administrators in the college or university.
4. A statement of your career goals. Make this short, to the point, and not overly ambitious. It would be absurd to indicate that you want to be president of General Motors. But it would be appropriate to indicate that you want an **entry-level job**—your first permanent job after leaving school—in the sales department of a major cosmetics company with the idea of becoming a district manager within two years.

Take your time preparing your credentials file. Make sure that it is complete, accurate, and attractive. Have someone else correct your grammar and spelling, and if you cannot type, have it professionally typed. Obtain your reference letters well in advance of any potential job interviews. Remember that the references you ask may be very busy. But you must be persistent in obtaining these very important letters. Don't just call on the phone; go visit your professors personally and explain to them who you are, what you want to do, how well you did in their classes, and what you need from them in terms of a letter of recommendation.

Highlight Do You Want Status?

Some people are worried about status, which can loosely be defined as a person's or thing's relative position as compared to the rest of the world. Donald Treiman, a sociologist, has devised a prestige ranking for over 500 international occupations that shows the status of various jobs. The ratings of some of these jobs, on a scale from 0 to 100, appear in Exhibit 25.1. Physicians and university professors rank the highest. Janitors and laborers rank at about the bottom, although Treiman found that people living on public assistance are at rock bottom.

Choosing an Occupation

There are numerous publications you can consult to obtain information on potential careers in business. Here are four general sources:

1. The *Encyclopedia of Careers and Vocational Guidance* is a two-volume work published by J. G. Ferguson Company of Chicago and distributed by Doubleday & Company. These two volumes contain general information on vocational testing, interviewing, and the like. In addition, there is information on jobs and professions that do not require college training.
2. The *Occupational Outlook for College Graduates* is an annual publication of the U.S. Department of Labor. It surveys the job outlook for college graduates and describes each profession in terms of training required, salaries, working conditions, and the nature of the work. This publication may help you avoid choosing a career for which there will be no demand in the future.

EXHIBIT 25.1 Prestige Rankings of Various Occupations

Occupation	Rating
University professors	78
Physicians	78
Lawyers	71
Professional accountants	68
Business executives	67
High school teachers	64
Journalists	55
Secretaries	53
Real estate agents	59
Bank tellers	58
Office clerks	43
Receptionists	38
Sales clerks	34
Truck drivers	33
Janitors	21
Laborers	19

Source: D. Treiman, *Occupational Prestige and Comparative Prospective*. New York: Academic Press, 1977.

Highlight Does It Pay to Go to College?

Some pretty strong evidence from the U.S. government indicates that it does pay to go to school. Exhibit 25.2 shows the lifetime earnings in 1981 dollars of men with various levels of education. The payoff for going to college, as opposed to just finishing high school, is an extra $370,314. Exhibit 25.3 uses another format to show the advantages of attending college.

EXHIBIT 25.2 Expected Lifetime Earnings for Men

Educational Level	Working Life (years)	Lifetime Earnings (1981 dollars)
Four years college	22–61.7	$1,199,113
Four years high school	18–61.4	828,799
Eight years grammar school	18–61.4	602,266

Based on U.S. Bureau of the Census *Current Population Reports,* Series P-60 data.

3. The *Occupational Thesaurus* may be obtained from Everett A. Teal, Lehigh University, Bethlehem, Pennsylvania. This two-volume work lists employment areas for which college majors are qualified. There are specific job-skill categories, arranged according to demand, for different industries.
4. The *College Placement Annual* is published by the College Placement Council, Inc., P.O. Box 2263, Bethlehem, Pennsylvania. It gives job information for college graduates and alphabetically lists all major private employers in the United States. Government agencies are also listed. A unique employment index lists employers by occupations that are needed in the region the employer serves.

EXHIBIT 25.3 Age-Earnings Profile for Selected Degree Holders

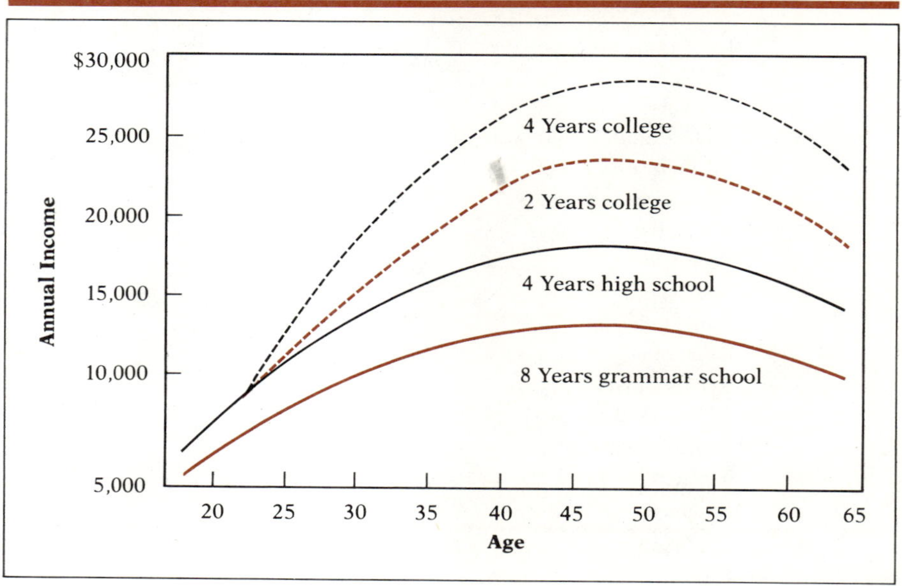

For specific information on business-related jobs, you can write to any of the following:

Air Transport Association of America
1709 New York Avenue NW
Washington DC 20006

American Advertising Federation
1225 Connecticut Avenue NW
Washington DC 20036

American Bankers Association
Bank Personnel Division
1120 Connecticut Avenue NW
Washington DC 20036

American Council of Life Insurance
277 Park Avenue
New York NY 10017

American Federation of Information Processing Societies
210 Summit Avenue
Montvale NJ 07645

American Hotel and Motel Association
Educational Institute
Stephan S. Nisbet Building
1407 South Harrison Road
East Lansing MI 48823

American Institute of Certified Public Accountants
1211 Avenue of the Americas
New York NY 10036

American Institute of Planners
1776 Massachusetts Avenue NW
Washington DC 20036

American Management Association
135 West 50th Street
New York NY 10020

American Personnel and Guidance Association
1607 New Hampshire Avenue NW
Washington DC 20009

American Society for Personnel Administration
19 Church Street
Berea OH 44017

Association for Computing Machinery
1133 Avenue of the Americas
New York NY 10036

Association of University Programs in Health Administration
1755 Massachusetts Avenue NW
Washington DC 20036

Business-Professional Advertising Association
205 East 52nd Street
New York NY 10017

Direct Mail/Marketing Educational Foundation
6 East 43rd Street
New York NY 10003

Financial Executives Institute
633 Third Avenue
New York NY 10017

Independent Insurance Agents of America
85 John Street
New York NY 10038

Institute of Internal Auditors
International Headquarters
249 Maitland Avenue
Altamonte Springs FL 32701

National Association of Accountants
919 Third Avenue
New York NY 10022

National Association of Life Underwriters
1922 F Street NW
Washington DC 20006

National Automobile Dealers Association
Career Booklet
8400 Westpark Drive
McLean VA 22101

National Consumer Finance Association
1000 16th Street NW
Washington DC 20036

National Institute for the Food Service Industry
120 South Riverside Plaza
Chicago IL 60606

National Society of Public Accountants
1717 Pennsylvania Avenue NW
Washington DC 20006

Public Relations Society of America
PRSA Career Guidance
845 Third Avenue
New York NY 10022

Society of Actuaries
208 South LaSalle Street
Chicago IL 60604

CAREER CLUSTERS

Some people know when they enter college exactly what they are going to be and therefore what they need to study. But for those who don't know which business career to take, the appropriate approach might be to look at a **career cluster**—a group of related jobs.

The first step you might take is to look at employment projections and trends in *Occupational Outlook.* You might find that in 1986 there is going to be a high demand for accountants and computer programmers. Of course, the entry-level jobs in those areas require specific skills and knowledge, but all of them require a certain basic background—business knowledge and skills. If you believe you might be interested in such a career cluster, you could take general business courses and then specialize in several specific possibilities.

To get a better idea of what career clustering is all about, you might look at the Winter 1973 issue of *Occupational Outlook Quarterly.* The article on page 17 describes the fifteen career clusters that the U.S. Office of Education has identified. Two of these clusters are business and office jobs and marketing and distribution jobs.

INFORMATION ON SPECIFIC JOBS

There are many places to find information on specific jobs that you might qualify for, some of which are listed here:

1. *College or university placement centers* Virtually every college and university has some type of placement center. For college students, this might be the first place to look for job information. Placement centers have career consultants and vocational guidance counselors, as well as facilities for interviews between prospective graduates and recruiters from major firms and government agencies.
2. *State employment agencies* All fifty states have state employment offices operating in conjunction with the U.S. Employment Service of the Department of Labor. They charge no fee and make placements in all types of jobs. Some even provide computer job matching. Many of the 1,800 state employment offices provide free career guidance and aptitude tests.
3. *Specialized placement services* Employers seeking women and women seeking jobs may consult special job-matching services. The Catalyst National Network (14 E. 60th Street, New York NY 10022) provides listings and resumes of managerial and professional applicants. The Talent Search Skills Bank (Office of Voluntary Programs, Equal Opportunity Commission, 1800 G Street NW, Washington DC 20506) maintains a file on minority female applicants and their skills. The National Federation of Business and Professional Women's Clubs, Inc. (2012 Massachusetts Avenue NW, Washington DC 20036) operates a talent bank to help women find positions in educational institutions, private industry, and government.
4. *"Help wanted" ads in newspapers and journals* Virtually every newspaper in the country has "help wanted" ads listing vacancies for various jobs. Vacancies are also listed in trade and professional jour-

nals. Since they usually require that you apply by mail, an impressive resume is imperative.

5. *Private employment agencies* You can register with an agency and wait to be called or apply directly to one for a job that it has advertised in a periodical. Agencies generally require you to sign a contract that obligates you to pay a fee if you are placed by them. Read these contracts carefully: You may, for example, owe the agency the fee even if you are fired after one week. Agency fees run from 5 to 15 percent of annual starting salaries. In upper-income job brackets, agency fees can sometimes be 30 percent. For guidance on agencies in your chosen field, look at *Employment Directions* (National Employment Association, 2000 K Street NW, Washington DC 20006), which lists agencies by specialty in forty-nine states and five foreign countries.

Preparing a Winning Resume

PRESENTATION

For almost all job applications, you must submit a **resume.** Because the personnel officer in a corporation must read thousands of resumes every year, it behooves you to do your best. Remember, your resume is an advertisement for yourself.

Since your resume is, in large part, bait for the interview, it need not be an entire dossier that includes letters of recommendation. Nor should it list your every accomplishment, information about your outside interests, or the backgrounds of your parents.

Your resume should be on one or more sheets of paper, preferably high-quality rag bond. A good resume is usually typed or printed. Remember, the appearance of a resume is like the appearance you will make for an interview: First impressions count.

FORMAT

You needn't write a resume as if it were an application for college. In other words, don't put the word *NAME* before your name; the fewer headlines, the better. But you can divide your resume into sections, such as education, experience, publications, honors, awards, and special interests.

You should list your work experiences in a separate section either in reverse chronological order or according to functional headings, such as sales, teaching, or administration.

In the education section, list appropriate institutional degrees and certificates. If you went to college, you need not mention high school, unless it was a special kind. If you transferred to three or four different colleges, you need not list all of them—only the one you received your degree from. Otherwise, a prospective employer might think you are unstable.

Exhibit 25.4 shows one possible format for your resume. The format you use, however, should show *you* off to best advantage.

EXHIBIT 25.4 Sample Resume

PERSONAL INFORMATION

Pat J. Duncan 3026 27th Avenue South Minneapolis, Minnesota 55465 (612) 338-7326	Date of Birth: 9/23/60 Health is Excellent

EDUCATION

Ramsey County Community College	Associate of Arts in Business (1979)
Midwest State University	Bachelor of Business Administration (1981)

Overall Grade Point Average 2.65 on 4.0 scale.

EXTRACURRICULAR ACTIVITIES

Photography Club 1979-80
Debating Team 1979-80
Swimming Team 1980-81

WORK EXPERIENCE

Dates	Employer	Duties
June 1978-August 1978	Sammy's Pizza Place Minneapolis	Cashier
Sept. 1978-August 1979	The Clothes Line Minneapolis	Salesperson
Sept. 1978-Present	The Clothes Line Minneapolis	Accounts Clerk (part time)

REFERENCES

References and Academic credentials are availabe upon request from the following sources:

Career Planning Office Ramsey County Community College St. Paul, Minnesota 55102	Career Opportunity Center Midwest State University Minneapolis, Minnesota 55465

Other references may be obtained by writing:

Professor James Haslow Business Department Ramsey County Community College St. Paul, Minnesota 55102	Professor Sandra Mason Business Administration Midwest State University Minneapolis, Minnesota 55465

Business in Action

PORTFOLIO VI: YOUR FUTURE IN BUSINESS

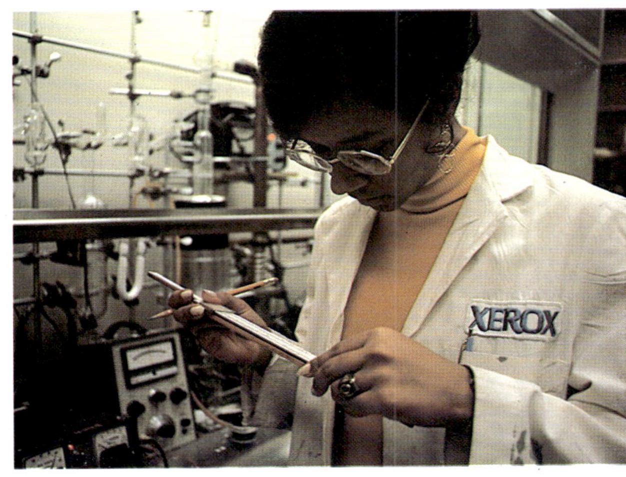

BUNDESBAHN
ALTSTOFFE
ALTPAPIER
MÜLL
BKE-LAGER
ÖLE-FETTE
TRI-PERLAGER

Pantone Letraset

Being Interviewed

Assuming that your resume gets you an interview, there are certain pointers that can improve your job chances. The personnel officer of a company interviews many prospective employees. You must somehow convince the interviewer that you are as good as or better than anyone who is being considered for a given job. Basically, you must use the interview to convince prospective employers that you can fulfill their needs. In order to do that, you must find out beforehand about the job requirements, the company, and if possible, your prospective interviewer.

Here are some specific suggestions for a successful interview:

- Be on time.
- Come with a list of your qualifications.
- Always maintain eye contact and listen attentively.
- Be honest and frank, but do not make derogatory remarks about a previous employer.
- Let your interviewer offer you information on benefits, salary, and agency fees (if any).
- Decide in advance that you want the offer. It is better to have more options than less.
- Find out what you need to learn about your potential employer as well as what they need to learn about you.
- Dress appropriately. First impressions are important!

Prior to the interview, you should find out some facts about your potential employer. This can be done by looking at some of the following sources:

- *Moody's Manuals*
- *Fitch Corporation Manuals*
- *Thomas' Register of American Manufacturers*
- *MacRae's Blue Book*
- Company annual reports

Some Final Pointers on Job Hunting

Remember that the key to success in job hunting is motivation. If you really want a job, you will follow some of the suggestions just mentioned. If you feel that you need more professional advice, consider seeking the services of a professional resume writer, who is generally associated with a private employment-counseling firm. If you need help with interviews, practice with a friend or with someone who works in the placement center at your college or university. Without a doubt, serious job hunting requires an effort.

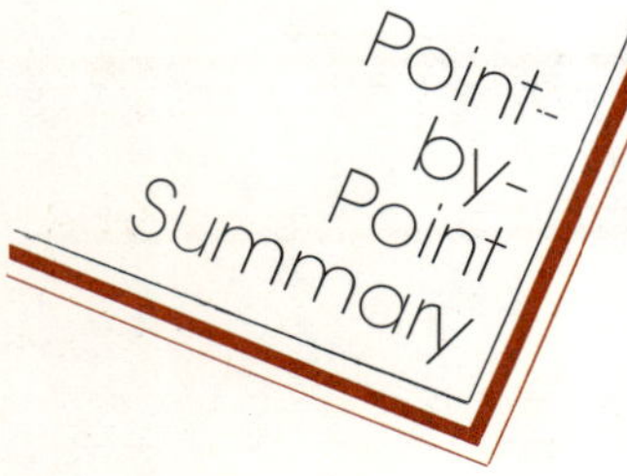

- One way to find out whether your goals and values are consistent is to use the Systems Interactive Guidance Information computer program. This can be done through your local college or university career guidance office.
- Every credentials file should have a complete transcript of your academic record, information about you (a resume), letters of recommendation, and a statement of your career goals (which should be short).
- There are numerous publications you can consult for information on career outlooks. A large number of organizations also provide specific information on business-related jobs.
- When you are actually looking for a job, you can go to your college or university placement center, a state employment agency, specialized placement services, and private employment agencies. Don't forget "help wanted" ads too.
- A winning resume must be brief and to the point.
- Every interviewee should be on time, maintain eye contact with the interviewer, be honest and frank, obtain information on a potential employer ahead of time, and dress appropriately.

1. How would it be possible to pick a career that is inconsistent with your values?
2. Make out a sample statement of your career goals that might go into your credentials file. Does it adequately provide a potential employer with information on where you want to go?
3. Look up a career you might plan on in *Occupational Outlook Quarterly,* published by the Bureau of Labor Statistics. Have you chosen a "good" career?
4. Under what circumstances would you continue studying for an occupation even when you knew that there would be an excess supply of potential workers in that occupation?

APPLICATION

When people think of spaceships and space shuttles, the name Rockwell often comes to the fore. Indeed, Rockwell has been one of the primary manufacturers of rocket engines so vital to America's space program, and Rockwell Space Systems Group and Rockadyne Division began work on the space shuttle more than a decade ago. Rockwell is currently developing the world's first reusable rocket engine for the world's first reusable space ship.

A DIVERSIFIED COMPANY

Rockwell International is known primarily for its rockets, but it has four diverse business segments—automotive, aerospace, electronics, and general industries.

Automotive

With sales of over $2 billion, the Automotive Division of Rockwell International is far from small. It is one of the leading suppliers of components for heavy-duty truck and off-highway equipment. Additionally, it has a new branch called the Automotive Technical Center, through which it hopes to expand its participation in the huge passenger-car, light-truck, and international markets.

To reduce fuel consumption and weight, original-equipment manufacturers are turning to electronic controls and lightweight components for their vehicles.

Rockwell International Corporation

Rockwell International produces and sells many electronically controlled products, as well as new plastic and aluminum components, to meet these requirements. For example, it has developed an aluminum version of a truck tandem axle that saves ninety pounds compared to its steel counterpart. And it has developed an electronic monitoring system called Trip Master, which assists vehicle users in reducing maintenance costs and improving fuel economy.

Recently, the Automotive Division has expanded its manufacturing program to Frankfurt, Germany, where it has a brake facility, and to Great Britain and France, where it manufactures mechanical devices for passenger cars. It has also entered licensing agreements with a company in Korea for axle manufacturing and is considering other joint ventures in Europe.

Aerospace

In addition to the space shuttle and space transportation system, Rockwell's Aerospace Division is currently working on four operational shuttlecraft under a contract from the National Aeronautics and Space Administration. This division is also working on unmanned satellite programs, the most important of them for the Department of Defense. Rockwell has used its rocket technology to design and develop water-propulsion systems for the Navy. Finally, it continues to work on the B-1 strategic aircraft and to work for civilian commercial aviation manufacturers, specifically the Boeing Company. With sales approaching $2 billion, Aerospace is indeed an important part of Rockwell International.

Electronics

With sales only a little less than for Aerospace, the Electronics Division of Rockwell International is growing rapidly. It has developed a huge research and development organization for air-transport avionics, which allowed Rockwell International to win contracts from Boeing for fully digital autopilot systems and flight instrument

systems for the new 757s and 767s. It also delivered control systems to Lockheed. These systems are expected to aid in cutting fuel consumption by 3 percent (which is a lot for a jet airliner). Special control systems designed by the Electronics Division are available to some 350,000 business and private aircraft used everywhere in the world.

Telecommunications is another part of Rockwell's electronics business. Digital microwave systems have been ordered by seventeen of the twenty-three Bell Telephone operating companies.

This division has so many other products that it would be impossible to discuss them all. Perhaps one of the most significant, however, is the bubble memory, which greatly expands the memory capacity of minicomputers and microcomputers.

General Industries

Last but not least of the Rockwell divisions is General Industries, which accounts for slightly more than $1 billion of gross sales a year. General Industries businesses are engaged in manufacturing and marketing high-speed printing presses; energy-generation and environmental control systems for utilities; components for oil, gas, and nuclear industries; power tools; and textile machinery products. General Industries operates forty-two plants and employs more than 23,000 men and women in nineteen countries.

CAREER OPPORTUNITIES

According to recruiting brochures given out by Rockwell International, "it's amazing what a college business grad can do at Rockwell." Business graduates participate in financial planning, help Rockwell comply with an array of government laws and regulations, and participate in marketing and communications programs. Because of this variety, we'll concentrate on one possible career—management of purchasing and materials.

Purchasing Positions

The hierarchy of purchasing positions tells you right away that there is room for advancement (see Exhibit 25.5). The entry-level job is that a buyer engages in are as follows:

1. Edits requisitions and confers with departments regarding requirements, specifications, quantity and quality of merchandise, and delivery requirements. Recommends substitutes where a savings in cost and improved delivery will result.
2. Solicits and analyzes quotations for new or nonstandard items. Negotiates with suppliers to obtain most favorable terms of purchase. Recommends or approves awarding of contracts or purchase orders, ensuring that all purchases comply with

EXHIBIT 25.5 Hierarchy of Purchasing Positions at Rockwell

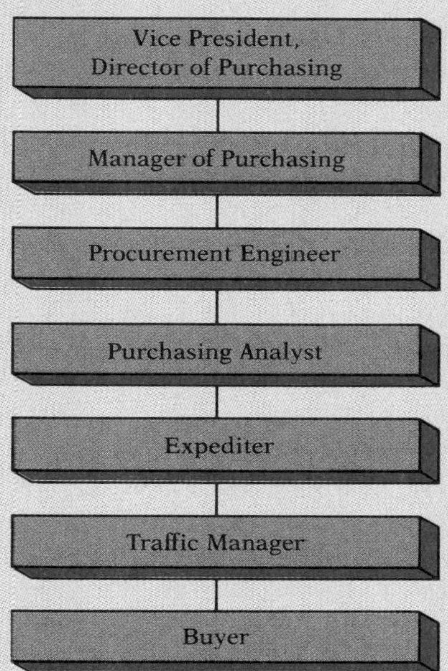

government regulations and accepted trade practices.

3. Interviews suppliers and their representatives personally and maintains close contact by correspondence, telephone, and plant visits.
4. Arranges with appropriate subcontractors to fabricate special equipment to company blueprints. Checks blueprints to ensure freedom from accidental errors and completeness of information so that the supplier can comply with special requirements.
5. Carries out necessary followup and expediting activities to ensure delivery as required by production schedules.
6. Serves in an advisory capacity to assist other departments in obtaining proper specifications, quotations, delivery terms, and costs.
7. May examine and approve all invoices covering purchase orders placed.
8. Handles adjustments with suppliers involving replacement of materials not conforming to purchase specifications, return of material declared surplus as a result of engineering changes, cancellations of orders, and so on. Prepares shipping orders and ensures that appropriate credit is received.
9. Maintains an appropriate file of catalogs, price lists, and the like to assist departments in obtaining the latest information about new products.

Within this general set of tasks, there are several specific categories (see Exhibit 25.6).

EXHIBIT 25.6 Buyer Categories at Rockwell

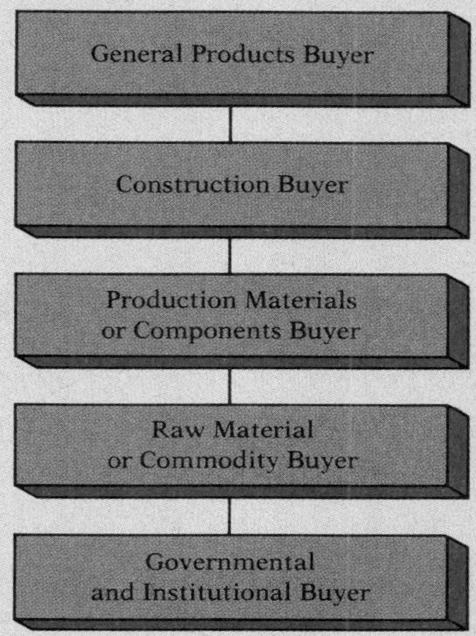

Training

Rockwell assumes that the entry-level buyer has had business courses in general economics, accounting, commercial law, statistics, computer applications, marketing, sales forecasting, production planning and control, industrial purchasing, and traffic management. However, education for a purchasing career doesn't stop there. Every department in Rockwell International has a training program for members of the purchasing department. Their methods range from the very informal method of observing buyers at work and assisting them under close supervision to formally organized courses of instruction, used in the larger companies within Rockwell International.

Additionally, new purchasing agents (and older ones) are asked to attend seminars, conferences, and institutes conducted periodically around the country. Many of the Rockwell International companies subsidize tuition costs for those studying for graduate degrees.

Pathway to the Future

A career in purchasing is not a dead end. In fact, purchasing offers at least as many pathways to top management as do other major functional areas in business concerns. Entry-level workers in purchasing who do not aspire to top-level management responsibility can look forward to a progression from buyer to traffic manager, expediter, purchasing analyst, and finally, manager of purchasing.

And For the Community College Graduate

Just about everything we've described for career opportunities for Rockwell International applies to the community college graduate in business or technical fields. Additional training and perhaps a few more years' experience are required for the A.A. or A.S. degree holder before advancement, but the advancement is definitely possible.

FOR DISCUSSION

1. Do you think Rockwell International would be better off if the cold war intensified?
2. Why does Rockwell International provide the auto pilot systems for the new Boeing 757s and 767s? Why doesn't Boeing make them itself?

CREDITS

COLOR PHOTOS

Opening section Page one: upper left, courtesy of Borroughs Corporation; upper right, H. Armstrong Roberts; lower, courtesy of Exxon. Page two: top, H. Armstrong Roberts; lower left, courtesy of Sperry; lower right, courtesy of Levi Strauss & Co. Page three: upper left, courtesy of Xerox Corporation; upper right, Ted Horowitz—The Image Bank; lower, H. Armstrong Roberts. Page four: upper left, Ted Horowitz—The Image Bank; upper right, courtesy of Levi Strauss & Co.; middle left, William Rivelli—The Image Bank; lower, courtesy of Xerox Corporation. Page five: upper, courtesy of Xerox Corporation; lower left, Pete Turner—The Image Bank; lower right, courtesy of Republic Steel. Page six: upper, Alex Webb—Magnum; lower, courtesy of Xerox Corporation. Page seven: upper, courtesy of Exxon; lower left, courtesy of Western Electric; lower right, courtesy of Armco. Page eight: upper, courtesy of IBM.

Portfolio I Page one: upper right, courtesy of Xerox Corporation; lower, courtesy of Sperry. Page two: upper, H. Armstrong Roberts; lower left, L. H. Jawitz—The Image Bank; lower right, Mark Godfrey—Magnum. Page three: upper, courtesy of Gulf Oil Corporation; lower, courtesy of Marathon Oil Company. Page four: upper, J. Rawle—Stock, Boston; lower left, Raoul Hackel—Stock, Boston; lower right, courtesy of Xerox Corporation.

Portfolio II Page one: left, J. Rawle—Stock, Boston; lower right, Gabe Palmer—The Image Bank. Page two: upper, courtesy of Xerox Corporation; lower left, Edith Haun—Stock Boston; lower right, Gerhard Gscheidle—The Image Bank. Page three: upper left, courtesy of Xerox Corporation; upper right, courtesy of Republic Steel; lower, courtesy of Xerox Corporation. Page four: upper, courtesy of Bethlehem Steel; lower, Gabe Palmer—The Image Bank.

Portfolio III Page one: upper left, Richard Kalvar—Magnum; upper right, Gabe Palmer—The Image Bank; lower, H. Armstrong Roberts. Page two: upper, courtesy of Levi Strauss & Co.; lower left, courtesy of Avon Products, Inc.; lower right, Alvis Upitis—The Image Bank. Page three: upper left, courtesy of Levi Strauss & Co.; upper right, courtesy of Levi Strauss & Co.; lower, courtesy of Levi Strauss & Co. Page four: left, H. Armstrong Roberts; upper right, Ron Benvenisti—Magnum; middle right, courtesy of Armco; lower right, courtesy of Western Electric.

Portfolio IV Page one: upper left, William Rivelli—The Image Bank; upper right, David Hamilton—The Image Bank; lower, L. Fried—The Image Bank. Page two: upper, H. Armstrong Roberts; lower, courtesy of Merrill Lynch & Company, Inc. Page three: upper, Costa Manos—Magnum; lower, Alvis Upitis—The Image Bank. Page four: upper left, H. Armstrong Roberts; upper right, H. Armstrong Roberts; lower, courtesy of Armco.

Portfolio V Page one: upper left, Burt Glinn—Magnum; upper right, Pete Turner—The Image Bank; lower, courtesy of Marathon Oil Company. Page two: lower, courtesy of Burroughs Corporation. Page three: upper, courtesy of Sperry. Page four: lower left, courtesy of Sperry; lower right, Robert Witkowski—The Image Bank.

Portfolio VI Page one: left, Don Carroll—The Image Bank; upper right, G. Champlong—The Image Bank; lower right, courtesy of Xerox Corporation. Page two: upper, courtesy of Burroughs Corporation; lower, H. Armstrong Roberts. Page three: upper, H. Armstrong Roberts; lower left, courtesy of Xerox Corporation; lower right, courtesy of Avon Products, Inc. Page four: upper left, courtesy of Xerox Corporation; upper right, courtesy of Xerox Corporation; lower, Gabe Palmer—The Image Bank.

BLACK AND WHITE PHOTOS

p. xxii, George Malave—Stock Boston; p. 3, Historical Pictures Service, Inc., Chicago; p. 11, Historical Pictures Service, Inc., Chicago; pp. 18 and 19, courtesy Anheuser-Busch Companies, Inc.; p. 21, Mark Godfrey—Magnum; p. 25, The Bettmann Archive; pp. 43 and 44, courtesy of General Dynamics Corporation; p. 47, Bruce Kliewe—Jeroboam; p. 70, courtesy of United Technologies; p. 75, Stock, Boston; p. 99, courtesy of Bethlehem Steel Corporation; p. 102, Milton Feinberg—Stock, Boston; p. 105, Stephen L. Feldman—Photo Researchers, Inc.; p. 127, courtesy of Republic Steel Corporation; p. 131, Elliot Erwitt—Magnum; p. 159, Donald Dietz—Stock, Boston; p. 176, courtesy of American Metal Treating Company; p. 179, Gene Daniels—Black Star; p. 201, Peeter Vilms—Jeroboam; p. 220, courtesy of Dow Chemical Company; p. 223, Georg Gerster—Rapho/Photo Researchers, Inc.; p. 242, courtesy of IBM; p. 244, Stock, Boston; p. 247, Leonard Freed—Magnum; pp. 267 and 268, courtesy of The Procter & Gamble Company; p. 271, Janet Fries—ICON; p. 285, courtesy of Bristol-Myers Company; p. 289, Paul Sequeira—Rapho/Photo Researchers, Inc.; p. 307, courtesy of The Coca-Cola Company; p. 309, Barbara Alper—Stock, Boston; p. 331, courtesy Huntington National Bank; p. 332, Bruce Davidson—Magnum; p. 335, Bettye Lane—Photo Researchers; p. 358, courtesy of Bank of America; p. 361, courtesy Bethlehem Steel Corporation; p. 387, James R. Holland—Stock, Boston; p. 412, courtesy of Merrill Lynch & Company; p. 415, Ray Ellis—Photo Researchers; p. 434, courtesy Xerox Corporation; p. 436, Robert Burroughs—Jeroboam; p. 439, Bruce Kliewe—Jeroboam; p. 457, courtesy of Marathon Oil Company; p. 461, Ellis Herwig—Stock, Boston; pp. 466, 467, 468, 469 and 473, courtesy of IBM; p. 487, Suzanne Arms—Jeroboam; p. 504, courtesy of Gulf Oil Corporation; p. 509, Philip Jon Bailey—Stock, Boston; p. 525, courtesy of Hewlett-Packard Company; p. 529, Jules Zalon—The Image Bank; p. 552, courtesy of Ford Motor Company; p. 555, Cary Wolinsky—Stock, Boston; p. 572, courtesy of Digital Equipment Corporation; p. 575, Julie O'Neil—Stock, Boston.

GLOSSARY

Absolute advantage Economic condition that occurs when one nation can produce a good with fewer economic resources, at less cost, than other nations.

Accountability Requirement that a person with authority and responsibility be held accountable for any action.

Accounting The process of analyzing and recording each event that effects an organization's financial position and periodically summarizing and reporting these entries in financial statements.

Account receivable Money owed to the company by a customer, resulting from the purchase of a product or service from the company on credit.

Accrual basis A method of accounting where a financial transaction is recognized in the time period in which it occurred rather than when cash is disbursed or collected as under the cash basis.

Achievement theories One of several approaches to motivation of individuals. Achievement theories are based on the assumption that some people have a greater need to achieve than others and that this "need to achieve" will motivate the person.

Acid test Measure of a firm's ability to pay its current debts on very short notice; quick ratio.

Acquisition Occurs when one company purchases another company. Acquisitions are frequently made for the purpose of vertical integration, which involves the purchase of companies that operate in earlier or later stages of a common production process.

Activity ration One family of ratios used to analyze financial statements, measure how efficiently a company uses its resources (assets), e.g. inventory and accounts receivable. Examples include inventory turnover (cost of goods sold/inventory), and the accounts receivable collection period (accounts receivable/sales per day).

Actuary mathematician Calculates and assigns a numerical value for a given risk.

Administrative law Decision by a government agency that becomes binding unless overturned by a court.

Advertising Any form of nonpersonal, paid promotion of products or ideas usually directed toward a large number of people.

Affirmative action Programs created by the government which force employers to comply with the Equal Employment Opportunity Act. These programs require employers to establish hiring goals for minorities to ensure that an effort is made to get them employed.

Agency shop A formal arrangement between labor and management under which all employees pay union dues and receive the same benefits, regardless of whether or not they belong to the union.

Agents Facilitate buying and selling; do not take title to goods.

Agent wholesaler Person whose primary function is to help producers distribute their products for a fee or commission.

American Federation of Labor (AFL) After the decline of the Knights of Labor, the American Federation of Labor was formed in 1886 to organize and unite the skilled workers' unions. The AFL avoided political party ties, maintained the autonomy of each national union, and registered only one national union per craft. Under the leadership of Samual Gompers, the AFL used the strike as its main weapon, and despite unfavorable court rulings and depressions the AFL successfully grew to over 5 million members by 1920. It later merged with the CIO.

Annual report Provides an overview of a company's progress during the past year and serves as the primary medium of communication between the company and its investors. An annual report usually includes the president's letter to shareholders summarizing the company's accomplishments and future plans, an operations review analyzing operations by segment, the financial statements and auditor's opinion, and a statistical summary of key information over the past five to ten years.

Appellate court A court of review, that is, a court that reviews the decisions and findings of lower courts.

Arbitrator Third party to a labor dispute who makes a binding decision.

Arithmetic/logic unit The part of the computer system which executes all arithmetical computations and logical operations.

Array List of numbers arranged by size.

Articles of incorporation Outline the name, address, and purpose of a corporation in addition to the names and addresses of the initial board of directors, as well as the amount of capital to be put into the corporation.

Assembly language An intermediate machine language used to program computers.

Assets The economic resources owned by the organization. They include current assets, such as cash, accounts receivable inventories, and marketable securities, and fixed assets, such as land, buildings, and machinery.

"Assistant to" positions Provide training and development for employees through short, temporary assignments to upper management, exposing the employees to specialized aspects of the firm's operations.

Attitudinal survey Determines what people think about something. People's attitudes are determined through the use of questionnaires and interviews.

Auction company Provides facility in which buyer and seller can complete transaction.

Auditor's opinion The written statement by an independent accounting firm after reviewing a company's financial statements which evaluates the accuracy and fairness of the financial information presented in the statements. It is usually included in the annual report with the financial statements.

Authority A manager's right to guide and direct the actions of employees and to make decisions.

Automatic data processing Mechanically aided manual data processing.

Balance of payments Monetary difference between the amounts a country earns and the amounts a country spends.

Balance of trade The quantitative difference between the amounts of exports and the amounts of imports of a country.

Balance sheet Presents a company's financial position at a particular point in time, such as the end of the year. It indicates the company's assets, liabilities, and equity.

Bargaining in good faith Refers to the National Labor Relations Act requirement that both parties in a labor dispute must attempt to negotiate fairly and consistently toward an agreement before resorting to strikes or work stoppages.

Barrier to entry A natural or artificial impediment to entry into an industry, e.g., high capital cost, need for a government-provided license, economies of scale.

Barter The exchange of commodities for commodities without the use of a medium of exchange such as money.

Bear Investor who believes the stock market will decline.

Bill of exchange A written document, from one person to another, unconditionally ordering the receiver to pay a specific amount to the third party.

Bill of materials A breakdown of the kinds and amounts of raw materials required to manufacture one unit of a finished product. The bill of materials is based on the material quantity standards.

Binding arbitration If negotiations in a labor dispute reach a stalemate, either party may seek binding arbitration under which the issue is decided by a neutral third party after hearing arguments from both sides. The arbitrator's decision is final and both sides must abide by it.

Bit The basic unit of information in a computer; it enables the computer to distinguish between one and zero.

Blue-sky law Popular name for various state laws enacted to protect the public from securities frauds.

Board of directors The people who control the corporation; they are elected by the stockholders. The board of directors typically hire the president, vice-president, and other corporation officers.

Bond A type of security which is an evidence of a debt owed by the issuing company or government to the receiver. Typically it states that a specified payment will be made at periodic intervals and that a certain principle will be paid off at a specified date.

Book value Value of a stock in the company's records; can be calculated by dividing the number of shares into the net worth (value of common stock plus retained earnings).

Boycott Union bargaining tactic whereby it tries to get people or other organizations to refuse to deal with the company.

Break-even point Number and price of units required to be produced if firm is to remain in business.

Broker Agent who handles the public's orders to buy and sell securities, commodities, or other property.

Budget A formal dollar-quantified statement of an organization's expected performance, i.e., what resources will be required to implement the plans developed by management. Budgets are useful for planning, allocating and controlling resources.

Bull Investor who believes the stock market will rise.

Bureaucracy Organizational model used primarily for large scale operations like government, in which each individual's duties and responsibilities are fixed and limited by a chain of command, a firm system of rules and standards that cover how work is performed, employment based on technical qualifications, and protection from arbitrary dismissal.

Burglary The unlawful entry into a building with the attempt to commit theft.

Business Means of exchanging goods, services, or money for profit.

Business life cycle Process of inception, growth, and demise of the viability of a particular business enterprise.

Call Otherwise known as a call option, an investor buys, for a certain premium, the right to purchase 100 shares of a particular common stock at a specified period of time.

Capital Synonymous with money.

Capital cost The basic start-up cost to get a firm going.

Capital expenditure Investments a company makes in purchasing its fixed assets, such as property, plant, equipment, or long-term research and development.

Capital gain The positive difference between the sale price and the purchase price of any asset.

Capital good Industrial good, including fixed plant and production equipment.

Capitalism An economic system in which individuals can own and utilize virtually all resources, subject to minimal restrictions.

Capitalist An individual who provides capital for businesses.

Capital loss The negative difference between the sale price and the purchase price of any asset.

Career cluster A group of related jobs one of which may suit the individual in question.

Case law Law based on the decisions of courts handed down in written cases.

Cash account An investor's account at a brokerage firm in which securities are purchased for cash only.

Cash-and-carry wholesaler Services small retailers; does not deliver or grant credit.

Cash basis A method of accounting where a financial transaction is recognized only when there is either a receipt or disbursement of cash.

Cash discount Part of the terms of credit in a company's collection policies, which refers to the discount given to customers for paying the company within a fixed period of time.

Cashier's check A negotiable instrument drawn by a bank on itself.

Casuality insurance Covers loss to specified property.

Cathode-ray tube (CRT) A visual display device that receives electrical impulses and translates them into a picture on a television-like screen.

Cease-and-desist order An administrative or judicial order commanding a business firm to cease conducting the activities which the agency or court has deemed "unfair deceptive trade practices."

Census A survey conducted by the U.S. Government every ten years of all the people in the United States.

Central bank The head of any monetary or banking system, e.g., the Federal Reserve in the United States; a banker's bank.

Centralization The traditional organization model in which decision-making authority and responsibility are concentrated in the hands of top management.

Central processing unit (CPU) The main frame of a computer system, it is composed of the control unit, the arithmetic/logic unit, and the primary storage unit.

Certified check A check drawn by an individual on his own account but bearing a guarantee by a bank that the bank will pay the check regardless of whether the drawer's account contains adequate funds at the time the check is presented for payment.

Chain of command The official reporting relationships between individuals in an organization (it is commonly depicted by an organizational chart).

Charter of incorporation The certificate of incorporation obtained from the state in which the articles and an application for the certificate have been filed. It is usually signed by the secretary of state and allows the corporation to legally do business in that state.

Checking account balance The amount of undisbursed funds remaining in a checking account that can be withdrawn on demand.

Clayton Act (1914) Designed to break apart trusts and monopolies; however, with the rising antiunion sentiment, the Supreme Court applied the Clayton Act to unions and ruled that injunctions could be issued against union activities, which led to a decline in unionism during the 1920's.

Closed shop A formal arrangement between labor and management under which anyone hired must already be a union member. The closed shop is illegal in its pure form.

Closely held corporation A corporation like any other, except the shares of which belong to members of a family or to relatively few people who are known personally to each other. In some states, closely held corporations have less stringent reporting rules than regular corporations.

COBOL (Common Business Oriented Language) Computer language specifically developed to facilitate business data-processing procedures.

Coinsurance A requirement that policyholder buy insurance equal to a certain percentage of the replacement value of the property.

Collateral The property or assets which back up a company's borrowings. If the company defaults on its debt, the creditor takes possession of the company's property or assets pledged as collateral.

Collection period Part of the terms of credit in a company's collection policies, the length of time a customer is allowed to pay for a purchase.

Collective bargaining The process used to resolve conflict between employees and management, whereby employees join together to bargain as a unit; and any agreement reached applies to all employees.

Commercial bank A bank that has the ability to accept demand deposits, or checking accounts.

Commercial paper A form of short-term financing which consists of a short-term promissory note or I.O.U. issued by the company without any collateral. Commercial paper is typically issued only by large companies having minimal risk of default.

Commission agents Serve agricultural producers by selling at best price less commission.

Common carrier A transportation company that offers its services to the general public; government regulations control operations of this type of company.

Common law That body of law developed in English and American courts not attributable to a legislature.

Common property Property which is owned by everyone (or owned by no one). To be contrasted with private property.

Common stock A security that indicates the real ownership in a corporation. It is not a legal obligation for the firm and does not have a maturity. It has the last claim on dividends each year and assets in the event of firm liquidation.

Communism Economic system in which the government rigidly controls all of the nation's economic resources.

Company-owned wholesaler Wholesaler established by manufacturer to cut costs.

Comparative advantage Economic condition that occurs when one nation can produce a good relatively more efficiently than other goods.

Competition The effort of two or more businesses to win the trade of a particular market population by offering the most attractive products and the easiest means of procuring these goods.

Competitive advantage What a firm does best; a determination of basic strengths which can help promote and sell a target product.

Competitive bidding Firms promise to provide goods or services to specifications for a set price; firm offering lowest price usually selected.

Complementary goods Products which perform only part of a complete cycle of operations; for example, washers and dryers.

Computer Electronic machines that accept data and manipulate it mathematically to solve problems and produce new information; its power is derived from its speed, accuracy and memory.

Computer graphics A computerized visual aid constructed by a computer which gives a large-scale representation of data in a relatively compact and more easily interpreted form; for example, the CAT Scan as an alternative to repeated x-rays.

Computer hardware Electronic and mechanical elements of a computer, used to read, store, process, and provide data.

Computer modeling Complex problem solving with the aid of a high speed computer; the computer weighs any number of input factors and provides a quick, concise analysis within the bounds of a given equation or program.

Computer software Computer programs supplied by the manufacturer to accomplish such tasks as scheduling jobs through the machine, sorting computer records, and organizing and maintaining internal computer files.

Concentrated product strategy The decision to promote one particular product in lieu of all others in the hope of becoming known and sought after for that single line.

Congress of Industrial Organizations (CIO) Since the AFL organized skilled craft workers only, the Congress of Industrial Organizations (CIO) was formed in 1935 to represent industrial and semi-skilled or unskilled workers. After being denied access to the AFL, the CIO, led by John Lewis of the United Mine Workers, quickly grew to national prominence. A fierce rivalry developed between the AFL and the CIO until the two unions merged in 1955.

Consideration That which motivates the exchange of promises in a contractual agreement. Consideration is necessary to make any contract legally binding. This is a term that can refer to anything of value.

Constant dollar accounting An approach to preparing financial statements which attempts to measure the impact of inflation (measured by the consumer price index) on the company's financial statements. Major companies are required to report their financial statements as restated using constant dollar accounting.

Consumer goods Products that will be used by the general public; products that will not be used to manufacture other products.

Consumerism Social movement by American consumers in opposition to the perceived disinterest and irresponsibility of manufacturers.

Contests Games offering prizes to customers or would-be customers.

Contract A set of promises constituting an agreement between parties, giving each a legal duty to the other and also the right to seek remedy for the breach of the promises owed to each other.

Contract carrier A transportation company that carries products on a selective basis for a limited number of customers; not permitted to solicit business from the general public.

Contract law The law pertaining to the formation, carrying out, and breach of contracts.

Controlling One of the major functions of management; the process of comparing actual results to the originally planned results, and correcting any significant differences to ensure that plans are successfully completed.

Control unit Directs the sequence of operations in the computer.

Convenience goods Basic necessity products which are purchased and used on a regular basis, such as soaps, toilet tissue, deodorants.

Conversion process The flow of inputs (material, labor, overhead) through the production process to the completion of finished products. At each step, value is added to basic input, thus increasing the utility of the final product.

Convertible preferred stock Security that can be exchanged, at the option of the holder, for a lesser security, generally common stock in the issuing firm.

Cooperative Business organization in which a group of owners band together to operate the business.

Corporation A legal fiction, or artificial being, with a distinct existence that is separate from the human beings who control it.

Cost-oriented approach Price of production determines cost of item.

Coupons Discount vouchers to attract cost-conscious buyers.

C.P.A. (Certified Public Accountant) The certificate is given to accountants by the American Institute of CPAs after passage of a uniform examination and two years of experience.

Craft union Union made up of people with a craft or trade, such as carpenters, bricklayers, or plumbers.

Credentials file A file usually kept at the placement office of a college or university in which all of the information pertaining to the past activities of a job candidate are kept.

Credit insurance Covers losses arising out of debts to a firm.

Credit policy The amount of trade credit a company will allow and to whom the company will allow the credit. The credit policy will affect sales, bad debts, and the investment in accounts receivable.

Criminal law The law that governs and defines those actions which subject the convicted offender to punishment imposed by the state. Criminal law involves actions deemed illegal by the state, not by private persons.

Cumulative voting Voting system that allows stockholders to accumulate the total votes they are allowed to cast and to cast them for one or more candidates.

Currency In the United States, the medium of exchange which consists of paper bills and coins.

Current assets The company's cash and assets that can be readily converted to cash; current assets usually consists of cash, marketable securities, accounts receivable, and inventories.

Current liabilities A company's debts which must be paid off within one year; current liabilities are usually shown separately on the balance sheet, and include short-term notes payable, accounts payable, income taxes, and payroll and other accruables.

Cutthroat pricing In principle, pricing designed to drive a competitor out of business. Typically cutthroat pricing involves pricing below cost.

Debenture A type of bond that is backed only by the general credit of a corporation rather than by a specific lien on particular assets of the corporation.

Debt capital Funds borrowed from the creditors of a business.

Debt financing The sale of bonds as a long term source of funds. Debt financing requires the periodic payment of interest and the repayment of the loan on a fixed maturity date, and therefore involves the risk that the company may not be able to meet these fixed obligations.

Decentralization The organization model in which decision-making authority is dispersed throughout the organization in the form of autonomous units (profit centers), each responsible to a central headquarters for its performance.

Decision theory A set of concepts and techniques to aid managers in decision-making when there are a number of alternatives to choose from and uncertainty surrounds each alternative.

Decision tree A common form of analysis in decision theory involving a methodical presentation of alternatives, and the conditions surrounding them, in the form of tree to aid in decision-making.

Deductible Amount not paid on a claim.

Delegation Process by which authority is distributed throughout a business.

Demand deposit Another name for a checking account; a deposit in a commercial bank the balance of which can be withdrawn on demand.

Demand-oriented pricing Price set by intensity of value consumers place on product.

Demographics The results of statistical analysis of human populations in regard to size and density, age and sex distribution, ethnic backgrounds, educational levels, income levels or religious affiliation which is then applied to marketing strategy.

Demonstration Authentication of product claims to stimulate sales.

Departmentalization The process of grouping activities and employees into separate identifiable areas of the organization (departments), each headed by a manager who is responsible for his department's performance.

Depreciation The estimated decline in the useful value of an asset over a period of time due to wear and tear. Depreciation can not be estimated with certainty, but is approximated using various standard methods.

Descriptive statistics Data organized, summarized, and presented in a form that a manager may find useful in decision-making.

Differentiated product strategy Systematic plan which strives to sell a product which meets specific market needs, such as geographics or income level of the population for which the product is intended.

Directing One of the major functions of management, directing is the process of supervising and guiding employees to implement plans and achieve goals. It involves motivating individuals to do their best, leading them, and communicating with them so that they know what to do.

Direct observation A technique for collecting data by direct observing and recording the opinions, behavior, and actions of people.

Discount rate The rate that the Federal Reserve charges to member banks for borrowed reserves.

Dividend Payment made by a company to its stockholders as a distribution of the company's profits, thus providing the stockholders with a return on their investment.

Draft Any negotiable instrument drawn on any person (including a bank) which orders that person to pay a certain sum of money. A check is a draft.

Drop-shippers Collect retail orders for manufacturers for direct shipment to retailers.

Electronic data processing (EDP) The electronic collection and manipulation of data.

Electronic funds transfer system (EFTS) A checkless money transfer system in which sums of money are transferred from one account to another simply by means of magnetic signals.

Electronic mail Transmission of a written message via interconnecting computers in lieu of communication by the conventional mail services; computer can be selectively programmed to transmit certain categories of information automatically to various branches in the system to facilitate large scale information transmission and exchange.

Embargo Restriction of trade between two countries for political or ideological reasons.

Embezzlement The fraudulent appropriation of money or other property by a person to whom the money or property has been entrusted.

Empirical management The management school of thought which attempts to understand management by analyzing what tasks managers actually do. It advocates learning about management by doing and observing the activities of other managers.

Encryption The use of secret codes to protect business from having ideas or processes stolen by competitors who may be eavesdropping over the telecommunications system.

Entrepreneur The individual who undertakes the risks of organizing production, the return for which is profit.

Entry-level job That job which new two-year or four-year college graduates can aspire to and from which a career can be launched.

Environment of business All of the factors that can influence a business' success or failure.

Environmental impact statement A statement that under law must be made by various government agencies and others when a proposed action is to be taken that will adversely affect the environment in any way.

Equal Employment Opportunities Act (EEO) (1972) Designed to ensure that minorities and women have an equal chance at getting jobs and to eliminate discrimination in hiring practices. EEO is enforced through affirmative action programs.

Equilibrium price The price from which there is no tendency to change once it is established.

Equity The owners' or stockholders' investment in the organization. Equity arises from direct investment by the owners, such as purchasing stock, and from profits retained in the organization.

Equity capital Capital raised by a firm by the sale of common stock.

Equity financing The issuance of stock as a long-term source of funds. Equity financing offers the firm flexibility since dividend payments are optional and there is no maturity date on stock, but it also extends voting rights and control to more owners.

Esteem need In Maslow's need hierarchy, the need for self-respect and respect from others.

Exchange The act of willingly trading one item for another.

Exclusive distribution strategy Distribution rights granted to small number of retailers; e.g., automobile distributors.

Executive perks (perquisites) A form of supplementary benefits made available to employees as they move up the management ladder. They include status symbols like bigger offices and benefits like company autos, club memberships, legal counseling, and investment counseling.

Expectation theory Based on the assumption that individuals will be more highly motivated to take some action if they expect the result from taking that action to be sufficiently better than the result from not taking it.

Expected loss The likelihood of a certain event occuring as determined by the laws of probability.

Expenses The resources used by the organization to provide goods or services (and generate revenue). Expenses include the cost of goods sold, such as materials, labor, and factory overhead; administrative expenses, such as salaries of the president and management; selling expenses, such as advertising costs and sales commissions; and interest paid on money borrowed by the organization.

Exporting Sending a product to another country in order to enter their market without making a substantial investment.

Extensive problem solving Exploring all the possibilities before making an important or expensive purchase; shopping around for the best possible deal.

External data Data obtained from sources outside the business.

Family life cycle An analysis of the ages and number of members in a family unit in order to help predict purchasing habits and to then decide which product will meet that projected demand.

Fidelity bond Insures against dishonesty by an employee.

Fiduciary money Any money that is not commodity money or "backed" by some commodity that can be redeemed and exchanged. Fiduciary money involves people having faith that the money is usable in the payment of all debts.

Finance A discipline concerned with the acquisition and management of a company's money to support its operations and expenditures. Finance involves determining the amount, source and best use of a company's money.

Financial accounting The process of developing a set of financial statements that provide a historical record of what financial events have occurred during a given period of time. Financial accounting attempts to satisfy the informational needs of external users, such as investors, government agencies, special interest groups, and the public.

Financial manager A financial manager is responsible for the acquisition, investment (use), and management of the firm's money. The financial manager may be the owner or president in smaller firms, or a treasurer, controller, or vice president of finance in larger firms.

Financial statements The end result of the financial accounting process. They summarize and report the entries made in a company's financial records over a period of time. The two key financial statements are the balance sheet and the income statement.

Fire insurance Protection against loss by fire, including damage by water and smoke.

First generation computer Such computers as the IBM 650, which utilized vacuum tube memory and circuitry.

Fixed assets The company's assets which can not be readily converted into cash, consisting primarily of the company's investment in property, plant, and equipment. Fixed assets are usually the primary income-producing assets, generally have long lives, and normally represent the company's largest investments.

Fixed costs Costs, such as mortgage payments, unchanged by production, wages, material, or service costs.

Floating exchange rate A daily fluctuating currency exchange rate, which reflects the relative value of particular unit of currency based upon the supply and demand of a currency.

Flowchart Device for visually describing by symbols and interconnecting lines, the structure and sequence of operations of a computer program.

Forgery The false or unauthorized signature of a document, or false making of a document, with the intent to defraud.

Formal organization The official lines of authority, responsibility, and communication between individuals in a company, commonly depicted by the organizational chart.

Form utility Power of a product or service to satisfy wants; created when raw inputs are converted into a finished-product.

FORTRAN (Formula Translation) Widely used computer language designed to solve scientific, mathematical, and business problems.

Fractional reserve banking system A system in which depository institutions are not required to keep 100 percent of their deposits on reserve in the form of currency or reserves at the central bank.

Franchise A system for distributing goods or services under a known name even though the business is operated by an independent owner. The owner pays the fachisor a fee for the right to use its name and for technical assistance.

Franchisee Person licensed by a franchisor to sell its products or services in a specified territory under a franchising contract.

Franchisor Person or company that licenses franchises to sell its products or services.

Free-form organization Organizational model in which the form structure, departments and positions are deemphasized and replaced with operating units consisting of changing blends of personnel.

Free trade Unrestricted trade between countries irrespective of the impact of such trade on home industries.

Fringe benefits Non-monetary, or additional, benefits that employees of a company receive, e.g., medical insurance at reduced or zero cost, below-cost group life insurance, etc.

Full-service wholesaler Holds title to goods he sells retailers.

Functional authority Authority of a service department to establish policies which *must* be followed by the employees in a particular area of the company.

General-jurisdiction trial court A court that can hear all cases arising under state law, except those expressly assigned to specialized courts, such as small claims and justice of the peace courts. These courts are also called district courts and common pleas courts.

Generally accepted accounting principles (GAAP) The guidelines for financial accounting which specify what information should be reported in financial statements and how it should be reported. GAAP are established primarily by the Financial Accounting Standards Board, and by the Securities and Exchange Commission.

General-merchandise wholesaler Handles large assortment of non-perishable goods.

General partner Owner in a partnership with full rights and responsibilities whose actions are legally binding on all partners.

Goal A target to be accomplished in a particular time period.

Grapevine The informal channel of communication within an organization. The grapevine may pass information upward, downward, crosswise, or randomly throughout the organization regardless of the formal channels of communication which follow the organization structure and chain of command.

Grievance Complaint about a job that creates dissatisfaction or discomfort, made by an employee or the union.

Guild The earliest form of labor organization in the U.S., dating back to 1648. They were formed to protect employees' jobs from immigrants by enforcing high manufacturing standards. Early guilds were organized at the local level, which limited their bargaining power.

Hawthorne studies Western Electric Company experiments of the 1930's, conducted to determine the impact of the work environment on employee productivity.

Higher-level language The most sophisticated programming languages, getting to be more like human languages.

Human-behavior management The management school of thought, which focuses on understanding what motivates individuals to work, why individuals behave in certain ways in certain situations, and how a manager's actions affect worker behavior.

Human relations How companies treat and manage their employees in an attempt to promote worker and organizational effectiveness.

Human resource management The process of controlling, directing, and motivating employees in an attempt to achieve the firms goals and objectives without sacrificing the employees' needs.

Hygiene factors In Herzberg's psychological theory of motivation, hygiene factors are those job-related factors whose presence will have no impact on employee motivation, although lack of them may result in job dissatisfaction.

Hypothesis A statement about what should happen if certain actions or events take place. These statements are usually presented in an "if. . . .then" format and are usually proven to be correct through some type of testing procedure.

Import Good or service bought by one nation from other nations.

Impulse purchase Buying a product on the spur of the moment; purchase which is not necessarily based upon rational decision making but more commonly upon whim.

Income statement One of the key financial statements which shows the organization's financial progress over a given period of time. The income statement summarizes the organization's revenues and expenses, and calculates the profit or loss according to the equation: Revenues − expenses = Profit (or Loss).

Industrial distributor Marketing intermediary in an industrial channel that serves the same function as the wholesaler in the consumer channel of distribution.

Industrial union Union composed of workers in a particular company or industry, regardless of occupation.

Inferential statistics Data drawn from some information base, but they do not include all possible information. They allow the user to infer a conclusion about an entire group without having to take the time or money to survey the entire group.

Inferior trial court A specialized type of court with limited jurisdiction of subject matter, such as divorces, traffic, and small claims courts.

Inflation Economic situation in which costs for goods and services increase or the purchasing power of a nation decreases.

Informal organization A structural system of communication and relationships created by groups of people with common interests. It cuts across formal organization lines often developing its own leaders, policies, and procedures.

Information overload Too much information bombarding an executive or decision maker rendering it difficult to discern what is important from the deluge of information; a situation which can lead to inertia in decision making.

Injunction Court order that prohibits the defendant from engaging in certain activities. For example, an employer may get an injunction that orders employees not to strike.

Inland marine insurance Broad type of insurance generally covering articles that may be transported from one place to another or such items of transportation as bridges and tunnels.

Input Data and instructions given the computer.

Inside information Information that has not yet been made public about the future profitability of a corporation.

Insurable interest You can only insure property which you own and which, if damaged, lost, or stolen, will cause you financial loss.

Insurable risk Insurance principle that requires a risk to meet certain broad tests in order to be insurable.

Intangible asset Asset with no physical substance; asset that exists as a legal right acquired by the firm.

Intensive distribution strategy Large number of retail outlets for convenience goods.

Interest The charge paid by the company for borrowing money, thus providing the lendor with a return on his money. Interest payments are mandatory, fixed amounts typically made periodically on specific dates during the life of the debt.

Internal data Obtained from records within a business that relate to the operation of that business.

International Monetary Fund An international exchange policing agency which was supposed to discourage the payments of debts with paper currency rather than with gold, or else to urge a country to reduce its exchange rate, if it were using highly inflated currency which was not commensurate with its gold holdings.

Inventory control Maintaining adequate supplies for production while keeping the costs of carrying inventory down.

Inventory turnover Financial ratio that measures the number of times a firm's inventory was sold in a period of time.

Job analysis The process of preparing job descriptions and specifications for an organization.

Job description Based on the definition of individual jobs (obtained through job design). The job description is a written description of the basic responsibilities and tasks of someone in that job. The job description includes such information as job title, organizational position and relationships, specific duties, and relation to other jobs.

Job design The process of dividing all of the tasks to be performed by the organization into distinct, manageable units (jobs). It differentiates between jobs but at the same time ensures that the jobs are integrated and coordinated so that the firm's total task is efficiently accomplished.

Job enrichment A practical method for motivating employees, particularly production workers, by upgrading their jobs to provide more responsibility more meaningful work, and more recognition to the employee.

Job evaluation Comparing one job with other jobs to develop an equitable wage and salary program.

Job rotation Consists of moving an employee through different positions within an organization to expose the employee to a broad range of operations and opportunities. Job rotation is used for the effective placement of the employee in the right position, and for developing potential managers by providing an understanding of the various functions of the firm.

Job security The protection of an employee against firing or lay-off. It is one of the goals commonly sought by unions for their members. Job security provisions usually include specific lay-off procedures, for example by a seniority system, or instead of laying off some workers, the company will reduce all workers' hours by a fixed percentage.

Job specification Is a written statement of the qualifications required of an employee to hold a specific job. This would include such factors as education, experience, training, mental ability, and physical skills.

Joint venture Similar to a partnership, except that actual management is delegated to one person and the venture lasts for a short time.

Knights of Labor The first national organization designed to unite and coordinate all of the individual unions. It extended membership to both skilled and unskilled workers. After a successful strike against the Wabash Railroad in the mid-1880's, the Knights of Labor grew to over 700,000 workers. But the conflicting interests of its diverse members led to its rapid decline a few years later.

Labor efficiency standards Predetermined production standards which indicate the numbers of direct labor hours needed to manufacture one unit of finished product. They are typically based on time-and-motion studies, which time production workers as they manufacture the product.

Labor union Group of employees joined together to achieve goals that deal with existing employment condition.

Laissez-faire Literally "leave alone." A hands-off attitude to be taken by the government.

Landrum-Griffith Act (1959) Labor-management reporting and disclosure act passed to prevent corrupt union practices. It guaranteed members certain rights or participation in union affairs, helped to regulate union elections, and provided for financial accountability of unions.

Larceny The act of taking another's personal property unlawfully.

Law of demand Quantity demanded of a commodity is inversely related to its price: a higher price yields a smaller quantity demanded than a lower price.

Law of large numbers The larger the sample of a given phenomenon statistically analyzed, the greater the certainty of the prediction.

Law of supply The quantity supplied is positively related to price; a higher price elicits a higher quantity supplied.

Leadership A person's ability to direct others and to positively affect their behavior.

Leasing A form of intermediate-term financing used to acquire fixed assets, in which the company is permitted to use the asset over an extended period of time in exchange for periodic lease payments. Leasing represents an alternative to borrowing to buy an asset, which enables the company to avoid the risk of the asset becoming obsolete.

Legal tender Any money or currency which must be accepted by law in payment of any debt, public or private.

Leverage The amount of debt a company uses to finance its assets. The amount of leverage increases with the amount of debt. Leverage is usually measured by leverage ratios, such as the debt ratio (notes payable plus long-term liabilities/total assets).

Leverage ratios One family of ratios used in analyzing financial statements; measure how much debt a company uses to finance its assets. The primary leverage ratio is the debt ratio.

Liabilities The debts owed by an organization to its creditors. They include current liabilities, such as notes payable, trade accounts payable, income taxes, and accrued payrolls; and long-term liabilities, such as loans due in future years.

Liability insurance Protection against claims for damage or injury to persons.

License To permit or authorize use of a brand name or technology.

Life insurance Protection against the loss of individuals in whom one has an insurable interest.

Light pen Mechanism to enter data directly into computer by utilizing light-emitting cell of pen on visual display screen.

Limited-function wholesalers Provide limited services; examples are drop shippers, truck jobbers, and cash-and-carry wholesales *(q.v.)*

Limited partnerships Partnership with at least one general partner and one or more limited partners, who are liable for loss only to the amount of their investment.

Limited problem solving The decision to purchase a product based on the comparison of several factors, such as price, relative quantity, brand name, style, color, type of warranty or subsequent servicing available.

Limit order An investor instructs his broker to buy or sell a security at a specified market price.

Line authority The most basic, fundamental type of authority. It is the direct authority of a manager to plan, direct and control the activities of subordinates at the next lower organizational level.

Line of credit An agreement between a company and a bank under which the company can borrow money from the bank at any time up to a predetermined credit limit.

Liquidity The firm's ability to pay its bills and obligations when they come due. Maintaining liquidity by ensuring that the firm has sufficient cash on hand is one of the primary jobs of the financial manager, and is essential to the firm's survival.

Liquidity ratios One family of ratios used in analyzing financial statements which measure the short-run solvency of a company, i.e. its ability to pay current bills from cash and current assets. Examples include the current ratio (current assets/current liabilities), and the quick ratio (current assets minus inventories/current liabilities).

List price What a company says it wants for its products.

Local spot Advertising time on radio or TV purchased to reach local customers.

Lockout Management pressure tactic that involves denying employees access to their place of employment.

Long-term liabilities A company's debts which are not due in the current year but in a future period. Long-term liabilities are usually shown separately in the liabilities section of the balance sheet.

Loss Occurs when an organization's expenses exceed its revenues over a period of time, as indicated on the organization's income statement. Losses decrease the owner's equity in the organization.

Loss leader An item priced at a specially low price to attract customers to the store.

Machine language A combination of zero and 1; the only language a computer can execute directly.

Magnetic ink Printed characters can be read by machine and humans. Has proved extremely useful in check processing.

Maintenance factor Results in job satisfaction but isn't classified as a motivator in Herzberg's work motivation model. Some of the maintenance factors are pay, working conditions, status, and job security.

Malpractice insurance Type of public liability insurance that provides doctors with protection against lawsuits over negligence or mistakes.

Management The process of achieving organizational objectives through individuals, machines, materials, and money.

Management accounting Attempts to satisfy the informational needs of a company's internal management. It supplements the information provided by financial account in the financial statements.

Management by objectives (MBO) One of the practical techniques widely used by management to motivate employees, particularly white-collar workers. MBO consists of the manager and employee jointly setting goals; determining job duties, establishing a plan of action, and measuring standards of performance; and periodically reviewing progress toward the goals.

Management information system (MIS) A formal network using computer capabilities to provide the most useful and correct information to the appropriate manager at the right time.

Management style Refers to a basis for classifying leadership according to the *willingness* of the leader to share his decision-making power. For example, Lewin, Lippit and White identified three management styles: autocratic, in which the leader makes all decisions; laissez-faire, in which members of the group make decisions; and democratic, in which decision-making is shared between the leader and the group.

Management work station A central location which is in computer communication with all of the arteries of a firm; an efficient base of operations from which the manager can make corporate decisions.

Managerial grid Developed by Blake and Mouton, classifies leadership along two dimensions: concern for people and concern for production. Five basic leadership styles are identified, representing combinations of different levels of the two attributes; for example a "9,1" manager shows maximum concern for production and minimum concern for people.

Margin account An investor's account in a brokerage firm in which a portion of the necessary funds for purchasing securities is borrowed from the brokerage firm.

Marketable security A short-term (less than one year) investment made by a company using excess cash available from fluctuations in business activity. An investment in marketable securities will yield interest to the company and can quickly be converted back into cash when needed. Examples include U.S. Treasury securities, commercial paper, and certificates of deposit.

Marketing Satisfying people's needs and wants and the organization's profit objectives by efficiently promoting and distributing goods, services, and concepts, subject to the constraints in the marketing environment.

Marketing channels The various paths a product may follow from the manufacturer to the customer.

Marketing concept Philosophy that consumer preferences for goods and services have significant impact on what is to be supplied in the market.

Marketing mix Combination of elements—product, its price, promotional activities, and distribution channels—that affect the selling of a product.

Market order An investor instructs his broker to buy or sell a security at the next available market price.

Market price The price the consumer pays.

Market segment Classifications of possible customers for various goods which is arrived at by a linear analysis from most general market to the most specific.

Market value Prevailing price paid by buyers to sellers of a stock.

Mass production A manufacturing approach in which a large number of homogeneous units are manufactured in a routine, standardized fashion. The pattern of product flow in mass production can be sequential, parallel, or selective.

Material price standard Predetermined production standards which indicate the unit price of each type of raw material needed to manufacture the finished product. Price standards are typically based on vendor price quotations and historical experience.

Material quantity standard Predetermined production standards which indicate the amount of each type of raw material that should be required to manufacture one unit of finished product. They are typically based on the original engineering specifications, and may take the form of a bill of materials.

Matrix organization The organization model in which temporary project teams are formed within functional lines of authority to work on particular jobs, after which the team is disbanded and individuals are reassigned to other projects.

Mean The arithmetic average of a series of numbers.

Median The middle score in a set of numbers.

Mediation Attempt by a third party to get the two parties in a labor dispute to reach an agreement or settle an issue.

Merchant cities Centers where commerce flourished.

Merger A joining together of two separate firms into one firm.

Metric measurement Measurement system based primarily on the meter. Three of its six base units are the meter (length), kilogram (weight), and second (time).

Microprocessor A miniaturized solid state electronic circuit.

Mode The most frequent value in a set of numbers.

Model A mathematical or graphical representation of a real-world situation.

Money Any asset that is widely accepted as a payment for debts, as a medium of exchange, as a store of purchasing power, and as a unit of accounting.

Money capital The money that is typically put together for the use of forming or expanding a business.

Monopolistic competition An industrial, or market, structure in which numerous competitors each have a small amount of market power due to distinct brand names, etc.

Monopoly One person or group in control of one particular product or process to the exclusion of all other contenders; the state of having no competitors who can threaten your hold on a specific market.

Mortgage bond A bond that is secured by a specific real asset, such as a building or land.

Motivation The underlying reasons for an individual's behavior. Employee motivation is a determinant of productivity, and is therefore essential to organizational success.

Motivator factor In Herzberg's psychological theory of motivation, motivator factors are those job-related factors whose presence will increase employee motivation.

Multinational corporation A corporation which has a home country for its main base and has a network of auxillary operations in other countries.

Mutual company Nonprofit organizations owned by policyholders.

Mutual fund An investment company that continually buys or sells to investors shares of ownership in its portfolio, which is simply made up of the shares of ownership of other companies.

National Labor Relations Act (NLRA) (or Wagner Act) Freed unionism and collective bargaining from judicial haranguing in an attempt to put labor back on its feet during the great depression of the 1930's. It established the National Labor Relations Board to oversee the safe development of unions, and allowed workers the right to strike to gain better wages and working conditions.

National Labor Relations Board (NLRB) Was established under the National Labor Relations Act to oversee the safe development of unionism. The NLRB determined what union activities to organize employees were permissable and what employer activities against unionism were unfair labor practices.

National spot Advertising time on radio or TV purchased from different networks and independent stations to reach national audience.

Need hierarchy Maslow's need hierarchy describes the needs that human beings try to satisfy, arranged in order of importance from the lowest-order primary needs (food, shelter, sex), to security needs (safety, protection), to social needs (friendship), and to the highest order needs (esteem, self-realization). Management can motivate employees by providing an environment that allows them to satisfy their needs, but once a need is satisfied, it is no longer a motivator.

Negotiated price Price arranged between buyer and seller based on specific features of item.

Net income (earnings) A company's profit after income taxes, commonly shown on the annual income statement. It is computed as revenues minus income taxes.

Network advertisement Radio or TV time purchased for simultaneous advertisement to national audience.

No-fault insurance Does not require that fault be determined in an automobile accident in order for an injured party to collect. Victims are compensated by their own insurance companies.

Non store retailing House-to-house sales, vending machines, and mail-order sales are examples of retailing without the use of stores.

Objective Specific result or target to be reached by a certain time.

Occupational Safety and Health Act (OSHA) (1970) Designed to ensure that workers have healthy and safe work environments. OSHA inspectors verify that work sites meet federal standards, and impose fines on employers who fail to meet those standards.

Ocean marine insurance Covers all types of vessels and any liabilities associated with them or their cargoes.

Odd-figure pricing A form of psychological pricing in which the price is set at an add number to enhance the value of the item in the consumer's perceptions. For example, item is priced at 97¢ instead of $1.00.

Odd lot Amount of stock less than a round lot, one to ninety-nine shares.

Oligopoly Few sellers; an industrial situation in which there are several sellers that dominate the market and are therefore interdependent.

On-the-job training Training for a job under close supervision. The supervisor manages, observes, and evaluates the trainee.

Open market operations Purchase and sale of U.S. Government bonds on the open market by the Federal Reserve System.

Open shop Exists when employees are free to choose whether or not to join a union, with no management effort against unionism, and no union effort to force employees to join.

Operational management The traditional management school of thought, fathered by Henri Fayol, which attempts to develop principles of how managers *should* perform the general functions of planning, organizing, commanding, coordinating, and controlling.

Operational planning Short-range planning that involves setting short-range goals and developing a specific course of action to meet those goals.

Operations research A discipline that uses quantitative analysis in decision making and an interdisciplinary, team approach to solving business problems.

Opportunity cost Profits which cannot be earned because the income-producing asset has been lost.

Optical-character recognition Electronic scanner which can read numbers, letters, and other characters.

Option An option to either buy at a specific price or sell at a specific price a hundred shares of a particular common stock within a specified time period.

Organization The coordination of individuals, each performing different tasks, to achieve a common goal. Organizations vary in structure, environment, and purpose, each of which effects the type of individuals attracted to the organization, how they act within it, and how effectively it accomplishes its goals.

Organizational chart Illustrates the official reporting relationships among individuals in a company and details how the company organizes its activities.

Organizational climate The quality of the environment within the organization and the impact of this climate on employees.

Organization development (OD) Instead of focusing on individual employees, organizational development programs attempt to improve overall organizational effectiveness through a planned program of change aimed at improving the interpersonal relationships of employees. OD utilizes many techniques, including MBO, job enrichment, and the managerial grid.

Organizing One of the major functions of management, organizing is the process of coordinating the work effort of employees and assigning work activities to accomplish the company's goals.

Output What the computer says to the operator.

Over-the-counter market The market for stocks that are not traded on the major exchanges.

Owner's equity Things of value that the owner or owners have invested in the business.

Parallel flow production A pattern of product flow in mass production in which different products go through different, separate processes to manufacture components which are then brought together in a final process. For example, in the auto industry, subcomponents of a car (frame, engine, trim) are manufactured separately and then finally brought together to assemble the car.

Participation theories One of several approaches to the motivation of individuals, these theories are based on the assumption that employees will be more highly motivated to properly execute decisions if they are involved in making the decisions.

Partnership A type of business organization in which two or more individuals join together for the purpose of conducting a business.

Par value The face amount of an instrument of value, such as the monetary value assigned to each share of stock in the charter of a corporation.

Penetration strategy Low initial price set on item to gain quick market acceptance.

Percentage-of-sales approach Certain amount of sales revenue allotted for promotion.

Performance appraisal The evaluation of employees on a regular, periodic basis. They provide positive reinforcement through praise of the employee's strengths, and suggestions for improvement through constructive criticism of the employee's weaknesses.

Performance standards The yardsticks by which both managers and employees can measure their performance. They are a part of the overall performance appraisal system, and cover such key characteristics as reliability, ability to follow orders, congeniality, work habits, attitude, and loyalty.

Personal property Any property which can be moved; any property that is not real property (see real property).

Personal selling Advertising brings the customer to the product; the salesman sells it.

Personnel management Process of accomplishing organizational objectives by continually acquiring, retaining, developing, and properly using human resources.

Physical distribution Movement of products from producer to consumer.

Physiological need Biological need for such things as food, air, water.

Picketing Walking around a plant or office building with signs informing the public and other employees that the employer is unfair.

Piecework Compensating employees on the basis of number of units produced instead of on the basis of time.

Plan A course of action designed to accomplish stated goals.

Planned progression Training and developing potential managers by moving them through different jobs and managerial positions within the organization. Planned progression is similar to job rotation but has a longer time perspective.

Planning One of the major functions of management, planning is the process of setting goals for the organization and developing strategies to meet them.

Plant layout The decision of what equipment is needed, how should it be arranged within the plant, and how work should flow through the plant. It attempts to provide effective utilization of space and equipment and to avoid bottlenecks and ensure efficient flow of materials through the plant.

Plant location Decision of where a company should locate a new production plant. It is affected by such factors as the proximity to suppliers and customers, availability of effective transportation, and the costs of doing business in a particular area (taxes, utilities).

Point-of-purchase promotion A display by the cash register.

Preemptive right Gives holders of common stock the first chance to buy additional issues of common stock on a basis proportional to the number of shares they hold.

Preferential shop In a preferential shop, members of the recognized union are given preferential treatment by management, particularly in the area of initial hiring. However, many of the preferential advantages given to union members are currently illegal under the Taft-Hartley Act.

Preferred stock A security that indicates financing obtained from investors by a corporation. It is not a legal obligation for the firm. It does not have a maturity, but pays a fixed dividend each year. It has preferred position over common stock, both for dividends and for assets in the event of firm liquidation.

Premium Payment made to insurer to bear specific risk.

Press release Information about new products made available to local and national advertising media.

Prestige pricing A high price justified by reputation and expertise

Price Value of a product to consumers, converted into dollars and cents.

Price discrimination Selling different units of identical products at different prices.

Price war Reciprocal lowering of prices to lure customers from competing firms.

Primary storage unit Holds all data and instructions necessary for processing.

Privacy Act of 1974 An act of Congress to protect individuals from being victimized by the computerized composite picture of their financial and personal lives. Individuals now have the right to know the contents of their data files which are held by federal agencies. The data is also supposed to be used only for its original purpose and is supposed to be true insofar as the agency can determine.

Private carrier A company that owns and operates its own transportation system for the purpose of moving its own goods; not permitted to carry goods of another company.

Private enterprise An economic system in which individuals are allowed to use their resources—labor and capital—in any way they see fit.

Private property Right of an individual to possess and use property for personal pleasure or profit, within limits prescribed by law.

Probability The likelihood of an event occuring as determined by statistical analysis.

Producer's goods Products which are used to make other products and are purchased for industrial use.

Product The output of a production process, created from such inputs as labor, materials, and equipment. May be tangible, like a car, or intangible, like the legal service provided by a lawyer.

Production Process of transforming inputs into goods and services that people and organizations want or need.

Production control Activities that support the production process, through aggregate production planning, production scheduling, and inventory control.

Production era One of three stages of marketing development in the U.S. (1865–1930); focused on manufacturing efficiency.

Production management The process by which an organization converts inputs like equipment, labor, and raw materials into finished products.

Production schedule Indicates what products will be produced, when they will be produced, in what volumes, and what labor and materials will be required. The production schedule is designed to meet production targets based on the sales forecast. The production schedule is the primary document implementing the production process.

Production standard Predetermined figures which indicate the amounts and kinds of labor skills and materials which should be required to manufacture one unit of product. Production standards include material quantity, material price, labor efficiency, and wage-rate standards.

Productive capacity Whether the company has enough machinery, tools, personnel, and factory space to manufacture what is required.

Productivity The relationship between output (goods and services) and input (labor, material, and capital).

Product life cycle The time span between the inception of a product and its demise with each stage in the interim requiring specialized marketing strategies and attention to anticipated strengths and weaknesses.

Product line The various components of the general product which are designed to appeal to varied types of customer needs, desires and demands.

Product mix The sum total of all the different product lines that a company carries; if one product does not satisfy a buyer's need, then the hope is that another will; analogous to species differentiation in biology which ensures survival through the development of members which adapt to the particular environment.

Profit The net earnings of an organization, calculated as the excess of revenues over expenses over a period of time, and shown on the income statement. Profits increase the owners' equity in the organization.

Profitability ratios One family of ratios used in analyzing financial statements, measure a company's profit in relation to its assets and sales. Examples include return on assets (net earnings/total assets), profit margin (net earnings/net sales), and return on equity (net earnings/shareholders' investment).

Profit centers Independent, autonomous operating units in a decentralized organization.

Program The sequence of instructions fed into a computer in order to enable it to carry out a process.

Promissory note A promise to pay a specific sum under the conditions of place, time, and other circumstances as agreed.

Promotion The generation of sales.

Promotional price Price of item lowered for specific period in order to increase sales.

Protective tariff Tariffs which are imposed in order to indirectly promote local products by making the import more expensive.

Proxy Legal form that assigns the right to vote to another person or persons.

Psychological theories One of several approaches to motivation of individuals, these theories focus on employees, jobs, attitudes, and occupations rather than organizational elements. For example, Herzberg suggested that factors such as money and working conditions do not motivate employees, but challenging work and recognition do positively motivate employees.

Publicity Developing awareness of products and services.

Public relations Maintenance of firm's image, dissemination of information, and cultivation of customers.

Pull strategy Promotional efforts directed at final consumer.

Purchasing function Determining when, from whom, and how to acquire the raw materials needed for production at the least cost.

Pure risk Provides only the chance of a loss.

Push strategy Promotional efforts directed at marketing channels.

Put A type of option in which an investor buys, for a certain premium, the right to sell 100 shares of a particular common stock at a specified price within a specified period of time.

Quality control An approach to production control in which the product is inspected at various stages of the manufacturing process. If problems are discovered during an inspection, management can correct the problems before further work is done. Quality control inspections are usually made on a random sample of products, rather than every single unit of product.

Quantitative analysis An approach to decision-making which encourages decision makers to identify all relevant data and then to express problems in mathematical or graphical form.

Quantity discount Reduced price for volume purchase.

Quotas A proportional part or share of goods that may be imported into the country.

Random sample A survey where the participants are chosen by chance from the population.

Random walk A situation in which the future movement of anything, such as the price of a share of stock, cannot be predicted by simply using information on past movements of the price of that stock.

Ratio analysis One of the tools used to analyze financial statements. It involves comparing certain types of financial information to compute ratios which provide an additional perspective of the organization's financial health. Such ratios include profitability ratios, liquidity ratios, leverage ratios, and activity ratios.

Real property Property consisting of land and buildings thereon which are stationary, as opposed to personal property, which can be moved (see personal property).

Reserve requirements The requirements that depository institutions keep a specified percentage of their deposits on reserve either in the form of vault currency or reserves at district federal reserve banks.

Responsibility A manager being accountable for the performance of the operations and employees under his authority, i.e. if a manager has the authority over how a job gets done, he has the responsibility for results.

Resume A short account of one's career and qualifications prepared typically by an applicant for a new position.

Retail cooperative Wholesale company set up by group of retailers.

Retailer Marketing intermediary that sells directly to final consumers.

Retained earnings Also called corporate savings; those earnings that corporations reinvest (do not give out as dividends).

Retirement Employee's exit from a firm at the end of their working life.

Return on investment (ROI) Measured as profits divided by total investment. Otherwise known as the profitability of an investment.

Revenue The resources, primarily cash, coming into an organization as a result of goods sold or services rendered. Revenue also includes interest earned on bank accounts or on bonds, and cash dividends received from investments.

Revenue tariff Duties imposed on costly luxury items which are usually imported goods.

Right-to-work laws State laws which make union shops illegal. These laws provide that two people doing the same job must be paid the same wage, even if one is not a union member. Georgia, Texas, Florida, and Arizona have right-to-work laws.

Risk Chance of loss or injury.

Risk management Concern with those situations where potential loss is coupled with no chance of potential gain.

Robbery Theft from a person accompanied by assault and/or battery.

Round lot Unit of trading on a stock exchange, usually 100 shares.

Salary Compensation to an employee on a weekly, biweekly or monthly basis.

Sales branch Producer-owned wholesaler that also serves as a base for sales representatives and stocks a small inventory of products and parts.

Sales office A producer-owned wholesaler that rarely stocks inventory.

Sales promotion Efforts to promote sales by means other than advertisements and personal selling; e.g., point of purchase displays, or free samples.

Sample survey A polling of a statistically representative segment of a given population, the results of which can facilitate marketing strategies.

Satellite-based communications network Nearly instantaneous large scale transmission of information via satellite to the economic advantage of the company.

Scientific management The management approach, originally proposed by Frederick Taylor, of developing management principles based on scientifically proven axioms.

Second generation computer Computer utilizing transistors.

Secondary data Published by other businesses, trade associations, and government.

Security A certificate issued by a government or a business to obtain needed financing from investors. Principal securities are stocks and bonds.

Selective distribution strategy Number of retailers limited by manufacturer.

Selection flow production A pattern of product flow in mass production in which manufactured items go through different combinations and sequences of processes to manufacture different products. For example, in meat processing, some of the product goes directly to packaging, some goes to smoking and then to packaging, and some goes to grinding and then to packaging for sale to consumers.

Self-insurance Business absorbs its own losses.

Sequential flow production A pattern of product flow in mass production in which each product goes through the same set of operations in the same sequence. It usually exists in companies making uniform products such as bread, refined ores and metals, sugar, beverages, and chemicals.

Shopping goods Products that necessitate that the customer spend time and effort before purchasing; purchase decision based upon considered comparison of cost and quality of like or different products.

Short-term working capital Money that is usually used to finance inventory that turns over rapidly, or to pay bills while waiting for receivables to be collected.

Single-line wholesaler Handle few product lines, e.g., paint, clothing.

Skimming Initial high price to recoup development costs.

Small business Normally, a business with sales under $25 million, less than 100 employees and assets of less than $10 million.

Small Business Administration (SBA) A U.S. Government organization created to assist small businesses.

Socialism An economic system in which the major factors of production are owned by the government.

Social responsibility Requires that business consider the social consequences of its actions in addition to the economic consequences.

Social-system management The management school of thought which focuses on understanding the psychology of group behavior and how groups affect the managing process.

Sole proprietorship A form of business organization in which there is only one individual who owns that business.

Span of control The number of employees that a manager supervises.

Speciality goods Products that the customer insists upon by brand name; the product has become known as the best of its kind, and the consumer will accept no substitute.

Speciality wholesalers Handle limited product line, generally requiring technical or specialized knowledge.

Speculative risk Offers the possibility of either gain or loss.

Staff authority The advisory authority of a service department to provide assistance, support and advice to other managers upon request, but the staff person has no direct authority to make the line manager follow the advice.

Staffing One of the major functions of management, staffing is the process of getting the best possible people to work for the organization. It involves recruiting and hiring qualified individuals, developing their skills, appraising their performance, and compensating and promoting them based on their performance.

Standard labor cost The total cost of direct labor required to manufacture one unit of finished product. It is obtained by multiplying the labor efficiency standard by the wage-rate standard for each process and then summing the products.

Standard material cost The total cost of raw materials needed to manufacture one unit of finished product. It is obtained by multiplying the material quantity standard by the material price standard for each raw material and then summing the products.

Statistical analysis A mathematical model based upon probability which gives an objective picture of various factors and is used to predict sales trends.

Statistics The mathematics of the collection, organization and interpretation of numerical data.

Statute law Law that is enacted by a legislative body. Also called statutory law.

Stock A type of security that indicates real ownership in the assets of a corporation.

Stock company A business (whose product is insurance) owned by stockholders.

Stop-loss order An order to sell a specified stock whenever the market price hits or falls below a specified price. Also called a stop order.

Strategic planning Long-range planning which involves setting long-range goals and developing a general course of action to meet those goals.

Strict liability Legal doctrine requiring a showing that a specific manufacture or design led to an injury. This doctrine led to a rapid increase in product liability suits against business.

Subchapter S corporation A type of corporation that is taxed much like a partnership. It is also known as a tax-option corporation. All profits and losses of the Subchapter S corporation are passed through to the individual shareholders.

Suggestion selling Encouraging the purchase of complementary items along with the original product.

Superstore Wide range of offerings to meet most customers needs.

Supplementary benefits The various forms of compensation given to employees in addition to basic wages. Examples include workers compensation insurance and unemployment insurance (required by law); life, health, and accident insurance; vacation days, sick days and personal holidays; and profit-sharing, bonuses, and executive perks.

Surety bond Insures against the failure of a firm to meet its contractual agreements.

Survey An approach to data collection in which information of interest to the researcher is acquired from people through the use of interviews, questionnaires, and so on.

Sweepstakes Sales promotion by offering customer chance to win prize.

Survey of buyer intentions A low cost method of determining whether a product is marketable in a particular area; a polling of prospective buyer population which will provide valuable information about the purchasing disposition of a prospective new territory.

Taft-Hartley Act (1947) Amended the National Labor Relations Act; was passed in reaction to the growing number of strikes, coercion of employees, and other union abuses which resulted from the rivalry between the AFL and CIO (It restored some power to management in labor disputes by recognizing that unions could also be guilty of unfair labor practices in their attempts to organize employees.)

Target market The market that appears most promising or lucrative in terms of highest and most probable profit margins.

Tariffs Government taxes imposed on imported goods.

Task force Temporary ad hoc committee formed to accomplish a particular job after which the task force is disbanded. Allows the organization to bring together individuals with the specific skills needed for each new task or problem.

Taylorism The management theories of Frederick Taylor, who founded the scientific management school of thought.

Teleconferencing Simultaneous world-wide verbal and visual communication among decision makers in a firm via computers and satellite communication networks which saves valuable time and money for the company.

Term insurance Insurance with premium set for specific period; does not build cash value.

Term loan A type of intermediate-term financing in which the company borrows money from a bank under a formal agreement with a fixed maturity date and interest rate. The company is usually required to back up the term loan with collateral, such as property or assets.

Test market Offering a new product at a sale price to a selected group of buyers within the parameters of the target market population in order to predict success of the product in its present form.

Theory of comparative advantage A theory advanced by David Ricardo which compares the feasibility of producing a particular product by comparing the number of hours of labor required to produce it with the country's efficiency in producing other goods, thereby indicating which goods to specialize in.

Theory X The traditional management view of employees described by Douglas McGregor in THE HUMAN SIDE OF

ENTERPRISE. It assumes that the average person has an inherent dislike for work and will avoid it if possible, and management must therefore maintain close supervision and control over employees.

Theory Y The counterapproach to the Theory X. It recognizes the human need for self-fulfillment and ego satisfaction and that people exercise self-direction and self-control in the service of objectives they are committed to.

Third generation computers Utilize solid-state technology and integrated circuits.

Third securities market A market in which large brokerage firms bypass organized exchanges in order to buy and sell blocks of stock.

Time deposit A deposit which, in principle, cannot be obtained on demand, but rather for which thirty days' notice of intent to withdraw must be given.

Time series study A prediction of sales based upon past sales data and pattern.

Title Legal ownership of goods.

Title insurance Protects owners of buildings and land against the claims of previous owners.

Tort A civil wrong (as opposed to criminal) not arising from the breaking of a contract.

Total cost Fixed costs plus variable costs.

Trade acceptance A draft drawn by the seller of goods on the purchaser and accepted by such purchaser. It represents the purchaser's promise to pay.

Trade credit A form of short-term financing used to buy goods from suppliers. Trade credit consists of open accounts payable and notes payable to the supplier which are created when the supplier allows the company an extended period of time to pay for its purchases.

Trade discount Percentage off list price to wholesalers.

Trait theory Assumes that there are certain physical and psychological traits that differentiate a leader from the group, and attempts to identify these leadership traits by studying recognized leaders.

Travelers check A check drawn by the issuing bank upon itself which is accepted by the act of issuance. As with a cashier's check, the bank is secondarily liable.

Truck-jobbers Sell perishable goods to small retailers.

Underemployment When an individual has qualifications which exceed the requirements of his job.

Undifferentiated product strategy Marketing plan which will appeal to most buyers; mass marketing; planning based on the assumption that buyer needs are fairly homogeneous for this product.

Unemployment The number or percentage of people who are not working but are between the legal working ages of 16 to 65 and are seeking employment. Unemployed people include people between jobs and those who are on a temporary or seasonal layoff, but exclude those who are chronically unemployed and not looking for jobs.

Unfair labor practice An illegal tactic used by an employer to block a union's attempt to organize his employees (under the National Labor Relations Act) or an illegal tactic used by a union in its attempt to organize employees (under the Taft-Hartley Act).

Union shop A formal agreement between labor and management under which all newly hired employees are required to join the company's union. Union shops are illegal in states which have passed right-to-work laws.

Universal product code (UPC). A form of optical character recognition carried on many grocery items. The combination of lines is read by a laser beam in the input unit and an impulse is sent from the cash register to the computer.

Utility Power of a good or service to satisfy wants or needs.

Variable costs Costs, such as for material and labor, which change with number of units produced.

Vertical integration A type of merger between two firms that are at two separate positions in the production process, e.g., the purchase by an electric utility of its supplier of coal; the purchase of a retail chain of shoe stores by a manufacturer of shoes.

Wage-rate standard Predetermined production standards which indicate the expected wage per hour for each production worker. They are typically based on union contracts and salary schedules established by the personnel department.

Wages The basic form of compensation of employees for the performance of their jobs. Wages are generally determined by the individual employee's productivity, qualifications, and worth to the firm. Wages may also be affected by government regulations like the minimum wage law, or by unions through collective bargaining.

Wagner Act Labor law, passed in 1935, that spells out employer practices that are unfair to labor and that created the National Labor Relations Board.

Wheel of retailing Concept describing the retailing cycle, in which new retailers enter a market to compete with established retailers by offering lower prices.

Whole life insurance Insurance with set premiums which builds cash value which can be borrowed against, or, on maturity, be paid to insured.

Wholesaler Marketing intermediary that buys products from producers and sells them to other wholesalers, retailers, or industrial users.

Wholesaler-sponsored voluntary chain Retailers organized by wholesaler.

Worker's compensation Protection against claims of injury to employees.

Working capital A company's current assets. Cash or assets which can be readily converted into cash. It includes cash, marketable securities, accounts receivable and inventories, and must be managed to ensure that the company has enough cash to pay its bills and enough inventory to satisfy customer needs.

Yield Return on an investment

Zero population growth (ZPG) Birth rate (2.1 children per couple) that provides only for the replacement of each couple.

INDEX